THE SOCIAL ARCHAEOLOGY OF THE LEVANT

The volume offers a comprehensive introduction to the archaeology of the southern Levant (modern-day Israel/Palestine/Jordan) from the Paleolithic period to the Islamic era, presenting the past with chronological changes from hunter-gatherers to empires. Written by an international team of scholars in the fields of archaeology, epigraphy, and bioanthropology, the volume presents central debates around a range of archaeological issues, including gender, ritual, the creation of alphabets and early writing, biblical periods, archaeometallurgy, looting, and maritime trade. Collectively, the essays also engage diverse theoretical approaches to demonstrate the multivocal nature of studying the past. Significantly, *The Social Archaeology of the Levant* updates and contextualizes major shifts in archaeological interpretation.

Dr. Assaf Yasur-Landau is an associate professor at the University of Haifa, a Fulbright Scholar, and head of the laboratory for Coastal Archaeology and Underwater Survey. He co-directs the Tel Kabri excavations and the Tel Dor underwater excavations. His book, *The Philistines and Aegean Migration in the Late Bronze Age* (Cambridge University Press), has appeared in English (2010; 2014) and Spanish (2012).

Dr. Eric H. Cline is a professor of classics and anthropology in the Department of Classical and Near Eastern Languages and Civilizations and director of the Capitol Archaeological Institute at The George Washington University, in Washington, DC. A Fulbright Scholar, National Geographic Explorer, and NEH Public Scholar, Dr. Cline has authored, co-authored, or edited a total of eighteen books to date, of which four have won awards, including the Biblical Archaeology Society's "Best Popular Book on Archaeology" award (2001, 2009, and 2011) and the American Schools of Oriental Research's "Nancy Lapp Award for Best Popular Book" in 2014.

Dr. Yorke M. Rowan is a research associate professor at The Oriental Institute of The University of Chicago. A Fulbright Scholar in Jordan and an NEH Fellow at the W. F. Albright Institute of Archaeological Research in Jerusalem, he co-directs two field projects, the Eastern Badia Archaeological Project (Jordan), and the Galilee Prehistory Project (Israel).

THE SOCIAL ARCHAEOLOGY OF THE LEVANT

FROM PREHISTORY TO THE PRESENT

Edited by

ASSAF YASUR-LANDAU
University of Haifa

ERIC H. CLINE
The George Washington University

YORKE M. ROWAN
The University of Chicago

CAMBRIDGE
UNIVERSITY PRESS

University Printing House, Cambridge CB2 8BS, United Kingdom

One Liberty Plaza, 20th Floor, New York, NY 10006, USA

477 Williamstown Road, Port Melbourne, VIC 3207, Australia

314–321, 3rd Floor, Plot 3, Splendor Forum, Jasola District Centre, New Delhi – 110025, India

79 Anson Road, #06–04/06, Singapore 079906

Cambridge University Press is part of the University of Cambridge.

It furthers the University's mission by disseminating knowledge in the pursuit of education, learning, and research at the highest international levels of excellence.

www.cambridge.org
Information on this title: www.cambridge.org/9781107156685
DOI: 10.1017/9781316661468

© Cambridge University Press 2019

This publication is in copyright. Subject to statutory exception and to the provisions of relevant collective licensing agreements, no reproduction of any part may take place without the written permission of Cambridge University Press.

First published 2019

A catalogue record for this publication is available from the British Library.

Library of Congress Cataloging-in-Publication Data
NAMES: Yasur-Landau, Assaf, editor. | Cline, Eric H., editor. | Rowan, Yorke M., editor.
TITLE: The social archaeology of the Levant : from prehistory to the present / edited by Assaf Yasur-Landau, Eric H. Cline, Yorke Rowan.
DESCRIPTION: Cambridge ; New York, NY : Cambridge University Press, 2019. | Includes bibliographical references and index.
IDENTIFIERS: LCCN 2018018454 | ISBN 9781107156685 (hardback) |
SUBJECTS: LCSH: Middle East–History. | Middle East–Antiquities. | Social archaeology–Middle East.
CLASSIFICATION: LCC DS62 .S63 2019 | DDC 956–dc23
LC record available at https://lccn.loc.gov/2018018454

ISBN 978-1-107-15668-5 Hardback

Cambridge University Press has no responsibility for the persistence or accuracy of URLs for external or third-party internet websites referred to in this publication and does not guarantee that any content on such websites is, or will remain, accurate or appropriate.

CONTENTS

List of Figures   *page* ix
List of Tables   xiii
List of Contributors   xv
Foreword   xvii
    Thomas E. Levy
Acknowledgments   xxix
List of Abbreviations   xxxi

    PROLOGUE   1
    Yorke M. Rowan, Assaf Yasur-Landau, and Eric H. Cline

PART ONE   7

1   THE LOWER AND MIDDLE PALEOLITHIC OF THE SOUTHERN LEVANT   9
    Gary O. Rollefson

2   AN ANTHROPOLOGICAL REVIEW OF THE UPPER PALEOLITHIC IN THE SOUTHERN LEVANT   29
    Anna Belfer-Cohen and Nigel Goring-Morris

3   THE FORAGER–FARMER TRANSITION IN THE SOUTHERN LEVANT (CA. 20,000–8,500 CAL. BP)   47
    Natalie D. Munro and Leore Grosman

4   GETTING IT TOGETHER: THE CREATION OF COMMUNITY IN THE NEOLITHIC   67
    Bill Finlayson

5   FIRE AND SOCIETY IN THE EASTERN MEDITERRANEAN: A DIACHRONIC VIEW WITH A MICROARCHAEOLOGICAL FOCUS   86
    Ruth Shahack-Gross

TABLE OF CONTENTS

6 IT'S A SMALL WORLD: WORK, FAMILY LIFE, AND COMMUNITY IN THE LATE NEOLITHIC 98
Edward B. Banning

7 THE SPIRITUAL AND SOCIAL LANDSCAPE DURING THE CHALCOLITHIC PERIOD 122
Yorke M. Rowan

8 USING ARCHAEOBOTANICAL REMAINS TO MODEL SOCIAL, POLITICAL, AND ECONOMIC CHANGES DURING THE CHALCOLITHIC PERIOD IN THE SOUTHERN LEVANT 146
Philip Graham

PART TWO 161

9 THE SOUTHERN LEVANT DURING THE EARLY BRONZE AGE I–III 163
Meredith S. Chesson

10 CONTINUITY, INNOVATION, AND CHANGE: THE INTERMEDIATE BRONZE AGE IN THE SOUTHERN LEVANT 183
Susan L. Cohen

11 MIX 'n' MATCH: THE BIOARCHAEOLOGY OF COMMINGLED REMAINS 199
Susan Guise Sheridan

12 THE MIDDLE BRONZE AGE CANAANITE CITY AS A DOMESTICATING APPARATUS 224
Assaf Yasur-Landau

13 CUNEIFORM WRITING IN BRONZE AGE CANAAN 245
Yoram Cohen

14 "CANAAN IS YOUR LAND AND ITS KINGS ARE YOUR SERVANTS": CONCEPTUALIZING THE LATE BRONZE AGE EGYPTIAN GOVERNMENT IN THE SOUTHERN LEVANT 265
Shlomo Bunimovitz

PART THREE 281

15 THE "CONQUEST" OF THE HIGHLANDS IN THE IRON AGE I 283
David Ilan

TABLE OF CONTENTS

16 IRON AGE I PHILISTINES: ENTANGLED IDENTITIES IN A
    TRANSFORMATIVE PERIOD   310
    Aren M. Maeir

17 MOVING BEYOND KING MESHA: A SOCIAL ARCHAEOLOGY
    OF IRON AGE JORDAN   324
    Benjamin W. Porter

18 A SOCIAL ARCHAEOLOGY OF THE KINGDOM OF JUDAH:
    TENTH–SIXTH CENTURIES BCE   337
    Avraham Faust

19 PHASES IN THE HISTORY OF THE KINGDOM OF ISRAEL   354
    Daniel M. Master

20 THE ALPHABET COMES OF AGE: THE SOCIAL CONTEXT OF
    ALPHABETIC WRITING IN THE FIRST MILLENNIUM BCE   371
    Christopher A. Rollston

PART FOUR   391

21 PEOPLE, MATERIAL CULTURE, AND ETHNO-RELIGIOUS
    REGIONS IN ACHAEMENID PALESTINE   393
    Oren Tal

22 LAND/HOMELAND, STORY/HISTORY: THE SOCIAL
    LANDSCAPES OF THE SOUTHERN LEVANT FROM
    ALEXANDER TO AUGUSTUS   410
    Andrea M. Berlin

23 THE EFFECTS OF EMPIRE ON DAILY LIFE IN THE PROVINCIAL
    EAST (37 BCE–313 CE)   438
    Alexandra L. Ratzlaff

24 THE SOCIAL ARCHAEOLOGY OF THE SOUTHERN LEVANT
    IN THE BYZANTINE PERIOD: RETHINKING
    THE MATERIAL EVIDENCE   458
    Itamar Taxel

25 RURAL COMMUNITIES AND LABOR IN THE MIDDLE
    ISLAMIC-PERIOD SOUTHERN LEVANT   478
    Ian W. N. Jones

TABLE OF CONTENTS

26 SOCIETY IN THE FRANKISH PERIOD — 492
Rabei G. Khamisy

PART FIVE — 507

27 THEMES AND PATTERNS IN HUMAN–ANIMAL INTERACTIONS: HUNTING, DOMESTICATION, AND LIVESTOCK HUSBANDRY — 509
Nimrod Marom

28 FINDING A WORLD OF WOMEN: AN INTRODUCTION TO WOMEN'S STUDIES AND GENDER THEORY IN BIBLICAL ARCHAEOLOGY — 522
Stephanie L. Budin

29 SOCIAL ARCHAEOLOGY IN THE LEVANT THROUGH THE LENS OF ARCHAEOMETALLURGY — 536
Erez Ben-Yosef and Sariel Shalev

30 THE ARCHAEOLOGY OF MARITIME ADAPTATION — 551
Assaf Yasur-Landau

PART SIX — 571

31 THE IMPACT OF RADIOCARBON DATING AND ABSOLUTE CHRONOLOGY IN THE HOLY LAND: A SOCIAL ARCHAEOLOGICAL PERSPECTIVE — 573
Felix Höflmayer and Katharina Streit

32 ITINERANT OBJECTS: THE LEGAL LIVES OF LEVANTINE ARTIFACTS — 594
Morag M. Kersel

33 ARCHAEOLOGY, MUSEUMS, AND THE PUBLIC IN JORDAN: 100 YEARS OF EDUCATION — 613
Arwa Badran

EPILOGUE — 634
Assaf Yasur-Landau, Yorke M. Rowan, and Eric H. Cline

Index — 639

FIGURES

1.1	The location of principal Lower Paleolithic sites	page 10
1.2	(a) Middle Acheulian bifaces from Jebel Uwaynid; and (b) a Late Acheulian bifacial cleaver from 'Ain al-Assad	13
1.3	Middle Acheulian bifaces from 'Uyun al-Qadim	14
1.4	(a) Large Late Acheulian bifacial cleaver from 'Ain Sawda; and (b) Late Acheulian Micoquian piercer from 'Ain Sawda	17
1.5	The location of principal Middle Paleolithic sites	19
1.6	Middle Paleolithic knives from Trench 3 at 'Ain Sawda	21
2.1	Distributions of: (a) Initial Upper Paleolithic; (b) Ahmarian; and (c) Levantine Aurignacian, Atlitian, and Arqov/Divshon sites in the Levant	32
2.2	Characteristic core and tool types	33
2.3	Tool distributions in relation to combustion features through the Boqer Tachtit sequence	35
2.4	(a) Nahal Zin, (b) Erq el-Ahmar, (c) massive fire pit at Qadesh Barnea 501 (Ahmarian), and (d) incised ocher-smeared slab and equid pendants (insets) from Hayonim Cave and split-base point from Kebara Cave (Levantine Aurignacian)	36
3.1	Map of the southern Levant including sites mentioned in the text and their chronological periods	49
3.2	From left to right, a wild oat grain, a wild oat awn, and a wild barley grain from House 11 at PPNA Gilgal	52
3.3	Three plastered skulls recovered *in situ* from the Middle PPNB site of Yiftahel	59
3.4	Faunal evidence for ritual feasting from the Late Natufian burial site of Hilazon Tachtit	59
6.1	A map of the southern Levant indicating Late Neolithic sites	99
6.2	A plan of Yarmoukian courtyard Complex H at Sha'ar Hagolan	102
6.3	(a) A map of the Wadi Rabah site of Tabaqat al-Bûma during Phase LN2; and (b) a map of activity areas (Clusters 1–4) identified in the G34 structure (Phase LN3) through micro-refuse	103
6.4	Examples of a Yarmoukian clay figurine (on the left) and a "pebble" figurine (on the right) from Sha'ar Hagolan	105
6.5	Examples of Yarmoukian pottery sherds	109
7.1	Selected Chalcolithic sites	124
7.2	Site plan of Bir es-Safadi, southern section	127
7.3	Flint tools	129
7.4	Basalt vessels	130

7.5	Ceramic vessels	131
7.6	Copper artifacts from the Nahal Mishmar hoard	133
7.7	Burial caves at Givʻatayim, numbers 1 and 7	135
7.8	Ceramic ossuaries	136
8.1	Carbonized wood versus carbonized animal dung at Tel Tsaf, Shiqmim, and Marj Rabba	150
8.2	The cultivars from Tel Tsaf	151
8.3	The cultivars from Shiqmim	151
8.4	The cultivars from Marj Rabba	151
9.1	Map with EB IA–EB III sites	164
9.2	Reconstruction of residential contexts at EB III Numayra	175
9.3	A large clay bin filled with carbonized emmer wheat from the final occupational phase of EB III Numayra	176
10.1	Map of the southern Levant showing Intermediate Bronze Age sites	184
10.2	Architecture from Khirbet Iskander Area B, Phase A	187
10.3	Map of Intermediate Bronze Age sites in the Negev	188
10.4	Plan of circular structures from Area A at Beʼer Resisim	189
10.5	Sample of Intermediate Bronze Age ceramics from the burial caves at Jebel Qaʻaqir (not to scale)	191
11.1	Map of the southern Levant with sites discussed and modern capitals labeled	200
11.2	The bioarchaeological model	201
12.1	Megiddo Stratum XIII	229
12.2	Megiddo Stratum XII	231
12.3	Megiddo Stratum XI	233
12.4	Plan and reconstruction of the Tel Dan gate	234
12.5	Plan of Hazor, with MB II symmetrical ("Syrian") temples in Areas A and H, and a "Syrian" gate in Area K	235
13.1	Sites associated with cuneiform writing in Canaan during the Bronze Age	248
14.1	Egyptian vessels from Jaffa	267
14.2	Ramesses II gate from Jaffa	269
14.3	Lid of an anthropoid coffin from Beth Shean	270
14.4	The Mekal Stele from Beth Shean	275
15.1	A selection of key Iron Age I highland material culture	285
17.1	The Mesha Stele	325
17.2	Map of Khirbat al-Mudayna denoting Buildings 100 through 800, (1) a tower, (2) a moat, (3) a possible gate, (4) a paved pathway, and (5) a courtyard	327
17.3	Iron Age II fortifications on Dhibanʼs southeast corner	329
17.4	Busayra (ancient Bozrah), the Edomite administrative capital, looking south over the acropolis	332
18.1	Jerusalem in the late Iron Age	340
18.2	Settlement hierarchy in the kingdoms of Judah and Israel	341
18.3	Plan of the northwestern quarter at Tell Beit Mirsim	342
18.4	The kingdom of Judah: differences in the quality of buildings	343
18.5	A typical four-room house (the governorʼs residency at Tel Eton)	347

LIST OF FIGURES

18.6	A typical Judahite tomb from Gibeon	350
19.1	Key excavations in the Northern Kingdom of Israel	358
21.1	Selection of Phoenician coins	397
21.2	Philistian coins	398
21.3	Philistian denominations as demonstrated by a coin type from Ashdod	399
21.4	Selection of Philistian coins	399
21.5	Selection of anepigraphic Samarian coins	401
21.6	Samarian denominations: (top) *rb' šql*, (center) *m'h*, and (bottom) half *m'h*	401
21.7	Selection of epigraphic Samarian coins: (top) *šmryn*, (center) *bdyḥbl*, and (bottom) *wny*	402
21.8	Selection of Judahite coins	403
21.9	Edomite *rb' šqln*	406
22.1	The Sanctuary of Pan (Banias) at Mount Hermon	412
22.2	Administrative Building at Kedesh	413
22.3	Third-century BCE imported household goods from Tel Dor	416
22.4	Civic sealings from the archive of the Administrative Building at Kedesh	419
22.5	A Tanit sealing from the archive of the Administrative Building at Kedesh	420
22.6	Hellenistic sanctuary and fortified enclosure on Mount Gerizim	421
22.7	Household pottery from late second-century BCE Jerusalem	423
22.8	A reconstruction of the painted plastered wall in the dining room from the villa at Tel Anafa (ca. 100 BCE)	424
23.1	The "Mona Lisa of the Galilee"	440
23.2	First-century CE Jewish ossuaries	443
23.3	Palestinian Bag Jar and Gaza Jar	445
23.4	Mold-made discus lamp with a goat and a tree from Israel	446
23.5	Camp F at Masada	448
23.6	The remnants of the Roman aqueduct at Caesarea Maritima	452
23.7	The hypocausts under the floor of the Herodian-period bath at Masada	454
24.1	At Yavneh-Yam, an amphora, storage jar, and cooking pot reused as sunken storage facilities in a room's floor	465
24.2	At Yavneh-Yam, (1, 2) amphora bases, one with a drilled hole, reused as stoppers; and (3) an upper section of a storage jar, reused as a funnel	466
24.3	A plan of the watchtower/booth and selected ceramic finds from Nahal Yattir	467
24.4	Winepress and selected ceramic and metal finds at Tirat Karmel	469
24.5	A plan of the fort and two spindle whorls found in it at Yotvata	472
25.1	Map of Islamic-period sites mentioned in the text	479
25.2	HMGPW jug from Khirbat Nuqayb al-Asaymir	485
27.1	Animal domestication from a southern Levantine perspective	513
29.1	Location of main copper ore districts of the southern Levant and other places mentioned in the text	540
29.2	Generalized early Iron Age (twelfth–ninth centuries BCE) *chaînes opératoires* for copper production in the Aravah Valley	542
29.3	Copper content in slag from the Aravah Valley	542
30.1	Interactions in a harbor scene, tomb of Kenamun	554
31.1	Modeled radiocarbon determinations for Tel Yarmouth	579

31.2	Modeled radiocarbon determinations for Tell Fadous-Kfarabida	581
31.3	Modeled phase transitions for Tel Rehov	585
31.4	Modeled radiocarbon determinations for Khirbet Qeiyafa	586
32.1	Plan of Bab adh-Dhra' Shaft Tomb A 72	597
32.2	A typical Early Bronze Age tomb group from Bab adh-Dhra'	598
32.3	Early Bronze Age vessel at The Oriental Institute from Bab adh-Dhra' Tomb Group A 72NW	603
32.4	Looters' tools at the Early Bronze Age site of Fifa	606
32.5	Buff-colored Early Bronze Age pots	607
32.6	Early Bronze Age pot from the "age of the patriarchs and matriarchs" in a Jerusalem shop window	608
33.1	The first display of Neolithic statues from 'Ain Ghazal	625
33.2	Inside the Archaeological Museum of Jordan	626
33.3	Students observing and discussing images on pottery theater tickets	627
33.4	Students trying on Roman togas with the help of their teacher	627

TABLES

1.1	Southern Levant Lower and Middle Paleolithic chronometric dates from Tabun Cave	*page* 15
3.1	Chronology of Epipaleolithic and Pre-Pottery Neolithic periods in the southern Levant	48
5.1	Types of fuels used in the operation of hearths (Paleolithic to historic periods) and ovens (historic periods)	91
6.1	Very preliminary sketch of the chronology for the main "periods" in the seventh and sixth millennia BCE	100
8.1	The total number of samples, specimens, and taxa at Tel Tsaf, Shiqmim, and Marj Rabba	149
8.2	Fuel choice at Tel Tsaf, Shiqmim, and Marj Rabba, given in milliliters (ml)	150
8.3	A summary of the archaeobotanical remains found at Tel Tsaf, Shiqmim, and Marj Rabba	153
9.1	Early Bronze Age IA–III characteristics and chronology	165
9.2	Characteristics of EB IB–III slow urbanism or townism	179
11.1	A sampling of sites with commingled interments of at least 50 individuals in Israel, Palestine, and Jordan	203
11.2	Time periods for study sites, as determined for each excavation	205
15.1	Selected radiocarbon dates from terminal Late Bronze Age III/early Iron I contexts	286
15.2	Radiocarbon dates from middle Iron Age I contexts	287
15.3	Radiocarbon dates from late Iron Age I contexts	287
24.1	Summary of ceramics' reuse practices in Late Roman, Byzantine, and Early Islamic Palestine	461
27.1	A schematic summary showing the evolution of domestication, livestock husbandry, and hunting over time	515
29.1	Iron Age socio-technological systems in the Aravah Valley	544
33.1	List of 18 archaeological museums in Jordan	624

TABLES

1.1	Southern Levant Lower and Middle Paleolithic chronometric dates from Tabun Cave	*page* 15
3.1	Chronology of Epipaleolithic and Pre-Pottery Neolithic periods in the southern Levant	48
5.1	Types of fuels used in the operation of hearths (Paleolithic to historic periods) and ovens (historic periods)	91
6.1	Very preliminary sketch of the chronology for the main "periods" in the seventh and sixth millennia BCE	100
8.1	The total number of samples, specimens, and taxa at Tel Tsaf, Shiqmim, and Marj Rabba	149
8.2	Fuel choice at Tel Tsaf, Shiqmim, and Marj Rabba, given in milliliters (ml)	150
8.3	A summary of the archaeobotanical remains found at Tel Tsaf, Shiqmim, and Marj Rabba	153
9.1	Early Bronze Age IA–III characteristics and chronology	165
9.2	Characteristics of EB IB–III slow urbanism or townism	179
11.1	A sampling of sites with commingled interments of at least 50 individuals in Israel, Palestine, and Jordan	203
11.2	Time periods for study sites, as determined for each excavation	205
15.1	Selected radiocarbon dates from terminal Late Bronze Age III/early Iron I contexts	286
15.2	Radiocarbon dates from middle Iron Age I contexts	287
15.3	Radiocarbon dates from late Iron Age I contexts	287
24.1	Summary of ceramics' reuse practices in Late Roman, Byzantine, and Early Islamic Palestine	461
27.1	A schematic summary showing the evolution of domestication, livestock husbandry, and hunting over time	515
29.1	Iron Age socio-technological systems in the Aravah Valley	544
33.1	List of 18 archaeological museums in Jordan	624

TABLES

1.1	Southern Levant Lower and Middle Paleolithic chronometric dates from Tabun Cave	page 15
3.1	Chronology of Epipaleolithic and Pre-Pottery Neolithic periods in the southern Levant	48
5.1	Types of fuels used in the operation of hearths (Paleolithic to historic periods) and ovens (historic periods)	91
6.1	Very preliminary sketch of the chronology for the main "periods" in the seventh and sixth millennia BCE	100
8.1	The total number of samples, specimens, and taxa at Tel Tsaf, Shiqmim, and Marj Rabba	149
8.2	Fuel choice at Tel Tsaf, Shiqmim, and Marj Rabba, given in milliliters (ml)	150
8.3	A summary of the archaeobotanical remains found at Tel Tsaf, Shiqmim, and Marj Rabba	153
9.1	Early Bronze Age IA–III characteristics and chronology	165
9.2	Characteristics of EB IB–III slow urbanism or townism	179
11.1	A sampling of sites with commingled interments of at least 50 individuals in Israel, Palestine, and Jordan	203
11.2	Time periods for study sites, as determined for each excavation	205
15.1	Selected radiocarbon dates from terminal Late Bronze Age III/early Iron I contexts	286
15.2	Radiocarbon dates from middle Iron Age I contexts	287
15.3	Radiocarbon dates from late Iron Age I contexts	287
24.1	Summary of ceramics' reuse practices in Late Roman, Byzantine, and Early Islamic Palestine	461
27.1	A schematic summary showing the evolution of domestication, livestock husbandry, and hunting over time	515
29.1	Iron Age socio-technological systems in the Aravah Valley	544
33.1	List of 18 archaeological museums in Jordan	624

CONTRIBUTORS

Arwa Badran, MA International Cultural Heritage Program, Archaeology Department, Durham University, United Kingdom

Edward B. Banning, Department of Anthropology, University of Toronto, Canada

Anna Belfer-Cohen, The Institute of Archaeology, The Hebrew University of Jerusalem, Israel

Erez Ben-Yosef, Jacob M. Alkow Department of Archaeology and Ancient Near Eastern Cultures, Tel Aviv University, Israel

Andrea M. Berlin, Department of Archaeology, Boston University, USA

Stephanie L. Budin, Independent researcher, USA

Shlomo Bunimovitz, Jacob M. Alkow Department of Archaeology and Ancient Near Eastern Cultures, Tel Aviv University, Israel

Meredith S. Chesson, Department of Anthropology, University of Notre Dame, USA

Eric H. Cline, Department of Classical and Near Eastern Languages and Civilizations, The George Washington University, USA

Susan L. Cohen, Department of History and Philosophy, Montana State University, USA

Yoram Cohen, Jacob M. Alkow Department of Archaeology and Ancient Near Eastern Cultures, Tel Aviv University, Israel

Avraham Faust, The Martin (Szusz) Department of Land of Israel Studies and Archaeology, Bar-Ilan University, Israel

Bill Finlayson, Council for British Research in the Levant, United Kingdom

Nigel Goring-Morris, The Institute of Archaeology, The Hebrew University of Jerusalem, Israel

Philip Graham, Department of Anthropology, University of Connecticut, USA

Leore Grosman, Institute of Archaeology, The Hebrew University of Jerusalem, Israel

Felix Höflmayer, Institute for Oriental and European Archaeology, Austrian Academy of Sciences, Austria

David Ilan, Nelson Glueck School of Biblical Archaeology, Hebrew Union College–Jewish Institute of Religion, Israel

Ian W. N. Jones, Levantine and Cyber-Archaeology Laboratory, University of California, San Diego, USA

Morag M. Kersel, Department of Anthropology, DePaul University, USA

Rabei G. Khamisy, The Zinman Institute of Archaeology, University of Haifa, Israel

Aren M. Maeir, The Martin (Szusz) Department of Land of Israel Studies and Archaeology, Bar-Ilan University, Israel

Nimrod Marom, Laboratory of Archaeozoology, The Zinman Institute of Archaeology, University of Haifa, Israel

Daniel M. Master, Department of Biblical & Theological Studies, Wheaton College, USA

Natalie D. Munro, Department of Anthropology, University of Connecticut, USA

Benjamin W. Porter, Phoebe A. Hearst Museum of Anthropology, University of California, Berkeley, USA

Alexandra L. Ratzlaff, Department of Maritime Civilizations, Laboratory for Coastal Archaeology and Underwater Survey, University of Haifa, Israel

Gary O. Rollefson, Department of Anthropology, Whitman College, USA

Christopher A. Rollston, Department of Classical and Near Eastern Languages and Civilizations, The George Washington University, USA

Yorke M. Rowan, The Oriental Institute of The University of Chicago, USA

Ruth Shahack-Gross, Department of Maritime Civilizations, Leon H. Charney School of Marine Sciences, University of Haifa, Israel

Sariel Shalev, The Zinman Institute of Archaeology, University of Haifa, Israel

Susan Guise Sheridan, Department of Anthropology, University of Notre Dame, USA

Katharina Streit, The Institute of Archaeology, The Hebrew University of Jerusalem, Israel

Oren Tal, Jacob M. Alkow Department of Archaeology and Ancient Near Eastern Cultures, Tel Aviv University, Israel

Itamar Taxel, Pottery Specializations Branch, Archaeological Research Department, Israel Antiquities Authority, Israel

Assaf Yasur-Landau, Department of Maritime Civilizations, Leon H. Charney School of Marine Sciences, University of Haifa, Israel

FOREWORD
Past Forward: The Social Archaeology of the Levant

When the distinguished anthropological archaeologist Kent Flannery kindly wrote an introduction to the 1998 version of my edited book, *The Archaeology of Society in the Holy Land*, he began by saying, "I once bet $100 that the Old Testament would never meet the New Archaeology. Now, thanks to the authors of this volume, I have lost my bet" (1998: xvii). I think it is fair to say that over the past several decades, Levantine archaeology has indeed met processual and social archaeology (and other archaeologies!), and embraced it in so many positive dimensions as reflected in this Cambridge University Press book. However, I'm not a gambler, so I won't make a bet on how *The Social Archaeology of the Levant: From Prehistory to the Present* successfully moves the field forward as we near the end of the second decade of the twenty-first century. This will be up to the readers of Assaf Yasur-Landau, Eric Cline, and Yorke Rowan's impressive edited volume, perhaps best done in a future blog discussion. To measure the book's success, I believe readers should consider five interrelated research themes that Levantine archaeologists must focus on to make our field relevant as we move forward. These include: (1) social archaeology and transdisciplinary research, (2) science and historical biblical archaeology, (3) cyber-archaeology and the information technology revolution, (4) high-precision dating, and (5) climate and environmental change. Below are some reflections that may and may not have been achieved in the wide-ranging book in your hands, and where we might go in the future. For me, social archaeology aims at the "big picture" of what happens in society, how it happened, how it changes, and how it is reflected in the archaeological (material culture) record. It is not about historical individuals in the archaeological record (they are so hard to identify there), but rather social archaeology goes from the static archaeological record (to borrow Lewis Binford's [1983] metaphor) to the dynamics of culture. With this model, it is possible to perhaps place historical figures or their acts in the archaeological record in the context of trying to explain culture change through time. To generate new data and new interpretive models of the past, the best approach is one rooted in transdisciplinary research, that is, basically team science. Accordingly, researchers contribute their unique expertise to the transdisciplinary project but work outside of their own discipline. By taking a true team approach, transdisciplinary researchers work outside their "comfort zone," transcend their own discipline, and work with others to understand the complexity of a given problem.

SOCIAL ARCHAEOLOGY AND TRANSDISCIPLINARY RESEARCH

To succeed in "pushing the envelope" of scientific advancement in the archaeology of the southern Levant (and science and archaeology is the way to go), large grants are needed from organizations, such as the National Science Foundation (NSF) in the United States, the Israel Science Foundation, the European Research Council (ERC), TED Prize, the National Research Council Canada, the Austrian Academy of Sciences, and other large funding organizations to bring researchers together on specific research problems. Some of these large projects have helped move research in new positive directions that fulfill the aims of social archaeology. They also transcend the historical particularist story of archaeology in the Holy Land by making our field an important contributor to global archaeology as witnessed in Levantine archaeology publications that appear in journals such as *Nature*, *Proceedings of the National Academy of Science*, *PLOS ONE*, and many others. By working closely together as teams on an archaeological, paleoenvironmental, or ancient historical problem, where specialist studies are not relegated to the appendices of archaeological monographs but rather play a fully integrated role in the formulation of the project research design, new and exciting advances in theory and method can be achieved.

SCIENCE AND HISTORICAL BIBLICAL ARCHAEOLOGY

The European Research Council Advanced Grant, entitled "Reconstructing Ancient Israel: The Exact and Life Sciences Perspective" and awarded to Israel Finkelstein and Steve Weiner, involved about forty researchers and had a very positive impact on helping to move historical biblical archaeology toward the adoption of science-based methods for investigating a field that was traditionally dominated by an historical particularist perspective focused on the Old Testament/Hebrew Bible (Finkelstein, Weiner, and Boaretto 2015). This transdisciplinary project expanded beyond the periods closely linked to the Hebrew Bible (Middle Bronze to Iron Ages [ca. 2,200–586 BCE]) and included Early Bronze Age studies linked to the first urban revolution in the Levant through later periods. Research advances in geoarchaeology (Shahack-Gross and Finkelstein 2015), epigraphy (Faigenbaum-Golovin et al. 2016), archaeometallurgy (Yahalom-Mack et al. 2014), ancient DNA (Meiri et al. 2013), paleoclimate (Langgut, Finkelstein, and Litt 2013; Langgut et al. 2014; 2015), radiocarbon dating (Mazar and Bronk Ramsey 2010; Toffolo et al. 2014), and foodways (zooarchaeology [Sapir-Hen et al. 2013], paleobotany) were achieved, helping move the field beyond the confines of the important but narrow field of biblical archaeology, so that science and historical biblical archaeology now play a role in global archaeology. By funding doctoral students and post-docs, this grant has been a positive force in changing the character of Israeli archaeology (whose research dominates the field of Levantine archaeology today) from a nationalist endeavor to one that intersects with the global community for periods most closely linked to historical biblical archaeology.

The University of California, San Diego NSF Integrative Graduate Education and Research Traineeship (IGERT) grant mentioned below marshaled together a transdisciplinary team of archaeologists, radiocarbon dating specialists, paleomagnetic dating specialists, computer scientists, Egyptologists, archaeometallurgists, and others to tackle the problem of the rise of Iron Age complex societies in the region of biblical Edom in southern Jordan as seen through the lens of ancient metallurgical craft specialization. The work in southern Jordan has been carried out in collaboration with Mohammad Najjar for over 20 years. While this transdisciplinary research project aimed at creating "cultural heritage engineers," excitement grew in great part around the application of information technology and telecommunications to the field of archaeology and, in particular, Levantine archaeology, where the main field sites for applying these methods took place. This inspired me to lead our team in helping to develop the nascent field of "cyber-archaeology" (Levy et al. 2010; Levy 2013).

As Levantine archaeologists move forward, melding science-based research with the social investigation of the traditional domain of biblical archaeology, a more pragmatic approach is needed. Working with a number of empirical Levantine archaeologists, I proposed that we "re-brand" this subfield of Levantine archaeology "historical biblical archaeology" (Levy 2010; Levy [ed.] 2010) and embed it with new advances in cyber-archaeology. This is rooted more in an inductive approach to material culture data, where patterns in time and space reveal the realities of what happened in the past.

CYBER-ARCHAEOLOGY AND THE INFORMATION TECHNOLOGY REVOLUTION

Cyber-archaeology is a relatively new field that melds archaeology with computer science, engineering, and the natural sciences, taking advantage of continuing developments in information technology and telecommunications. However, it is the anthropological, archaeological, and historical questions that drive cyber-archaeology. Transdisciplinary research teams at the University of California, San Diego, led by me and my research collaborators, Thomas DeFanti and Falko Kuester, have been able to develop new tools for digital data capture, curation, analyses, and dissemination of archaeological data in high-resolution 2D and 3D virtual reality platforms, the Internet, and high-speed fiber optic networks. The stimuli for this transdisciplinary research have been two major research grants: a NSF grant (2010–2015) for Training, Research and Education in Engineering for Cultural Heritage Diagnostics (TEECH), where most of the archaeological testing took place in Jordan's biblical Edom region; and a University of California Office of the President (UCOP) Catalyst Grant titled "At-Risk World Heritage and the Digital Humanities" that brought together four University of California archaeologists working in the Middle East to apply the cyber-archaeology model to at-risk sites in the most vulnerable places of the region today.

The cyber-archaeology workflow developed by the team has had a positive influence on Levantine archaeology for on-site data recording using a real-time GIS data recording program called ArchField (Smith and Levy 2012; 2014; Smith et al. 2015) and a web-based excavation database called *ArchaeoSTOR* (Matsui et al. 2012; Gidding et al. 2013; Gidding, Levy, and DeFanti 2014). Solutions to "Big Data" problems, such as MedArchNet and the *Digital Archaeology Atlas of the Holy Land* (with Steve Savage), were developed that provide an online geo-spatial database for over 40,000 sites, including metadata from the Lower Paleolithic to Ottoman period to facilitate spatial analyses and conservation of sites (Savage and Levy 2014) (https://daahl.ucsd.edu/DAAHL/). We have partnered with the Israel Antiquities Authority, who has provided all their Israel Survey data and that of greater Jerusalem for the DAAHL database. To help ASOR's Cultural Heritage Initiatives in the Middle East, TerraWatchers, an online crowd-sourcing program, was developed to monitor at-risk sites in the Levant and Iraq (Savage, Johnson, and Levy 2017). This involved rigorous training of undergraduate students in how to interpret satellite imagery for evidence of site damage. The development of permanent archaeological data repositories at research universities through the Digital Collections model (cf. https://library.ucsd.edu/dc/collection/bb41653353) and CAVEbase (McFarland et al. 2017), a university research library-based online program to store and access 3D images, videos, and models for viewing in large-scale virtual reality or personal virtual reality devices, make these data freely available to researchers and the public (Knabb et al. 2014).[1] Both of these virtual reality platforms help to "democratize" public access to at-risk heritage sites in the Middle East. As described here, advances in cyber-archaeology have helped Levantine archaeology play an important role in global issues of cultural heritage conservation, curation, and new ways of analyzing data to solve social archaeology issues.

HIGH-PRECISION DATING

Levantine archaeology has been a key player in the adoption and implementation of high-precision radiocarbon dating and Bayesian analyses. This has been used in two rather diametrically opposed ways: to "prove" the validity of different chronological paradigms, for example, a traditional "high" chronology or alternative "low" chronology for the Iron Age tenth century BCE, which is linked to issues concerning the historicity of biblical kings (David and Solomon); or measuring rates of culture change in the southern Levant, and how more precise dating frameworks relate to processes of change. Chronological debates using high-precision radiocarbon dating are not limited to the Iron Age and have emerged for Early Bronze Age research with issues concerning the rise of urbanism, as well as the Late Bronze Age in the eastern Mediterranean that focuses on the Thera eruption and its relationship with regional chronologies in Greece, Egypt, and the Levant. Major long-term archaeological research projects in Israel and Jordan have devoted significant funding to solving chronological problems and represent important achievements over the past two decades; these need to be continued as an integral part of all future research to test archaeological models from whatever theoretical perspective.

The key to establishing accurate chronologies is to treat all archaeological sites with the excavation methodology used in prehistory – that is, have no preconceived chronological preconception, such as the "low" chronology for the Iron Age of the southern Levant (e.g., Finkelstein 2005). A case in point for applying this objective approach is our deep-time study of ancient mining and metallurgy in the Feinan copper ore resource zone of southern Jordan that spans the Neolithic to medieval Islamic periods (Levy and Najjar 2007). From 1997 to 2001, our work concentrated primarily on the Pre-Pottery Neolithic B to Early Bronze Age IV periods. In 2002, we began work on the Iron Age and assumed that the prevailing chronological model was correct: The Iron Age in southern Jordan (biblical Edom) began very late in the seventh and sixth centuries BCE, and there was no evidence of earlier tenth–twelfth-century BCE occupation in lowlands of Edom and Feinan. Our excavations followed the methodology of pre- and proto-historic archaeology – careful stratigraphic excavations and large open-air exposures to achieve a social picture of Iron Age metalworking populations in the region (Levy, Najjar, and Ben-Yosef 2014). Material culture, including ceramics, scarabs, and other classes of artifacts, were typologically classified and spatially studied according to locus and stratum, and carefully dated with over 130 high-precision radiocarbon dates coupled with Bayesian analyses (Levy et al. 2008; Levy, Najjar, and Ben-Yosef 2014) and paleomagnetic dating methods (Ben-Yosef et al. 2008; 2009). After the first season of excavation at the massive copper production site of Khirbat en-Nahas, we were surprised to find that occupation (by local Edomite populations) peaked during the tenth and ninth centuries BCE, when copper production and building activities were carried out on an industrial scale (Levy et al. 2004). By the time the final publication appeared for our Iron Age studies in Fayan (Levy et al. 2014), the data provided conclusive evidence that the social organization of these local tenth–ninth-century BCE Iron Age polities went beyond the chiefdom level of social integration and was closest to small-scale, archaic state-level societies.

Using this same excavation, recording, and analytical methodology, Erez Ben-Yosef's (2016) team, working in Israel's Timna' Valley, has defined the same chronological framework for Iron Age copper production sites there – some 105 km south of contemporary Feinan. Working on the Early Bronze Age of the Arabah/Aravah Valley, Ben-Yosef's team and ours collaborated to define a new chronology or chronological paradigm for this period in this part of the southern Levant (Ben-Yosef et al. 2016). This high-precision radiocarbon dating project supported the new Early Bronze Age chronology for the greater southern Levant and was spear-headed by Johanna Regev (Regev et al. 2012; Regev, Miroschedji, and Boaretto 2012). New advances in Levantine archaeology chronological studies that couple a variety of methods, such as radiocarbon dating (Levy et al. 2008), paleomagnetic dating (Ben-Yosef et al. 2008), optically stimulated luminescence dating (Davidovich et al. 2014), uranium-thorium dating (Cramer et al. 2017), Bayesian analyses, and others methods, will provide social archaeologists with more accurate ways of measuring social change than was previously possible.

CLIMATE AND ENVIRONMENTAL CHANGE

Today, one of the most pressing international problems is the issue of climate and environmental change, and Levantine archaeologists and their transdisciplinary teams are contributing to this international research effort (Issar and Zohar 2007; Rosen 2007; McMichael 2012; Langgut, Finkelstein, and Litt 2013; Smith and Zeder 2013; Langgut et al. 2015; Ramsey, Rosen, and Nadel 2017). This is an area of research to which only archaeology is capable of contributing the appropriate datasets that integrate human and environmental systems across time and space.[2] The southern Levant, situated as a land bridge between the continents of Africa and Asia, has always been the focal point of social, economic, and environmental interaction. To test the resilience of social groups to climate and environmental change from the Pleistocene to Holocene, the coastal settings (Sideris et al. 2017; Levy et al. 2018; Lazar et al. 2018) of archaeological sites in the Levant and eastern Mediterranean will provide the ideal locus for examining these issues in "deep-time." In many respects, the last great frontier for exploration, especially with regard to climate and environmental change, are the coastal and submerged landscapes of the Holocene. For the southern Levant, this means the eastern Mediterranean stretching across the Sinai Desert to the Red Sea region. Land and sea projects, such as those carried out in the Gulf of Corinth in Greece (Levy et al 2018), micro-contextual analyses associated with ancient wrecks (Demesticha 2018), and the shallow bays around Tel Dor on Israel's Mediterranean coast (Lazar et al. 2017) provide models for moving in this direction.

CONCLUDING THOUGHTS

Time and space are archaeology's most precious commodities. The control of time through high-precision radiocarbon dating, artifact typologies using advances in the application of mathematics and informatics for more precise relative dating, and new developments in other radiometric methods, such as uranium-thorium dating, provide the essential time-scales for measuring social interaction at the local, regional, and trans-regional levels to investigate the social archaeology of the southern Levant. The control of space – that is, the context of archaeological phenomenon that gives ultimate meaning to the archaeological record – is achieved through advances in digital data capture, curation, and dissemination to facilitate accurate analyses and comparative studies that lead to understanding the dynamics of ancient societies. Where then are the new frontiers of social archaeology in the Holy Land? Geographically, the changing and evolving submerged coastal zones provide *terra incognita* for discovering "lost" archaeological periods and the investigation of global issues of climate and environmental change. Terrestrially, while hundreds of archaeological surveys and excavations have taken place in the Levant and neighboring areas, new insights can be achieved by improving the spatial and temporal resolution of our observations by carrying out more intensive field surveys over smaller geographic distances with the aim of achieving 100 percent coverage to provide better databases for model testing. Similarly, rather than "go large" with extensive excavations, as we move into the future, why not "go micro" with smaller excavation areas, but with the aim of retrieving much larger microarchaeological data samples related to ancient economy and trade, social organization, ideology and religion, subsistence, and technology in relation to changes in climate and environment through time? Another challenge is how can we integrate archaeological legacy data given the advances in dating, data capture, curation, analyses, and dissemination noted above?

Thomas E. Levy
San Diego, California, USA

NOTES

[1] To help make this a reality, the project installed six-panel 3D display systems at four University of California campus libraries and museums in San Diego, Merced, Berkeley, and Los Angeles (http://ucsdnews.ucsd.edu/pressrelease/new_3_d_cavekiosk_at_uc_san_diego_brings_cyber_archaeology_to_geisel).

2 Perhaps the most famous case was presented for ancient agricultural methods related to run-off farming in the Negev Desert in the late 1950s and early 1960s and the reconstruction of Nabataean farms in the central Negev (Evenari et al. 1961; Evenari, Shanan, and Tadmor 1982).

REFERENCES

Ben-Yosef, E. 2016. Back to Solomon's Era: Results of the First Excavations at "Slaves' Hill" (Site 34, Timna, Israel). *BASOR* 376: 169–98.

Ben-Yosef, E.; Gidding, A.; Tauxe, L.; Davidovich, U.; Najjar, M.; and Levy, T. E. 2016. Early Bronze Age Copper Production Systems in the Northern Arabah Valley: New Insights from Archaeomagnetic Study of Slag Deposits in Jordan and Israel. *JAS* 72: 71–84.

Ben-Yosef, E.; Tauxe, L.; Levy, T. E.; Shaar, R.; Ron, H.; and Najjar, M. 2009. Archaeomagnetic Intensity Spike Recorded in High Resolution Slag Deposit from Historical Biblical Archaeology Site in Southern Jordan. *EPSL* 287: 529–39.

Ben-Yosef, E.; Tauxe, L.; Ron, H.; Agnon, A.; Avner, U.; Najjar, M.; and Levy, T. E. 2008. A New Approach for Geomagnetic Archaeointensity Research: Insights on Ancient Metallurgy in the Southern Levant. *JAS* 35: 2863–79.

Binford, L. R. 1983. *In Pursuit of the Past: Decoding the Archaeological Record*. New York: Thames & Hudson.

Cramer, K. L.; O'Dea, A.; Clark, T. R.; Zhao, J.-X.; and Norris, R. D. 2017. Prehistorical and Historical Declines in Caribbean Coral Reef Accretion Rates Driven by Loss of Parrotfish. *Nature Communications* 8. doi:10.1038/ncomms14160.

Davidovich, U.; Goldsmith, Y.; Porat, R.; and Porat, N. 2014. Dating and Interpreting Desert Structures: The Enclosures of the Judean Desert, Southern Levant, Re-Evaluated. *Archaeometry* 56: 878–97.

Demesticha, S. 2018. Cutting a Long Story Short? Underwater and Maritime Archaeology in Cyprus. *JEMAHS* 6: 62–78.

Evenari, M.; Shanan, L.; and Tadmor, N. 1982. *The Negev — The Challenge of a Desert*. 2nd ed. Cambridge, MA: Harvard University Press.

Evenari, M.; Shanan, L.; Tadmor, N.; and Aharoni, Y. 1961. Ancient Agriculture in the Negev. *Science* 133: 976–96.

Faigenbaum-Golovin, S.; Shaus, A.; Sober, B.; Levin, D.; Na'aman, N.; Sass, B.; Turkel, E.; Piasetzky, E.; and Finkelstein, I. 2016. Algorithmic Handwriting Analysis of Judah's Military Correspondence Sheds Light on Composition of Biblical Texts. *PNAS* 113: 4664–9.

Finkelstein, I. 2005. A Low Chronology Update: Archaeology, History and Bible. In *The Bible and Radiocarbon Dating: Archaeology, Text and Science*, ed. T. E. Levy and T. F. G. Higham. London: Equinox: 31–42.

Finkelstein, I.; Weiner, S.; and Boaretto, E. 2015. Preface — The Iron Age in Israel: The Exact and Life Sciences Perspectives. *Radiocarbon* 57: 197–206.

Gidding, A.; Levy, T. E.; and DeFanti, T. A. 2014. ArchaeoSTOR: The Development and Utilization of a Web-Based Database for the Field and Lab. *NEA* 77: 198–202.

Gidding, A.; Matsui, Y.; Levy, T. E.; DeFanti, T. A.; and Kuester, F. 2013. ArchaeoSTOR: A Data Curation System for Research on the Archeological Frontier. *Future Generation Computer Systems* 29: 2117–27.

Issar, A. S., and Zohar, M. 2007. *Climate Change: Environment and History of the Near East.* 2nd ed. Berlin: Springer.

Knabb, K. A.; Schulze, J. P.; Kuester, F.; DeFanti, T. A.; and Levy, T. E. 2014. Scientific Visualization, 3D Immersive Virtual Realtiy Environments, and Archaeology in Jordan and the Near East. *NEA* 77: 228–32.

Langgut, D.; Finkelstein, I.; and Litt, T. 2013. Climate and the Late Bronze Collapse: New Evidence from the Southern Levant. *TA* 40: 149–75.

Langgut, D.; Finkelstein, I.; Litt, T.; Neumann, F. H.; and Stein, M. 2015. Vegetation and Climate Changes during the Bronze and Iron Ages (∼3600–600 BCE) in the Southern Levant Based on Palynological Records. *Radiocarbon* 57: 217–35.

Langgut, D.; Neumann, F. H.; Stein, M.; Wagner, A.; Kagan, E. J.; Boaretto, E.; and Finkelstein, I. 2014. Dead Sea Pollen Record and History of Human Activity in the Judean Highlands (Israel) from the Intermediate Bronze into the Iron Ages (∼2500–500 BCE). *Palynology* 38: 280–302.

Lazar, M.; Engoltz, K.; Basson, U.; and Yasur-Landau, A. 2018. Water Saturated Sand and a Shallow Bay: Combining Coastal Geophysics and Underwater Archaeology in the South Bay of Tel Dor. *QI* 473A: 112–19.

Levy, T. E. 1998. *The Archaeology of Society in the Holy Land.* NAAA. London: Leicester University Press.

——— 2010. The New Pragmatism: Integrating Anthropological, Digital, and Historical Biblical Archaeologies. In *Historical Biblical Archaeology and the Future: The New Pragmatism,* ed. T. E. Levy, 3–42. London: Equinox.

——— 2013. Cyber-Archaeology and World Cultural Heritage: Insights from the Holy Land. *Bulletin of the American Academy of Arts & Sciences* 66: 26–33.

Levy, T. E., ed. 2010. *Historical Biblical Archaeology and the Future: The New Pragmatism.* London: Equinox.

Levy, T. E.; Adams, R. B.; Najjar, M.; Hauptmann, A.; Anderson, J. D.; Brandl, B.; Robinson, M. A.; and Higham, T. 2004. Reassessing the Chronology of Biblical Edom: New Excavations and ^{14}C Dates from Khirbat en-Nahas (Jordan). *Antiquity* 78: 863–79.

Levy, T. E.; Higham, T.; Bronk Ramsey, C.; Smith, N. G.; Ben-Yosef, E.; Robinson, M.; Münger, S.; Knabb, K.; Schulze, J. P.; Najjar, M.; and Tauxe, L. 2008. High-Precision Radiocarbon Dating and Historical Biblical Archaeology in Southern Jordan. *PNAS* 105: 16460–5.

Levy, T. E., and Najjar, M. 2007. Ancient Metal Production and Social Change in Southern Jordan: The Edom Lowlands Regional Archaeology Project and Hope for a UNESCO World Heritage Site in Faynan. In *Crossing Jordan: North American Contributions to the Archaeology of Jordan,* ed. T. E. Levy, P. M. M. Daviau, R. W. Younker, and M. Shaer, 97–105. London: Equinox.

Levy, T. E.; Najjar, M.; and Ben-Yosef, E., eds. 2014. *New Insights into the Iron Age Archaeology of Edom, Southern Jordan: Surveys, Excavations and Research from the University of California, San Diego — Department of Antiquities of Jordan, Edom Lowlands Regional Archaeology Project (ELRAP).* 2 vols. MonArch 35. Los Angeles: The Cotsen Institute of Archaeology Press.

Levy, T. E.; Najjar, M.; Higham, T.; Arbel, Y.; Muniz, A.; Ben-Yosef, E.; Smith, N. G.; Beherec, M.; Gidding, A.; Jones, I. W. N.; Frese, D.; Smitheram, C.; and Robinson, M. 2014. Excavations at Khirbat en-Nahas, 2002–2009: An Iron Age Copper Production Center in the Lowlands of Edom. In *New Insights into the Iron Age*

Archaeology of Edom, Southern Jordan: Surveys, Excavations and Research from the University of California, San Diego — Department of Antiquities of Jordan, Edom Lowlands Regional Archaeology Project (ELRAP), Vol. 1, ed. T. E. Levy, M. Najjar, and E. Ben-Yosef, 89–245. MonArch 35. Los Angeles: The Cotsen Institute of Archaeology Press.

Levy, T. E.; Petrovic, V.; Wypych, T.; Gidding, A.; Knabb, K.; Hernandez, D.; Smith, N. G.; Schulz, J. P.; Savage, S. H.; Kuester, F.; Ben-Yosef, E.; Buitenhuys, C.; Barrett, C. J.; Najjar, M.; and DeFanti, T. 2010. On-Site Digital Archaeology 3.0 and Cyber-Archaeology: Into the Future of the Past — New Developments, Delivery and the Creation of a Data Avalanche. In *Cyber-Archaeology*, ed. M. Forte, 135–53. BAR International Series 2177. Oxford: Archaeopress.

Levy, T. E.; Sideris, T.; Howland, M.; Liss, B.; Tsokas, G.; Stambolidis, A.; Fikos, E.; Vargemezis, G.; Tsourlos, P.; Georgopoulos, A.; Papatheodorou, G.; Garaga, M.; Christodoulou, D.; Norris, R.; Rivera-Collazo, I.; and Liritzis, I. 2018. At-Risk World Heritage, Cyber, and Marine Archaeology: The Kastrouli–Antikyra Bay Land and Sea Project, Phokis, Greece. In *Cyber-Archaeology and Grand Narratives: Digitial Technology and Deep-Time Perspectives on Culture Change in the Middle East*, ed. T. E. Levy and I. W. N. Jones, 143–234. OWA. New York: Springer.

Matsui, Y.; Gidding, A.; Levy, T. E.; Kuester, F.; and DeFanti, T. A. 2012. ArchaeoSTOR Map: Publishing Archaeological Geodata on the Web. In *COM.Geo '12: Proceedings of the 3rd International Conference on Computing for Geospatial Research and Applications, Washington, D.C., USA, July 01–03, 2012*. ACM International Conference Proceedings Series. New York: Association for Computing Machinery.

Mazar, A., and Bronk Ramsey, C. 2010. A Response to Finkelstein and Piasetzky's Criticism and "New Perspective." *Radiocarbon* 52: 1681–8.

McFarland, C.; DeFanti, T.; Levy, T. E.; and Kuester, F. 2017. CAVEBase: Preserving and Accessing Digital Cultural Heritage through 3D Virtual Reality Environments; Case Studies from the Eastern Mediterranean. Presented at the Annual Meeting of ASOR, Boston, MA.

McMichael, A. J. 2012. Insights from Past Millennia into Climatic Impacts on Human Health and Survival. *PNAS* 109: 4730–7.

Meiri, M.; Huchon, D.; Bar-Oz, G.; Boaretto, E.; Horwitz, L. K.; Maeir, A. M.; Sapir-Hen, L.; Larson, G.; Weiner, S.; and Finkelstein, I. 2013. Ancient DNA and Population Turnover in Southern Levantine Pigs — Signature of the Sea Peoples Migration? *Scientific Reports* 3. doi:10.1038/srep03035.

Ramsey, M. N.; Rosen, A. M.; and Nadel, D. 2017. Centered on the Wetlands: Integrating New Phytolith Evidence of Plant-Use from the 23,000-Year-Old Site of Ohalo II, Israel. *AA* 82: 702–22.

Regev, J.; Miroschedji, P. de; and Boaretto, E. 2012. Early Bronze Age Chronology: Radiocarbon Dates and Chronological Models from Tel Yarmuth (Israel). *Radiocarbon* 54: 505–24.

Regev, J.; Miroschedji, P. de; Greenberg, R.; Braun, E.; Greenhut, Z.; and Boaretto, E. 2012. Chronology of the Early Bronze Age in the South Levant: New Analysis for a High Chronology. *Radiocarbon* 54: 525–66.

Rosen, A. M. 2007. *Civilizing Climate: Social Responses to Climate Change in the Ancient Near East*. Lanham, MD: AltaMira.

Sapir-Hen, L.; Bar-Oz, G.; Gadot, Y.; and Finkelstein, I. 2013. Pig Husbandry in Iron Age Israel and Judah: New Insights Regarding the Origin of the "Taboo." *ZDPV* 129: 1–20.

Savage, S. H.; Johnson, A.; and Levy, T. E. 2017. TerraWatchers, Crowdsourcing, and At-Risk World Heritage in the Middle East. In *Heritage and Archaeology in the DigitalAge: Acquisition, Curation, and Dissemination of Spatial Cultural Heritage Data*, ed. M. L. Vincent, V. M. López-Menchero Bendicho, M. Ioannides, and T. E. Levy, 67–77. Quantitative Methods in the Humanities and Social Sciences. New York: Springer.

Savage, S. H., and Levy, T. E. 2014. DAAHL — The Digital Archaeological Atlas of the Holy Land: A Model for Mediterranean and World Archaeology. *NEA* 77: 243–7.

Shahack-Gross, R., and Finkelstein, I. 2015. Settlement Oscillations in the Negev Highlands Revisited: The Impact of Microarchaeological Methods. *Radiocarbon* 57: 253–64.

Sideris, A.; Liritzis, I.; Liss, B.; Howland, M. D.; and Levy, T. E. 2017. At-Risk Cultural Heritage: New Excavations from the Mycenaean Site of Kastrouli, Phokis, Greece. *Mediterranean Archaeology and Archaeometry* 17: 271–85.

Smith, B. D., and Zeder, M. A. 2013. The Onset of the Anthropocene. *Anthropocene* 4: 8–13.

Smith, N. G.; Howland, M.; and Levy, T. E. 2015. Digital Archaeology Field Recording in the 4th Dimension: ArchField C++ a 4D GIS for Digital Field Work. In *2015 Digital Heritage International Congress (2015 Digital Heritage) Federating the 21st Int'l VSMM, 13th Eurographics GCH: Plus Special Sessions from CIPA ICOMOS/ISPRS Special Heritage Documentation Worskhop, CAA Fall Symposium, 7th Int'l Meeting Arqueólogica 2.0, Space2Place, Archeo Virtual, ICOMOS Digital Interpretation Panel, EU Projects, et al., 28 Sep–2 Oct 2015, Granada, Spain*, Vol. 2, 251–8. Piscataway, NJ: IEEE.

Smith, N. G., and Levy, T. E. 2012. Real-Time 3D Archaeological Field Recording: ArchField, an Open-Source GIS System Pioneered in Jordan. *Antiquity Project Gallery*. http://antiquity.ac.uk/projgall/smith331/ (accessed December 5, 2017).

———. 2014. ArchField in Jordan: Real-Time GIS Data Recording for Archaeological Excavations. *NEA* 77: 166–70.

Toffolo, M. B.; Arie, E.; Martin, M. A. S.; Boaretto, E.; and Finkelstein, I. 2014. Absolute Chronology of Megiddo, Israel, in the Late Bronze and Iron Ages: High-Resolution Radiocarbon Dating. *Radiocarbon* 56: 221–44.

Yahalom-Mack, N.; Galili, E.; Segal, I.; Eliyahu-Behar, A.; Boaretto, E.; Shilstein, S.; and Finkelstein, I. 2014. New Insights into Levantine Copper Trade: Analysis of Ingots from the Bronze and Iron Ages in Israel. *JAS* 45: 159–77.

ACKNOWLEDGMENTS

We would like to thank Asya Graf, who first proposed this project, and Beatrice Rehl, who saw it through to completion at Cambridge University Press. In addition, we would like to thank Heather Heidrich, copy editor extraordinaire, for all of her assistance in shepherding this through the editorial process. Finally, we would like to thank Tom Levy and David Schloen, who were both consulted during initial stages of this project, the anonymous peer reviewers who agreed that this would be a worthwhile project for the press to publish, and all of the contributors for their commitment to the project and for adhering to the time limits, word limits, and topic limits that we set in place for them. Last, but by no means least, we would like to thank our families for putting up with us while we devoted our efforts to this project, often at the expense of time spent with them.

ABBREVIATIONS

AA	*American Antiquity*
AAA	Approaches to Anthropological Archaeology
AAS	*Archaeological and Anthropological Science*
AASOR	Annual of the American Schools of Oriental Research
ABD	*Anchor Bible Dictionary*, ed. D. N. Freedman. 6 vols. New York: Doubleday, 1992.
ABRL	Anchor Bible Reference Library
ABS	Archaeology and Biblical Studies
ACM	Association for Computing Machinery
ACOR	American Center for Oriental Research
ADAJ	*Annual of the Department of Antiquities of Jordan*
ADPV	Abhandlungen des Deutschen Palästina-Vereins
AEKIIEJ	Archaeological Expedition to Khirbat Iskandar and Its Environs, Jordan
AF	*Altorientalische Forschungen*
AHL	*Archaeology & History in the Lebanon*
AIA	Archaeological Institute of America
AJA	*American Journal of Archaeology*
AJPA	*American Journal of Physical Anthropology*
AmAnth	*American Anthropologist*
ANESSup	Ancient Near Eastern Studies Supplement
ANET	*Ancient Near Eastern Texts Relating to the Old Testament*, ed. J. B. Pritchard. 3rd ed. Princeton: Princeton University Press, 1969.
ANGSBAJ	Annual of the Nelson Glueck School of Biblical Archaeology, Jerusalem
AO	Archiv für Orientforschung
AOAT	Alter Orient und Altes Testament
APAAA/ APAAA	Archeological Papers of the American Anthropological Association
ARA	*Annual Review of Anthropology*
ARC	Center for Archeological Research and Consultancy
ARCP	Centre for Archeological Research and Consultancy Publications
ARGHG	*Annual Review of Genomics and Human Genetics*
ASOR	American Schools of Oriental Research
ASORAR	American Schools of Oriental Research Archaeological Reports
ASORDS	American Schools of Oriental Research Dissertation Series
ASPRB	American School of Prehistoric Research Bulletin

ASPRMS	American School of Prehistoric Research Monograph Series
BA	*Biblical Archaeologist*
BAH	Bibliothèque archéologique et historique
BANEA	The British Association of Near East Archaeology
BAR	British Archaeological Reports
BAR	*Biblical Archaeology Review*
BASOR	*Bulletin of the American Schools of Oriental Research*
BCA	Blackwell Companions to Anthropology
BCH	*Bulletin du correspondence héllenique*
BCSMS	*Bulletin of the Canadian Society for Mesopotamian Studies*
BEO	*Bulletin d'études orientales*
BICS	*Bulletin of the Institute of Classical Studies*
BIHP	Bioarchaeological Interpretations of the Human Past
BMSAES	*British Museum Studies in Ancient Egypt and Sudan*
BSA	*Bulletin on Sumerian Agriculture*
BSAJ	British School of Archaeology in Jerusalem
BST	Bioarchaeology and Social Theory
BSVAP	Beth-Shean Valley Archaeological Project
CA	*Current Anthropology*
CAARI	Cyprus American Archaeological Research Institute
CAH	*The Cambridge Ancient History*
CAIOP	Center for Archaeological Investigations Occasional Papers
CAJ	*Cambridge Archaeological Journal*
CANE	*Civilizations of the Ancient Near East*, ed. J. M. Sasson. 4 vols. New York: Scribner, 1995. Repr. in 2 vols. Peabody, MA: Hendrickson, 2006.
CBRL	Council for British Research in the Levant
CCEM	Contributions to the Chronology of the Eastern Mediterranean
CCRFJ	Cahiers du Centre de Recherche Français de Jérusalem
CER	*Comparative Education Review*
CHANE	Culture and History of the Ancient Near East
CMAO	Contributi e materiali di archeologia orientale
CNRS	Centre National de la Recherche Scientifique
CRSAIBL	*Comptes rendus des séances de l'Académie des Inscriptions et Belles-Lettres*
CWA	Cambridge World Archaeology
DG	Denkschriften der Gesamtakademie
DJD	Discoveries in the Judaean Desert
EA	*Evolutionary Anthropology*
EEHKJ	Excavations and Explorations in the Hashemite Kingdom of Jordan
EJA	*Estonian Journal of Archaeology*
EnArch	*Environmental Archaeology*
EPS	*Earth and Planetary Science*
EPSL	*Earth and Planetary Science Letters*
ERAUL/ *ERAUL*	Études et recherches archéologiques de l'Université de Liège

LIST OF ABBREVIATIONS

ErIsr	*Eretz-Israel*
ESI	*Excavations and Surveys in Israel*
FIA	Fundamental Issues in Archaeology
FRLLEA	Final Reports of the Leon Levy Expedition to Ashkelon
GA	Gender and Archaeology
HA–ESI	*Hadashot Arkheologiyot–Excavations and Surveys in Israel*
HE	*Human Evolution*
HSM	Harvard Semitic Monographs
HSMP	Harvard Semitic Museum Publications
HSS	Harvard Semitic Studies
HTR	*Harvard Theological Review*
HUCA/ HUCA	Hebrew Union College Annual
IAA	Israel Antiquities Authority
ICA	Interdisciplinary Contributions to Archaeology
ICAANE	International Congress on the Archaeology of the Ancient Near East
ICARDA	International Center for Agricultural Research in the Dry Areas
ICOM	International Council of Museums
IEJ	*Israel Exploration Journal*
IES	Israel Exploration Society
IFPO	Institut Français du Proche-Orient
IJNA	*The International Journal of Nautical Archaeology*
IJO	*International Journal Osteoarchaeology*
IJP	*International Journal of Paleopathology*
INJ	*Israel Numismatic Journal*
INR	*Israel Numismatic Research*
IOS	*Israel Oriental Studies*
ISEMRI	Institute for the Study of Earth and Man Reports of Investigations
JAA	*Journal of Anthropological Archaeology*
JAE	*Journal of Arid Environments*
JAEI	*Journal of Ancient Egyptian Interconnections*
JAJSup	Journal of Ancient Judaism Supplements
JAMT	*Journal of Archaeological Method and Theory*
JAOS	*Journal of the American Oriental Society*
JAR	Journal of Archaeological Research
JARCE	*Journal of the American Research Center in Egypt*
JAS	*Journal of Archaeological Science*
JBL	*Journal of Biblical Literature*
JCHPS	The Jaffa Cultural Heritage Project Series
JCS	*Journal of Cuneiform Studies*
JDS	Judean Desert Studies
JEMAHS	*Journal of Eastern Mediterranean Archaeology and Heritage Studies*
JFA	*Journal of Field Archaeology*
JFS	*Journal Forensic Sciences*
JHE	*Journal of Human Evolution*

JHG	*Journal of Human Genetics*
JHS	*Journal of Hellenistic Studies*
JIPS	*Journal of The Israel Prehistoric Society*
JMA	*Journal of Mediterranean Archaeology*
JNES	*Journal of Near Eastern Studies*
JoE	*Journal of Ethnobiology*
JRAIGBI	*Journal of the Royal Anthropological Institute of Great Britain and Ireland*
JRASup	Journal of Roman Archaeology Supplementary Series
JSA	*Journal of Social Archaeology*
JSJ	*Journal for the Study of Judaism*
JSJSup	Supplements to the Journal for the Study of Judaism
JSOT/*JSOT*	Journal for the Study of the Old Testament
JSOTSup	Journal for the Study of the Old Testament Supplement Series
JSP	Judea and Samaria Publications
JSSEA	*Journal of the Society for the Study of Egyptian Antiquities*
JWH	*Journal of World History*
JWP	*Journal of World Prehistory*
KAI	*Kanaanäische und aramäische Inschriften*, ed. H. Donner and W. Röllig. Wiesbaden: Harrassowitz, 1966–1969.
KMFS	Kelsey Museum Fieldwork Series
KTU	*Die keilalphabetischen Texte aus Ugarit*, ed. M. Dietrich, O. Loretz, and J. Sanmartín. Münster: Ugarit-Verlag, 2013. 3rd enl. ed. of *KTU: The Cuneiform Alphabetic Texts from Ugarit, Ras Ibn Hani, and Other Places*, ed. M. Dietrich, O. Loretz, and J. Sanmartín. Münster: Ugarit-Verlag, 1995.
LA	Levantine Archaeology
LAA	Late Antique Archaeology
LAAA	*Liverpool Annals of Archaeology and Anthropology*
LCL	Loeb Classical Library
LibAnn	*Liber Annuus*
LSS	Levant Supplementary Series
LSTS	Library of Second Temple Studies
MASCA	Museum Applied Science Center for Archaeology
MASup	Mediterranean Archaeology Supplement
MBE	*Molecular Biology and Evolution*
MIM	McDonald Institute Monographs
MMA	Monographs in Mediterranean Archaeology
MonArch	Monumenta Archaeologica
MSR	*Mamlūk Studies Review*
MSSMNIA	Monograph Series of the Sonia and Marco Nadler Institute of Archaeology
MTCRPFJ	Mémoires et travaux du Centre de Recherches Préhistoriques Français de Jérusalem
MWA	Monographs in World Archaeology
NAAA	New Approaches in Anthropological Archaeology
NDA	New Directions in Archaeology

LIST OF ABBREVIATIONS

NEA	*Near Eastern Archaeology*
NEAEHL	*The New Encyclopedia of Archaeological Excavations in the Holy Land*, ed. E. Stern. 5 vols. Jerusalem: IES; Carta; New York: Simon & Schuster, 1993–2008.
NINEP	The Netherlands Institute for the Near East Publications
OBO	Orbis Biblicus et Orientalis
OEANE	*The Oxford Encyclopedia of Archaeology in the Near East*, ed. E. M. Meyers. 5 vols. New York: Oxford University Press, 1997.
OIP	Oriental Institute Publications
OIS	Oriental Institute Seminars
OJA	*Oxford Journal of Archaeology*
OLA	Orientalia Lovaniensia Analecta
OWA	One World Archaeology
PAe	Probleme der Ägyptologie
PEF	Palestine Exploration Fund
PEFA	Palestine Exploration Fund Annual
PEQ	*Palestine Exploration Quarterly*
PNAS	Proceedings of the National Academy of Sciences
PPS	Proceedings of the Prehistoric Society
Qad	Qadmoniot
QI	Quaternary International
QSR	Quaternary Science Reviews
RAAO	*Revue d'assyriologie et d'archéologie orientale*
RB	*Revue biblique*
REA	Research in Economic Anthropology
REDSPJ	Reports of the Expedition to the Dead Sea Plain, Jordan
RlA	*Reallexikon der Assyriologie*, ed. E. Ebeling, B. Meissner, and O. Edzard. Berlin: de Gruyter, 1928–
ROSAPAT	Rome "La Sapienza" Studies on the Archaeology of Palestine & Transjordan
SA	Social Archaeology
SAHL	Studies in the Archaeology and History of the Levant
SAM	Sheffield Archaeological Monographs
SAOC	Studies in Ancient Oriental Civilization
SBFCMa	Studium Biblicum Franciscanum Collectio Maior
SBFCMi	Studium Biblicum Franciscanum Collectio Minor
SBL	Society of Biblical Literature
SBT	Studien zu den Boğazköy Texten
SCA	Smithsonian Contributions to Anthropology
SEG	Supplementum Epigraphicum Graecum
SENEPSE	Studies in Early Near Eastern Production, Subsistence, and Environment
SEQ	*Studi per l'ecologia del Quaternario*
SER	Salvage Excavation Reports
SHAJ	*Studies in the History and Archaeology of Jordan*
SHCANE	Studies in the History and Culture of the Ancient Near East
SSAA	Sheffield Studies in Aegean Archaeology

SSAI	Smithsonian Series in Archaeological Inquiry
STDJ	Studies on the Texts of the Desert of Judah
TA	*Tel Aviv*
TPAH	Turning Points in Ancient History
TPR	*Town Planning Review*
UF	*Ugarit-Forschungen*
UMM	University Museum Monographs
UZKOAI	Untersuchungen der Zweigstelle Kairo des Österreichischen Archäologischen Institutes
VHA	*Vegetation History and Archaeobotany*
VT	*Vetus Testamentum*
VTSup	Vetus Testamentum Supplements
WA	*World Archaeology*
WAW	Writings from the Ancient World
WAWSup	Writings from the Ancient World Supplement
WMARENEP	Wellcome-Marston Archaeological Research Expedition to the Near East Publications
YPA	*Yearbook of Physical Anthropology*
ZAVA	*Zeitschrift für Assyriologie & Vorderasiatische Archäologie*
ZAW	*Zeitschrift für die alttestamentliche Wissenschaft*
ZDPV	*Zeitschrift des Deutschen Palästina-Vereins*
ZPE	*Zeitschrift für Papyrologie und Epigraphik*

PROLOGUE

YORKE M. ROWAN, ASSAF YASUR-LANDAU,
AND ERIC H. CLINE

What does archaeology do? Why do so many people, whether professionals, avocational, or the public, profess such a keen interest in archaeology? And what is the object of archaeological study? The rather simple definition of archaeology – that it is a discipline that offers a unique perspective on human history and culture extending from the recent past back into pre-recorded time – is sufficient but perhaps a bit banal. Instead, maybe we should say that archaeology approaches big questions about where we came from and why we changed: from the major changes, such as the emergence of anatomically modern humans, the origins of agriculture, and the rise of states, to the details and patterns of daily life – how people worshipped, mourned their dead, organized themselves, or traded in mundane and precious items. For some, the "big" generalized questions are the challenge, while for others, particular questions (e.g., who built this monument and how?) are of greater interest. This tension between different objectives – whether cultural evolution, linear historical narratives, or particular groups and individuals – reflects the disciplinary background, field training, national heritage, and other characteristics of each scholar.

The questions asked, and how scholars approach them, reflect these and many other factors, whether the research project is located in Southwest Asia, North America, or Mongolia. Particularly in an area such as the southern Levant, where fundamental discoveries concerning early humans, the agricultural revolution, and biblical lands all meet and contend for recognition, relevance and funding, our own recognition that we express ourselves through how we conceptualize society and history seems profoundly significant. This particular appreciation of the "social" underscores one of the fundamental motivations for this volume. Equally important, however, is the need for an updated volume that incorporates chronological narratives with thematic issues that have expanded tremendously in recent years.

Tom Levy's edited volume *The Archaeology of Society in the Holy Land* (1995; 1998) incorporated processual and historical approaches to archaeology during the 1990s. Spanning the Paleolithic period to the British Mandate, it represented a distinct effort to break with traditional cultural-historical approaches to the archaeology of the region.

However, it has now been over twenty years since Levy's volume first appeared. Tremendous additions to the available archaeological record in the interim necessitate a reevaluation of both the data and the ways in which we understand the ancient world. New or improved analytical methods from life and earth sciences, such as organic residue analysis, more readily accessible analytical procedures for pottery and metal provenience studies, and improved accelerator mass spectrometry (AMS) radiocarbon dating, are transforming archaeological practices. Coupled with the accessibility of data acquisition through satellites, unpiloted aerial vehicles (drones), and the affordability of software, archaeology is undergoing something of a revolution in recording methods.

In the archaeology of the Levant, however, these innovative methods have been used in the last decade primarily as a means to support chronological arguments about the political history of the Iron Age or other traditional debates related to the historicity of biblical traditions. It is high time that these analytical methods are enlisted to alter the way in which we look at ancient societies, rather than simply serving as a technocratic panacea for addressing difficult, uncomfortable questions. Archaeological theory, which has also transformed, provides new vistas and sharpened critiques with which to envision past social shifts and fundamental changes to human society. Theory also leads to reevaluating the origins of archaeological practice and the potential for interpretations based on unexamined modern assumptions and perspectives.

The increasing interest in the archaeology of gender, household archaeology, and public archaeology, to name but a few themes, demonstrates a revitalized and dynamic field once dominated primarily by cultural-historical narratives. In contrast to the 1990s, when interest in anthropological and archaeological method and theory was paramount worldwide, the past decade has been dominated by a revival of (neo-) historical biblical archaeology, and advances in theory have been only infrequently applied to interpreting archaeological remains of the Bronze and Iron Ages, as well as later periods.

The aim of this volume, therefore, is to present research that connects analytical data to the lives of ancient people through the use of theoretical frameworks. It goes beyond the usual political and military history, especially since such volumes continue to appear apace, by providing fresh perspectives on ancient communities and societies in different periods, focusing on the construction of social points of view.

This perspective involves incorporating views from the bottom up, rather than from the top down. For example, we encouraged our contributors of historical periods to consider the lives of farmers and families rather than just kings, courtiers, and the narratives recorded by their scribes. By involving ideas and elements such as gender, ethnicity, identity, or household archaeology, materiality, and agency, we hope that engagement with broader themes will provide fresh perspective, at a variety of scales, to the more usual range of data discussed in previous volumes by other authors and editors.

However, we need to provide some definitions at the outset, because "social archaeology" can mean different things to different people. For example, Lynn Meskell and Robert Preucel (2006), as well as Ian Hodder (2007), have carefully summarized different iterations of social archaeology. Although the "social" was conceptualized as part of the "cultural" in the processual archaeology of the 1970s and 1980s, it was envisioned as a system ultimately subordinate to economy, technology, and the environment. Colin Renfrew (1973; 1982; 1984) was an early processual proponent of social archaeology, proposing a more expansive perspective of the social. He conceived social archaeology as the reconstruction of ancient social organization, ranking, empires, and systems. Reaching beyond the work of other processual scholars' interests in social ranking and exchange, he was explicitly interested in ethnicity and identity. Renfrew argued against the functionalist and technological determinism of processualist perspectives, contending that religious beliefs and practices were also fundamental to society. These rather broad issues continue to be relevant to archaeologists today, including those studying the ancient world of the southern Levant.

Broadly speaking, the critique of positivism, and functionalism in particular, led various intellectual movements, such as structuralist, Marxist, and cognitive archaeologies (typically lumped together in the archaeological literature as "post-processualist"), to reject the notion that hypotheses were independently and objectively testable. Rather than working with objectively derived data and "middle-range" theories that could be tested and meet positivist principles, scholars recognized that archaeology is a destructive science that could not replicate results. Post-processual archaeologists took this in a number of different directions. For example, many archaeologists adopted a hermeneutic approach, which recognizes that interpretation of data is perceived through the experience, prior knowledge, and personal perspective of the scholar (Ricœur 1971; Thomas 2000). Rather than a belief that there is some socially neutral and objective state for the researcher, this perspective allows for the possibility that the experience of the scholar will influence their interpretation of the past.

In addition, Hodder and others recognized that processual archaeologists prioritized the economic or environment over the "religious," for example. This reflects a certain implicit preference for *a priori* categories, which in turn reflects Western belief in these categories as necessarily paramount to an objective understanding. The challenge to this opened up a variety of perspectives on understanding the past that emphasized what Hodder originally termed "contextual archaeology" (1982) and that contributed to "post-processualist archaeology" (e.g., Shanks and Tilley 1987), as mentioned above. From this point of view, social archaeology refers to "the ways in which we express ourselves through the things that we make and use, collect and discard, value or take for granted, and seek to be remembered by" (Hall 2001, cited in Meskell and Preucel 2006: 3). Moreover, this version of social archaeology recognizes that every form of political economy requires its own history and past narrative, and therefore archaeology becomes implicated in nationalism and globalization (Meskell and Preucel 2006: 3). In these ways, this version of social archaeology, particularly as discussed by Hodder (2007) and Meskell and Preucel (2006), differs from earlier expositions on social versus cultural, or the social versus social organization, as found in earlier iterations of social archaeology. Archaeology as a current social practice, integrated in modern politics, power relations, economics, and identity, cannot be divorced from critique or self-reflexive insights. There is no reason to cast archaeologists as shallow caricatures, as mere agents of the state, for they are also members of communities, tourists, concerned citizens with humanistic intentions (Baram and Rowan 2004: 14).

We believe that the need for a new volume with a wide diachronic scope is even more acute since the focus of archaeological investigation in the Levant continues to be heavily tilted toward the Late Bronze through Iron Ages. These periods in particular witness the importance of understanding archaeology as a social practice in the modern world – one that is embedded in contemporary power relations and thus deserving of scrutiny. While the renaissance of pragmatic or neo-biblical archaeology, sometimes theoretically aware, has revolutionized the study of this period, it is high time to present a synthetic work with a broader temporal viewpoint. Thus, the aim of this volume is to present vistas on ancient societies in the southern Levant (generally defined as including southern Syria and Lebanon, Israel, the Palestinian Autonomous Authority, Jordan, and the Sinai Peninsula) from the Paleolithic to nearly the modern era.[1] The contributions are organized into a number of major parts, linked together thematically and chronologically.

Part One includes the first hominins in the southern Levant and the earliest human societies. This includes the earliest recognition of the controlled use of fire, Neanderthals and *Homo sapiens*, and the biocultural impact of the transition of hunter-gatherer societies to increasingly sedentary communities with control over domesticated plants and animals, as well as the beginning of craft specialization.

Part Two introduces the urban societies of the Bronze Age, stressing the nonlinear processes of urbanization and collapse of urban communities, and also illuminates aspects of connectivity, ritual, literacy, and economy in both cities and rural sites. Bioarchaeology and archaeobotanical studies underscore methodological approaches that are still growing in the region.

Part Three focuses on the lives of people during the era of the local kingdoms of the Iron Age. Changes in identity, ethnicity, and even political economy are investigated from the point of view of individuals, household and kinship groups, and communities, while historical texts are viewed and appreciated as complementary evidence for reconstructing social lives in the kingdom of Judah, Israel, Philistia, and the kingdoms of Transjordan.

Part Four sees the reach of empires impacting the lives of people under their rule, and the rise of Christianity and Islam in turn fundamentally altering the perspective of those living in the region continuing into the modern age.

Part Five switches gears and examines key diachronic themes in the archaeology of the Levant, including women, metallurgy, livestock, shipwrecks, and harbors, enabling a bird's-eye view of social processes spanning millennia without the constraints of division into archaeological periods.

Part Six then examines the impact of modern technology on the "doing" of archaeology, such as radiocarbon analysis and, equally important, the impact of the ancient world on modern politics, heritage, economy, and identity, and the influence of the modern world on our understanding of and teaching about ancient societies.

We hope and anticipate that this book will be of use and interest to scholars, graduate and undergraduate students, and the broader educated public. Our goal was to produce a volume sophisticated enough for introductory graduate courses on Near Eastern archaeology, yet accessible to undergraduate students in courses dedicated to "Archaeology of the Holy Land," "Archaeology of Israel," or similar courses, as well as members of the general public.

NOTES

[1] When compilation of this volume began, we hoped to achieve a balance between the northern and southern Levant. Over time the content evolved, becoming more focused on the southern Levant. Rather than change the focus – and, thus, the title – we decided to let *The Social Archaeology of the Levant* stand and simply acknowledge the concentration on the southern Levant of this volume here in the Prologue.

REFERENCES

Baram, U., and Rowan, Y. M. 2004. Archaeology after Nationalism: Globalization and the Consumption of the Past. In *Marketing Heritage: Archaeology and the Consumption of the Past*, ed. Y. M. Rowan and U. Baram, 3–23. Walnut Creek, CA: AltaMira.

Hall, M. 2001. Social Archaeology and the Theatres of Memory. *JSA* 1: 50–61.

Hodder, I. 1982. *Symbols in Action: Ethnoarchaeological Studies of Material Culture*. New Studies in Archaeology. Cambridge: Cambridge University Press.

―― 2007. The "Social" in Archaeological Theory: An Historical and Contemporary Perspective. In *A Companion to Social Archaeology*, ed. L. Meskell and R. W. Preucel, 23–42. Oxford: Blackwell.

Levy, T. E., ed. 1995. *The Archaeology of Society in the Holy Land*. New York: Facts on File.

―― 1998. *The Archaeology of Society in the Holy Land*. NAAA. New York: Facts on File.

Meskell, L., and Preucel, R. W., eds. 2007. *A Companion to Social Archaeology*. Oxford: Blackwell.

Renfrew, C. 1973. *Social Archaeology: An Inaugural Lecture Delivered at the University, 20th March, 1973*. Southampton: University of Southampton.

―― 1982. *Towards an Archaeology Mind: An Inaugural Lecture Delivered before the University of Cambridge on 30 November 1982*. Cambridge: Cambridge University Press.

―― 1984. *Approaches to Social Archaeology*. Edinburgh: Edinburgh University Press.

Ricœur, P. 1971. The Model of the Text: Meaningful Action Considered as a Text. *Social Research* 38: 529–62.

Shanks, M., and Tilley, C. 1987. *Social Theory and Archaeology*. Cambridge: Polity.

Thomas, J., ed. 2000. *Interpretive Archaeology: A Reader*. London: Leicester University Press.

PART ONE

ONE

THE LOWER AND MIDDLE PALEOLITHIC OF THE SOUTHERN LEVANT

GARY O. ROLLEFSON

The early evolution of human ancestry occurred in Africa, and sometime near the Plio-Pleistocene boundary members of *Homo erectus* grade first ventured outside the African continent. The migration must have passed through southwestern Asia, marking the beginning of a long and gradual evolution both physically and culturally in what is today the southern Levant. Although evidence for the earliest emergence into the region is rare, recent advances in chronometric dating have placed the changing trajectories of both cultural and physical evolution on firmer foundations. The ensuing developments have become more numerous, continuous, and understandable during the Lower and Middle Paleolithic periods through the disappearance of Archaic *Homo sapiens* at the beginning of the Upper Paleolithic, some 45,000 years ago.

THE LOWER PALEOLITHIC PERIOD IN THE SOUTHERN LEVANT

The Early Lower Paleolithic/Early Acheulian

The discovery of hominin occupation in the cave at Dmanisi in the Caucasus in Georgia, dated to about 1.8 million years ago (Lordkipanidze et al. 2013), has important implications for the initial presence of hominins in the Levant, since it is likely that the emergence of *Homo erectus* grade from its African homeland would have passed through this part of southwestern Asia.

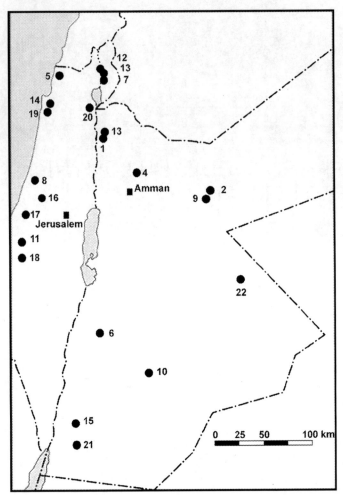

1.1. The location of principal Lower Paleolithic sites discussed in this chapter: (1) Abu el-Khas; (2) Azraq Oasis ('Ain al-Assad, 'Ain Soda, C-Spring, Druze Marsh); (3) Berekhat Ram; (4) Dauqara; (5) Evron Quarry; (6) Fjayj; (7) Gesher Benot Ya'aqov; (8) Holon; (9) Jebel Uwaynid; (10) al-Jafr Basin; (11) Kfar Menachem; (12) Ma'ayan Barukh; (13) Mashari'a; (14) Misliya Cave; (15) Qalka; (16) Qesem Cave; (17) Revadim; (18) Bizat Ruhama; (19) Tabun; (20) 'Ubeidiya; (21) Wadi Rum; and (22) Wadi as-Sirhan. (Map by G. O. Rollefson. Courtesy of the 'Ain al-Assad Archaeological Project.)

At the present time, the earliest solid evidence for early hominin habitation in the Levant is at 'Ubeidiya (Fig. 1.1:20), where *Homo erectus*–grade exploitation of an African type of fauna has been dated to 1.2–1.6 million years ago (by reversed polarity, faunal inventory, and an electron spin resonance [ESR] date), so earlier evidence should exist somewhere in the southern Levantine region. The earliest layers at 'Ubeidiya contain lithic assemblages that are similar to Olduvai Bed II (with the same age range) and are "large enough to suggest that they may indicate the presence of an early group of hominins that did not produce bifaces" (Bar-Yosef and Belmaker 2011:

1321). Assemblages higher in the stratigraphy are techno-typologically Early Acheulian, with the use of the hard hammer technique to produce relatively crudely fashioned bifaces and trihedrals in addition to other core-and-flake tools.

In a small sounding at Evron Quarry (Fig. 1.1:5), a limited collection of stratified artifacts without bifaces was dated by ESR (Porat and Ronen 2002) and paleomagnetism to ca. 1.0 million years ago, although nearby there were non-stratified bifaces of Early Acheulian aspect (Bar-Yosef and Belmaker 2011: 1324). On the eastern side of the Jordan Valley, Linda Villiers collected samples from a large redeposited surface site at Abu el-Khas (Fig. 1.1:1). There appeared to be two groups, one of which was Late Acheulian, but the other in her estimation shares techno-typological affinities with the Early Acheulian at 'Ubeidiya and the later site at Latamne in Syria (Villiers 1983: 34).

Bizat Ruhama (Fig. 1.1:18) is an intriguing locus of a rich "microlithic" assemblage (Zaidner, Ronen, and Burdukiewicz 2003) without bifaces that Ofer Bar-Yosef and Miriam Belmaker assign to a "core-and-flake" industry that, according to thermoluminescence (TL) and paleomagnetism probably falls between 990,000 and 850,000 years ago (2011: 1324). A site in the Dauqara Formation (Fig. 1.1:4) on the banks of the Zarqa River in Jordan has also produced a "core-and-flake" assemblage of 243 artifacts of Lower Paleolithic aspect, including one chopper but no bifaces (Parenti et al. 1997). In view of the associated remains of *Mammuthus meridionalis*, Claude Guérin dates the formation (and thus the artifacts) to about 1 million years ago (Parenti et al. 1997: 20). The authors suggest that the industry may be much older and might represent "a more advanced phase than the 'Ubeidiya Developed Olduwan" (Parenti et al. 1997: 19). In 2015, Fabio Parenti and his team excavated a new locality nearby and encountered another core-and-flake assemblage with choppers (but no bifaces) that may be considerably older in view of the stratigraphic position in the Dauqara Formation (F. Parenti, pers. comm., 2015).

Elsewhere in Jordan, Norman Whalen and Christopher Kolly identified thirty-eight Lower Paleolithic surface sites on the western reaches of the Wadi as-Sirhan (Fig. 1.1:22). Based on the presence or absence of bifaces and the degree of weathering, the collections were assigned to the "Early Acheulian" or the "Middle Acheulian," although the former term was due to the absence of bifaces "in the lowest levels of the Early Acheulian at ... Ubeidiya [sic]" (Whalen and Kolly 2001: 13). No firm evidence of an Early Pleistocene age was found. In the red sandstone canyons of Wadi Rum and its adjacent vicinity (Fig. 1.1:21), several surface sites have been assigned to the Early Acheulian based on morphology, manufacturing technique, and weathering (Fabiano and Primiceri 2001; Succi Fabiani 2001).

The Middle Acheulian

Middle Acheulian sites are as rare in the southern Levant as those assigned to the Early Acheulian period. Perhaps the most widely known is Gesher Benot Ya'aqov (Fig. 1.1:7), located on the eastern side of the present Jordan River, though during its occupation it was on the shore of a lake (Bar-Yosef and Belmaker 2011: 1324). Despite the locally abundant flint resources, the Middle Acheulian assemblage of basalt cleavers (among other bifaces) was manufactured on stout flakes in a way common in Africa but nowhere else in the southern Levant; there is speculation that this might represent an Early Pleistocene incursion of a group of African hunters into the southern Levant (Goren-Inbar and Saragusti 1996). In contrast to most Middle Acheulian sites throughout Africa and Eurasia, there is evidence that fire was well controlled by the *Homo erectus*–grade inhabitants (Alperson-Afil 2008). Potassium-argon dating and paleomagnetic studies indicate a date of ca. 0.9 million years ago (Shea 2010: 58).

Elsewhere in the Jordan Valley, there are reports of Middle Acheulian bifaces and other artifacts in two localities at Mashari'a (Fig. 1.1:13) based on the large size of the pieces, as well as their location in a formation that underlies Late Acheulian material (Macumber 1992; Macumber and Edwards 1997). Below Jebel Uwaynid (Fig. 1.1:9), in a drainage leading to the Azraq paleolake in eastern Jordan, numerous eroded bifaces of large dimensions and bearing hard hammer technique (Fig. 1.2) also indicate a Middle Acheulian presence (Rollefson 1984).

In the 'Uyun al-Qadim area in the northeastern edge of the al-Jafr Basin (Fig. 1.1:10) in southern Jordan, Philip Wilke, Leslie Quintero, and Jason Rech surveyed seven densely concentrated surface assemblages dominated by bifacial cleavers in what was a wetland environment fed by springs emanating from the eastern escarpment (Wilke, Quintero, and Rech 2010). Four of the sites (J-25, J-83, J-92, and J-140) produced very large bifacial cleavers coarsely fashioned from local flint nodules that contrasted in technique and size from other assemblages that were smaller and demonstrated more refined production skills (Fig. 1.3). For these reasons, the researchers assigned the assemblages to the Middle Acheulian (Quintero and Wilke 2014: 16).

Three surface sites in the Wadi Rum area (see Fig. 1.1:21) have been assigned to the Middle Acheulian based on geochronological circumstances and techno-typology, including one at the base of Jebel al-Hattiya and two others on terraces along the Wadi Harad (Belmonte et al. 1992; Pollarolo 2003; Succi Fabiani and Fabiano 2004).

The Late Acheulian

Late Acheulian sites are numerous throughout the southern Levant, and the assemblages show considerable diversity in terms of the use of Levallois techniques to produce blades, flakes, and points, as well as tool production

LOWER AND MIDDLE PALEOLITHIC

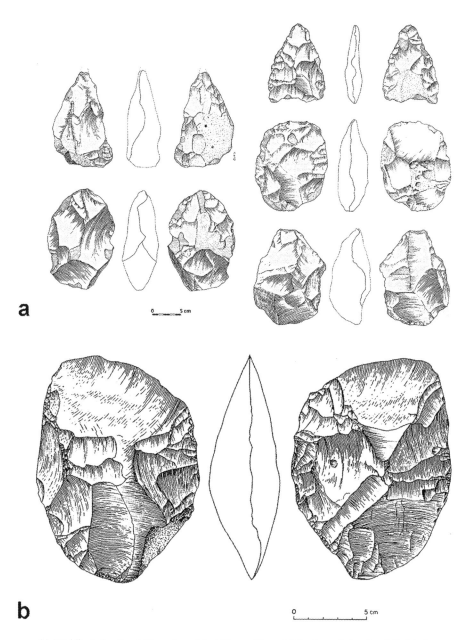

1.2. (a) Middle Acheulian bifaces from Jebel Uwaynid; and (b) a Late Acheulian bifacial cleaver from 'Ain al-Assad. (Drawings by B. Byrd. Courtesy of the Jebel Uwaynid and 'Ain al-Assad Archaeological Projects.)

and discard during the latter part of the Middle Pleistocene, particularly between ca. 400,000 and 250,000 years ago.

Deep stratified cave deposits at Tabun (Fig. 1.1:19) have provided useful records of changes in lithic production during the Late Acheulian and even through the Middle Paleolithic. Chronometric dating using optically stimulated

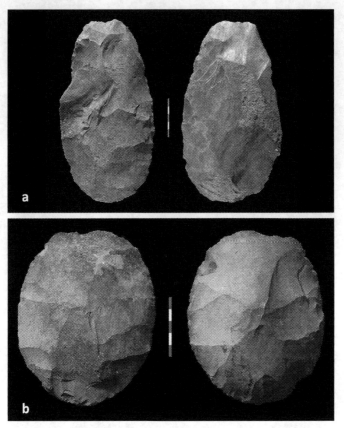

1.3. Middle Acheulian bifaces from 'Uyun al-Qadim: (a) one from Site J-92; and (b) one from Site J-140. (Photos by G. O. Rollefson. Courtesy of the Jafr Prehistoric Archaeology Project.)

luminescence, TL, uranium series, and ESR have provided estimates of absolute dates, although the results of the different approaches are not always compatible with each other. A good case in point is the long sequence at Tabun, where TL dates on burned flint fit the stratigraphic order fairly well (Table 1.1), but ESR results were consistently significantly younger by tens of thousands of years (Mercier and Valladas 2003: fig. 2). Of particular importance here is the customary use of the Tabun sequence to "date" other assemblages based on technotypology, particularly during the Middle Paleolithic (see below).

A major distinction during the Late Acheulian is the presence of the Acheulo-Yabrudian complex along the Mediterranean coast of Israel and Lebanon and into the highlands of southern Syria, characterized by interfingered layers of assemblages with bifaces (Acheulian), Yabrudian (scraper-rich assemblages with scant or absent numbers of bifaces), and a blade-rich Amudian/Pre-Aurignacian industry (Jelinek 1982). Outside of this narrow strip, there is only a Late Acheulian industry in the Jordan Valley and across the entirety of the Jordanian countryside. The Acheulo-Yabrudian complex clearly has roots in the

TABLE 1.1. *Southern Levant Lower and Middle Paleolithic chronometric dates from Tabun Cave based on TL assays (after Mercier and Valladas 2003: tables 1, 2) compared with ESR dates (Grün et al. 1991).*

TL Dates		ESR Early Uptake	ESR Linear Uptake
Unit/Layer	Mean Age (Years Ago)	Age (Years Ago)	Age (Years Ago)
Unit I/C	165,000 ± 16,000	ca. 124,000	ca. 145,000
Unit II/D	196,000 ± 21,000	–	–
Unit V/D	222,000 ± 27,000	–	–
Unit IX/D	256,000 ± 26,000	–	–
Unit X/Ea	267,000 ± 22,000	–	–
Unit XI/Ea	264,000 ± 28,000	–	–
Unit XII/Eb	324,000 ± 31,000	180,000 ± 32,000	195,000 ± 37,000
Unit XIII/Ed	302,000 ± 27,000	149,000 ± 17,000	191,000 ± 28,000
Probable top of F	247,000 ± 27,000	–	–
Top F/Bottom Ed	317,000 ± 36,000	–	–
Bottom of F	315,000 ± 20,000	–	–
Bottom of F	324,000 ± 22,000	–	–
Bottom XIV/Bed 80	415,000 ± 27,000	–	–

earlier Late Acheulian of the coastal strip, but why this development occurred only in this restricted region remains enigmatic. The impetus to develop a scraper-rich industry and a relatively delicate bladelike industry is not known; but, whatever the reason, populations elsewhere did not answer the same call.

The Acheulo-Yabrudian complex was first noted at Tabun (Garrod and Bate 1937) and Yabrud in Syria (Rust 1950); new excavations at Tabun greatly refined the understanding of the complex, which was renamed the Mugharan Tradition (Jelinek 1982). Although found at Jamal Cave (Weinstein-Evron et al. 1999) in the Wadi al-Mughara, only 100 m downslope from Tabun, and at Zuttiyeh (Schwarzc, Goldberg, and Blackwell 1980) in the Galilee area, stunning new evidence of the Acheulo-Yabrudian comes from Qesem Cave (Fig. 1.1:16) (e.g., Gopher et al. 2005). Here, a 7.5 m stratigraphic section of this complex has been investigated since 2001, and the results have been exhilarating in terms of the scope of data relevant to the intensity and duration of recurrent occupation of the site.

While the beginning of the Late Acheulian outside of the Acheulo-Yabrudian complex has not been established by chronometric dating, the beginning and end of the Acheulo-Yabrudian has been defined on the basis of several methods, although once again there is some disagreement among some dates. Avi Gopher and his team (2010) used uranium-thorium dating to produce fifty-four dates for speleothems from Qesem Cave that spanned a general range of 400,000 years ago at the beginning of the sequence and 200,000 years ago at the end. This general range is supported by uranium-thorium dates above the Acheulo-Yabrudian layer at Jamal Cave, and although there are serious discrepancies in the results of various methods used at Tabun, there are also patterns that generally coincide with the uranium-thorium dates from Qesem Cave (Gopher et al. 2010: 653–4; Rink et al. 2004).

Areas where the Acheulo-Yabrudian complex has not been found evidently witness a continuation of the earlier Late Acheulian trajectory of changes in stone tool manufacture. The Late Acheulian layer of Arthur Jelinek's Unit XIV (which is near the beginning of the sequence and beneath the Acheulo-Yabrudian layers) has a TL date of 415,000 ± 27,000 years ago (Mercier et al. 2000: 732), which fits the stratigraphy of the site, and the beginning of the Acheulo-Yabrudian layers above it at Tabun and Qesem Cave. (This does not, on the other hand, provide a firm date for the beginning of the Late Acheulian.) The end of the Late Acheulian at Holon (Fig. 1.1:8) has been dated by ESR to 215,000 ± 30,000 years ago (Porat et al. 2002), indicating that the Late Acheulian spans the range of time of the Acheulo-Yabrudian phenomenon.

The Late Acheulian *sensu stricto* at Revadim (Fig. 1.1:17) and Holon (see Fig. 1.1:8) appears to have little evidence of the use of Levallois techniques (Marder et al. 1999: table 2; Chazan 2000: 14), a situation that also characterizes the Late Acheulian of Tabun (Jelinek 1982: table 1). The situation is very different in the eastern desert of Jordan, where the Levallois indices at 'Ain Sawda are quite high (Rollefson, Quintero, and Wilke 2006: 66), as they are in the Azraq ad-Druze marsh deposits (Nowell 2014: 28) and at Spring C in the southern oasis of Azraq al-Shishan (Copeland 1989; 1991). The combination of high bifacial cleaver content (Fig. 1.4), as well as the intensive use of Levallois techniques, led Lorraine Copeland to propose the term "Desert Wadi Acheulian" for the eastern assemblages (Copeland 1988: 68–9; Copeland and Hours 1988: 303).

In view of the high Levallois content in Late Acheulian sites in the Jordan Valley at Ma'ayan Barukh (Ronen et al. 1980) and to the east of the rift, including Berekhat Ram (Goren-Inbar 1985), Fjayj (Rollefson 1981), Qalka (Fig. 1.1:15) (Henry 1995), and the al-Jafr and Azraq sites (Rollefson, Quintero, and Wilke 2006; Quintero, Wilke, and Rollefson 2007: tables 1, 2; Quintero and Wilke 2014), there seems to be some cultural "boundary" between the coastal region of the southern Levant and the interior of the region, a cultural separation strongly supported by the elevated bifacial cleaver counts in the east (e.g., Rollefson, Quintero, and Wilke 2005; 2006). Bar-Yosef (1987) stressed the importance of a Levantine corridor that facilitated movement of populations and ideas out of Africa and into southwestern Asia. The identification and characterization of the eastern Jordanian Late Acheulian sites could signal the presence of another corridor that followed a series of shallow wetland basins[1]

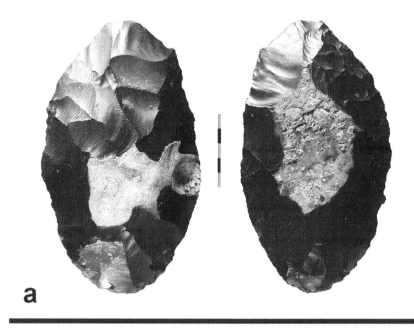

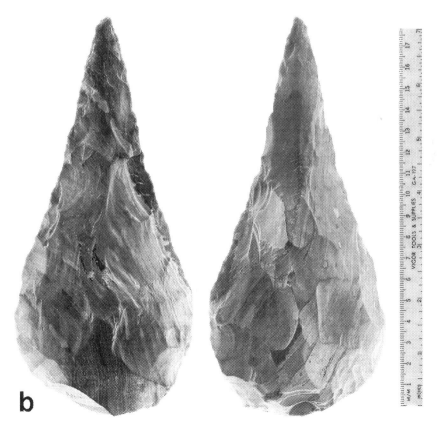

1.4. (a) Large Late Acheulian bifacial cleaver from 'Ain Sawda; and (b) Late Acheulian Micoquian piercer from 'Ain Sawda (Photo [a] by G. Rollefson. Photo [b] by L. Quintero, P. Wilke, J. Quintero, and G. O. Rollefson. Courtesy of the 'Ain Sawda Archaeological Project.)

from Mudawwara in southern Jordan through the basins of al-Jafr, al-Jinz, al-Hasa, and Azraq in the north (Quintero, Wilke, and Rollefson 2007).

THE MIDDLE PALEOLITHIC

Chronometric dates for the end of the Lower Paleolithic provide a *terminus post quem* for the beginning of the Middle Paleolithic period, which in the southern Levant, is comprised only of the Levantine Mousterian. Acknowledging the problems with the various chronometric methods mentioned earlier, there seems to be a rough consensus that the "boundary" between the Acheulo-Yabrudian and the Levantine Mousterian in the coastal region of the southern Levant occurred about 250,000–200,000 years ago (Porat et al. 2002; Mercier et al. 2007: 1075; Gopher et al. 2010: 644; Valladas et al. 2013: 592).

The replacement of the Acheulo-Yabrudian with the Levantine Mousterian was relatively sudden and, in a sense, startling. Bifaces were no longer produced, and the techniques of producing flakes, blades, and points was dominated by the Levallois techniques, a tradition that was virtually absent in the latest Late Acheulian on the coast. The new industrial complex was so distinctive in almost every way that it seems to have been because of the "arrival of a new population ... associated with either Neandertals ... from Europe ... or with [Early Anatomically Modern Humans] that were evolving in Africa"[2] (Valladas et al. 2013: 592).

Where did the new industry originate? Certainly, there are few indications that the Acheulo-Yabrudian produced any heirs in the southern Levant. In view of the heavy reliance on Levallois techniques in the Levantine Mousterian, a logical ancestral candidate would be a Late Acheulian industry with a focus on Levallois techniques, and this scenario would surely look to the area east of the Jordan Valley. The highest probability of likely ancestral lithic candidates would be those that demonstrated similarities closest to the earliest non-biface Mousterian industries in the coastal area, and this would be found at 'Ain Sawda in the Azraq Oasis of eastern Jordan.

Liliane Meignen has determined Layers E and F at Hayonim (Fig. 1.5:5) to be Early Levantine Mousterian, similar to Tabun Layer D, as well as with the Hummalian tradition at el Kowm in Syria (cf. Copeland 1985), a non-biface (and thus post-Acheulian) industry (Meignen 2011). The blade domination of the tool blanks is similar at both sites, and the illustrations of retouched, pointed blades shows very close parallels; the same is true (Fig. 1.6) of one of the Middle Paleolithic layers at 'Ain Sawda (Fig. 1.5:2) in the Azraq Oasis (Rollefson, Quintero, and Wilke in press).

Tabun Cave (Fig. 1.5:11) produced a deep sequence of Levantine Mousterian developments that are commonly used as landmarks for cross-referencing other Middle Paleolithic sites in the southern Levant. Three major

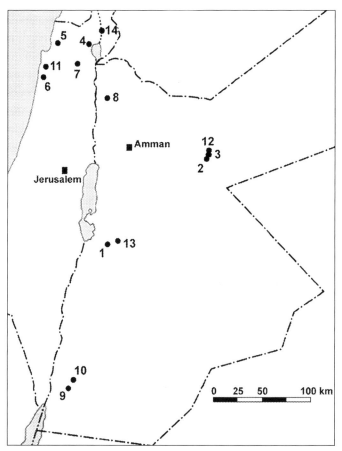

1.5. The location of principal Middle Paleolithic sites discussed in this chapter: (1) 'Ain Difla; (2) 'Ain Sawda; (3) Azraq ad-Druze; (4) Amud and Zuttiyeh; (5) Hayonim Cave; (6) Kebara Cave; (7) Qafzeh; (8) al-Rasafa; (9) Tor Faraj; (10) Tor Sabiha; (11) Wadi al-Mughara (Skhul, Tabun, el-Wad); (12) Wadi 'Uniqiya; (13) WHS 621; and (14) Nahal Manayaheem Outlet. (Map by G. O. Rollefson.)

stages (Tabun D, C, and B [also known as Early, Middle, and Late Levantine Mousterian, or Phase 1, Phase 2, and Phase 3]) are used for comparisons (e.g., Copeland 1975; Culley, Popescu, and Clark 2013) that generally correlate to two glacial periods with an intervening interglacial (Shea 2001: 47).

In terms of settlement patterns, the assertion that "most Mousterian Levantine sites are located within the present distribution of the Mediterranean woodland ecotone" (Meignen et al. 2006: 162) requires some modification based on recent field work. The observation might pertain to the territory west of the Jordan Valley, but surveys and excavations east of the rift have shown considerable numbers of sites in present-day steppe and desert landscapes. 'Ain Difla (of the Tabun D facies) is a long and deep but shallow rock-shelter in Wadi al-'Ali, a tributary to the Wadi al-Hasa. Faunal remains – though very fragmentary – consisted solely of wild ass (*Equus hemionus*) and gazelle (*Gazella* sp.), a combination indicative of cool steppic or semidesert conditions (Clark et al. 1988: 235). This conclusion is bolstered by pollen data, dominated by steppe vegetation that included Noaea-type chenoams and grasses; even the minor pollen types were xerophytic types (Clark et al. 1997: 89).

WHS 621 (Fig. 1.5:13) is one of several large open-air Levantine Mousterian sites about 15 km southeast of Site 634. WHS 621 extends over 0.4 ha and is densely covered with Middle Paleolithic material that has not been significantly disturbed (Clark et al. 1988: 215). The site is located on the edge of what was a broad wetland basin. Faunal remains included *Equus caballus*, *E. hemionus*, and *Bos primigenius*, all of which are consistent with a grassland steppe (Clark et al. 1988: 225). The lithic industry does not fit comfortably into a single stage of the Tabun sequence, showing Levallois point length-to-width ratios similar to Tabun B or C, but other indices are consistent with Tabun D (Clark et al. 1988: 221).

Levantine Mousterian sites are found throughout the wadi systems in Jordan, including those drainages in the eastern desert. Site WE-2 (Fig. 1.5:12) in Wadi 'Uniqiya ("Enoqiya" in the original survey report by Francis Hours [1989]), a small drainage emptying eventually into the Azraq mudpan, was located along the edge of a small playa and sampled by intensive surface collection by Michael Bisson and his team (2014). The flat topography suggested a low probability of significant postdepositional movement and damage to artifacts. Levallois flakes numbered three to one compared to Levallois blades, and nine to one compared to Levallois points (Bisson et al. 2014: table 2). Levallois points are very rare in the collection, but the researchers note that the laminarity of the cores and detached pieces would indicate a Tabun D affiliation (Bisson et al. 2014). One undamaged flake was found *in situ* associated with a carbonate sample that was dated using the uranium-thorium method to between 106,000 and 146,000 years ago, which is too late for a Tabun D ascription. They caution that available flint resources are distant and mostly tabular, so blade production is affected as much (if not more) by the characteristics of the cores than anything else (Bisson et al. 2014: 46). Not surprisingly, no faunal remains were found in direct association, although *Equus* sp., *Bos* sp., and *Camelus* sp. remains were found, all indicating a steppe environment (Bisson et al. 2014: 38).

Climatic conditions contributing to the paleolake at the Azraq Oasis (in South Azraq [also called Azraq al-Shishan] and in North Azraq [also known as Azraq ad-Druze (Fig. 1.5:3)]) fluctuated greatly during the past 200,000 years, periodically providing marshy shores that would have attracted large game and thus hunters as well. These periods of refugia included substantial occupation levels in both the northern and southern areas of the oasis during the Middle Paleolithic, particularly during Marine Isotope Stages 5 and early 4 (Cordova et al. 2013: 108).

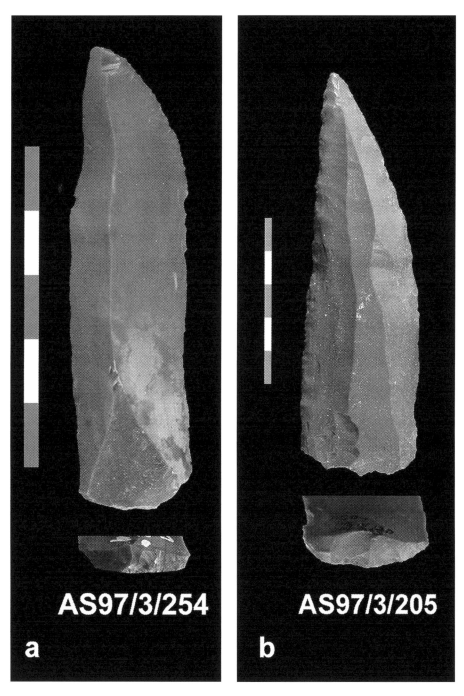

1.6. Middle Paleolithic knives from Trench 3 at 'Ain Sawda: (a) a retouched Levallois blade; and (b) a blade with truncated faceted platform. (Photos by G. O. Rollefson. Courtesy of the 'Ain Sawda Archaeological Project.)

Mention has already been made of the Levantine Mousterian strata at 'Ain Sawda, a once freshwater, spring-fed pool in the southern Azraq Oasis (see Fig. 1.5:2). Although the uppermost Middle Paleolithic layers were sparse in terms of Levallois (or any other) material, the Levallois points were relatively short and broad; however, the sample is too small to claim some association with the Tabun sequence. The principal Mousterian layers (Trenches 3 and 4, with the largest samples) were consistently high in laminarity for Levallois blades and points, and the similarity with the Tabun D assemblage is strong (Rollefson, Quintero, and Wilke in press: table 8). Faunal remains – except for teeth – were sparse in the Middle Paleolithic layers, although skeletal remains of *Bos* sp. and a partial skull of *Equus* cf. *hydruntinus* were found in Trench 3, and a molar of a probable *Elephas namadicus* came from the Mousterian layer in Trench 1 (Dirks, Watson, and Schnurrenberger 1998).

The site of al-Rasafa (Fig. 1.5:8) is located in the northern Jordan Valley at an altitude of -37 m, where Middle Paleolithic hunters could have monitored game on the shore of Lake Lisan below (Shea 1998). Four test pits produced a sizeable sample of cores, tools, and debitage; the Levallois Index (IL) was remarkably high at 30.5 (Shea 1998: table 3). More than 200 Levallois flakes, points, and blades were recovered. No materials suitable for chronometric dating were found, and the midpoint width-to-midpoint thickness ratios for whole flakes and length-to-width ratios for points were contradictory in terms of characterizing the assemblage according to the Tabun definitions (Shea 1998: 47; cf. Jelinek 1982), so it is unclear where the site ranges during the Middle Paleolithic period.

Another Levantine Mousterian site occurs in Israel about 65 km north of al-Rasafa. The Nahal Manayaheem Outlet (Fig. 1.5:14) is a briefly occupied hunting camp on the eastern shore of paleolake Lake Hula (Sharon and Oron 2014). A relatively small assemblage of about 1,200 Levantine Mousterian artifacts was recovered in five excavation seasons. The relative frequencies and diversity of tool types are remarkable in that tools account for 34.3 percent of the inventory (very high) and very low frequencies of scrapers (7 percent of the tools; Levallois items and other points make up 12.2 percent of the tools). Furthermore, unretouched debitage and cores are very low in relative frequencies (67 percent) (Sharon and Oron 2014: 173). The sediment containing the artifacts has been optically stimulated luminescence dated to about 65,000 years ago (Sharon and Oron 2014: 169; cf. Kalbe et al. 2014: 144).

Research in Israel's arid Negev Desert in the 1970s led to the recognition of an Early Levantine Mousterian settlement pattern that consisted of long-term base camps from which teams of people would radiate out to temporary extraction camps, where hunting, gathering, and quarrying activities took place (Marks 1981: 296–8). This "radiating base camp" pattern was supplanted in the generally cool and dry Upper Paleolithic period when most settlements were temporary, and high mobility characterized this opportunistic "circulating" settlement pattern.

In the Wadi Hisma of southern Jordan, where landscapes and climatic conditions resemble those of the Negev, excavations at two Late Levantine Mousterian sites (ca. 55,000 years ago) indicated that a transhumant combination of both the radiating and circulating settlement patterns existed (Henry 1998). Tor Faraj (Fig. 1.5:9) is a rock shelter at ca. 1,000 m elevation that produced stratified deposits of artifacts of relatively high density and a diversity of tool types and appears to have been inhabited during the cold season for long periods of time; however, the rock-shelter was abandoned during the warm season when the occupants retreated to higher elevations, such as the temporary opportunistic camp at Tor Sabiha (Fig. 1.5:10), some 250 m higher (Henry 1998: 31–3). This kind of elevational transhumance took advantage of differing climatic conditions and consequent resource availabilities.

None of the Middle Paleolithic sites in Jordan has produced hominin fossils, but skeletal evidence has come from sixteen sites in Israel, all caves or rock-shelters; the preservation of many of the finds is poor and incomplete (Shea 2001: 43). Nevertheless, the population contains the earliest examples of the emergence of anatomically modern humans out of Africa into southwestern Asia, a region that was still populated by Neanderthals. *Homo* sp. indet. is associated with all three phases of the Levantine Mousterian, including Early Middle Paleolithic/Tabun D-type Levantine Mousterian assemblages from Hayonim Level E, Misliya Unit II, and 'Ain Difla; Middle Levantine Mousterian/Tabun C-type in Tabun Unit I; and Late Levantine Mousterian/Tabun B-type at Kebara VI–XII, Tor Faraj C, and Tor Sabiha C (Shea 2003: table V). The relatively complete skeletal remains and elements are robust and typical of the *Homo sapiens neanderthalensis* subspecies. It is in Skhul B and Qafzeh XVII–XXIV that the presence of well-preserved, anatomically modern human skeletons appeared (seven adults and three juveniles at the former, and four adults and two juveniles at the latter [Shea 2001: 43]) in the milieu of the Middle Levantine Mousterian/Tabun C-type phase (Shea 2003: 346), dated to between 92,000 and 120,000 years ago (Shea 2003: fig. 6).

This poses an intriguing puzzle. If the Skhul and Qafzeh populations are traceable to one degree or another (First-generation immigrants? Third generation? Tenth generation?) to some part of Africa, where and when did they adopt the Middle Levantine Mousterian/Tabun C-type tradition? There is no apparent record of the industry in northeastern Africa, suggesting that they discarded their native lithic tradition and learned a new one. It is widely held that population levels and densities were such that interactions between the two subspecies of *Homo sapiens* must have been infrequent; however, in order to develop the skills of a new technique and new inventory of tool types, there must have been close and persistent contact at some time for the novel approach of tool manufacture to have been transferred.

Another interesting aspect to ponder deals with gene flow between the two subspecies, now that it is clear that interbreeding occurred (e.g., Green et al. 2010). Much of the original Neanderthal contribution to the first hybrids has possibly/probably disappeared due to evolutionary forces. But one wonders how the original hybrids might have compared to the Skhul and Qafzeh individuals.

NOTES

1 These basins were originally considered to be paleolakes (cf. Schuldenrein and Clark 1994), but recent research shows the basins to be wetlands or springs fed by groundwater discharge (Rech et al. 2013).
2 Of course, the question of the sudden appearance of a confined distribution of the Acheulo-Yabrudian complex at ca. 400,000 years ago might also be attributed to population movements from some unknown region (Garrod 1970: 228; Gopher et al. 2005: 88; Shimelmitz, Barkai, and Gopher 2011: 477).

REFERENCES

Alperson-Afil, N. 2008. Continual Fire-Making by Hominins at Gesher Benot Ya'aqov, Israel. *QSR* 27: 1733–9.
Bar-Yosef, O. 1987. Pleistocene Connexions between Africa and Southwest Asia: An Archaeological Perspective. *African Archaeological Review* 5 (1): 29–38.
Bar-Yosef, O., and Belmaker, M. 2011. Early and Middle Pleistocene Faunal and Hominins Dispersals through Southwestern Asia. *QSR* 30: 1318–37.
Belmonte, A.; Fabiani, L.; Mercatanti, L.; Rustioni, M.; and Vianello, F. 1992. L'Acheuleano medio di Jebel el Hattiya nella Giordania meridionale. *SEQ* 14: 15–31.
Bisson, M. S.; Nowell, A.; Cordova, C. E.; Poupart, M.; Pokines, J.; and Ghaleb, B. 2014. WE-2: The Middle Paleolithic of the Wādī al-'Unqiyya Revisited. In *Jordan's Prehistory: Past and Future Research*, ed. B. Finlayson and G. O. Rollefson, 35–47. Amman: Department of Antiquities of Jordan.
Chazan, M. 2000. Typological Analysis of the Lower Paleolithic Site of Holon, Israel. *JIPS* 30: 7–32.
Clark, G. A.; Lindly, J.; Donaldson, M. L.; Garrard, A.; Coinman, N.; Schuldenrein, J.; Fish, S. K.; and Olszewski, D. 1988. Excavations at Middle, Upper and Epipalaeolithic Sites in the Wadi Hasa, West-Central Jordan. In *The Prehistory of Jordan: The State of Research in 1986*, Part 1, ed. A. N. Garrard and H. G. K. Gebel, 209–85. BAR International Series 396 (1). Oxford: BAR.
Clark, G. A.; Schuldenrein, J.; Donaldson, M. L.; Schwarcz, H. P.; Rink, W. J.; and Fish, S. K. 1989. Analysis of the Paleolithic Artifacts from the Sounding of A. Garrard at C-Spring, 1985 Season. In *The Hammer on the Rock: Studies in the Early Paleolithic of Azraq, Jordan*, Vol. 2, ed. L. Copeland and F. Hours, 325–90. BAR International Series 540 (2). Oxford: BAR.

1997. Chronostratigraphic Contexts of Middle Paleolithic Horizons at 'Ain Difla Rockshelter (WHS 634), West-Central Jordan. In *The Prehistory of Jordan II: Perspectives from 1997*, ed. H. G. K. Gebel, Z. Kafafi, and G. O. Rollefson, 77–100. SENEPSE 4. Berlin: Ex Oriente.

Copeland, L. 1975. The Middle and Upper Paleolithic of Lebanon and Syria in the Light of Recent Research. In *Problems in Prehistory: North Africa and the Levant*, ed. F. Wendorf and A. Marks, 317–50. Dallas: Southern Methodist University Press.

1985. The Pointed Tools of Hummal 1a (El Kowm, Syria). *Cahiers de l'Euphrate* 4: 177–89.

1988. Environment, Chronology and Lower-Middle Paleolithic Occupations of the Azraq Basin, Jordan. *Paléorient* 14 (2): 66–75.

1991. The Late Acheulean Knapping-Floor at C-Spring, Azraq Oasis, Jordan. *Levant* 23: 1–6.

Copeland, L., and Hours, F. 1988. The Paleolithic in North Central Jordan: An Overview of Survey Results from the Upper Zarqa and Azraq 1982–1986. In *The Prehistory of Jordan: The State of Research in 1986*, Part 2, ed. A. N. Garrard and H. G. K. Gebel, 287–309. BAR International Series 396 (2). Oxford: BAR.

Cordova, C. E.; Nowell, A.; Bisson, M.; Ames, C. J. H.; Pokines, J.; Chang, M.; and al-Nahar, M. 2013. Interglacial and Glacial Desert Refugia and the Middle Paleolithic of the Azraq Oasis, Jordan. *QI* 300: 94–110.

Culley, E. V.; Popescu, G.; and Clark, G. A. 2013. An Analysis of the Compositional Integrity of the Levantine Mousterian Facies. *QI* 300: 213–33.

Dirks, W.; Watson, R.; and Schnurrenberger, D. 1998. Preliminary Account of Pleistocene Mammals from 'Ain Soda, Azraq Basin, Jordan. *Journal of Vertebrate Paleontology Abstracts* 18 (3): 38A–39A.

Fabiano, M., and Primiceri, P. 2001. L'Acheuleano inferiore di Giabal el Issua nella Giordania meridionale. *SEQ* 23: 9–41.

Garrod, D. A. E. 1970. Pre-Aurignacian and Amudian: A Comparative Study of the Earliest Blade Industries of the Near East. In *Frühe Menschheit und Umwelt*, Vol. 1: *Archäologische Beiträge*, ed. K. Gripp, R. Schütrumpf, and H. Schwabedissen, 224–9. Fundamenta A2 (1). Cologne: Böhlau.

Garrod, D. A. E., and Bate, D. M. A. 1937. *The Stone Age of Mount Carmel: Excavations at the Wady el-Mughara*, Vol. 1. Oxford: Clarendon.

Gopher, A.; Ayalon, A.; Bar-Matthews, M.; Barkai, R.; Frumkin, A.; Karkanas, P.; and Shahack-Gross, R. 2010. The Chronology of the Late Lower Paleolithic in the Levant Based on U–Th Ages of Speleothems from Qesem Cave, Israel. *Quaternary Geochronology* 5: 644–56.

Gopher, A.; Barkai, R.; Shimelmitz, R.; Khalaily, M.; Lemorini, C.; Hershkovitz, I.; and Stiner, M. 2005. Qesem Cave: An Amudian Site in Central Israel. *JIPS* 35: 69–92.

Goren-Inbar, N. 1985. The Lithic Assemblage of the Berekhat Ram Acheulian Site, Golan Heights. *Paléorient* 11 (1): 7–28.

Goren-Inbar, N., and Saragusti, I. 1996. An Acheulian Biface Assemblage from Gesher Benot Ya'aqov, Israel: Indications of African Affinities. *JFA* 23: 15–30.

Green, R. E.; Krause, J.; Briggs, A. W.; Maricic, T.; Stenzel, U.; Kircher, M.; Patterson, N.; Li, H.; Zhai, W.; Fritz, M. H.-Y.; Hansen, N. F.; Durand, E. Y.; Malaspinas, A.-S.; Jensen, J. D.; Marques-Bonet, T.; Alkan, C.; Prüfer, K.; Meyer, M.; Burbano, H. A.; Good, J. M.; Schultz, R.; Aximu-Petri, A.; Butthof, A.; Höber, B.; Höffner, B.; Siegemund, M.; Weihmann, A.; Nusbaum, C.; Lander, E. S.; Russ, C.; Novod, N.;

Affourtit, J.; Egholm, M.; Verna, C.; Rudan, P.; Brajkovic, D.; Kucan, Ž.; Gušic, I.; Doronichev, V. B.; Golovanova, L. V.; Lalueza-Fox, C.; de la Rasilla, M.; Fortea, J.; Rosas, A.; Schmitz, R. W.; Johnson, P. L. F.; Eichler, E. E.; Falush, D.; Birney, E.; Mullikin, J. C.; Slatkin, M.; Nielsen, R.; Kelso, J.; Lachmann, M.; Reich, D.; and Pääbo, S. 2010. A Draft Sequence of the Neandertal Genome. *Science* 328 (5979): 710–22.

Grün, R.; Stringer, C. B.; and Schwarcz, H. B. 1991. ESR Dating of Teeth from Garrod's Tabun Cave Collection. *JHE* 20: 231–48.

Henry, D. O. 1998. The Middle Paleolithic of Jordan. In *The Prehistoric Archaeology of Jordan*, ed. D. Henry, 23–38. BAR International Series 705. Oxford: BAR.

——, ed. 1995. *Prehistoric Cultural Ecology and Evolution: Insights from Southern Jordan*. New York: Plenum.

Hours, F. 1989. The Lithic Industries of Wadi Enoqiyya. In *The Hammer on the Rock: Studies in the Early Paleolithic of Azraq, Jordan*, Vol. 2, ed. L. Copeland and F. Hours, 403–50. BAR International Series 540 (2). Oxford: BAR.

Jelinek, A. J. 1982. The Tabun Cave and Paleolithic Man in the Levant. *Science* 216 (4553): 1369–75.

Kalbe, J.; Sharon, G.; Porat, N.; Zhang, C.; and Mischke, S. 2014. Geological Setting and Age of the Middle Paleolithic Site of Nahal Mahanayeem Outlet (Upper Jordan Valley, Israel). *QI* 331: 139–48.

Lordkipanidze, D.; Ponce de León, M. S.; Margvelashvili, A.; Rak, Y.; Rightmire, G. P.; Vekua, A.; and Zollikofer, C. P. E. 2013. A Complete Skull from Dmanisi, Georgia, and the Evolutionary Biology of Early *Homo*. *Science* 342 (6156): 326–31.

Macumber, P. G. 1992. The Geological Setting of Palaeolithic Sites at Tabaqat Fahl, Jordan. *Paléorient* 18 (2): 31–44.

Macumber, P. G., and Edwards, P. C. 1997. Preliminary Results from the Acheulian Site of Mashari'a 1, and a New Stratigraphic Framework for the Lower Paleolithic of the East Jordan Valley. In *The Prehistory of Jordan II: Perspectives from 1997*, ed. H. G. K. Gebel, Z. Kafafi, and G. O. Rollefson, 23–43. SENEPSE 4. Berlin: Ex Oriente.

Marder, O.; Khalaily, H.; Rabinovitz, R.; Gvirtzman, G.; Wieder, M.; Porat, N.; Ron, H.; Bankirer, R.; and Saragusti, I. 1999. The Lower Paleolithic Site of Revadim Quarry: Preliminary Finds. *JIPS* 28: 21–53.

Marks, A. E. 1981. The Middle Paleolithic of the Negev, Israel. In *Préhistoire du Levant*, ed. J. Cauvin and P. Sanlaville, 287–98. Paris: CNRS.

Meignen, L. 2011. The Contribution of Hayonim Cave Assemblages to the Understanding of the So-Called Early Levantine Mousterian. *ERAUL* 126: 85–100.

Meignen, L.; Bar-Yosef, O.; Speth, J. D.; and Stiner, M. C. 2006. Middle Paleolithic Settlement Patterns in the Levant. In *Transitions before the Transition: Evolution and Stability in the Middle Paleolithic and Middle Stone Age*, ed. E. Hovers and S. L. Kuhn, 149–69. ICA. New York: Springer.

Mercier, N., and Valladas, H. 2003. Reassessment of TL Age Estimates of Burnt Flints from the Paleolithic Site of Tabun Cave, Israel. *JHE* 45: 401–9.

Mercier, N.; Valladas, H.; Froget, L.; Joron, J.-L.; Reyss, J.-L.; Weiner, S.; Goldberg, P.; Meignen, L.; Bar-Yosef, O.; Belfer-Cohen, A.; Chech, M.; Kuhn, S. L.; Stiner, M. C.; Tillier, A.-M.; Arensburg, B.; and Vandermeersch, B. 2007. Hayonim Cave: A TL-Based Chronology for This Levantine Mousterian Sequence. *JAS* 34: 1064–77.

Mercier, N.; Valladas, H.; Froget, L.; Joron, J.-L.; and Ronen, A. 2000. Datation par thermoluminescence de la base du gisement paléolithique de Tabun (Mont Carmel, Israël). *EPS* 330: 731–8.

Nowell, A. 2014. Reversals of Fortune: Neandertals and Modern Humans in the Levantine Middle Paleolithic, a View from the Druze Marsh, North Azraq (Jordan). In *Jordan's Prehistory: Past and Future Research*, ed. B. Finlayson and G. O. Rollefson, 23–34. Amman: Department of Antiquities of Jordan.

Parenti, F.; al-Shiyab, A. H.; Santucci, E.; Kafafi, Z.; and Palumbo, G., with an appendix by Guérin, C. 1997. Early Acheulean Stone Tools and Fossil Faunas from the Dauqara Formation, Upper Zarqa Valley, Jordanian Plateau. In *The Prehistory of Jordan II: Perspectives from 1997*, ed. H. G. K. Gebel, Z. Kafafi, and G. O. Rollefson, 7–22. SENEPSE 4. Berlin: Ex Oriente.

Pollarolo, L. 2003. L'Acheuleano medio sui terrazzi di Uadi el Harad nella Girodania meridionale. *SEQ* 25: 23–36.

Porat, N.; Chazan, M.; Schwarcz, H. P.; and Horwitz, L. K. 2002. Timing of the Lower to Middle Paleolithic Boundary: New Dates from the Levant. *JHE* 43: 107–22.

Porat, N., and Ronen, A. 2002. Luminescence and ESR Age Determinations of the Lower Paleolithic Site Evron Quarry, Israel. *Advances in ESR Applications* 18: 123–30.

Quintero, L., and Wilke, P. 2014. Ayoun Qedim: Middle Pleistocene Hunting Patterns at a Box Canyon Oasis in al-Jafr Basin, Jordan. In *Jordan's Prehistory: Past and Future Research*, ed. B. Finlayson and G. O. Rollefson, 9–21. Amman: Department of Antiquities of Jordan.

Quintero, L. A.; Wilke, P.; and Rollefson, G. O. 2007. An Eastern Jordan Perspective on the Lower Paleolithic of the "Levantine Corridor." *SHAJ* 9: 157–66.

Rech, J. A.; Pigati, J. S.; al-Kuisi, M.; and Bright, J. 2013. The Rise and Fall of Late Pleistocene Paleolakes in Southern Jordan. *Geological Society of America Abstracts* 45: 680.

Rink, W. J.; Schwarcz, H. P.; Ronen, A.; and Tsatskin, A. 2004. Confirmation of a near 400 ka Age for the Yabrudian Industry at Tabun Cave, Israel. *JAS* 31: 15–20.

Rollefson, G. O. 1981. The Late Acheulian Site at Fjaje, Wadi el-Bustan, Southern Jordan. *Paléorient* 7 (1): 5–21.

———. 1984. A Middle Acheulian Surface Site in the Wadi Uweinid, Eastern Jordan. *Paléorient* 10 (1): 127–33.

Rollefson, G. O.; Quintero, L. A.; and Wilke, P. J. 2005. The Acheulian Industry in the al-Jafr Basin of Southeastern Jordan. *JIPS* 35: 53–68.

———. 2006. Late Acheulian Variability in the Southern Levant: A Contrast of the Western and Eastern Margins of the Levantine Corridor. *NEA* 69: 61–72.

———. In press. Excavations at 'Ayn Sawda, Azraq Wetlands Reserve, Eastern Jordan. *ADAJ*.

Ronen, A.; Ohel, M. Y.; Lamdan, M.; and Assaf, A. 1980. Acheulean Artifacts from Two Trenches at Ma'ayan Barukh. *IEJ* 30: 17–33.

Rust, A. 1950. *Die Höhlernfunde von Jabrud, Syrien*. Offa-Bücher 8. Neumünster: Wachholz.

Schuldenrein, J., and Clark, G. A. 1994. Landscape and Prehistoric Chronology of West-Central Jordan. *Geoarchaeology* 9: 31–55.

Schwarcz, H. P.; Goldberg, P.; and Blackwell, B. 1980. Uranium Series Dating of Archaeological Sites in Israel. *Israel Journal of Earth Sciences* 29: 157–65.

Sharon, G., and Oron, M. 2014. The Lithic Tool Arsenal of a Mousterian Hunter. *QI* 331: 167–85.

Shea, J. J. 1998. Ar-Rasfa, a Stratified Middle Paleolithic Open-Air Site in Northwest Jordan: A Preliminary Report on the 1997 Excavation. *ADAJ* 42: 41–52.

———. 2001. The Middle Paleolithic: Early Modern Humans and Neandertals in the Levant. *NEA* 64: 38–64.

2003. The Middle Paleolithic of the East Mediterranean Levant. *JWP* 17: 313–94.

2010. Stone Age Visiting Cards Revisited: A Strategic Perspective on the Lithic Technology of Early Hominin Dispersal. In *Out of Africa I: The First Hominin Colonization of Eurasia*, ed. J. G. Fleagle, J. J. Shea, F. E. Grine, A. L. Baden, and R. E. Leakey, 47–64. Vertebrate Paleobiology and Paleoanthropology. Dordrecht: Springer.

Shimelmitz, R.; Barkai, R.; and Gopher, A. 2011. Systematic Blade Production at Late Lower Paleolithic (400–200 kyr) Qesem Cave, Israel. *JHE* 61: 458–79.

Succi Fabiani, L. 2001. Due siti dell'Acheuleano medio/arcaico nella Giordania meridionale. *SEQ* 23: 57–67.

Succi Fabiani, L., and Fabiano, M. 2004. L'Acheuleano medio del bacino idrografico di Uadi Harad (Giordania meridionale). *SEQ* 26: 41–55.

Valladas, H.; Mercier, N.; Hershkovitz, I.; Zaidner, Y.; Tsatskin, A.; Yeshurun, R.; Vialettes, L.; Joron, J.-L.; Reyss, J.-L.; and Weinstein-Evron, M. 2013. Dating the Lower to Middle Paleolithic Transition in the Levant: A View from Misliya Cave, Mount Carmel, Israel. *JHE* 65: 585–93.

Villiers, L. E. 1983. Final Report on Paleolithic Sampling at Abu al-Khas, North Jordan. *ADAJ* 27: 27–44.

Weinstein-Evron, M.; Tsatskin, A.; Porat, N.; and Kronfeld, J. 1999. ^{230}Th/^{234}U Date for the Acheulo-Yabrudian Layer in the Jamal Cave, Mount Carmel, Israel. *South African Journal of Science* 95: 186–8.

Whalen, N. M., and Kolly, C. M. 2001. Survey of Acheulean Sites in the Wadi as-Sirhan Basin, Jordan, 1999. *ADAJ* 45: 11–18.

Wilke, P. J.; Quintero, L. A.; and Rech, J. A. 2010. The Acheulian Occupations at 'Uyun al-Qadim, al-Jafr Basin, Jordan: A Progress Summary. *ADAJ* 54: 423–41.

Zaidner, Y.; Ronen, A.; and Burdukiewicz, J.-M. 2003. L'industrie microlithique du Paléolithique inférieur de Bizat Ruhama, Israël. *L'Anthropologie* 107: 203–22.

TWO

AN ANTHROPOLOGICAL REVIEW OF THE UPPER PALEOLITHIC IN THE SOUTHERN LEVANT

ANNA BELFER-COHEN AND NIGEL GORING-MORRIS

The Upper Paleolithic coincides with the spread of modern humans (*Homo sapiens sapiens*) all over the globe, becoming the only living human species on earth. This is clearly the case in Western Europe, where prehistoric research originated, dictating until recently Eurocentric interpretations of local developments elsewhere. Indeed, local Neanderthal populations there supposedly were replaced with little or no interbreeding by the modern human newcomers. Yet, ongoing research on the Paleolithic sequence in other parts of the world – especially in the Levant – has revealed that the interactions between indigenous populations and groups arriving from Africa were more complex than previously believed. The presence of modern humans (anatomically speaking) in the Levant dates back as far as ca. 90,000 cal. BP, that is, during the Middle Paleolithic, more or less contemporaneous with or predating local Neanderthal groups, both represented by the Mousterian (Arensberg and Belfer-Cohen 1998; Teyssandier 2008; Teyssandier, Bon, and Bordes 2010; Zilhão 2013; 2014, with references).

Geneticists agree that the Levant is also the region where interbreeding between Neanderthals and modern humans took place, assumed to occur earlier than, or just at what is considered as, the beginnings of the Upper Paleolithic (e.g., Gibbons 2016; Kuhlwilm et al. 2016, with references). Without going into the broad implications of these findings in regards to human evolution, that is, definition of a human species, modern behavior, cognitive abilities, and so forth, clearly one can state that from the very beginning of the Levantine Upper Paleolithic local human groups were modern humans, originating from earlier and later waves of migration out of Africa. Thus, one may assume that the basics of their social conduct were within the known range of extant human behavior.

Traditionally, the local Upper Paleolithic is considered to last about 25,000 years (from ca. 50,000 to 25,000 cal. BP), comprising several archaeological traditions/cultures of mobile foragers (Belfer-Cohen and Goring-Morris 2014a). In the following, we attempt to evaluate the (scant) evidence available concerning socio-cultural developments in the region, integrating existing data to infer subsistence, behavioral, and social adaptations, including settlement patterns, spatial organization of activities, material cultural innovations, and so forth.

CHRONOLOGICAL FRAMEWORK

Dating the beginnings of the Upper Paleolithic in southwestern Asia is hotly debated; this stems from differences of opinion concerning the role played by the Levant in the dispersion routes of modern humans and the diffusion of novel ideas out of Africa throughout the world. Was the Levant the first stop of *Homo sapiens sapiens* en route to Eurasia? If and how many of the innovations introduced to Eurasia were first observed or even initiated in the Levant? The route(s) of dispersal from Africa and the initial appearance of modern humans in Eurasia are focal issues of ongoing paleo-anthropological studies, including the "Nile Valley-Levant" and "Horn of Africa-Saudi Arabia" options (Groucutt et al. 2015, with references).

Recent ^{14}C charcoal dating series from Kebara Cave, Mount Carmel indicate that the Initial Upper Paleolithic emerged by ca. 50,000 cal BP (Rebollo et al. 2011). Further north, at the key rock-shelter site of Ksar Akil, two independent ^{14}C date sets on marine mollusks indicate the inception of the Initial Upper Paleolithic there at either ca. 43,000/42,000 cal. BP or 45,900 cal. BP (Bosch et al. 2015a, 2015b; Douka et al. 2013; Douka, Higham, and Bergman 2015).[1] While debate is ongoing as to which of the date sets is more robust, we tend to accept the earlier dates, placing the Levant in a focal position in regards to the route of this out-of-Africa dispersion with all the implications entailed. Additionally, recent radiometric dating of a modern human cranium from Manot Cave in Galilee[2] (ca. 50,000–60,000 uncal. BP [Hershkovitz et al. 2015]) raises the possibility of an even earlier date for the Middle Paleolithic/Upper Paleolithic transition.

The Levantine Upper Paleolithic ends with the emergence of the Epipaleolithic complexes (ca. 25,000 cal. BP), coinciding with the onset of the Last Glacial Maximum climatic episode. By contrast, the traditional Eurocentric subdivision of the Paleolithic correlates the end of the Upper Paleolithic with the end of the last glaciation and the Pleistocene–Holocene transition, ca. 10,000 years ago (Goring-Morris and Belfer-Cohen 2017). This issue, the end of the Upper Paleolithic in the Levant, has also been debated; initially the Epipaleolithic period was part of the Upper Paleolithic sequence (Garrod 1934; 1957; Neuville 1934; 1951), separated in the 1960s into two distinctive archaeological periods based on chipped-stone assemblage characteristics (Bar-Yosef 1970; Perrot 1968). Subsequently, this paradigm was challenged based on factors relating to social organization, subsistence adaptations, and the very validity of the arguments for this division (Gilead 1984). Still, there is a broad consensus today recognizing major differences between the Upper Paleolithic and the Epipaleolithic that justify their separation, for example, tempo of cultural developments, demographic growth, and increasing territoriality, among others (Goring-Morris, Hovers, and Belfer-Cohen 2009).

THE ARCHAEOLOGICAL CULTURES (FIGS. 2.1 AND 2.2)

Initial Upper Paleolithic

The configuration of the South Levantine chipped-stone assemblages at the beginning of the Upper Paleolithic indicates the presence of several distinctive variants, prominent ones being the "Emiran" and "Ksar Akil Phase 1," the chronological relationships between them being rather opaque (Belfer-Cohen and Goring-Morris 2014a). There is a general tendency for Initial Upper Paleolithic assemblages to display typological changes *prior* to technological developments compared to the preceding Mousterian. New tool forms appeared, such as the distinctive chamfered pieces (mostly at Lebanese sites) and bifacially thinned Emireh points, as well as quantities of endscrapers and burins, the last two being rare in Middle Paleolithic assemblages (Newcomer 1968–1969; Volkman and Kaufman 1983). Lagging behind was the shift from the surficial Levallois flaking method to narrow-fronted serial blade production (Belfer-Cohen and Goring-Morris 2007). Such developments are most clearly illustrated at the site of Boqer Tachtit in the central Negev, portraying four short-term sequential occupations, each with systematic refitting studies (Volkman 1983; 1989).

In addition to techno-typological changes, the spatial configurations of the four brief occupation levels, in terms of the numbers of fire pits and hearths and their relations to the chipped-stone assemblages, may reflect shifts in

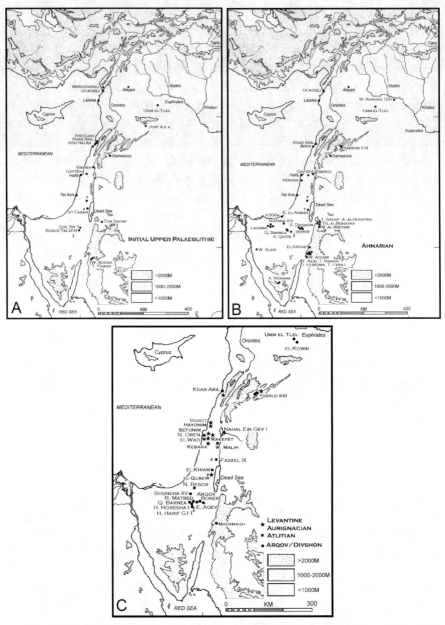

2.1. Distributions of: (a) Initial Upper Paleolithic; (b) Ahmarian; and (c) Levantine Aurignacian, Atlitian, and Arqov/Divshon sites in the Levant. (Drawn by N. Goring-Morris.)

behavioral patterns (Fig. 2.3) (Marks 1983; Marks and Friedel 1977). It was suggested that the more ephemeral Upper Paleolithic levels mirrored a shift from Middle Paleolithic logistical "radiating" home bases to more "circulating" mobile Upper Paleolithic settlement patterns, that is, a shift from collectors to foragers (Binford 1980; see below).

UPPER PALEOLITHIC

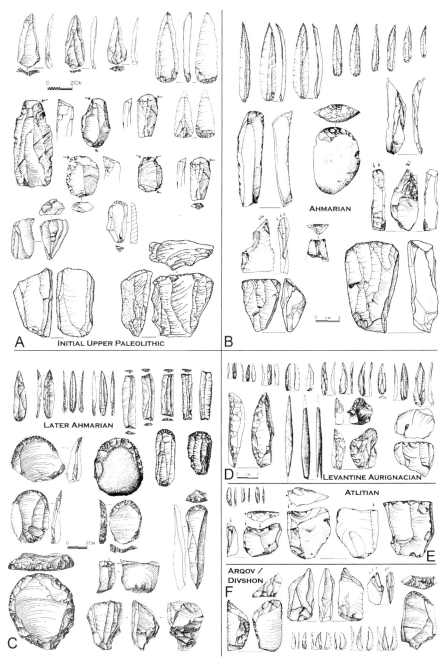

2.2. Characteristic core and tool types of: (a) Initial Upper Paleolithic; (b) Ahmarian; (c) Later Ahmarian; (d) Levantine Aurignacian; (e) Atlitian; and (f) Arqov/Divshon. (Compiled by N. Goring-Morris.)

The Early Upper Paleolithic

The Ahmarian. A direct development from Initial Upper Paleolithic to Ahmarian (ca. 46,000/42,000–31,000/29,000 cal. BP) is documented in the earlier occupation levels at Boqer on the other bank of Nahal Zin, immediately opposite Boqer Tachtit (Fig. 2.4a). This is reflected in the techno-typological characteristics of the lithic assemblages (Marks 1983). It apparently continues through to the Late Upper Paleolithic. Geographically, the Ahmarian is pan-Levantine (Goring-Morris and Belfer-Cohen 2018), being recognized in cave and rock-shelter sites throughout the Mediterranean zone, as well as in the semiarid eastern and southern margins, where it is mostly characterized by open-air sites (Figs. 2.1b and 2.4b).

Ahmarian lithic assemblages display a certain degree of techno-typological variability, some being regional, some chronological (see Fig. 2.2b and 2.2c). In general, the characteristic technology focused upon the serial production of symmetrical, convergent blade/bladelets from narrow-fronted cores, commonly retouched into el-Wad points that were used as both projectiles and perforators (Becker 2003). Larger tools, that is, scrapers and burins, often derive from initial setting up of the cores or from core tablets (Goring-Morris and Davidzon 2006). Blade/bladelet blanks tend to be more gracile in assemblages from the semiarid margins, indicating differences in raw material procurement and treatment. Most finds are limited to the lithic assemblages, although occasional grinding slabs, bone tools, ocher, and dentalia are found.

The Levantine Aurignacian. There has been considerable confusion concerning the term "Aurignacian," as it was originally used as a synonym for the whole Upper Paleolithic sequence. As research advanced, it became apparent that, in Western Europe (especially France, where it was originally defined), the oldest facies of this taxon, the "Proto-Aurignacian" and "Aurignacian 0," actually closely resemble the Levantine Ahmarian and differ significantly from the following "Aurignacian I," considered as the classical phase of this entity (Conard and Bolus 2006; Teyssandier 2008; Teyssandier, Bon, and Bordes 2010; Zilhão 2014, with references).

The Levantine Aurignacian, in its restricted definition (see chapters in Bar-Yosef and Zilhão 2006), portrays characteristics of the European "Aurignacian I" and postdates its European counterparts (dated to ca. 39,000–33,000 cal. BP), though it was probably of much shorter duration (Barzilai, Hershkovitz, and Marder 2016; Belfer-Cohen and Goring-Morris 2014b; Lengyel et al. 2006; Otte, Shidrang, and Flas 2012). It is represented by a limited number of assemblages deriving from caves and rock-shelters located in a circumscribed, mostly coastal area within the Mediterranean zone, and most occupations are quite limited in size. Accordingly, it seems to represent a brief phenomenon of distinctly nonlocal

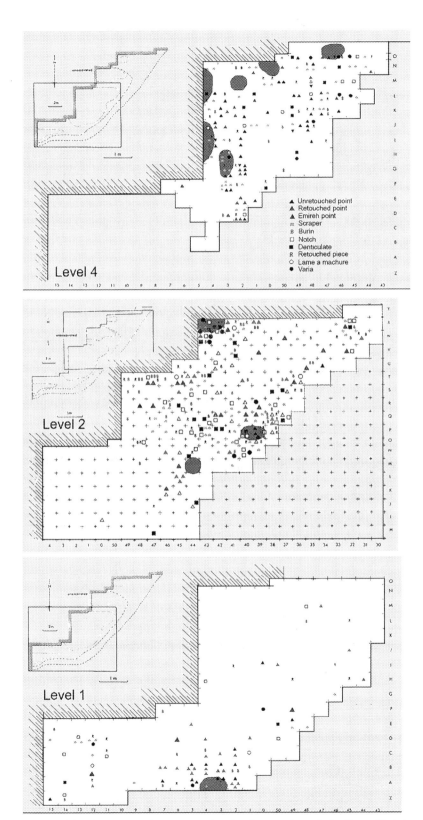

2.3. Tool distributions in relation to combustion features through the Boqer Tachtit sequence. Note that Level 1 is earliest (after Marks 1983). (Drawn by N. Goring-Morris.)

2.4. (a) Nahal Zin, looking south, showing the relative locations of Boker Tachtit (Initial Upper Paleolithic), Boqer (Ahmarian), and Sde Divshon (Ahmarian); (b) Erq el-Ahmar; (c) massive fire pit at Qadesh Barnea 501 (Ahmarian); and (d) incised ocher-smeared slab and equid pendants (insets) from Hayonim Cave and split-base point from Kebara Cave (Levantine Aurignacian). (Photos [a–c] by N. Goring-Morris. Photo [d] by Z. Radovan. Courtesy of the archives of The Institute of Archaeology, The Hebrew University of Jerusalem.)

derivation in terms of the techno-typological lithic and bone tool characteristics; indeed, similar to those of "Aurignacian 1" (see references above).

When found in stratigraphic association, the Levantine Aurignacian overlies Ahmarian occupations, for example, Ksar Akil (Douka et al. 2013; Williams and Bergman 2010), Yabrud (Bachdach 1982; Rust 1950), Manot (Barzilai, Hershkovitz, and Marder 2016), and Kebara (Bar-Yosef et al. 1996) (for a general overview, see Mellars 2006), although there are also sites where the Aurignacian is the only Upper Paleolithic entity found, for example, Hayonim Cave (Belfer-Cohen and Bar-Yosef 1981), Raqefet Cave (Lengyel et al. 2006), and Sefunim Cave (Ronen 1984) (see Fig. 2.1c).[3]

The chipped-stone technology features the production of thick flake/blade blanks for modification into a variety of carinated scrapers and burins; there is also some blade/bladelet production, most of the latter deriving from carination, often as twisted (*Dufour*) bladelets with inverse semi-abrupt retouch (see Fig. 2.2d). Another distinctive feature is the presence of relatively abundant worked bone, antler, and horn core artifacts, such as bi-points, points, and awls (Goring-Morris and Belfer-Cohen 2006). The rare presence of distinctive "split-base" points (Fig. 2.4d) characteristic of the Western European "Aurignacian I" strengthens the likelihood that the Levantine Aurignacian represents a relatively brief intrusion of European groups from the northwest (Bar-Yosef 2007; Belfer-Cohen and Goring-Morris 2014b).

Other distinctive material culture remains with a European flavor include incised stone plaques, ungulate teeth pendants (see Fig. 2.4d), raptors' wings, and so forth (Belfer-Cohen and Bar-Yosef 1981; R. Rabinovich, pers. comm., 2017; Tejero et al. 2018).

Later Upper Paleolithic

This period is represented by two new, still poorly dated entities, namely the Atlitian in the Mediterranean zone and the Arqov/Divshon industry in the south, especially the Negev (Belfer-Cohen and Goring-Morris 2014a) (see Figs. 2.1 and 2.2d). They appear in both open-air and rock-shelter sites. The Atlitian is characterized by thick flake production with a heavy emphasis on concave truncated burins; the Arqov/Divshon entity, also flake oriented, features numerous lateral carinated burins and scrapers (Williams 2003). When found in stratigraphic contexts, they mostly postdate both the Ahmarian and Levantine Aurignacian. Thus, the Atlitian at Ksar Akil overlies the Aurignacian levels and predates the Epipaleolithic entities (Bergman 1987), while in Boqer the Arqov/Divshon level is found above Ahmarian ones (Marks 1983).

DISCUSSION

During the earlier stages of the Upper Paleolithic, there were few dramatic changes in lifeways from the preceding Middle Paleolithic. It was suggested that differences in the intensity and nature of occupation reflect a shift from the Middle Paleolithic radiating "logistical" adaptation (i.e., semisedentary, to a degree) to a much more mobile "circular" one in the Upper Paleolithic (Marks 1983; Marks and Friedel 1977); but, humans continued to subsist on foraging in small groups, and population densities remained low. Still, it is clear that the magnitude of movements grew at an extent and tempo unknown previously. During the Upper Paleolithic, these occurred at variable scales: large-scale pan-regional movements with population replacement and/or assimilation; intra-regional movements of specific bands sharing mating networks within annual subsistence rounds; and fission/fusion processes of specific bands. All of this without considering the influence of dynamic environmental differences and changes. For example, Ahmarian blade/bladelet blanks and tools are more gracile in the semiarid margins than their more robust Mediterranean zone counterparts. Could this reflect more mobile adaptations over vast swathes of the landscape within the steppic margins, as opposed to more restricted movements by bands based in the more mesic woodland areas? While hunting was undoubtedly a major pursuit, it seems that the vegetal component of the Upper Paleolithic diet is difficult to evaluate. Based on the nutritional profiles of ethnographic hunter-gatherers, vegetal foods should comprise ca. 60–80 percent of the diet (Binford 2001; Speth 2010, with references). This aspect of the dietary input is hardly, if at all, visible within the local Upper Paleolithic record, with the exception of a few grinding stones and slabs. Rather, the composition of Upper Paleolithic lithic assemblages and micro-wear studies primarily reflect hunting, butchering, and hide-working activities (Becker 2003). Still, recent evidence for plant manipulation and cultivation at the early Epipaleolithic Ohalo II site (ca. 24,000 cal. BP), with its unusual preservation of organic remains, should serve as a cautionary tale concerning the systematic exploitation of vegetal resources during the Paleolithic (Snir et al. 2015).

There is a broad consensus that the Upper Paleolithic "package" diffused out of Africa via southwestern Asia into Europe in the form of actual population movements. This may have occurred during the Initial Upper Paleolithic (the Emiran) and/or somewhat later during the Early Upper Paleolithic (i.e., Ahmarian), with archaeological evidence for features of both entities present in southeastern Europe (e.g., Škrdla 2003; Tsanova 2008; Tsanova et al. 2012). In addition, the Levantine Aurignacian provides compelling evidence for subsequent migration in the opposite direction – "on-the-rebound" (Bar-Yosef and Belfer-Cohen 2010; Belfer-Cohen and Goring-Morris 2014b; Tejero et al. 2016).

The Middle Paleolithic/Upper Paleolithic shift is recognized primarily by the lithic assemblages; as noted above, it appears that typological changes preceded technological developments. The meaning and significance of this trend is hotly debated, since it pertains to issues, such as what entails modern behavior? And are there observable, quantifiable differences between the behavior of modern humans, representing the Upper Paleolithic, versus the preceding Middle Paleolithic populations, indicating differences in cognition and mental abilities (e.g., Hovers and Belfer-Cohen 2005; 2013)? While the appearance and use of bone tools, ocher, ostrich eggshell, and marine mollusks have often been cited as indicators of modern human behavior (Conard 2010, with references), they all appear sporadically in the Levantine Middle Paleolithic[4] and are not especially abundant components of Upper Paleolithic occupations in the Levant. Specific behavioral changes between the Middle Paleolithic and the Initial Upper Paleolithic, as reflected in the material culture, site patterning, environmental exploitation, and so forth are ultimately rather scant.

Most Upper Paleolithic sites were small, rarely exceeding 75–125 m^2. The situation regarding the intensity of Upper Paleolithic occupation within many Mediterranean zone caves and rock-shelters is not entirely clear; still, these spatially constrained occupations do appear to have been less intensively settled than during the Middle Paleolithic (Bar-Yosef et al. 1996; Belfer-Cohen and Bar-Yosef 1981).

Most *in situ* Ahmarian occupations in the semiarid margins were short-term, ephemeral occupations, commonly containing one or more large fire pits and closely associated hearths (see Fig. 2.4c) (Goring-Morris and Belfer-Cohen 2018, with references).[5] A notable exception is Sde Divshon (D27b), which, though partially deflated, was more extensive and also contained a more balanced toolkit, indicating multiple activities and multiple occupations, more reminiscent of a Middle Paleolithic base camp (see Fig. 2.4a) (Ferring 1976; 1984). Indeed, a shift was observed at Boqer Tachtit, from a single hearth with distinct and disparate activity areas in the lowest level (1) (i.e., similar to the Middle Paleolithic Rosh Ein Mor base camp), to multiple fire pits and hearths, each with its associated full suite of tool types in the latest level (4) (see Fig. 2.3). There is also extensive intra-level refitting of lithic artifacts within each level, indicating contemporaneity of the distinct activity areas associated with the fire pits (Marks 1983). A similar picture emerges from lithic conjoins between Abu Noshra I and VI, located ca. 200 m from one another at the edge of a marsh in southern Sinai (Becker 2003: 135), demonstrating the absolute contemporaneity of the two occupations. This may provide hints concerning the possible presence of diffuse encampments (of nuclear families?) of the band in relatively close proximity to one another, thus providing a degree of privacy.

The phenomenon of multiple small hearths was also observed within the spatially restricted Aurignacian occupation layers at Hayonim Cave, not recorded in previous Middle Paleolithic levels there; certainly, most other Levantine Aurignacian occupations, for example, Yabrud and Sefunim, were spatially limited (Belfer-Cohen and Bar-Yosef 1981).

Indeed, given all the above, in behavioral terms, it appears that the more mobile Upper Paleolithic bands returned repeatedly to the same locality (i.e., palimpsests), with the encampment sometimes comprising what we, as archaeologists, commonly define as different sites. Such bands comprised smaller units (nuclear families?) that, in setting up camp together, sometimes spatially segregated themselves from one another as separate, independent social units.

Since both Upper Paleolithic site and group sizes were small, there had to have existed intergroup social networks in order to ensure a viable genetic pool; only thus could Upper Paleolithic populations sustain the long-term survival/existence of the discrete entity comprising groups sharing a common history and cultural traditions. Such a genetic pool requires a minimum of ± 250 individuals. If, as seems likely, band sizes were on the order of ± 25 individuals, intergroup contacts entailing ± 10 other bands would be required to enable such gene flow, whether seasonally, annually, or over the course of several years.[6]

Similar to the Middle Paleolithic, Levantine Upper Paleolithic populations were sparsely distributed, such that a high degree of mobility over large regions would have been mandatory. There are occasional indications that likely reflect the scale, direction, and nature of these long-distance connections – as with the example of later Ahmarian Boqer BE Levels III–V in the central Negev and Thalab al-Buhayra in Wadi Hasa 110 km away on the plateau east of the rift valley, the typological configurations of the respective assemblages being strikingly similar (Coinman 2003; Jones, Marks, and Kaufman 1983) (see Fig. 2.2c).

Another issue awaiting future research concerns relationships between the various Upper Paleolithic entities. Especially intriguing is the relationship between the Ahmarians and the Aurignacians. Although no Aurignacian has been recovered to date from the semiarid areas, Ahmarian assemblages were recovered in the Mediterranean zone, sometimes in relatively close proximity to the Aurignacians. Lithic assemblages of the latter include the el-Wad point in small numbers, presently considered to be the lithic marker of the Ahmarian. Dorothy Garrod (1953: 25) had already written that perhaps this should be considered as the local endemic contribution, being "hardly known in the west [i.e., Europe]." Still, the el-Wad point is quite a simple artifact, with similar items known from preceding and succeeding lithic industries. Indeed, the smaller, thinner, and more aerodynamic el-Wad points (versus the Mousterian and Emireh points of the Initial Upper Paleolithic) may indicate technological innovations, such as the *atlatl* (spear-thrower) and/or bow and arrow (Bergman and Newcomer 1983).

Unfortunately, we are limited in our speculations *vis-à-vis* the identity and relationship(s) between the various groups/cultures to the lithic assemblages comprising most of the material remains. Thus, ornaments, which are considered as social and group identity markers (Kuhn and Stiner 2007), are a rare commodity in the Upper Paleolithic and even when recovered are common, being available to all (e.g., dentalia shells). The Levantine Aurignacian is indeed the only cultural entity that is conspicuous among the local Upper Paleolithic entities.

In summary, Levantine Upper Paleolithic adaptations indicate low densities of small, dispersed, highly mobile bands moving within the diverse landscapes of both the Mediterranean and semiarid zones. These groups had to be in contact in order to retain the viable genetic pool, common to the entity they comprised. We are in the dark in regards to the intragroup structure of these bands. Can one begin to talk about evidence for nuclear families as the basic unit of the group? The same can be said concerning the nature of intergroup ties. Did all group members know or were they aware of all the other members within their common mating network? One has to assume that on occasion they did encounter strangers, that is, people of different entities, as in the case of the Ahmarian and Aurignacian, living cheek-to-cheek for some millennia.

Still, although the data on the ground are scant, the Levantine Upper Paleolithic represents humble but pivotal beginnings for subsequent developments, with a greater emphasis on group identity and increasing territoriality within southwestern Asia; this subsequently culminated in the transition to the sedentary complex hunter-gatherers/cultivators of the Late Epipaleolithic and the Neolithic to come.

NOTES

1 It should be noted that the beginning of the Initial Upper Paleolithic coincides with limits of the latest ^{14}C dating methods. In addition, dating marine mollusks is widely recognized as being problematic.
2 It was recovered with no direct stratigraphic context.
3 The Ahmarian continued to develop in the semiarid and arid margins coevally with the intrusion of the Levantine Aurignacian into the Mediterranean zone.
4 Not to mention in coeval contexts in Africa (e.g., Henshilwood et al. 2011).
5 This contrasts with what is known from the Middle Paleolithic levels in many sites, where there was continuous use of a central fireplace through multiple Middle Paleolithic occupations, one level after another.
6 Seemingly different means of networking were employed with the emergence of the Epipaleolithic (ca. 24,000 cal. BP), when there is evidence for greater territoriality of groups and the appearance of major annual aggregation sites for the disparate groups. With the appearance of the Late Epipaleolithic Natufian complex and the beginnings of sedentism and hamlets, another different mechanism was employed (Belfer-Cohen and Goring-Morris 2011; Maher 2016).

REFERENCES

Arensburg, B., and Belfer-Cohen, A. 1998. Sapiens and Neandertals: Rethinking the Levantine Middle Paleolithic Hominids. In *Neandertals and Modern Humans in Western Asia*, ed. T. Akazawa, K. Aoki, and O. Bar-Yosef, 311–22. New York: Plenum.

Bachdach, J. 1982. *Das Jungpaläolithikum von Jabrud in Syrien*. PhD diss., University of Cologne.

Bar-Yosef, O. 1970. *The Epi-Palaeolithic Cultures of Palestine*. PhD diss., The Hebrew University of Jerusalem.

2007. The Archaeological Framework of the Upper Paleolithic Revolution. *Diogenes* 54 (2): 3–18.

Bar-Yosef, O.; Arnold, M.; Mercier, N., Belfer-Cohen, A.; Goldberg, P.; Housley, R.; Laville, H.; Meignen, L.; Vogel, J. C.; and Vandermeersch, B. 1996. The Dating of the Upper Paleolithic Layers in Kebara Cave, Mt Carmel. *JAS* 23: 297–306.

Bar-Yosef, O., and Belfer-Cohen, A. 2010. The Levantine Upper Palaeolithic and Epipalaeolithic. In *South-Eastern Mediterranean Peoples between 130,000 and 10,000 Years Ago*, ed. E. A. A. Garcea, 144–67. Oxford: Oxbow.

Bar-Yosef, O., and Zilhão, J., eds. 2006. *Towards a Definition of the Aurignacian: Proceedings of the Symposium Held in Lisbon, Portugal, June 25–30, 2002.* Trabalhos de arqueologia 45. Lisbon: Instituto Português de Arqueologia; Cambridge, MA; American School of Prehistoric Research, Peabody Museum, Harvard University.

Barzilai, O.; Hershkovitz, I.; and Marder, O. 2016. The Early Upper Palaeolithic Period at Manot Cave, Western Galilee, Israel. *JHE* 31: 85–100.

Becker, M. S. 2003. Spatial Patterning in the Upper Palaeolithic: A Perspective from the Abu Noshra Sites. In *More than Meets the Eye: Studies on Upper Palaeolithic Diversity in the Near East*, ed. A. N. Goring-Morris and A. Belfer-Cohen, 134–50. Oxford: Oxbow.

Belfer-Cohen, A., and Bar-Yosef, O. 1981. The Aurignacian in Hayonim Cave. *Paléorient* 7 (2): 19–42.

Belfer-Cohen, A., and Goring-Morris, A. N. 2007. From the Beginning: Levantine Upper Palaeolithic Cultural Change and Continuity. In *Rethinking the Human Revolution: New Behavioural and Biological Perspectives on the Origin and Dispersal of Modern Humans*, ed. P. Mellars, K. Boyle, O. Bar-Yosef, and C. Stringer, 199–206. MIM. Cambridge: McDonald Institute for Archaeological Research.

2011. Becoming Farmers: The Inside Story. *CA* 52 (suppl. 4): S209–20.

2014a. The Upper Palaeolithic and Earlier Epi-Palaeolithic of Western Asia. In *The Cambridge World Prehistory*, Vol. 3: *West and Central Asia and Europe*, ed. A. C. Renfrew and P. G. Bahn, 1381–407. Cambridge: Cambridge University Press.

2014b. On the Rebound – A Levantine View of Upper Palaeolithic Dynamics. In *Modes de contacts et de déplacements au Paléolithique eurasiatique: Actes du Colloque international de la commission 8 (Paléolithique supérieur) de l'UISPP, Université de Liège, 28–31 mai 2012*, ed. M. Otte and F. Le Brun-Ricalens, 27–36. ERAUL 140; ArchéoLogiques 5. Liège: University of Liège; Luxembourg: Centre National de Recherche Archéologique, Musée National d'Histoire et d'Art.

Bergman, C. A. 1987. *Ksar Akil, Lebanon: A Technological and Typological Analysis of the Later Palaeolithic Levels of Ksar Akil*, Vol. 2: *Levels XIII–VI*. BAR International Series 329. Oxford: BAR.

Bergman, C. A., and Newcomer, M. H. 1983. Flint Arrowhead Breakage: Examples from Ksar Akil, Lebanon. *JFA* 10: 238–43.

Binford, L. R. 1980. Willow Smoke and Dogs' Tails: Hunter-Gatherer Settlement Systems and Archaeological Site Formation. *AA* 45: 4–20.

2001. *Constructing Frames of Reference: An Analytical Method for Archaeological Theory Building Using Ethnographic and Environmental Data Sets*. Berkeley: University of California Press.

Bosch, M. D.; Mannino, M. A.; Prendergast, A. L.; O'Connell, T. C.; Demarchi, B.; Taylor, S. M.; Niven, L.; van der Plicht, J.; and Hublin, J.-J. 2015a. New Chronology for Ksâr 'Akil (Lebanon) Supports Levantine Route of Modern Human Dispersal into Europe. *PNAS* 112: 7683–8.

2015b. Reply to Douka et al.: Critical Evaluation of the Ksâr 'Akil Chronologies. *PNAS* 112: E7035.

Coinman, N. R. 2003. The Upper Paleolithic of Jordan: New Data from the Wadi al-Hasa. In *More than Meets the Eye: Studies on Upper Palaeolithic Diversity in the Near East*, ed. A. N. Goring-Morris and A. Belfer-Cohen, 151–70. Oxford: Oxbow.

Conard, N. J. 2010. Cultural Modernity: Consensus or Conundrum? *PNAS* 107: 7621–2.

Conard, N. J., and Bolus, M. 2006. The Swabian Aurignacian and Its Place in European Prehistory. In *Towards a Definition of the Aurignacian: Proceedings of the Symposium Held in Lisbon, Portugal, June 25–30, 2002*, ed. O. Bar-Yosef and J. Zilhão, 211–39. Trabalhos de arqueologia 45. Lisbon: Instituto Português de Arqueologia; Cambridge, MA; American School of Prehistoric Research, Peabody Museum, Harvard University.

Douka, K.; Bergman, C. A.; Hedges, R. E. M.; Wesselingh, F.P. T.; and Higham, T. F. G. 2013. Chronology of Ksar Akil (Lebanon) and Implications for the Colonization of Europe by Anatomically Modern Humans. *PLOS ONE* 8 (9): e72931. https://doi.org/10.1371/journal.pone.0072931 (accessed September 26, 2017).

Douka, K.; Higham, T. F. G.; and Bergman, C. A. 2015. Statistical and Archaeological Errors Invalidate the Proposed Chronology for the Site of Ksar Akil. *PNAS* 112: E7034.

Ferring, C. R. 1976. Sde Divshon: An Upper Paleolithic Site on the Divshon Plain. In *Prehistory and Paleoenvironments in the Central Negev, Israel*, Vol. 1: *The Avdat/Aqev Area, Part 1*, ed. A. E. Marks, 99–206. ISEMRI 2 (1). Dallas: Southern Methodist University Press.

——— 1984. Intrasite Spatial Patterning: Its Role in Settlement Pattern – Subsistence Systems Analysis. In *Intrasite Spatial Analysis in Archaeology*, ed. H. J. Hietala, 116–126. NDA. Cambridge: Cambridge University Press.

Garrod, D. A. E. 1934. The Stone Age of Palestine. *Antiquity* 8 (30): 133–50.

——— 1953. The Relations between South-West Asia and Europe in the Later Palaeolithic Age. *JWH* 1: 13–38.

——— 1957. Notes sur le Paléolithique superieur du Moyen Orient. *Bulletin de la Société Préhistorique Française* 54: 439–46.

Gibbons, A. 2016. Five Matings for Moderns, Neandertals. *Science* 351 (6279): 1250–1.

Gilead, I. 1984. Is the Term "Epipaleolithic" Relevant to Levantine Prehistory? *CA* 25: 227–9.

Goring-Morris, A. N., and Belfer-Cohen, A. 2006. A Hard Look at the "Levantine Aurignacian": How Real Is the Taxon? In *Towards a Definition of the Aurignacian: Proceedings of the Symposium Held in Lisbon, Portugal, June 25–30, 2002*, ed. O. Bar-Yosef and J. Zilhão, 297–314. Trabalhos de arqueologia 45. Lisbon: Instituto Português de Arqueologia; Cambridge, MA; American School of Prehistoric Research, Peabody Museum, Harvard University.

——— 2017. The Early and Middle Epipalaeolithic of Cisjordan. In *Quaternary of the Levant: Environments, Climate Change, and Humans*, ed. Y. Enzel and O. Bar-Yosef, 639–50. Cambridge: Cambridge University Press.

——— 2018. The Ahmarian in the Context of the Earlier Upper Palaeolithic in the Near East. In *The Middle and Upper Paleolithic Archeology of the Levant and Beyond*, ed. Y. Nishiaki and T. Akazawa, 87–104. Replacement of Neanderthals by Modern Humans Series. Singapore: Springer.

Goring-Morris, A. N., and Davidzon, A. 2006. Straight to the Point: Upper Paleolithic Ahmarian Lithic Technology in the Levant. *Anthropologie* 44: 93–111.

Goring-Morris, A. N.; Hovers, E.; and Belfer-Cohen, A. 2009. The Dynamics of Pleistocene Settlement Patterns and Human Adaptations in the Levant: An Overview. In *Transitions in Prehistory: Essays in Honor of Ofer Bar-Yosef*, ed. J. J. Shea and D. E. Lieberman, 187–254. ASPRMS. Oxford: Oxbow.

Groucutt, H. S.; Petraglia, M. D.; Bailey, G.; Scerri, E. M. L.; Parton, A.; Clark-Balzan, L.; Jennings, R. P.; Lewis, L.; Blinkhorn, J.; Drake, N. A.; Breeze, P. S.; Inglis, R. H.;

Devès, M. H.; Meredith-Williams, M.; Boivin, N.; Thomas, M. G.; and Scally, A. 2015. Rethinking the Dispersal of *Homo sapiens* out of Africa. *EA* 24: 149–64.

Henshilwood, C. S.; d'Errico, F.; van Niekerk, K. L.; Coquinot, Y.; Jacobs, Z.; Lauritzen, S.-E.; Menu, M.; and García-Moreno, R. 2011. A 100,000-Year-Old Ochre-Processing Workshop at Blombos Cave, South Africa. *Science* 334 (6053): 219–22.

Hershkovitz, I.; Marder, O.; Ayalon, A.; Bar-Matthews, M.; Yasur, G.; Boaretto, E.; Caracuta, V.; Alex, B.; Frumkin, A.; Goder-Goldberger, M.; Gunz, P.; Holloway, R. L.; Latimer, B.; Lavi, R.; Matthews, A.; Slon, V.; Bar-Yosef Mayer, D.; Berna, F.; Bar-Oz, G.; Yeshurun, R.; May, H.; Hans, M. G.; Weber, G. W.; and Barzilai, O. 2015. Levantine Cranium from Manot Cave (Israel) Foreshadows the First European Modern Humans. *Nature* 520: 216–19.

Hovers, E., and Belfer-Cohen, A. 2005. "Now You See It, Now You Don't" – Modern Human Behavior in the Middle Paleolithic. In *Transitions before the Transition: Evolution and Stability in the Middle Paleolithic and Middle Stone Age*, ed. E. Hovers and S. L. Kuhn, 295–304. ICA. New York: Springer.

———. 2013. On Variability and Complexity: Lessons from the Levantine Middle Paleolithic Record. *CA* 54 (suppl. 8): S337–57.

Jones, M.; Marks, A. E.; and Kaufman, D. 1983. Boker: The Artifacts. In *Prehistory and Paleoenvironments in the Central Negev, Israel*, Vol. 3: *The Avdat/Aqev Area, Part 3*, ed. A. E. Marks, 283–332. ISEMRI 2 (3). Dallas: Southern Methodist University Press.

Kuhlwilm, M.; Gronau, I.; Hubisz, M. J.; de Filippo, C.; Prado-Martinez, J.; Kircher, M.; Fu, Q.; Burbano, H. A.; Lalueza-Fox, C.; de la Rasilla, M.; Rosas, A.; Rudan, P.; Brajkovic, D.; Kucan, Ž.; Gušic, I.; Marques-Bonet, T.; Andrés, A. M.; Viola, B.; Pääbo, S.; Meyer, M.; Siepel, A.; and Castellano, S. 2016. Ancient Gene Flow from Early Modern Humans into Eastern Neanderthals. *Nature* 530: 429–33.

Kuhn, S. L., and Stiner, M. C. 2007. Body Ornamentation as Information Technology: Towards an Understanding of the Significance of Early Beads. In *Rethinking the Human Revolution: New Behavioural and Biological and Perspectives on the Origins and Dispersal of Modern Humans*, ed. P. Mellars, K. Boyle, O. Bar-Yosef, and C. Stringer, 45–54. MIM. Cambridge: McDonald Institute for Archaeological Research.

Lengyel, G.; Boaretto, E.; Fabre, L.; and Ronen, A. 2006. New AMS ^{14}C Dates from the Early Upper Paleolithic Sequence of Raqefet Cave, Mount Carmel, Israel. *Radiocarbon* 48: 253–8.

Maher, L. A. 2016. A Road Well Travelled? Exploring Terminal Pleistocene Hunter-Gatherer Activities, Networks and Mobility in Eastern Jordan. In *Fresh Fields and Pastures New: Papers Presented in Honor of Andrew M. T. Moore*, ed. K. T. Lillios and M. Chazan, 55–82. Leiden: Sidestone.

Marks, A. E., ed. 1983. *Prehistory and Paleoenvironments in the Central Negev, Israel*, Vol. 3: *The Avdat/Aqev Area*, Part 3. ISEMRI 2 (3). Dallas: Southern Methodist University Press.

Marks, A. E., and Friedel, D. A. 1977. Prehistoric Settlement Patterns in the Avdat/Aqev Area. In *Prehistory and Paleoenvironments in the Central Negev, Israel*, Vol. 2: *The Avdat/Aqev Area, Part 2, and the Har Harif*, ed. A. E. Marks, 131–58. ISEMRI 2 (2). Dallas: Southern Methodist University Press.

Mellars, P. 2006. A New Radiocarbon Revolution and the Dispersal of Modern Humans in Eurasia. *Nature* 439: 931–5.

Newcomer, M. H. 1968–1969. The Chamfered Pieces from Ksar Akil (Lebanon). *Bulletin of the Institute of Archaeology* 8–9: 177–91.

Neuville, R. 1934. Le préhistorique de Palestine. *RB* 43: 237–59.
———. 1951. *Le paléolithique et le mésolithique du desert de Judée*. Archives de l'Institut de Paléontologie Humaine Mémoire 24. Paris: Masson.
Otte, M.; Shidrang, S.; and Flas, D., eds. 2012. *The Aurignacian from Yafteh Cave and Its Context (2005–2008 Excavations)*. ERAUL 132. Liège: University of Liège.
Perrot, J. 1968. La préhistoire palestinienne. In *Supplement au dictionnaire de la Bible*, Vol. 8, 286–446. Paris: Letougey & Ane.
Rebollo, N. R.; Weiner, S.; Brock, F.; Meignen, L.; Goldberg, P.; Belfer-Cohen, A.; Bar-Yosef, O.; and Boaretto, E. 2011. New Radiocarbon Dating of the Transition from the Middle to the Upper Paleolithic in Kebara Cave, Israel. *JAS* 38: 2424–33.
Ronen, A., ed. 1984. *The Sefunim Prehistoric Sites: Mount Carmel, Israel*. BAR International Series 230. Oxford: BAR.
Rust, A. 1950. *Die Höhlenfunde von Jabrud, Syrien*. Vor- und Frühgeschichtliche Untersuchungen aus dem Museum vorgeschichtlicher Altertümer in Kiel, n.F. 8. Neumunster: Wachholtz.
Škrdla, P. 2003. Comparison of Boker Tachtit and Stránská skála MP/UP Transitional Industries. *JIPS* 33: 37–73.
Snir, A.; Nadel, D.; Groman-Yaroslavski, I.; Melamed, Y.; Sternberg, M.; Bar-Yosef, O.; and Weiss, E. 2015. The Origin of Cultivation and Proto-Weeds, Long before Neolithic Farming. *PLOS ONE* 10 (7): e0131422. https://doi.org/10.1371/journal.pone.0131422 (accessed September 26, 2017).
Speth, J. D. 2010. *The Paleoanthropology and Archaeology of Big-Game Hunting: Protein, Fat, or Politics?* ICA. New York: Springer.
Tejero, J.-M.; Belfer-Cohen, A.; Bar-Yosef, O.; Gutkin, V.; and Rabinovich, R. 2018. Symbolic Emblems of the Levantine Aurignacians as a Regional Entity Identifier (Hayonim Cave, Lower Galilee, Israel). *PNAS* 115: 5145–50.
Tejero, J.-M.; Yeshurun, R.; Barzilai, O.; Goder-Goldberger, M.; Hershkovitz, I.; Lavi, R.; Schneller-Pels, N.; and Marder, O. 2016. The Osseous Industry from Manot Cave (Western Galilee, Israel): Technical and Conceptual Behaviours of Bone and Antler Exploitation in the Levantine Aurignacian. *QI* 403: 90–106.
Teyssandier, N. 2008. Revolution or Evolution: The Emergence of the Upper Paleolithic in Europe. *WA* 40: 493–519.
Teyssandier, N.; Bon, F.; and Bordes, J.-G. 2010. Within Projectile Range: Some Thoughts on the Appearance of the Aurignacian in Europe. *JAR* 66: 209–29.
Tsanova, T. 2008. *Les débuts du Paléolithique supérieur dans l'Est des Balkans: Réflexion à partir e l'étude taphonomique et techno-économique des ensembles lithiques des sites de Bacho Kiro (couche 11), Temnata (couches VI et 4) et Kozarnika (niveau VII)*. BAR International Series 1752. Oxford: Archaeopress.
Tsanova, T.; Zwyns, N.; Eizenberg, L.; Teyssandier, N.; Le Brun-Ricalens, F.; and Otte, M. 2012. Le plus petit dénominateur commun: Réflexion sur la variabilité des ensembles lamellaires du Paléolithique supérieur ancien d'Eurasie; Un bilan autour des exemples de Kozarnika (est des Balkans) et Yafteh (Zagros central). *L'Anthropologie* 116: 469–509.
Volkman, P. W. 1983. Boker Tachtit: Core Reconstructions. In *Prehistory and Paleoenvironments in the Central Negev, Israel*, Vol. 3: *The Avdat/Aqev Area, Part 3*, ed. A. E. Marks, 123–90. ISEMRI 2 (3). Dallas: Southern Methodist University Press.
———. 1989. *Boker Tachtit: The Technological Shift from the Middle to the Upper Paleolithic in the Central Negev, Israel*. Ann Arbor, MI: University Microfilms International.

Volkman, P. W., and Kaufman, D. 1983. A Reassessment of the Emireh Point as a Possible Type Fossil for the Technological Shift from the Middle to the Upper Palaeolithic in the Levant. In *The Mousterian Legacy: Human Biocultural Change in the Upper Pleistocene*, ed. E. Trinkaus, 35–51. BAR International Series 164. Oxford: BAR.

Williams, J. K. 2003. An Examination of Upper Palaeolithic Flake Technologies in the Marginal Zone of the Levant. In *More Than Meets the Eye: Studies on Upper Palaeolithic Diversity in the Near East*, ed. A. N. Goring-Morris and A. Belfer-Cohen, 196–208. Oxford: Oxbow.

Williams, J. K., and Bergman, C. A. 2010. Upper Paleolithic Levels XIII–XVI (A and B) from the 1937–1938 and 1947–1948 Boston College Excavations and the Levantine Aurignacian at Ksar Akil, Lebanon. *Paléorient* 36 (2): 117–61.

Zilhão, J. 2013. Neandertal-Modern Human Contact in Western Eurasia: Issues of Dating, Taxonomy, and Cultural Associations. In *Dynamics of Learning in Neanderthals and Modern Humans,* Vol. 1: *Cultural Perspectives*, ed. T. Akazawa, Y. Nishiaki, and K. Aoki, 21–57. Replacement of Neanderthals by Modern Humans Series. Tokyo: Springer.

2014. The Upper Palaeolithic of Europe. In *The Cambridge World Prehistory*, Vol. 3: *West and Central Asia and Europe*, ed. A. C. Renfrew and P. G. Bahn, 1753–85. Cambridge: Cambridge University Press.

THREE

THE FORAGER–FARMER TRANSITION IN THE SOUTHERN LEVANT (CA. 20,000–8,500 CAL. BP)

NATALIE D. MUNRO AND LEORE GROSMAN

The forager–farmer transition has received abundant attention due to its alteration of foundational aspects of human societies. In the southern Levant, the transition was a gradual process, characterized by momentous changes in human economic, social, and ritual life. Here, we review the current state of research on the transition to agriculture in the southern Levant, focusing on the interconnectedness of economic, social, and ritual factors. Due to the limitations of space, we review only the most essential elements, including the emergence of plant and animal domestication, settlement distribution and sedentism, community organization and accompanying social change, and the ritual activities that reflect new ideologies designed to smooth these changes.

Despite ample research attention, there is little agreement over which terminology best describes the transition to agriculture and the definition of commonly used terms. Here, we use "forager–farmer transition" and "transition to agriculture" to refer to the more inclusive aspects of the process – those that integrate economy, society, and world view. We describe the more specific biological changes that occur in plants and animals across the transition to agriculture as the process of domestication. For animals, we use the terms "control," "management," and "domestication" (see definitions below) to describe increasing levels of human intervention in animal movement, mortality, and reproduction. For plants, we use "gathering" for the collection of plants in the wild, "cultivation" to describe the tending of morphologically wild plants (often called "pre-domestication cultivation"), and "domestication" for the

TABLE 3.1. *Chronology of Epipaleolithic and Pre-Pottery Neolithic periods in the southern Levant*

Chronology	Years cal. BP
Early Epipaleolithic	21,500–17,000
Middle Epipaleolithic	17,000–15,000
Late Epipaleolithic	15,000–11,500
Early Natufian	15,000–13,000
Late Natufian	13,000–11,500
Pre-Pottery Neolithic A	11,500–10,500
Early Pre-Pottery Neolithic B	10,500–10,000
Middle Pre-Pottery Neolithic B	10,000–9,500
Late Pre-Pottery Neolithic B	9,500–8,700

cultivation of plants that have undergone morphological change as a result of human selection.

We use the Epipaleolithic through Pre-Pottery Neolithic chronology to frame our discussion (Table 3.1). Although the Epipaleolithic begins more than 10,000 years before the Neolithic, its inclusion allows us to observe the conditions from which agriculture emerged and to address how and why questions about the transition itself. Although several cultural entities have been identified within the Epipaleolithic, we use a general subdivision of this period (Early, Middle, Late) so that we can talk broadly about overarching trends. Only in the Late Epipaleolithic when there is a striking leap in cultural complexity, do we refer to more specific cultural entities (Early and Late Natufian) to consider cultural change at higher resolution. Our discussion ends with the termination of the Pre-Pottery Neolithic, by which time plants and animals were fully domesticated, and agricultural economies became entrenched. Our chronological periods are based on a summary of radiocarbon dates derived from archaeological layers that share agreed on material characteristics, typifying each period (Maher, Banning, and Chazan 2011; Grosman 2013) (see Table 3.1 and Fig. 3.1).

ECONOMIC CHANGE

Plant Domestication

Opinion over the rate, geographic origin, and process of domestication in Southwest Asia is currently divided. The discussion revolves around two primary models, the core-area origin hypothesis (reviewed in Abbo and Gopher 2017; see also Bar-Yosef 2017) and the multiregional hypothesis (Willcox 2005; Asouti 2010; Fuller, Asouti, and Puruganan 2012; Allaby et al. 2015).

The core-area origin hypothesis emerged shortly before the turn of the last millennium (Lev-Yadun, Gopher, and Abbo 2000; Honne and Heun 2009;

3.1. Map of the southern Levant including sites mentioned in the text and their chronological periods. (Map by N. Klein.)

Abbo and Gopher 2017). It postulates that a single geographic area, the Karaçadag region of southeastern Anatolia, was home to the rapid domestication of the eight founder crops (einkorn wheat, emmer wheat, barley, chickpea, lentil, pea, bitter vetch, flax). The core area was identified based on the intersection of the distributions of the wild progenitors of all eight species (Lev-Yadun, Gopher, and Abbo 2000). Genetic, archaeological, and archaeobotanical data have been assembled to support the hypothesis. Key supporting evidence includes amplified fragment length polymorphism (AFLP) analysis of domestic einkorn and emmer wheat that most closely match the wild varieties from the Karaçadag region (Heun et al. 1997; Özkan et al. 2002). Manfred Heun and his colleagues (1997) data also support a monophyletic origin for einkorn, although this has been contested (Kilian et al. 2007).

The core-area origin hypothesis is also supported by archaeobotanical and radiocarbon data from southeastern Anatolian sites (Cafer Höyük, Cayönü, Nevali Çori) that document an *in situ* transformation from wild to domestic (van Zeist and Roller 1991–1992; Moulins 1993; Pasternak 1998; Gopher, Abbo, and Lev-Yadun 2002). Another overview of archaeobotanical and radiocarbon data by Ofer Bar-Yosef (2017) for the Upper and Middle Euphrates River Valley proposes an adjacent/overlapping core area. Stefan Kozlowski and Olivier Aurenche (2005) also emphasize the centrality of the Karaçadag region, naming it "the golden triangle" based on the convergence of diverse artifact types (lithics, ground stone, symbolic items) from east and west Fertile Crescent traditions.

Based on the supporting data, proponents of the core-area origin hypothesis argue that domestication happened only once in a single location. They describe it as a rapid, intentional, human-directed process that was based on a deep knowledge of the qualities of wild crop progenitors and ultimately domestic plants. Once domesticated, the crops spread as a complex throughout Southwest Asia and beyond.

The multiregional hypothesis presents a strongly contrasting scenario, purporting that multiple pathways to domestication were followed over a broad swath of Southwest Asia. Proponents of this hypothesis emphasize a gradual rather than a rapid pace of change, describing the beginning of cultivation as a protracted process that emerged over the course of millennia (Willcox 2005; Asouti 2010; Fuller, Willcox, and Allaby 2011). The process was strongly influenced by local ecological and social conditions. It included dead ends, frequent stops and starts, variation in its pace and character, and, at times, the movement and replacement of crops from other regions. Initial domestication is viewed partially as an unintended outcome that was propelled by human modification of the environment (niche construction) as groups settled into increasingly permanent communities (Fuller, Willcox, and Allaby 2011; Fuller, Asouti, and Purugganan 2012).

The multiregional model emerged out of the long-term research programs of scholars working with the rich archaeobotanical and radiocarbon records from the Upper Euphrates River Valley. The appearance of large quantities of wild einkorn in less than ideal habitats beyond the natural distribution of their wild progenitor is cited as evidence for the slow pace of change (Willcox, Fornite, and Herveux 2008), as is the gradual increase in the frequency of domestic traits in cereal assemblages (Fuller 2007; Fuller and Allaby 2009; Purugganan and Fuller 2011; Tanno and Willcox 2012). In particular, they document the slow emergence of key domestication traits in wheat and barley, such as a flexible rachis and increased grain size, over a period of 2,000–4,000 years (Fuller and Allaby 2009). The appearance of weed complexes provides additional evidence for cultivation in diverse locations across the northern and southern Levant.

In the southern Levant, plant remains are poorly preserved in most Epipaleolithic sites. An exception is the large assemblage of archaeobotanical remains from the water-logged Early Epipaleolithic site of Ohalo II, which predates the accepted onset of cultivation by more than 10,000 years. Despite the early date, wild grasses (wild wheat, barley, oats) comprise one-third of the archaeobotanical assemblage, articulation scars indicating domestic-type flexible rachises are common, and thirteen species of proto-weeds that thrive in disturbed environments are present. Nevertheless, domestic barley does not emerge at Ohalo II or in later Epipaleolithic sites in the region; thus, the assemblage is interpreted as a domestication dead end (Snir et al. 2015). Unfortunately, at present, the archaeobotanical evidence from Late Epipaleolithic sites (Natufian) is too scant to distinguish the intensive harvesting of wild cereals from cultivation (15,000–11,500 cal. BP).

Instead, in a key synthesis of archaeobotanical data from Early Epipaleolithic through Late Pre-Pottery Neolithic B (PPNB) sites, Ehud Weiss and his colleagues (2004) argue that the broad resource spectrum that typifies the Late Epipaleolithic faunal record is also true of plants, although it appears somewhat earlier. During the Early Epipaleolithic, costly small-grained grasses, that yield low returns despite high processing costs, are abundant at Ohalo II. These costly seeds point to intensive resource use. Ultimately, these were replaced by larger-grained wild cereals leading up to their cultivation and, ultimately, their domestication (Weiss et al. 2004). Supporting secondary evidence – sickle blades and abundant ground-stone tools used to harvest and process cereals – support the importance of larger-grained cereals by the Late Epipaleolithic (Wright 1994).

High frequencies of cereals beyond what could be expected to be harvested in the wild provide the first widespread evidence for cultivation in the PPNA (11,500–10,500 cal. BP) (Weiss, Kislev, and Hartmann 2006; Melamed, Plitmann, and Kislev 2008). The most compelling evidence comes from the

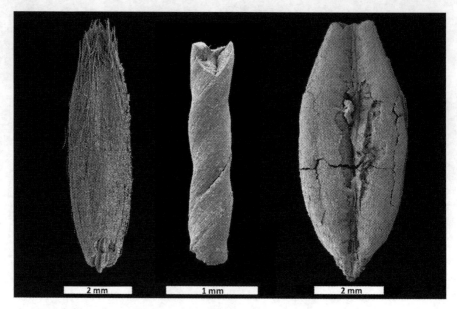

3.2. From left to right, a wild oat grain, a wild oat awn, and a wild barley grain from House 11 at PPNA Gilgal. The enormous numbers of these plant parts at the site suggest that the seeds were sown, indicating pre-domestication cultivation (after Weiss, Kislev, and Hartmann 2006: fig. on p. 1609). (Courtesy of E. Weiss.)

Jordan Valley sites of Netiv Hagdud (Kislev, Bar-Yosef, and Gopher 1986) and especially Gilgal (Noy 1989) – where massive concentrations of hundreds of thousands of charred barley and oat seeds were recovered from a single architectural feature (Weiss, Kislev, and Hartmann 2006) (Fig. 3.2). Likewise, Yoel Melamed, Uzi Plitmann, and Mordechai Kislev (2008) suggest that large numbers of rambling vetch (*Vicia peregrine*) seeds from the site of Netiv Hagdud could not have been efficiently collected in the wild. Instead, they propose that the legumes were harvested alongside barley from cultivated fields. The harvest of large quantities of wild grains precedes morphological evidence for plant domestication by up to 1,000 years in the southern Levant (Fuller, Willcox, and Allaby 2011).

The first definitive evidence for full-fledged plant domestication in the southern Levant appears in the Middle PPNB and becomes widespread by the Late PPNB. Domestic barley grains from Tell Aswad are the earliest directly dated specimens (10,300–10,000 cal. BP) (Willcox 2005). Barley recovered from Middle PPNB Jericho and Nahal Hemar was clearly domesticated based on morphological features, including high proportions of flexible rachis types. In the 1980s and 1990s, it was widely agreed that barley was first domesticated in the southern Levant, but this has fallen out of favor in recent years (Weiss, Kislev, and Hartmann 2006). Nevertheless, a recent ancient DNA sequence derived from 6,000-year-old domestic barley, discovered at a dry Chalcolithic cave site (Yoram

Cave) close to the Dead Sea, is most similar to varieties of barley from the southern Levant and Egypt – breathing new life into an old hypothesis (Mascher et al. 2016).

In summary, the archaeobotanical record from the southern Levant provides evidence for intensive cereal exploitation and potentially even dead-end cultivation dating back to the Early Epipaleolithic. Cultivation was widespread in the PPNA and was followed by full-fledged domestication by the Middle PPNB. Although some early cultigens were likely replaced by crops from other areas, Pre-Pottery Neolithic cultivation and harvesting strategies ultimately impacted and modified cereal plants (i.e., through seed bed competition and unintentional selection of plants with flexible rachises), even if they did not transform directly into the domestic species that ultimately came to dominate agricultural economies in the Levant.

Animal Domestication

In Southwest Asia, the first animal domesticates were sheep (*Ovis aries*) and goat (*Capra hircus*) (10,000–10,500 cal BP), followed by pig (*Sus scrofa*) and then cattle (*Bos taurus*). Like for plants, the picture for animal domestication has become increasingly multifaceted over the past twenty years. Importantly, recent research has emphasized the long-term aspect of domestication by focusing on the lesser-known, more elusive human–animal interactions that define the early stages. This includes human control over the physical movement of animals through translocation and/or constraint of their physical movement, as well as animal management (Zeder 2006; Vigne et al. 2011; Sapir-Hen et al. 2016). Initial human control over animals is best detected by increased frequencies of domestic progenitors in archaeological assemblages and/or their occurrence outside their natural range. Animal management is even more invasive and adds the targeted culling of specific age and sex groups to increase production efficiency (Zeder 2006). Management can be detected in mortality profiles dominated by juvenile males and adult females. Management differs from domestication, which also involves human control over reproduction and ultimately causes morphological change through human selection and/or reproductive isolation.

As with plants, the widely accepted earliest dates for animal management derive from a group of sites in southeastern Anatolia (ca. 10,500–10,200 cal. BP for sheep at Nevali Çori [Peters, von den Driesch, and Helmer 2005], Çayönü [Hongo et al. 2005], and Cafer Höyük [Helmer 2008]), hinting at a core-area domestication scenario. However, new research has pushed back the timing of animal domestication in surrounding regions so that they are nearly contemporaneous – thus, increasingly supporting a multiregional scenario. For example, Mary Stiner and her colleagues (2014) found widespread evidence for sheep dung and inflated proportions of very young sheep remains in layers dating before 10,200 cal. BP at Aşıklı Höyük in central Anatolia, a region long considered peripheral to the emergence of animal domestication. Likewise, Melinda Zeder and Brian Hesse (2000) tracked increased proportions of juvenile males at Ganj Dareh in the eastern Fertile Crescent (9,900 cal. BP). Finally, although it is widely accepted that domestic animals appeared in the southern Levant from 500 up to 1,000 years later than in the north, new data indicate elevated frequencies of all three domestic progenitor species (goat, cattle, pig) as early as the Early PPNB (10,500–10,000 cal. BP) (Meier, Goring-Morris, and Munro 2016; Sapir-Hen et al. 2016; Munro et al. 2018).

Other recent work emphasizes the protracted nature of animal domestication. The most compelling is the transport of wild and domestic progenitor species over at least 69 km of open sea to the island of Cyprus (10,400–10,200 cal BP). This provides unequivocal evidence that humans knew how to control and manipulate morphologically wild animal taxa at a time when animal management was just emerging in the northern Levant (Vigne et al. 2011). The protracted nature of the process is further supported by multiple lines of zooarchaeological evidence indicating that domestication emerges out of an intensive hunting regime in the southern Levant (Stiner, Munro, and Surovell 2000; Munro 2004; Munro et al. 2018); increased investment in more costly, low-ranked taxa (especially hares, ground birds, and waterfowl) reflects a decline in foraging efficiency over the course of the Epipaleolithic, culminating in the PPNA. This trend reverses in the Early PPNB as small game and adult and juvenile gazelles begin to trade off with wild goat, pig, and cattle (Meier, Goring-Morris, and Munro 2016; Sapir-Hen et al. 2016; Munro et al. 2018; see also below).

Two competing hypotheses have long dominated the discourse on animal domestication in the southern Levant. These include a receiver scenario, in which domestic animals were imported from the north, and an autochthonous domestication model. The receiver model relies on the fact that sheep are not native to the southern Levant and thus had to be imported from the north (Wasse 2002; Bar-Yosef 2017). Nevertheless, managed goats appear earlier than sheep and are native to the region.

Liora Horwitz and her colleagues (1999; see also Horwitz 2003) support their local domestication scenario with primary data from sites in the southern Levant, namely the Mediterranean hills and Jordan Valley. They recovered higher than expected proportions of juvenile male goats, animals with reduced body size, and increased frequencies of goat at the expense of wild ungulates in archaeozoological assemblages by the Middle PPNB. A similar argument was presented for 'Ain Ghazal in the Jordan Valley

(Rollefson and Köhler-Rollefson 1993; von den Driesch and Wodtke 1997). New work in the Mediterranean hills (Meier, Goring-Morris, and Munro 2016; Sapir-Hen et al. 2016; Munro et al. 2018) supports this scenario, citing increased frequencies of domestic progenitors in sync with the decline in intensive hunting that typified the Epipaleolithic and PPNA periods. Stepwise declines in hunting intensity as measured by decreased dietary breadth and increased proportions of high-ranked game (in this case, the wild progenitors of domestic goat, pig, and cattle) suggest early manipulation of local herd populations prior to the appearance of demographic and morphological change in the Early PPNB (Munro et al. 2018). Domestic sheep do not appear in the southern Levant until ca. 9,200 cal. BP (Horwitz and Ducos 1998).

The route to cattle and pig domestication is less well known than for caprines and in some ways favors a core-region domestication model. The earliest dates for pig management derive from sites in southeastern Anatolia. Anton Ervynck and his colleagues (2001) provide evidence for a gradual reduction in pig molar size and average body size over time, as well as an increase in the proportion of juvenile pigs at Çayönü by the channeled phase (10,500–10,200 cal. BP). Daniel Helmer's 2008 study of the same site agrees with this early date (10,300 cal. BP). The morphological and demographic evidence is supported by genetic data (Bollongino et al. 2012). Domestic pigs appear much later in the eastern Fertile Crescent (9,000 cal. BP [Flannery 1983]) and in the southern Levant. Although some claim they may have arrived as early as 9,000 cal. BP (Horwitz et al. 1999), others argue that convincing morphological evidence for domestic pigs is present in the region only by ca. 8,000 cal. BP (Marom and Bar-Oz 2013).

A reduction in body-size sexual dimorphism in the Early PPNB layer of the Euphrates Valley sites of Halula and Dja'de el-Mughara (Helmer et al. 2005; Helmer and Gourichon 2008) provides the earliest evidence for human intervention in cattle production. Nevertheless, domestic cattle arise much later in other parts of Southwest Asia. Results from a recent metastudy of eighty-five zooarchaeological assemblages reveal that small-sized domestic cattle appeared quite suddenly in the eastern Fertile Crescent – the lack of transitional assemblages in the periods preceding their appearance suggests the importation of cattle from the west (Arbuckle et al. 2016). Despite the increased focus on wild cattle in human diets from the Early PPNB onward in the southern Levant, clear evidence for domestication also develops quite late there. An increase in the frequency of cattle with smaller body sizes occurs by about 8,500 cal. BP (Davis 1982; Horwitz and Ducos 2005). Nimrod Marom and Guy Bar-Oz (2013) argue that cattle domestication emerges from a period of intensive hunting based on the high proportions of juvenile cattle at PPNC Sha'ar Hagolan.

SEDENTISM AND SETTLEMENT

Economic change went hand-in-hand with shifts in social organization related to increasing site permanence that culminated in the formation of permanent agricultural villages. During the Epipaleolithic, sites were located in a wide range of habitats, including Mediterranean forests and semiarid desert fringes (Grosman and Munro 2017). The largest sites were located in the better-watered Mediterranean hills; thus, it is not surprising that this region became the locus of more permanent settlement in the Early Natufian. In the Late Natufian, human populations in the Mediterranean hills became more mobile, potentially due to cooling related to the Younger Dryas climatic event (Hartman et al. 2016). Some folks likely relocated to the more climatically stable Jordan Valley, where wild cereals were sufficiently abundant to support large sedentary communities, such as Nahal 'Ein Gev II (Grosman et al. 2016; Hartman et al. 2016).

The process of animal and plant domestication is tightly linked to the gradual emergence of fully sedentary communities and associated reorganization across the Epipaleolithic–Pre-Pottery Neolithic boundary. Although a few early examples of aggregated, semipermanent communities date back to the Early Epipaleolithic (Ohalo II [Nadel and Werker 1999], Kharaneh IV [Maher et al. 2012]), the broader regional trend is toward larger and more permanent hunter-gatherer communities over the course of the Epipaleolithic (Goring-Morris and Belfer-Cohen 2008). An especially abrupt increase in the scale of site occupation occurs in the Early Natufian with the appearance of more permanent architectural features; commensal animal taxa; on-site human burials; increased average site size; deeper archaeological deposits; and non-transportable, heavy-duty processing tools (Grosman and Munro 2017). This trend continues into the Pre-Pottery Neolithic phases, culminating with mega-sites in the Late PPNB.

Increasing sedentism was enabled by changing economics that allowed humans to live in the same location for longer periods of time. Foraging efficiency decreased gradually over the course of the Paleolithic and Epipaleolithic periods (Stiner, Munro, and Surovell 2000) as the balance between human populations and high-ranked resources shifted. By the Early Natufian, growing human populations crossed a threshold that made the exploitation of low-ranked but high-yielding plant and animal species feasible (Munro 2004). Although these resources were costly to procure, they were resilient to intensive harvesting and provided large quantities of storable food. Once it became feasible to add these more costly resources to the diet, humans could occupy a single location for longer periods of time without exhausting local environments – thus, it became efficient to settle down into more sedentary communities (Codding and Bird 2015). As human populations began to grow and the landscape became more crowded, the cost of moving increased. People became more tethered to permanent locations and ultimately further intensified resource use by domesticating plants and animals.

Increased sedentism in the southern Levant is associated with a rise in symbolic activity, likely linked to territorial behavior as soon as the Early Natufian. The relative abundance of various ornament types varies across Late Epipaleolithic sites, suggesting that people from different sites were using specific symbols to express group identity (Belfer-Cohen and Bar-Yosef 2000), an effective strategy for alleviating the scalar stress brought on by living in landscapes with increasing population density.

COMMUNITY ORGANIZATION AND SOCIAL CHANGE

The increase in human populations, as well as site permanence and size across the transition to agriculture, required that communities be reorganized to accommodate associated social changes (Goring-Morris and Belfer-Cohen 2008). Shifts in community organization are clearly visible in the diversification of architectural features throughout the Epipaleolithic and the PPNA. The resulting variation reflects increasingly differentiated use of space, a rise in communal architecture, and new site functions and activities (Stordeur 1998; Kuijt and Finlayson 2009; Finlayson et al. 2011; Meier, Goring-Morris, and Munro 2017). Semipermanent huts with brush superstructures were the norm in Early Epipaleolithic communities and functioned primarily as shelters (Nadel and Werker 1999; Maher et al. 2012). By the Early Natufian, round stone structures with multiple functions become commonplace and concentrated, especially at sites in the Mediterranean zone and the Jordan Valley, while features such as built hearths and graves, as well as slab-lined floors become increasingly diverse and numerous (Goring-Morris and Belfer-Cohen 2008). Space is further differentiated in the PPNA, and communal structures appear (Finlayson et al. 2011). Communal spaces likely played a variety of roles, including storage; activity areas for mundane tasks, such as food processing; and ritual practice. It is not until the PPNB that clearer divisions between public and private space emerge (Finlayson et al. 2011).

As agriculture became more entrenched in the Late PPNB and the size of human populations and habitation sites grew, living spaces in agricultural communities became increasingly more compartmentalized (Kuijt 2000). Population packing increased up until the Late PPNB, culminating in the mega-sites. This is accompanied by a shift in the positioning of architectural features such as doorways that closed off household spaces to public view over time. Brian Byrd (1994) interprets this as evidence for the emergence of private property.

RITUAL PRACTICE AND IDEOLOGY

Significant community reorganization required new methods for integrating human social groups. Thus, it is not surprising that an intensification of ritual practice went hand-in-hand with the social and economic changes described here. An early example of ritual intensification includes the appearance of caches of symbolic items at Early Epipaleolithic Kharaneh IV, a complex seasonal aggregation site that was more intensively occupied than contemporaneous communities (Maher et al. 2012). By the Early Epipaleolithic period, the growing importance of ritual practice is epitomized by the surge in human burials and a diversification of burial practices sometimes associated with symbols (i.e., ornaments, figurines, and animal remains). Specialized ritual sites for human burial first emerge in the Late Natufian, notably at the site of Hilazon Tachtit, which lacked the remnants of domestic activity but contained skeletal parts from at least twenty-eight individuals, including one female shaman (Grosman, Munro, and Belfer-Cohen 2008). Other Late Natufian sites fit this pattern, as they provide more evidence for burials than domestic activity (Raqefet Cave, Nahal Oren, Hayonim Cave [Grosman and Munro 2017]).

Ritual practice intensified significantly in the Pre-Pottery Neolithic phases. The aspects that have drawn the most attention concern the burial and reburial of the dead and associated rituals (Kuijt 2000; 2001). Like the Late Epipaleolithic populations who went before, early Neolithic people commonly reopened graves after burial and removed specific body parts, especially skulls, some of which were plastered, modeled, and painted with facial features (Kuijt 2001). Groups of both plastered and unplastered skulls were reburied in caches at several early Neolithic sites (Fig. 3.3). This flourishing of ritual activity has been interpreted as a strategy to cope with the massive sociocultural changes that accompanied the transition to agriculture and village life (Verhoeven 2002).

Ritual practices accompanied the burial and reburial of human bodies (Kuijt 2001; Grosman and Munro 2016). These included feasting with the dead, evidenced first at Late Natufian Hilazon Tachtit (Munro and Grosman 2010) (Fig. 3.4) and continuing into the Pre-Pottery Neolithic periods at Kfar HaHoresh and other sites (Horwitz and Goring-Morris 2004; Twiss 2008; Meier, Goring-Morris, and Munro 2017). Intensified ritual activity likely provided an essential social glue for communities undergoing gradual but significant change. Ritual undoubtedly served a range of purposes from promoting group solidarity and consolidating social power to marking social identity at a time when social circles were increasing in size, scale, and permanence.

DISCUSSION

As more data accumulates, the spatial-temporal landscape of plant and animal domestication is becoming an increasingly complex mosaic that centers less and less on southeastern Anatolia. New evidence suggests a more multiregional picture that includes local domestication trajectories in many regions. Similar coevolutionary processes occurred across a broad area but played out differently on a local scale. Greater emphasis on process has documented the

3.3. Three plastered skulls recovered *in situ* from the Middle PPNB site of Yiftahel (from Slon et al. 2014: fig. 2 [CC BY 4.0 (https://creativecommons.org/licenses/by/4.0/)]).

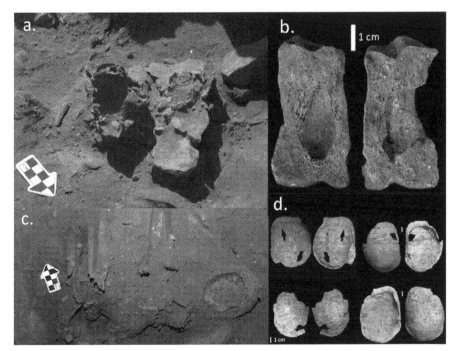

3.4. Faunal evidence for ritual feasting from the Late Natufian burial site of Hilazon Tachtit. (a) Articulated *Bos* lumbar vertebra from Structure B; (b) butchered *Bos* first phalanx from Structure B; (c) complete tortoise carapaces interred among the skeletal remains of a human burial in Structure A; and (d) complete tortoise carapaces recovered from a human burial in Structure A. (Photos by G. Hartman and N. D. Munro.)

protracted nature of domestication and increasingly its early stages, which are more difficult to detect in the archaeological record. Although arguments in defense of the core area model still abound, there is growing consensus that the multiregional model provides a better fit for the data (Fuller, Willcox, and Allaby 2011; Zeder 2011; Fuller, Asouti, and Purugganan 2012; Arbuckle 2014; Munro et al. 2018). Likewise, recent research suggests that the pathways to domestication are more complex than previously thought. They include false starts and dead ends and variation in the process from crop to crop and animal to animal in response to local ecological and social conditions. Current evidence also suggests multiple pathways to domestication, both in plants and animals, across a broad swath of Southwest Asia.

The appearance of a new economic way of life, marked by the recovery of domestic plants and animals from the archaeological record, does not signal the beginning of the agricultural transition. Instead, it marks a late stage or an end point in a much larger transformation in cultural dynamics that began during the Epipaleolithic. Although the path was uneven and, at times, nonlinear, and variable in pace, the 10,000-year process leading up to the Neolithic was essential in setting the stage for the successful adoption of a dramatically different economic strategy.

Associated social change included the intensification of intra-community organization, demonstrated by the increasingly formalized and differentiated use of space, waste management, and the privatization of property. Like the evidence for plant and animal domestication, social and ideological change manifested differently across Southwest Asia with a myriad of local traditions that were often connected by common symbolic themes (Belfer-Cohen and Goring-Morris 2014; Meier, Goring-Morris, and Munro 2017). These socio-economic transformations were accompanied by intensified and increasingly public ritual activity, which provided the essential social glue for communities experiencing gradual but significant change. Ritual served a range of purposes from promoting group solidarity, consolidating social power, and marking social identity at a time when social circles were increasing in size, scale, and permanence.

ACKNOWLEDGMENTS

Special thanks to Jackie Meier for her constructive comments on an earlier draft of this chapter; to Gideon Hartman, Hamoudi Khalaily, and Ehud Weiss for providing permission to print photos; and to Noa Klein for her careful work drafting Fig. 3.1. We also thank the editors, Assaf Yassur-Landau, Eric Cline, and especially Yorke Rowan, and the copy editor, Heather Heidrich, for their assistance and patience during the publication process.

REFERENCES

Abbo, S., and Gopher, A. 2017. Near Eastern Plant Domestication: A History of Thought. *Trends in Plant Science* 22: 491–511.

Allaby, R. G.; Kistler, L.; Gutaker, R. M.; Ware, R.; Kitchen, J. L.; Smith, O.; and Clarke, A. C. 2015. Archaeogenomic Insights into the Adaptation of Plants to the Human Environment: Pushing Plant–Hominin Co-Evolution Back to the Pliocene. *JHE* 79: 150–7.

Arbuckle, B. S. 2014. Pace and Process in the Emergence of Animal Husbandry in Neolithic Southwest Asia. *Bioarchaeology of the Near East* 8: 53–81.

Arbuckle, B. S.; Price, M. D.; Hongo, H.; and Öksüz, B. 2016. Documenting the Initial Appearance of Domestic Cattle in the Eastern Fertile Crescent (Northern Iraq and Western Iran). *JAS* 72: 1–9.

Asouti, E. 2010. Beyond the "Origins of Agriculture": Alternative Narratives of Plant Exploitation in the Neolithic of the Middle East. In *Proceedings of the 6th International Congress of the Archaeology of the Ancient Near East, 5 May–10 May 2009, "Sapienza," Università di Roma,* Vol. 1: *Near Eastern Archaeology in the Past, Present and Future – Heritage and Identity – Ethnoarchaeological and Interdisciplinary Approach: Results and Perspectives – Visual Expression and Craft Production in the Definition of Social Relations and Status,* ed. P. Matthiae, F. Pinnock, L. Nigro, and N. Marchetti with the collaboration of L. Romano, 189–202. Wiesbaden: Harrassowitz.

Bar-Yosef, O. 2017. Multiple Origins of Agriculture in Eurasia and Africa. In *On Human Nature: Biology, Psychology, Ethics, Politics, and Religion,* ed. M. Tibayrenc and F. J. Ayala, 297–331. Amsterdam: Elsevier; Academic.

Belfer-Cohen, A., and Bar-Yosef, O. 2000. Early Sedentism in the Near East: A Bumpy Ride to Village Life. In *Life in Neolithic Farming Communities: Social Organization, Identity, and Differentiation,* ed. I. Kuijt, 19–37. FIA. New York: Kluwer Academic/Plenum.

Belfer-Cohen, A., and Goring-Morris, A. N. 2014. North and South – Variable Trajectories of the Neolithic in the Levant. In *Settlement, Survey, and Stone: Essays on Near Eastern Prehistory in Honour of Gary Rollefson,* ed. B. Finlayson and C. Makarewicz, 61–71. Berlin: Ex Oriente.

Bollongino, R.; Burger, J.; Powell, A.; Mashkour, M.; Vigne, J.-D.; and Thomas, M. G. 2012. Modern Taurine Cattle Descended from Small Number of Near-Eastern Founders. *MBE* 29: 2101–4.

Byrd, B. F. 1994. Public and Private, Domestic and Corporate: The Emergence of the Southwest Asian Village. *AA* 59: 639–66.

Codding, B. F., and Bird, D. W. 2015. Behavioral Ecology and the Future of Archaeological Science. *JAS* 56: 9–20.

Davis, S. J. M. 1982. Climatic Change and the Advent of Domestication: The Succession of Ruminant Artiodactyls in the Late Pleistocene–Holocene in the Israel Region. *Paléorient* 8 (2): 5–15.

Driesch, A. von den, and Wodtke, U. 1997. The Fauna of 'Ain Ghazal, a Major PPN and Early PN Settlement in Central Jordan. In *The Prehistory of Jordan II: Perspectives from 1997,* ed. H. G. K. Gebel, Z. Kafafi, and G. O. Rollefson, 511–56. SENEPSE 4. Berlin: Ex Oriente.

Ervynck, A.; Dobney, K.; Hongo, H.; and Meadow, R. 2001. Born Free? New Evidence for the Status of *Sus scrofa* at Neolithic Çayönü Tepesi (Southeastern Anatolia, Turkey). *Paléorient* 27 (2): 47–73.

Finlayson, B.; Mithen, S. J.; Najjar, M.; Smith, S.; Maričević, D.; Pankhurst, N.; and Yeomans, L. 2011. Architecture, Sedentism, and Social Complexity at Pre-Pottery Neolithic A WF16, Southern Jordan. *PNAS* 108: 8183–8.

Flannery, K. V. 1983. Early Pig Domestication in the Fertile Crescent: A Retrospective Look. In *The Hilly Flanks and Beyond: Essays on the Prehistory of Southwestern Asia; Presented to Robert J. Braidwood*, ed. T. C. Young Jr., P. E. L. Smith, and P. Mortensen, 163–88. SAOC 36. Chicago: The Oriental Institute of The University of Chicago.

Fuller, D. Q. 2007. Contrasting Patterns in Crop Domestication and Domestication Rates: Recent Archaeobotanical Insights from the Old World. *Annals of Botany* 100: 903–24.

Fuller, D. Q., and Allaby, R. G. 2009. Seed Dispersal and Crop Domestication: Shattering, Germination and Seasonality in Evolution under Cultivation. In *Fruit Development and Seed Dispersal*, ed. L. Ostergaard, 238–95. Annual Plant Reviews 38. Oxford: Wiley-Blackwell.

Fuller, D. Q.; Asouti, E.; and Purugganan, M. D. 2012. Cultivation as Slow Evolutionary Entanglement: Comparative Data on Rate and Sequence of Domestication. *VHA* 21: 131–45.

Fuller, D. Q.; Willcox, G.; and Allaby, R. G. 2011. Cultivation and Domestication Had Multiple Origins: Arguments against the Core Area Hypothesis for the Origins of Agriculture in the Near East. *WA* 43: 628–52.

Gopher, A.; Abbo, S.; and Lev-Yadun, S. 2002. The "When," the "Where" and the "Why" of the Neolithic Revolution in the Levant. *Documenta Praehistorica* 28: 49–62.

Goring-Morris, A. N., and Belfer-Cohen, A. 2008. A Roof over One's Head: Developments in Near Eastern Residential Architecture across the Epipalaeolithic–Neolithic Transition. In *The Neolithic Demographic Transition and Its Consequences*, ed. J.-P. Bocquet-Appel and O. Bar-Yosef, 239–86. New York: Springer.

Grosman, L. 2013. The Natufian Chronology Scheme – New Insights and Their Implications. In *Natufian Foragers in the Levant: Terminal Pleistocene Social Changes in Western Asia*, ed. O. Bar-Yosef and F. R. Valla, 622–37. International Monographs in Prehistory, Archaeological Series 19. Ann Arbor, MI: International Monographs in Prehistory.

Grosman, L., and Munro, N. D. 2016. A Natufian Ritual Event. *CA* 57: 311–31.

——— 2017. The Natufian Culture: The Harbinger of Food-Producing Societies. In *Quaternary of the Levant: Environments, Climate Change and Humans*, ed. Y. Enzel and O. Bar-Yosef, 699–708. Cambridge: Cambridge University Press.

Grosman, L.; Munro, N. D.; Abadi, I.; Boaretto, E.; Shaham, D.; Belfer-Cohen, A.; and Bar-Yosef, O. 2016. Nahal Ein Gev II, a Late Natufian Community at the Sea of Galilee. *PLOS ONE* 11 (1): e0146647. https://doi.org/10.1371/journal.pone.0146647 (accessed May 2, 2018).

Grosman, L.; Munro, N. D.; and Belfer-Cohen, A. 2008. A 12,000-Year-Old Shaman Burial from the Southern Levant (Israel). *PNAS* 105: 17665–9.

Hartman, G.; Bar-Yosef, O.; Brittingham, A.; Grosman, L.; and Munro, N. D. 2016. Hunted Gazelles Evidence Cooling, but not Drying, during the Younger Dryas in the Southern Levant. *PNAS* 113: 3997–4002.

Helmer, D. 2008. Révision de la faune de Cafer Höyük (Malatya, Turquie): Apports des méthodes de l'analyse des mélanges et de l'analyse de Kernel à la mise en évidence de la domestication. In *Archaeozoology of the Near East VIII: Proceedings of the Eighth*

International Symposium on the Archaeozoology of Southwestern Asia and Adjacent Areas, Lyon, June 28–July 1, 2006, ed. E. Vila, L. Gourichon, A. M. Choyke, and H. Buitenhuis, 169–95. Travaux de la Maison de l'Orient et de la Méditerranée 49. Lyon: Maison de l'Orient et de la Méditerranée.

Helmer, D., and Gourichon, L. 2008. Premières données sur les modalités de subsistance à Tell Aswad (Syrie, PPNB moyen et récent, Néolithique céramique ancien) – Fouilles 2001–2005. In *Archaeozoology of the Near East VIII: Proceedings of the Eighth International Symposium on the Archaeozoology of Southwestern Asia and Adjacent Areas, Lyon, June 28–July 1, 2006*, ed. E. Vila, L. Gourichon, A. M. Choyke, and H. Buitenhuis, 119–51. Travaux de la Maison de l'Orient et de la Méditerranée 49. Lyon: Maison de l'Orient et de la Méditerranée.

Helmer, D.; Gourichon, L.; Monchot, H.; Peters, J.; and Saña Segui, M. 2005. Identifying Early Domestic Cattle from Pre-Pottery Neolithic Sites on the Middle Euphrates Using Sexual Dimorphism. In *First Steps of Animal Domestication: New Archaeozoological Approaches; Proceedings of the 9th Conference of the International Council of Archaeozoology, Durham, August 2002*, ed. J.-D. Vigne, J. Peters, and D. Helmer, 86–95. Oxford: Oxbow.

Heun, M.; Schäfer-Pregl, R.; Klawan, D.; Castagna, R.; Accerbi, M.; Borghi, B.; and Salamini, F. 1997. Site of Einkorn Wheat Domestication Identified by DNA Fingerprinting. *Science* 278 (5341): 1312–14.

Hongo, H.; Meadow, R. H.; Öksüz, B.; and İlgezdi, G. L. 2005. Sheep and Goat Remains from Cayönü Tepesi, Southeastern Anatolia. In *Archaeozoology of the Near East VI: Proceedings of the Sixth International Symposium on the Archaeozoology of Southwestern Asia and Adjacent Areas, London, August 30–September 1, 2002*, ed. H. Buitenhuis, A. M. Choyke, L. Martin, L. Bartosiewicz, and M. Mashkour, 112–23. ARCP 123. Groningen: ARC.

Honne, B. I., and Heun, M. 2009. On the Domestication Genetics of Self-Fertilizing Plants. *VHA* 18: 269–72.

Horwitz, L. K., with a contribution by O. Lernau. 2003. Temporal and Spatial Variation in Neolithic Caprine Exploitation Strategies: A Case Study of Fauna from the Site of Yiftah'el (Israel). *Paléorient* 29 (1): 19–58.

Horwitz, L. K., and Ducos, P. 1998. An Investigation into the Origins of Domestic Sheep in the Southern Levant. In *Archaeozoology of the Near East III: Proceedings of the Third International Symposium on the Archaeozoology of Southwestern Asia and Adjacent Areas*, ed. H. Buitenhuis, L. Bartosiewicz, and A. M. Choyke, 80–94. ARCP 18. Groningen: ARC.

2005. Counting Cattle: Trends in Neolithic *Bos* Frequencies from the Southern Levant. *Revue de paléobiologie, Genève* 10: 209–24.

Horwitz, L. K., and Goring-Morris, A. N. 2004. Animals and Ritual during the Levantine PPNB: A Case Study from the Site of Kfar Hahoresh, Israel. *Anthropozoologica* 39: 165–78.

Horwitz, L. K.; Tchernov, E.; Ducos, P.; Becker, C.; von den Driesch, A.; Martin, L.; and Garrard, A. 1999. Animal Domestication in the Southern Levant. *Paléorient* 25 (2): 63–80.

Kilian, J.; Whitehead, D.; Horak, J.; Wanke, D.; Weinl, S.; Batistic, O.; D'Angelo, C.; Bornberg-Bauer, E.; Kudla, J.; and Harter, K. 2007. The AtGenExpress Global Stress Expression Data Set: Protocols, Evaluation and Model Data Analysis of UV-B Light, Drought and Cold Stress Responses. *The Plant Journal* 50: 347–63.

Kislev, M. E.; Bar-Yosef, O.; and Gopher, A. 1986. Early Neolithic Domesticated and Wild Barley from the Netiv Hagdud Region in the Jordan Valley. *Israel Journal of Botany* 35: 197–201.

Kozlowski, S. K., and Aurenche, O. 2005. *Territories, Boundaries and Cultures in the Neolithic Near East.* BAR International Series 1362. Oxford: Archaeopress.

Kuijt, I. 2000. People and Space in Early Agricultural Villages: Exploring Daily Lives, Community Size, and Architecture in the Late Pre-Pottery Neolithic. *JAA* 19: 75–102.

——— 2001. Place, Death, and the Transmission of Social Memory in Early Agricultural Communities of the Near Eastern Pre-Pottery Neolithic. *APAAA* 10: 80–99.

Kuijt, I., and Finlayson, B. 2009. Evidence for Food Storage and Predomestication Granaries 11,000 Years Ago in the Jordan Valley. *PNAS* 106: 10966–70.

Lev-Yadun, S.; Gopher, A.; and Abbo, S. 2000. The Cradle of Agriculture. *Science* 288 (5471): 1602–3.

Maher, L. A.; Banning, E. B.; and Chazan, M. 2011. Oasis or Mirage? Assessing the Role of Abrupt Climate Change in the Prehistory of the Southern Levant. *CAJ* 21: 1–30.

Maher, L. A.; Richter, T.; Macdonald, D.; Jones, M. D.; Martin, L.; and Stock, J. T. 2012. Twenty Thousand-Year-Old Huts at a Hunter-Gatherer Settlement in Eastern Jordan. *PLOS ONE* 7 (2): e31447. https://doi.org/10.1371/journal.pone.0031447 (accessed May 2, 2018).

Marom, N., and Bar-Oz, G. 2013. The Prey Pathway: A Regional History of Cattle (*Bos taurus*) and Pig (*Sus scrofa*) Domestication in the Northern Jordan Valley, Israel. *PLOS ONE* 8 (2): e55958. https://doi.org/10.1371/journal.pone.0055958 (accessed May 2, 2018).

Mascher, M.; Schuenemann, V. J.; Davidovich, U.; Marom, N.; Himmelbach, A.; Hübner, S.; Korol, A.; David, M.; Reiter, E.; Riehl, S.; Schreiber, M.; Vohr, S. H.; Green, R. E.; Dawson, I. K.; Russell, J.; Kilian, B.; Muehlbauer, G. J.; Waugh, R.; Fahima, T.; Krause, J.; Weiss, E.; and Stein, N. 2016. Genomic Analysis of 6,000-Year-Old Cultivated Grain Illuminates the Domestication History of Barley. *Nature Genetics* 48: 1089–93.

Meier, J. S.; Goring-Morris, A. N.; and Munro, N. D. 2016. Provisioning the Ritual Neolithic Site of Kfar HaHoresh, Israel at the Dawn of Animal Management. *PLOS ONE* 11 (11): e0166573. https://doi.org/10.1371/journal.pone.0166573 (accessed May 2, 2018).

——— 2017. Aurochs Bone Deposits at Kfar HaHoresh and the Southern Levant across the Agricultural Transition. *Antiquity* 91 (360): 1469–83.

Melamed, Y.; Plitmann, U.; and Kislev, M. E. 2008. *Vicia peregrina*: An Edible Early Neolithic Legume. *VHA* 17: 29–34.

Moulins, D. de. 1993. Les restes de plantes carbonisées de Cafer Höyük. *Cahiers de l'Euphrate* 7: 191–234.

Munro, N. D. 2004. Zooarchaeological Measures of Hunting Pressure and Occupation Intensity in the Natufian: Implications for Agricultural Origins. *CA* 45 (suppl. 4): S5–34.

Munro, N. D.; Bar-Oz, G.; Meier, J. M.; Sapir-Hen, L.; Stiner, M. C.; and Yeshurun, R. 2018. The Emergence of Animal Management in the Southern Levant. *Scientific Reports* 8: article no. 9279. https://www.nature.com/articles/s41598-018-27647-z (accessed August 15, 2018).

Munro, N. D., and Grosman, L. 2010. Early Evidence (*ca.* 12,000 B.P.) for Feasting at a Burial Cave in Israel. *PNAS* 107: 15362–6.

Nadel, D., and Werker, E. 1999. The Oldest Ever Brush Hut Plant Remains from Ohalo II, Jordan Valley, Israel (19,000 BP). *Antiquity* 73 (282): 755–64.

Noy, T. 1989. Gilgal I – A Pre-Pottery Neolithic Site, Israel: The 1985–1987 Seasons. *Paléorient* 15 (1): 11–18.

Özkan, H.; Brandolini, A.; Schäfer-Pregl, R.; and Salamini, F. 2002. AFLP Analysis of a Collection of Tetraploid Wheats Indicates the Origin of Emmer and Hard Wheat Domestication in Southeast Turkey. *MBE* 19: 1797–1801.

Pasternak, R. 1998. Investigations of Botanical Remains from Nevali Çori PPNB, Turkey: A Short Interim Report. In *The Origins of Agriculture and Crop Domestication: Proceedings of the Harlan Symposium, 10–14 May 1997, Aleppo, Syria*, ed. A. B. Damania, J. Valkoun, G. Willcox, and C. O. Qualset, 170–7. Aleppo: ICARDA.

Peters, J.; von den Driesch, A.; and Helmer, D. 2005. The Upper Euphrates-Tigris Basin: Cradle of Agro-Pastoralism? In *First Steps of Animal Domestication: New Archaeozoological Approaches; Proceedings of the 9th Conference of the International Council of Archaeozoology, Durham, August 2002*, ed. J.-D. Vigne, J. Peters, and D. Helmer, 96–124. Oxford: Oxbow.

Purugganan, M. D., and Fuller, D. Q. 2011. Archaeological Data Reveal Slow Rates of Evolution during Plant Domestication. *Evolution* 65: 171–83.

Rollefson, G. O., and Köhler-Rollefson, I. 1993. PPNC Adaptations in the First Half of the 6th Millennium B.C. *Paléorient* 19 (1): 33–42.

Sapir-Hen, L.; Dayan, T.; Khalaily, H.; and Munro, N. D. 2016. Human Hunting and Nascent Animal Management at Middle Pre-Pottery Neolithic Yiftah'el, Israel. *PLOS ONE* 11 (7): e015696. https://doi.org/10.1371/journal.pone.0156964 (accessed May 2, 2018).

Slon, V.; Sarig, R.; Hershkovitz, I.; Khalaily, H.; and Milevski, I. 2014. The Plastered Skulls from the Pre-Pottery Neolithic B Site of Yiftahel (Israel) – A Computed Tomography-Based Analysis. *PLOS ONE* 9 (2): e89242. https://doi.org/10.1371/journal.pone.0089242 (accessed May 2, 2018).

Snir, A.; Nadel, D.; Gorman-Yaroslavski, I.; Melamed, Y.; Sternberg, M.; Bar-Yosef, O.; and Weiss, E. 2015. The Origin of Cultivation and Proto-Weeds, Long before Neolithic Farming. *PLOS ONE* 10 (7): e0131422. https://doi.org/10.1371/journal.pone.0131422 (accessed May 2, 2018).

Stiner, M. C.; Buitenhuis, H.; Duru, G.; Kuhn, S. L.; Mentzer, S. M.; Munro, N. D.; Pöllath, N.; Quade, J.; Tsartsidou, G.; and Özbaşaran, M. 2014. A Forager–Herder Trade-Off, from Broad-Spectrum Hunting to Sheep Management at Aşıklı Höyük, Turkey. *PNAS* 111: 8404–9.

Stiner, M. C.; Munro, N. D.; and Surovell, T. A. 2000. The Tortoise and the Hare: Small Game Use, the Broad-Spectrum Revolution, and Paleolithic Demography. *CA* 41: 39–73.

Stordeur, D., with a contribution by T. Margueron. 1998. Espace naturel, espace construit à Jerf el Ahmar sur l'Euphrate. In *Espace naturel, espace habité en Syrie du nord (10e–2e millénaires av. J.-C.); Actes du colloque tenu à l'Université Laval (Québec) du 5 au 7 mai 1997*, ed. M. Fortin and O. Aurenche, 93–107. Travaux de la Maison de l'Orient et de la Méditerranée 28. Lyon: Maison de l'Orient et de la Méditerranée.

Tanno, K.-I., and Willcox, G. 2012. Distinguishing Wild and Domestic Wheat and Barley Spikelets from Early Holocene Sites in the Near East. *VHA* 21: 107–15.

Twiss, K. C. 2008. Transformations in an Early Agricultural Society: Feasting in the Southern Levantine Pre-Pottery Neolithic. *JAA* 27: 418–42.

Verhoeven, M. 2002. Ritual and Ideology in the Pre-Pottery Neolithic B of the Levant and Southeast Anatolia. *CAJ* 12: 233–58.

Vigne, J.-D.; Carrère, I.; Briois, F.; and Guilaine, J. 2011. The Early Process of Mammal Domestication in the Near East: New Evidence from the Pre-Neolithic and Pre-Pottery Neolithic in Cyprus. *CA* 52 (suppl. 4): S255–71.

Wasse, A. 2002. Final Results of an Analysis of the Sheep and Goat Bones from Ain Ghazal, Jordan. *Levant* 34: 59–82.

Weiss, E.; Kislev, M. E.; and Hartmann, A. 2006. Autonomous Cultivation before Domestication. *Science* 312 (5780): 1608–10.

Weiss, E.; Wetterstrom, W.; Nadel, D.; and Bar-Yosef, O. 2004. The Broad Spectrum Revisited: Evidence from Plant Remains. *PNAS* 101: 9551–5.

Willcox, G. 2005. The Distribution, Natural Habitats and Availability of Wild Cereals in Relation to Their Domestication in the Near East: Multiple Events, Multiple Centres. *VHA* 14: 534–41.

Willcox, G.; Fornite, S.; and Herveux, L. 2008. Early Holocene Cultivation before Domestication in Northern Syria. *VHA* 17: 313–25.

Wright, K. I. 1994. Ground-Stone Tools and Hunter-Gatherer Subsistence in Southwest Asia: Implications for the Transition to Farming. *AA* 59: 238–63.

Zeder, M. A. 2006. Archaeological Approaches to Documenting Animal Domestication. In *Documenting Domestication: New Genetic and Archaeological Paradigms*, ed. M. A. Zeder, D. G. Bradley, E. Emshwiller, and B. D. Smith, 171–80. Berkeley: University of California Press.

——— 2011. The Origins of Agriculture in the Near East. *CA* 52 (suppl. 4): S221–35.

Zeder, M. A., and Hesse, B. 2000. The Initial Domestication of Goats (*Capra hircus*) in the Zagros Mountains 10,000 Years Ago. *Science* 287 (5461): 2254–7.

Zeist, W. van, and de Roller, G. J. 1991–1992. The Plant Husbandry of Aceramic Cayönü, S.E. Turkey. *Palaeohistoria* 33–34: 65–96.

FOUR

GETTING IT TOGETHER
The Creation of Community in the Neolithic

BILL FINLAYSON

There is a consistent trope that underlies our understanding of the Neolithic – it was a sharp break with our hunter-gatherer past that concerns a shift to people like us and represents, in some way, the start of real human history (Hodder 1990; 2001; Cauvin 2000; Renfrew 2003; 2007; Watkins 2004), in particular, of societies we would recognize as close to our own (Watkins 2005). This fracture from the Paleolithic hunter-gatherer past assumes a rapid and radical shift in the nature of human society at the start of the Neolithic, and the narrative of rapid change underpins many possible revolutions (the Neolithic [Childe 1951], agricultural [Barker 2006], sedentary [Renfrew 2003], symbolic [Cauvin 1994], or cognitive [Watkins 2005] revolutions), even though it has become increasingly apparent that the Neolithic process is extremely long, and that many Neolithic innovations in Southwest Asia can be pushed deep back in time (Finlayson 2013).

Despite arguments for such a long Neolithic, the Early Aceramic Neolithic at the start of the Holocene continues to be perceived as the real point of departure from previous hunting and gathering lifestyles. Given this context and the importance given to social changes as a driving factor within the overall transition, assessing the evidence behind the enduring trope of radical and rapid social change becomes critical. Most social archaeological approaches have concerned high-level models trying to provide general theories and histories for the Southwest Asian Neolithic. These models are based on two essential assumptions. The first, despite a lack of historical, geographical, environmental, or chronological proximity, is a dependence on broad-scale ethnographic analogy, where a move from egalitarian hunter-gatherers to non-egalitarian, complex foraging and farming societies, and then the emergence of chiefdoms provides the context for transformation (Bar-Yosef 2001). Unfortunately, such a framework places a heavy hand on our ability to study the largely non-analogous contexts of Late Pleistocene and Early Holocene societies (Finlayson 2011). Natufian, Pre-Pottery Neolithic A (PPNA), and even many Pre-Pottery Neolithic B (PPNB) societies were supported by low-level food production economies that have few parallels in the modern world. It is therefore inappropriate to commence analysis on the premise of oppositions between farmers and hunter-gatherers, which insists on exaggerating the differences between large, settled farming communities and hunter-gatherers living in small highly mobile groups on the basis of a heavy reliance on ethnographic analogy, despite the non-analogous context of modern hunter-gatherers (Finlayson 2013).

The second assumption is that population increased with the development of large sedentary communities, invested in fixed economic resources, which locked residence in one place. Neolithic settlements are characterized as sedentary communities described as "villages" (Byrd 2005). These villages were inhabited by people who dwelled in houses, and these houses represented a new concept of home, and, through the emergence of households, of structuring Neolithic society. These large village communities are interpreted as having driven the social, cognitive, and symbolic changes that occurred. This set of domestic constructions is integral to the concept that Neolithic people are modern and like us. Even the nature of personhood is believed to have changed, where before the Neolithic hunter-gatherers were part of nature, and in the Neolithic the self-contained individual, facing the external world, was born (Hodder 1999). Jacques Cauvin's (2000) position was clear: Neolithic people created the world as we know it. Our evidence for community-scale, sedentary permanence, and the ideas of house and home, is at best patchy and requires careful assessment.

While the subsistence shift from hunting and gathering to farming remains the defining attribute of the Neolithic, it is intimately bound up with these social changes. The subsistence economic transition is part of the same extended Neolithic process, comprising a long period of low-level food production before farming economies emerged late in the process (Smith 2001; Zeder 2009; 2011; Finlayson 2013). In this chapter, I will question the inferential sequence behind the social interpretations, covering settlement, scale of population, and the identification of houses and homes, to reassess the commonly deployed building blocks used in Neolithic social archaeology, to consider how appropriate they may be, and to deploy the archaeological evidence as our primary means of understanding Neolithic society.

NEOLITHIC SOCIETY

The Sedentary Village: Population and Sedentism

The Neolithic is routinely considered as part of a longer pattern of population increase, visible in the proliferation of large coresident communities. The process is seen to have commenced in the Epipaleolithic and, despite significant climate change, especially the Younger Dryas and the Holocene, the increase in scale of settlement and overall population is thought to have been a constantly upward trend (Bar-Yosef and Belfer-Cohen 1989; Henry 1989; Kuijt 2000; Sterelny and Watkins 2015). Kim Sterelny and Trevor Watkins have argued that there was a rapid increase in sedentism when "the capacity to form and sustain the new, large, permanently coresident communities of the end of the Pleistocene and the beginning of the Holocene took hyper-sociality and super-cooperation to new levels" (2015: 677). The social and ideological transformations that have been used to characterize the Neolithic are substantially based on the appearance of these large sedentary communities (Childe 1951; Hodder 1990; Belfer-Cohen and Bar-Yosef 2000; Cauvin 2000; Barker 2006; Zeder 2009). However, Nigel Goring-Morris and Anna Belfer-Cohen (2011: fig 2) show a considerable fluctuation in site distribution densities over time, and it is clear that within the overall trend there is much local variation in population increase and distribution.

Sedentary behavior has been argued to have deep Epipaleolithic roots, going back to at least 22,000 years ago in the Levant, with the construction of shelters at sites, such as Ohalo II and Kharaneh IV (Nadel 2003; Maher, Richter, and Stock 2012). However, these early shelters do not provide an architecturally built environment in the manner that emerges in the Natufian (ca. 14,900–11,750 cal. BP). While the shelters of the earlier Epipaleolithic remain relatively ephemeral, Natufian settlements were composed of structures built for more than just shelter and incorporated an increasing range of architectural features, and even included large – presumably communal – buildings, as at 'Ain Mallaha (Perrot 1966). Although the case for Natufian sedentism and collective storage may well have been overstated (cf. Olszewski 1991 and Bar-Yosef 1998), it remains the case that the architecture at Early Natufian (14,900–13,700 cal. BP) settlements is a scale order more material than earlier constructions. The Late Natufian (13,700–11,750 cal. BP) was assumed to represent a return to greater mobility during the Younger Dryas in what has been described as a "bumpy-ride" to sedentism (Belfer-Cohen and Bar-Yosef 2000; Bar-Yosef 2001), with a parallel return from emergent hierarchy to a more egalitarian society (Kuijt 1996); however, recent excavations at Nahal 'Ein Gev II show that at least some Natufian communities maintain far greater continuity between the Early Natufian and the Neolithic (Grossman et al. 2016).

The increase in investment in place goes hand-in-hand with the emergence of low-level food producing economies. This process continues into the Early Aceramic Neolithic, with a few PPNA (12,000–10,500/10,300) settlements, such as Netiv Hagdud, Gilgal, and Dhra', representing an increase in settlement size in the Early Holocene (Bar-Yosef and Gopher 1997; Finlayson et al. 2003; Bar-Yosef, Goring-Morris, and Gopher 2010). PPNA Jericho, with its wall and tower, appears even more substantial (Kenyon and Holland 1981). The development of these new settlements in a time when food production was still extremely limited confirms that the growth of increasingly sedentary communities was not simply a consequence of food production but was integral to the Neolithic transition.

The emergence of these settlements should not be used to presume the existence of a bucolic landscape filled first with Natufian hamlets and then Neolithic villages, commonly used terms that carry substantial cultural baggage. Even the more neutral terminology of "large, permanently co-resident community" (Watkins 2015) is problematic, as it assumes that both scale and permanence are important factors in these early settlements. The scale of the settlement at Jericho and the physical permanence provided by its monumental architecture are not typical. Even at Jericho, it is possible that the highly visible monumental tower may have been placed on the periphery of the site because it was related to external, regional relations, and perhaps to the use of the location for periodic aggregation, rather than the internal structuring of community. In terms of scale, beyond the relatively small number of large sites, most Natufian and PPNA sites remain small, unlikely to reach the 150-person threshold that is thought to require more elaborate social organization than the small-scale societies typical of hunter-gatherers (Zeder 2015). In the southern Levant, substantial settlement scale does not truly pick up until late in the aceramic sequence, most notably in the large Late PPNB (9,200–8,700 cal. BP) sites of the Jordanian plateau, for example, 'Ain Ghazal (Rollefson 1997), es-Sifiya (Mahasneh 1997), Basta (Gebel, Nissen, and Zaid 2006), and 'Ain Jammam (Waheeb and Fino 1997). Even these sites appear to have been a relatively short-lived adaptation before settlements mostly returned to being small scale in the Late (or Pottery) Neolithic.

While we can assume that investment in place is continuing to develop through the Natufian and Neolithic, it is unlikely that most Early Neolithic populations had become entirely sedentary. Architectural developments do not, of themselves, indicate permanence of people, even if it confirms patterns of return (Boyd 2006). In the PPNA, for example at WF16 and Dhra', we have evidence of abandonment of individual buildings during the lifespan of the overall settlement, while at Middle PPNB (10,300–9,200 cal. BP) Shkārat Msaied, the blocking of doorways has suggested periodic absences from the site (Finlayson et al. 2003; Finlayson and Mithen 2007; Jensen in press). In the

PPNB and Pottery Neolithic, sites in the al-Jafr Basin and the eastern Badia in Jordan suggest that there were still at least segments of the population who remained seasonally mobile (e.g., Fujii 2009; Rollefson, Rowan, and Wasse 2014). The research focus on large, archaeologically rich sites may distort the nature of our evidence, where throughout Southwest Asia, large permanent settlements appear to be exceptional, and, in general, community identity appears to be constructed before large-scale permanent settlement becomes the norm.

House and Home

Identifying houses at Neolithic sites is generally understood as a matter of common sense, including the key attributes of standard forms of construction and design, size, and internal features, especially hearths (Baird 2011; Banning 2011; Düring and Marciniak 2005). As the huts and shelters of the early Epipaleolithic become more permanent constructions made of mud or stone rather than brushwood, they become described as houses. However, many of the structures labeled as "houses" in the PPNA are no more substantial, and indeed are often less so than their Natufian predecessors. The "maisons" at Hatula (Lechevalier and Ronen 1994) are particularly ephemeral and compare poorly with Natufian sites, such as 'Ein Mallaha or Nahal 'Ein Gev II.

Watkins (1990) argued strongly that the Neolithic was where the idea of home began. He followed the work of Peter Wilson (1988) on the significance of domestic space and clearly expressed a perception that is often left implicit in the designation of structures as houses (Watkins 1990; Streleny and Watkins 2015). There is an understanding that the basic architectural unit in settlements is for residential shelter – the direct descendent of the Early Epipaleolithic hut. The small circular or elliptical structures that characterize the early stages of the Neolithic are widely interpreted as homes for nuclear families, while the later, larger rectilinear houses are interpreted as homes for larger households (Flannery 1972; 2002; Byrd 1994; 2000; Kuijt 1996). Kent Flannery's key southern Levantine case study in 1972 was Beidha, now known as a rather late example of circular architecture that continues to be employed in southern Jordan in the Middle PPNB, during a period when rectilinear architecture had begun to characterize the Middle PPNB elsewhere in the southern Levant. However, at Beidha and the contemporary neighboring Middle PPNB site of Shkārat Msaied, the circular form is employed differently from its use in earlier PPNA architecture in the same region. This is not a matter of individual structure design, rather in the Middle PPNB settlements, the circular structures now appear as relatively standard forms repeated across the site, and the architecture, circular or rectilinear, begins to fit our commonsense understanding of what a house should look like. The transformation is not complete, for example, Middle PPNB structures at Beidha may have continued to have separate storage cells external to the house, but large stone bins inside the entrances to buildings at Shkārat Msaied suggest that some storage functions may have begun to be internalized within the houses (Kinzel 2013), potentially reflecting a greater sense of family, rather than community and ownership. This diversity of design between the two sites reinforces the possibility that the Middle PPNB may have been a key transformational period (Banning and Byrd 1987), as the diversity may reflect the transition in process. The development of buildings recognizable as houses continues into the Late PPNB, with increased standardization, compartmentalization, and incorporation of functions, such as storage within the house.

Recent excavations in southern Jordan have provided more evidence that the "house" may develop slowly in the Neolithic. At the PPNA sites at Dhra', WF16, and el-Hemmeh, it appears that the default identification of structures as houses may be premature, as many structures appear to have been designed for specific functions, such as storage, workshops, mortuary spaces, and larger communal buildings, all potentially shared community facilites (Kuijt and Finlayson 2009; Finlayson et al. 2011; Makarewicz and Finlayson 2018). Reappraisal of other southern Levantine sites suggests that nonresidential buildings may have been present at other settlements, such as at Netiv Hagdud and Gilgal I (Kuijt and Finlayson 2009). Combined with the ephemeral nature of many PPNA houses, this suggests that the significance of house and home within a built environment as an early step in the process of becoming Neolithic has been overstated.

Pre-Pottery Neolithic burial practices provide another means to explore social organization. There is general agreement that burial rituals are important for reproducing social structure and providing a social regulatory function among the living (Belfer-Cohen 1995; Boyd 2001). PPNA mortuary practices include the partial burial of bodies and the secondary manipulation of bones by adding and subtracting different skeletal parts, which has suggested that burial is not used to commemorate dead individuals, but that mortuary practices sublimated individual identity. Within the context of subfloor burial practices, such burial practices may have played a role in identifying the ownership of a house with a lineage, reinforcing the idea of "home" in the PPNA (Watkins 1990). However, subfloor burial is only one of many burial practices used in the Neolithic, and many floors have no associated burials, so the correlation between subfloor burial with house and home in the PPNA is problematic at best. Recent discoveries of an apparent mortuary structure with seated burials in individual cists at the site of el-Hemmeh in Jordan confirms the considerable diversity in burial practice, which requires a considerable reevaluation of the role of the dead in the southern Levantine Neolithic (Makarewicz and Rose 2011; Makarewicz and Finlayson 2018).

Households

Most social archaeological approaches to the Neolithic have focused on the household as the basic building block of Neolithic society, but there has been limited discussion of how these households first emerged (e.g., Kuit 2000; Hodder and Cessford 2004; Watkins 2008; Kuijt et al. 2011). In practice, it appears that the emphasis on households is a simple response to the archaeological identification of houses and perhaps should not be applied to the PPNA at all. Ian Kuijt (2000) has developed Claude Lévi-Strauss's (1983) concept of *sociétés à maison* and adapted it to Aceramic Neolithic contexts, but mainly to the Middle PPNB. If we accept this correlation of house with household, it is possible that households may have begun to emerge – perhaps at various places around the southern Levant – during the Middle PPNB when the complex mortuary practices of burial, secondary burial, skull removal, skull plastering, display, and handling became a marked feature. Kuijt has proposed that these mortuary practices were central to the deconstruction of individuality and the creation of lineages and households (1996; 2000; 2008). There is still some evidence for the earlier PPNA communal ethos continuing into the Middle PPNB, at least in southern Jordan, where communal architecture is evident in both the central mortuary building at Shkārat Msaied (Kinzel 2013), and in the large Building 37 at Beidha (Makarewicz and Finlayson 2018). It is notable that the practice of skull plastering does not extend to these sites in southern Jordan, suggesting significant differences in social practices in this part of the Levant (Makarewicz and Finlayson 2018). New forms of integration may have also developed, as at the possible regional funerary site of Kfar HaHoresh, which is located near contemporary typical Middle PPNB settlements such as Yiftahel, but lacks both their normal domestic contexts and their landscape context (Goring-Morris 2000). Such regional integration sites may be a response to the rise of autonomous households, as these become a divisive factor in community integration (Byrd 1994; Rollefson 2005)

By the Late PPNB, many of the traits thought to indicate the presence of increasingly autonomous households have emerged, in particular, the partitioning of houses to create increased privacy and facilities for storage, often in basements that would have been well concealed from public view and access (Byrd and Banning 1988). The large multi-roomed structures, perhaps epitomized by the "Basta House" (Gebel, Nissen, and Zaid 2006), appear as good evidence for the sort of house society that Kuijt has proposed. However, these appear after the demise of the complex Middle PPNB mortuary practices that Kuijt (2000) sees as a means of actively promoting house societies used in much of the southern Levant. Instead, the final stage of the mortuary practices may have concerned wider community integration, and the household may not have been a significant component of these rituals. Marc Verhoeven (2002) has suggested an even later date for the emergence of households, arguing that the much less complex primary inhumations within buildings that are found in the Pottery Neolithic may have been intended to emphasize individual households, in contrast to the practices associated with skull removal and plastering, or the mortuary structures of Beidha, el-Hemmeh, and Shkārat Msaied.

An alternative for Neolithic mortuary practices and the removal of individuality is that they were designed to resist the emergence of hierarchies and preserve the egalitarian structure of hunter-gatherer society. Kuijt (1996) argued that burial practices in the Late Natufian and PPNA indicate deliberate attempts to prevent or limit the emergence of hierarchical power, a resistance that continued into the Middle PPNB. He developed this approach by suggesting that Pre-Pottery Neolithic mortuary practices, especially the use of secondary burial, were public performances scheduled in advance to foster community participation and identity. However, despite anthropological models and arguments put forward that the Neolithic was at least in part driven by hyper-agents or aggrandizers (Hayden 2004), there is no clear evidence for pressures toward such increasingly hierarchical societies or the emergence of identifiable aggrandizers.

An additional argument that has been used to support ideas of property and lineage pertaining to households is the repeated reconstruction of Neolithic buildings, one atop the last (e.g., Düring 2007). The associated presence of subfloor burials has further suggested that the ancestors were used to legitimize the development of the lineage and, therefore, the household. These practices are, however, regionally very distinct; while they occur in Anatolia, where there is much better evidence for households, they are not typical of the southern Levant, where buildings were often relocated between phases or modified to serve different purposes, suggesting that such household and lineage concerns were not so central to southern Levantine society as in the north. Indeed, in contrast, the flexibility and repurposing of architecture that seems commonplace in the southern Levantine PPNA may be a means to expressly limit the development of lineages of power. Throughout the process of transformation, it is important to note that there is no single, uniform Neolithic across Southwest Asia, rather a series of regional expressions.

Shared Architecture

If individual houses are not always the dominant and standard architectural component of settlements, buildings that support some level of shared activity appear relatively frequently. PPNA architecture, in particular, appears to focus extensively on shared facilities, including storage buildings, presumably at least in part for the increased harvest of cultivated wild crops (Kuijt and Finlayson 2009), food processing shelters, workshops, community mortuary structures

(Makarewicz and Rose 2011), and large-scale communal buildings, such as the tower at Jericho and the communal building at WF16, which both appear likely to have supported visible public ritual, as well as other communal activities (Finlayson et al. 2011). These shared and communal buildings all represent different functions within the community, but the emphasis appears to be strongly on maintaining community cohesion. While Ofer Bar-Yosef (2001) interprets communal building efforts as requiring leadership by a headman and therefore as evidence for emergent hierarchies, communal public storage may rather have played an important role in enforcing communal sharing of resources and preventing the development of household resource accumulation. Sterelny and Watkins (2015) see shared storage as an expression of community cooperation and complete trust. In contrast, Flannery (1972) had seen the presence of publicly located storage as a mechanism for enforcing sharing, with reference to the mechanisms used by modern hunter-gatherers to enforce sharing. These two interpretations are not necessarily mutually exclusive; the importance of the principle of sharing can be expressed at the same time that it is enforced.

Describing buildings as "communal" does not mean that they had to be able to accommodate an entire community at a single time. With the exception of the rare monumental structures, most are not large enough to have been used for activities involving participation by an entire community. Rather, "communal" refers to their use for the community. While they include the largest structures present, other buildings are relatively small but served a communal function, such as communal grain stores. Some buildings may have served as places to meet, but with access restricted to specific groups within the community, such as those formed by gender, age status, or task group. A few communal buildings, for example, in the PPNA the large amphitheater-like communal structure at WF16 could have provided a venue for performance, a powerful means to develop community identity. The prevalence of this wide variety of communal and shared buildings in the PPNA suggests that together they played an important role in the social construction of these communities prior to the development of households. The scale and location of some PPNA communal structures in the southern Levant on the margins of the settlements, such as the tower at Jericho or perhaps the communal building at WF16, suggest that their purpose goes beyond the site-based community, and that these structures provided a venue for wider group integration.

Subsequently, during the course of the PPNB, the range of communal buildings appears to reduce and becomes increasingly centered on the role of communal architecture as meeting or ritual space, as many of the task-specific, shared buildings become incorporated within the larger compartmentalized houses. Both Brian Byrd (1994; 2000) and Gary Rollefson (2005) have interpreted this shift at Beidha and 'Ain Ghazal as a means to counter the increasingly divisive pressures of the developing autonomous households. These potential ritual structures remain rare and differ in their nature from site to site. Unusual, and therefore interpreted as non-domestic, buildings have been identified in Middle PPNB Jericho (Kenyon and Holland 1981), and structures interpreted as sanctuaries were built just outside the Beidha settlement (Kirkbride 1968). The Late PPNB ritual structures at 'Ain Ghazal remain unique, so far not seen at any other Late PPNB site. They have been interpreted as playing an integrative role, with the smaller buildings within the settlement representing lineage cult buildings, while the larger temples at the edge of the settlement have been seen as belonging to the entire community (Rollefson 2000; 2005). The PPNB aggregation and the ritual site of Kfar HaHoresh may represent a location dedicated to regional integration (Goring-Morris 2000). Nahal Hemar Cave, where a rich collection of Middle or Late PPNB ritual paraphernalia was preserved, has been proposed as ritually significant, as it was located at the intersection between different tribal territories (Bar-Yosef and Alon 1988). This interpretation is highly speculative and is based largely on the location of the cave at a geographical or ecotonal intersection.

Middle PPNB integrative mortuary rituals were presumably not strong enough to integrate larger Late PPNB communities with the increasingly autonomous households becoming divisive forces within the larger communities (Rollefson 2005). The role of the skull cult and the use of plaster statues may therefore have been replaced by rituals that reinforced community integrity, when "[m]onument-building and the continual expression of collective memory seem to have become central preoccupations of social life." (Sterelny and Watkins 2015: 681). It is not clear how this really happened, as apart from at 'Ain Ghazal, monumental buildings become very rare in the Late PPNB. However, collective action, behavioral norms, and ideological infrastructure would presumably have been vital during the Late PPNB as communities grew larger, and it is possible that the emerging households are providing the locus for structuring society. The larger ritual buildings of 'Ain Ghazal continue the PPNA practice of being located on the periphery of the settlement (Bar-Yosef 2001), which again questions whether they relate more to regional or inter-community relations rather than within community organization.

The Nature of Community

Although the development of increasingly sedentary communities was a slow process, it appears likely that the coresident community would have become central to social organization, rather than the kinship-based social groups associated with mobile hunter-gatherers and more temporary dwelling spaces

(Watkins 1990; Hodder and Cessford 2004; Gerritsen 2006). The built environment is where community is expressed, as it creates the spaces where social interaction takes place within the routines of daily practice (Bourdieu 1973; 1977; Giddens 1984). Shared and communal buildings, especially in the PPNA, confirm the importance of the built environment to social reproduction. Shared values are part of the structure of the community, and various mechanisms, from shared storage to communal ritual, appear likely to have served to create and sustain a sense of community. The strength of the community in structuring society may help to explain the trend through the Aceramic Neolithic for increasingly permanent and large settlements.

Communal buildings, especially the larger ones, would have been important to the construction and reconstruction of community. Their construction and maintenance were probably major communal collaborative projects that may have played a role in bringing a community together, possibly as much as their ongoing function and use. They may not have functioned on a permanent basis, and seasonal repair and refurbishment may have been a part of mechanisms to encourage aggregation, as seems likely in the case of WF16. These structures had the potential to include a role for performance, and Watkins (2011: 32) has suggested that the emergence of a new mode of social life seen in large, permanently coresident settlements created "arenas for ritual acts," where the drama of ritual was a powerful means for social integration and the creation of communal social forces. The desire to reinforce community identity may also explain why Early Neolithic sites are so tightly bound, densely built up within confined areas, sometimes further isolated by walls, as a material representation of their community. The wall at Jericho may have given that community a sense of separation from its neighbors as strong as geographical distance (Naveh 2003). The mortuary practices of the Middle PPNB may have replaced the role of PPNA communal buildings in much of the southern Levant, providng a venue for communal, performative practices.

Another strong characteristic of Pre-Pottery Neolithic settlements is their diversity. Throughout the southern Levant, there are differences between subregions and, indeed, between individual sites. This further suggests that community was an important level of social organization – each community not only provided strong integrative measures to hold itself together but marked out its individual identity through differences with other communities. While diversity between Late PPNB settlements shows that individual community identity continued to be important, the internalization of food storage and processing within the large houses of the substantial Late PPNB settlements suggest that the collective communal nature of the much smaller PPNA and Middle PPNB settlements had transformed to a household level. This is in contrast to Sterelny and Watkins (2015), who have argued that a commitment to cooperation was behind the ability to live together in large permanent settlements, with the need for collective action increasing during the Neolithic. The emergence of autonomous households and the end of substantial communal projects, such as the Jericho tower, argue against this. The large temple buildings at 'Ain Ghazal are the only Late PPNB example of substantial community projects that may have provided an overarching community identity.

While each settlement may have had its own identity, communities are neither isolated from each other, nor necessarily internally homogenous. Despite the marked inter-site and interregional diversity within the southern Levant, there is much that is held in common in terms of material culture (especially the diagnostic points and the naviform bipolar technology in the PPNB), general architectural trends, innovation and adaption in subsistence, and ritual behavior. Equally, certainly in the Early Aceramic Neolithic, it appears clear that the population at individual sites would have required wider marriage networks to make them viable. Coupled with a recognition that most settlements were not fully sedentary, and that much economic – and, therefore, social – activity took place in the landscape between sites, suggests the structures that created and maintained community were located within a heterogeneous and fluid wider social environment.

Agency in the Neolithic

If Early Aceramic Neolithic society was founded on the idea of community where economic choices, daily practice, and ritual behavior intersect in social lives, is it possible to understand how that community was constructed if not through houses and households (Finlayson and Makarewicz 2017)? I have argued that one route may be through collective agency (Finlayson 2010). Agency has received little attention in discussions of the Early Neolithic in Southwest Asia and mostly appears only in the background to discussions of what plastered skulls and plaster figurines may represent in the sense of individuals or generic ancestors. Agency is usefully considered here as the power behind human choice and decision-making, where knowledgeable agents construct their social worlds while being conditioned and constrained by that world (Barrett 1988; 2000). However, agency does not necessarily correlate with Neolithic individuals. Early attempts to consider agency as pertaining to the individual (e.g., Hodder 1999) by representing modernist Western-empowered individuals missed the Early Neolithic socio-cultural context (Fowler 2000; Gero 2000). Agency does not emerge as a set of attributes that are the property of individuals but, through the social context of culture, history, gender, age, and lineage, reproducing community identity (Gardner 2007). People derive their sense of identity through relationships, and the elaborate kinship structures of many recent hunter-gatherer societies reflect ways of identifying people, not so much as individuals, but as parts of a whole to which the sense of individuality is absent or subservient. The collective body can be stable, such as kin or gender groups, but can include groups that progress, such as age sets; are transformative, such as marriage relationships; or temporary and task-specific, such as groups of herders, harvesters, or hunters, assembling daily, weekly, or seasonally, with variable composition.

Although there is some very tentative evidence for the emergence of individuality in the later Neolithic (Hodder 2011), there is little archaeological evidence for the concept of the individual in the Aceramic Neolithic of the southern Levant. Indeed, mortuary practices such as skull removal, secondary burial practices, and remodeling of skulls without their mandibles all appear designed to reduce individuality. In contrast, there is much better evidence for community action, which may equate with community identity (Finlayson 2010; Finlayson and Makarewicz 2017). Early Neolithic communities were highly integrated through daily practices associated with their shared and communal architecture, and through a complex suite of mortuary practices. These will have constantly confirmed membership of community and identity. It is more pragmatic to consider community as a way to approach agency in the Early Neolithic transition where communities become organizations that are, in effect, unitary actors with identities that emerge from their shared behavior (DiMaggio and Powell 1991).

NEOLITHIC SOCIAL CHANGE

While Melissa Zeder has argued it is only a "vocal minority" (2015: 698) who advocate that social changes are central to the Neolithic, social change effectively plays two major roles integral to the Neolithic transformation. It is a primary driver for the adoption of a new food-producing economy and as a means to cope with the demographic increase and changes in concepts of the relationship between people and the world that flowed from the new resource base. While many of the features associated with traditional small-scale farming are seen equally in complex hunter-gatherer societies, low-level food production requires changes in social practice, especially around the investment in place and storage, and as farming develops, these become more significant with more land clearance, soil maintenance, ownership issues, and water provision (Bender 1985). Farming economies, or subsistence economies reliant on storage, clearly require new conflict resolution mechanisms. Reliance on stored produce also likely necessitates changes to the sharing economies of mobile hunter-gatherers. The assumption that increasingly large, permanent settlements were a feature of the Early Neolithic and that these drive developments underlies most social archaeologies of the Neolithic. Increasing sedentism and commitment to place with investment in resources and facilities has been widely recognized as requiring major changes in social organization; as people lose the ability to move away from conflict that provides one option for resolution among mobile hunter-gatherers. However, these settlements emerge very slowly and are mostly a temporary expression of the Neolithic, not consistently replicated through time or space. The social transformations that took place during the Neolithic are clearly vitally significant to human development, but they were not entirely novel; rather, they are an expression of longstanding trends that accelerate from the Natufian onward.

Integration is likely to have been an important aspect of Early Neolithic society, fostered by strong community identities, needed especially if populations were not fully sedentary. The communal architecture that was ubiquitous in the PPNA is concerned with varying levels of social integration, from intercommunity public social interaction, supported by the largest and most monumental structures, to smaller structures that suggest some exclusivity for the collective group who could meet within. The strength of the mechanisms that developed to hold together the small communities typical of the Natufian and PPNA may have continued to develop, creating the social mechanism that led to the formation of the extremely large sites of the Late PPNB, which were unlikely to have been sustainable in the longer term. The diversity of the Natufian and Neolithic communities that was created by the strong sense of community identity may help to explain the development of a decentralized Neolithic, where developments arise in multiple locations throughout the Neolithic world (Rollefson and Gebel 2004).

REFERENCES

Baird, D. 2011. Comment on "So Fair a House: Göbekli Tepe and the Identification of Temples in the Pre-Pottery Neolithic of the Near East." *CA* 52: 641–2.

Banning, E. B. 2011. So Fair a House: Göbekli Tepe and the Identification of Temples in the Pre-Pottery Neolithic of the Near East. *CA* 52: 619–20.

Banning, E. B., and Byrd, B. F. 1987. Houses and the Changing Residential Unit: Domestic Architecture at PPNB 'Ain Ghazal, Jordan. *PPS* 53: 309–25.

Bar-Yosef, O. 1998. The Natufian Culture in the Levant, Threshold to the Origins of Agriculture. *EA* 6: 159–77.

2001. From Sedentary Foragers to Village Hierarchies: The Emergence of Social Institutions. In *The Origin of Human Social Institutions*, ed. W. G. Runciman, 1–38. Proceedings of the British Academy 110. Oxford: Oxford University Press.

Bar-Yosef, O., and Alon, D. 1988. Nahal Hemar Cave. *'Atiqot* 18: 1–81.

Bar-Yosef, O., and Belfer-Cohen, A. 1989. The Origins of Sedentism and Farming Communities in the Levant. *JWP* 3: 447–98.

Bar-Yosef, O., and Gopher, A. 1997. *An Early Neolithic Village in the Jordan Valley*, Part 1: *The Archaeology of Netiv Hagdud*. ASPRB 44. Cambridge, MA: Peabody Museum of Archaeology and Ethnology, Harvard University.

Bar-Yosef, O.; Goring-Morris, N.; and Gopher, A., eds. 2010. *Gilgal: Early Neolithic Occupations in the Lower Jordan Valley; The Excavations of Tamar Noy*. ASPRMS. Oxford: Oxbow.

Barker, G. 2006. *The Agricultural Revolution in Prehistory: Why Did Foragers Become Farmers?* Oxford: Oxford University Press.

Barrett, J. C. 1988. Fields of Discourse: Reconstituting a Social Archaeology. *Critique of Anthropology* 7: 5–16.

— 2000. A Thesis on Agency. In *Agency in Archaeology*, ed. M.-A. Dobres and J. E. Robb, 61–8. London: Routledge.

Belfer-Cohen, A. 1995. Rethinking Social Stratification in the Natufian Culture: The Evidence from Burials. In *The Archaeology of Death in the Ancient Near East*, ed. S. Campbell and A. Green, 9–16. Oxbow Monographs 51. Oxford: Oxbow.

Belfer-Cohen, A., and Bar-Yosef, O. 2000. Early Sedentism in the Near East: A Bumpy Ride to Village Life (13,000–8,000 BP). In *Life in Neolithic Farming Communities: Social Organization, Identity, and Differentiation*, ed. I. Kuijt, 19–37. FIA. New York: Kluwer Academic/Plenum.

Bender, B. 1985. Prehistoric Developments in the American Midcontinent and in Brittany, Northwest France. In *Prehistoric Hunter-Gatherers: The Emergence of Cultural Complexity*, ed. T. D. Price and J. A. Brown, 21–57. Studies in Archaeology. Orlando: Academic.

Bourdieu, P. 1973. The Berber House. In *Rules and Meaning: The Anthropology of Everyday Knowledge*, ed. M. Douglas, 25–54. Penguin Modern Sociology Readings. Harmondsworth: Penguin.

— 1977. *Outline of a Theory of Practice*. Cambridge Studies in Social Anthropology 16. Cambridge: Cambridge University Press.

Boyd, B. 2001. The Natufian Burials from el-Wad, Mount Carmel: Beyond Issues of Social Differentiation. *JIPS* 31: 185–200.

— 2006. On "Sedentism" in the Later Epipalaeolithic (Natufian) Levant. *WA* 38: 164–78.

Byrd, B. F. 1994. Public and Private, Domestic and Corporate: The Emergence of the Southwest Asian Village. *AA* 59: 639–66.

— 2000. Households in Transition: Neolithic Social Organization within Southwest Asia. In *Life in Neolithic Farming Communities: Social Organization, Identity, and Differentiation*, ed. I. Kuijt, 63–98. FIA. New York: Kluwer Academic/Plenum.

— 2005. Reassessing the Emergence of Village Life in the Near East. *JAR* 13: 231–90.

Byrd, B. F., and Banning, E. B. 1988. Southern Levantine Pier Houses: Intersite Architectural Patterning during the Pre-Pottery Neolithic B. *Paléorient* 14 (1): 65–72.

Cauvin, J. 1994. *Naissance des divinités, naissance de l'agriculture: La révolution des symboles au Néolithique*. Empreintes de l'homme. Paris: CNRS.

— 2000. *The Birth of the Gods and the Origins of Agriculture*. New Studies in Archaeology. Cambridge: Cambridge University Press.

Childe, V. G. 1951. *Man Makes Himself*. New York: New American Library of World Literature.

DiMaggio, P. J., and Powell, W. W. 1991. Introduction. In *The New Institutionalism in Organizational Analysis*, ed. W. W. Powell and P. J. DiMaggio, 1–20. Chicago: The University of Chicago Press.

Düring, B. S. 2007. The Articulation of Houses at Neolithic Çatalhöyük, Turkey. In *The Durable House: House Society Models in Archaeology*, ed. R. Beck, 130–53. Southern Illinois University Carbondale Center for Archaeological Investigations Occasional

Paper 35. Carbondale: Center for Archaeological Investigations, Southern Illinois University.

Düring, B. S., and Marciniak, A. 2005. Households and Communities in the Central Anatolian Neolithic. *Archaeological Dialogues* 12: 165–87.

Finlayson, B. 2010. Agency in the Pre-Pottery Neolithic A. In *The Development of Pre-State Communities in the Ancient Near East: Studies in Honour of Edgar Peltenburg*, ed. D. Bolger and L. C. Maguire, 141–6. Themes from the Ancient Near East BANEA Publication Series 2. Oxford: Oxbow.

2011. Archaeology, Evidence and Anthropology: Circular Arguments in the Transition from Foraging to Farming. In *The Principle of Sharing: Segregation and Construction of Social Identities at the Transition from Foraging to Farming; Proceedings of a Symposium Held on 29th–31st January 2009 at the Albert-Ludwigs-University of Freiburg, Hosted by the Department of Near Eastern Archaeology*, ed. M. Benz, 19–34. SENEPSE 14. Berlin: Ex Oriente.

2013. Imposing the Neolithic on the Past. *Levant* 45: 133–48.

Finlayson, B.; Kuijt, I.; Arpin, T.; Chesson, M.; Dennis, S.; Goodale, N.; Kadowaki, S.; Maher, L.; Smith, S.; Schurr, M.; and McKay, J. 2003. Dhra', Excavation Project, 2002 Interim Report. *Levant* 35: 1–38.

Finlayson, B., and Makarewicz, C. 2017. The Construction of Community in the Early Neolithic of Southern Jordan. In *Neolithic Corporate Identities*, ed. M. Benz, H. G. K. Gebel, and T. F. Watkins, 91–106. SENEPSE 20. Berlin: Ex Oriente.

Finlayson, B., and Mithen, S. J. 2007. *The Early Prehistory of Wadi Faynan, Southern Jordan: Archaeological Survey of Wadis Faynan, Ghuwayr and al-Bustan and Evaluation of the Pre-Pottery Neolithic A Site of WF16*. LSS 4; Wadi Faynan Series 1. Oxford: Oxbow.

Finlayson, B.; Mithen, S. J.; Najjar, M.; Smith, S.; Maričevic, D.; Pankhurst, N.; and Yeomans, L. 2011. Architecture, Sedentism, and Social Complexity at Pre-Pottery Neolithic A WF16, Southern Jordan. *PNAS* 108: 8183–8.

Flannery, K. V. 1972. The Origins of the Village as a Settlement Type in Mesoamerica and the Near East: A Comparative Study. In *Man, Settlement, and Urbanism*, ed. P. J. Ucko, R. Tringham, and G. W. Dimbleby, 23–53. London: Duckworth.

2002. The Origins of the Village Revisited: From Nuclear to Extended Households. *AA* 67: 417–33.

Fowler, C. 2000. The Individual, the Subject, and Archaeological Interpretation: Reading Luce Irigaray and Judith Butler. In *Philosophy and Archaeological Practice: Perspectives for the 21st Century*, ed. C. Holtorf and H. Karlsson, 107–33. Göteborg: Bricoleur.

Fujii, S. 2009. Wadi Abu Tulayha: A Preliminary Report on the Summer 2008 Final Field Season of the Jafr Basin Prehistoric Project, Phase 2. *ADAJ* 53: 173–210.

Gardner, A. 2007. Introduction: Social Agency, Power, and Being Human. In *Agency Uncovered: Archaeological Perspectives on Social Agency, Power, and Being Human*, ed. A. Gardner, 1–15. Walnut Creek, CA: Left Coast.

Gebel H. G. K.; Nissen, H. J.; and Zaid, Z., eds. 2006. *Basta II: The Architecture and Stratigraphy*. Bibliotheca Neolithica Asiae Meridionalis et Occidentalis; Monograph of the Faculty of Archaeology and Anthropology 5. Berlin: Ex Oriente.

Gero, J. M. 2000. Troubled Travels in Agency and Feminism. In *Agency in Archaeology*, ed. M.-A. Dobres and J. E. Robb, 34–9. Malden, MA: Blackwell.

Gerritsen, F. 2006. Archaeological Perspectives on Local Communities. In *A Companion to Archaeology*, ed. J Bintliff, 141–54. Oxford: Blackwell.

Giddens, A. 1984. *The Constitution of Society: Outline of the Theory of Structuration.* Cambridge: Polity.

Goring-Morris, A. N. 2000. The Quick and the Dead: The Social Context of Aceramic Neolithic Mortuary Practices as Seen from Kfar HaHoresh. In *Life in Neolithic Farming Communities: Social Organization, Identity, and Differentiation*, ed. I. Kuijt, 103–36. FIA. New York: Kluwer Academic/Plenum.

Goring-Morris, A. N., and Belfer-Cohen, A. 2011. Neolithization Processes in the Levant: The Outer Envelope. *CA* 52 (suppl. 4): S195–208.

Grosman, L.; Munro, N. D.; Abadi, I.; Boaretto, E.; Shaham, D.; Belfer-Cohen, A.; and Bar-Yosef, O. 2016. Nahal Ein Gev II, a Late Natufian Community at the Sea of Galilee. *PLOS ONE* 11 (1): e0146647.

Hayden, B. 2004. Sociopolitical Organization in the Natufian: A View from the Northwest. In *The Last Hunter-Gatherers in the Near East*, ed. C. Delage, 263–308. BAR International Series 1320. Oxford: Hedges.

Henry, D. O. 1989. *From Foraging to Agriculture: The Levant at the End of the Ice Age.* Philadelphia: University of Pennsylvania Press.

Hodder, I. 1990. *The Domestication of Europe: Structure and Contingency in Neolithic Societies.* SA. Oxford: Blackwell.

——— 1999. *The Archaeological Process: An Introduction.* Oxford: Blackwell.

——— 2001. Symbolism and the Origins of Agriculture in the Near East. *CAJ* 11: 107–12.

——— 2011. An Archaeology of the Self: The Prehistory of Personhood. In *In Search of Self: Interdisciplinary Perspectives on Personhood*, ed. J. W. Van Huyssteen and E. P. Weibe, 50–69. Grand Rapids, MI: Eerdmans.

Hodder, I., and Cessford, C. 2004. Daily Practice and Social Memory at Çatalhöyük. *AA* 69: 17–40.

Jensen, C. H. In press. Three Years of Excavation at the PPNB Site Shaqarat Mazyad, Southern Jordan. In *Proceedings of the Third International Congress on the Archaeology of the Ancient Near East, Paris, 2002*, ed. J.-C. Margueron, P. de Miroschedji, and J. P. Thalmann. Winona Lake, IN: Eisenbrauns.

Kenyon, K. M., and Holland, T. A. 1981. *Excavations at Jericho*, Vol. 3: *The Architecture and Stratigraphy of the Tell.* 2 vols. London: BSAJ.

Kinzel, M. 2013. *Am Beginn des Hausbaus: Studien zur PPNB-Architektur von Shkārat Msaied und Baʿja in der Petra-Region, Südjordanien.* SENEPSE 17. Berlin: Ex Oriente.

Kirkbride, D. 1968. Beidha 1967: An Interim Report. *PEQ* 100: 90–6.

Kuijt, I. 1996. Negotiating Equality through Ritual: A Consideration of Late Natufian and Prepottery Neolithic A Period Mortuary Practices. *JAA* 15: 313–36.

——— 2000. Keeping the Peace: Ritual, Skull Caching, and Community Integration in the Levantine Neolithic. In *Life in Neolithic Farming Communities: Social Organization, Identity, and Differentiation*, ed. I. Kuijt, 137–64. FIA. New York: Kluwer Academic/Plenum.

——— 2008. The Regeneration of Life: Neolithic Structures of Symbolic Remembering and Forgetting. *CA* 49: 171–97.

Kuijt, I., and Finlayson, B. 2009. New Evidence for Food Storage and Predomestication Granaries 11,000 Years Ago in the Jordan Valley. *PNAS* 106: 10966–70.

Kuijt, I.; Guerrero, E.; Molist, M.; and Anfruns, J. 2011. The Changing Neolithic Household: Household Autonomy and Social Segmentation, Tell Halula, Syria. *JAA* 30: 502–22.

Lechevalier, M., and Ronen, A., eds. 1994. *Le gisement de Hatoula en Judée occidentale, Israël: Rapport de fouilles 1980–1988*. MTCRPFJ 8. Paris: Paléorient.

Lévi-Strauss, C. 1983. *The Way of the Masks*. Trans. S. Modelski, from French. London: Cape.

Mahasneh, H. 1997. Es-Sifiya: A Pre-Pottery Neolithic B Site in the Wadi el-Mujib, Jordan. In *The Prehistory of Jordan II: Perspectives from 1997*, ed. H. G. K. Gebel, Z. Kafafi, and G. O. Rollefson, 203–14. SENEPSE 4. Berlin: Ex Oriente.

Maher, L. A.; Richter, T.; and Stock, J. T. 2012. The Pre-Natufian Epipaleolithic: Long-Term Behavioral Trends in the Levant. *EA* 21: 69–81.

Makarewicz, C., and Finlayson, B. 2018. Constructing Community in the Neolithic of Southern Jordan: Quotidian Practice in Communal Architecture. *PLOS ONE* 13 (6): e0193712. https://doi.org/10.1371/journal.pone.0193712 (accessed August 20, 2018).

Makarewicz, C., and Rose, K. 2011. Early Pre-Pottery Neolithic Settlement at el-Hemmeh: A Survey of the Architecture. *Neo-Lithics* 2011 (1): 23–9.

Nadel, D. 2003. The Ohalo II Brush Huts and the Dwelling Structures of the Natufian and PPNA Sites in the Jordan Valley. *Archaeology, Ethnology & Anthropology of Eurasia* 1 (13): 34–48.

Naveh, D. 2003. PPNA Jericho: A Socio-Political Perspective. *CAJ* 13: 83–96.

Olszewski, D. I. 1991. Social Complexity in the Natufian? Assessing the Relationship of Ideas and Data. In *Perspectives on the Past: Theoretical Biases in Mediterranean Hunter-Gatherer Research*, ed. G. A. Clark, 322–40. Philadelphia: University of Pennsylvania Press.

Perrot, J. 1966. Le gisement Natoufien de Mallaha (Eynan), Israël. *L'Anthropologie* 70: 437–84.

Renfrew, C. 2003. *Figuring It Out: What Are We? Where Do We Come from? The Parallel Vision of Artists and Archaeologists*. New York: Thames & Hudson.

——— 2007. *Prehistory: The Making of the Human Mind*. London: Weidenfeld & Nicolson.

Rollefson, G. O. 1997. Changes in Architecture and Social Organization at 'Ain Ghazal. In *The Prehistory of Jordan II: Perspectives from 1997*, ed. H. G. K. Gebel, Z. Kafafi, and G. O. Rollefson, 287–307. SENEPSE 4. Berlin: Ex Oriente.

——— 2000. Ritual and Social Structure at Neolithic 'Ain Ghazal. In *Life in Neolithic Farming Communities: Social Organization, Identity, and Differentiation*, ed. I. Kuijt, 165–90. FIA. New York: Kluwer Academic/Plenum.

——— 2005. Early Neolithic Ritual Centers in the Southern Levant. *Neo-Lithics* 2005 (2): 3–13.

Rollefson, G. O., and Gebel, H. G. K. 2004. Towards New Frameworks: Supra-Regional Concepts in Near Eastern Neolithization. *Neo-Lithics* 2004 (1): 21–2.

Rollefson, G. O.; Rowan, Y. M.; and Wasse, A. 2014. The Late Neolithic Colonization of the Eastern Badia of Jordan. *Levant* 46: 285–301.

Smith, B. D. 2001. Low-Level Food Production. *JAR* 9: 1–43.

Sterelny, K., and Watkins, T. F. 2015. Neolithization in Southwest Asia in a Context of Niche Construction Theory. *CAJ* 25: 673–91.

Verhoeven, M. 2002. Transformations of Society: The Changing Role of Ritual and Symbolism in the PPNB and the PN in the Levant, Syria and South-East Anatolia. *Paléorient* 28 (1): 5–13.

Waheeb, M., and Fino, N. 1997. 'Ayn el-Jammam: A Neolithic Site near Ras el-Naqb, Southern Jordan. In *The Prehistory of Jordan II: Perspectives from 1997*, ed. H. G. K. Gebel, Z. Kafafi, and G. O. Rollefson, 215–20. SENEPSE 4. Berlin: Ex Oriente.

Watkins, T. F. 1990. The Origins of House and Home? *WA* 21: 336–47.

2004. Architecture and "Theatres of Memory" in the Neolithic of Southwest Asia. In *Rethinking Materiality: The Engagement of Mind with the Material World*, ed. E. DeMarrais, C. Gosden, and C. Renfrew, 97–106. MIM. Cambridge: McDonald Institute for Archaeological Research.

2005. The Neolithic Revolution and the Emergence of Humanity: A Cognitive Approach to the First Comprehensive World-View. In *Archaeological Perspectives on the Transmission and Transformation of Culture in the Eastern Mediterranean*, ed. J. Clarke, 84–88. LSS 2. Oxford: Oxbow.

2008. Ordering Time and Space: Creating a Cultural World. In *Proceedings of the 5th International Congress on the Archaeology of the Ancient Near East, Madrid, 3–8 April 2006*, Vol. 3, ed. J. M. Córdoba, M. Molist, M. C. Pérez, I. Rubio, and S. Martínez, 647–59. Madrid: Centro Superior de Estudios sobre el Oriente Próximo y Egipto, Universidad Autónoma de Madrid.

2011. Opening the Door, Pointing the Way. *Paléorient* 37 (1): 29–38.

2015. The Cultural Dimension of Cognition. *QI* 405A: 91–7.

Wilson, P. J. 1988. *The Domestication of the Human Species*. New Haven, CT: Yale University Press.

Zeder, M. 2009. The Neolithic Macro-(R)evolution: Macroevolutionary Theory and the Study of Culture Change. *JAR* 17: 1–63.

2011. The Origins of Agriculture in the Near East. *CA* 52 (suppl. 4): S221–235.

2015. Comment on "Neolithization in Southwest Asia in a Context of Niche Construction Theory." *CAJ* 25: 698–700.

FIVE

FIRE AND SOCIETY IN THE EASTERN MEDITERRANEAN

A Diachronic View with a Microarchaeological Focus

RUTH SHAHACK-GROSS

The role of fire in human society has been central for millennia. This source of energy provides light, warmth, protection from predators, and the ability to cook, clear organic matter indoors and outdoors, and carry out certain technologies that depend on high temperature (i.e., pyrotechnologies). Some of these possibilities have been utilized by humans since the Lower Paleolithic (ca. 1.4–0.25 million years before present in the southern Levant). Apart from the beneficial attributes fire had, and still has, in human life, it may also incur unwanted damage. In the following chapter, I will outline the social, utilitarian, and devastating aspects of the long-lasting interaction between humans and fire. All of these subjects are well represented in the archaeological record of the eastern Mediterranean. Below, I provide a review that focuses on the microarchaeological and material aspects (*sensu* Weiner 2010) related to fire and society, along with examples from research conducted primarily in Israel.

FIRE AS A FORMATIVE FORCE IN HUMAN EVOLUTION: THE PALEOLITHIC PERIOD

Early use of fire by Paleolithic hominins is central to understanding human evolution, and much has been written on the subject (see reviews in Roebroeks and Villa 2011; Gowlett and Wrangham 2013; and Dunbar and Gowlett 2014). Current evidence seems to suggest that the earliest use of fire by hominins is found in South Africa at ca. 1.0 million years BP (Berna et al.

2012); however, a later date cannot be ruled out (Dunbar and Gowlett 2014). Accepting this, the use of fire by hominins seems to have spread out from Africa through the Levantine Corridor, thus placing the eastern Mediterranean in an important geographic location that allows us to trace the development of the use of fire during the Paleolithic period.

Evidence for early use of fire in the eastern Mediterranean has been reported from the Lower Paleolithic Acheulian site of Gesher Benot Ya'aqov, dated to ca. 780,000 years BP (Goren-Inbar et al. 2004; Alperson-Afil and Goren-Inbar 2010, with references). The site, located on the shore of the paleo-lake Hula, includes several occupation levels rich in lithic artifacts and faunal and floral remains. Na'ama Goren-Inbar and her colleagues (2004) identified the use of fire based on concentrations of flint micro-debitage and the presence of charred botanic remains. This was supported by evidence for heat-damaged flint artifacts (Alperson-Afil, Richter, and Goren-Inbar 2017). Another study identified the early use of fire through heat-damaged flint in Lower Paleolithic levels at Tabun Cave, dated to ca. 400,000 years ago (Shimelmitz et al. 2014).

Using a set of microarchaeological tools, Panagiotis Karkanas and his colleagues (2007) identified large amounts of wood ash associated with burnt bones along the stratigraphic sequence of the Lower Paleolithic Amudian site of Qesem Cave, while continued excavations at the same site revealed the earliest known superimposed hearth, dating to ca. 300,000 years before present (Shahack-Gross et al. 2014). The emerging picture is that by about 300,000–400,000 years ago (and possibly earlier), hominins in the eastern Mediterranean had full control over fire, a picture that accords with evidence from other parts of the world (Roebroeks and Villa 2011).

The ability to control fire, that is, set fire at will in any location, had immense implications for human evolution. It is argued that the ability to use fire as a source of warmth enabled hominins to extend their territories to cold latitudes, and the ability to cook allowed for more caloric energy to be freed from the gut and invested in the development of the brain (Wrangham et al. 1999). The latter, in turn, contributed to the development of cohesive social relationships, the enlargement of hominin group sizes, and the development of language (Dunbar and Gowlett 2014). Indeed, there is evidence at Qesem Cave for hearth-side activities, which imply increased social interactions among the hominins that inhabited it (Stiner, Gopher, and Barkai 2011). By the end of the Lower Paleolithic, the hearth served as a central place for complex socioeconomic activities.

Evidence for the use of fire in the Middle Paleolithic, starting some 250,000 years ago, is abundant in the eastern Mediterranean. It includes large amounts of wood ash, burnt bones, and single-layered and superimposed hearths, mostly found in cave sites, such as at Tabun, Kebara, and Hayonim (Albert et al. 1999; 2000). The social centrality of the hearth in this period is highlighted by the potential for the development of complex communication via language or otherwise that may have included conversation, gossip, storytelling, singing, and possibly long-distance signaling. R. I. M. Dunbar and J. A. J. Gowlett (2014) propose that the control over fire resulted in prolonged light, which caused a change in the circadian clock of hominins, as well as extended work days (as social activity centered nocturnally around the hearth); this allowed for the collection of more food and thus the enlargement of hominin group sizes. In turn, this resulted in increased social complexity. In addition to the intensive use of fire at cave sites, evidence for the differential use of space by hominins emerged at several sites, such as Amud Cave (Alperson-Afil and Hovers 2005). The use of fire for small-scale utilitarian purposes, such as the preparation of pigments using heat, was reported, for example, at Skhul Cave (Salomon et al. 2012). Fuel materials throughout the Middle Paleolithic record were dominated by wood with evidence for the use of grass, possibly for the initial lighting of fires (Albert et al. 1999; 2000; Madella et al. 2002). Cave sites thus appear to have been intensively inhabited and used as base camps for domestic activities.

Open-air sites dating to the Middle Paleolithic present a different picture. A few small single-layered hearths have been identified in open-air sites, for example, at Far'ah II (Gilead and Grigson 1984). At the Mousterian site of Nesher-Ramla, which formed within a karst depression, several small hearths have been identified and associated with burnt bones, as well as an area that seems to have functioned as an ash dump (Friesem, Zaidner, and Shahack-Gross 2014). This site is located in a geomorphic landform that is intermediate between sheltered and open-air sites, and this is probably one of the reasons why it includes vast evidence for fire (Zaidner et al. 2016). The current observations raise the question whether the scant evidence for hearths in fully open-air Middle Paleolithic sites, such as on flood plains, indicate that hominins did not use fire in the open, or that remains after fire use – notably ash and bones, which are soluble in slightly acidic conditions – were not preserved in the open. This subject is a matter for ongoing (e.g., Stahlschmidt et al. 2018) and future research.

The use of fire at Upper Paleolithic sites in the eastern Mediterranean has not been studied extensively. Steve Weiner and his colleagues (2015) recently reported a new method by which they were able to show that the knapping properties of flint found in Manot Cave were manipulated by heat. Rosa-Maria Albert and her colleagues (2003) reported that fuel in Natufian hearths is dominated by wood but includes large amounts of grass. Sporadic evidence for utilizing fire for the manipulation of geogenic raw materials for the production of lime plaster emerges in the terminal Upper Paleolithic (i.e., the Natufian period [Kingery, Vandiver, and Prickett 1988]).

FIRE AND TECHNOLOGICAL INNOVATION: THE NEOLITHIC PERIOD TO PRESENT

The transition from hunter-gatherer foraging to an agricultural way of life in the eastern Mediterranean was accompanied by a distinct change in human manipulation of geogenic materials. This change starts with the manipulation of soils and sediments in the preparation of and building with sun-dried mud bricks (e.g., at Gilgal and Netiv Hagdud [Bar-Yosef 1995]) and the intensive activities related to the production of lime plaster (e.g., at Yiftahel and Kfar Hahoresh [Goren and Goldberg 1991; Goren and Goring-Morris 2008]). The production of lime, ceramics, metals, and glass have been conducted using fire installations, such as open fires, fire pits, ovens, furnaces, and kilns. Certain activities necessitated specific tool kits, such as crucibles and wax models.[1] Below, I summarize recent developments related to the identification and characterization of lime plaster, as well as insights gained from the micro-archaeological study of materials associated with cooking ovens.

Lime plaster is produced through the calcination of limestone and/or chalk ($CaCO_3$ in the form of the mineral calcite) at high temperatures. Yuval Goren and Nigel Goring-Morris (2008) have shown that calcination can be achieved through prolonged pit firing. Lime (CaO) readily reacts with moisture and atmospheric carbon dioxide, and, upon consolidation, reforms as $CaCO_3$ (also in the form of the mineral calcite). Therefore, distinguishing between pulverized limestone/chalk and lime plaster when they are found in the form of floors or wall plaster at archaeological sites cannot rely on chemical or mineralogical composition as they are the same – $CaCO_3$ in the form of the mineral calcite. One possible way of differentiation is using petrographic microscopy; yet, identification is not always clear-cut despite certain petrographic guidelines (e.g., Karkanas 2007). It has been noted that lime plaster forms as extremely small crystals of the mineral calcite (Kingery, Vandiver, and Prickett 1988). Such crystals are not as well developed as larger geogenic calcite crystals in limestone and chalk, and are thus less ordered on the atomic level. Lior Regev and his colleagues (2010) were able to develop a method based on infrared spectroscopy that makes it possible to distinguish between pyrogenic and geogenic calcites. This method is frequently used for various case studies at archaeological sites in the eastern Mediterranean. For example, Nurith Goshen and her colleagues (2017) conducted a study of plaster materials in the Middle Bronze Age palace at Tel Kabri using both infrared spectroscopy and petrography. They were able to accurately distinguish between pyrogenically produced lime plaster and unheated geogenic plaster, the latter prepared from pulverization and pressing of chalk. Furthermore, they have shown that lime plaster was used only in special contexts in the monumental architecture of the palace at Kabri.

The use of pulverized and pressed chalk was also identified in Early Bronze Age Megiddo (Friesem and Shahack-Gross 2013), Middle and Late Bronze Age Lachish (Shimron 2004), and Iron Age Tell eṣ-Ṣafi/Gath (Shahack-Gross in press) and Tel Eton (my unpublished data). Using unheated plaster that has an external appearance similar to that of lime plaster raises interesting questions regarding the impact of chalk quarrying and lime production on the environment, as well as the investment required in terms of a work force and the degree of craft specialization required to conduct such construction projects in antiquity. More research into these topics will contribute much new knowledge.

Carrying out pyrotechnological activities involves the use of specific installations. Fire installations dating to the Neolithic and later periods are often less studied with the aid of microarchaeological techniques than prehistoric hearths. Installations such as ovens and kilns are rather visible archaeologically; yet, recent advancements in microarchaeology have shown that small, seemingly unimpressive features in Bronze and Iron Age contexts may, in fact, relate to metallurgical activities (e.g., Berna et al. 2007; Eliyahu-Behar et al. 2009; 2012; Yahalom-Mack et al. 2017). In more visible fire installations, such as ovens, research mostly focused on macroscopic attributes, such as shape and size, and only recently have there been studies conducted on these features using microarchaeological techniques. Shira Gur-Arieh and her colleagues (2014) have shown that it is possible to determine the placement of fuel – whether within or around an installation – and by that distinguish *tannur* (internal fueling) from *tabun* (external fueling). They have also shown that the highest temperature recorded on oven walls does not correspond to cooking temperature, which is always lower (Gur-Arieh et al. 2013).

Microarchaeological studies of ash remaining within or next to fire installations are useful for determining fuel sources, and thus socioeconomic choices and/or tradition. Furthermore, it may highlight the relationship between humans and their environment. As stated above, wood was the major fuel constituent in Paleolithic hearths. The rarity of microarchaeological studies at Neolithic sites creates a gap in our knowledge of fuel materials in this important period of transition from hunting and gathering to cultivation and domestication (Table 5.1). As early as the Chalcolithic, dung is identified as another fuel material (Katz et al. 2007), which accords well with other lines of evidence for the use of secondary herd products in this period. Research of fuel constituents at several Bronze and Iron Age sites in central and northern Israel revealed that both wood and dung have been used for fuel in domestic hearths and ovens (Gur-Arieh et al. 2014). In the arid zones, dung is a fuel constituent in Iron Age IIA sites in the Negev highlands (Shahack-Gross and Finkelstein 2008) while wood was used in the

TABLE 5.1. *Types of fuels used in the operation of hearths (Paleolithic to historic periods) and ovens (historic periods). References focus on results from microarchaeological studies, that is, studies of ash and phytoliths.*

Period	Type of Fuel in Hearths and Ovens	References	Sites
Lower Paleolithic	Wood (and bones?)	Karkanas et al. 2007	Qesem Cave
		Shahack-Gross et al. 2014	Qesem Cave
Middle Paleolithic	Wood with small amounts of grass (the latter as tinder?)	Albert et al. 1999	Tabun Cave
		Albert et al. 2000	Kebara Cave
		Madella et al. 2002	Amud Cave
Upper Paleolithic	Wood and large amounts of grass	Albert et al. 2003	Hayonim Cave, Natufian
Neolithic	?	—	—
Chalcolithic	Wood and dung	Katz et al. 2007	Nahal Grar
Bronze Age	Wood and dung	Gur-Arieh et al. 2014	Megiddo
	Wood	Dunseth et al. 2018	'Ein Ziq
Iron Age		Gur-Arieh et al. 2014	Megiddo, Tell eṣ-Ṣafi/Gath, Qubur el-Walaydah
	Wood and dung	Shahack-Gross and Finkelstein 2008	Atar Haroa
Persian	?	—	—
Hellenistic	?	—	—
Roman	?	—	—
Byzantine	?	—	—
Islamic	?	—	—

large (central) Intermediate Bronze Age sites in the same region (Dunseth, Finkelstein, and Shahack-Gross 2018). The study of fuel constituents from fire installations dating to periods later than the Iron Age in the eastern Mediterranean has not yet been published (to my knowledge). The manipulation of raw materials using fire is still far from being thoroughly explored from the point of view of fire installation technology and fueling.

FIRE AS A DESTRUCTIVE FORCE: THE BRONZE AND IRON AGES

The sections above highlighted the formative and utilitarian aspects in the relationship between humans and fire. Yet, fire may also be devastating when it is either set purposefully or goes out of human control, such as in conflagration events that seem to be part of the history of almost any ancient city in the Near East. Field identification of destruction events in Bronze and Iron Age sites in Israel relies on criteria such as presence of crashed vessels (rather than pottery sherds) on floors covered by ash, sometimes including charred materials, and sometimes overlain by accumulation of stone and/or mud-brick collapse to various thicknesses. Such destruction layers are often interpreted to be associated with violent human activities that include arson (i.e., conquests); however, the possibility of accidental fire – especially when only part(s) of settlements appear burnt – is also considered. Understanding the destruction event itself may be achieved via a study of the imprint left by high temperature on various materials, using microarchaeological techniques. Below, I summarize the microarchaeological approach in the study of the thermal behavior of mud bricks as a key material in the reconstruction of building technologies, areas of ignition, and fire-path spread during conflagration events.

The construction of permanent settlements since the Neolithic seems to have been based on sun-dried mud bricks with or without stone (the latter could have been wall foundations, whole walls, pavements, etc.). Sun-dried mud bricks are prepared by mixing soil/sediment with dry vegetal matter, often straw or chaff. The vegetal temper both decreases the specific density of the bricks and acts as a binder to the sediment, which reinforces the brick's tensile strength. These properties make sun-dried mud bricks good construction materials (Binici, Aksogan, and Shah 2005). Yet, this mechanical advantage may also incur a disadvantage when such bricks are exposed to fire. A recent experimental study found that when heated, the vegetal component in chaff-tempered mud bricks ignites and causes the brick to burn at temperatures that are higher than their environment as much as 100°C (Forget et al. 2015). Furthermore, the more chaff a mud brick includes, the higher and longer it will burn (Forget et al. 2015). Therefore, the ignition of sun-dried mud brick structures may be devastating. For example, Francesco Berna and his colleagues (2007) reconstructed the heating of mud bricks to as much as 1,000°C in an Iron Age IIA destruction event at Tel Dor, while Regev and his team (2015) identified temperatures in the range of over 800°C at the possible area of ignition in a late Iron Age IIA sector of Megiddo. It is interesting to note that despite the fact that chaff-tempered mud-brick structures are essentially "fire traps," this technology persisted up to the Hellenistic/Roman period, only then did pre-fired mud bricks start to be commonly utilized.

Dvory Namdar and her colleagues (2011) raised the possibility of construction with pre-fired mud bricks as early as the Iron Age IIA (ninth century

BCE) at Tell eṣ-Ṣafi/Gath. From the energetic point of view, the thermal properties of chaff-tempered mud bricks make them easier to burn in kilns as less external fuel is needed. In addition, pre-fired mud bricks are even lighter in weight than sun-dried bricks and have higher compressive strengths (i.e., suitable for building multi-storied houses), though they have lower tensile strength (i.e., less resistant to earthquakes). While the advantages and disadvantages of building with sun-dried versus pre-fired mud bricks are clear, archaeological research has yet to establish what technology was being used during different periods in the past.

The key to deciphering what technology was used in Bronze and Iron Age mud-brick construction may lie in large-scale spatial analysis of specific destruction events. Theoretically, based on forensic fire investigation guidelines (e.g., Harrison 2013), ignition within a closed space, such as a mud-brick house, will result in the accumulation of heat at the higher parts of the internal surface of walls. At the same time, it is expected that lower courses and the outer faces of walls will show minimal exposure to heat. Mud bricks in wall segments may thus provide important information about fire intensity in space. The first to explore this were Mathilde Forget and her colleagues (2015), who carried out a large-scale study of mud bricks associated with the destruction of Canaanite Megiddo at the end of the Iron Age I (end of the eleventh century BCE). They showed that a certain wall segment was exposed to heat from one cardinal direction, and its central part was not exposed to temperatures above 500°C. This pattern suggests that the construction at Late Iron Age I Megiddo was done using sun-dried mud bricks, which ignited as whole wall units during the destruction event. More recently, an archaeomagnetic study of several wall segments from this destruction event confirmed that construction utilized sun-dried mud bricks (Shahack-Gross et al. in press). Additionally, Igor Kreimerman and I (in press) showed experimentally the heat patterns that form across mud-brick walls and mud-plastered roofs, while Kreimerman (pers. comm., 2018) identified such patterns in Bronze Age Tel Lachish. Further studies of this sort should be conducted at different destruction layers in various sites in the eastern Mediterranean before we can create a full picture of building traditions and technologies, thus shedding new, interesting, and important light on the work of fire during destruction events.

CONCLUSION

Future studies should seek to document contextual information on hearths and ovens, *vis-à-vis* microarchaeological and other types of studies on fuel sources, organization, and the use of space. At the same time, archaeologists should continue to study the role of fire in building technology and destruction events. All will shed more light on the place of fire within the lifeways of the past.

NOTE

1 For detailed information on the production of lime, ceramics, metals, and glass, see Goffer 2007.

REFERENCES

Albert, R. M.; Bar-Yosef, O.; Meignen, L.; and Weiner, S. 2003. Quantitative Phytolith Study of Hearths from the Natufian and Middle Palaeolithic Levels of Hayonim Cave (Galilee, Israel). *JAS* 30: 461–80.

Albert, R. M.; Lavi, O.; Estroff, L.; Weiner, S.; Tsatskin, A.; Ronen, A.; and Lev-Yadun, S. 1999. Mode of Occupation of Tabun Cave, Mt Carmel, Israel during the Mousterian Period: A Study of the Sediments and Phytoliths. *JAS* 26: 1249–60.

Albert, R. M.; Weiner, S.; Bar-Yosef, O.; and Meignen, L. 2000. Phytoliths in the Middle Palaeolithic Deposits of Kebara Cave, Mt Carmel, Israel: Study of the Plant Materials Used for Fuel and Other Purposes. *JAS* 27: 931–47.

Alperson-Afil, N., and Goren-Inbar, N. 2010. *The Acheulian Site of Gesher Benot Ya'aqov*, Vol. 2: *Ancient Flames and Controlled Use of Fire*. Vertebrate Paleobiology and Paleoanthropology. Dordrecht: Springer.

Alperson-Afil, N., and Hovers, E. 2005. Differential Use of Space in the Neandertal Site of Amud Cave, Israel. *Eurasian Prehistory* 3 (1): 3–22.

Alperson-Afil, N.; Richter, D.; and Goren-Inbar, N. 2017. Evaluating the Intensity of Fire at the Acheulian Site of Gesher Benot Ya'aqov – Spatial and Thermoluminescence Analyses. *PLOS ONE* 12 (11): e0188091. https://doi.org/10.1371/journal.pone.0188091 (accessed August 20, 2018).

Bar-Yosef, O. 1995. Earliest Food Producers – Pre-Pottery Neolithic (8000–5500). In *The Archaeology of Society in the Holy Land*, ed. T. E. Levy, 190–204. NAAA. London: Leicester University Press.

Berna, F.; Behar, A.; Shahack-Gross, R.; Berg, J.; Boaretto, E.; Gilboa, A.; Sharon, I.; Shalev, S.; Shilstein, S.; Yahalom-Mack, N.; Zorn, J. R.; and Weiner, S. 2007. Sediments Exposed to High Temperatures: Reconstructing Pyrotechnological Processes in Late Bronze and Iron Age Strata at Tel Dor (Israel). *JAS* 34: 358–73.

Berna, F.; Goldberg, P.; Horwitz, L. K.; Brink, J.; Holt, S.; Bamford, M.; and Chazan, M. 2012. Microstratigraphic Evidence of *In Situ* Fire in the Acheulean Strata of Wonderwerk Cave, Northern Cape Province, South Africa. *PNAS* 109 (20): E1215–20.

Binici, H.; Aksogan, O.; and Shah, T. 2005. Investigation of Fibre Reinforced Mud Brick as a Building Material. *Construction and Building Materials* 19: 313–18.

Dunbar, R. I. M., and Gowlett, J. A. J. 2014. Fireside Chat: The Impact of Fire on Hominin Socioecology. In *Lucy to Language: The Benchmark Papers*, ed. R. I. M. Dunbar, C. Gamble, and J. A. J. Gowlett, 277–96. Oxford: Oxford University Press.

Dunseth, Z. C.; Finkelstein, I.; and Shahack-Gross, R. 2018. Intermediate Bronze Age Subsistence Practices in the Negev Highlands, Israel: Macro- and Microarchaeological Results from the Sites of Ein Ziq and Nahal Boqer 66. *JAS: Reports* 19: 712–26.

Eliyahu-Behar, A.; Regev, L.; Shilstein, S.; Weiner, S.; Shalev, Y.; Sharon, I.; and Berg, J. 2009. Identifying a Roman Casting Pit at Tel Dor, Israel: Integrating Field and Laboratory Research. *JFA* 34: 135–51.

Eliyahu-Behar, A.; Yahalom-Mack, N.; Shilstein, S.; Zukerman, A.; Shafer-Elliott, C.; Maeir, A. M.; Boaretto, E.; Finkelstein, I.; and Weiner, S. 2012. Iron and Bronze Production in Iron Age IIA Philistia: New Evidence from Tell es-Safi/Gath. *JAS* 39: 255–67.

Forget, M. C. L.; Regev, L.; Friesem, D. E.; and Shahack-Gross, R. 2015. Physical and Mineralogical Properties of Experimentally Heated Chaff-Tempered Mud Bricks: Implications for Reconstruction of Environmental Factors Influencing the Appearance of Mud Bricks in Archaeological Conflagration Events. *JAS: Reports* 2: 80–93.

Friesem, D., and Shahack-Gross, R. 2013. Area J, Part 5: Analyses of Sediments from the Level J-4 Temple Floor. In *Megiddo V: The 2004–2008 Seasons*, Vol. 1, ed. I. Finkelstein, D. Ussishkin, and E. H. Cline, 143–7. MSSMNIA 31. Winona Lake, IN: Eisenbrauns.

Friesem, D. E.; Zaidner, Y.; and Shahack-Gross, R. 2014. Formation Processes and Combustion Features at the Lower Layers of the Middle Palaeolithic Open-Air Site of Nesher Ramla, Israel. *QI* 331: 128–38.

Gilead, I., and Grigson, C. 1984. Far'ah II: A Middle Paleolithic Open-Air Site in the Northern Negev, Israel. *PPS* 50: 71–97.

Goffer, Z. 2007. *Archaeological Chemistry*. 2nd ed. Chemical Analysis 170. Hoboken, NJ: Wiley-Interscience.

Goren, Y., and Goldberg, P. 1991. Petrographic Thin Sections and the Development of Neolithic Plaster Production in Northern Israel. *JFA* 18: 131–40.

Goren, Y., and Goring-Morris, A. N. 2008. Early Pyrotechnology in the Near East: Experimental Lime-Plaster Production at the Pre-Pottery Neolithic B Site of Kfar HaHoresh, Israel. *Geoarchaeology* 23: 779–98.

Goren-Inbar, N.; Alperson, N.; Kislev, M. E.; Simchoni, O.; Melamed, Y.; Ben-Nun, A.; and Werker, E. 2004. Evidence of Hominin Control of Fire at Gesher Benot Ya'aqov, Israel. *Science* 304 (5671): 725–7.

Goshen, N.; Yasur-Landau, A.; Cline, E. H.; and Shahack-Gross, R. 2017. Palatial Architecture under the Microscope: Production, Maintenance, and Spatiotemporal Changes Gleaned from Plastered Surfaces at a Canaanite Palace Complex, Tel Kabri, Israel. *JAS: Reports* 11: 189–99.

Gowlett, J. A. J., and Wrangham, R. W. 2013. Earliest Fire in Africa: Towards Convergence of Archaeological Evidence and the Cooking Hypothesis. *Azania* 48: 5–30.

Gur-Arieh, S.; Mintz, E.; Boaretto, E.; and Shahack-Gross, R. 2013. An Ethnoarchaeological Study of Cooking Installations in Rural Uzbekistan: Development of a New Method for Identification of Fuel Sources. *JAS* 40: 4331–47.

Gur-Arieh, S.; Shahack-Gross, R.; Maeir, A. M.; Lehmann, G.; Hitchcock, L. A.; and Boaretto, E. 2014. The Taphonomy and Preservation of Wood and Dung Ashes Found in Archaeological Cooking Installations: Case Studies from Iron Age Israel. *JAS* 46: 50–67.

Harrison, K. 2013. The Application of Forensic Fire Investigation Techniques in the Archaeological Record. *JAS* 40: 955–9.

Karkanas, P. 2007. Identification of Lime Plaster in Prehistory Using Petrographic Methods: A Review and Reconsideration of the Data on the Basis of Experimental and Case Studies. *Geoarchaeology* 22: 775–96.

Karkanas, P.; Shahack-Gross, R.; Ayalon, A.; Bar-Matthews, M.; Barkai, R.; Frumkin, A.; Gopher, A.; and Stiner, M. C. 2007. Evidence for Habitual Use of Fire at the End of the Lower Paleolithic: Site-Formation Processes at Qesem Cave, Israel. *JHE* 53: 197–212.

Katz, O.; Gilead, I.; Bar (Kutiel), P.; and Shahack-Gross, R. 2007. Chalcolithic Agricultural Life at Grar, Northern Negev, Israel: Dry Farmed Cereals and Dung-Fueled Hearths. *Paléorient* 33 (2): 101–16.

Kingery, W. D.; Vandiver, P. B.; and Prickett, M. 1988. The Beginnings of Pyrotechnology, Part 2: Production and Use of Lime and Gypsum Plaster in the Pre-Pottery Neolithic Near East. *JFA* 15: 219–44.

Kreimerman, I., and Shahack-Gross, R. In press. Understanding Conflagration of One-Story Mud-Brick Structures: An Experimental Approach. *AAS*.

Madella, M.; Jones, M. K.; Goldberg, P.; Goren, Y.; and Hovers, E. 2002. The Exploitation of Plant Resources by Neanderthals in Amud Cave (Israel): The Evidence from Phytolith Studies. *JAS* 29: 703–19.

Namdar, D.; Zukerman, A.; Maeir, A. M.; Katz, J. C.; Cabanes, D.; Trueman, C.; Shahack-Gross, R.; and Weiner, S. 2011. The 9th Century BCE Destruction Layer at Tell es-Safi/Gath, Israel: Integrating Macro- and Microarchaeology. *JAS* 38: 3471–82.

Regev, L.; Cabanes, D.; Homsher, R.; Kleiman, A.; Weiner, S.; Finkelstein, I.; and Shahack-Gross, R. 2015. Geoarchaeological Investigation in a Domestic Iron Age Quarter, Tel Megiddo, Israel. *BASOR* 374: 135–57.

Regev, L.; Poduska, K. M.; Addadi, L.; Weiner, S.; and Boaretto, E. 2010. Distinguishing between Calcites Formed by Different Mechanisms Using Infrared Spectrometry: Archaeological Applications. *JAS* 37: 3022–9.

Roebroeks, W., and Villa, P. 2011. On the Earliest Evidence for Habitual Use of Fire in Europe. *PNAS* 108: 5209–14.

Salomon, H.; Vignaud, C.; Coquinot, Y.; Beck, L.; Stringer, C.; Strivay, D.; and D'Errico, F. 2012. Selection and Heating of Colouring Materials in the Mousterian Level of es-Skhul (c. 100 000 Years BP, Mt. Carmel, Israel). *Archaeometry* 54: 698–722.

Shahack-Gross, R. In press. Micromorphological Insights into Construction Materials and Their Manufacture Technology at Tell es-Safi/Gath. In *Tell it in Gath: Studies in the History and Archaeology of Israel: Essays in Honor of A. M. Maeir on the Occasion of His Sixtieth Birthday*, ed. I. Shai, J. Chadwick, L. Hitchcock, A. Dagan, and J. Uziel. Ägypten und Altes Testament. Münster: Ugarit-Verlag.

Shahack-Gross, R.; Berna, F.; Karkanas, P.; Lemorini, C.; Gopher, A.; and Barkai, R. 2014. Evidence for the Repeated Use of a Central Hearth at Middle Pleistocene (300 ky ago) Qesem Cave, Israel. *JAS* 44: 12–21.

Shahack-Gross, R., and Finkelstein, I. 2008. Subsistence Practices in an Arid Environment: A Geoarchaeological Investigation in an Iron Age Site, the Negev Highlands, Israel. *JAS* 35: 965–82.

Shahack-Gross, R.; Shaar, R.; Hassul, E.; Ebert, Y.; Forget, M.; Nowaczyk, N.; Marco, S.; Finkelstein, I.; and Agnon, A. In press. Fire and Collapse: Untangling the Formation of Destruction Layers Using Archaeomagnetism. *Geoarchaeology*.

Shimelmitz, R.; Kuhn, S. L.; Jelinek, A. J.; Ronen, A.; Clark, A. E.; and Weinstein-Evron, M. 2014. "Fire at Will": The Emergence of Habitual Fire Use 350,000 Years Ago. *JHE* 77: 196–203.

Shimron, A. E. 2004. Selected Plaster and Glassy Samples. In *The Renewed Archaeological Excavations at Lachish (1973–1994)*, Vol. 5, ed. D. Ussishkin, 2620–55. MSSMNIA 22. Tel Aviv: Emery and Claire Yass Publications in Archaeology.

Stahlschmidt, M. C.; Nir, N.; Greenbaum, N.; Zilberman, T.; Barzilai, O.; Ekshtain, R.; Malinsky-Buller, A.; Hovers, E.; and Shahack-Gross, R. 2018. Geoarchaeological Investigation of Site Formation and Depositional Environments at the Middle Palaeolithic Open-Air Site of 'Ein Qashish, Israel. *Journal of Paleolithic Archaeology* 1: 32–53.

Stiner, M. C.; Gopher, A.; and Barkai, R. 2011. Hearth-Side Socioeconomics, Hunting and Paleoecology during the Late Lower Paleolithic at Qesem Cave, Israel. *JHE* 60: 213–33.

Weiner, S. 2010. *Microarchaeology: Beyond the Visible Archaeological Record.* New York: Cambridge University Press.

Weiner, S.; Brumfeld, V.; Marder, O.; and Barzilai, O. 2015. Heating of Flint Debitage from Upper Palaeolithic Contexts at Manot Cave, Israel: Changes in Atomic Organization Due to Heating Using Infrared Spectroscopy. *JAS* 54: 45–53.

Wrangham, R. W.; Jones, J. H.; Laden, G.; Pilbeam, D.; and Conklin-Brittain, N. 1999. The Raw and the Stolen: Cooking and the Ecology of Human Origins. *CA* 40 (5): 567–94.

Yahalom-Mack, N.; Eliyahu-Behar, A.; Martin, M. A. S.; Kleiman, A.; Shahack-Gross, R.; Homsher, R. S.; Gadot, Y.; and Finkelstein, I. 2017. Metalworking at Megiddo during the Late Bronze and Iron Ages. *JNES* 76: 53–74.

Zaidner, Y.; Frumkin, A.; Friesem, D.; Tsatskin, A.; and Shahack-Gross, R. 2016. Landscapes, Depositional Environments and Human Occupation at Middle Paleolithic Open-Air Sites in the Southern Levant, with New Insights from Nesher Ramla, Israel. *QSR* 138: 76–86.

SIX

IT'S A SMALL WORLD
Work, Family Life, and Community in the Late Neolithic

EDWARD B. BANNING

As compared to the Pre-Pottery Neolithic (PPN) B, there has been little work on the social characteristics of Late Neolithic communities in the southern Levant. This is surprising given the social-evolutionary theoretical underpinnings of some of this research; PPNB societies are often interpreted as pre-urban precursors of later urban societies; yet, there is a disjunction between the PPNB and more complex political forms of the Late Chalcolithic or Early Bronze Age II. This inevitably leads some to treat the end of PPNB as a failure. A history of research in which scholars long considered the Levantine Pottery Neolithic a "dark age" has contributed to a lack of attention, but recent research is beginning to reveal it as a period of rapid social, technological, and economic change with sites known to occur in most geographical regions of the southern Levant (Fig. 6.1).

Now that we are past treating the Late Neolithic of the southern Levant as a *hiatus* of regional abandonment (Kenyon 1957: 79; Vaux 1966: 510–13; Perrot 1968), scholars have increasingly turned their attention to the social and economic dynamics of Late Neolithic cultures and their variants. Growing amounts and types of evidence have improved our capacity for hypotheses about the nature of and changes in family structure, community organization, and intercommunity networks.

While there is no space here for details of the Late Neolithic's chronotypology, the broad consensus is to characterize the two millennia that followed the PPNB by units variously considered cultures or periods (Table 6.1). The

WORK, FAMILY LIFE, AND COMMUNITY IN THE LATE NEOLITHIC 99

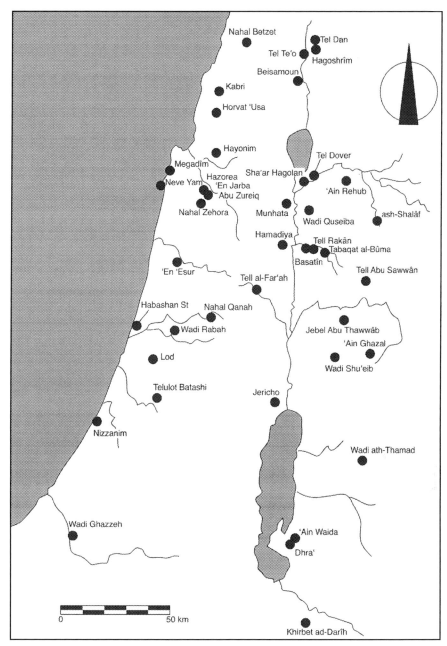

6.1. A map of the southern Levant indicating Late Neolithic sites. (Map by E. B. Banning.)

PPNC was clearly transitional from the Late PPNB and in many respects fits better with its successors than its predecessors. The Yarmoukian followed with a broad distribution and similarities to Byblos' *Néolithique Ancien*. Jericho IX (or Lodian) may have coexisted with the Yarmoukian for some time, although it is more poorly dated and its spatial distribution is more restricted. It may also

TABLE 6.1. *Very preliminary sketch of the chronology for the main "periods" in the seventh and sixth millennia BCE. All dates are in calibrated radiocarbon years, and the ranges indicate the current uncertainty about the period boundaries, as well as potential overlaps and transitions (cf. Banning 2007).*

Culture/Period	Began	Ended	Key Sites
Pre-Ghassulian	5100–4900 cal. BCE	4600–4400 cal. BCE	Tel Tsaf, Tel 'Ali
Wadi Rabah	5800–5600 cal. BCE	5100–4900 cal. BCE	Munhata, Nahal Zehora, 'En Jarba
Jericho IX	6000–5500 cal. BCE	5700–5400 cal. BCE	Jericho, Lod
Yarmoukian	6500–6400 cal. BCE	5900–5800 cal. BCE	Sha'ar Hagolan, Beisamoun
PPNC	7000–6800 cal. BCE	6500–6400 cal. BCE	'Ain Ghazal
Late PPNB	7300–7100 cal. BCE	7000–6800 cal. BCE	'Ain Ghazal, Beisamoun

overlap with the Wadi Rabah culture, which tends to have a northerly distribution and is sometimes classified as Early Chalcolithic. The Qatifian (5200–4750 cal. BCE) and Besorian (ca. 4750–4400 cal. BCE) are identified only in the south, the latter contemporary with entities conventionally considered Chalcolithic and probably best grouped with them. Meanwhile, the Badia of eastern Jordan and southeastern Syria seems to have had its own Late Neolithic culture – as yet unnamed – while assemblages from some sites do not fit neatly into any of these categories.

FAMILY STRUCTURE AND HOUSEHOLDS

For Aristotle (*Pol.* 1.3.12; cf. Engels 1884), it was axiomatic that the natural social and economic unit was a household led by a man as the primary decision maker, including a subservient wife, several children, and slaves, while its main rationale was the acquisition of property. Some anthropological characterizations of households, while broader in some respects, also focus on their economic role and emphasize senior men and the basic functions of production, redistribution, reproduction, and transmission of property, roles, and titles (e.g., Wilk and Rathje 1982).

As for the PPNB (e.g., Byrd 2000), most scholars investigating social aspects of the Late Neolithic have, like Aristotle, assumed that a nuclear family led by a man was the building block of social relationships in this period. While the generally small size of probable houses and the way these structures are distributed on sites seem consistent with this interpretation, it is not without problems.

Where architecture is our main source of evidence for households, it is necessary to make some assumptions about how architecture "maps on" to social arrangements (Banning 2010). It is not a trivial matter to decide the likely spatial boundaries of a household, even if households occupied spatially contiguous spaces, let alone when they did not (Wilk and Rathje 1982: 620). To be confident that we are identifying household spaces correctly, we must do more than assume that all the space in a building, let alone all the space we happen to have excavated in a portion of a site, corresponds with a single household (Banning and Chazan 2006: 5–7). In addition, the gendered aspect of families and households has not received adequate attention in studies that focus on this period (Hendon 2006; cf. Meyers 2003). The archaeological assumption of a normative household as consisting of a heterosexual man and woman with several children is now under attack (e.g., Dowson 2006: 93–9).

Rather than focus exclusively on architecture, we must integrate architectural evidence with the features, artifacts, micromorphology, and microremains in and around the structures that might provide clues to how spaces were used and who may have used them, or at least how differentiated people's roles may have been and at what scale differentiation occurred. In addition, we should consider skeletal, mortuary, and other sources of evidence for the roles of age and gender in social status and division of labor.

Yosef Garfinkel and David Ben-Shlomo (Garfinkel and Ben-Shlomo 2002; Garfinkel 2006) have suggested that the Yarmoukian community at Sha'ar Hagolan had extended-family households, mainly on architectural evidence for redundant groupings of rooms around common courtyards (Fig. 6.2). The basic unit in the scenario they describe is a presumed nuclear family that occupied a two-room architectural unit, with one living room and one paved room for storage. The arrangement of these two-room units around courtyards in which some common activities took place leads them to infer the bottom two tiers of a decision-making hierarchy. The implication is that one two-room unit belonged to a more senior branch of an extended family, whose head made decisions for, or at least represented, the entire courtyard group in the community.

It is not clear whether individual structures in a later site, such as Tabaqat al-Bûma (Fig. 6.3), constitute single-room houses associated with small households, or whether groupings of these small buildings were like rooms of a larger house, tied together by unroofed space where many domestic tasks took place. In Sha'ar Hagolan, the neatly circumscribed architectural groupings and repetitive nature of the constituent units make a stronger case that the social boundaries have been identified correctly. However, we should be mindful of several scenarios that could account for larger residential units, and the snapshots of buildings that archaeologists recover are the culmination of complex histories of architectural and household change (Banning 1996a; Banning and Byrd 1987). It is noteworthy that the resulting collective social groups would not likely have operated collectively in all of their activities, which also brings into question whether they operated collectively in all aspects of

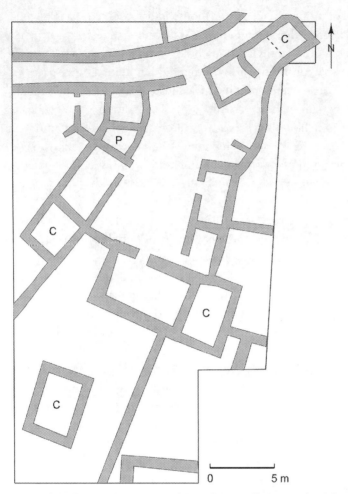

6.2. A plan of Yarmoukian courtyard Complex H at Sha'ar Hagolan (after Garfinkel 2006). "C" marks cobbled spaces, and "P" paved spaces that were probably storage rooms. (Drawing by E. B. Banning.)

production, redistribution, reproduction, and transmission of property, roles, and titles. The presence of such things as grinding stones in the courtyards indeed suggests that some economic activities were shared; yet, the repetition of hearths and especially storage rooms in the individual units suggest that redistribution and transmission of property were *not* exclusively communal.

Property

As Kent Flannery (1972) points out, control over access to storage is a clue to whether nuclear families or some larger social unit controlled property. In the Late Neolithic, probable storage facilities were not centralized but dispersed among domestic units, often in very standardized ways. As we have seen at

WORK, FAMILY LIFE, AND COMMUNITY IN THE LATE NEOLITHIC

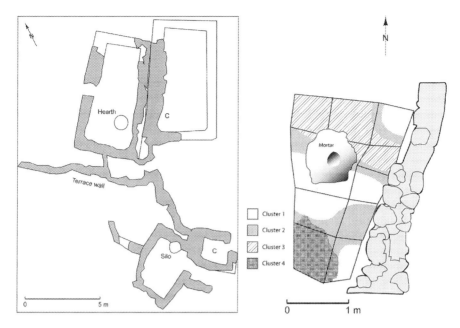

6.3. (a) A map of the Wadi Rabah site of Tabaqat al-Bûma during Phase LN2; and (b) a map of activity areas (Clusters 1–4) identified in the G34 structure (Phase LN3) through micro-refuse (after Ullah, Duffy, and Banning 2015). (Map by E. B. Banning.)

Shaʻar Hagolan, pairs of rooms that we may plausibly associate with nuclear families each have a paved room that was probably for storage and had significant capacity (see Fig. 6.2). This is different from the compounds that Flannery discusses, in which the huts associated with courtyards were not occupied by nuclear families, but rather by individual yet related adults and their children, and storage facilities were at least partly shared by the whole compound. Although it remains likely that occupants of the two-room units identified at Shaʻar Hagolan cooperated with the other members of their courtyard group in some respects – perhaps in agricultural and construction tasks, for example, they appear to have divided up foodstuffs and property – they may have jointly accumulated and stored it in their private spaces.

This kind of arrangement may be consistent with the "house societies" (*sociétés à maison*) that Claude Lévi-Strauss (1982) proposed. In this type of society, "houses" are social groups that may not live in the same building (but often do) and use the house building as a metaphor for their group and a setting for ritual and competitive display. Houses have flexible, generally non-unilineal descent systems and emphasize the transmission of titles, names, iconic symbols, and other heritable items between generations. Property in house societies can vary in its ownership and control, with the house itself, or more often its chief, perhaps controlling the largest share of property, but individual house members also potentially having their own shares. In a preindustrial society like those of the Late Neolithic, a major element of property would be storable foodstuffs; at present, we have no way of knowing whether the courtyard groups owned land.

In Wadi Rabah-related sites, it is not at all obvious that anything like the Sha'ar Hagolan pattern persisted. For example, quite small stone-lined silos and one clay-lined silo are associated with several residential buildings at Tabaqat al-Bûma (see Fig. 6.3), while at Wadi Rabah (Kaplan 1958) and some other sites, paved platforms may be the bases of storage facilities. Some of these likely storage features are outdoors, but we lack clearly defined courtyards to suggest whether their use was communal or private.

Throughout the Late Neolithic, the likely storage facilities appear to be associated with individual, fairly small buildings, as would be consistent with control by a nuclear-family household although not conclusively demonstrating one. We have no examples of unusually large or centrally located storage that might point to communal ownership and redistribution.

However, the presence of at least some facilities and heavy ground-stone artifacts in the shared courtyards at Sha'ar Hagolan suggest that some kinds of property were shared among the people associated with each courtyard (Garfinkel and Ben-Shlomo 2002). It also seems likely that courtyards would have sheltered livestock at night; whether ownership of these herds was communal or private and herded and penned cooperatively remains unknown.

Gender and Labor

Past hypotheses about Neolithic social organization have usually presented one of three views about gender relations. One is that Neolithic societies were idyllic communities that valued feminine nurturing and worshiped a "Mother Goddess." Another is that the Neolithic was a loss of innocence when women began to take on the burden of agricultural and domestic drudgery, while a third is that gender roles have deep evolutionary roots in the Pleistocene, with men responsible for hunting and group protection and women for gathering and child-rearing (cf. Murdock and Provost 1973). Most likely, none of these scenarios is very realistic as the role of gender in society, subsistence, and ideology is very context-specific, while most studies have suffered from the influences that social hierarchies of the recent past impose on our ethnographic and archaeological practice and the subjects of those studies (Leacock 1978; Peterson 2006; 2010).

The predominant interpretation of human figurines in the Neolithic has been through the lens of fertility and the Mother Goddess (Gimbutas 1974). More recent scholarship has suggested that the interpretations of these figurines

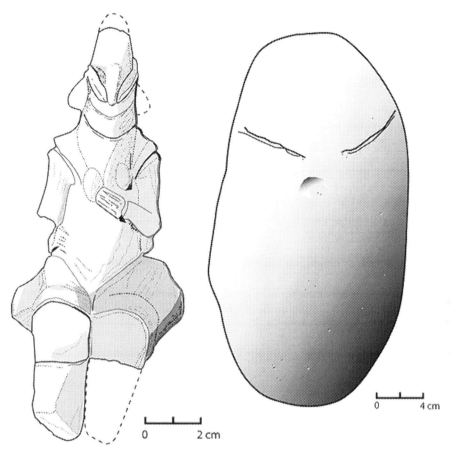

6.4. Examples of a Yarmoukian clay figurine (on the left) and a "pebble" figurine (on the right) from Sha'ar Hagolan (after Garfinkel, Korn, and Miller 2002: fig. 13.11, 13.27). (Drawing by K. Abu Jayyab and E. B. Banning.)

as evidence for matriarchy or idyllic gender relations do themselves constitute a type of gender stereotyping rooted in our own culture's preconceptions about female nurturing (Conkey and Tringham 1995; Meskell 1995; Hamilton et al. 1996; Tringham and Conkey 1998; Lesure 2002). So what, if anything, can these figurines tell us about women or gender in the Late Neolithic?

Few archaeological projects have collected data explicitly with the purpose of interpreting gendered roles or activities in Late Neolithic contexts (but see Naveh and Gopher 2012). Yarmoukian clay figurines with broad hips, understated appendages, pointed heads, and "cowry" eyes (Fig. 6.4) bear some similarity to Samarran and Ubaid figurines in Mesopotamia and are typically interpreted in the Mother Goddess framework. However, the gendered aspect of these figurines is actually somewhat ambiguous and, perhaps, intentionally so. Avi Gopher and Estelle Orrelle (1996), for example, suggest that many of the clay figurines combine phallic imagery with vulva-like eyes, presenting androgynous, trickster, or sexually contradictory signals that could have figured in *rites de passage* and changes in the roles of reproduction and children as society became more fully agricultural. Symbolic aspects of pottery may have been similarly ambiguous, becoming more so as the frequency of figurines declined over the sixth millennium (Orrelle and Gopher 2000; Gibbs 2013). As clay figurines are scattered in a wide array of domestic and refuse contexts (Miller 2002), generally broken, they may have been involved in household-scale rituals, but their meaning is debatable. The simple pebble figurines are more ambiguous still in their sexual characteristics but could still have involved similar sorts of symbolism.

Another potential source of evidence for gender relations, especially gendered aspects of labor, is the activity area (Flannery 1972). It is difficult to associate activity areas with gender roles without assuming exactly the stereotypes we should challenge, but some kinds of spatial analysis can at least help identify the degree of spatial differentiation of activities that were potentially structured by gender and age. Sources of evidence for the use of space in various activities include the distribution of features, macroscopic tools, and microscopic and chemical residues.

Seiji Kadowaki's (2007) analysis of built environment, lithics, and site-formation processes at the Wadi Rabah farmstead site of Tabaqat al-Bûma in Wadi Ziqlab from ca. 5700 to 5100 cal. BCE depended mainly on the site-formation processes that created the archaeological deposits and the macro-artifacts, especially lithics, that occurred within them. This allowed him to identify probable locations of primary and secondary refuse, and locations where flint tool production and maintenance took place. He suggests that the small site's inhabitants consisted at first of two or three small households that shared common outdoor activity spaces, but the households became more segregated and independent over time. While the plan of buildings at this site is in stark contrast to those at Sha'ar Hagolan, Kadowaki argues that the use of shared open space by more than one household in the early phases of the former is like the use of courtyards in the latter. Social groups at this site cooperated in some tasks but operated separately in others.

Macroscopic artifacts as found in Neolithic sites often occur in refuse-disposal contexts rather than in contexts of use, although occasionally either their large size has led them to be left in place or at least a few artifacts from the last use of a room before its abandonment were too worthless to warrant removal. In many cases, microscopic and chemical residues are likely more telling with respect to persistent or habitual uses of space.

In one example from the same site that Kadowaki examined, spatial analysis of microscopic bits of basalt, bone, pottery, shell, seeds, charcoal, coprolites, insect carapaces, and flint microflakes reveals distinct activity areas on house floors (Ullah 2009; 2012; Ullah, Duffy, and Banning 2015). In one room, activities appear to have been structured with reference to a circular plastered hearth and a probable doorway. Evidence for food preparation was more common near the hearth, while evidence for sweeping and activities, like flint-knapping, that would have required good light, was more common near the probable doorway. In the other room, the most obvious feature was a large limestone mortar, and the evidence indicates that grinding involving basalt (not just limestone) tools took place south of the mortar, while food preparation, including animal foods, took place to its north. A small area with higher densities of micro-ceramics south of the mortar may have been the locus of the use or storage of pottery. While we cannot confidently associate any of these areas with any particular social or gendered group, we can say that activities were spatially structured in a way that could have, and probably did, depend at least in part on gender and age distinctions.

Mortuary evidence for the Late Neolithic is slim, and burial practice shows little basis for inferring gender differences, but the bones themselves have some potential. Jane Peterson's (2002; 2010; cf. Molleson 2007) attempt to identify gendered differences in physical activities of musculoskeletal stress on skeletons has some traction for other periods but suffers from a dearth of evidence for the Late Neolithic. She notes that the transition from the Natufian to the earlier Neolithic entailed greater changes for men than women, as hunting became less important and men probably became more deeply involved in horticultural and food-processing tasks. We would expect this trend to have continued, and perhaps intensified, in the Late Neolithic, when such hunting paraphernalia as projectile points became rarer than in PPNB.

Hunting did not disappear entirely in the Late Neolithic, but hunting parties, possibly dominated by or exclusive to men, may have become more important for their social and ideological significance than their nutritional contributions. Despite the rarity of projectile points at most sites, faunal remains continue to show at least low levels of hunted animals. In the Badia, the system of "kites" – extensive stone-built game traps used for catastrophic kills of gazelle – continued in use (Helms and Betts 1987), and the inherently communal nature of this hunting method, along with the scale of the kill, made gazelle hunting an inherently social occasion. In the Mediterranean region, hunting parties were likely smaller and focused on more solitary animals, such as deer and wild boar, but would still have led to social contexts of consumption that, while not necessarily feasts, would sometimes have involved more than just individual nuclear families.

Meals and Culinary Arts

Since food-sharing is arguably at the heart of household arrangements, evidence for feasting and dining is of great archaeological interest. Recently, archaeologists have focused on feasts – the relatively infrequent dining events that involved more than immediate family and typically marked important occasions – rather than daily meals that were the social glue on a small scale. Both are important, but here we focus on normal meals in households. Daily consumption of food in a social setting is one of the primary socializing contexts in any society (Bourdieu 1970; Klarich 2010).

Archaeologists have long devoted research to the nutritional and especially caloric implications of ancient foodways but have largely neglected cuisine and taste, despite their importance in most societies (Goody 1982; Barkow et al. 2001). Katherine Wright (2000) has studied the likely impact of changing cuisine on social relations in the earlier Neolithic, noting frequent evidence for preparation and consumption of food in semipublic areas, such as house porches, in Middle PPNB, but its increasing privatization in Late PPNB. This trend likely continued into the Late Neolithic, given our evidence for food preparation within courtyards in the Yarmoukian and within rooms in Wadi Rabah.

The Late Neolithic has several indications that dining and entertaining were important. The most obvious of these is pottery. A large proportion of the vessels consists of what are almost certainly serving vessels – small and large bowls, platters, and small jars that would be appropriate for the consumption of food and drink (Fig. 6.5) – and these also tend to be the focus of surface decoration. There are also indications for a growing variety of food-preparation techniques. Deep but somewhat open jar-like vessels are suitable as cooking pots for boiling gruels, stews, and soups, but there are sometimes flat-bottomed pan-like vessels that could be used for frying and, at some sites, V-shaped bowls and pans potentially suitable for baking. The increasing variety of pottery and heat-related features in Wadi Rabah sites appears to herald the ascendance of new cooking methods.

The high densities of what could be fire-cracked rock at PPNB, Yarmoukian, and some Wadi Rabah sites might indicate that stone boiling and earth roasting persisted alongside these new methods. Concentrations of angular stones, mostly limestone and dolomite, frequently line or fill pits, some of which could have served as earth ovens, but are also spread on surfaces to create platforms or discard cleanouts from cooking. As Danny Rosenberg and Nurit Shtober's (2010) work at Beisamoun shows that many of the stones were intentionally flaked and not necessarily fire-cracked, it is premature to associate all these stone concentrations with stone boiling or earth roasting, even if some may have served in that fashion.

Macrobotanical evidence from Late Neolithic sites is rarer than for the earlier Neolithic, and this may in itself suggest changes in culinary practices that altered the probability of preservation. The staples of subsistence continued to be emmer and einkorn wheat, two-row hulled barley, lentils, and fava beans. At

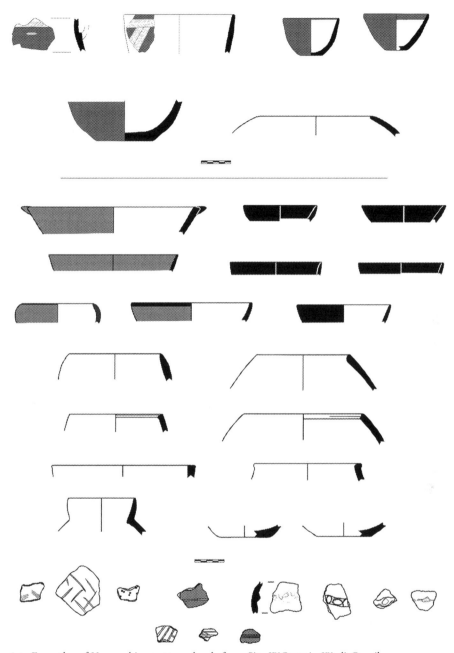

6.5. Examples of Yarmoukian pottery sherds from Site WQ117 in Wadi Quseiba (on the top) and Wadi Rabah-related pottery (on the bottom) from Jawafat Shaban in Wadi al-Bîr, northern Jordan. (Drawing by K. Abu Jayyab.)

least from the PPNC onward, we have reports of almond, carob, date, fig, flax, grape, and olive (e.g., Kafafi 1988; Muheisen et al. 1988; Galili et al. 1993: 152; Allen 2002; Caracuta et al. 2014). Even though they are not typically represented in archaeobotanical reports, such potential seasonings as bay leaf, capers, mint, oregano, sage, and thyme are ubiquitous in the southern Levant and could have been used to flavor dishes; many of them also have medicinal properties.

Although direct evidence is still controversial to non-existent (Gregg et al. 2009; Nieuwenhuyse et al. 2015), it is possible that Late Neolithic cuisine also took advantage of dairy products, such as yogurt and clarified butter, and sweeteners, such as honey and fruit syrups. However, dairying was likely relatively unimportant at this time, as zooarchaeological evidence is more consistent with a focus on meat production (Wasse 2002).

As settlement became more dispersed in the Late Neolithic, cuisine and hospitality may have played a more important role in forging and maintaining social relationships, encouraging economic sharing across and between communities, and accumulating prestige (Banning 2001: 154).

COMMUNITY ORGANIZATION: HIERARCHY OR HETERARCHY?

Garfinkel and Ben-Shlomo (2002; 2006) argue that Sha'ar Hagolan provides evidence for a Yarmoukian three-tiered social hierarchy. They interpret the somewhat grid-like street system and the communal well as evidence for decision-making at the community level and the clustering of house units around shared courtyards as an indication of decision making at the next level of extended-family households. At the bottom are the families in individual house units, each with its own storage room and living room. They go on to argue that these hierarchical relationships, and particularly what they view as community planning, may be indications of early urbanism.

Garfinkel and Ben-Shlomo make strong points about the likelihood of communal decision-making at large sites such as Sha'ar Hagolan, which was probably at about the same level as in the large Late PPNB sites. However, we should not overstate the need for (coercive) hierarchy in such decisions. For example, well-organized street systems, including ones that have grid-like structure, can develop from the multiple local decisions of interacting neighbors (Banning 1996b), especially if the early house compounds in the settlement sprang up next to existing pathways and trails. Similarly, the digging of wells, which occurred at several Late Neolithic sites (e.g., Gopher 2012), no doubt involved cooperation among households but not necessarily coordination by a village chief or council. In historical times, well digging and well cleaning in the upper Volta Basin of Ghana, for example, were usually activities for men from several neighboring households but sometimes the work of slaves or, in recent times, specialist contractors (Okoro 2003).

As mentioned above, feasting has attracted a lot of archaeological attention in the last decade for the light it might shed on ancient communities (Twiss 2008; Hayden 2014). Archaeologists have often assumed either that feasting was an integrative solidarity-building mechanism to mitigate conflict and fission as Neolithic communities became large and complex (e.g., Kuijt 2000), that they provided a "levelling mechanism" to prevent large wealth disparities between households or level out temporal variations in food availability (cf. Suttles 1968), or that they presented the opportunity for some households or aggrandizing individuals to gain wealth or prestige at the expense of others (e.g., Hayden 1990; 2001). Most likely, feasts had multiple and complex motivations (Twiss 2008) but were fundamentally social occasions. Garfinkel (2003), for example, has explored the iconographic evidence for the dancing that probably accompanied them, noting the prevalence of dancing in groups, rather than pairs, in the Late Neolithic.

The likelihood that many of the "desert kites" were operative during the Late Neolithic suggests that large groups in the Badia, at least, cooperated in hunting gazelle and then shared the meat, perhaps in a feast. Although they could have preserved meat by drying or smoking, it would help to cement ties between the cooperating hunting groups to consume some of it in a celebratory manner.

Another potential sign of Late Neolithic feasting is the presence of roasting pits or "earth ovens," which would have been suitable for cooking large amounts of meat. This is one possible interpretation for pits filled with stones and ashy sediment, some of them stone-lined or covered with flat stones, found at Beisamoun, Nahal Yarmut, and elsewhere (Khalaily 2011; cf. Twiss 2008).

Community Mortuary Practices

Mortuary practices in the Late Neolithic differed in several ways from those of the PPNB. Intramural burial of adults became much less common, and intramural burial of infants and children more common. Late Neolithic communities also discontinued the PPNB practice of curating skulls, with a few possible Yarmoukian exceptions (Perrot 1968; Simmons et al. 2001; Banning 2009).

Human remains, especially of adults, are rarely found at Late Neolithic sites, most likely because interment usually took place elsewhere. Those found in settlements tend to be in simple pits, sometimes covered with stones, or in small stone-lined cists covered with flat stones. These are either primary burials in flexed or semi-flexed position of one, two, or three individuals, or secondary burials, with human remains sometimes mixed with bones of other animals (e.g., Gopher and Eshed 2012). By the time of the Wadi Rabah settlements, fetuses and children were sometimes buried in jars, on large sherds, or in disused silos. Although artifacts sometimes occur in grave deposits, clear grave goods, such as groups of intact vessels, are rare.

Off-site cemeteries, although rarely found, may have been the normal burial places for adults, given the scarcity of adult burials in settlement sites. This may not have been a new feature, but the Late Neolithic provides better evidence for off-site cemeteries than does PPNB. The earliest Neolithic level at Tabaqat al-Bûma provides a glimpse of a likely cemetery of Yarmoukian date, with two large, limestone cist graves with slab covers (Banning, Rahimi, and Siggers 1994; Banning, Gibbs, and Kadowaki 2011); others may occur in unexcavated parts of this level. In one cist, two jars, a large ceramic bowl, two small bowls or lids, a stone bowl, and a stone palette or grinding slab accompanied the poorly preserved remains of two adults. In the other cist were a subadult woman and an infant wearing a dentalium-shell necklace.

The submerged Wadi Rabah site of Neve Yam has similar cist graves in an area apparently dedicated to mortuary activities some 50 m south of the settlement (Galili et al. 2009). Most of the burials were in well-built cists, some still covered by slabs, and most were primary burials of adults and children, although children were often in simple pit graves. None of the graves excavated contained grave goods, but there were possible ritual facilities, such as hearths, pits, paved surfaces, and post holes, and some concentrations of plant remains, such as lentils, barley grains, peas, and horse beans, that may have been offerings.

Late Neolithic ideas surrounding death and burial were different than in the PPNB. Despite the remains of three adults under a house floor at 'En Jarba (Arensburg 1970), Late Neolithic communities appear to have rejected the close association between certain deceased individuals – often described as "ancestors" – and particular house structures. This possibly reflected substantive changes in political leadership.

REGIONAL INTEGRATION AND INTERACTION

As knowledge of the spatial distribution of Late Neolithic sites is spotty, distributions of distinct artifact styles, especially among pottery, and exchange in exotic goods, such as obsidian, tend to be our main evidence for social connections between settlements.

The distribution of artifact, and particularly pottery, styles continues to provide the basis for much synthesis of Neolithic social organization at the regional scale, with cultures defined mainly on the basis of ceramic forms and decorative features (Gopher and Gophna 1993; Garfinkel 1999; Gilead 2007). While similarities and differences in material culture may be related to social interactions that encouraged the spread of some traits and localization of others, we need not assume that sets of these traits have distinct borders in space-time or that form and decoration are the only relevant aspects of style. Alternatives include considering the *chaînes opératoires* – the "recipes" and sequences of production steps and associated gestures and knowledge – and to see them as spreading (or not) through networks of social interaction and communities of learning.

Kevin Gibbs (2008) argues that subtle differences in the *chaînes opératoires* of fabrics, vessel construction, and decoration of pottery, in conjunction with other similarities and differences in the manufacture of sickle elements (Kadowaki et al. 2008), demonstrate that the contemporary and neighboring settlements of al-Basatîn, al-Aqaba, and Tabaqat al-Bûma in Wadi Ziqlab had different but overlapping communities of practice during the sixth millennium cal. BCE. They produced vessels and sickle elements that looked much the same but were often made through different sequences of procedures or movements. In others, as in some classes of pottery, there were more marked differences in surface treatment that would have been obvious and perhaps meant to signal social difference. Variation in clay sources and tempering recipes were also evident, and the minority recipes probably identify vessels that were brought to the sites from elsewhere. Some, for example, have fabrics similar to one of the fabric groups at Munhata (Goren 1992). These sites shared an overall idea of what pots should look like, but potters learned how to achieve this goal in various ways.

Although sites vary in size, evidence for regional hierarchy with central places (Christaller 1933) is wanting for the Late Neolithic. While we find some very large settlements such as 'Ain Ghazal and Sha'ar Hagolan, especially in the Yarmoukian, and a majority of small ones, there is no evidence that the larger sites "ruled" or exploited smaller ones, or even provided them with services. Many kinds of settlement systems, not only hierarchies, can lead to settlement differentiation. The small settlements could be agricultural or resource-extraction stations used seasonally, or autonomous hamlets and villages that maintained only loose relationships with each other and the large settlements to find marriage partners, exchange exotic resources, and engage in some rituals. That large Yarmoukian sites are dense with well-built rectilinear architecture, while many of the smaller ones instead have circular or oval huts or pit houses and considerable open space (e.g., Garfinkel 1992: 20–5; Bienert and Vieweger 2000; Banning et al. 2015), hints at social or functional differences; yet, even small sites sometimes contain many figurines, our most visible sign of ritual activity. Our only strong evidence for regional centers (see below) entails sites toward the end of our period that were well connected in trade networks.

One possibility is that clusters of small settlements operated as an extended community. Surveys for Late Neolithic sites in Wadi Ziqlab found many small sites, interpreted as an extensive network (Banning 2001; 2004; Kadowaki et al. 2008). These share many aspects of material culture and have overlapping carbon dates but also exhibit significant differences, such as the presence of substantial rectilinear architecture at Tabaqat al-Bûma, while only stone platforms and rare circular structures at al-Basatîn. Dispersing population along easily traversed routes that crosscut habitat zones would have facilitated access to resources that occur differentially across those zones, labor-sharing during harvest times that vary by altitude, and other activities that demanded larger work groups (Wilk and Rathje 1982: 623; Banning and Siggers 1997).

However, we should also consider the possibility of less amicable intercommunity relations. One possible interpretation of some ground-stone objects that began to appear at the time of the Wadi Rabah settlements is that they are mace-heads and sling stones (Rosenberg 2009; 2010), which suggests warfare. Our lack of strong evidence for interpersonal violence may be due to our tiny sample size of adult burials. Such violence did occur at least occasionally elsewhere in the Near East at this time, as at Domuztepe in Turkey (Carter, Campbell, and Gauld 2003; Whitcher Kansa et al. 2009), where more than 10,000 bone fragments from at least thirty-six people and animals provide evidence for feasting, including cannibalism, after a catastrophic kill. We cannot be certain what motivated those killings and have no basis to generalize to the Levant, but it suggests one possible interpretation for the isolated and burned human bones at some of our Late Neolithic sites, sometimes mixed with animal bones, and usually just interpreted as bones accidentally burnt (e.g., Gopher and Eshed 2012: 1401). Unlike some sites in Iraq, we have no evidence for Late Neolithic fortifications in the southern Levant.

Evidence for long-distance contacts comes in the form of materials, finished artifacts, and stylistic concepts for artifacts. For millennia, obsidian and shell were two materials that traveled great distances from their sources. While the distribution of obsidian at Late Neolithic sites is spotty, some sites were very well connected to the distribution network for this valued material. Hagoshrim in northern Israel was particularly well supplied with obsidian from central and eastern Turkey, especially during its Wadi Rabah phase (Schechter et al. 2013). This, in conjunction with the site's stamp seals, chlorite vessels, and Halaf-type ornaments (Rosenberg, Getzov, and Assaf 2010; Getzov 2011), argues for its likely role as a regional manufacture and distribution center.

While archaeological attention to long-distance contacts in this period have tended to focus on the north (Kaplan 1960), it is clear that Mediterranean links with the Badia were also important. It seems likely that the now-desert regions of Jordan and southeastern Syria became populated by Neolithic hunter-gatherers during Middle and Late PPNB, when a relatively moist climate made the Badia more appealing than it is today; however, there has been debate on the nature of the relationship between these two regions in the millennia that followed. Some researchers, notably Ilse Köhler-Rollefson (1992), have argued that the same people seasonally occupied both

Mediterranean villages, such as 'Ain Ghazal, and the Badia sites as a means of relieving grazing pressure. The competing theory is that the occupants of the Badia were a distinct population that retained a hunting-gathering lifeway longer than their counterparts near the Mediterranean but eventually adopted herding (Byrd 1992). Dawn Cropper's (2006) analysis of the Late Neolithic lithic technologies of these two regions favors the second hypothesis: Despite some similarities, there are fundamental differences in the reduction strategies in the two regions that are not explicable by such mundane factors as raw materials, indicating that the knappers belonged to distinct communities of practice. However, there is good evidence for exchange between these two regions in the form of tabular knives (Baird 1993; Cropper 2006), manufactured in the Badia but found in low frequencies in Mediterranean villages, and both finished beads and the stone and shell raw materials for beads (Wright and Garrard 2003). Similarly specialized lithic production occurred in the Sinai and Negev (Goring-Morris, Gopher, and Rosen 1994).

CONCLUSIONS

Although there has been progress, our understanding of Late Neolithic society is still rudimentary. While we need to be cautious, it appears likely that small households of nuclear families were the most common building block of Late Neolithic society. These sometimes were linked closely to other households with which they shared some spaces, communal tasks, and communal meals. Spatial analysis indicates that the activities of households were spatially structured, but it is premature to associate particular tasks with any gender and musculoskeletal evidence is still lacking, although it seems likely that the Late Neolithic continued the trend, begun in PPNB, of converging male and female tasks.

There is little evidence for hierarchical community organization but some cooperation both within settlements and among neighboring ones with respect to marriage partners, infrastructure, labor bottlenecks, and possibly hunting and herd management. Mace-heads probably became status symbols in the Chalcolithic, but there is no strong evidence for ranking in the Late Neolithic.

Regional integration was minimal in the Late Neolithic, but members of some communities interacted with both neighboring and far-flung populations in order to exchange some kinds of highly valued materials, such as obsidian, shell, chlorite, and some finished goods. Exchanges of ideas, tastes, and styles often accompanied these material transfers. Those who were well connected in these networks may have had advantageous positions as society moved further, during the Chalcolithic, toward social and economic stratification.

ACKNOWLEDGMENTS

I thank Yorke Rowan, Assaf Yasur-Landau, and Eric Cline for their invitation to participate in this volume; Khaled Abu Jayyab, Kevin Gibbs, and Julia Pfaff, for some of the illustrations; and the Social Sciences and Humanities Research Council of Canada.

REFERENCES

Allen, S. E. 2002. Palaeoethnobotany: Preliminary Results. In *Sha'ar Hagolan*, Vol. 1: *Neolithic Art in Context*, ed. Y. Garfinkel and M. A. Miller, 236–46. Qedem 9. Oxford: Oxbow.

Arensburg, B. 1970. The Human Remains from 'Ein el-Jarba. *BASOR* 197: 49–52.

Baird, D. 1993. *Neolithic Chipped Stone Assemblages from the Azraq Basin, Jordan, and the Significance of the Arid Zones of the Southern Levant*. PhD diss., University of Edinburgh.

Banning, E. B. 1996a. Houses, Compounds and Mansions in the Prehistoric Near East. In *People Who Lived in Big Houses: Archaeological Perspectives on Large Domestic Structures*, ed. G. Coupland and E. B. Banning, 165–85. MWA 27. Madison, WI: Prehistory Press.

——— 1996b. Pattern or Chaos? New Ways of Looking at "Town Planning" in the Ancient Near East. In *Debating Complexity: Proceedings of the 26th Annual Chacmool Conference*, ed. D. A. Meyer, P. Dawson, and D. Hanna, 510–18. Calgary: Archaeological Association of the University of Calgary.

——— 2001. Settlement and Economy in Wādī Ziqlāb during the Late Neolithic. *SHAJ* 7: 149–55.

——— 2004. Changes in Spatial Organization of the Transjordanian Settlements from Middle PPNB to Late Neolithic. In *Central Settlements in Neolithic Jordan: Proceedings of a Symposium Held in Wadi Musa, Jordan, 21.–25. of July 1997*, ed. H.-D. Bienert, H. G. K. Gebel, and R. Neef, 215–32. SENEPSE 5. Berlin: Ex Orient.

——— 2007. Wadi Rabah and Related Assemblages in the Southern Levant: Interpreting the Radiocarbon Evidence. *Paléorient* 33 (1): 77–101.

——— 2009. From Out of Left Field: Excavations in the South Field, 'Ain Ghazal. In *Modesty and Patience: Archaeological Studies and Memories in Honour of Nabil Qadi "Abu Salim,"* ed. H. G. K. Gebel, Z. Kafafi, and O. al-Ghul, 18–23. Monographs of the Faculty of Archaeology and Anthropology. Irbid: Yarmouk University; Berlin: Ex Oriente.

——— 2010. Houses, Households, and Changing Society in the Late Neolithic and Chalcolithic of the Southern Levant. *Paléorient* 36 (1): 49–87.

Banning, E. B., and Byrd, B. F. 1987. Houses and the Changing Residential Unit: Domestic Architecture at PPNB 'Ain Ghazal, Jordan. *PPS* 53: 309–25.

Banning, E. B., and Chazan, M. 2006. Structuring Interactions, Structuring Ideas: Domestication of Space in the Prehistoric Near East. In *The Domestication of Space: Construction, Community, and Cosmology in the Late Prehistoric Near East*, ed. E. B. Banning and M. Chazan, 5–14. SENEPSE 12. Berlin: Ex Oriente.

Banning, E. B.; Gibbs, K.; and Kadowaki, S. 2011. Changes in Material Culture at Late Neolithic Tabaqat al-Bûma, in Wadi Ziqlab, Northern Jordan. In *Culture, Chronology and the Chalcolithic: Theory and Transition*, ed. J. L. Lovell and Y. M. Rowan, 36–60. LSS 9. Oxford: Oxbow.

Banning, E. B.; Gibbs, K.; Ullah, I.; Hitchings, P.; Abu Jayyab, K.; Edwards, S.; and Rhodes, S. 2015. Archaeological Excavations in Wadi Quseiba and Wadi al-Bîr, Northern Jordan. *Antiquity Project Gallery*. http://antiquity.ac.uk/projgall/banning344 (accessed December 15, 2016).

Banning, E. B.; Rahimi, D.; and Siggers, J. 1994. The Late Neolithic of the Southern Levant: Hiatus, Settlement Shift or Observer Bias? The Perspective from Wadi Ziqlab. *Paléorient* 20 (2): 151–64.

Banning, E. B., and Siggers, J. 1997. Technological Strategies at a Late Neolithic Farmstead in Wadi Ziqlab, Jordan. In *Prehistory of Jordan II: Perspectives from 1997*, ed. H. G. K. Gebel, Z. Kafafi, and G. O. Rollefson, 319–31. SENEPSE 4. Berlin: Ex Oriente.

Barkow, J. H.; Taslim, N. A.; Hadju, V.; Ishak, E.; Attamimi, F.; Silwana, S.; Dachlan, D. M.; Ramli; and Yahya, A. 2001. Social Competition, Social Intelligence, and Why the Bugis Know More about Cooking than about Nutrition. In *The Origin of Human Social Institutions*, ed. W. G. Runciman, 119–47. Proceedings of the British Academy 110. Oxford: Oxford University Press.

Bienert, H.-D., and Vieweger, D. 2000. Archaeological Excavations at the Late Neolithic Site of ash-Shallaf in Northern Jordan: A Preliminary Report on the Second Season 1999. *ADAJ* 44: 109–18.

Bourdieu, F. 1970. La maison Kabyle ou le monde Renversé. In *Échanges et communications: Mélanges offerts à Claude Lévi-Strauss à l'occasion de son 60ème anniversaire*, Vol. 2, ed. J. Pouillon and P. Maranda, 739–58. Studies in General Anthropology 5. The Hague: Mouton.

Byrd, B. F. 1992. The Dispersal of Food Production across the Levant. In *Transitions to Agriculture in Prehistory*, ed. A. B. Gebauer and T. D. Price, 49–61. MWA 4. Madison, WI: Prehistory Press.

——— 2000. Households in Transition: Neolithic Social Organization within Southwest Asia. In *Life in Neolithic Farming Communities: Social Organization, Identity, and Differentiation*, ed. I. Kuijt, 63–102. FIA. New York: Kluwer Academic/Plenum.

Caracuta, V.; Weiss, E.; van den Brink, E. C. M.; Liran, R.; Vardi, J.; and Barzilai, O. 2014. From Natural Environment to Human Landscape: New Archaeobotanical Data from the Neolithic Site of Nahal Zippori 3, Lower Galilee. *Neo-Lithics* 2014 (1): 33–41.

Carter, E.; Campbell, S.; and Gauld, S. 2003. Elusive Complexity: New Data from Late Halaf Domuztepe in South Central Turkey. *Paléorient* 29 (2): 117–33.

Christaller, W. 1933. *Die zentralen Orte in Süddeutschland: Eine ökonomisch-geographische Untersuchung über die Gesetzmässigkeit der Verbreitung und Entwicklung der siedlungen mit städtischen Funktionen*. Jena: Fischer.

Conkey, M. W., and Tringham, R. E. 1995. Archaeology and the Goddess: Exploring the Contours of Feminist Archaeology. In *Feminisms in the Academy*, ed. D. C. Stanton and A. J. Stewart, 199–247. Ann Arbor: The University of Michigan Press.

Cropper, D. N. 2006. *Bridging the Gap between the Mediterranean Region and the Badia: Lithic Technology in Late Neolithic Jordan*. PhD diss., University of Sydney.

Dowson, T. A. 2006. Archaeologists, Feminists, and Queers: Sexual Politics in the Construction of the Past. In *Feminist Anthropology: Past, Present, and Future*, ed. P. L. Geller and M. K. Stockett, 89–102. Philadelphia: University of Pennsylvania Press.

Engels, F. 1884. *Der Ursprung der Familie, des Privateigenthums und des Staats: Im Anschluss an Lewis H. Morgan's Forschungen*. Hottingen-Zürich: Schweizerische Genossenschaftsbuchdruckerei.

Flannery, K. V. 1972. The Origins of the Village as a Settlement Type in Mesoamerica and the Near East: A Comparative Study. In *Man, Settlement, and Urbanism*, ed. P. J. Ucko, R. Tringham, and G. W. Dimbleby, 23–53. London: Duckworth.

Galili, E.; Eshed, V.; Rosen, B.; Kislev, M. E.; Simchoni, O.; Hershkovitz, I.; and Gopher, A. 2009. Evidence for a Separate Burial Ground at the Submerged Pottery Neolithic Site of Neve-Yam, Israel. *Paléorient* 35 (1): 31–46.

Galili, E.; Weinstein-Evron, M.; Hershkovitz, I.; Gopher, A.; Kislev, M.; Lernau, O.; Horwitz, L. K.; and Lernaut, H. 1993. Atlit-Yam: A Prehistoric Site on the Sea Floor off the Israeli Coast. *JFA* 20: 133–57.

Garfinkel, Y. 1992. *The Pottery Assemblages of the Shaʻar Hagolan and Rabah Stages of Munhata (Israel)*. CCRFJ 6. Paris: Paléorient.

——— 1999. *Neolithic and Chalcolithic Pottery of the Southern Levant*. Qedem 39. Jerusalem: The Institute of Archaeology, The Hebrew University of Jerusalem.

——— 2003. *Dancing at the Dawn of Agriculture*. Austin: University of Texas Press.

——— 2006. The Social Organization at Neolithic Shaʻar Hagolan. The Nuclear Family, the Extended Family and the Community. In *Domesticating Space: Construction, Community, and Cosmology in the Late Prehistoric Near East*, ed. E. B. Banning and M. Chazan, 103–11. SENEPSE 12. Berlin: Ex Oriente.

Garfinkel, Y., and Ben-Shlomo, D. 2002. Architecture and Village Planning in Area E. In *Shaʻar Hagolan*, Vol. 1: *Neolithic Art in Context*, ed. Y. Garfinkel and M. Miller, 55–70. Qedem 9. Oxford: Oxbow.

Garfinkel, Y.; Korn, N.; and Miller, M. A. 2002. Art from Shaʻar Hagolan: Visions of a Neolithic Village in the Levant. In *Shaʻar Hagolan*, Vol. 1: *Neolithic Art in Context*, ed. Y. Garfinkel and M. Miller, 188–208. Qedem 9. Oxford: Oxbow.

Getzov, N. 2011. Seals and Figurines from the Beginning of the Early Chalcolithic Period at Ha-Gosherim. *ʻAtiqot* 67: 1–26 (Hebrew; English summary on pp. 81*–83*).

Gibbs, K. 2008. *Understanding Community: A Comparison of Three Late Neolithic Pottery Assemblages from Wadi Ziqlab, Jordan*. PhD diss., University of Toronto.

——— 2013. Late Neolithic Pottery and Ambiguous Symbols in the Southern Levant. *Paléorient* 39 (2): 69–84.

Gilead, I. 2007. The Besorian: A Pre-Ghassulian Cultural Entity. *Paléorient* 33 (1): 33–49.

Gimbutas, M. 1974. *The Gods and Goddesses of Old Europe, 7000 to 3500 BC: Myths, Legends and Cult Images*. London: Thames & Hudson.

Goody, J. 1982. *Cooking, Cuisine, and Class: A Study in Comparative Sociology*. Themes in Social Sciences. Cambridge: Cambridge University Press.

Gopher, A. 2012. Locus 54, a Yarmukian Seepage "Well" or Cistern. In *Village Communities of the Pottery Neolithic Period in the Menashe Hills, Israel: Archaeological Investigations at the Sites of Naḥal Zehora*, Vol. 1, ed. A. Gopher, 292–314. MSSMNIA 29. Tel Aviv: Emery and Claire Yass Publications in Archaeology.

Gopher, A., and Eshed, V. 2012. Burials and Human Skeletal Remains from Nahal Zehora II in PN Perspective. In *Village Communities of the Pottery Neolithic Period in the Menashe Hills, Israel: Archaeological Investigations at the Sites of Naḥal Zehora*, Vol. 3, ed. A. Gopher, 1389–1412. MSSMNIA 29. Tel Aviv: Emery and Claire Yass Publications in Archaeology.

Gopher, A., and Gophna, R. 1993. Cultures of the Eighth and Seventh Millennia BP in the Southern Levant: A Review for the 1990s. *JWP* 7: 297–353.

Gopher, A., and Orrelle, E. 1996. An Alternative Interpretation for the Material Imagery of the Yarmukian, a Neolithic Culture of the Sixth Millennium BC in the Southern Levant. *CAJ* 6: 255–79.

Goren, Y. 1992. Petrographic Study of the Pottery Assemblage of Munhata. In *The Pottery Assemblage of the Sha'ar Hagolan and Rabah Stages of Munhata (Israel)*, ed. Y. Garfinkel, 329–60. CCRFJ 6. Paris: Paléorient.

Goring-Morris, N.; Gopher, A.; and Rosen, S. 1994. The Neolithic Tawailan Cortical Knife Industry of the Negev. In *Neolithic Chipped Stone Industries from the Fertile Crescent: Proceedings of the First Workshop on PPN Chipped Lithic Industries, Seminar für Vorderasiatrische Altertumskunde, Free University of Berlin, 29th March–2nd April, 1993*, ed. H. G. K. Gebel and S. K. Kozlowski, 511–24. SENEPSE 1. Berlin: Ex Oriente.

Gregg, M. W.; Banning, E. B.; Gibbs, K.; and Slater, G. F. 2009. Subsistence Practices and Pottery Use in Neolithic Jordan: Molecular and Isotopic Evidence. *JAS* 36: 937–46.

Hamilton, N.; Marcus, J.; Haaland, G.; Haaland, R.; and Ucko, P. J. 1996. Can We Interpret Figurines? *CAJ* 6: 281–307.

Hayden, B. 1990. Nimrods, Piscators, Pluckers, and Planters: The Emergence of Food Production. *JAA* 9: 31–69.

   2001. Fabulous Feasts: A Prolegomenon to the Importance of Feasting. In *Feasts: Archaeological and Ethnographic Perspectives on Food, Politics, and Power*, ed. M. Dietler and B. Hayden, 23–64. SSAI. Washington, DC: Smithsonian Institution Press.

   2014. *The Power of Feasts: From Prehistory to the Present*. Cambridge: Cambridge University Press.

Helms, S., and Betts, A. 1987. The Desert "Kites" of the Badiyat esh-Sham and North Arabia. *Paléorient* 13 (1): 41–67.

Hendon, J. A. 2006. The Engendered Household. In *Handbook of Gender and Archaeology*, ed. S. M. Nelson, 171–98. GA. Lanham, MD: AltaMira.

Kadowaki, S. 2007. *Changing Community Life at a Late Neolithic Farmstead: Built Environments and the Use of Space at Tabaqat al-Bûma in Wadi Ziqlab, Northern Jordan*. PhD diss., University of Toronto.

Kadowaki, S.; Gibbs, K.; Allentuck, A.; and Banning, E. B. 2008. Late Neolithic Settlement in Wadi Ziqlab, Jordan: al-Basatîn. *Paléorient* 34 (1): 105–29.

Kafafi, Z. 1988. Jebel Abu Thawwab: A Pottery Neolithic Village in North Jordan. In *The Prehistory of Jordan*, Vol. 1, part 1: *The State of Research in 1986*, ed. A. N. Garrard and H. G. K. Gebel, 451–71. BAR International Series 396 (1). Oxford: Archaeopress.

Kaplan, J. 1958. Excavations at Wadi Rabah. *IEJ* 8: 149–60.

   1960. The Relation of the Chalcolithic Pottery of Palestine to Halafian Ware. *BASOR* 159: 32–6.

Kenyon, K. M. 1957. *Digging Up Jericho*. London: Benn.

Khalaily, H. 2011. Nahal Yarmut: A Late Pottery Neolithic Site of the Wadi Rabah Culture, South of Nahal Soreq. *'Atiqot* 67 (1): 1*–29*.

Klarich, E. A. 2010. Behind the Scenes and into the Kitchen: New Directions for the Study of Prehistoric Meals. In *Inside Ancient Kitchens: New Directions in the Study of Daily Meals and Feasts*, ed. E. Karich, 1–16. Boulder: University of Colorado Press.

Köhler-Rollefson, I. 1992. A Model for the Development of Nomadic Pastoralism on the Transjordan Plateau. In *Pastoralism in the Levant: Archaeological Materials in Anthropological Perspectives*, ed. O. Bar-Yosef and A. Khazanov, 11–18. MWA 10. Madison, WI: Prehistory Press.

Kuijt, I. 2000. People and Space in Early Agricultural Villages: Exploring Daily Lives, Community Size, and Architecture in the Late Pre-Pottery Neolithic. *JAA* 19: 75–102.

Leacock, E. 1978. Women's Status in Egalitarian Society: Implications for Social Evolution. *CA* 19: 247–75.

Lesure, R. G. 2002. The Goddess Diffracted: Thinking about the Figurines of Early Villages. *CA* 43: 587–610.

Lévi-Strauss, C. 1982. *The Way of the Masks.* Trans. S. Modelski, from French. London: Cape.

Meskell, L. 1995. Goddesses, Gimbutas and "New Age" Archaeology. *Antiquity* 69 (262): 74–86.

Meyers, C. M. 2003. Engendering Syro-Palestinian Archaeology: Reasons and Resources. *NEA* 66: 185–97.

Miller, M. A. 2002. The Function of the Anthropomorphic Figurines: A Preliminary Analysis. In *Sha'ar Hagolan,* Vol. 1: *Neolithic Art in Context,* ed. Y. Garfinkel and M. Miller, 221–33. Qedem 9. Oxford: Oxbow.

Molleson, T. I. 2007. Bones of Work at the Origins of Labour. In *Archaeology and Women: Ancient and Modern Issues,* ed. S. Hamilton, R. D. Whitehouse, and K. I. Wright, 185–98. Publications of the Institute of Archaeology, University College London. Walnut Creek, CA: Left Coast.

Muheisen, M.; Gebel, H. G. K.; Hanns, C.; and Neef, R. 1988. Excavations at 'Ain Rahub, a Final Natufian and Yarmoukian Site near Irbid (1985). In *The Prehistory of Jordan,* Vol. 1, part 1: *The State of Research in 1986,* ed. A. N. Garrard and H. G. K. Gebel, 472–502. BAR International Series 396 (1). Oxford: Archaeopress.

Murdock, G. P., and Provost, C. 1973. Factors in the Division of Labor by Sex: A Cross-Cultural Analysis. *Ethnology* 12: 203–25.

Naveh, D., and Gopher, A. 2012. Gender Relations as Reflected by Spatial Distribution of Material Culture Assemblages. In *Village Communities of the Pottery Neolithic Period in the Menashe Hills, Israel: Archaeological Investigations at the Sites of Naḥal Zehora,* Vol. 3, ed. A. Gopher, 1416–48. MSSMNIA 29. Tel Aviv: Emery and Claire Yass Publications in Archaeology.

Nieuwenhuyse, O. P.; Roffet-Salque, M.; Evershed, R. P.; Akkermans, P. M. M. G.; and Russell, A. 2015. Tracing Pottery Use and the Emergence of Secondary Product Exploitation through Lipid Residue Analysis at Late Neolithic Tell Sabi Abyad (Syria). *JAS* 64: 54–66.

Okoro, J. 2003. Research on Water and Slaves in Salaga. *Nyame Akuma* 59: 45–53.

Orrelle, E., and Gopher, A. 2000. The Pottery Neolithic Period: Questions about Pottery Decoration, Symbolism, and Meaning. In *Life in Neolithic Farming Communities: Social Organization, Identity, and Differentiation,* ed. I. Kuijt, 295–308. FIA. New York: Kluwer Academic/Plenum.

Perrot, J. 1968. La Préhistoire palestinienne. In *Supplément au Dictionnaire du la Bible,* Vol. 8, 286–446. Paris: Letouzey & Ané.

Peterson, J. D. 2002. *Sexual Revolutions: Gender and Labor at the Dawn of Agriculture.* GA 4. Walnut Creek, CA: AltaMira.

——— 2006. Gender in Early Farming Societies. In *Handbook of Gender in Archaeology,* ed. S. M. Nelson, 537–570. GA. Lanham, MD: AltaMira.

——— 2010. Domesticating Gender: Neolithic Patterns from the Southern Levant. *JAA* 29: 249–64.

Rosenberg, D. 2009. Flying Stones – The Slingstones of the Wadi Rabah Culture of the Southern Levant. *Paléorient* 35 (2): 99–112.

2010. Early Maceheads in the Southern Levant: A "Chalcolithic" Hallmark in Neolithic Context. *JFA* 35: 204–216.

Rosenberg, D.; Getzov, N.; and Assaf, A. 2010. New Light on Long-Distance Ties in the Late Neolithic/Early Chalcolithic Near East: The Chlorite Vessels from Hagoshrim, Northern Israel. *CA* 51: 281–93.

Rosenberg, D., and Shtober, N. 2010. The Stone Component of the Pits and Pavements. In *An Early Pottery Neolithic Occurrence at Beisamoun, the Hula Valley, Northern Israel: The Results of the 2007 Salvage Excavation*, ed. D. Rosenberg, 19–34. BAR International Series 2095. Oxford: Archaeopress.

Schechter, H. C.; Marder, O.; Barkai, R.; Getzov, N.; and Gopher, A. 2013. The Obsidian Assemblage from Neolithic Hagoshrim, Israel: Pressure Technology and Cultural Influence. In *Stone Tools in Transition: From Hunter-Gatherers to Farming Societies in the Near East*, ed. F. Borrell, J. J. Ibáñez, and M. Molist, 509–27. Barcelona: Universitat Autònoma de Barcelona.

Simmons, A. H.; al-Nahar, M.; Rollefson, G. O.; Cooper, J.; Kafafi, Z.; Köhler-Rollefson, I.; Mandel, R. D.; and Durand, K. R. 2001. Wadi Shu'eib, a Large Neolithic Community in Central Jordan: Final Report of Test Investigations. *BASOR* 321: 1–39.

Stekelis, M. 1972. *The Yarmukian Culture of the Neolithic Period*. Jerusalem: Magnes.

Suttles, S. 1968. Coping with Abundance: Subsistence on the Northwest Coast. In *Man the Hunter*, ed. R. B. Lee and I. Devore, 56–68. Chicago: Aldine.

Tringham, R., and Conkey, M. 1998. Rethinking Figurines: A Critical View from Archaeology of Gimbutas, the "Goddess" and Popular Culture. In *Ancient Goddesses: The Myths and the Evidence*, ed. L. Goodison and C. Morris, 22–45. Wisconsin Studies in Classics. Madison: University of Wisconsin Press.

Twiss, K. C. 2008. Transformations in an Early Agricultural Society: Feasting in the Southern Levantine Pre-Pottery Neolithic. *JAA* 27: 418–42.

Ullah, I. I. T. 2009. Within-Room Spatial Analysis of Activity Areas at Late Neolithic Ṭabaqat al-Būma, Wādī Ziqlāp, al-Kūra, Jordan. *SHAJ* 10: 87–95.

2012. Particles of the Past: Microarchaeological Spatial Analysis of Ancient House Floors. In *New Perspectives on Household Archaeology*, ed. B. J. Parker and C. P. Foster, 123–38. Winona Lake, IN: Eisenbrauns.

Ullah, I. I. T.; Duffy, P. R.; and Banning, E. B. 2015. Modernizing Spatial Micro-Refuse Analysis: New Methods for Collecting, Analyzing, and Interpreting the Spatial Patterning of Micro-Debris from House-Floor Contexts. *JAMT* 22: 1238–62.

Vaux, R. de. 1966. Palestine during the Neolithic and Chalcolithic Periods. *CAH* 1 (1): 499–538.

Wasse, A. 2002. Final Results of an Analysis of the Sheep and Goat Bones from 'Ain Ghazal, Jordan. *Levant* 34: 59–82.

Whitcher Kansa, S.; Gauld, S. C.; Campbell, S.; and Carter, E. 2009. Whose Bones Are Those? Preliminary Comparative Analysis of Fragmented Human and Animal Bones in the "Death Pit" at Domuztepe, a Late Neolithic Settlement in Southeastern Turkey. *Anthropozoologica* 44: 159–72.

Wilk, R. R., and Rathje, W. L. 1982. Household Archaeology. *American Behavioral Scientist* 25: 617–39.

Wright, K. I. 2000. The Social Origins of Cooking and Dining in Early Villages of Western Asia. *PPS* 66: 89–121.

Wright, K. I., and Garrard, A. N. 2003. Social Identities and the Expansion of Stone Bead-Making in Neolithic Western Asia: New Evidence from Jordan. *Antiquity* 77 (296): 267–84.

SEVEN

THE SPIRITUAL AND SOCIAL LANDSCAPE DURING THE CHALCOLITHIC PERIOD

YORKE M. ROWAN

During the Chalcolithic period, villages that continued Neolithic traditions expanded across much of Palestine and Transjordan. Communities held in common similar mixed economies based on agriculture and animal husbandry (sheep, goat, pigs, cattle), with people living in hamlets and villages of rectilinear houses including storage structures and hearths oriented around courtyards (Levy 1998; Rowan and Golden 2009). The spread of these communities across the landscape suggests a rapidly increasing population, with some larger villages (between 6 to 12 ha). A variety of house sizes are found within these villages and hamlets, but there is a lack of palaces or other centralized controls of the staple economy. Most food and goods are produced locally, whether wheat, chickpea, lentil, or barley, and animal husbandry primarily reflects local environmental conditions (sheep, goat, and cattle, with pigs in less arid zones). Some pottery and flint were moved between a few sites,[1] but most quotidian objects were produced and consumed locally.

Viewed against those fundamentals, the Chalcolithic period is often considered something of an enigma in the archaeology of the southern Levant. Advanced metallurgical skills in copper and gold to produce exotic ritual objects, labor-intensive creation of intricate bowls of basalt, basalt pillar figurines, carved items of ivory, and mace-heads of exotic stone and copper all attest to a vested interest in the production, distribution, and exchange of exogenous, socially valued, and rare items that were uncommon to most households (Ilan and Rowan 2011; Levy 1998). Alongside these technological advances and material changes, the rise of intensive investment in the extended secondary treatment of the human corpse provides an intriguing complement to the exotic elements of material culture and possibly part of an explanatory inspiration and linkage to their purpose. With the secondary treatment of human skeletal remains came the novel and extraordinary ossuaries (bone containers), sometimes idiosyncratically decorated with human and animal features, painted, and interred in caves, carved cavities, and built structures. Without contemporaneous parallels in nearby lands, the virtual explosion of exotic goods linked to ritualized activities, particularly burial practices, indicates an indigenous shift in outlook. This is rarely explored as an overarching perspective that provides insight into the key shifts in beliefs that distinguish the period in contrast to the preceding and subsequent time periods in the southern Levant.

Current research on the southern Levant during the Chalcolithic period is at a key juncture. Rather than debate the degree of complexity in social organization, scholars are asking different questions, in particular, regarding how to understand the social, ritual, and economic lives of people living over 6,000 years ago. There remains no consensus on where the Chalcolithic fit within neo-evolutionary types (whether egalitarian or chiefdom), but it is increasingly unlikely that a centralized political organization exerted substantial power beyond a few larger villages. Nonetheless, the notable presence of items with exotic origins or intensive labor requirements underscores the non-egalitarian nature of socioeconomic organizational complexity. A compelling part of this change is the evidence that ritual practice dramatically increases during the Chalcolithic in comparison to the preceding Late Neolithic period. How ritual practice and religious belief intertwined with increasing complex socioeconomic organization remains a central unanswered question.

DEFINING THE PERIOD: CHRONOLOGY, SUBSISTENCE, AND SETTLEMENT

The "Classic Chalcolithic" of the southern Levant (or the "Developed Chalcolithic" [Joffe and Dessel 1995]) is typically identified within the area of modern Israel, Palestine, and the western highland zones of modern Jordan. Also known as the Ghassulian, after Teleilat el-Ghassul, the type site located on the northeastern shore of the Dead Sea in Jordan (Fig. 7.1), the Chalcolithic is sometimes equated with the Ghassulian culture and treated by some as a subset or an archaeological culture. Defined by rectilinear architecture of mud brick or stone; pottery forms, such as churns, cornets, holemouth jars, and V-shaped bowls; and flint tools, such as axes and adzes, sickle blades, and "tabular" fan scrapers made of thin cortical flakes, the Ghassulian Chalcolithic apparently heralds an expansion in settlements and population (Gilead 2011; Gošić and Gilead 2015). In the more arid zones of eastern Jordan and the south of Israel,

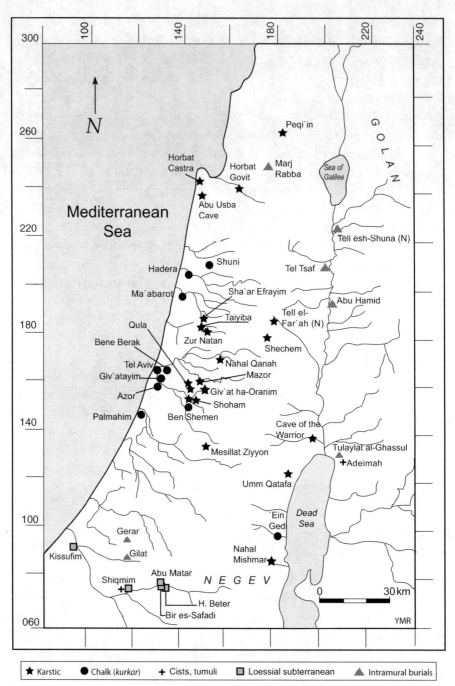

7.1. Selected Chalcolithic sites. (Map by Y. M. Rowan.)

Jordan, and Sinai, the Chalcolithic is difficult to identify or correlate due to the rarity of diagnostic material culture dating to the traditional chronological framework, ca. 4500–3600 BCE. To the north, few assemblages are identified to the period with confidence, although some parallels are possible at Byblos

(Dunand 1973) and possibly Sidon-Dakerman (Saideh 1979). Thus, the boundaries of the normative Chalcolithic period, or what will be termed the "Classic Chalcolithic," seem circumscribed, although this may reflect modern political borders.

Material culture defining the Chalcolithic period exhibits continuity with the preceding Late Neolithic and subsequent Early Bronze Age (Rowan and Golden 2009). Subdivisions of the period into phases or cultures differ from project to project and between scholars. For brevity's sake, the various proposed subdivisions and cultures are not summarized here (but see Rowan and Golden 2009, and Banning 2007); however, a traditional perspective characterizes the core period to extend from about 4500 BCE to approximately 3600 BCE. More recent radiocarbon dates push the earliest phases to at least around 4700–4600 BCE. Some scholars refer to this as the "Late Chalcolithic." Traditionally, the Wadi Rabah is considered Late Neolithic, but some now designate this as "Early Chalcolithic" (Garfinkel 1999). The period between Wadi Rabah and the start of the Classic Chalcolithic is then termed the "Middle Chalcolithic" (Garfinkel 1999) or the post-Wadi Rabah–pre-Ghassulian by others (PoWR-PG) (see Gopher 2012). This poorly represented transitional period has no diagnostic features and few dates; it seems to represent subregional groups primarily limited to northern Israel and the Jordan Valley. These groups or phases seem more similar to Wadi Rabah and other Late Neolithic entities than to the Classic Chalcolithic. Whether or not Wadi Rabah and PoWR-PG groups should be designated Late Neolithic or Chalcolithic may seem a semantic distinction, but the differences are significant, meaningful, and allow us to distinguish the Classic Chalcolithic (including the Ghassulian) from earlier Neolithic groups/cultures/entities (Gilead 2011). For the present discussion, the normative definition of the Classic Chalcolithic is the period between the early fifth millennium BCE to the end of the first quarter of the fourth millennium BCE.

A number of characteristics differentiate the Chalcolithic from earlier groups. Like the earlier Neolithic, the Chalcolithic period was primarily agropastoral with virtually no significant reliance on hunting except in the most marginal arid zones, where dating is typically problematic (see Rosen 2011). The domestication of the olive may have allowed for oil production to expand greatly, possibly as a commodity for exchange (Lovell 2002). A general intensification of cereals and legumes seems clear, and an increase in storage capacity is visible before the Chalcolithic. The expansion of Chalcolithic settlements into more peripheral areas, such as the Golan and Negev, were probably enabled through the adoption of check dams and floodwater farming in the Negev (Levy 1998: 230; Levy and Alon 1987).

Patterns of animal husbandry are broadly similar to those of the Late Neolithic entities, relying upon domesticated sheep, goat, and cattle, with the addition of pigs where the environment allowed for their higher moisture requirements (Grigson 1998; Price et al. 2013). Caroline Grigson (1998: 251) argues that although sheep and goats dominate most faunal assemblages of Chalcolithic sites, cattle contribute at least 50 percent of the meat. Within the environmental constraints that might allow different frequencies of domesticated animals, the general model is one of sedentary villages with an important element of limited transhumant pastoralism that includes some hunting in a very limited role.

At the same time, cattle probably played a significant role in the secondary products revolution. Skeletal morphology, pathology, and age-class patterns of cattle indicate their use in plowing (Sherratt 1981). Extensive evidence for spinning in the form of bone tools and spindle whorls, coupled with herding strategies, may indicate wool production (Grigson 2006) more than milk production, although some would argue all spinning and weaving equipment was used for flax (Levy and Gilead 2013).

Chalcolithic settlements are distributed more widely than during the previous Late Neolithic, albeit this may be based on a perceived lacunae in Late Neolithic sites. Late Neolithic sites are now documented in the arid zones of the Negev (Rosen et al. 2007) and the eastern Black Desert of Jordan (Rollefson, Rowan, and Wasse 2014; Rowan et al. 2015), as well as the Mediterranean zones. Nevertheless, Chalcolithic sites increase in number and size, best recognized in areas with methodical surveys (Levy 1987; Levy and Alon 1987). Large villages are known, particularly in the Jordan Valley (Teleilat el-Ghassul, Abu Hamid), and the Beersheva region (Shiqmim, Bir es-Safadi, Abu Matar) and more recently, in the north (Marj Rabba [Rowan and Kersel 2014], 'Ein Assawir [Yannai 2006]). There are other smaller sites, but their relationship to larger settlements is unclear.

Building sizes can vary; still, there is little indication of elite structures or formal temple constructions within these settlements. Villages in the northern Negev, however, include subterranean complexes excavated into the hard-packed sediments meters below the surface (Fig. 7.2). These interlinked underground pits, tunnels, and chambers sometimes include underground mud-brick or stone walls and human burials. Living underground seems improbable because the earthen roofs would collapse easily; nevertheless, some were semi-subterranean and could have been used for domestic purposes. Storage seemed to be a strong motivation for the intense amount of work necessary to dig underground. Whether this was a defensive measure or intended for a specific part of the population is unclear. When first identified and excavated, Jean Perrot (1955; 1984) considered them a pioneer phase, built by seminomadic pastoralists as an adaptation to the hot arid environment. Thomas Levy (1998; Levy et al. 1991) suggested that they served as storage and defensive complexes. Isaac Gilead (1994) argued that they were used contemporaneously with the aboveground architecture.

SPIRITUAL AND SOCIAL LANDSCAPE DURING THE CHALCOLITHIC

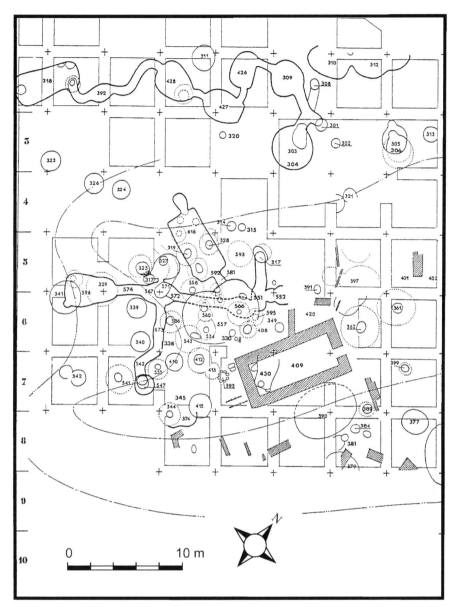

7.2. Site plan of Bir es-Safadi, southern section. Rectilinear architecture on surface is shaded; curvilinear lines represent subterranean features (from Commenge Pellerin 1990; fig. 2a). (Adapted by Y. M. Rowan.)

But the subterranean features had another, possibly secondary function. Articulated skeletons and fragmentary human remains were found within the extensive subterranean features at Shiqmim (Levy et al. 1991). Burials were placed in subterranean chambers and, in at least one example, interred behind a wall closing a chamber off, with a basalt vessel placed at the base (Rowan and Ilan 2013: 101). This suggests that the subterranean features found in the northern Negev Chalcolithic villages served a mortuary function. These may have been the original resting place for the primary inhumation, with reburial in grave circles above the village (Rowan and Ilan 2013). Groups of grave circles on the chalk hills overlooked Shiqmim village on the wadi terrace below. Presumably, these once had a superstructure, possibly of mud brick. Most included disarticulated, poorly preserved, commingled remains. Associated artifacts in the grave circles were few. The secondary treatment of human burials is discussed below.

MATERIAL CULTURE AND PRODUCTION

Chalcolithic flint, pottery, and ground-stone production show continuity with earlier Neolithic traditions, but there are significant changes and innovations. New tool types are introduced and previously minor forms become increasingly significant. Perforated flint discs, some featuring radial spikes, are introduced in the north and Jordan Valley (Rosenberg and Shimelmitz 2017) and date to the Classic Chalcolithic (Fig. 7.3a). Likewise, so-called tabular scrapers (large cortical flakes [Fig. 7.3b]) and bifacial core tools (Fig. 7.3c, d) increase in quantity dramatically, although both existed in the Late Neolithic. The production of blades, primarily for sickles (Fig. 7.3e), continues with minor differences, but large prismatic blades, similar to the Early Bronze Age "Canaanean" blades, appear during the Chalcolithic (Bar and Winter 2010; Rowan and Levy 1994; but see Milevski, Fabian, and Marder 2011). There are indications of more standardized, controlled production of some chipped-stone items, specifically bifacial core tools (adzes, axes, chisels) at the Wadi Ghazzeh sites (Rosen 1997: 104; Roshwalb 1981). Sickle blades, in particular, are increasingly standardized, at least at the Beersheva Basin sites. At Beit Eshel, large quantities ("tens of thousands") contained all stages of blade production, from core to blades, including hammerstones and anvils (Gilead, Davidzon, and Vardi 2010: 224). This significant find suggests some level of specialized production for sickle blades.

Ground-stone artifacts include typical agricultural implements, such as hand stones, grinding slabs, pestles, mortars, and a variety of expedient cobbles and pebbles, typically made of locally available rock. Less common artifacts, such as mace-heads, palettes, violin-shaped figurines, and pendants, are typically made of nonlocal rock selected for qualities of hardness, color, or workability, indicating a level of prestige value (Rowan and Golden 2009). Bowls manufactured of basalt become a hallmark of the period (Fig. 7.4) and are found in small quantities (Amiran and Porat 1984; Rowan 1998). Simple forms of basalt bowls and mortars are found at sites located in basaltic areas, such as the Golan (see Fig. 7.4f, g); however, at sites more distant from sources, they are typically finely worked, sometimes intricately, and often found in burial caves (see

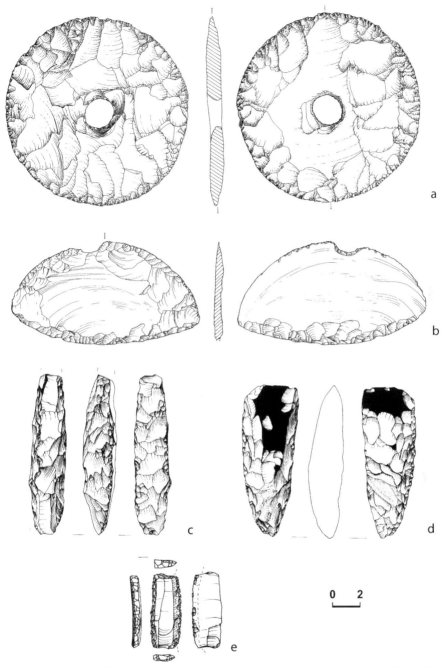

7.3. Flint tools: (a) perforated disc from Golan (from Noy 1998: pl. LIV.1; courtesy of the IAA); (b) fan scraper (from Noy 1998: pl. XLVI.4; courtesy of the IAA); (c) chisel (from Barkai 2004: fig. 7.11:2; courtesy of the Institute of Archaeology of Tel Aviv University); (d) adze (from Barkai 2004: fig. 7.7:2; courtesy of the Institute of Archaeology of Tel Aviv University); and (e) sickle blade (from Noy 1998: pl. LX.14; courtesy of the IAA). (Compiled by Y. M. Rowan.)

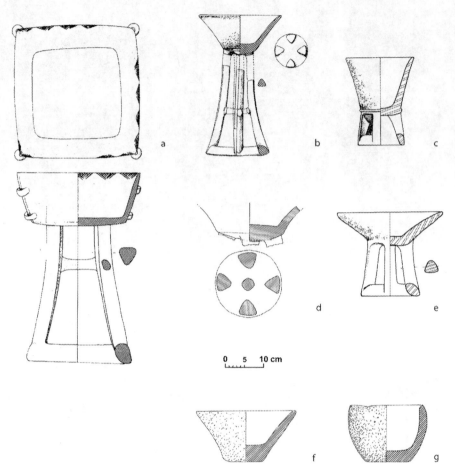

7.4. Basalt vessels: (a) unique pedestaled square vessel from Giv'at ha-Oranim (from Scheftelowitz 2004: fig. 4.7:3; courtesy of the Institute of Archaeology of Tel Aviv University); (b) pedestaled vessel from Peqi'in, with extra interior support (from van den Brink, Rowan, and Braun 1999: fig. 9); (c) pedestaled fenestrated stand from Wadi Zeita; (d) pedestaled bowl fragment with interior extra support from Nahal Qanah (from Gopher and Tsuk 1996: fig. 4.16:3; courtesy of the Institute of Archaeology of Tel Aviv University); (e) pedestaled vessel (after Perrot, Zori, and Reich 1967: fig. 13.1); (f) flared flat base bowl from Golan (from Epstein 1998: pl. 34.9; courtesy of the IAA); and (g) convex bowl from Golan (from Epstein 1998: pl. 36.4; courtesy of the IAA). (Compiled by Y. M. Rowan.)

Fig. 7.4a–e) (van den Brink, Rowan, and Braun 1999). The difficulty of manufacturing these bowls, the technical skill, and the distance to transport such a heavy material indicates that the creators were highly skilled; yet, their variability and low numbers argue against full-time specialists (Rowan 2014a: 229).

Technological advances in pottery production are evident (Fig. 7.5), with a slow wheel used for some vessels (V-shaped bowls in particular) and components of other vessels (Commenge 2006: 403–7). Specific ceramic forms were exchanged between sites in a few cases (Roux 2003), and new forms, such as the cornet, spoon, and ossuaries, were invented. Local clays remained the

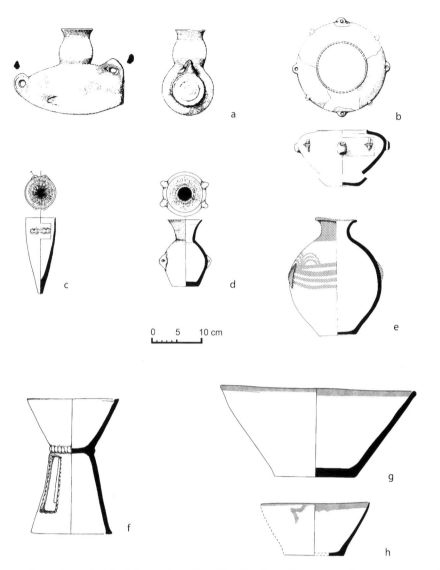

7.5. Ceramic vessels: (a) miniature churn from Kissufim (from Goren 2002: fig. 4.5:3; courtesy of the IAA); (b) amphoriskos from Kissufim (from Goren 2002: fig. 4.4:4; courtesy of the IAA); (c) goblet from Grar (from Gilead and Goren 1995: fig. 4.8:4; courtesy of the Ben-Gurion University of the Negev); (d) jar from Grar (from Gilead and Goren 1995: fig. 4.15:5; courtesy of the Ben-Gurion University of the Negev); (e) jar from Kissufim (from Goren 2002: fig. 4.4:5; courtesy of the IAA); (f) pedestaled fenestrated stand from Golan (from Epstein 1998: pl. 22.1; courtesy of the IAA); and (g, h) open bowls from Giv'at ha-Oranim (from Scheftelowitz 2004: fig. 3.4:6, 9; courtesy of the Institute of Archaeology of Tel Aviv University). (Compiled by Y. M. Rowan.)

primary choice for vessel manufacture, although this requires an expanded and more thorough study. Standardization of some forms is also apparent in contrast to Late Neolithic pottery, and manufacturing techniques integrated the use of the wheel. This suggests that wheel use was not an effort toward greater efficiency.

In addition to these significant changes in the quotidian elements of material culture, the technological skills involved in metal production, from ore extraction to the lost-wax casting method, was a new and dramatic industry for the creation of largely symbolic, nonfunctional items. Whereas other craft production technologies required various levels of expertise, there is little doubt that specialists were necessary for the copper smelting that began during the Chalcolithic (or slightly earlier [see the copper awl from Tel Tsaf (Garfinkel et al. 2014)]). Copper items are often grouped into two general categories: tools, such as adzes, axes, and awls cast in open molds; and prestige objects, such as mace-heads, standards, "crowns," and vessels cast in lost-wax molds (Fig. 7.6). The former is usually cast using oxide-rich ores, while the latter is usually manufactured using what Jonathan Golden (2010) terms "complex metals," copper with arsenic, antimony, and nickel. Although there are exceptions where prestige items were created with relatively pure copper, it remains largely accurate. Complex metals were preferred for the lost-wax casting technique because of fluidity, lower melting point, and superior appearance; yet, they were used for the less functional objects, which would have benefited from the hardness (Rowan and Golden 2009).

Evidence for smelting is best documented at the northern Negev sites of Shiqmim and Abu Matar, Israel, where chemical composition (as well as structure and texture) indicate that the ores were from the Wadi Feinan, Jordan. Some complex metals, however, were derived from more distant and as-yet unidentified regions, possibly in Transcaucasia, Azerbaijan, Syria, or Sinai. Whether originating in Feinan or further afield, ores were nonlocal, difficult to acquire, and worked by people with a skill most people did not hold. Nevertheless, the evidence for household-based copper manufacturing in the Negev argues against centralized workshops or attachment to elite supports, at least using the southern Levantine ores (Golden, Levy, and Hauptmann 2001). The locale for the production of complex metal artifacts, however, is not well attested (Levy and Shalev 1989).

In 1961, the spectacular discovery of more than 400 copper objects in a reed mat secreted in a sheer cliff-face cave 250 m above Nahal Mishmar (Bar-Adon 1980) dramatically shifted our understanding of the copper artifact repertoire. The hundreds of copper standards, mace-heads, vessels, and tools (see Fig. 7.6) led most scholars to agree that the objects were associated with ritual or "cultic" practices (possibly not in the cave). Why they were hidden in this remote and inaccessible cave is unclear. Pessaḥ Bar-Adon (1980: 202) posited that the hoard came from a nearby temple, and David Ussishkin (1980) proposed the 'Ein Gedi sanctuary, 10.5 km north of the cave. Others saw them as similar to commodities of traders or smithies (Gates 1992; Tadmor 1989). Yosef Garfinkel (1994) suggested that the deposit was

SPIRITUAL AND SOCIAL LANDSCAPE DURING THE CHALCOLITHIC

7.6. Copper artifacts from the Nahal Mishmar hoard: (a) cylinder decorated with birds, horns, and knobs (not to scale; dia. 16.8 cm); (b) horn-shaped object with birds and knobs; (c) hollow standard, piriform head (Bar-Adon 1980: 108); (d) chisel (Bar-Adon 1980: 166); and (e) basket handled jars (Bar-Adon 1980: 159, 160, 161). (Photos by C. Amit. Courtesy of the IAA.)

like a *genizeh*, a repository for worn out ritual objects no longer suitable for ceremonial uses. Possibly, they were collected from multiple places to avoid an external threat, or they may have been part of the interment of primary inhumations found inside the cave not far from the deposit (Ilan 1994). Surprisingly, the possible connection to the human burials was largely ignored or missed until recently (Rowan and Ilan 2013), possibly because the deposit is so incredibly rich. The iconography of the artifacts found in the cave may denote mortuary associations and regeneration or rebirth (Ilan and Rowan 2015; Moorey 1988). Other caves with secondary deposits, such as Peqi'in, Nahal Qanah, and Shoham (North), include rich associated finds, although only a few are copper. Whatever the reason for the secluded deposit from Nahal Mishmar, this extraordinary hoard provides insights into technology and symbolism that would have been lacking based on the rare copper finds from other sites.

DEATH AND THE NUMINOUS

The variety of ways to bury the dead expands dramatically during the Chalcolithic. As in previous periods, intramural burials continue during the Chalcolithic, usually single primary interments. This includes infants and fetuses in jars (Mallon, Koeppel, and Neuville 1934; Smith et al. 2006: 335, 338–9), continuing an earlier practice of the Neolithic. Intramural primary multiple burials are also known, typically within sites (e.g., Gilat [Levy et al. 2006; Smith et al. 2006] and Shiqmim [Levy and Alon 1987: fig. 6.1, 6.17a, b]) but also occurring in caves (e.g., Nahal Mishmar). However, the period introduced fundamentally different mortuary activities that extended the burial process, increased the production and burial of mortuary and prestige goods, and established the preference for subterranean spaces for the dead. These alterations reflect an essential shift in world view and perception of how to handle corpses, and imply dramatically different expressions of concerns about the proper treatment of the dead.

Caves, subterranean chambers, and cist graves become common places for the dead during the Chalcolithic. Whether subterranean or above ground, most of these extramural cemeteries were for secondary burials – that is, the exhumation and reburial of the skeleton. Many, particularly those in caves, were placed in clay or stone ossuaries for reburial. The vast majority of the ossuaries were located in caves of the central coastal plain and the piedmont of Israel and Palestine (van den Brink 1998). This includes deep karstic caves, such as Nahal Qanah and Peqi'in, as well as cavities hollowed out in the local softer bedrock (chalk [*kurkar*]) in the piedmont zone paralleling the coastal plain (Fig. 7.7). The furthest east any ossuaries are found come from Shechem

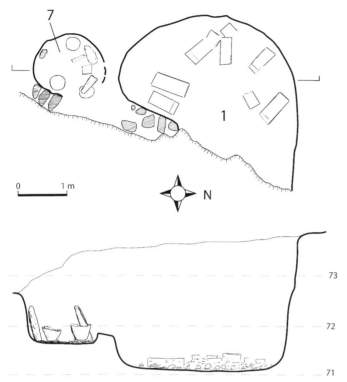

7.7. Burial caves at Giv'atayim, numbers 1 and 7; (top) plan and (bottom) section (after Sussman and Ben-Arieh 1966: fig. 3). (Drawing by Y. M. Rowan.)

(Clamer 1977), while the most northerly were found in the Upper Galilean cave of Peqi'in.

Perrot and Daniel Ladiray (1980) identified three types of Chalcolithic ossuaries: boxes (tubs), structures (so-called houses), and jars. These are primarily ceramic, although stone tubs are also recovered. We can add another fourth style: open ceramic bowls and jars (Rowan 2014b: 105). The most common type is the structural ossuary (Rowan and Ilan 2013: 89), which is most frequently decorated, painted, and modeled with plastic elements (Fig. 7.8a, c, e). Most are painted, often with a prominent Ghassulian nose and eyes, sometimes with breasts (Fig. 7.8d). Peqi'in, the northern karstic cave, had the largest number recovered from a single site, which included features previously unknown in the repertoire of ossuaries (Shalem, Gal, and Smithline 2013), such as modeled and painted ears, painted hair, modeled arms and hands, and mouths. Most appear human, although a few seem more zoomorphic (e.g., Shalem, Gal, and Smithline 2013: 76, fig. 4.66–78, 4.134). Jar ossuaries (Fig. 7.8b) may represent either grain silos (Bar-Yosef and Ayalon 2001) or a chrysalis (Nativ 2008). No matter what the form, the underpinning concept seems to be one intended to expedite regeneration (Rowan and Ilan 2013: 90).

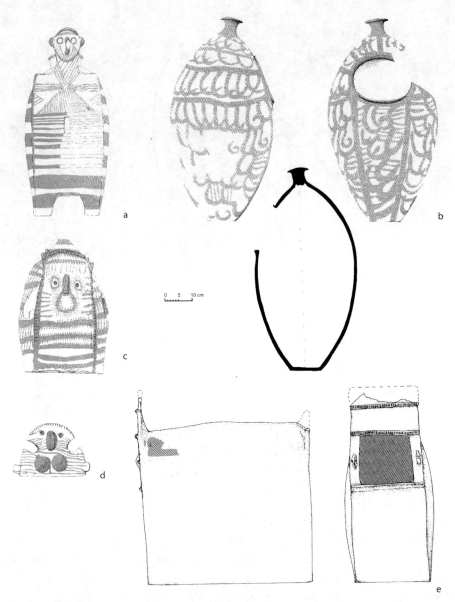

7.8. Ceramic ossuaries: (a) ossuary facade from Peqi'in (from Gal, Smithline, and Shalem 1999: fig. 1; courtesy of the IAA); (b) jar ossuary from Kissufim (from Goren 2002: fig. 4.12; courtesy of the IAA); (c, d) anthropomorphic ossuary facades from Peqi'in (from Gal, Smithline, and Shalem 1999: figs. 5, 7; courtesy of the IAA); and (e) box ossuary from Shoham (North) Cave 2 (from van den Brink 2005: fig. 4.5; courtesy of the IAA). (Compiled by Y. M. Rowan.)

There appears to be a slight regional element to ossuaries (Nativ 2014), and this may be true of burial practices, although neither is very strictly bound. The more arid regions have clusters of grave circles or cists (e.g., Adeimah, Nahal Sekher, Shiqmim, Palmahim). The cemetery burials at Shiqmim may have come from other villages and hamlets as well. Whereas most ossuaries and secondary cave burials are found in the central coast and piedmont, primary burials in caves are occasionally discovered. The Judean Desert, in particular, includes caves with primary burials. The remarkable primary articulated burial of an adult male was uncovered in the "Cave of the Warrior," with a 7 m woven linen shroud, a bow with arrows, prismatic blades, a wooden bowl, and sandals, all treated with powdered red ocher (Schick 1998). Other Judean Desert cave burials are noted, but many were either looted or only examined cursorily. The Judean Desert caves, the Nahal Mishmar hoard, the 'Ein Gedi sanctuary complex, and the springs in the desert may have been interrelated parts of the extended mortuary process, part of a funerary landscape (Ilan and Rowan 2015).

The primacy of secondary burial in caves during the Chalcolithic signals a fundamental transformation in practice and belief that contrasts strongly with the earlier Neolithic. Because the preference is for secondary burial in designated – often remote – subterranean spaces (whether natural or manufactured), the extended mortuary process would have a protracted presence in the lives of people (Rowan and Ilan 2013). This extended ritual cycle increased the desire, or necessity, and the amount of time required to create or collect funerary goods to accompany the interment, particularly with secondary burials.

RITUAL SITES AND RITUAL PRODUCTION

Scholars familiar with the Chalcolithic period of the southern Levant know of its intriguing iconography: the fantastic wall murals from Teleilat el-Ghassul (Drabsch 2015), the zoomorphic and anthropomorphic aspects of ossuaries and vessels, and the evocative metal found at Nahal Mishmar. Coupled with both formal and expedient ritual spaces (Seaton 2008), these expressive symbolic aspects of the period contrast sharply with the previous Late Neolithic and the subsequent Early Bronze Age.

Many scholars would agree that much of this paraphernalia represents something related to spiritual belief and ritual practices. One site widely accepted as a formal ritual complex is 'Ein Gedi. On a remote promontory overlooking the Dead Sea to the east, 'Ein Gedi consists of four primary architectural components: a courtyard, two broad rooms, and a "gatehouse" (Ussishkin 1980: fig. 1). A shallow circular stone feature in the courtyard center may have held a tree or was a shallow pit. The large (19.7 × 5.5 m) main rectilinear building has a stone bench abutting the wall interior. Opposite the entrance, a semicircular stone feature abuts the northern wall, with a nonlocal limestone drum (or altar) found nearby (Ussishkin 1980: fig. 11). A ceramic bull or ram with two churns on its back was recovered in the vicinity. In the floor of the broad room, small shallow pits contained ash, charcoal, and fragments of vessels. One complete fenestrated, pedestaled bowl, like those commonly found in secondary burial contexts, was found turned over atop two ruminant horns. Many other horns were also found in these pits, as were other fenestrated, pedestaled bowls (at least nine) and the base of cornets. Other finds included pendants, beads, and most surprising, a fragment of a predynastic Egyptian alabaster jar, a unique item for the Chalcolithic. Whether a temple (Gilead 2002), sanctuary (Levy 1998; Levy et al. 2006), or shrine (Mazar 2000; Ussishkin 1980), scholarly consensus is that the 'Ein Gedi complex is a specialized ritual complex.

A more complex site posited as ritual in nature is Gilat. Architecture there included round and rectangular buildings primarily of mud brick, large hearths, and small stone features. An extraordinary number of pits cut through these features, and most artifacts were found within pits and fills. The artifact assemblage included two well-known ceramic figurines, the Gilat Lady and the Ram with Cornets. The diverse ceramic repertoire included miniature versions of standard Chalcolithic vessels and rare vessel types, such as tubular beakers, chalices, and the unusual "torpedo jars" – a large, thick walled cylindrical vessel that may have been used to transport olive oil (Burton and Levy 2006). Like at 'Ein Gedi, large numbers of ceramic cornets and fenestrated, pedestaled stands were found; the latter were also created of basalt, a nonlocal material (Rowan et al. 2006). Most ceramic vessels were produced locally, although some were made with nonlocal clays (Goren 1995: 295; 2006: 371). Obsidian, extremely rare at Chalcolithic sites, originated with different sources in Anatolia (Yellin, Levy, and Rowan 1996). A variety of prestige items were manufactured of exogenous rock, including palettes, spindle whorls, and mace-heads, all of which occur in greater numbers than other sites in the southern Levant (Rowan et al. 2006). Another Chalcolithic hallmark, the violin-shaped figurines primarily made of nonlocal rock, are more numerous than at all other sites combined (Commenge 2006).

The rich artifact assemblage and large number of burials may explain one of the central functions of what was interpreted as a central pilgrimage site by the original excavators (Levy 2006). A minimum of ninety individuals were estimated to have been found in a variety of contexts, including fills, pits, and silos (Smith et al. 2006). Burials were apparently primary, although many were scattered bones and otherwise disturbed. In a large shallow mud-brick-lined pit (or silo), nine complete individuals were buried on top of a layer of animal bones and sherds, which were above the paved floor of the structure (Levy et al. 2006: fig. 5.20). Associated with the structure, a mud-lined pit contained a complete fenestrated basalt stand and burned gazelle horn cores (Levy et al. 2006: fig. 5.21). The burned gazelle horn cores are reminiscent of the ruminant horns at 'Ein Gedi and parallel the surprising find of burned gazelle phalanges at Marj Rabba, possibly also associated with human remains (Price et al. 2016).

Burial density at Gilat is extraordinarily high relative to other Chalcolithic sites, reflecting its ritual function (Rowan and Ilan 2007: 251). Together with the material culture, the mortuary aspect distinguishes it from typical cemeteries and villages. The concentration of human remains and evocative symbolic artifacts suggests that the two were intertwined in mortuary rites, one of the central roles fulfilled by this site. Perhaps this represents an additional permutation of a ritual economy (Sabloff 2008; Spielmann 2008), driven by the extended mortuary process.

SYNTHESIS: SOCIAL TRANSFORMATIONS IN THE FIFTH TO EARLY FOURTH MILLENNIA BCE

Rapid technological change, settlement expansion, and increased population size during the Chalcolithic period hint at fundamental changes in the social lives of people living in the southern Levant. The diverse nature of ritual practice, secondary burial processes and the attendant equipment, and ceremonial structures attest to a new and creative approach to living and confronting death. Much of this ritual practice and the economy serving it is recognizably new in contrast to the Late Neolithic. At the same time, this appears neither codified nor homogenous. Different lines of evidence drawing from burial practices and ritual spaces argue against permanent, formal religious authorities (Rowan and Ilan 2012). Ritual practice was not simply a tool that elites controlled, but was present in the daily social lives of people. The feasting pit at Marj Rabba, an early Chalcolithic site in the Lower Galilee, is a good example (Hill, Price, and Rowan 2016).

The Chalcolithic underwent a period of rapid and critical change, one that involved the production of socially valued goods, partially in order to meet the needs of a more demanding ritual cycle. One aspect of this ritual cycle was tied, at least to some extent, to the protracted mortuary treatment that involved burial, exhumation, and subsequent reburial with special equipment in predetermined communal loci, which occurred well after biological death. At the same time, ritual knowledge and performance appears to have operated in several different spheres, including intervillage local practice, more formal sanctuaries, and pilgrimage to distant places. The very presence of these multiple ritual performance places suggests that there was probably a modification of religious belief itself (Fogelin 2007; Ilan and Rowan 2012), although our ability to analyze and discuss prehistoric religious belief and practice continues, ultimately, to rely on definitions of religion as the irrational aspects of the past (Fowles 2013: 4–12).

There remains a great deal to understand about how this dramatic change in social lives and networks affected, or were affected by, other aspects of society, such as political and economic spheres of activity. Our understanding of what role leadership and power had in these different intersecting aspects of daily life remain obscure. Tackling those issues will require more refined chronological and regional outlines in order to establish comparative frameworks for the entire area.

NOTE

1 E.g., for pottery, between the northern Negev and Jordan Valley, see Roux 2003. For flint, possibly from eastern Jordan, see Müller-Neuhof 2013.

REFERENCES

Amiran, R., and Porat, N. 1984. The Basalt Vessels of the Chalcolithic and Early Bronze Age I. *TA* 11: 11–19.

Banning, E. B. 2007. Time and Tradition in the Transition from Late Neolithic to Chalcolithic: Summary and Conclusions. *Paléorient* 33 (1): 137–42.

Bar, S., and Winter, H. 2010. Canaanean Flint Blades in Chalcolithic Context and the Possible Onset of the Transition to the Early Bronze Age: A Case Study from Fazael 2. *TA* 37: 33–47.

Bar-Adon, P. 1980. *The Cave of the Treasure: The Finds from the Caves in Nahal Mishmar.* JDS. Jerusalem: IES.

Bar-Yosef, O., and Ayalon, E. 2001. Chalcolithic Ossuaries—What Do They Imitate and Why? *Qad* 121: 34–43 (Hebrew).

Barkai, R. 2004. The Chalcolithic Lithic Assemblage. In *Giv'at ha-Oranim: A Chalcolithic Site*, ed. N. Scheftelowitz and R. Oren, 87–109. SER 1. Tel Aviv: Tel Aviv University.

——— 2005. The Ceramic Ossuaries. In *Shoham (North): Late Chalcolithic Burial Caves in the Lod Valley, Israel*, ed. E. C. M. van den Brink and R. Gophna, 27–46. IAA Reports 27. Jerusalem: IAA.

Brink, E. C. M. van den. 1998. An Index to Chalcolithic Mortuary Caves in Israel. *IEJ* 48: 165–73.

Brink, E. C. M. van den; Rowan, Y. M.; and Braun, E. 1999. Pedestalled Basalt Bowls of the Chalcolithic: New Variations. *IEJ* 49: 161–83.

Burton, M., and Levy, T. E. 2006. Organic Residue Analysis of Selected Vessels from Gilat—Gilat Torpedo Jars. In *Archaeology, Anthropology and Cult: The Sanctuary at Gilat, Israel*, ed. T. E. Levy, 849–62. AAA. London: Equinox.

Clamer, C. 1977. A Burial Cave near Nablus (Tell Balata). *IEJ* 27: 48.

Commenge, C., with a contribution by T. E. Levy and E. Kansa 2006. Gilat's Ceramics: Cognitive Dimensions of Pottery Production. In *Archaeology, Anthropology and Cult: The Sanctuary at Gilat, Israel*, ed. T. E. Levy, 394–506. AAA. London: Equinox.

Commenge-Pellerin, C. 1990. *La poterie de Safadi (Beershéva) au IVe millénaire avant l'ère chrétienne.* CCRFJ 5. Paris: Paléorient.

Drabsch, B. 2015. *The Mysterious Wall Paintings of Teleilat Ghassul, Jordan in Context.* Monographs of the Sydney University Teleilat Ghassul Project 3. Oxford: Archaeopress.

Dunand, M. 1973. *Fouilles de Byblos V: L'architecture, les tombes, le matériel domestique des origines néolithiques à l'avènement urbain.* 2 vols. Paris: Maisonneuve.

Epstein, C. 1998. *The Chalcolithic Culture of the Golan.* IAA Reports 4. Jerusalem: IAA.

Fogelin, L. 2007. The Archaeology of Religious Ritual. *ARA* 36: 55–71.
Fowles, S. M. 2013. *An Archaeology of Doings: Secularism and the Study of Pueblo Religion.* Santa Fe, NM: School for Advanced Research Press.
Gal, Z.; Smithline, H.; and Shalem, D. 1999. New Iconographic Aspects of Chalcolithic Art: Preliminary Observations on Finds from the Peqi'in Cave. *'Atiqot* 37: 1–16.
Garfinkel, Y. 1994. Ritual Burial of Cultic Objects: The Earliest Evidence. *CAJ* 4: 159–88.
―― 1999. *Neolithic and Chalcolithic Pottery of the Southern Levant.* Qedem 39. Jerusalem: The Institute of Archaeology, The Hebrew University of Jerusalem.
Garfinkel, Y.; Klimscha, F.; Shalev, S.; and Rosenberg, D. 2014. The Beginning of Metallurgy in the Southern Levant: A Late 6th Millennium CalBC Copper Awl from Tel Tsaf, Israel. *PLOS ONE* 9 (3): e92591. https://doi.org/10.1371/journal.pone.0092591 (accessed May 9, 2018).
Gates, M.-H. 1992. Nomadic Pastoralists and the Chalcolithic Hoard from Nahal Mishmar. *Levant* 24: 131–9.
Gilead, I. 1994. The History of the Chalcolithic Settlement in the Nahal Beer Sheva Area: The Radiocarbon Aspect. *BASOR* 296: 1–13.
―― 2002. Religio-Magic Behavior in the Chalcolithic Period of Palestine. In *Aharon Kempinski Memorial Volume: Studies in Archaeology and Related Disciplines*, ed. S. Ahituv and E. D. Oren, 103–28. Beer-Sheva: Ben-Gurion University of the Negev.
―― 2011. Chalcolithic Culture History: Ghassulian and Other Entities in the Southern Levant. In *Culture, Chronology and the Chalcolithic: Theory and Transition*, ed. J. L. Lovell and Y. M. Rowan, 12–24. LSS 9. Oxford: Oxbow.
Gilead, I.; Davidzon, A.; and Vardi, J. 2010. The Ghassulian Sickle Blades Workshop of Beit Eshel, Beer Sheva, Israel. In *Lithic Technology in Metal Using Societies: Proceedings of a UISPP Workshop, Lisbon, September 2006*, ed. B. V. Eriksen, 221–30. Jutland Archaeological Society Publications 67. Højbjerg: Jutland Archaeological Society.
Gilead, I., and Goren, Y. 1995. The Pottery Assemblage from Grar. In *Grar, a Chalcolithic Site in the Northern Negev*, ed. I. Gilead, 137–221. Beer-Sheva 7. Beer-Sheva: Ben-Gurion University of the Negev Press.
Golden, J. M. 2010. *Dawn of the Metal Age: Technology and Society during the Levantine Chalcolithic.* London: Equinox.
Golden, J. M.; Levy, T. E.; and Hauptmann, A. 2001. Recent Discoveries Concerning Ancient Metallurgy at the Chalcolithic (ca. 4000 BC) Village of Shiqmim, Israel. *JAS* 9: 951–63.
Gopher, A. 2012. *Village Communities of the Pottery Neolithic Period in the Menashe Hills, Israel: Archaeological Investigations at the Sites of Nahal Zehora.* MSSMNIA 29. Tel Aviv: Emery and Claire Yass Publications in Archaeology, Institute of Archaeology, Tel Aviv University.
Gopher, A., and Tsuk, T. 1996. *The Nahal Qanah Cave: Earliest Gold in the Southern Levant.* MSSMNIA 12. Tel Aviv: Institute of Archaeology, Tel Aviv University.
Goren, Y. 1995. Shrines and Ceramics in Chalcolithic Israel: The View through the Petrographic Microscope. *Archaeometry* 37: 287–305.
―― 2002. The Pottery Assemblage. In *Kissufim Road: A Chalcolithic Mortuary Site*, ed. Y. Goren and P. Fabian, 21–41. IAA Reports 16. Jerusalem: IAA.
―― 2006. The Technology of the Gilat Pottery Assemblage: A Reassessment. In *Archaeology, Anthropology and Cult: The Sanctuary at Gilat, Israel*, ed. T. E. Levy, 369–93. AAA. London: Equinox.

Gošić, M., and Gilead, I. 2015. Casting the Sacred: Chalcolithic Metallurgy and Ritual in the Southern Levant. In *Defining the Sacred: Approaches to the Archaeology of Religion in the Near East*, ed. N. Laneri, 161–75. Oxford: Oxbow.

Grigson, C. 1998. Plough and Pasture in the Early Economy of the Southern Levant. In *The Archaeology of Society in the Holy Land*, ed. T. E. Levy, 245–68. NAAA. London: Leicester University Press.

——— 2006. Farming? Feasting? Herding? Large Mammals from the Chalcolithic of Gilat. In *Archaeology, Anthropology and Cult: The Sanctuary at Gilat, Israel*, ed. T. E. Levy, 215–319. AAA. London: Equinox.

Hill, A. C.; Price, M. D.; and Rowan, Y. M. 2016. Feasting at Marj Rabba, an Early Chalcolithic Site in the Galilee. *OJA* 35: 127–40.

Ilan, D. 1994. Temples, Treasures and Subterranean Villages: Death's Dominion in the Chalcolithic of Canaan. Presented at the Annual Meeting of ASOR, Chicago, IL.

Ilan, D., and Rowan, Y. M. 2011. Deconstructing and Recomposing the Narrative of Spiritual Life in the Chalcolithic of the Southern Levant (4500–3700 BC). In *Beyond Belief: The Archaeology of Religion and Ritual*, ed. Y. M. Rowan, 89–113. APAAA 21. Hoboken, NJ : Wiley-Blackwell.

——— 2015. The Judean Desert as a Chalcolithic Necropolis. *JMA* 28: 171–94.

Joffe, A. H., and Dessel, J. P. 1995. Redefining Chronology and Terminology for the Chalcolithic of the Southern Levant. *CA* 36: 507–18.

Levy, J., and Gilead, I. 2013. The Emergence of the Ghassulian Textile Industry in the Southern Levant Chalcolithic Period (c. 4500–3900 BCE). In *Textile Production and Consumption in the Ancient Near East: Archaeology, Epigraphy, Iconography*, ed. M.-L. Nosch, H. Koefoed, and E. A. Strand, 26–44. Ancient Textiles Series 12. Oxford: Oxbow.

Levy, T. E. 1998. Cult, Metallurgy and Rank Societies—Chalcolithic Period (ca. 4500–3500 BCE). In *The Archaeology of Society in the Holy Land*, ed. T. E. Levy, 226–44. NAAA. London: Leicester University Press.

Levy, T. E., ed. 1987. *Shiqmim I: Studies Concerning Chalcolithic Societies in the Northern Negev Desert, Israel (1982–1984)*. 2 vols. BAR International Series 356. Oxford: BAR.

Levy, T. E., and Alon, D. 1987. Settlement Patterns along the Nahal Beersheva–Lower Nahal Besor: Models of Subsistence in the Northern Negev. In *Shiqmim I: Studies Concerning Chalcolithic Societies in the Northern Negev Desert, Israel (1982–1984)*, Vol. 1, ed. T. E. Levy, 45–138. BAR International Series 356 (1). Oxford: BAR.

Levy, T. E.; Alon, D.; Grigson, C.; Holl, A.; Goldberg, P.; Rowan, Y. M.; and Smith, P. 1991. Subterranean Settlement in the Negev Desert, c. 4500–3700 BC. *National Geographic Research & Exploration* 7: 394–413.

Levy, T. E.; Alon, D.; Rowan, Y. M.; and Kersel, M. M. 2006. The Sanctuary Sequence: Excavations at Gilat, 1975–77, 1989, 1990–92. In *Archaeology, Anthropology and Cult: The Sanctuary at Gilat, Israel*, ed. T. E. Levy, 95–212. AAA. London: Equinox.

Levy, T. E., and Shalev, S. 1989. Prehistoric Metalworking in the Southern Levant: Archaeometallurgical and Social Perspectives. *WA* 20: 352–72.

Lovell, J. L. 2002. Shifting Subsistence Patterns: Some Ideas about the End of the Chalcolithic in the Southern Levant. *Paléorient* 28 (1): 89–102.

Mallon, A.; Koeppel, R.; and Neuville, R. 1934. *Teleilat Ghassul I: Compte rendu des fouilles de l'Institut Biblique Pontifical, 1929–32*. Scripta Pontificii Instituti Biblici 87. Rome: Pontifical Biblical Institute.

Mazar, A. 2000. A Sacred Tree in the Chalcolithic Shrine at En-Gedi: A Suggestion. *Bulletin of the Anglo-Israel Society* 18: 31–6.

Milevski, I.; Fabian, P.; and Marder, O. 2011. Canaanean Blades in Chalcolithic Contexts of the Southern Levant? In *Culture, Chronology and the Chalcolithic: Theory and Transition*, ed. J. L. Lovell and Y. M. Rowan, 149–59. LSS 9. Oxford: Oxbow.

Moorey, P. R. S. 1988. The Chalcolithic Hoard from Nahal Mishmar, in Context. *WA* 20: 171–89.

Müller-Neuhof, B. 2013. SW-Asian Late Chalcolithic/EB Demand for "Big Tools": Specialised Flint Exploitation Beyond the Fringes of Settled Regions. *Lithic Technology* 38: 220–36.

Nativ, A. 2008. A Note on Chalcolithic Ossuary Jars: A Metaphor for Metamorphosis. *TA* 35: 209–14.

―― 2014. *Prioritizing Death and Society: The Archaeology of Chalcolithic and Contemporary Cemeteries in the Southern Levant*. AAA. Durham: Acumen.

Noy, T. 1998. The Flint Artifacts. In *The Chalcolithic Culture of the Golan*, ed. C. Epstein, 269–99. IAA Reports 4. Jerusalem: IAA.

Perrot, J. 1955. The Excavations at Tell Abu Matar, near Beersheba. *IEJ* 5: 17–40, 73–84, 167–89.

―― 1984. Structures d'habitat, mode de vie et environnement: Les villages souterrains des pasteurs de Beershéva, dans le sud d'Israël, au IVe millénaire avant l'ère chrétienne. *Paléorient* 10 (1): 75–96.

Perrot, J., and Ladiray, D. 1980. *Tombes à ossuaires de la région côtière palestinienne au IVe millénaire avant l'ère chrétienne*. MTCRPFJ 1. Paris: Paléorient.

Perrot, J.; Zori, N.; and Reich, Y. 1967. Neve Ur, un nouvel aspect du Ghassoulien. *IEJ* 17: 201–32.

Price, M. D.; Buckley, M.; Kersel, M. M.; and Rowan, Y. M. 2013. Animal Management Strategies during the Chalcolithic in the Lower Galilee: New Data from Marj Rabba (Israel). *Paléorient* 39 (2): 183–200.

Price, M. D.; Hill, A. C.; Rowan, Y. M.; and Kersel, M. M. 2016. Gazelles, Liminality, and Chalcolithic Ritual: A Case Study from Marj Rabba, Israel. *BASOR* 376: 7–27.

Rollefson, G.; Rowan, Y. M.; and Wasse, A. 2014. The Late Neolithic Colonization of the Eastern Badia of Jordan. *Levant* 46: 285–301.

Rosen, S. A. 1997. *Lithics after the Stone Age: A Handbook of Stone Tools from the Levant*. Walnut Creek, CA: AltaMira.

―― 2011. Desert Chronologies and Periodization Systems. In *Culture, Chronology and the Chalcolithic: Theory and Transition*, ed. J. L. Lovell and Y. M. Rowan, 71–83. LSS 9. Oxford: Oxbow.

Rosen, S. A.; Bocquentin, F.; Avni, Y.; and Porat, N. 2007. Investigations at Ramat Saharonim: A Desert Neolithic Sacred Precinct in the Central Negev. *BASOR* 346: 1–27.

Rosenberg, D., and Shimelmitz, R. 2017. Networks of Prestige Item Exchange and the Role of Perforated Flint Objects in the Late Chalcolithic of the Southern Levant. *CA* 58: 295–306.

Roshwalb, A. F. 1981. *Protohistory in the Wadi Ghazzeh: A Typological and Technological Study Based on the Macdonald Excavations*. PhD diss., University of London.

Roux, V. 2003. A Dynamic Systems Framework for Studying Technological Change: Application to the Emergence of the Potter's Wheel in the Southern Levant. *JAMT* 10: 1–30.

Rowan, Y. M. 1998. *Ancient Distribution and Deposition of Prestige Objects: Basalt Vessels during Late Prehistory in the Southern Levant*. PhD diss., The University of Texas at Austin.

———. 2014a. The Southern Levant (Cisjordan) during the Chalcolithic Period. In *The Oxford Handbook of the Archaeology of the Levant, c. 8000–332 BCE*, ed. M. L. Steiner and A. E. Killebrew, 223–36. Oxford: Oxford University Press.

———. 2014b. The Mortuary Process in the Chalcolithic Period. In *Masters of Fire: Copper Age Art from Israel*, ed. M. Sebbanne, O. Misch-Brandl, and D. M. Master, 100–13. New York: Institute for the Study of the Ancient World; Princeton: Princeton University Press.

Rowan, Y. M., and Golden, J. M. 2009. The Chalcolithic Period of the Southern Levant: A Synthetic Review. *JWP* 22: 1–92.

Rowan, Y. M., and Ilan, D. 2007. The Meaning of Ritual Diversity in the Chalcolithic of the Southern Levant. In *Cult in Context: Reconsidering Ritual in Archaeology*, ed. D. Barrowclough and C. Malone, 249–54. Oxford: Oxbow.

———. 2013. The Subterranean Landscape of the Southern Levant during the Chalcolithic Period. In *Sacred Darkness: A Global Perspective on the Ritual Use of Caves*, ed. H. Moyes, 87–107. Boulder: University Press of Colorado.

Rowan, Y. M., and Kersel, M. M. 2014. New Perspectives on the Chalcolithic Period in the Galilee: Investigations at the Site of Marj Rabba. In *Material Culture Matters: Essays on the Archaeology of the Southern Levant in Honor of Seymour Gitin*, ed. J. R. Spencer, R. A. Mullins, and A. J. Brody, 221–37. Winona Lake, IN: Published on behalf of the W. F. Albright Institute of Archaeology by Eisenbrauns.

Rowan, Y. M., and Levy, T. E. 1994. Proto-Canaanean Blades of the Chalcolithic Period. *Levant* 26: 167–74.

Rowan, Y. M.; Levy, T. E.; Alon, D.; and Goren, Y. 2006. Gilat's Ground Stone Assemblage: Stone Fenestrated Stands, Bowls, Palettes and Related Artifacts. In *Archaeology, Anthropology and Cult: The Sanctuary at Gilat*, ed. T. E. Levy, 575–684. AAA. London: Equinox.

Rowan, Y. M.; Rollefson, G. O.; Wasse, A.; Abu-Azizeh, W.; Hill, A. C.; and Kersel, M. M. 2015. The "Land of Conjecture": New Late Prehistoric Discoveries at Maitland's Mesa and Wisad Pools, Jordan. *JFA* 40: 176–89.

Sabloff, J. A. 2008. Considerations of Ritual Economy. In *Dimensions of Ritual Economy*, ed. E. C. Wells and P. A. McAnany, 269–77. REA 27. Bingley: Emerald.

Saideh, R. 1979. Fouilles de Sidon-Dakerman: L'agglomération chalcolithique. *Berytus* 27: 29–55.

Scheftelowitz, N. 2004. The Pottery Assemblage. In *Giv'at Ha-Oranim: A Chalcolithic Site*, ed. N. Scheftelowitz and R. Oren, 37–58. SER 1. Tel Aviv: Tel Aviv University.

Schick, T. 1998. *The Cave of the Warrior: A Fourth Millennium Burial in the Judean Desert, Israel*. IAA Reports 5. Jerusalem: IAA.

Seaton, P. 2008. *Chalcolithic Cult and Risk Management at Teleilat Ghassul: The Area E Sanctuary*. Monographs of the Sydney University Teleilat Ghassul Project 2; BAR International Series 1864. Oxford: Archaeopress.

Shalem, D.; Gal, Z.; and Smithline, H. 2013. *Peqi'in: A Late Chalcolithic Burial Site, Upper Galilee, Israel*. Land of Galilee 2. Jerusalem: Ostracon.

Sherratt, A. G. 1981. Plough and Pastoralism: Aspects of the Secondary Products Revolution. In *Patterns of the Past: Studies in Honour of David Clarke*, ed. I. Hodder, G. Isaac, and N. Hammond, 261–305. Cambridge: Cambridge University Press.

Smith, P.; Zagerson, T.; Sabari, P.; Golden, J. M.; Levy, T. E.; and Dawson, L. 2006. Death and the Sanctuary: The Human Remains from Gilat. In *Archaeology, Anthropology and Cult: The Sanctuary at Gilat, Israel*, ed. T. E. Levy, 327–66. AAA. London: Equinox.

Spielmann, K. A. 2008. Crafting the Sacred: Ritual Places and Paraphernalia in Small-Scale Societies. In *Dimensions of Ritual Economy*, ed. E. C. Wells and P. A. McAnany, 37–72. REA 27. Bingley: Emerald.

Sussman, V., and Ben-Arieh, S. 1966. Ancient Burials in Giv'atayim. *'Atiqot* 3: 27–39 (Hebrew; English summary on p. 4*).

Tadmor, M. 1989. The Judean Desert Treasure from Nahal Mishmar: A Chalcolithic Traders' Hoard? In *Essays in Ancient Civilization Presented to Helene J. Kantor*, ed. A. Leonard Jr. and B. B. Williams, 249–61. SAOC 47. Chicago: The Oriental Institute of The University of Chicago.

Ussishkin, D. 1980. The Ghassulian Shrine at En-Gedi. *TA* 7: 1–44.

Yannai, E. 2006. *'En Esur ('Ein Asawir) I: Excavations at a Protohistoric Site in the Coastal Plain of Israel*. IAA Reports 31. Jerusalem: IAA.

Yellin, J.; Levy, T. E.; and Rowan, Y. M. 1996. New Evidence on Prehistoric Trade Routes: The Obsidian Evidence from Gilat, Israel. *JFA* 23: 361–8.

EIGHT

USING ARCHAEOBOTANICAL REMAINS TO MODEL SOCIAL, POLITICAL, AND ECONOMIC CHANGES DURING THE CHALCOLITHIC PERIOD IN THE SOUTHERN LEVANT

PHILIP GRAHAM

In late prehistory, as during the earlier Neolithic period, agriculture formed the base of the economic system. In order to understand the complex social and political economic changes that took place during late prehistory, it is essential to understand how people got their food and how agricultural tasks were organized at the household and site levels. More than just helping us know what people were eating in the past, archaeobotanical remains enable us to better understand the significant changes that took place during later prehistory. During the Neolithic, plants and animals were domesticated for the first time, and the imposition of an agricultural regime as a fundamental part of daily life began a process of gradually increasing social, political, and economic complexity that accelerated during the subsequent Chalcolithic period (Tzori 1958; Banning 2002). In the southern Levant, the period between the Neolithic and the Bronze Age is called the Chalcolithic, or "Copper Stone Age." The Chalcolithic is important because it was a time of social, political, and economic change, marking the transition of small egalitarian villages of the Neolithic into the first territorial states during the Bronze Age (Yakar 1985; Hanbury-Tenison 1986; Gilead 1988; Golden 1998; Bourke 2001; Rowan and Golden 2009;). Relatively little was known about the agricultural system of the Chalcolithic. Fortunately, recent studies have begun to provide information about Chalcolithic agriculture that, in turn, helps us to better understand the social and political changes taking place during this period.

The botanical remains from three Chalcolithic sites were analyzed with the goal of understanding the agricultural system of the Chalcolithic and how this system may have facilitated increasingly complex political structures. The three sites chosen, Tel Tsaf in the Jordan River Valley, Marj Rabba in the Galilee region, and Shiqmim in the Negev Desert, each represent a different environmental region within the Levant. The hope was that the data from these three Chalcolithic sites would enable us to understand the different agricultural strategies used to adapt to different environmental conditions.[1]

BACKGROUND

Tel Tsaf is located in the Jordan River Valley (Gophna 1979; Garfinkel et al. 2007). The area around Tel Tsaf is characterized by Irano-Touranian vegetation and receives approximately 300 mm of rainfall a year (Liphschitz 1988). The cutoff for successfully engaging in rain-fed agriculture is 200 mm of precipitation a year, putting Tel Tsaf firmly in the zone of successful rain-fed agriculture (Issar and Zohar 2004). At Tel Tsaf, the fertile soil, numerous springs, and proximity to the Jordan River make this productive agricultural land that continues to be used to grow crops today. The eighteen large grain silos excavated at Tel Tsaf attest to the region's productivity during the Chalcolithic (Garfinkel, Ben-Shlomo, and Kuperman 2009).

Marj Rabba is located in the Galilee region and falls within the Mediterranean vegetation zone (Rowan and Kersel 2014). This type of biome typically has wet winters and warm, dry summers. The region would have received ample amounts of precipitation to conduct rain-fed agriculture (Heusinkveld et al. 2004). Marj Rabba is located in the uplands with no obvious nearby year-round source of water. The inhabitants of Marj Rabba had no other option but to engage in rain-fed agriculture.

Shiqmim is located on the border of two climatic zones, positioning its inhabitants to take advantage of a wide variety of resources (Levy and Alon 1985). Irano-Taurian flora dominates approximately six miles to the north of Shiqmim, while six miles south, Saharo-Arabian flora prevails (Levy and Goldberg 1987). The site is within the 150 mm a year precipitation isohyet, making it difficult to grow crops there without some kind of water management system. The site's location adjacent to a wadi was instrumental in the inhabitant's success at maintaining an agricultural regime (Kislev 1987).

CHALCOLITHIC AGRICULTURE

Scholars cite various changes that have been documented for this period, including new stone tool technologies; larger settlements; distinctive ceramics; the exploitation of new resources as evidenced by, for example, butter churns;

and the metallurgical technology that gives the period its name (Gilead 1988; Golden 1998; Levy 1998; Bourke 2001; Rowan and Golden 2009). Also widely debated is the sociopolitical organization of the period with arguments ranging from chiefdoms to egalitarian villages, to some form of politically complex but unranked society, such as sodalities. Archaeobotany is useful here because ethnographic evidence suggests that each of these types of sociopolitical organization require different levels of surplus production in order to support the system (Childe 1950; Carneiro 1970; Redman 1978; Wittfogel 1981; Stein and Rothman 1994; Earle 1997). For example, innovations such as water management systems, even on a small scale, may necessitate some kind of community leadership to organize the timing, as well as the labor necessary to complete the project.

The data from Tel Tsaf, Marj Rabba, and Shiqmim suggest that the changes begun during the Neolithic were facilitated during the Chalcolithic by an agricultural economy undergoing a period of intensification where new agricultural techniques and methods were being introduced, enabling greater food production. The results of these innovations were fully realized during the Early Bronze Age, when the first territorial states emerged in the region. A more complex agro-economy necessitates more complex political and social structures in order to manage the agricultural fields, as well as the postharvest processing and storage of comestibles (Stevens 2003).

The analysis of the composition of botanical remains throughout an archaeological site enables an understanding of how agricultural tasks were organized and carried out on both a site-wide and individual household level. Individual versus site-based organization of agricultural tasks can potentially act as a proxy for the complexity of political or social organizational structures (Stevens 2003). When this type of analysis is carried out at sites from the Neolithic, Chalcolithic, and Early Bronze periods, the timing of these changes can be better understood, which is important in understanding the role changing agricultural systems in other areas of development, such as craft specialization, metallurgy, and, eventually, highly stratified societies.

DATA ANALYSIS

Biases

Each of the datasets discussed suffer from certain biases; thus, they have to be understood as part of an interpretation process. Comparing archaeobotanical data between sites is notoriously difficult but necessary in order to investigate trends. One major source of bias in the data is the preservation of the archaeobotanical remains. Plant remains typically preserve via carbonization, which can render them sensitive to destruction (Boardman and Jones 1990; Jupe 2003; Braadbaart et al. 2004; Braadbaart and van Bergen 2005). For example,

TABLE 8.1. *The total number of samples, specimens, and taxa at Tel Tsaf, Shiqmim, and Marj Rabba.*

	Tel Tsaf	Shiqmim	Marj Rabba
Total number of samples	92	18	121
Total number of specimens	3,506	34,801	268
Total number of taxa	67	98	37

of the three sites discussed here, the preservation at Marj Rabba was very poor. Even though a large number of samples were collected, the remains from Marj Rabba yielded relatively little data (Table 8.1). The preservation at Marj Rabba was impacted by the high level of bioturbation observed at the site during excavation and the lack of pyric features recovered.

Archaeobotanical assemblages can be biased by the number of samples collected and the density of carbonized remains recovered. The density of carbonized remains is determined, in part, by the number of pyric features sampled. For example, both Tel Tsaf and Shiqmim have excellent preservation and more samples came from Tel Tsaf. However, most of the Tel Tsaf samples and all but one of the Marj Rabba samples do not come from pyric contexts, while almost all of the Shiqmim samples had some evidence of burning or contained waste from pyric features.

Fuel Choice

In Southwest Asia, wood and animal dung are the two types of fuel commonly encountered (Miller 1984). Fuel preference has been used as a proxy for the availability of wood in ancient environments (Miller 1985). Dung can also provide information about how animals were fed and weed seeds found in dung can provide information about the local environment (Anderson and Ertug-Yaras 1998). At Tel Tsaf, Shiqmim, and Marj Rabba, the preference was for wood (Fig. 8.1; Table 8.2).

At Tel Tsaf, the pattern of fuel use is clear; all of the pyric features contained only carbonized wood with no evidence of carbonized animal dung. The carbonized animal dung recovered at Tel Tsaf comes from non-pyric contexts, such as the contents of a buried jar. A previous study on wood remains at Tel Tsaf found pistachio, oak, poplar, tamarisk, olive, and jujube (Liphschitz 1988). These identifications are consistent with the environment around Tel Tsaf and are evidence that wood was available near the site in antiquity.

At Marj Rabba, the pattern of fuel use is much less clear due to the overall poor preservation. The single pyric feature excavated at Marj Rabba, a hearth, contained mostly unidentifiable ash and only a very small amount of highly fragmented wood. These pieces were too small to attempt any identification.

TABLE 8.2. *Fuel choice at Tel Tsaf, Shiqmim, and Marj Rabba, given in ml.*

	Tel Tsaf	**Shiqmim**	**Marj Rabba**
Wood	873.16	87.85	6.42
Carbonized dung	1.38	50.73	0.3

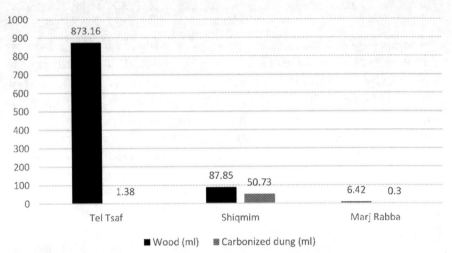

8.1. The amount of carbonized wood versus carbonized animal dung at Tel Tsaf, Shiqmim, and Marj Rabba, illustrating fuel preference at each site. (Graph by P. Graham.)

The excellent preservation at Shiqmim provided a clear picture of fuel use. Most of the carbonized wood, the majority of which has preliminarily been identified as tamarisk, came from ash pits, which are hypothesized to be dumps for products associated with smelting. The animal dung, by contrast, is found almost exclusively in domestic contexts, such as hearths within house structures. There is also evidence that metallurgy was taking place at Shiqmim (Levy and Alon 1985; Golden, Levy, and Hauptmann 2001). Smelting typically requires high temperatures, and wood burns at a higher temperature than animal dung. Given the available paleoenvironmental data, wood was likely not available in large quantities around Shiqmim. One way of interpreting the fuel data from Shiqmim is that the inhabitants were practicing an optimized fuel strategy, where wood fuel was reserved largely for smelting, and animal dung was used for domestic activities, such as cooking and heating.

Cultivars

Barley is the primary cultivar at Tel Tsaf and Shiqmim, while emmer wheat predominates at Marj Rabba (Figs. 8.2–8.4). Much of the barley found at Tel Tsaf comes from a single grain silo. Since only a few silos were sampled for botanical remains, we cannot assume that barley was the primary cultivar. Certainly, the

ARCHAEOBOTANICAL REMAINS TO MODEL CHALCOLITHIC CHANGES 151

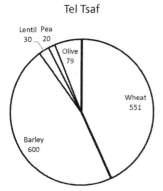

8.2. The cultivars from Tel Tsaf. (Chart by P. Graham.)

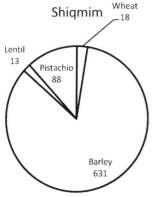

8.3. The cultivars from Shiqmim. (Chart by P. Graham.)

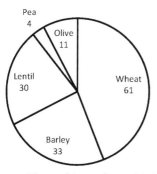

8.4. The cultivars from Marj Rabba. (Chart by P. Graham.)

large amount of emmer that was also recovered from Tel Tsaf, especially from domestic contexts, indicates that wheat was also very important.

Historically, barley was often grown in order to feed animals (Charles 1996; Jones 1998). At Shiqmim – the only one of these three sites where large quantities of animal dung were recovered – there is no correlation between the presence of dung and the presence of barley. This suggests that barley may not have been a major component of animal food at Shiqmim, or it was used only seasonally.

Lentils were recovered from all three sites and pea was found at Tel Tsaf and Marj Rabba. There are known factors that bias the preservation and recovery of cereals over legumes, so it is difficult to assess the importance of legumes relative to cereals since cereals are typically overrepresented and legumes typically underrepresented. Other important economic taxa include olive at Tel Tsaf and Marj Rabba, and pistachio at Shiqmim.

The timing of the domestication of cultivated fruits, such as olive, has been widely debated (Breton et al. 2009; Liphschitz et al. 1991). By the Early Bronze Age, the presence of olive oil installations, pottery vessels with oil residue, and ceramic oil lamps attest to a robust olive oil industry. During the Chalcolithic, the question is to what degree these resources were being exploited.

The timing of the widespread cultivation of olive is currently being studied. The key switch is from sexual reproduction, where there are variable genetics, to vegetative reproduction – this leads to the maintenance of preferred genotypes (Breton et al. 2009). Whether olive was cultivated or not during the Chalcolithic is not clear, but olive was actively being exploited during the period. At some Chalcolithic sites, such as Rasm Harbush, there is evidence that olives were being crushed and pressed for small-scale oil extraction (Epstein 1993). At other sites, such as Tel Tsaf, where there is no evidence of oil pressing, although olive was likely part of the diet.

AGRICULTURAL INTENSIFICATION DURING THE CHALCOLITHIC

Of the three sites discussed here, the remains from Marj Rabba are too poorly preserved to offer any archaeobotanical evidence for intensification. However, the well-preserved archaeobotanical remains from Tel Tsaf and Shiqmim both show evidence of a robust agricultural system (Table 8.3). The archaeological evidence illustrates that the Chalcolithic was a period of change and transition where new technologies were innovated, and we suggest that the agricultural system should be viewed within this paradigm of innovation.

Tel Tsaf

The archaeobotanical data from Tel Tsaf is compelling; the twenty-one silo structures illustrate that large amounts of grain were being stored (Garfinkel et al. 2007). The carbonized plant remains recovered from the silos are relatively free of processing debris and, instead, contain sizable amounts of *Lolium* and other wild grasses that are of a similar size to domesticated wheat and barley (Graham 2014). Chris Stevens (2003) argues that how crops were stored can be used as a proxy for the availability of labor. Because harvest is a busy time, a community's labor resources are stressed. Cereal grains must be harvested and dried before being put into storage. Cereal processing, which follows a series of stages that are largely similar throughout the world, requires additional labor that may not always be available at harvest time (Hillman 1984; Jones 1984). Stored clean grains may suggest a greater availability of labor, since it takes significantly more time to process and clean cereals before placing them in storage. The removal of mimic weeds, like *Lolium*, is typically one of the final stages of cereal processing, suggesting that the storage of relatively clean grains at Tel Tsaf may have required a higher level of social organization.[2]

The inhabitants of Tel Tsaf appear to have been growing large amounts of food, and this suggests an agricultural system that is becoming increasingly sophisticated. There are two broad types of strategies that can be used to grow more food – intensification and extensification. Intensification is a strategy whereby inhabitants attempt to produce a larger amount of food per acre, while extensification means bringing more land under cultivation. Perhaps the most powerful evidence of extensification at Tel Tsaf comes from Austin Hill's (2011) evidence for cattle being used for traction. If cattle were being used to pull plows, this would reduce the labor costs of agriculture and enable Tel Tsaf's inhabitants to bring more land under cultivation.

TABLE 8.3. *A summary of the archaeobotanical remains found at Tel Tsaf, Shiqmim, and Marj Rabba.*

	Tel Tsaf	Shiqmim	Marj Rabba
Grasses			
Triticum sp.	551	18	61
Hordeum sp. (Cultivated, Straight, or Twisted)	600	631	33
Legumes			
Vicia ervilia	3	0	3
Lens culinaris	30	13	30
Pisum sativum	20	0	4
Trees			
Olea europaea	79	0	11
Cereal chaff/Processing debris			
Rachis	18	7,760	25
Spikelet Forks	318	287	9
Glume Bases	363	337	3
Culm Fragments	67	24,819	11
Wild taxa	1,441	928	77
Total number of specimens	3,490	34,793	267

While using animals to pull plows has obvious benefits, it also necessitates changes to the agricultural system. Plowing helps accelerate the loss of soil fertility. Plowed fields can typically only grow cereal crops for two to three years before the field's fertility is exhausted (Duiker and Beegle 2006). Strategies to mitigate fertility loss and restore fertility include growing a beneficial cover crop during periods when the fields are lying fallow and adding dung fertilizer to the field to help add nutrients back into the soil.

While relatively small amounts of dung were recovered in the macrobotanical samples, the micromorphology from Tel Tsaf showed that dung was present in some areas of the site but not in pyric features (Hubbard 2010). If dung was being curated at the site but not used for fuel, one hypothesis for an alternative use for the dung is as fertilizer. In an agricultural regime where plowing was regularly employed, dung fertilizer would have played an important part in maintaining the fertility of agricultural fields. Other important strategies for helping to maintain soil fertility include rotating the fields through a fallow regime and growing beneficial cover crops (Heichel 1987). In the archaeobotanical remains, the wild taxa are dominated by weedy legumes, such as *Scorpiurus* species. These legumes are beneficial cover crops that also serve as excellent browse for ruminant animals (Maymone, Dattilo, and Mazziotti di Celso 1953; Pülschen 1992; Abbate et al. 2010).

Shiqmim

The lack of rainfall at Shiqmim means that successful agriculture could only be practiced with the assistance of some kind of water management system, such as irrigation. Like the example discussed above about storing clean grain, water management systems also demand a higher level of social organization to manage the labor involved in creating and maintaining the irrigation system. In her study of the phytolith remains at Shiqmim, Arlene Rosen (1987) argued that the remains suggested the site's inhabitants employed run-off irrigation. In this type of spate irrigation, water would have been diverted from the nearby wadi adjacent to the site for agricultural production. In many parts of the world, spate irrigation is a low-cost strategy to successfully grow crops in a dry environment (van Steenbergen 1997). This type of irrigation does not necessarily leave standing water in agricultural fields as much of it is absorbed into the sediment. The dominance of barley at Shiqmim could possibly be explained as an adaptation to the local environment, since barley is more tolerant of salt, something that can build up in agricultural soils over time when irrigation is practiced (Young 2001; Fischbeck 2002; Grando and Gómez Macpherson 2005; Mehari, Schultz, and Depeweg 2006).

CONCLUSION

The Chalcolithic period in the Levant has widely been viewed as a period of change and development, and the evidence from Shiqmim and Tel Tsaf suggest that the agricultural system of this period should be viewed as part of this paradigm of change. In many ways, innovations in the agricultural system can be viewed as an extension of the secondary products revolution, which also began during this period and saw people increasingly exploiting secondary products from animals, such as milk (Sherratt 1981; Grigson 2000; Fall, Falconer, and Lines 2002; Miller 2003; Isaakidou 2006; Greenfield 2010). At Tel Tsaf, the use of animal traction would have resulted in a large increase in agricultural yields. This innovation would have required further changes to the agricultural economy, perhaps including the use of fertilizer and cover cropping, to boost fertility. At Shiqmim, the site's inhabitants may have experimented with a water management system to maximize their agricultural output in a relatively dry environment. The organization of fuel, where dung was perhaps used in domestic contexts and wood for metallurgy, further demonstrates a sophisticated understanding of how to optimize plant resources.

We hypothesize that the agricultural revolution that took place during the Neolithic was followed by what may be termed an "intensification revolution" during the Chalcolithic, where farmers, increasingly comfortable with agriculture, optimize their systems to grow more crops. One important contribution that archaeobotany can make to our understanding of the Chalcolithic is whether or not a changing social and political system was driving changes in the agro-economy, leading to increased production, or if surplus agricultural production happened first, and then the presence of increasingly large surpluses provided communities the opportunity to develop increasingly complex political structures. The archaeobotanical remains from more Chalcolithic sites will need to be analyzed further to answer this question and better understand the role that agriculture played in the development of complex societies.

ACKNOWLEDGMENTS

I would like to thank Alexia Smith for allowing me to use the collections at the University of Connecticut and for her advice and help at all stages of my research. I am deeply indebted to Yosef Garfinkel for allowing me to work on the Tel Tsaf project and analyze the archaeobotanical remains as well as to the project's staff, especially David Ben-Shlomo and Michael Friekman. I also want to thank Tom Levy for allowing me to work on the Shiqmim archaeobotanical samples, as well as Morag Kersel and Yorke Rowan for allowing me to work on the Marj Rabba material and for their advice and support. I am also grateful to the staff of the Galilee Prehistory Project, especially Joyce Fountain and Ani Marty. Without their support, this research would not have been possible. Finally, I would like to thank Austin "Chad" Hill. Our many discussions and collaborations were instrumental to the development of the ideas presented in this chapter.

NOTES

1 For more information about the botanical remains at Tel Tsaf, see Graham 2014. The botanical reports for Shiqmim and Marj Rabba are forthcoming.
2 For a longer discussion of social complexity and agriculture at Tel Tsaf, see Graham 2014.

REFERENCES

Abbate, V.; Maugeri, G.; Cristaudo, A.; and Gresta, F. 2010. *Scorpiurus muricatus* L. subsp. *subvillosus* (L.) Thell., a Potential Forage Legume Species for a Mediterranean Environment: A Review. *Grass and Forage Science* 65 (1): 2–10.

Anderson, S., and Ertug-Yaras, F. 1998. Fuel Fodder and Faeces: An Ethnographic and Botanical Study of Dung Fuel Use in Central Anatolia. *EnArch* 1: 99–109.

Banning, E. B. 2002. Consensus and Debate on the Late Neolithic and Chalcolithic of the Southern Levant. *Paléorient* 28 (2): 148–55.

Boardman, S., and Jones, G. 1990. Experiments on the Effects of Charring on Cereal Plant Components. *JAS* 17: 1–11.

Bourke, S. J. 2001. The Chalcolithic Period. In *The Archaeology of Jordan*, ed. B. MacDonald, R. Adams, and P. Bienkowski, 107–62. LA 1. Sheffield: Sheffield Academic.

Braadbaart, F., and van Bergen, P. F. 2005. Digital Imaging Analysis of Size and Shape of Wheat and Pea upon Heating under Anoxic Conditions as a Function of the Temperature. *VHA* 14: 67–75.

Braadbaart, F.; Boon, J. J.; van der Horst, J.; and van Bergen, P. F. 2004. Laboratory Simulations of the Transformation of Peas as a Result of Heating: The Change of the Molecular Composition by DTMS. *Journal of Analytical and Applied Pyrolysis* 71: 997–1026.

Breton, C.; Terral, J.-F.; Pinatel, C.; Médail, F.; Bonhomme, F.; and Bervillé, A. 2009. The Origins of the Domestication of the Olive Tree. *Comptes rendus biologies* 332: 1059–64.

Carneiro, R. L. 1970. A Theory of the Origin of the State. *Science* 169 (3947): 733–8.

Charles, M. 1996. Fodder from Dung: The Recognition and Interpretation of Dung-Derived Plant Material from Archaeological Sites. *EnArch* 1: 111–22.

Childe, V. G. 1950. The Urban Revolution. *TPR* 21 (1): 3–17.

Duiker, S. W., and Beegle, D. B. 2006. Soil Fertility Distributions in Long-Term No-Till, Chisel/Disk and Moldboard Plow/Disk Systems. *Soil and Tillage Research* 88: 30–41.

Earle, T. K. 1997. *How Chiefs Come to Power: The Political Economy in Prehistory*. Stanford: Stanford University Press.

Epstein, C. 1993. Oil Production in the Golan Heights during the Chalcolithic Period. *TA* 20: 133–46.

Fall, P. L.; Falconer, S. E.; and Lines, L. 2002. Agricultural Intensification and the Secondary Products Revolution along the Jordan Rift. *Human Ecology* 30: 445–82.

Fischbeck, G. 2002. Contribution of Barley to Agriculture: A Brief Overview. In *Barley Science: Recent Advances from Molecular Biology to Agronomy of Yield and Quality*, ed. G. A. Slafer, J. L. Molina-Cano, R. Savin, J. L. Araus, and I. Romagosa, 1–14. New York: Food Products Press.

Garfinkel, Y.; Ben-Shlomo, D.; Freikman, M.; and Vered, A. 2007. Tel Tsaf: The 2004–2006 Excavation Seasons. *IEJ* 57: 1–33.

Garfinkel, Y.; Ben-Shlomo, D.; and Kuperman, T. 2009. Large-Scale Storage of Grain Surplus in the Sixth Millennium BC: The Silos of Tel Tsaf. *Antiquity* 83 (320): 309–25.

Gilead, I. 1988. The Chalcolithic Period in the Levant. *JWP* 2: 397–443.

Golden, J. M. 1998. *The Dawn of the Metal Age: Social Complexity and the Rise of Copper Metallurgy during the Chalcolithic in the Southern Levant, circa 4500–3500 B.C.* PhD diss., University of Pennsylvania.

Golden, J. M.; Levy, T. E.; and Hauptmann, A. 2001. Recent Discoveries Concerning Chalcolithic Metallurgy at Shiqmim, Israel. *JAS* 28: 951–63.

Gophna, R. 1979. Tel Tsaf – A Chalcolithic Settlement on the Banks of the Jordan. *Qad* 12: 54–6 (Hebrew).

Graham, P. 2014. Archaeobotanical Remains from Late 6th/Early 5th Millennium BC Tel Tsaf, Israel. *JAS* 43: 105–10.

Grando, S., and Gómez Macpherson, H. 2005. *Food Barley: Importance, Uses and Local Knowledge*. Aleppo: ICARDA.

Greenfield, H. J. 2010. The Secondary Products Revolution: The Past, the Present and the Future. *WA* 42: 29–54.

Grigson, C. 2000. The Secondary Products Revolution? Changes in Animal Management from the Fourth to the Fifth Millennium, at Arjoune, Syria. In *Archaeology of the Near East IV: Proceedings of the Fourth International Symposium on the Archaeozoology of Southwestern Asia and Adjacent Areas*, Part B, ed. M. Mashkour, A. M. Choyke, H. Buitenhuis, and F. Poplin, 12–28. ARCP 32. Groningen: Centre for Archeological Research and Consultancy.

Hanbury-Tenison, J. W. 1986. *The Late Chalcolithic to Early Bronze I Transition in Palestine and Transjordan*. BAR International Series 311. Oxford: BAR.

Heichel, G. H. 1987. Legume Nitrogen: Symbiotic Fixation and Recovery by Subsequent Crops. In *Energy in Plant Nutrition and Pest Control*, ed. Z. R. Helsel, 63–80. Energy in World Agriculture 2. Amsterdam: Elsevier.

Heusinkveld, B. G.; Jacobs, A. F. G.; Holtslag, A. A. M.; and Berkowicz, S. M. 2004. Surface Energy Balance Closure in an Arid Region: Role of Soil Heat Flux. *Agricultural and Forest Meteorology* 122: 21–37.

Hill, A. C. 2011. *Specialized Pastoralism and Social Stratification – Analysis of the Fauna from Chalcolithic Tel Tsaf, Israel*. PhD diss., University of Connecticut.

Hillman, G. C. 1984. Interpretation of Archaeological Plant Remains: The Application of Ethnographic Models from Turkey. In *Plants and Ancient Man: Studies in Palaeoethnobotany*, ed. W. van Zeist and W. A. Casparie, 1–41. Rotterdam: Balkema.

Hubbard, E. M. 2010. Livestock and People in a Middle Chalcolithic Settlement: A Micromorphological Investigation from Tel Tsaf, Israel. *Antiquity* 84 (326): 1123–34.

Isaakidou, V. 2006. Ploughing with Cows: Knossos and the Secondary Products Revolution. In *Animals in the Neolithic of Britain and Europe*, ed. D. Serjeantson and D. Field, 95–112. Neolithic Studies Group Seminar Papers 7. Oxford: Oxbow.

Issar, A. S., and Zohar, M. 2004. *Climate Change: Environment and Civilization in the Middle East*. Berlin: Springer.

Jones, G. 1984. The Interpretation of Archaeological Plant Remains: Ethnographic Models from Greece. In *Plants and Ancient Man: Studies in Palaeoethnobotany*, ed. W. van Zeist and W. A. Casparie, 43–61. Rotterdam: Balkema.

― 1998. Distinguishing Food from Fodder in the Archaeobotanical Record. *EnArch* 1: 95–98.

Jupe, M. 2003. *The Effects of Charring on Pulses and Implications for Using Size Change to Identify Domestication in Eurasia*. BA thesis, University College London.

Kislev, M. D. 1987. Chalcolithic Plant Husbandry and Ancient Vegetation at Shiqmim. In *Shiqmim I: Studies Concerning Chalcolithic Societies in the Northern Negev Desert, Israel (1982–1984)*, Vol. 1, ed. T. E. Levy, 251–79. BAR International Series 356 (1). Oxford: BAR.

Levy, T. E. 1998. Cult, Metallurgy and Rank Societies – Chalcolithic Period (ca. 4500–3500 BCE). In *The Archaeology of Society in the Holy Land*, ed. T. E. Levy, 226–44. NAAA. London: Leicester University Press.

Levy, T. E., and Alon, D. 1985. Shiqmim: A Chalcolithic Village and Mortuary Centre in the Northern Negev. *Paléorient* 11 (1): 71–83.

Levy, T. E., and Goldberg, P. 1987. The Environmental Setting of the Northern Negev. In *Shiqmim I: Studies Concerning Chalcolithic Societies in the Northern Negev Desert, Israel (1982–1984)*, Vol. 1, ed. T. E. Levy, 1–22. BAR International Series 356 (1). Oxford: BAR.

Liphschitz, N. 1988. Analysis of the Botanical Remains from Tel Tsaf. *TA* 15: 52–4.

Liphschitz, N.; Gophna, R.; Hartman, M.; and Biger, G. 1991. The Beginning of Olive (*Olea europaea*) Cultivation in the Old World: A Reassessment. *JAS* 18: 441–53.

Maymone, B.; Dattilo, M.; and Mazziotti di Celso, P. 1953. Ricerche sulla produttività della leguminosa *Scorpiurus muricata* L. var. *Subvillosa* L.: Pregevole foraggera dei prati naturali e dei pascoli meridionali. *Annali della Sperimentazione Agraria* 7: 1289–329.

Mehari, A.; Schultz, B.; and Depeweg, H. 2006. Salinity Impact Assessment on Crop Yield for Wadi Laba Spate Irrigation System in Eritrea. *Agricultural Water Management* 85: 27–37.

Miller, L. J. 2003. Secondary Products and Urbanism in South Asia: The Evidence for Traction at Harappa. In *Indus Ethnobiology: New Perspectives from the Field*, ed. S. A. Weber and W. R. Belcher, 251–326. Lanham, MD: Lexington.

Miller, N. F. 1984. The Interpretation of Some Carbonized Cereal Remains as Remnants of Dung Cake Fuel. *BSA* 1: 45–7.

― 1985. Paleoethnobotanical Evidence for Deforestation in Ancient Iran: A Case Study of Urban Malyan. *Journal of Ethnobiology* 5: 1–19.

Pülschen, L. 1992. Effects of Two Underseed Species, *Medicago polymorpha* L. and *Scorpiurus muricatus* L., on the Yield of Main Crop (Durum Wheat) and Subsequent Crop (Teff) under Humid Moisture Regimes in Ethiopia. *Journal of Agronomy and Crop Science* 168: 249–54.

Redman, C. L. 1978. *The Rise of Civilization: From Early Farmers to Urban Society in the Ancient Near East*. San Francisco: Freeman.

Rosen, A. M. 1987. Phytolith Studies at Shiqmim. In *Shiqmim I: Studies Concerning Chalcolithic Societies in the Northern Negev Desert, Israel (1982–1984)*, Vol. 1, ed. T. E. Levy, 243–50. BAR International Series 356 (1). Oxford: BAR.

Rowan, Y. M., and Golden, J. M. 2009. The Chalcolithic Period of the Southern Levant: A Synthetic Review. *JWP* 22: 1–92.

Rowan, Y. M., and Kersel, M. M. 2014. New Perspectives on the Chalcolithic Period in the Galilee: Investigations at the Site of Marj Rabba. In *Material Culture Matters: Essays on the Archaeology of the Southern Levant in Honor of Seymour Gitin*, ed. J. R. Spencer, R. A. Mullins, and A. J. Brody, 221–37. Winona Lake, IN: Published on behalf of the W. F. Albright Institute of Archaeology by Eisenbrauns.

Sherratt, A. 1981. Plough and Pastoralism: Aspects of the Secondary Products Revolution. In *Pattern of the Past: Studies in Honour of David Clarke*, ed. I. Hodder, G. Isaac, and N. Hammond, 261–305. Cambridge: Cambridge University Press.

Steenbergen, F. van. 1997. Understanding the Sociology of Spate Irrigation: Cases from Balochistan. *JAE* 35: 349–65.

Stein, G., and Rothman, M. S. 1994. *Chiefdoms and Early States in the Near East: The Organizational Dynamics of Complexity*. MWA 18. Madison, WI: Prehistory.

Stevens, C. J. 2003. An Investigation of Agricultural Consumption and Production Models for Prehistoric and Roman Britain. *EnArch* 8: 61–76.

Tzori, N. 1958. Neolithic and Chalcolithic Sites in the Valley of Beth-Shan. *PEQ* 90: 44–51.

Wittfogel, K. A. 1981. *Oriental Despotism: A Comparative Study of Total Power*. New York: Vintage.

Yakar, J. 1985. *The Later Prehistory of Anatolia: The Late Chalcolithic and the Early Bronze Age*. 2 vols. BAR International Series 268. Oxford: BAR.

Young, B. 2001. Barley: The Versatile Crop. *Ethnobotanical Leaflets* 2001 (1): Article 1.

PART TWO

NINE

THE SOUTHERN LEVANT DURING THE EARLY BRONZE AGE I–III

MEREDITH S. CHESSON

URBANISM, TOWNISM, OR SOMETHING ENTIRELY DIFFERENT?

During the southern Levantine Early Bronze Age (EB) I–III (ca. 3600–2400 BCE), people embarked upon an extraordinary and fascinating regional and cultural endeavor spanning approximately 1,200 years. This project reorganized earlier Chalcolithic cultural lifeways in crucial political, economic, and social realms (Y. M. Rowan, this volume). While still relying on agropastoralism, craft production, and trade as the economic basis for life, they transformed their social, political, and physical geographies of the region, inventing fortified and walled settlements in which power and authority resided in control over land, water, animal, and labor resources, and the resultant staple products (Philip 2008; Braemer et al. 2009; Greenberg 2014). Moreover, EB IB–III society encompassed a fascinating diversity in the expression of regional trends, technologies, and material goods emerging from local histories and networks, geographies, and resources.

With more than a century of research into the EB I–III, researchers from a wide range of theoretical perspectives have characterized its culture with a variety of political and economic models, including secondary states, chiefdoms, kingdoms, dynamic corporate villages, networks of heterarchical communities, and city-states. Regardless of the researchers' chosen models, all interpretations and arguments revolve, in one way or another, around the question of ancient urbanism. Very generally, scholars posit that EB I–III

9.1. Map with EB IA–EB III sites mentioned in this chapter. (Map by M. S. Chesson.)

society was the earliest attempt at urban development, experimentation, and engagement in the region. This scholarly dialogue continues today, with some scholars questioning the focus on cities and others defending this view (Miroschedji 1999; 2009; Chesson and Philip 2003; 2008; Rast and Schaub 2003; Greenberg et al. 2006; Fisher 2008; Braemer 2011; Chesson 2015). Interestingly, this dialogue often emerges from the situated knowledge of the scholar: Those based at large fortified settlements (such as Tel Yarmouth, Khirbat as-Zeraqon, or Tel Beth Yerah) lean toward characterizations of urban society, while others working at smaller-scale sites (such as Bab adh-Dhra' and Numayra) see a greater diversity in scales of complexity (Fig. 9.1).

Regardless of the label, the key to understanding EB I–III society relies on our ability to understand a regional endeavor emerging from locally sourced social and economic tools and resources at hand. These localized foundations create diversity in the scale and specific material expression of the four major EB I–III transformations (Table 9.1):

TABLE 9.1. *Early Bronze Age IA–III characteristics and chronology.*

	Trait	EB IA (3600–3300 BCE)	EB IB (3300–3100 BCE)	EB II (3100–2900 BCE)	EB III (2900–2500 BCE)
Organization and scales of communities	Settlement pattern	Dispersed hamlets and farmsteads throughout valleys, coastal plain, and interior plateaus and hills	Establishment of hamlets and villages, ranging in size from small to very large in agriculturally rich areas, as well as in desertic areas	Population aggregation widespread into walled or fortified communities throughout the region; placemaking evident and common	Widespread population aggregation and placemaking; continued occupation of some sites, reoccupation of some abandoned sites and establishment of new fortified sites
	Site sizes	<1 ha	<1–30 ha	1–25 ha	1–25 ha
	Settlement organization	Clusters of residential buildings and courtyards	Clusters of residential buildings and courtyards	Fortified or walled settlements, sometimes with semblance of planning (markets, streets, nonresidential spaces)	Fortified or walled settlements, sometimes with semblance of planning (markets, streets, and nonresidential spaces)
Social and economic practices	Economic base	Agriculture, pastoralism, viticulture, and orchard fruits	Intensification of agricultural, pastoral, and orchard production to feed larger villages	Intensification of agricultural, pastoral, and orchard production to feed larger communities; exchange within region evident with ceramics and foodstuffs	Intensification of agricultural, pastoral, and orchard production to feed larger communities; exchange within region evident with ceramics and foodstuffs
	Social and economic differentiation	No significant markers of differentiation or differential access to material or immaterial resources (including labor)	No significant material markers of differential access to goods, but organization of intensification of staple good production suggests management structures	Varies: Limited evidence in residential contexts, but implications for differential power with large ritual and administrative complexes at larger sites, likely	Varies: Limited evidence in residential contexts, but implications for differential power with large ritual and administrative complexes at larger sites, likely

(cont.)

TABLE 9.1. (cont.)

Trait	EB IA (3600–3300 BCE)	EB IB (3300–3100 BCE)	EB II (3100–2900 BCE)	EB III (2900–2500 BCE)
Social and economic practices		with greater control over labor resources	revolves around access to labor, land, and water resources to produce staple products (foodstuffs, tools, containers, buildings)	revolves around access to labor, land, and water resources to produce staple products (foodstuffs, tools, containers, buildings)
Mortuary practices	Diverse practices, depending on location, including secondary burials in shaft and cist tombs, rock-cut tombs, and dolmens and cairns	Diverse practices (secondary and primary), depending on location, including dolmen fields, cemeteries of shaft tombs, circular charnel houses, and rock-cut tombs	Few large cemeteries of rock-cut tombs and charnel houses	Few large cemeteries of rock-cut tombs and charnel houses
Nonlocal connections and networks	Goods of nonlocal materials found in mortuary contexts, including carnelian beads, alabaster mace-heads, and shell bracelets (connections looking to the south)	Significant Egyptian presence (people and products) in certain settlements, with suggestions of direct involvement with Egyptians or their factors in exchange networks	Widespread withdrawal of Egyptian presence and reduction of goods made from nonlocal resources; goods of nonlocal resources (metal weapons and beads, mother of pearl pendants, carnelian and lapis beads) found in mortuary contexts	Widespread withdrawal of Egyptian presence and reduction of goods made from non-local resources; presence of Kura-Uraxes migrants in Tel Beth Yerah; goods of non-local resources (metal weapons and beads, mother of pearl pendants, carnelian and lapis beads) found in mortuary contexts
Craft specialization	Limited and part-time, at best (perhaps seasonal production of many crafts, including pottery, metal	Limited and part-time (perhaps seasonal production of crafts, including pottery), which includes traders, vintners,	Largely part-time (perhaps seasonal production of crafts, including pottery), which includes traders, vintners, potters, farmers,	Limited and part-time (perhaps seasonal production of crafts, including pottery), which includes traders, vintners,

166

		objects, and chipped stone tools)	potters, farmers, herders, and weavers	herders, and weavers; emergence of ceramic specialists in some areas (North Canaanite Metallic Ware and Arad ceramic industries)	potters, farmers, herders, and weavers; ceramic specialization with Khirbet Kerak Ware?
Civic governance and political structures	Fortification systems and enclosures	None	Debated: Walls around some settlements but not most	Yes	Yes
	Hydraulic systems	None	Irrigation in fields and orchards; water catchment systems for settlements	Irrigation in fields and orchards; water catchment systems for settlements	Irrigation in fields and orchards; water catchment systems for settlements, including tunnels to water table
	Administrative or nonresidential spaces	None	None	Yes	Yes
	Ritual spaces	Few cemeteries and more isolated tombs or small concentrations of tombs; dolmen fields	Few within settlements, few cemeteries	Few cemeteries	Temples, few cemeteries

1. widespread population into fortified settlements;
2. intensification of agricultural, pastoral, viticultural, and orchard production, including development of irrigation and water collection technologies, as well as terracing and widespread anthropogenic landscape change;
3. construction of nonresidential architectural spaces, such as storerooms, administrative complexes, and palaces; and
4. increasing social differentiation, most likely on the level of groups, seen in mortuary practices and the largest fortified settlements.

Diversity is a key issue here as we track the emergence and development of the EB I–III cultural endeavor throughout the region, from the eastern and northern desert areas surrounding Jawa and Labwe, to Tel Beth Yerah by the Sea of Galilee, to Arad in the Negev, and to Numayra on the southeastern Dead Sea Plain in Jordan (Amiran et al. 1978; Amiran and Ilan 1996; Betts 1991; Greenberg et al. 2006; al-Maqdissi and Braemer 2006; Braemer et al. 2010; Chesson 2012; Chesson and Goodale 2014; Müller-Neuhof and Abu-Azizeh 2016). Regardless of how we label this long-term phenomenon and how it finds material expression in different geographic locations and at different scales, the trends above are shared throughout the region (see Fig. 9.1). This chapter provides a concise overview of the social, economic, and political emergence of this cultural project, which I characterize as slow urbanism, through time by subperiods: the EB IA, EB IB, EB II, and EB III. The time periods listed are intended as general guides, because each subperiod started and ended at different places at varying times over the 1,200-year span of the EB I–III. While different areas embarked on participation in this cultural project at varying times, radiocarbon analyses show that they all seem to abandon it around 2,500 cal. BCE (Regev et al. 2012).

EB IA (3600–3300 BCE): DISPERSAL AND STAPLE PRODUCTS

Archaeological evidence for the EB IA includes both settlement and mortuary sites located within modern Israel, Palestine, Jordan, southern Lebanon, and southern Syria. All habitation sites were small hamlets or farmsteads dispersed across the countryside in a variety of ecological zones, with evidence of mobility that might have been linked to seasonal patterns of agropastoral enterprises and exchange patterns (e.g., Jawa in the eastern desert of Jordan and Tall Umm Hammad in the eastern Jordan Valley, Yiftahel in the Lower Galilee) (Betts 1991; 1992; Braun 1997). These settlements showed no evidence for economic, political, or social differentiation based on differential access to resources, labor, or nonlocal exchange networks.

Cemeteries of rock-cut or cist tombs, as well as dolmen fields, on both sides of the Jordan Valley offer another line of evidence for investigating the nature of social, political, and economic complexity during the EB IA (Kenyon 1960; Schaub and Rast 1989; Chesson 2001; Ilan 2002; Ortner and Fröhlich 2008; Fraser 2015). The largest excavated and published (to varying degrees) cemeteries were Jericho and a series of EB IA cemeteries on the southeastern Dead Sea Plain (Bab adh-Dhra', Fifa, and an-Naqa). Bab adh-Dhra' offers the largest and best published examples from this transitional period, with rock-cut shaft tombs and the deposition of defleshed individuals with burial goods in secondary ceremonies (Schaub and Rast 1989; Rast 1999; Chesson 2007; Ortner and Fröhlich 2008). Gillian Bentley and Victoria Perry's analysis of dental morphology (2008) demonstrates that individuals buried within a shaft tomb were more likely to be genetically related to each other than when compared between shaft tombs at Bab adh-Dhra'. These data suggest that kin groups acted as key organizational units in the EB IA people who established the cemetery. Analysis of grave goods in EB IA shaft tombs at Bab adh-Dhra' demonstrates little social differentiation in terms of access to local and nonlocal resources, but it does show economic connections with Egypt in the form of beads and mace-heads made from carnelian and alabaster, respectively, both materials with the closest sources in the Sinai, as well as *conus* shell bracelets from the Red Sea. These southeastern Dead Sea Plain cemeteries were not associated with any neighboring EB IA settlements, and EB IA tombs contain the remains of secondary burials – we have no evidence for primary mortuary practices, suggesting that people traveled with the defleshed skeletal remains of their dead to bury them at Bab adh-Dhra' and the neighboring cist-tomb cemeteries at an-Naqa and Fifa. Over the past several decades, researchers have suggested that these cemeteries serviced nomadic EB IA herders who were not linked to any sedentary settlements in the region. However, no data exist to deny or affirm linkages with nomadic groups or with any EB IA settlements north of the Dead Sea, west of the Wadi Aravah, or to the east on the Kerak Plateau. At best, we can state that we do not know where these people came from and therefore cannot ascertain whether they were fully sedentary, fully nomadic, transhumant, or making their livings with some combination of pastoralism, agriculture, and orchards.

The most striking difference between the previous Chalcolithic period and the EB IA culture emerges from the widespread shift from prestige goods, embodying power and authority, to a focus on staple products in both settlement and cemetery contexts. This transformation established the foundation for increasing social, economic, and political differentiation that reached its apex in the EB III at the largest sites in the region. The EB IA focus on staple products, produced through local land, water, and labor resources, grounded the diverse expressions of later economic, political, and social differentiation within the broader regional project beginning in the EB IB and culminating at the end of the EB III.

EB IB (3300–3100 BCE): EARLY PLACEMAKING AND INTENSIFICATION OF STAPLE GOODS PRODUCTION

Similar to the EB IA, archaeologists can examine both settlement and cemetery contexts to investigate the nature of social, economic, and political structures in EB IB society. The EB IB enacted a watershed moment during the late fourth millennium BCE with the emergence of widespread population aggregation into very large (up to 30 ha) villages (or even towns?) in agriculturally rich areas (e.g., Tall ash-Shuna North, Megiddo), as well as small villages and hamlets in other areas (Finkelstein, Ussishkin, and Halpern 2000). The establishment of very large villages represents efforts at placemaking by EB IB people and assuredly involved civic governance structures to manage the population density and the necessity of feeding and supporting large communities with local natural and labor resources. Moreover, this placemaking signals some cultural package of ideas encouraging, cajoling, or even coercing people to leave their small farmsteads and hamlets to move their families into these large communities.

In order to feed these large populations, people intensified production of food and craft stuffs. Paleo-ethnobotanical evidence from EB IB habitation sites demonstrates the widespread development and use of irrigation technologies at small and large settlements with fruit, flax, and cereal crops (e.g., Ras an-Numayra) (White, Chesson, and Schaub 2014). Graham Philip (2016) and his colleagues suggest that in order to feed these larger populations, laborers were recruited from the countryside surrounding large villages, such as Tall ash-Shuna North and Megiddo, and this control over these staple land, water, and labor resources enabled the development of civic governance structures overseeing the local land, water, mineral, and animal resources. While the vast majority of excavated EB IB structures reveal residential contexts with little evidence for status differentiation, at the largest sites there are striking examples of nonresidential spaces that undoubtedly required social and political authority to manage and maintain. The EB IB temple at Megiddo provides the most striking example of this manifestation of power. Whether authority resided with ritual practitioners, civic and land managers, or an emerging group of people with greater access to staple resources and authority in these largest communities remains unclear. The vast majority of excavated EB IB settlements offer little evidence for hierarchical economic or political structures; therefore, we cannot argue for the widespread emergence of an elite faction of people regionally: Differentiation did not translate into hierarchy or pronounced variation in access to material resources (but perhaps the key to status lay in immaterial resources such as ritual or occupational knowledge, which do not survive in the archaeological record).

Interestingly, at some of these larger villages and select smaller settlements in southern Israel (e.g., 'En Besor), material evidence for connections with Egyptian exchange networks, and possibly Egyptian people themselves, exists. The nature, mechanics, rationale for, implications of, and intensity of an Egyptian presence during the EB IB, concomitant with increasing social and political differentiation and the eventual emergence of state-level society with Dynasty 0, continues to be heavily debated. In considering the establishment of larger EB IB communities and the development of civic governance and management bodies, some researchers suggest that Egyptian interest in the region drove or minimally encouraged population aggregation. Scholarly debates include both push and pull models involving Egyptian interests and presence in the southern Levant. Egyptian presence varies widely from none to extensive, and this diversity of involvement undermines any monolithic explanation and interpretation that works throughout the entire region.

Part-time craft specialization in a variety of tasks, including pottery, chipped stone tools, ground stone tools, metal objects, textiles, viticulture, farming, and trading, likely was organized by seasonal rhythms as well as cultural ones (such as kin groups and structures of knowledge transmission). Researchers examining mortuary contexts suggest that key cultural structuring forces, such as kinship, likely continued similarly from the earlier EB IA. Mortuary practices at Bab adh-Dhra', in particular, demonstrate increasingly diverse ways of treating the dead: They utilized earlier shaft tombs by refitting them, created new chambers off of previously established shafts, and built circular mud-brick charnel houses. They interred their dead in a mix of primary and secondary mortuary practices in the cemetery, and researchers have suggested that this diversity of mortuary rites accompanied a transformation of society in this region. At the end of the EB IB and the earliest part of EB II, people settled at Bab adh-Dhra' by establishing an unwalled village adjacent to the wadi, north of the cemetery.

The end of the EB IB witnessed the general withdrawal of the Egyptian presence and the abandonment of the largest villages (e.g., Megiddo, Tall as-Shuna North), heralding the establishment of walled and fortified settlements throughout the region with widespread population aggregation. Raphael Greenberg (2014) has suggested that the removal of Egyptian involvement in large and small ways offered a power vacuum in the region, into which stepped people and groups that held greater sway, power, and authority over staple resources. These factions enacted a large-scale transformation of the region by encouraging, forcing, or, at the very least, convincing people to abandon the countryside and move into large and small fortified settlements, a sweeping project of placemaking and anthropomorphic change of the physical and social landscapes.

EB II (3100–2900 BCE): WIDESPREAD PLACEMAKING AND FLORESCENCE OF LIFE IN FORTIFIED SETTLEMENTS

During the EB II, people adopted the cultural project of inventing and moving into fortified settlements throughout the region. Walled communities include all the hallmarks of this endeavor: fortification systems, ritual compounds, nonresidential administrative complexes or palaces, differing engagements with "urban" planning, intensification of food and craft production, and a significant absence of Egyptian or nonlocal presence and materials. In an interesting case of discontinuous settlement, people abandoned several large EB IB villages (including Megiddo, Tall as-Shuna North, and Beth Shean) and established new fortified settlements (e.g., Tall as-Sa'idiyeh). Other communities continued from the EB IB (e.g., Tel Arad, Tall Abu al-Kharaz, Tell el-Far'ah North), adding fortifications and structural elements common to many EB II settlements, including fortification systems, nonresidential spaces, and ritual compounds (e.g., Bab adh-Dhra', Tel Beth Yerah, Tall Abu al-Kharaz) (Vaux and Steve 1969; Tubb 1988; Tubb, Dorrell, and Cobbing 1996; Greenberg 2003; Fisher 2008).

Larger sites, such as Tel Beth Yerah and Tell el-Far'ah North, demonstrate material expressions of political and economic status differentiation with the need for management oversight, such as nonresidential and administrative complexes, "urban" planning and investment (grid orientation of some areas or paved streets), and ritual compounds. Localized histories and diversity of expression characterize this regional project, with significant differences in scales of communities, resource bases, and expressions of status differentiation and civic governance.

Researchers have argued that the ubiquitous aggregation into settlements necessitated a reorganization of the cultural rules governing property and usufructure of land, water, animal, and immaterial resources (such as ritual and craft knowledge, kinship, and economic links and relationships) (Chesson 2003; Philip 2008; Miroschedji 2009; Greenberg 2011; 2014). In order to feed and support larger populations living in walled towns, cities, and villages, civic governance structures needed to manage resources and people inside the settlement, as well as the lands and resources surrounding each community. Investment into infrastructure within and outside settlements included the establishment and maintenance of irrigation systems, orchards, terraces, roads, trackways, fortification walls and gates, administrative complexes, ritual compounds, and potentially even market spaces. Political, economic, and social power and authority were linked to staple goods and the control over land, labor, water, plant, and animal resources. Based on the discovery of very large platters, such as at Tall as-Sa'idiyeh, Greenberg (2014) suggests that feasting celebrations, based on the consumption of staple foodstuffs, was an important mechanism for consolidating and maintaining power.

Interestingly, seal impressions found exclusively on ceramic storage containers (presumably for staple goods such as grains, wine, olive oil, and other foodstuffs) seem to have been decorative in nature and were not used as economic or administrative tools. The EB II peoples adopted the practice of sealing but not the significances and implications common to Mesopotamian contexts. Similarly, the EB I and II people were clearly aware of the writing systems of their Egyptian and Mesopotamian neighbors but decided not to adopt this technology. Part of the EB I–III project involved an active and regional choice to forego writing in any capacity – economic, political, or social. Researchers have proposed a variety of explanations for the Early Bronze peoples' lack of writing and the partial adoption of sealing practices, ranging from economies of scale and the lack of necessity for managing the social, economic, and political structures in walled communities, to more social explanations of cultural isolationism after the departure of the Egyptian presence. Regardless of interpretation, it is clear that the Early Bronze peoples throughout the region decided to choose some elements of their neighbors' lifeways and to eschew others. This region-wide choice emphasizes their involvement in a project or endeavor to build a society with similar practices linking together communities grounded in their local histories and resources.

Craft specialization, encompassing all aspects of daily life, still seems to have been largely based in part-time or seasonal engagement. Nevertheless, cultivation of a wide variety of cultigens, viticulture, olives and fruits, and animal husbandry all required specialized knowledge and experience, encased in notions of tradition and proper knowledge transmission, and in many ways should be considered craft specialties similar to more traditional concepts of craft production of ceramics, bone and stone tools, textiles, and metal objects. Ceramic repertoires became more standardized in terms of forms, decorative treatments, and production sequences; yet, from the standpoint of Cathy Costin's (2001) definitions of specialization, the EB II potters, in general, fall short of that litmus test. However, Greenberg (2003) has proposed compelling evidence for the emergence of full-time ceramic specialists in the north (North Canaanite Metallic Ware) and the south (Arad's ceramic industry), and the production of oversized platters and other unusual vessels and technologies requiring specialized knowledge and production facilities also suggest another realm of ceramic specialization (see also Roux and Miroschedji 2009).

Analysis of mortuary practices in the region, with particular reference to published excavations at Jericho and Bab adh-Dhra', demonstrate a growing differentiation in group access to nonlocal goods. Rock-cut tombs at Jericho and stone and mud-brick charnel houses at Bab adh-Dhra' included human remains from secondary rites; large numbers of ceramic serving vessels; miniature ceramic vessels; carved bone objects; metal weapons; stone mace-heads and palettes; and beads from a wide variety of local and nonlocal resources. Generally, tombs and charnel houses lacked any cooking vessels or large storage jars. Burying the dead involved the deposition of serving vessels (presumably associated with mortuary ceremonies of prepared foodstuffs) but not vessels or tools associated with food production or long-term storage. This trend evokes arguments about competitive feasting within settlements as important activities to forge, cement, and maintain economic, social, and political alliances. Anthropologically, there is a large evidentiary base of examples of secondary mortuary rituals acting as crucial arenas for just these types of endeavors. If the EB II people continued the practice of burying their kin within these rock-cut tombs and charnel houses (as they did with the EB IA shaft tombs), then kinship remained a crucial organizing force in these communities. Notably, the analysis of these tombs and charnel houses cannot be easily divided into EB II and EB III phases due to the collective nature of the mortuary contexts. A general lack of absolute dating from these contexts hampers our ability to track changes in mortuary practices from the EB II through the EB III or even to know the chronological span of these rock-cut tombs and charnel houses, many of which contain artifact markers from both EB II and EB III within the same structure.

At the end of the EB II, people abandoned several large fortified communities, such as Arad, Tell el-Far'ah North, Tall Abu al-Kharaz, and Tall as-Sa'idiyeh. In some cases, former large EB IB settlements were reoccupied (Megiddo, Beth Shean, possibly Tall al-Handaquq South), while others were founded at the beginning of the EB III (e.g., Numayra, Khirbat as-Zeraqon). At several settlements, people weathered the transition from EB II to EB III (e.g., Tel Beth Yerah, Tel Yarmouth, Bab adh-Dhra'). The general continuity in practices of daily life in EB II and EB III settlements provides little evidence for this transition, which in many areas would have involved major population movements, even locally, to new homes. It is unclear if and how transfers of people to new settlements altered the control over land, water, and animal resources that provided the staple goods that formed the base for power and authority in both EB II and EB III communities. Moreover, the relative levels of continuity in everyday life, mortuary practices, and material culture give researchers a poor evidentiary basis for proposing reasons behind settlement abandonments, reoccupations, and the founding of new communities.

EB III (2900–2500 BCE): DIVERSE SCALES OF ECONOMY AND POLITICS, EVENTUAL AND UNIFIED DISSOLUTION

Generally, daily life continued apace, based on the same suite of agricultural, pastoral, orchard, craft production, architectural, and mortuary practices,

EARLY BRONZE AGE I–III

9.2. Reconstruction of residential contexts at EB III Numayra. (Reconstruction by E. Carlson. Courtesy of the Expedition to the Dead Sea Plain.)

dependent on the nature and extent of land, animal, and water resources surrounding EB III settlements (Fig. 9.2). Following the localized trends, settlements display varying degrees of evidence for social, economic, and political differentiation, evinced in ritual compounds, administrative compounds, palaces, and massive fortification systems. Many of these differences correlate with scales of economy and settlement and population density combined with resource bases. For instance, heavily fortified Tel Yarmouth (15 ha) featured an administrative complex, interpreted as a palace, and was located in a rich agricultural area with ample resources to support its population and the amassing of staple resources by certain factions of its community. Alternatively, Bab adh-Dhra' (4 ha) and neighboring Numayra (1 ha) were situated in a more marginal agricultural zone, and no evidence for an administrative complex or a palace were ever located by the excavators despite concerted efforts. Regardless of size, however, power and authority still rested in the ability to control staple goods, land, water, labor, and animal resources (Fig. 9.3).

Comparative analysis of residential contexts at several sites shows little evidence to support increasing status differentiation between household groups (Chesson 2003; Chesson and Goodale 2014). However, detailed analysis of three residential compounds at Numayra suggest that households may have specialized in particular economic practices such as viticulture, winemaking, and textile production – all forms of specialized knowledge and practices (Chesson, Schaub, and Rast in press). Moreover, Numayra offers evidence

9.3. A large clay bin filled with carbonized emmer wheat from the final occupational phase of EB III Numayra. (Courtesy of the Expedition to the Dead Sea Plain.)

for differential access to foodstuffs, such as chickpeas, which were imports to the community. These differences in goods, knowledge, and practices did not translate to traditional archaeological markers of differential access to status or power to form hierarchical rankings. Instead, they highlight that diversity underlies life within a single community, and heterarchical frameworks may be more useful for modeling social, economic, and political complexity within and between communities.

Tel Beth Yerah offers a fascinating example of differential knowledge and craft production with the arrival of migrants from the Kura-Uraxes region. Significant differences in agricultural and pastoral practices, ceramic vessel and figurine technologies and production, and foodways between Khirbet Kerak and indigenous community members draw sharp distinctions between the two groups residing in the community. Interestingly, Khirbet Kerak vessels traditionally were utilized chronologically as a marker of the EB III, but clearly they mark population migration and the integration of a very different cultural worldview, traditions, and peoples (Berger 2016; Iserlis 2016; Longford and Berger 2016; Paz and Rotem 2016). Moreover, they entered into the material record as a clear example of trade: Production of Khirbet Kerak vessels has been documented at a limited number of settlements in the central north, primarily at Tel Beth Yerah, but the vessels themselves are found throughout the region as far south as Bab adh-Dhraʻ, albeit in reduced numbers as the distance from Tel Beth Yerah increases.

The cemeteries at Bab adh-Dhraʻ and Jericho remain the most studied examples of EB III mortuary practices, and the addition of actual and imitation Khirbet Kerak vessels in rock-cut tombs and charnel houses also demonstrates the exchange of goods within the region, along with metal weapons, stone palettes and mace-heads, and beads and pendants made from extra-regional materials (such as alabaster, lapis, carnelian, gold, and ostrich eggs). In comparing Bab adh-Dhra' and Jericho, it seems that people continued to practice mortuary rites as localized versions of regional practices (Chesson 2015). In addition, the collective nature of the rock-cut tombs of Jericho and the charnel houses of Bab adh-Dhra' further supports the interpretation that any further social, economic, and political differentiation occurred at the level of groups, possibly kin groups, and not with individuals or single households.

Analysis of radiocarbon dates from a large number of EB III sites demonstrates that by 2500 BCE, the vast majority of these fortified communities were abandoned (Regev et al. 2012). A wide variety of explanations for the dissolution of EB III society has been offered by researchers over the last several decades. Arlene Rosen's (1995) argument, proposing that Early Bronze peoples were faced with climate change and increasing difficulties in feeding large populations, seems the most likely and intellectually persuasive. Regardless of when walled settlements were established, they all were abandoned by 2400 BCE – a process that likely began by 2500 BCE. Whatever social, economic, and political reasons encouraged or forced people to aggregate into these large walled settlements, those arguments no longer held sway, and life within these communities became unsupportable, physically and ideologically. The Early Bronze project of incipient small-scale urbanism, townism, or fortified village life ended in the mid-third millennium BCE.

DIVERSITY AND SLOW URBANISM

Researchers have proposed a wide variety of models of civic governance, and, in most cases, the scale and mechanics of the model are grounded in the EB II site(s) at which the archaeologist is based and his/her theoretical background. The diversity we see in economic and political models of life in EB II and EB III communities encompasses the archaeological record, as well as the theoretical positionality of the archaeologists themselves. Regardless of the model favored by researchers, the Early Bronze project of walled community life involved the following elements, all nested and nurtured within localized histories and resource bases:

1. widespread population aggregation and placemaking;
2. investment of social, economic, and political power in the control of staple products, and the ownership and usufructure of land, water, labor, and animal resources;

3. choice to regionally focus inward, with the withdrawal of Egyptian presence and influences, and to eschew writing and sealing technologies overall;
4. intensification of agricultural, pastoral, and orchard production with development of irrigation technologies and water control;
5. emergence of limited craft specialization, especially with ceramic production, in certain areas, and the maintenance of part-time or seasonal specialization of most crafts and productive activities, including farming, trading, and foodways;
6. exchange of materials, including ceramic vessels, foodstuffs, chipped-stone tools, and metal droplets, within the region; and
7. increasing social differentiation at the group level, which might relate to the reorganization of notions of kinship groups and relatedness especially linked to control over land, water, and labor resources.

Taken as an ideological package, these characteristics suggest that there existed a strong unifying notion of how to be an Early Bronze person residing in a fortified community that provided an underlying level of cohesion throughout the region: an EB IB–III material package that included architectural, artifactual, and mortuary practices binding people within the region together. Simultaneously, each community took this package, embraced it, and built upon it in a localized way. This intriguing and complex combination of diversity and similarities presents researchers with a thorny theoretical quandary: how to encompass the scalar differences and diversity of practices throughout the region, while arguing from a fairly cohesive set of daily practices. Archaeologists have unsurprisingly offered a wide variety of models to explain EB IB–III society, ranging from urban state-level society with city-states to heterarchically governed, dynamic corporate villages. I suggest here that, at best, the EB IB–III can be characterized by slow urbanism, or even by the neologism "townism," that can encompass the diverse expressions of this material package and ideological project (Table 9.2).

When this system dissolved, most people abandoned their walled towns to move back into small hamlets. However, there are a number of significant walled Intermediate Bronze Age (also called EB IV [2400–2000 BCE]) settlements east of the Jordan River, where EB III settlements generally were smaller and perhaps suffered less from the regional pressures that sped the abandonment of fortified communities and the broader Early Bronze project. Gaetano Palumbo (1990) and others have suggested that these smaller communities historically practiced a more diverse and resilient set of economic practices, grounded in local histories and resources, that allowed them to weather the climatic and social challenges better than their contemporaries at much larger and more densely populated settlements.

TABLE 9.2. *Characteristics of EB IB–III slow urbanism or townism.*

Large-Scale Thematic Trend	Specific Characteristics
Localized population aggregation and scalar variability	• Range of settlements (1–25 ha) and population density • Varying evidence for political differentiation linked to scalar issues and local histories (community size, nature and abundance of local resources, localized social and economic histories) • Heterarchical structures prevent consolidation of power by any one group in walled communities
Intensification of agropastoral staple food production to feed larger communities	• Intensification of production supported by irrigation and water management technologies • Economy and power grounded in staple goods firmly rooted in local resources and histories • Diverse storage technologies and contexts suggest both competing and cooperative systems for managing and distributing staple goods
Increasing but limited specialization of craft production and regionalism of certain crafts	• Increasing standardization of the suite of material culture, including forms, technologies, and decorative styles (especially ceramics) • Emergence of regional-specific craft goods (e.g., Khirbet Kerak vessels, North Canaanite Metallic Ware) • Regional exchange of crafts and agropastoral products differentially throughout the region
Reworking notions of kinship and corporate groups	• Little evidence for significant social differentiation in residential contexts that would translate to differential access in status and access to staple and nonlocal goods • Increasing differentiation and complexity at the group level in mortuary and nonresidential contexts • Kinship notions expand to form larger corporate groups, with larger factions linked by kinship, economics, religion, and residency, working to prevent power consolidation by any one group to form a clear elite faction

REFERENCES

Amiran, R., and Ilan, O. 1996. *Early Arad II: The Chalcolithic and Early Bronze IB Settlements and Early Bronze II City; Architecture and Town Planning; 6th–18th Seasons of Excavations, 1971–1978, 1980–1984*. Jerusalem: The Israel Museum; IES.

Amiran, R.; Paran, U.; Shiloh, Y.; Brown, R.; Tsafrir, Y.; and Ben-Tor, A. 1978. *Early Arad: The Chalcolitic [sic] Settlement and Early Bronze City; First–Fifth Seasons of Excavations 1962–1966*. JDS. Jerusalem: IES.

Bentley, G. R., and Perry, V. J. 2008. Dental Analyses of the Bab adh-Dhra' Human Remains. In *The Early Bronze Age I Tombs and Burials of Bâb edh-Dhrâ', Jordan*, ed. D. J. Ortner and B. Fröhlich, 281–96. REDSPJ 3. Lanham, MD: AltaMira.

Beigel, A. 2010. "Feeding Cities? – Preliminary Notes on the Provisioning of Animal Products. Paper presented at the 10th ICAANE, Vienna, Austria.

Betts, A.V.G. 1991. *Excavations at Jawa 1972–1986*. EEHKJ. Edinburgh: Edinburgh University Press.

——— 1992. *Excavations at Tell Um Hammad 1982–1984: The Early Assemblages (EB I–II)*. EEHKJ. Edinburgh: Edinburgh University Press.

Braemer, F. 2011. *Badia* and *Maamoura*, the Jawlan/Hawran Regions during the Bronze Age: Landscapes and Hypothetical Territories. *Syria* 88: 31–46.

Braemer, F.; Davtian, G.; Criaud, H.; and al-Maqdissi, M. 2010. Labwe: Une ville fortifiée du Bronze ancient dans le Leja. In *Hauran V: La Syrie du Sud du Néolithique a l'Antiquité tardive; Recherches récentes*, ed. M. al-Maqdissi, F. Braemer, and J.-M. Dentzer, 111–18. BAH 191. Beirut: IFPO.

Braemer, F.; Genequand, D.; Dumond Maridat, C.; Blanc, P.-M.; Dentzer, J.-M.; Gazagne, D.; and Wech, P. 2009. Long-Term Management of Water in the Central Levant: The Hawran Case (Syria). *WA* 41: 36–57.

Braun, E. 1997. *Yiftaḥ'el: Salvage and Rescue Excavations at a Prehistoric Village in Lower Galilee, Israel*. IAA Reports 2. Jerusalem: IAA.

Chesson, M. S. 2001. Embodied Memories of Place and People: Death and Society in an Early Urban Community. In *Social Memory, Identity and Death: Ethnographic and Archaeological Perspectives on Mortuary Rituals*, ed. M. S. Chesson, 100–13. APAAA 10. Arlington, VA: American Anthropological Association.

——— 2003. Households, Houses, Neighborhoods and Corporate Villages: Modeling the Early Bronze Age as a House Society. *JMA* 16: 79–102.

——— 2007. House, Town, Field, and Wadi: Economic, Political and Social Landscapes in Early Bronze Age Walled Communities of the Southern Levant. In *The Durable House: House Society Models in Archaeology*, ed. R. A. Beck Jr., 317–43. CAIOP 35. Carbondale: Center for Archaeological Excavations, Southern Illinois University Press.

——— 2012. Homemaking in the Early Bronze Age. In *New Perspectives in Household Archaeology*, ed. B. J. Parker and C. P. Foster, 45–79. Winona Lake, IN: Eisenbrauns.

——— 2015. Reconceptualizing the Early Bronze Age Southern Levant without Cities: Local Histories and Walled Communities of EB II–III Society. *JMA* 28: 51–79.

Chesson, M. S., and Goodale, N. 2014. Population Aggregation, Residential Storage and Socioeconomic Inequality at Early Bronze Age Numayra, Jordan. *JAA* 35: 117–34.

Chesson, M. S., and Philip, G. 2003. Tales of the City? "Urbanism" in the Early Bronze Age Levant from Mediterranean and Levantine Perspectives. *JMA* 16: 3–16.

Chesson, M. S.; Schaub, R. T.; and Rast, W. A. In press. *Excavations at the EB III Townsite and EB IB Site of Ras an-Numayra*. Winona Lake, IN: Eisenbrauns.

Costin, C. 2001. Craft Specialization Systems. In *Archaeology at the Millennium: A Sourcebook*, ed. G. M. Feinman and T. D. Price, 273–327. New York: Springer.

Finkelstein, I.; Ussishkin, D.; and Halpern, B. 2000. *Megiddo III: The 1992–1996 Seasons*. MSSMNIA 18. Tel Aviv: Emery and Claire Yass Publications in Archaeology, Institute of Archaeology, Tel Aviv University.

Fischer, P. M. 2008. *Tell Abu al-Kharaz in the Jordan Valley*, Vol. 1: *The Early Bronze Age*. DG 48; CCEM 16. Vienna: Austrian Academy of Sciences.

Fraser, J. A. 2015. *Dolmens in the Levant*. PhD diss., University of Sydney.

Greenberg, R. 2003. Early Bronze Age Megiddo and Bet Shean: Discontinuous Settlement in Sociopolitical Context. *JMA* 16: 17–32.

　2011. Travelling in (World) Time: Transformation, Commoditization, and the Beginnings of Urbanism in the Southern Levant. In *Interweaving Worlds: Systemic Interactions in Eurasia, 7th to the 1st Millennia BC; Papers from a Conference in Memory of Professor Andrew Sherratt, "What Would a Bronze Age World System Look Like? World Systems Approaches to Europe and Western Asia, 4th to 1st Millennia BC,"* ed. T. C. Wilkinson, S. Sherratt, and J. Bennet, 231–42. Oxford: Oxbow.

　2014. Introduction to the Levant in the Early Bronze Age. In *The Oxford Handbook of the Archaeology of the Levant, c. 8000–332 BCE*, ed. M. L. Steiner and A. E. Killebrew, 269–77. Oxford: Oxford University Press.

Greenberg, R.; Eisenberg, E.; Paz, S.; and Paz, Y. 2006. *Bet Yeraḥ: The Early Bronze Age Mound*, Vol. 1: *Excavations Reports, 1933–1986*. IAA Reports 30. Jerusalem: IAA.

Ilan, D. 2002. Mortuary Practices in Early Bronze Age Canaan. *NEA* 65: 92–104.

Iserlis, M. 2016. Technological Choices: Identifying Kura-Araxes Ceramic Technologies in the Levant. Presented at the 10th ICAANE, Vienna, Austria.

Kenyon, K. M. 1960. *Excavations at Jericho*, Vol. 1: *The Tombs Excavated in 1952–4*. London: BSAJ.

Longford, C., and Berger, A. 2016. Growing Complexity: Early Bronze Age Plant Economy of Tel Bet Yerah. Presented at the 10th ICAANE, Vienna, Austria.

Maqdissi, M., al-, and Braemer, F. 2006. Labwe (Syrie): Une ville du Bronze ancient du Levant Sud. *Paléorient* 32 (1): 113–24.

Miroschedji, P. de. 1999. Yarmuth: The Dawn of City-States in Southern Canaan. *NEA* 62: 2–19.

　2009. Rise and Collapse in the Southern Levant in the Early Bronze Age. *Scienze dell'Antichità* 15: 101–29.

Müller-Neuhof, B., and Abu-Azizeh, W. 2016. Milestones for a Tentative Chronological Framework for the Late Prehistoric Colonization of the Basalt Desert (North-Eastern Jordan). *Levant* 48: 220–35.

Ortner, D. J., and Fröhlich, B. 2008. *The Early Bronze Age I Tombs and Burials of Bâb edh-Dhrâʿ, Jordan*. REDSPJ 3. Lanham, MD: AltaMira.

Palumbo, G. 1990. *The Early Bronze Age IV in the Southern Levant: Settlement Patterns, Economy, and Material Culture of a "Dark Age."* CMAO 3. Rome: University of Rome, "La Sapienza."

Paz, S., and Rotem, Y. 2016. Urbanization and Domestic Life: The EB I–III Sequence at Tel Bet Yerah (2003–2015 Seasons of Excavation). Presented at the 10th ICAANE, Vienna, Austria.

Philip, G. 2008. The Early Bronze I–III Ages. In *The Archaeology of Jordan*, ed. B. MacDonald, R. Adams, and P. Bienkowski, 163–232. London: Equinox.

　2016. The Late 4th Millennium BC at Tell esh-Shuna North in Its Regional Context. Presented at the 10th ICAANE, Vienna, Austria.

Rast, W. A. 1999. Society and Mortuary Customs at Bab edh-Dhraʿ. In *Archaeology, History, and Culture in Palestine and the Near East: Essays in Memory of Albert E. Glock*, ed. T. Kapitan, 164–82. ASOR Books 3. Atlanta: Scholars.

Rast, W. A., and Schaub, R. T. 2003. *Bab edh-Dhrâ': Excavations at the Town Site (1975–81)*. REDSPJ 2. Winona Lake, IN: Eisenbrauns.

Regev, J.; Miroshedji, P. de; Greenberg, R.; Braun, E.; Greenhut, Z.; and Boaretto, E. 2012. Chronology of the Early Bronze Age in the Southern Levant: New Analysis for a High Chronology. *Radiocarbon* 54: 525–66.

Rosen, A. M. 1995. The Social Response to Environmental Change in Early Bronze Age Canaan. *JAA* 14: 26–44.

Roux, V., and Miroschedji, P. de. 2009. Revisiting the History of the Potter's Wheel in the Southern Levant. *Levant* 41: 155–73.

Schaub, R. T., and Rast, W. A. 1989. *Bab edh-Dhrâ': Excavations in the Cemetery Directed by Paul W. Lapp (1965–67)*. REDSPJ 1. Winona Lake, IN: Published for ASOR by Eisenbrauns.

Tubb, J. N. 1988. Tell es-Sa'idiyeh: Preliminary Report on the First Three Seasons of Renewed Excavations. *Levant* 20: 23–88.

Tubb, J. N.; Dorrell, P. G.; and Cobbing, F. J. 1996. Interim Report on the Eighth (1995) Season of Excavations at Tell es-Sa'idiyeh. *PEQ* 128: 16–40.

Vaux, R. de, and Steve, A. M. 1969. *Les fouilles de Tell el-Far'ah*. Tel Aviv: Tel Aviv University.

White, C. E.; Chesson, M. S.; and Schaub, R. T. 2014. A Recipe for Disaster: Emerging Urbanism and Unsustainable Plant Economies at Early Bronze Age Ras an-Numayra, Jordan. *Antiquity* 88 (340): 363–77.

TEN

CONTINUITY, INNOVATION, AND CHANGE

The Intermediate Bronze Age in the Southern Levant

SUSAN L. COHEN

The Intermediate Bronze Age in the southern Levant (ca. 2650–1950/1925 BCE)[1] (Fig. 10.1) presents numerous interpretative challenges. Until recently, many analyses have described the Intermediate Bronze Age as a "dark age," an "interlude," and as a short and rather obscure transitional period of regression and/or stagnation between two more significant and important eras of urban development and social progression (e.g., Mazar 1990; Gophna 1992; Dever 1998). However, continued excavation and publication of material from sites throughout the region, including evidence from ^{14}C analysis, have resulted in new understandings of the social and economic organization and history of the Intermediate Bronze Age. Rather than simply be relegated to a secondary position as an interlude in which human civilization languished without either innovation or progress, these new data indicate that the Intermediate Bronze Age was instead an era of considerable resilience, adaptation, flexibility, and change that built on previous social and cultural traditions while simultaneously laying the groundwork for new growth and development.

PREVIOUS WORK: TERMINOLOGY AND CHRONOLOGY

A bewildering plethora of terms, dates, approaches, and assumptions has plagued the study of the Intermediate Bronze Age from the outset.[2] In recent years, however, the various names for the period have narrowed to two sets of terminology in simultaneous use: "Early Bronze Age IV" and "Intermediate

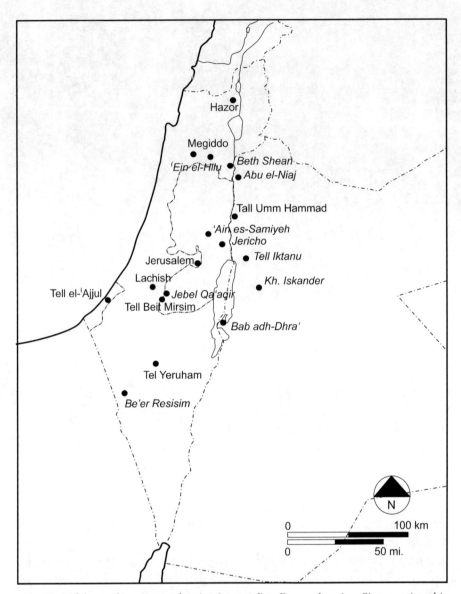

10.1. Map of the southern Levant showing Intermediate Bronze Age sites. Sites mentioned in the text are in italics. (Map by W. Więckowski.)

Bronze Age," each of which offer different assumptions and/or conclusions regarding relationships between this period and the eras preceding and following it, with accompanying inferences about social, cultural, and material developments. In many cases, the preference for employing one nomenclature over the other has divided along geographical lines, resulting from the regional changes so apparent in the period (see below), with EB IV more commonly used in reference to the eastern portions of the southern Levant (Palumbo

2008: 227), while the term "Intermediate Bronze Age" appears more frequently in connection with western regions.

Here, the term "Intermediate Bronze Age" is used, as it implies a connection with both the preceding Early Bronze Age and the following Middle Bronze Age throughout the southern Levant; yet, it also suggests an independence from the cultural signatures and developments notable for each of those eras. This then serves to emphasize the Intermediate Bronze Age as an independent phase in human development in the southern Levant. Ultimately, however, this terminological preference remains a semantic distinction, as the label of a period is of far less concern than is the understanding and analysis of the organization of the society that existed during that time.

In addition to terminological confusion, the chronology for the Intermediate Bronze Age also presents difficulties for the interpretation of the period. Until recently, general consensus was that the Intermediate Bronze Age was of relatively short duration, lasting at most two centuries, and thus the term "interlude" at least could be appropriate chronologically, if not culturally. However, recent ^{14}C data clearly indicate that the end of EB III must be raised by several centuries to ca. 2650 BCE (Regev et al. 2012; Höflmayer et al. 2014). Accordingly, this results in lengthening the time span attributed to the Intermediate Bronze Age. Rather than a relatively short duration of a mere two centuries, these new chronological data indicate that the Intermediate Bronze Age most probably lasted over half a millennium – at least 600 years – and possibly longer, depending on further analyses of both this era and data relating to the beginning of the Middle Bronze Age (Cohen 2012; 2017; Falconer and Fall 2016; 2017; Höflmayer 2017). Thus, based on chronology alone, it is clear that the Intermediate Bronze Age can no longer be considered simply as an interlude or transitional period. Instead, it must be examined as an independent era in its own right, with its own patterns of human habitation, settlement, and subsistence.

SOCIAL ORGANIZATION: SETTLEMENT, SITES, AND SUBSISTENCE

Most studies of the Intermediate Bronze Age tend to be in agreement regarding the strong local nature of society during this period, as the types of settlement, settlement patterns, and the accompanying subsistence strategies and associated material culture clearly differ regionally throughout the southern Levant (Richard and Long 2007). Until relatively recently, the majority of known sites dating to the Intermediate Bronze Age were those with exclusively mortuary remains, such as Jericho (Kenyon 1960; 1965), Jebel Qaʿaqir (Dever 2014), Dhahr Mirzbaneh (ʿAin es-Samiyeh) (Lapp 1966), and Beth Shean (Oren 1973), among others (see summary in Greenhut 1995). These, while providing valuable information regarding burial traditions and material culture, are also inherently limited by virtue of the time- and type-specific nature of mortuary remains in an archaeological context, and a data set composed almost exclusively of mortuary remains accordingly results in a dearth of information regarding other aspects of human settlement and activity.

In recent decades, however, continued excavation throughout the southern Levant has provided more data from sites with Intermediate Bronze Age settlement. Sites with occupational remains in Palestine and southern Jordan include Khirbet Iskander (Richard 2000; Richard and Long 2007; 2009; Richard et al. 2010), Umm el-Niaj (Falconer and Magness-Gardiner 1989), Tell Iktanu (Prag 2014), Bab adh-Dhra' (Rast and Schaub 2003), and 'Ein el-Hilu (Covello-Paran 2009), and excavations at each have revealed significant variation in settlement type and social and economic organization. This, in turn, has both encouraged the proliferation of models to describe Intermediate Bronze Age society and has led to differences in the postulated degrees of continuity and/or discontinuity with the preceding EB III, with the result that, depending on the site and region, the interpretations of dynamics of the "collapse" or shift from EB III to the Intermediate Bronze Age have varied considerably (Richard and Long 2007: 270; 2009: 91–4). Thus, rather than clear transitions, the numerous subregional sociocultural differences suggest instead "sloping horizons" (D'Andrea 2014a; 2014b: 153) between the Intermediate Bronze Age and the preceding and following eras in the southern Levant.

For example, excavations at Khirbet Iskander, located in modern Jordan, clearly reveal significant continuity with EB III, for example, evidence for year-round sedentary occupation, as well as indications of greater social complexity and some elite populations (Richard and Long 2009: 91) (Fig. 10.2). Three phases of continuous occupation were uncovered stratigraphically at Khirbet Iskander (Richard and Long 2010: 272–3), supported by the identification of three typo-chronological phases at the site as well (Richard and Long 2010: 275). Likewise, two building phases were uncovered at Tell Iktanu, and three at Tall Umm Hammad (Palumbo 2008: 238). These discoveries, and particularly the evidence from Khirbet Iskander, suggest that Intermediate Bronze Age occupation in Transjordan implemented more consistent and diverse occupational strategies, and retained a greater degree of permanent multiphase sedentary settlements based on agriculture than did the western portions of the southern Levant (Richard and Long 2009: 93; Richard 2010: 5).

This continuity of settlement from EB III to the Intermediate Bronze Age at sites in central Jordan is upheld by survey data (D'Andrea 2012: 44), and further support for the existence of both an agricultural and sedentary base utilized by the region's inhabitants comes from evidence for plant cultivation found at sites such as Abu el-Niaj and Bab adh-Dhra' (Palumbo 2008: 236, 251). The number of cultivated plant species found at Intermediate Bronze Age sites is

10.2. Architecture from Khirbet Iskander Area B, Phase A (redrawn after Richard and Long 2009: fig. 5).

smaller than those uncovered at sites in both the preceding and following eras – the more urban periods – which suggests that while Intermediate Bronze Age inhabitants may have had some sedentary bases, the production of agriculture remained limited. Regardless of scope, the presence of grapes and other fruits imply that at least some portion of the population remained sedentary throughout the year.

By contrast, excavation at the small village site of 'Ein el-Hilu in the Jezreel Valley revealed different socioeconomic organization, development, and overall subsistence strategies (Covello-Paran 2009). The site is best interpreted as a small hamlet that produced its own food and engaged in a mixed economy that resulted in a self-sufficiency for food production but produced little surplus (Covello-Paran 2009: 18–19). In addition, the lack of evidence for local pottery production suggests that the inhabitants of 'Ein el-Hilu participated in a larger regional economy for certain items, and some ceramics manufactured in Syria found at the site indicate participation in a longer-distance exchange network as well (Covello-Paran 2009: 18). The domestic nature and organization of the architecture at 'Ein el-Hilu, together with the distribution of artifacts, indicate that most activities occurred locally, at the household level, and there is no evidence that suggests hierarchy or complex social organization. Overall, the subsistence strategy represented at 'Ein el-Hilu reflects nonspecialized, village-based local activities (Covello-Paran 2009: 18), clearly different from those implemented at Khirbet Iskander.

Finally, the numerous small settlements uncovered in the Negev and northern Sinai represent yet another form of Intermediate Bronze Age

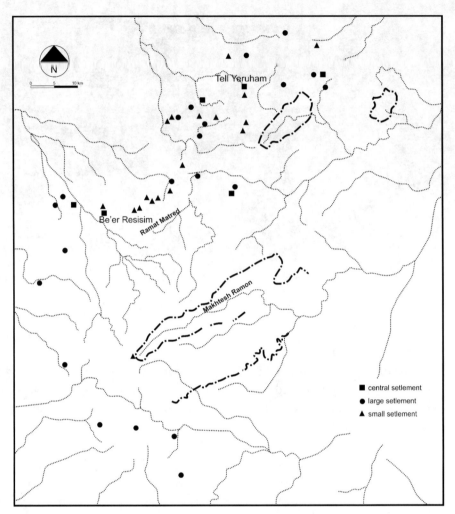

10.3. Map of Intermediate Bronze Age sites in the Negev (redrawn after Dever 2014: fig. 15.1).

socioeconomic organization and subsistence (Fig. 10.3). This increased and highly visible human presence in marginal areas and, particularly, desert regions – for example, north Sinai and the Negev – stands out as one of the defining characteristics of settlement during this period. Over 1,500 Intermediate Bronze Age sites have been identified in these areas (Haiman 2009: 38), and of these sites, the vast majority appear to have been temporary or inhabited for short periods only (Haiman 2009: 40); the distribution of the sites and, particularly, their location in relation to water sources suggest that they were not supported by permanent food production (Haiman 2009: 40). Excavations at the site of Be'er Resisim found numerous circular structures clustered around communal areas (Fig. 10.4) – some of which may have been for human shelter, while some functioned as enclosures for animals – which the

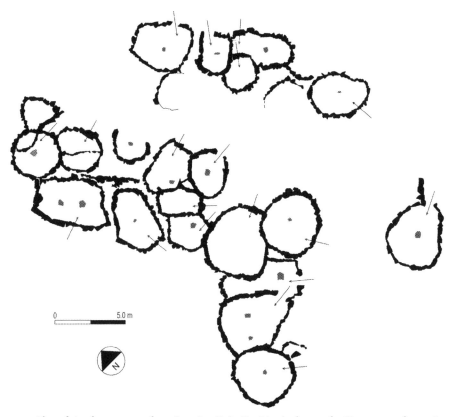

10.4. Plan of circular structures from Area A at Be'er Resisim (redrawn after Dever 2014: fig. 11.9).

excavator interpreted as the remains of winter campsites (Dever 2014: 229). The agglutinative architectural pattern at Be'er Resisim, together with the lack of monumental or public buildings or defensive walls, suggests both the lack of organized settlement planning as well as a relatively unstratified social structure (Dever 2014: 209). As with all other aspects of the period, interpretations of these sites in marginal regions in the extreme south vary widely regarding their role in Intermediate Bronze Age society and subsistence, ranging from association with metals production, transport, and trade (Goren 1996: 63; Haiman 1996; 2009; Kochavi 2009) (see below) to links with social, economic, and political organization and conditions in more settled regions of the southern Levant (Finkelstein and Perevolotsky 1990).

As this brief overview indicates, the settlement patterns, subsistence strategies, and likely degree of continuity from the Early Bronze Age revealed at excavation of sites in the eastern southern Levant differ significantly from those excavated in the western portions of the region (Richard and Long 2007; 2009), and both differ yet again from those in the more marginal regions of the extreme south. These variations have then influenced the contrasting scholarly interpretations and views of the Intermediate Bronze Age, and the corresponding degree of emphasis placed on sedentary occupation, nomadism, pastoralism, and various combinations of these different socioeconomic descriptions; this, in turn, has produced numerous competing – or at least often incompatible – models, each of which possesses certain interpretative advantages and drawbacks.[3] No single model seems appropriate to the entire region. Instead, these models serve to draw attention to the regionalism of Intermediate Bronze Age settlement in the southern Levant, characterized by a diverse array of subsistence strategies, consisting of nonspecialist village production, pastoral nomadism, localized herding, mixed economy herding, agriculture/horticulture, and participation in regional exchange networks.[4] The overwhelming conclusion that results from this variety of suggestions, foci, and emphases, therefore, is that southern Levantine society in the Intermediate Bronze Age consisted of a highly regionalized, sharply diversified, and strongly localized differing set of contemporary but not necessarily competing strategies, each designed to exploit the individual ecological niche in which each group was located.[5]

MATERIAL CULTURE, MORTUARY CUSTOMS, AND FOREIGN CONTACTS

The material culture of the Intermediate Bronze Age clearly reflects the regionalism so apparent in settlement patterns and subsistence strategies. This is especially visible in the ceramic remains found in mortuary contexts – long the primary evidence for analysis of the period as a whole – which contain a variety of styles and forms (Fig. 10.5).[6] As a result, the regionalism exhibited by the pottery assemblages stands out as perhaps the best known hallmark of the period, epitomized by William Dever's categorization of Intermediate Bronze Age ceramics into "families" (NC, CH, J, S, TR, possibly also C and AZ).[7] Once thought to illustrate chronological development within the Intermediate Bronze Age, most recent evaluations of these ceramic groups have noted that the different families provide further support for regionalism (see, e.g., Finkelstein 1991: 133; Richard 2000: *passim*; and D'Andrea 2012: 17). In addition, analyses of these different groups indicate that some forms exhibit clear continuity from the Early Bronze Age, while others show significant changes from the ceramics associated with the previous period, as illustrated, for example, by the assemblages at Tell Iktanu (Prag 2009: 83) and Khirbet Iskander (Richard et al. 2010) and confirmed further by a broad analysis of the ceramic corpus of Intermediate Bronze Age in its entirety (D'Andrea 2012; 2014a).

Overall, the mortuary customs reveal little evidence for strong social stratification.[8] Earlier scholarship supposed that the relative simplicity of burial customs then reflected the regression to a pastoral and/or nomadic way of life in the Intermediate Bronze Age following the collapse of EB III

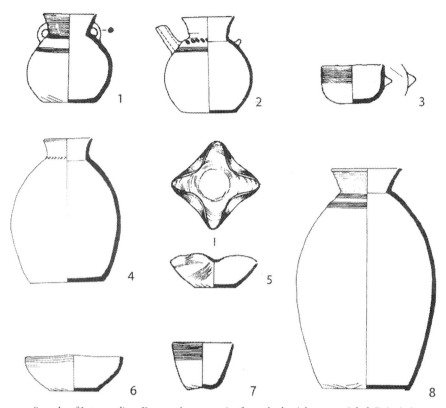

10.5. Sample of Intermediate Bronze Age ceramics from the burial caves at Jebel Qaʻaqir (not to scale) (adapted from Dever 2014: fig 2.88:4, 6; 2.89:7, 9, 11; 2.92:5; 2.93:1, 3).

urban culture (Dever 1987: 17). This approach cited the dominance of secondary burials found in Intermediate Bronze Age as supportive evidence, due to secondary burial reflecting postmortem movement of the body, which was then thought to be consistent with mortuary practices of non-sedentary peoples. However, further studies noted both the diversity of Intermediate Bronze Age mortuary traditions and the complexity of traditions reflected therein (Baxevani 1995: 95), suggesting that secondary burials and/or simplicity of burials need not necessarily be linked exclusively with nomadic peoples or seminomadic peoples. Although the Intermediate Bronze Age burials in the southern Levant do not suggest strong social stratification, it is not necessarily the case that they then must represent itinerant populations, especially given the evidence for mixed social-economic subsistence strategies at numerous sites, as discussed above.

The simplicity of the mortuary data hampers making determinations regarding religion and/or cultic practices of the Intermediate Bronze Age. Other than a silver cup found at ʻAin es-Samiyeh, no luxury or "elite" materials have been found in association with mortuary assemblages in the southern Levant. Evidence from animal remains and inscribed doorways found at the cemetery in Jebel Qaʿaqir provide some indication of cultic and/or ritual activity (Dever 2011: 95–6; 2014), but the evidence is limited and hence difficult to analyze. The presence of cups in the tomb assemblages suggests a rise in mortuary-related drinking activities, such as feasting and/or banqueting (Dever 2011: 95; Prag 2014: 396),[9] and Kay Prag (2014: 396) has proposed that the type and composition of the animal remains perhaps suggests a ritual emphasis on cattle.[10] Monoliths found in the household units at ʿEin el-Hilu (Covello-Paran 2009: 12) also indicate that some cultic activities occurred at the domestic level rather than in more hierarchically organized or centrally located spaces.

In general, evidence to date suggests that the Intermediate Bronze Age population in the southern Levant did not participate in long-distance trade to any significant degree (Palumbo 2008: 252). Other than the famed silver goblet found at ʿAin es-Samiyeh (see the discussion in Dever 2011: 97), there is little to no evidence of external trade in luxury goods or exotica. Overall, foreign contact remained limited in both scope and geography; Syrian influence extended only as far as the northern part of the southern Levant and the Jordan Valley, as illustrated by the presence of Syrian-produced and Syrian-inspired ceramics, such as those excavated at ʿEin el-Hilu (Covello-Paran 2009: 18).

By contrast, the international focus on the southern part of the southern Levant in the Intermediate Bronze Age was linked to Egypt and events there (e.g., Prag 2009: 87). The decentralization of authority in Egypt during the First Intermediate Period may have resulted in a shift in Egyptian activities in the southern portions of Palestine and the Sinai, particularly in relation to the acquisition of resources there, most notably copper. As such, the proliferation of sites and other evidence for human activity in the marginal regions of the southern Levant in the Intermediate Bronze Age as described above may be linked to the concurrent rise of local Levantine control over and/or participation in the copper trade (Goren 1996: 63; Haiman 1996; 2009; Kochavi 2009: 48). Although the limited – to date – number of sites with copper ingots or other copper remains at them (Finkelstein 1991: 131) hampers making this determination with certainty, it may be suggested that copper from the mines near Feinan, and perhaps also from other, more northern locations (see Prag 2014: 395), was transported across the Sinai and the northern Negev to Egypt. In addition to the possible proliferation of the copper trade, other evidence for sporadic participation in foreign trade with regions in the south comes from Red Sea shells found at Beʾer Resisim (Dever 2014: 209).

SUMMARY AND CONCLUSIONS: SOCIETY AND CULTURE IN THE INTERMEDIATE BRONZE AGE SOUTHERN LEVANT

By defining the Intermediate Bronze Age as "an interlude" (Dever 1998: 282; 2011: 89; Mazar 1990), a "crisis" of urban civilization (Gophna 1992: 126), or

10.5. Sample of Intermediate Bronze Age ceramics from the burial caves at Jebel Qa'aqir (not to scale) (adapted from Dever 2014: fig 2.88:4, 6; 2.89:7, 9, 11; 2.92:5; 2.93:1, 3).

urban culture (Dever 1987: 17). This approach cited the dominance of secondary burials found in Intermediate Bronze Age as supportive evidence, due to secondary burial reflecting postmortem movement of the body, which was then thought to be consistent with mortuary practices of non-sedentary peoples. However, further studies noted both the diversity of Intermediate Bronze Age mortuary traditions and the complexity of traditions reflected therein (Baxevani 1995: 95), suggesting that secondary burials and/or simplicity of burials need not necessarily be linked exclusively with nomadic peoples or seminomadic peoples. Although the Intermediate Bronze Age burials in the southern Levant do not suggest strong social stratification, it is not necessarily the case that they then must represent itinerant populations, especially given the evidence for mixed social-economic subsistence strategies at numerous sites, as discussed above.

The simplicity of the mortuary data hampers making determinations regarding religion and/or cultic practices of the Intermediate Bronze Age. Other than a silver cup found at 'Ain es-Samiyeh, no luxury or "elite" materials have been found in association with mortuary assemblages in the southern Levant. Evidence from animal remains and inscribed doorways found at the cemetery in Jebel Qaʻaqir provide some indication of cultic and/or ritual activity (Dever 2011: 95–6; 2014), but the evidence is limited and hence difficult to analyze. The presence of cups in the tomb assemblages suggests a rise in mortuary-related drinking activities, such as feasting and/or banqueting (Dever 2011: 95; Prag 2014: 396),[9] and Kay Prag (2014: 396) has proposed that the type and composition of the animal remains perhaps suggests a ritual emphasis on cattle.[10] Monoliths found in the household units at ʻEin el-Hilu (Covello-Paran 2009: 12) also indicate that some cultic activities occurred at the domestic level rather than in more hierarchically organized or centrally located spaces.

In general, evidence to date suggests that the Intermediate Bronze Age population in the southern Levant did not participate in long-distance trade to any significant degree (Palumbo 2008: 252). Other than the famed silver goblet found at ʻAin es-Samiyeh (see the discussion in Dever 2011: 97), there is little to no evidence of external trade in luxury goods or exotica. Overall, foreign contact remained limited in both scope and geography; Syrian influence extended only as far as the northern part of the southern Levant and the Jordan Valley, as illustrated by the presence of Syrian-produced and Syrian-inspired ceramics, such as those excavated at ʻEin el-Hilu (Covello-Paran 2009: 18).

By contrast, the international focus on the southern part of the southern Levant in the Intermediate Bronze Age was linked to Egypt and events there (e.g., Prag 2009: 87). The decentralization of authority in Egypt during the First Intermediate Period may have resulted in a shift in Egyptian activities in the southern portions of Palestine and the Sinai, particularly in relation to the acquisition of resources there, most notably copper. As such, the proliferation of sites and other evidence for human activity in the marginal regions of the southern Levant in the Intermediate Bronze Age as described above may be linked to the concurrent rise of local Levantine control over and/or participation in the copper trade (Goren 1996: 63; Haiman 1996; 2009; Kochavi 2009: 48). Although the limited – to date – number of sites with copper ingots or other copper remains at them (Finkelstein 1991: 131) hampers making this determination with certainty, it may be suggested that copper from the mines near Feinan, and perhaps also from other, more northern locations (see Prag 2014: 395), was transported across the Sinai and the northern Negev to Egypt. In addition to the possible proliferation of the copper trade, other evidence for sporadic participation in foreign trade with regions in the south comes from Red Sea shells found at Beʼer Resisim (Dever 2014: 209).

SUMMARY AND CONCLUSIONS: SOCIETY AND CULTURE IN THE INTERMEDIATE BRONZE AGE SOUTHERN LEVANT

By defining the Intermediate Bronze Age as "an interlude" (Dever 1998: 282; 2011: 89; Mazar 1990), a "crisis" of urban civilization (Gophna 1992: 126), or even, despite its current usage, an "intermediate" period, the era has been automatically relegated to a secondary position as a mere follower of or precursor to more presumably interesting and important things. In addition, the historic stress on the terminology of change rather than the actual nature of change then contributed to the proliferation of models that sought to fit the Intermediate Bronze Age and its peoples within holistic frameworks of societal types. Accordingly, until recently, the Intermediate Bronze Age has suffered from both an overabundance of labels and an excessive exceptionalization that has impeded examination of the growing body of data for the era.

In his seminal study of the Intermediate Bronze Age (EB IV), published in 1991 and thus already over twenty years old, Gaetano Palumbo (1991: 22) stated the need to examine this era as part of the greater culture of the Bronze Age in the southern Levant and noted that it was important to view the Intermediate Bronze Age as a product resulting from the previous EB III. Likewise, shortly thereafter, Dever pointed out that the presumed "darkness" of the era derived less from the reality of the situation than it was an expression of an "archaeological myopia" (1998: 295). In recent years, continued excavation of sites with Intermediate Bronze Age material has served to provide increasing visibility to the era and shed light on its connections to and differences from the Early and Middle Bronze Age periods proper. Both analyses of individual sites and broader synthetic studies have identified different phases within the Intermediate Bronze Age, described as decline/reorganization, consolidation/recovery, and growth (Richard and Long 2010: 278; D'Andrea 2014a: 278), which serve to counter long-standing views of the period as one of social, economic, and material stagnation.

Significantly, however, most – if not all – of the recent scholarship, including those that have identified phases and progression within the Intermediate Bronze Age (e.g., Richard and Long 2010; D'Andrea 2014a; Prag 2014), predate the most recent ^{14}C data that clearly indicate the Intermediate Bronze Age lasted far longer than previously supposed. As such, it is difficult to place these newly identified internal phases within the longer period, if only because the majority of the accompanying analysis of the relevant data was predicated on the shorter chronological span. In light of the lengthier duration of the period, however, the identification of these phases of development becomes even more compelling, as it is highly improbable that there would have been no fluctuations, changes, or adaptations in human development in the region for 600 years, especially given the changes and developments in sociopolitical organization in Egypt and the continuation of urbanized society in the northern Levant.

Instead of an interlude, the Intermediate Bronze Age must be viewed as a significant era of southern Levantine development in its own right (D'Andrea

2014b: 158). Rather than subsuming human society in the southern Levant during this period to one overarching social model, the variety and internal complexity of the period must be conceded, and the multiplicity of its contemporary organizational strategies analyzed independently. No one single or simple explanation may serve to explain an entire region and/or culture (Prag 2009: 82), especially given the variety and diversity in evidence that exists for the Intermediate Bronze Age, as outlined above, as well as its chronological longevity as recently determined.

Likewise, descriptions such as "dark age" and "discontinuous" must also be abandoned. The sheer variety of the ceramics, subsistence strategies, and other adaptations speak to the inherent creativity and regionalism that existed in the southern Levant. The data demonstrate independent development during the Intermediate Bronze Age, while certain regions and phases also exhibit clear continuity from EB III (Palumbo 1991), as well as continuity into Middle Bronze Age I (Cohen 2009; *contra* Dever 2014: 234). The Intermediate Bronze Age, therefore, may be best viewed as a period of change (Prag 2009: 87), and one that is, perhaps, more properly described as "different" (D'Andrea 2014a: 268).[11] Depending on the region, and, perhaps, the internal chronological phase as well, the peoples of the Intermediate Bronze Age in the southern Levant retained certain patterns of settlement, subsistence, and organization while simultaneously developing new ones as they adapted and reacted to new circumstances, suiting each to location and situation. Rather than a crisis, the Intermediate Bronze Age now may be better understood as a period of continuity and change, regression and progression, and innovation and conservatism.

NOTES

1 The chronology of the southern Levant in the third and second millennia BCE is currently the subject of intense debate, triggered by recent ^{14}C data that have raised the end of the Early Bronze Age (EB) III and suggest significant changes to both the beginning and end dates of the Middle Bronze Age. These changes obviously affect the chronology assigned to the Intermediate Bronze Age. The dates used in this chapter follow those established in Regev et al. 2012 and Höflmayer et al. 2014 for the beginning of the Intermediate Bronze Age (as discussed further below). Determination of the end of the Intermediate Bronze Age is linked to ongoing discussion about the beginning of the Middle Bronze Age (e.g., Cohen 2017; Falconer and Fall 2017; Höflmayer 2017) and, to date, is not yet fully resolved. The dates cited above thus remain approximate.
2 For recent overviews and discussions of the history of usage for varying terms, dates, and associated approaches, see, e.g., Bunimovitz and Greenberg 2006; Palumbo 2008; Richard 2010: 4; D'Andrea 2014a: 1–19, table 1; Dever 2014: 149; and Prag 2014, among many others. Older but still significant and pertinent syntheses of the history of scholarship on the Intermediate Bronze Age are Dever 1980 and Richard 1980.

3. For an assessment of the values of and problems with models of interpretation, see Dever (1998: 294): "the proliferation of models is sometimes self-serving, needlessly contentious, and tends towards fragmentation, rather than increasing and integrating our empirical knowledge of the past."
4. See, e.g., Dever's most recent assessment that the Intermediate Bronze Age consisted of a diversified subsistence economy, including herding of sheep and goats, hunting and gathering, and primitive dry farming (2014: 209).
5. The faunal evidence from the Intermediate Bronze Age also supports the perspective of regionalism, with various herding/animal husbandry strategies utilized in different environments (Horwitz 1989).
6. For an overview, see Dever 1987.
7. For recent discussions of the different ceramic families, see D'Andrea 2014a: 20–2 and Dever 2014: 149–50.
8. For detailed discussion/debate regarding stratification in Intermediate Bronze Age mortuary practices, see Shay 1983 and Palumbo 1987.
9. For a discussion of Syrian-inspired drinking customs and associated material culture, see Bunimovitz and Greenberg 2004; 2006.
10. Note, however, Liora Horwitz's (1989) discussion of the predominance of caprovines in Intermediate Bronze Age burials.
11. For more detailed discussion of this expression, see D'Andrea 2014a: 265–8.

REFERENCES

Baxevani, E. 1995. The Complex Nomads: Death and Social Stratification in EB IV Southern Levant. In *The Archaeology of Death in the Ancient Near East*, ed. S. Campbell and A. Green, 85–95. Oxbow Monograph 51. Oxford: Oxbow.

Bunimovitz, S., and Greenberg, R. 2004. Revealed in Their Cups: Syrian Drinking Customs in Intermediate Bronze Age Canaan. *BASOR* 334: 19–31.

2006. Of Pots and Paradigms: Interpreting the Intermediate Bronze Age in Israel/Palestine. In *Confronting the Past: Archaeological and Historical Essays on Ancient Israel in Honor of William G. Dever*, ed. S. Gitin, J. E. Wright, and J. P. Dessel, 23–31. Winona Lake, IN: Eisenbrauns.

Cohen, S. L. 2009. Continuities and Discontinuities: A Reexamination of the Intermediate Bronze Age–Middle Bronze Age Transition in Canaan. *BASOR* 354: 1–13.

2012. Synchronisms and Significance: Reevaluating Interconnections between Middle Kingdom Egypt and the Southern Levant. *JAEI* 4 (3): 1–8.

2017. Reevaluation of Connections between Egypt and the Southern Levant in the Middle Bronze Age in Light of the New Higher Chronology. *JAEI* 13 (1): 34–42.

Covello-Paran, K. 2009. Socio-Economic Aspects of an Intermediate Bronze Age Village in the Jezreel Valley. In *The Levant in Transition: Proceedings of a Conference Held at the British Museum on 20–21 April 2004*, ed. P. J. Parr, 9–20. PEFA 9. Leeds: Maney.

D'Andrea, M. 2012. The Early Bronze Age IV Period in South-Central Transjordan: Reconsidering Chronology through Ceramic Technology. *Levant* 44: 17–50.

2014a. *The Southern Levant in Early Bronze IV: Issues and Perspectives in the Pottery Evidence*. 2 vols. CMAO 17. Rome: University of Rome, "La Sapienza."

2014b. Townships or Villages? Remarks on the Middle Bronze IA in the Southern Levant. In *Proceedings of the 8th International Congress on the Archaeology of the Ancient Near East, 30 April–4 May 2012, University of Warsaw*, Vol. 1: *Plenary Sessions – Township and Villages – High and Low: The Minor Arts for the Elite and for the Populace*, ed. P. Bieliński, M. Gawlikowski, R. Koliński, D. Ławecka, A. Sołtysiak, and Z. Wygnańska, 151–72. Wiesbaden: Harrassowitz.

Dever, W. G. 1980. New Vistas on the EB IV ("MB I") Horizon in Syria-Palestine. *BASOR* 237: 35–64.

——— 1987. Funerary Practices in EB IV (MB I) Palestine: A Study in Cultural Discontinuity. In *Love & Death in the Ancient Near East: Essays in Honor of Marvin H. Pope*, ed. J. H. Marks and R. M. Good, 9–19. Guilford, CT: Four Quarters.

——— 1998. Social Structure in the Early Bronze Age IV Period in Palestine. In *The Archaeology of Society in the Holy Land*, ed. T. E. Levy, 282–96. NAAA. London: Leicester University Press.

——— 2011. Religion and Cult in Early Bronze Age IV Palestine. In *Daily Life, Materiality, and Complexity in Early Urban Communities of the Southern Levant: Papers in Honor of Walter E. Rast and R. Thomas Schaub*, ed. M. S. Chesson, 89–100. Winona Lake, IN: Eisenbrauns.

——— 2014. *Excavations at the Early Bronze IV Sites of Jebel Qa'aqir and Be'er Resisim*. SAHL 6. Winona Lake, IN: Eisenbrauns.

Falconer, S. E., and Fall, P. L. 2016. A Radiocarbon Sequence from Tell Abu en-Ni'aj, Jordan and Its Implications for Early Bronze IV Chronology in the Southern Levant. *Radiocarbon* 58: 615–47.

——— 2017. Radiocarbon Evidence from Tell Abu en-Ni'aj and Tell el-Hayyat, Jordan, and Its Implications for Bronze Age Levantine and Egyptian Chronologies. *JAEI* 13 (1): 7–19.

Falconer, S. E., and Magness-Gardiner, B. 1989. Bronze Age Village Life in the Jordan Valley: Archaeological Investigations at Tell el-Hayyat and Tell Abu en-Ni'aj. *National Geographic Research* 5: 335–47.

——— 1991. The Central Hill Country in the Intermediate Bronze Age. *IEJ* 41: 19–45.

Finkelstein, I., and Perevolotsky, A. 1990. Processes of Sedentarization and Nomadization in the History of Sinai and the Negev. *BASOR* 279: 67–88.

Gophna, R. 1992. The Intermediate Bronze Age. In *The Archaeology of Ancient Israel*, ed. A. Ben-Tor, 126–58. Trans. R. Greenberg, from Hebrew. New Haven, CT: Yale University Press; Tel Aviv: Open University of Israel.

Goren, Y. 1996. The Southern Levant in the Early Bronze Age IV: The Petrographic Perspective. *BASOR* 303: 33–72.

Greenhut, Z. 1995. EB IV Tombs and Burials in Palestine. *TA* 22: 3–46.

Haiman, M. 1996. Early Bronze Age IV Settlement Pattern of the Negev and the Sinai Deserts: View from Small Marginal Temporary Sites. *BASOR* 303: 1–32.

——— 2009. Copper Trade and Pastoralism in the Negev and Sinai Deserts in the EB IV. In *The Levant in Transition: Proceedings of a Conference Held at the British Museum on 20–21 April 2004*, ed. P. J. Parr, 38–42. PEFA 9. Leeds: Maney.

Höflmayer, F. 2017. A Radiocarbon Chronology for the Middle Bronze Age Southern Levant. *JAEI* 13 (1): 20–33.

Höflmayer, F.; Dee, M. W.; Genz, H.; and Riehl, S. 2014. Radiocarbon Evidence for the Early Bronze Age Levant: The Site of Tell Fadous-Kfarabida (Lebanon) and the End of the Early Bronze III Period. *Radiocarbon* 56: 529–42.

Horwitz, L. K. 1989. Sedentism in the Early Bronze IV: A Faunal Perspective. *BASOR* 275: 15–25.
Kenyon, K. M. 1960. *Excavations at Jericho,* Vol. 1: *The Tombs Excavated in 1952–4.* London: BSAJ.
———. 1965. *Excavations at Jericho,* Vol. 2: *The Tombs Excavated in 1955–8.* London: BSAJ.
Kochavi, M. 2009. The Intermediate Bronze Age (IBA) in the Negev, Forty Years Later. In *The Levant in Transition: Proceedings of a Conference Held at the British Museum on 20–21 April 2004,* ed. P. J. Parr, 43–8. PEFA 9. Leeds: Maney.
Lapp, P. W. 1966. *The Dhahr Mirzbâneh Tombs: Three Intermediate Bronze Age Cemeteries in Jordan.* Publications of the Jerusalem School 4. New Haven, CT: ASOR.
Mazar, A. 1990. *Archaeology of the Land of the Bible,* Vol. 1: *10,000–586 B.C.E.* ABRL. New York: Doubleday.
Oren, E. D. 1973. The Early Bronze IV Period in Northern Palestine and Its Cultural and Chronological Setting. *BASOR* 210: 20–37.
Palumbo, G. 1987. "Egalitarian" or "Stratified" Society? Some Notes on Mortuary Practices and Social Structure at Jericho in EB IV. *BASOR* 267: 43–59.
———. 1991. *The Early Bronze Age IV in the Southern Levant: Settlement Patterns, Economy, and Material Culture of a "Dark Age."* CMAO 3. Rome: University of Rome, "La Sapienza."
———. 2008. The Early Bronze IV. In *Jordan: An Archaeological Reader,* ed. R. B. Adams, 227–62. London: Equinox.
Prag, K. 2009. The Late Third Millennium in the Levant: A Reappraisal of the North–South Divide. In *The Levant in Transition: Proceedings of a Conference Held at the British Museum on 20–21 April 2004,* ed. P. J. Parr, 80–9. PEFA 9. Leeds: Maney.
———. 2014. The Southern Levant during the Intermediate Bronze Age. In *The Oxford Handbook of the Archaeology of the Levant, c. 8000–332 BCE,* ed. M. L. Steiner and A. E. Killebrew, 388–400. Oxford: Oxford University Press.
Rast, W. A., and Schaub, R. T. 2003. *Bab edh-Dhrâ' Excavations at the Town Site (1975–81).* REDSPJ 2. Winona Lake, IN: Eisenbrauns.
Regev, J.; Miroshedji, P. de; Greenberg, R.; Braun, E.; Greenhut, Z.; and Boaretto, E. 2012. Chronology of the Early Bronze Age in the Southern Levant: New Analysis for a High Chronology. *Radiocarbon* 54: 525–66.
Richard, S. 1980. Toward a Consensus of Opinion on the End of the Early Bronze Age in Palestine-Transjordan. *BASOR* 237: 5–34.
———. 2000. Chronology versus Regionalism in the Early Bronze IV: An Assemblage of Whole and Restored Vessels from the Public Building at Khirbet Iskander. In *The Archaeology of Jordan and Beyond: Essays in Honor of James A. Sauer,* ed. L. E. Stager, J. A. Greene, and M. D. Coogan, 399–417. HSMP; SAHL 1. Winona Lake, IN: Eisenbrauns.
———. 2010. Introduction. In *Khirbat Iskandar: Final Report on the Early Bronze IV Area C "Gateway" and Cemeteries,* ed. S. Richard, J. C. Long Jr., P. S. Holdorf, and G. Peterman, 1–20. ASORAR 14; AEKIIEJ 1. Boston: ASOR.
Richard, S., and Long, J. C., Jr. 2007. Khirbet Iskander: A City in Collapse at the End of the Early Bronze Age. In *Crossing Jordan: North American Contributions to the Archaeology of Jordan,* ed. T. E. Levy, P. M. M. Daviau, R. W. Younker, and M. Shaer, 269–76. London: Equinox.
———. 2009. Khirbet Iskander, Jordan and Early Bronze IV Studies: A View from a Tell. In *The Levant in Transition: Proceedings of a Conference Held at the British Museum on 20–21 April 2004,* ed. P. J. Parr, 90–100. PEFA 9. Leeds: Maney.

2010. Summary and Conclusions. In *Khirbat Iskandar: Final Report on the Early Bronze IV Area C "Gateway" and Cemeteries*, ed. S. Richard, J. C. Long Jr., P. S. Holdorf, and G. Peterman, 271–9. ASOR AR 14; AEKIIEJ 1. Boston: ASOR.

Richard, S.; Long, J. C., Jr.; Holdorf, P. S.; and Peterman, G., eds. 2010. *Khirbat Iskandar: Final Report on the Early Bronze IV Area C "Gateway" and Cemeteries*. ASORAR 14; AEKIIEJ 1. Boston: ASOR.

Shay, T. 1983 Burial Customs at Jericho in the Intermediate Bronze Age: A Componential Analysis. *TA* 10: 26–37.

ELEVEN

MIX 'n' MATCH
The Bioarchaeology of Commingled Remains

SUSAN GUISE SHERIDAN

This chapter will discuss the use of human skeletal collections from modern-day Israel, Palestine, and Jordan (Fig. 11.1) to demonstrate the potential of bioarchaeological reconstructions using mixed and fragmented (commingled) assemblages. I will provide a rationale for analyzing such collections – arguing that our dismissal of commingled remains has skewed a nuanced understanding of the ancient Levant. An overview of new methods, theories, and public interactions will be highlighted as well.

BIOARCHAEOLOGICAL MODEL

Bioarchaeology is the holistic synthesis of method and theory from biological anthropology and archaeology, drawing upon the humanities and natural and social sciences to explore the past 10,000–15,000 years of human history (Larsen 2015). A bioarchaeological approach can address questions of interest to Near Eastern archaeologists, using quantifiable data from the people themselves (bones and teeth), associated material culture, and modern social theory to inform reconstructions of: treatment of the dead (Porter and Boutin 2014); trade networks (Kaniewski et al. 2012); drivers of cultural change (Cline 2014); the role of women (Bolger 2008) and children (Leyerle 2002; 2013); violence (Gasperetti and Sheridan 2013); ethnicity (Gregoricka and Sheridan 2015); daily life (Chesson 2011); diet (Hill, Price, and Rowan 2016); and disease

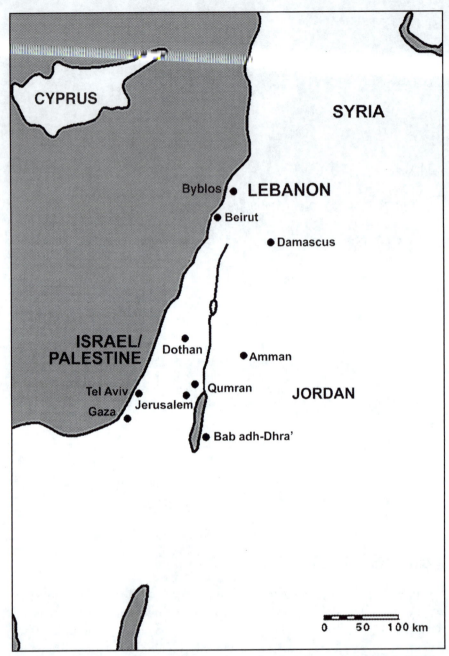

11.1. Map of the southern Levant with sites discussed and modern capitals labeled. (Map by S. G. Sheridan.)

(Perry 2012; Smith-Guzmán, Rose, and Kucken 2016) from past communities in the southern Levant.

Bioarchaeology views human remains "as biological specimens, as artifacts, and as symbols" (Martin and Harrod 2015: 117). Just as patterns of disease

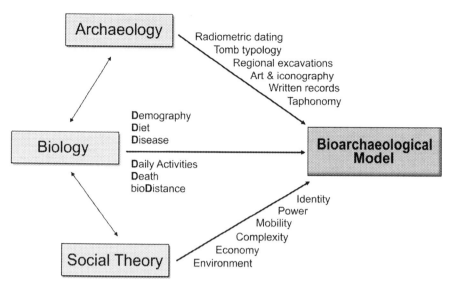

11.2. The bioarchaeological model. (Diagram by S. G. Sheridan.)

cannot be separated from the cultural context in which one exists, the symbol, myth, rituals, art, and technology of the past cannot be fully understood without an appreciation of our physiological restrictions. When biological information is merged with material remains, environmental constraints, and anthropological theory, a powerful tool becomes available (Sheridan 1999). Figure 11.2 illustrates the retrospective/prospective manner of bioarchaeology, where each component can draw from and contribute to the theories and interpretations of the others. A bioarchaeologist's contribution to this model – "the 6Ds of bioarchaeology" – includes forensic methods related to age, sex, and stature reconstruction to form a **D**emographic perspective; determination of foods consumed from the "menu" of available options for **D**iet reconstruction; differential diagnosis of **D**isease allowing assessment of morbidity and mortality; interpretation of a group's relationship to **D**eath via funerary practices; exploration of how people moved through the natural and built environment during **D**aily activities; and, the diversity/homogeneity of a community genetically (bio**D**istance) to address migration, exogamy, and ethnogenesis (Sheridan 2017).

COMMINGLING

In past excavations in the Levant, only portions of skeletons were collected (e.g., skulls and pelves) to permit basic demographic determinations related to age, sex, "race," stature, minimum number of individuals (MNI), and unique pathologies. Ancient Near Eastern human and non-human skeletal remains are often found in their original storage bags even decades after exhumation, housed in conditions far inferior to those provided artifacts, never having been analyzed. These practices have hinged bioarchaeological interpretations, subjugating many skeletal analyses to simple appendices of listed elements.

Compounding these concerns about excavation, curation, and/or a tendency toward typological studies, a larger worry involves a lack of recognition of the potential of commingled collections. A large number of Near Eastern skeletal assemblages are fragmented, mixed, and/or incomplete. Rivka Gonen (1992) noted that interring the bones of multiple individuals together was the predominant burial practice for most of Bronze Age Canaan and Middle Bronze and Iron Age Jordan. Abdulla al-Shorman and Ali Khwaileh (2011) reported numerous commingled collections, and Irit Yezerski (1999) discussed the importance of placing bones together in burials during the Iron Age, as ascribed in biblical passages (e.g., 2 Sam 17:23, 1 Kgs 13:31).

Mass graves resulting from disease or conflict (McMahon, Sołtysiak, and Weber 2011), generational reuse of family tombs (Ornter and Frohlich 2008; Sheridan et al. 2014), grouping bodies to free up land for agricultural use (McCreery 2002), or adherence to other cultural norms (Glencross 2011) explain some of the causes of commingling. Following burial, post-depositional processes can likewise produce admixture, such as the movement of bones by burrowing animals, agricultural/building practices, geological events, and flooding (Panakhyo and Jacobi 2016). Looting, poor excavation, curation, preservation, documentation, and storage can cause or exacerbate mixing (Lev-Tov and Maher 2001; Kersel and Chesson 2013). As a result, commingling is ubiquitous in Near Eastern bioarchaeology (Table 11.1), presenting limitations and advantages for research in the region.

SKELETAL COLLECTIONS

For this chapter, three large collections were used to demonstrate the potential that commingled assemblages offer our understanding of the ancient Levant. They include Early Bronze Age Bab adh-Dhra', Early Iron Age Tell Dothan, and Byzantine St. Stephen's monastery (Table 11.2).

Bab adh-Dhra'

This site is located southeast of the Dead Sea, just east of the Lisan Peninsula. It was occupied for approximately 2,500 years, offering arable land, a reliable water source, and access to wildlife (McCreery 2002). The human remains span the Early Bronze Age, representing the only large, well-excavated skeletal assemblage covering this period for all the southern Levant. While burials exhumed at Jericho may have also spanned the Early Bronze Age, the most

TABLE 11.1. *A sampling of sites with commingled interments of at least 50 individuals in Israel, Palestine, and Jordan. Time periods reflect the designation given in the cited references. Cremated remains are not included.*

Site	Location	Region	Period	MNI	References
Ashdod	Locus 1113	Israel/Palestine	Late 8th century BCE	2,434	Haas (1971)
Ashkelon	Sewer	Israel/Palestine	Late Roman–Early Byzantine	100	Smith and Kahila (1992)
Bab adh-Dhra'	A-22	Jordan, Dead Sea Plain	EB II–IV	~1,100	Sheridan et al. (2014)
Dothan, Tell	Tomb 1	Judean Hills, Israel/Palestine	Late Bronze–early Iron Ages	250–300	Cooley and Practico (1994); Gregoricka and Sheridan (2017)
Gezer	Burial Cave 10A	Judean foothills, Israel/Palestine	1450–1300 BCE	88	Seger (1988: 129–46)
Jebel al-Hawayah	Cave 4	Beqa'a Valley, Jordan	12th–11th centuries BCE	233	McGovern (1981; 1986)
	Cave B3		LB II	50	
	Burial cave		Iron Age	220	
Jericho	WH1	Israel/Palestine	Chalcolithic–Early Bronze Age	800	Kurth (1962)
	K2			300	Callaway (1963: 74)
Khirbat al-Khanazir	Al-Khanazir cemetery	Jordan, Dead Sea Plain	EB IV	258	Chesson and Schaub (2007)
Lachish	Cave 120	Coastal plain, Israel/Palestine	Iron Age	1,500	Risdon (1939); Tufnell (1958)

(cont.)

TABLE 11.1. (cont.)

Site	Location	Region	Period	MNI	References
Meiron	Kokhim	Upper Galilee, Israel/Palestine	1st century BCE–4th century CE	197	Meyers et al. (1981)
Mount Nebo	UCV-20	Jebel Hussein, Jordan	1000–586 BCE	750	Bloch-Smith (1992: 196)
	UCV-84		1000–586 BCE	250	Saller (1996)
St. Stephen's	Repository 6	Jerusalem	438–614 CE	250	Sheridan (1999)
Tell el-Far'ah South	201	Coastal plain, Israel/Palestine	10th century BCE	126	Gonen (1992: 184)
Tell en-Naṣbeh	Tomb 32	West Bank, Israel/Palestine	Mid-12th–mid-8th centuries BCE	"Massive number of individuals"	Bloch-Smith (2004: 82)
Tell eṣ-Ṣafi/Gath	Iron Age burial cave	Elah Valley, Israel/Palestine	Late Iron Age I/Iron Age II	70	Faerman et al. (2011)
Tel Halif	Burial cave	Kibbutz Lahav, Israel/Palestine	Iron Age	"Piled to the ceiling"	Biran and Gophna (1970: 152)

TABLE 11.2. *Time periods for study sites, as determined for each excavation.*

Site	Time Periods	Dates	Reference
Bab adh-Dhra'	Early Bronze Age IA	3500–3300 BCE	Rast and Schaub (2003)
	Early Bronze Age IB	3300–3100 BCE	
	Early Bronze Age II–III	3100–2300 BCE	
	Early Bronze Age IV	2300–2010 BCE	
Tell Dothan	Late Bronze Age IIA	1400–1300 BCE	Cooley and Practico (1994; 1995)
	Late Bronze Age IIB	1300–1200 BCE	
	Late Bronze Age IIB–Iron Age I	1300–1100 BCE	
	Early Iron Age I	1200–1100 BCE	
St. Stephen's	Byzantine period	438–614 CE	Sheridan and Gregoricka (2015)

complete surviving assemblage, housed at the Duckworth Museum in Cambridge, has *very* few representatives from the Early Bronze Age (EB) II–III occupation (Gasperetti 2013; Sheridan et al. 2014).

Mortuary practices, settlement, and subsistence patterns at Bab adh-Dhra' changed over time. Lower temperatures and higher rainfall coincided with seasonal campsites in the EB IA. A permanent campsite-village (e.g., mud-brick dwellings, intensified agriculture) characterized the EB IB at Bab adh-Dhra'. By the EB II, residential buildings and storage space grew, with the most construction at the height of the site's occupation during EB III. These communities are described as towns rather than urban centers, particularly when compared to the metropolises to the north in Mesopotamia and southeast in Egypt (Joffe 1993; McCreery 2002; Rast and Schaub 2003). Each period was marked by changing burial practices, from subterranean family chambers in the EB IA, to large, aboveground charnel houses in the period of greatest population size (EB II–III), to individual belowground graves when the population size markedly dropped in the EB IV.

Tell Dothan

This site is located in the West Bank's Judean hills, near the edge of the Dothan Valley. As with Bab adh-Dhra', arable land, reliable water, and plentiful fauna were available; plus, it was situated at the crossroads of international trade routes. The site was occupied from the Chalcolithic through Byzantine periods on a nearly continuous basis (Monson 2005). Although Dothan was a small regional center, it appears in several biblical and apocryphal passages (Gen 37:14–28; 2 Kgs 6:13–14; Jdt 3:9, 4:6, 7:3), indicating that it was known to early readers of these ancient texts (Monson 2005).

The site's commingled assemblage was found in a large family tomb (Cooley and Pratico 1994), representing a MNI of 250–300. Commingling likely resulted from the movement of burials to make room for new interments over generations (Free 1960; Cooley and Pratico 1994; 1995). A rich collection of faunal material (Lev-Tov and Maher 2001), along with hundreds of human teeth, comprise the extant collection. The tomb was dated to the Late Bronze through early Iron Ages based on ceramic typology; however, our recent radiocarbon dating of teeth narrowed tomb use to the very beginning of the Iron Age (Gregoricka and Sheridan 2017). The main focus of our bioarchaeological publications on the dental remains have been related to bioDistance and Death, given questions about the family nature of the tomb, and continuity versus conquest theories for this period (Lev-Tov and Maher 2001; Ullinger et al. 2005; Gregoricka and Sheridan 2017).

St. Stephen's Monastery

Byzantine St. Stephen's monastery in modern-day East Jerusalem was the largest monastic complex in the Holy Land for nearly 100 years (Price 1991). Empress Eudocia endowed the site to house the purported remains of the first martyr of Christianity (Stephen), dedicated in 438 CE (Clark 1982; Murphy-O'Connor 2008). However, the crypts below the monastery were hewn in the Iron Age (eighth–seventh centuries BCE) (Barkay and Kloner 1986; Barkay, Kloner, and Mazar 1994). The skeletal collection housed therein resulted from Byzantine reuse in the fifth–seventh centuries CE (Bautch et al. 2000). The bones date from the early sixth to mid-seventh centuries based on radiocarbon dating, artifacts commingled with the bones, Greek inscriptions found in the tomb complex, copious textual references, and considerable architectural evidence of a large Byzantine monastic occupation during a well-documented time frame (438–614 CE) (Sheridan 1999; Bautch et al. 2000). Analyses of demography (Sheridan 1999; Gregoricka and Sheridan 2012; Leyerle 2013); diet (Gregoricka and Sheridan 2012; 2013; Gregoricka, Sheridan, and Schirtzinger 2017); daily activities (Bautch 1999; Driscoll and Sheridan 2000; Sheridan 2017); death (Bautch et al. 2000); and biodistance (Ullinger 2002; Sheridan and Gregoricka 2015) have subsequently been published by our research group.

COMMINGLED COLLECTIONS

Christopher Knüsel and John Robb defined commingled assemblages as: "mixed deposits of disarticulated and often fragmented bones from multiple individuals; ... sometimes includes animal remains and/or artifacts" (2016: 3). This chapter will focus on human remains as is the norm for American bioarchaeology, with faunal assemblages falling under the purview of zooarchaeology.

Avoidance of commingled collections may have skewed a nuanced understanding of past human adaptation, focusing attention disproportionately on only a subset of well-preserved collections (Baustian, Osterholtz, and Cook 2014; Brickley and Buckberry 2015; Tung 2016). Growing acknowledgment of the prevalence of commingled collections can be seen in the explosion of publications addressing methodological and theoretical aspects of working with mixed and fragmented remains (Haglund and Sorg 2002; Adams and Byrd 2014; Osterholtz, Baustian, and Martina 2014; Osterholtz 2016; Sheridan 2017).

Standardization

A few basic considerations have been proposed to enhance standardization of data collection. First, Kathryn Baustian, Anna Osterholtz, and Della Collins Cook (2014) and Debra Martin and Osterholtz (2016) underscored the importance of laying out a clear methodology and ethical rationale prior to excavation/exhumation to ensure all involved have considered potential ramifications on the communities involved.

Maria Panakhyo and Keith Jacobi (2016) recommended rearticulation of skeletal elements to enhance the number of features available on a given bone. With large collections, we have adopted the practice of matching portions as elements are studied. For example, when all right femora portions are seriated according to specific features, the investigator is more likely to notice small details that aid in rejoining bones. This worked well for our massive Bab adh-Dhra' collection for numerous skulls and cranial segments in our study of violence (Gasperetti and Sheridan 2013).

Often the osteologist is asked for a MNI estimate upon exhumation. This is often a gross underestimation of the assemblage size, and Knüsel and Robb warned that despite "pressures from the site director, the MNI should never be interpreted as 'how many people were deposited at the site'" (2016: 7). I would caution that collections should also never be referred to as "populations," as they are not a full representation of the communities from which they drew (e.g., differential burial practices by age, sex, and status; migration and exogamy; removal of groups for war, influx of captives, etc.). Several methods have been adapted from zooarchaeology to estimate the number of individuals interred in a commingled setting. The most likely number of individuals (MLNI) estimate, utilizing osteometric sorting and pair matching, can prove useful even for large collections when bones and portions that are well preserved archaeologically are used (Adams and Koningsberg 2004; Thomas, Ubelaker, and Byrd 2013; Byrd and LeGarde 2014). We found that using the calcaneus and talus provided numerous non-metric landmarks for pair matching (Cruse 2002; 2003) and measurement points for osteometric sorting (Byrd

2008). For the large A22 charnel house at Bab adh-Dhra', the MNI from excavation reports was approximately 300; the MLNI increased that by nearly five times (Gregoricka, Sheridan, and Ullinger 2011). This is far more representative of the charnel house size, which may have had a second story (McCreery 2011), as well as the exceptional volume of material present (Sheridan et al. 2014). MLNI estimates for St. Stephen's tomb were approximately 250 individuals versus a MNI of 109, more in keeping with historical and archaeological records (Binns 1994; Chitty 1995) and the 15,000+ bone portions present (Sheridan and Gregoricka 2015).

Increasing appreciation for the study of commingling can be seen in recent books for bioarchaeologists. Osterholtz, Baustian, and Martin (2014) published an edited volume outlining new methods, followed by a volume on applying social theory to the analysis of these assemblages (Osterholtz 2016). Bradley Adams and John Byrd (2014) provided chapters about ethics, collection methods, and analytical techniques. Christopher Schmidt and Steve Symes (2015) focused on burned bone, with several chapters related to commingling. William Haglund and Marcella Sorg (2002) emphasized taphonomic considerations for mixed and fragmented bones. Specific to the ancient Near East, works by Donald Ortner and Bruno Frohlich (2008), Megan Perry (2012 [ed.]), Karina Croucher (2012), and Benjamin Porter and Alexis Boutin (2014) contain chapters about research with commingled collections.

6Ds of Bioarchaeology

The "osteological paradox" (Wood et al. 1992) requires that we keep the complexities of assessing health, frailty, stress, and fertility of the past in mind when studying bioarchaeological collections. Such limitations are magnified for mixed and fragmented bones. Calculating group patterns of ancient morbidity and mortality, a reliance on interdisciplinary contributions, employing techniques to limit duplication of results, careful attention to reducing interobserver error, and a willingness to reassess findings as new methods become available are all mechanisms to enhance "scrutiny of the contextual actors underlying an archaeological skeletal series" (Larsen 2015: 423). Below, I explore these constraints and the new methods to address them, using the 6Ds of bioarchaeology: **D**emography, **D**iet, **D**isease, **D**eath, **D**aily activities, and bio**D**istance (Sheridan 2017).

Demography. Demographic reconstruction involves creating a strong circumstantial case, complicated by commingling since multiple indicators from the same bone and/or individual are often not available. It does not preclude, however, exploring questions of human adaptation in the past, when wider categories and group patterns are used.

Many methods are being developed to counter demographic hurdles. Attempts to narrow the parameters needed for complex statistical tests have helped adapt new methods for commingling. For example, Lyle Konigsberg, Susan Frankenberg, and Helen Liversidge (2016) focused on singular traits (second mandibular molar, pubic symphysis); and Megan Brickley, Ana-Marie Dragomir, and Laura Lockau (2016) adapted transition analysis to utilize only two aspects of the auricular surface of the *os coxa*. Unfortunately, the EB II–III collection from Bab adh-Dhra' is too damaged to permit comparable examination. However, Rebecca Mayus (2017) applied the above to the St. Stephen's crania and *os coxae*, and found tentative support for the hypothesis that the majority of individuals interred at the monastery were indeed male, adding to previous demographic reconstructions for the collection (Sheridan 1999).

Diet. Stable isotopes in bone and teeth, oral hygiene indicators, dental wear, and dental calculus (hardened tartar) have all been utilized to reconstruct diet in the past. Specific tooth groups (e.g., molars) and types (e.g., lower left canines) can be used, making such studies possible for commingled collections. Archaeological evidence, such as pollen, food remnants, pottery, and subsistence patterns, permit considerable nuance for diet reconstruction. Near Eastern examples include Richard Evershed and colleagues' (2008) study of early herding and milk consumption in the Levant based on food residue on pottery and Simone Riehl, Reid Bryson, and Konstantin Pustovoytov's (2008) archaeobotanical study of the relationship between agriculture and climate change for Early and Middle Bronze Age Syria. We were able to determine the consumption of animal protein from Byzantine St. Stephen's commingled teeth using stable isotope analysis of enriched nitrogen ($\delta^{15}N$) in enamel (Gregoricka and Sheridan 2013) and subadult stable carbon ($\delta^{13}C$) isotopes in bone to determine weaning (Gregoricka and Sheridan 2012). We also analyzed $\delta^{13}C$ and $\delta^{15}N$ isotopes in enamel apatite, bone apatite, and bone collagen, providing "glimpses" of isotope incorporation in an individual's tissues during different stages of his/her life (Gregoricka, Sheridan, and Schirtzinger 2017). We thus estimated changing diet from childhood, through adolescence, to adulthood in the commingled collection, because mandibular portions with *in situ* molars remained together.

Group patterns of oral hygiene assessed from frequencies of dental caries, interproximal grooves, abscesses, and ante-mortem tooth loss also aid diet reconstruction. At Bab adh-Dhra', Jaime Ullinger (2010) found a significant increase in carious lesions and ante-mortem tooth loss with reduced molar wear with orchard cultivation, a pattern associated with eating soft sticky foods, such as dates (Ullinger, Sheridan, and Guatelli-Steinberg 2015).

Interproximal grooves are U-shaped indentations near the gum line caused by the use of a probe, by sucking grit through the teeth, or from processing non-dietary objects. They could not be assessed for the EB II–III collection given the required preservation of multiple *in situ* sequential teeth in a mandible. St. Stephen's yielded the necessary specimens; however, no grooves were found in that collection – a surprise given the very low incidence of carious lesions and calculous buildup, both potential indicators of good oral hygiene (Keegan 2009).

Pits and scratches on the enamel, viewed with scanning electron microscopy, can help distinguish consumption of hard versus soft foods. Analysis of microwear texture permits greater distinction between foods consumed, as seen in Rebecca Van Sessen and her colleagues' (2013) analysis of the Tell Dothan teeth. Texture patterns indicated that the inhabitants consumed less processed foods, with a more varied diet than later agriculturalists in the region. Such a study illustrated the ability to assess group patterns of diet, as the Dothan collection is composed of hundreds of disarticulated, commingled teeth gathered during sifting at excavation. In a substantial expansion of that study, Christopher Schmidt and his colleagues (in press) are assessing varation in dental microwear texture analysis (DMTA) from fifty archaeological sites to compare farmers, foragers, and pastoralists. We found differences in complexity and anisotropy in DMTA variables between the three subsistence strategies, further expanding the tools available for paleodietary reconstructions.

The use of tooth groups and types permits the analysis of dental calculus to assess oral health, utilizing microbes and small bits of food in tartar, as well as trapped phytoliths (minute mineralized particles of plants). A surprisingly low consumption of domesticated cereal phytoliths were found at Tell al-Raqa'i, Syria (Henry and Piperno 2008), and Baruch Arensburg's (1996) assessment of bacteria from dental calculus in Kebara Cave teeth helped identify features of the ancient microbiome. Haagen Klaus hypothesized that "syntheses of oral health data, stable isotope patterning, and microbiome composition could characterize ancient diets and health in highly detailed ways" (2014: 301).

Disease. Greater rigor in pathological description and diagnosis of past health requires the use of multiple sites on the skeleton (von Hunnius et al. 2006; Ortner 2012; Klaus 2015; Martin and Harrod 2015). For mixed and fragmented bones, it is imperative to remember: (1) many things that can kill a person do not leave traces on the skeleton; (2) bone can only react in a limited number of ways (formation and resorption); and (3) several mechanisms can cause similar pathological lesions.

For these reasons, we remained conservative in an assessment of violent trauma at Bab adh-Dhra' (Gasperetti and Sheridan 2013). We found many depressed cranial fractures located above the "hat brim line" (area above the eyebrows), a marker used to indicate interpersonal conflict in forensic settings (Kremer et al. 2008). However, the EB II–III inhabitants lived in terraced housing (Chesson and Schaub 2007), so we could not rule out accidental injury by items falling from above. Likewise, associated ulna and radii from the same individuals could not be articulated; thus, proper assessment of the cause of forearm breaks (accidental falls versus parrying blows) was not possible (Judd 2008). We did find numerous cranial and ulnar lesions compared to regional counterparts; however, when coupled with the broken, burned, and mixed nature of the collection, definitive interpretations of cause were hampered. We are currently finishing an expansion of the Matthew Gasperertti and Sheridan (2013) study to include individuals from three time periods (EB I–III) at Bab adh-Dhra' for a more finessed assessment of cranial depressed fractures before and after the construction of a large wall to enclose the town, between men and women, and to explore the possibility of recidivism (and thus, possibly, status).

New methods to assess quality of life and care of individuals have recently been developed (Tilley 2015; Tilley and Schrenck 2017). When possible, added depth in the understanding of ancient medical sophistication, community values, craft specialization, agency, and past definitions of illness results (Battles 2011). Lorna Tilley and Tony Cameron's (2014) "Index of Care" program presumes a perceived need for care; thus, in a bioarchaeological context marked impairment is required. For the commingled Byzantine St. Stephen's remains, only two people were candidates for such evaluation – one suffered from severe tarsal coalition (the fusion of multiple foot bones), the other from adult osteopetrosis or "stone bone" (excessive bone formation filling in marrow spaces). These pathologies are well documented in the clinical literature, allowing us to evaluate quality of life on a case-study basis. Both disorders cause considerable pain requiring long-term help, which is among the acknowledged behaviors seen in monastic communities of the period (Binns 1994).

Daily Activities. Increased interest in everyday life and embodiment theory has resulted in methods to interpret evidence of repetitive motion (Schader 2013). Analyses have used osteoarthritic changes (Walker et al. 2004), degenerative joint disease (Eshed et al. 2010), Schmorl's nodes of the vertebra (Faccia and Williams 2008), and cross-sectional geometry of the lower limb (Davies, Shaw, and Stock 2012). Diagnoses of specific activities have led to reconstructions, such as "thrower's elbow" (Villotte and Knüsel 2014), kayaking (Hawkey and Merbs 1995), fishing (Ponce 2010), archery (Thomas 2014), farming (Smith, Bar-Yosef, and Sillen 1984), and genuflection (Driscoll and Sheridan 2000). Robert Jurmain (1999) cautioned that age, sex, weight, and mechanical loading cannot be overlooked when diagnosing repetitive motion disorders;

for commingled collections, this situation is exacerbated by an inability to determine age beyond "adult" for single bones/fragments, let alone sex, weight, or loading. Thus, patterns across the collection must be evaluated.

New methods to assess fibrocartilagenous entheses (muscle/bone connections where cartilage formation has created fibrous tissue) are detected in archaeological remains (Villotte 2006; Havelková, Hladík, and Velemínský 2011) using porosity, calcification, and formation of extra bone (Mariotti, Facchini, and Giovanna Belcastro 2007; Villotte et al. 2010; Henderson et al. 2016). For St. Stephen's Monastery, lipping of the femoral and tibia condyles, marked indicators associated with muscles permitting deep flexion of the knee and ankle, and fusion of many first metatarsals and phalanges of the feet demonstrated a pattern of extreme degeneration of the articular surfaces for most adult males (Hawkey and Merbs 1995; Henderson et al. 2016). Texts describing prayer postures for the period and region yielded numerous examples of kneeling for worship, including multiple genuflections averaging 200–300 a day (Bautch 1999; Driscoll and Sheridan 2000). Sustained adherence to this dictate would indeed explain the severe pathologies noted. This example demonstrated that when features are examined as functional units (muscles and joints working together or in antagonism) across a large commingled collection, patterns for further exploration in the material or textual records can help explain a given phenomenon.

Death. The other "Ds of bioarchaeology" examine living processes, while this category recognizes that the treatment of the dead reveals much about how the individual was viewed in life. Status, gender, inequity, and relatedness can be examined by determining what death meant and to whom. Porter and Boutin's (2014) volume demonstrated the importance of this topic to Near Eastern studies. For Bab adh-Dhra', we explored changes in definitions of lineage related to the investment of tribute to the dead (Sheridan et al. 2014). Biological data and burial practices viewed in concert with archaeological evidence from EB I–IV allowed us to examine aspects of exclusivity, long-term familial investments, interpersonal dynamics, enhanced visibility of death, and other aspects of Bronze Age social structure. The nuance possible for such studies is reduced with commingled remains compared to discrete burials but still quite possible.

To further clarify interment practices, Knüsel and Robb (2016) argued for increased attention to funerary taphonomy to separate natural processes from human agency. By analyzing color changes from postmortem burning of the A22 charnel house at Bab adh-Dhra' and inventorying bone portions represented, we gleaned additional mortuary information about the EB II–III phase of habitation (Ullinger 2010; Ullinger and Sheridan 2015). Changes in color were assessed for bones representing different degrees of protection by soft tissue (distal humerus, frontal bone, ilium) to test whether bones were disarticulated prior to burning. Whether examining color quantitatively (CIELAB spectrophotometer method) or qualitatively (Munsell color charts), the frontal bones showed far greater burning than the ilia. There was no evidence of segregation of the crania from other body parts; therefore, the color differences may indicate that the ilia were still covered by tissue and/or articulated. We also divided the structure into sides and by core versus periphery. There was no significant difference by building side, but the core showed considerably hotter temperatures with the presence of possible incendiary materials (charred wood, burned linen). This corresponds to archaeological evidence of intense burning, including burned wooden beams and scorched bricks, in the center of the tomb in a single conflagration, not individual cremations prior to placement in the charnel house (Ullinger and Sheridan 2015).

BioDistance. Jane Buikstra, Frankenberg, and Konigsberg (1990) defined biological distance as the homogeneity/heterogeneity of groups separated by time and place. Non-metric traits of the teeth (Parras 2004), biogeochemical changes in stable isotope ratios (Perry et al. 2011), dental metrics (Pilloud and Larsen 2011), and ancient DNA (aDNA) analysis (Mardis 2008) have been used for such analyses. Again, specific tooth groups and types can be employed for these studies, thus permitting the determination of group patterns for commingled collections.

We compared dental non-metric traits from Tell Dothan and Lachish (southeast of Ashkelon) to determine whether the marked cultural change noted in the archaeological record between the Late Bronze and early Iron Ages in the southern Levant was the result of an influx of new groups (Ullinger et al. 2005). We found more similarities comparing the two sites, in contrast to comparisons with other Levantine, European, and North African locations, concluding that archaeological changes likely resulted from local environmental and social factors, not population replacement. As an expansion of that project, Lesley Gregoricka and I (2017) conducted an isotopic analysis of individuals from Tell Dothan and again found an absence of nonlocals, using $^{87}Sr/^{86}Sr$, $\delta^{18}O$, and $\delta^{13}C_{ap(VPDB)}$ values. Variations in these isotope ratios with local fauna are used to indicate migration (Sillen et al. 1998; Knudson 2011). This added to our argument against population replacement during the Late Bronze Age–Early Iron Age transition (Cline 2014).

aDNA studies of human gene flow through the Levantine corridor to understand the movements of human ancestors out of Africa (Olivieri et al. 2006), routes employed (Rowold et al. 2007), and the antiquity of indigenous populations (González et al. 2008) are of marked interest. Non-human faunal aDNA have provided corroborating information about human migration, such as the use of mitochondrial DNA (mtDNA) from ancient and modern pigs (Meiri et al. 2013), cattle (Götherström et al. 2005), goats (Kahila Bar-Gal et al. 2002), and sheep (Kahila Bar-Gal, Ducos, and Horwitz 2003) to follow domesticated animal movements and, by default, those of their human caretakers.

CONCLUSIONS

Working with commingled remains affords several advantages despite limitations. Mixed and fragmented collections compel a holistic approach, require broader questions about human adaptability, force the use of multiple morbidity and mortality indicators (Goodman 1993; Temple and Goodman 2014), oblige interdisciplinary cooperation, and catalyze the development of nuanced age and sex indicators. Greater incorporation of theory related to embodiment, power, structural violence, gender, niche construction, entanglement, and social identity are allowing greater synthesis with the humanities in developing nuanced reconstructions of past lifeways. Maintaining a realistic picture of what can be addressed using broken and mixed skeletal remains is of paramount importance; nevertheless, inclusion of these overlooked assemblages has allowed a fuller understanding of ancient Levantine lifeways than was possible with discrete burials alone.

The ancient Near East is where alphabetic writing, several forms of agriculture, and urbanism began, a region through which people have moved since at least the time of *Homo erectus*. The rapid improvement of physical and statistical methods, and the application of social theory have markedly improved in the past decade, permitting us to examine understudied collections. As long as one remains cognizant of the limitations, analyses of mixed and fragmentary assemblages using an expanded "toolbox" of methods will allow us to glean additional information from collections in the southern Levant with a depth and nuance not previously available. Enhanced focus on commingled assemblages will provide a fuller, more accurate view of ancient Levantine life by incorporating remains from sites previously avoided.

ACKNOWLEDGMENTS

Special thanks to Professors Eric Cline and Yorke Rowan for the opportunity to write this chapter. L'École Biblique et Archéologique Français and the Couvent St.-Étienne in Jerusalem, St. George's College in Jerusalem, Robert Cooley (Gordan-Conwell Theological Seminary), R. Thomas Schaub (Indiana University of Pennsylvania), and Donald Ortner (Smithsonian

Institution) provided access to the Byzantine St. Stephen's, Tell Dothan, and Bab adh-Dhra' skeletal collections. The William F. Albright Institute of Archaeological Research, L'École Biblique et Archéologique Français, and Augusta Victoria Hospital hosted many years of research on these collections while in Jerusalem.

REFERENCES

Adams, B. J., and Byrd, J. E., eds. 2014. *Commingled Human Remains: Methods in Recovery, Analysis, and Identification*. Amsterdam: Elsevier/Academic.

Adams, B. J., and Koningsberg, L. W. 2004. Estimation of the Most Likely Number of Individuals from Commingled Human Remains. *AJPA* 125: 138–51.

Arensburg, B. 1996. Ancient Dental Calculus and Diet. *HE* 11: 139–45.

Artin, G. 2010. The Necropolis and Dwellings of Byblos during the Chalcolithic Period: New Interpretations. *NEA* 73: 2–12

Barkay, G., and Kloner, A. 1986. Jerusalem Tombs from the Days of the First Temple. *BAR* 12 (2): 22–39.

Barkay, G.; Kloner, A.; and Mazar, M. 1994. The Northern Necropolis of Jerusalem during the First Temple Period. In *Ancient Jerusalem Revealed*, ed. H. Geva, 119–27. Jerusalem: IES.

Battles, H. 2011. Towards Engagement: Exploring the Prospects for an Integrated Anthropology of Disability. *Vis-à-Vis: Explorations in Anthropology* 11: 107–24.

Baustian, K. M.; Osterholtz, A. J.; and Cook, D. C. 2014. Taking Analyses of Commingled Remains into the Future: Challenges and Prospects. In *Commingled and Disarticulated Human Remains: Working toward Improved Theory, Method, and Data*, ed. A. J. Osterholtz, K. M. Baustian, and D. L. Martin, 265–74. New York: Springer.

Bautch, K. C.; Bautch, R. J.; Barkay, G.; and Sheridan, S. G. 2000. "The Vessels of the Potter Shall be Broken": Material Culture from the Tombs of St. Stephen's Monastery. *RB* 107: 561–90.

Bautch, R. J. 1999. On Bended Knee: Correlations Liturgical and Anthropological from a Fifth-Century Monastery. *Koinonia* 11: 155–67.

Binns, J. 1994. *Ascetics and Ambassadors of Christ: The Monasteries of Palestine, 314–631*. Oxford Early Christian Studies. Oxford: Clarendon.

Biran, A., and Gophna, R. 1970. An Iron Age Burial Cave at Tel Halif. *IEJ* 20: 151–69.

Bloch-Smith, E. 1992. *Judahite Burial Practices and Beliefs about the Dead*. JSOTSup 123; JSOT/ASOR Monograph Series 7. Sheffield: Sheffield Academic.

2004. Resurrecting the Iron I Dead. *IEJ* 54: 77–91.

Bolger, D., ed. 2008. *Gender through Time in the Ancient Near East*. Lanham, MD: AltaMira.

Brickley, M. B., and Buckberry, J. L. 2015. Picking Up the Pieces: Utilizing the Diagnostic Potential of Poorly Preserved Remains. *IJP* 8: 51–4.

Brickley, M. B.; Dragomir, A.-M.; and Lockau, L. 2016. Age-at-Death Estimates from a Disarticulated, Fragmented and Commingled Archaeological Battlefield Assemblage. *IJO* 26: 408–19

Buikstra, J. E.; Frankenberg, S. R.; and Konigsberg, L. W. 1990. Skeletal Biological Distance Studies in American Physical Anthropology: Recent Trends. *AJPA* 82: 1–7.

Byrd, J. E. 2008. Models and Methods for Osteometric Sorting. In *Recovery, Analysis, and Identification of Commingled Human Remains*, ed. B. J. Adams and J. E. Byrd, 199–220. Totowa, NJ: Humana.

Byrd, J. E., and LeGarde, C. 2014. Osteometric Sorting. In *Commingled Human Remains: Methods in Recovery, Analysis, and Identification*, ed. B. J. Adams and J. E. Byrd, 167–91. Amsterdam: Elsevier/Academic.

Callaway, J. A. 1963. Burials in Ancient Palestine: From the Stone Age to Abraham. *BA* 26: 73–91.

Chesson, M. S., ed. 2011. *Daily Life, Materiality, and Complexity in Early Urban Communities of the Southern Levant: Papers in Honor of Walter E. Rast and R. Thomas Schaub.* Winona Lake, IN: Eisenbrauns.

Chesson M. S., and Schaub, R. T. 2007. Death and Dying on the Dead Sea Plain: Fifa, Khirbat al-Khanazir, and Bab adh-Dhra' Cemeteries. In *Crossing Jordan: North American Contributions to the Archaeology of Jordan*, ed. T. E. Levy, P. M. M. Daviau, R. W. Younker, and M. Shaer, 253–60. London: Routledge.

Cheyney, M.; Brashler, J.; Boersma, B.; Contant, N.; DeWall, K.; Lane, M.; Smalligan, J.; and Vandern Berg, B. 2009. Umm al-Jimāl Cemeteries Z, AA, BB and CC: 1996 and 1998 Field Reports. *ADAJ* 53: 321–59.

Chitty, D. J. 1995. *The Desert a City: An Introduction to the Study of Egyptian and Palestinian Monasticism under the Christian Empire*. Crestwood, NY: St. Vladimir's Seminary Press.

Clark, E. A. 1982. Claims on the Bones of Saint Stephen: The Partisans of Melania and Eudocia. *Church History* 51: 141–56.

Cline, E. H. 2014. *1177 B.C.: The Year Civilization Collapsed*. TPAH. Princeton: Princeton University Press.

Cooley, R. E., and Pratico, G. 1994. Gathered to His People: An Archaeological Illustration from Tell Dothan's Western Cemetery. In *Scripture and Other Artifacts: Essays on the Bible and Archaeology in Honor of Philip J. King*, ed. M. D. Coogan, J. C. Exum, and L. E. Stager, 70–92. Louisville, KY: Westminster/John Knox.

———. 1995. Tell Dothan: The Western Cemetery, with Comments on Joseph Free's Excavations, 1953 to 1964. In *Preliminary Excavation Reports: Sardis, Bir Umm Fawakhir, Tell el-Umeiri, the Combined Caesarea Expeditions, and Tell Dothan*, ed. W. G. Dever, 147–90. New Haven, CT: ASOR.

Croucher, K. 2012. *Death and Dying in the Neolithic Near East*. Oxford: Oxford University Press.

Cruse, K. L. 2002. Commingled Prehistoric Skeletal Remains: An Undying Story. *Bios* 73: 120–6.

———. 2003. *Commingled Human Skeletal Remains: What's in a Number? The Implementation of the Lincoln/Petersen Index (LI) as a Method of Quantification*. Master's thesis, University of Cincinnati.

Davies, T.; Shaw, C.; and Stock J. 2012. A Test of a New Method and Software for the Rapid Estimation of Cross-Sectional Geometric Properties of Long Bone Diaphyses from 3D Laser Surface Scans. *AAS* 4: 277–90.

Driscoll, M. S., and Sheridan, S. G. 2000. Every Knee Shall Bend: A Biocultural Reconstruction of Liturgical and Ascetical Prayer in V–VII Century Palestine. *Worship* 74: 453–68.

Eshed, V.; Gopher, A.; Pinhasi, R.; and Hershkovitz, I. 2010. Paleopathology and the Origin of Agriculture in the Levant. *AJPA* 143: 121–33.

Evershed, R. P.; Payne, S.; Sherratt, A. G.; Copley, M. S.; Coolidge, J.; Urem-Kotsu, D.; Kotsakis, K.; Özdoğan, M.; Özdoğan, A. E.; Nieuwenhuyse, O.;

Akkermans, P. M. M. G.; Bailey, D.; Andeescu, R.-R.; Campbell, S.; Farid, S.; Hodder, I.; Yalman, N.; Özbaşaran, M.; Bıçakcı, E.; Garfinkel, Y.; Levy, T. E.; and Burton, M. M. 2008. Earliest Date for Milk Use in the Near East and Southern Europe Linked to Cattle Herding. *Nature* 455: 528–31.

Faccia, K. J., and Williams, R. C. 2008. Schmorl's Nodes: Clinical Significance and Implications for the Bioarchaeological Record. *IJO* 18: 28–44.

Faerman, M.; Smith, P.; Boaretto, E.; Uziel, J.; and Maeir, A. M. 2011. "...In Their Lives, and in Their Death...": A Preliminary Study of an Iron Age Burial Cave at Tell es-Safi, Israel. *ZDPV* 127: 29–48.

Free, J. P. 1960. The Seventh Season of Excavation at Dothan. *BASOR* 160: 6–15.

Gasperetti, M. A. 2013. *The Bioarchaeology of Agriculture in the Prehistoric Southern Levant*. PhD diss., University of Cambridge.

Gasperetti, M. A., and Sheridan, S. G. 2013. Cry Havoc: Interpersonal Violence at Early Bronze Age Bab edh-Dhra'. *AmAnth* 115: 388–410.

Glencross, B. A. 2011. Skeletal Injury across the Life Course: Towards Understanding Social Agency. In *Social Bioarchaeology*, ed. S. C. Agarwarl and B. A. Glencross, 390–409. Blackwell Studies in Global Archaeology 14. Chichester: Wiley-Blackwell.

Gonen, R. 1992. *Burial Patterns and Cultural Diversity in Late Bronze Age Canaan*. ASORDS 7. Winona Lake, IN: Eisenbrauns.

González, A. M.; Karadsheh, N.; Maca-Meyer, N.; Flores, C.; Cabrera, V. M.; and Larruga, J. M. 2008. Mitochondrial DNA Variation in Jordanians and Their Genetic Relationship to Other Middle East Populations. *Annals of Human Biology* 35: 212–31.

Goodman, A. H. 1993. On the Interpretation of Health from Skeletal Remains. *CA* 34: 281–8.

Götherström, A.; Anderung, C.; Hellborg, L.; Elburg, R.; Smith, C.; Bradley, D. G.; and Ellegren, H. 2005. Cattle Domestication in the Near East Was Followed by Hybridization with Aurochs Bulls in Europe. *Proceedings Royal Society London* B272: 2345–50.

Gregoricka, L. A., and Sheridan, S. G. 2012. Food for Thought: Isotopic Evidence for Dietary and Weaning Practices in a Byzantine Urban Monastery in Jerusalem. In *Bioarchaeology and Behavior: The People of the Ancient Near East*, ed. M. A. Perry, 138–64. BIHP. Gainesville: University Press of Florida.

2013. Ascetic or Affluent? Byzantine Diet at the Monastic Community of St. Stephen's, Jerusalem from Stable Carbon and Nitrogen Isotopes. *JAA* 32: 63–73.

2017. Continuity or Conquest? A Multi-Isotope Approach to Investigating Identity in the Early Iron Age of the Southern Levant. *AJPA* 162: 73–89.

Gregoricka, L. A.; Sheridan, S. G.; and Schirtzinger, M. 2017. Reconstructing Life Histories Using Multi-Tissue Isotope Analysis of Commingled Remains from St Stephen's Monastery in Jerusalem: Limitations and Potential. *Archaeometry* 59: 148–63.

Gregoricka, L. A.; Sheridan, S. G.; and Ullinger, J. M. 2011. MNI and MLNI in the Quantification of Commingled Skeletal Remains: Application to a Large-Scale Bronze Age Skeletal Collection. *AJPA* 144 (S52): 149.

Guy, P. L. O. 1938. *Megiddo Tombs*. OIP 33. Chicago: The University Chicago Press.

Haas, N. 1971. Anthropological Observations on the Skeletal Remains Found in Area D (1962–1963). In *Ashdod II/III: The Second and Third Seasons of Excavations 1963, 1965, Soundings in 1967*, ed. M. Dothan, 212–14. 'Atiqot 9–10. Jerusalem: Department of Antiquities.

Haglund, W. D., and Sorg, M. H., eds. 2002. *Advances in Forensic Taphonomy: Method, Theory and Archaeological Perspectives*. Boca Raton, FL: CRC.

Havelková, P.; Hladík, M.; and Velemínský, P. 2011. Entheseal Changes: Do They Reflect Socioeconomic Status in the Early Medieval Central European Population? (Mikulčice–Klášteřisko, Great Moravian Empire, 9th–10th Century). *IJO* 21: 237–51.

Hawkey, D. E., and Merbs, C. F. 1995. Activity-Induced Musculoskeletal Stress Markers (MSM) and Subsistence Strategy Changes among Ancient Hudson Bay Eskimos. *IJO* 5: 324–38.

Henderson, C. Y.; Mariotti, V.; Pany-Kucera, D.; Villotte, S.; and Wilczak, C. 2016. The New "Coimbra Method": A Biologically Appropriate Method for Recording Specific Features of Fibrocartilagenous Entheseal Changes. *IJO* 26: 925–32.

Henry, A. G., and Piperno, D. R. 2008. Using Plant Microfossils from Dental Calculus to Recover Human Diet: A Case Study from Tell al-Raqā'i, Syria. *JAS* 35: 1943–50.

Herr, L. G., and Clark, D. 2007. Tall al-'Umayri through the Ages. In *Crossing Jordan: North American Contributions to the Archaeology of Jordan*, ed. T. E. Levy, P. M. M. Daviau, R. W. Younker, and M. Shaer, 121–8. London: Routledge.

Hill, A. C.; Price, M. D.; and Rowan, Y. M. 2016. Feasting at Marj Rabba, an Early Chalcolithic Site in the Galilee. *OJA* 35: 127–40.

Hunnius, T. E. von; Roberts, C. A.; Boylston, A.; and Saunders, S. R. 2006. Histological Identification of Syphilis in Pre-Columbian England. *AJPA* 129: 559–66.

Joffe, A. H. 1993. *Settlement and Society in the Early Bronze Age I and II, Southern Levant: Complementarity and Contradiction in a Small-Scale Complex Society*. MMA 4. Sheffield: Sheffield Academic.

Jong, L. de. 2010. Performing Death in Tyre: The Life and Afterlife of a Roman Cemetery in the Province of Syria. *AJA* 114: 597–630.

Judd, M. A. 2008. The Parry Problem. *JAS* 35: 1658–66.

Jurmain, R. 1999. *Stories from the Skeleton: Behavioral Reconstruction in Human Osteology*. Interpreting the Remains of the Past 1. Amsterdam: Gordon & Breach.

Kahila Bar-Gal, G.; Ducos, P.; and Horwitz, L. K. 2003. The Application of Ancient DNA Analysis to Identify Neolithic Caprinae: A Case Study from the Site of Hatoula, Israel. *IJO* 13: 120–31.

Kahila Bar-Gal, G.; Khalaily, H.; Mader, O.; Ducos, P.; and Horwitz, L. K. 2002. Ancient DNA Evidence for the Transition from Wild to Domestic Status in Neolithic Goats: A Case Study from the Site of Abu Gosh, Israel. *Ancient Biomolecules* 4: 9–17.

Kaniewski, D.; Van Campo, E.; Boiy, T.; Terral, J. F.; Khadari, B.; and Besnard, G. 2012. Primary Domestication and Early Uses of the Emblematic Olive Tree: Palaeobotanical, Historical and Molecular Evidence from the Middle East. *Biological Reviews of the Cambridge Philosophical Society* 87: 885–99.

Keegan, K. 2009. *An Assessment of Diet and Dental Health at Byzantine St. Stephen's Monastery in Jerusalem*. Honors thesis, University of Notre Dame.

Kersel, M. M., and Chesson, M. S. 2013. Looting Matters: Early Bronze Age Cemeteries of Jordan's Southeast Dead Sea Plain in the Past and Present. In *The Oxford Handbook of the Archaeology of Death and Burial*, ed. S. Tarlow and S. Nilsson Stutz, 677–94. Oxford: Oxford University Press.

Klaus, H. D. 2014. Frontiers in the Bioarchaeology of Stress and Disease: Cross-Disciplinary Perspectives from Pathophysiology, Human Biology, and Epidemiology. *AJPA* 155: 294–308.

———. 2015. Paleopathological Rigor and Differential Diagnosis: Case Studies Involving Terminology, Description, and Diagnostic Frameworks for Scurvy in Skeletal

Remains. *IJP* (Online). https://doi.org/10.1016/j.ijpp.2015.10.002 (accessed June 26, 2017).

Knudson, K. J. 2011. Identifying Archaeological Human Migration Using Biogeochemistry: Case Studies from the South-Central Andes. In *Rethinking Anthropological Perspectives on Migration*, ed. G. S. Cabana and J. J. Clark, 231–47. Gainesville: University Press of Florida.

Knüsel, C. J., and Robb, J. 2016. Funerary Taphonomy: An Overview of Goals and Methods. *JAS* 10: 655–73.

Konigsberg, L. W.; Frankenberg, S. R.; and Liversidge, H. M. 2016. Optimal Trait Scoring for Age Estimation. *AJPA* 159: 557–76.

Kremer, C.; Racette, S.; Dionne, C. A.; and Sauvageau, A. 2008. Discrimination of Falls and Blows in Blunt Head Trauma: Systematic Study of the Hat Brim Line Rule in Relation to Skull Fractures. *JFS* 53: 716–19.

Kurth, G. 1962–1963. Der Wanderungsbegriff in Prähistorie/Kulturgeschichte unter palädemographischen und bevölkerungsbiologischen Gesichtspunkten: Mit besonderen Befunden von Nahostbefunden und -serien; Jericho/Tell es Sultan, Byblos, Khirokitia, Eridu. *Alt-Thüringen* 6: 1–21.

Larsen, C. S. 2015. *Bioarchaeology: Interpreting Behavior from the Human Skeleton*. 2nd ed. Cambridge Studies in Biological and Evolutionary Anthropology 69. Cambridge: Cambridge University Press.

Lev-Tov, J. S. E., and Maher, E. F. 2001. Food in Late Bronze Age Funerary Offerings: Faunal Evidence from Tomb 1 at Tell Dothan. *PEQ* 133: 91–110.

Leyerle, B. 2002. Children and Disease in a Sixth Century Monastery. In *What Athens Has to Do with Jerusalem: Essays on Classical, Jewish, and Early Christian Art and Archaeology in Honor of Gideon Foerster*, ed. L. V. Rutgers, 349–72. Interdisciplinary Studies in Ancient Culture and Religion 1. Leuven: Peeters.

2013. Children and "the Child" in Early Christianity. In *The Oxford Handbook of Childhood and Education in the Classical World*, ed. J. Evans Grubbs and T. Parkin with the assistance of R. Bell, 559–79. Oxford: Oxford University Press.

Mardis, E. R. 2008. Next-Generation DNA Sequencing Methods. *ARGHG* 9: 387–402.

Mariotti, V.; Facchini, F.; and Giovanna Belcastro, M. 2007. The Study of Entheses: Proposal of a Standardised Scoring Method for Twenty-Three Entheses of the Postcranial Skeleton. *Collegium Antropologicum* 31: 291–313.

Martin, D. L., and Harrod, R. P. 2015. Bioarchaeological Contributions to the Study of Violence. *AJPA* 156 (S59): 116–45.

Martin, D. L., and Osterholtz, A. J. 2016. Introduction. In *Theoretical Approaches to Analysis and Interpretation of Commingled Human Remains*, ed. A. J. Osterholtz, 1–4. BST. Cham: Springer.

Mayus, R. C. 2017. *Constructing Demographic Profiles in Commingled Collections: A Comparison of Methods for Determining Sex and Age-at-Death in a Byzantine Monastic Assemblage*. Master's thesis, The Ohio State University.

McCreery, D. W. 2002. Bronze Age Agriculture in the Dead Sea Basin: The Cases of Bâb edh-Dhrâ', Numeira and Tell Nimirin. In *"Imagining" Biblical Worlds: Studies in Spatial, Social and Historical Constructs in Honor of James W. Flanagan*, ed. D. M. Gunn and P. M. McNutt, 250–63. JSOTSup 359. Sheffield: Sheffield Academic.

2011. Agriculture and Religion at Bâb edh-Dhrâ', and Numeria during the Early Bronze Age. In *Daily Life, Materiality, and Complexity in Early Urban Communities of the*

Southern Levant: Papers in Honor of Walter E. Rast and R. Thomas Schaub, ed. M. S. Chesson, 77–88. Winona Lake, IN: Eisenbrauns.

McGovern, P. E. 1981. The Baq'ah Valley, Jordan. Test Soundings of Cesium Magnetometer Anomalies. *MASCA Journal* 1: 214–17.

———. 1986. *The Late Bronze and Early Iron Ages of Central Transjordan: The Baq'ah Valley Project, 1977–1981.* UMM 65. Philadelphia: University Museum of Archaeology and Anthropology, University of Pennsylvania.

McMahon, A.; Sołtysiak, A.; and Weber, J. 2011. Late Chalcolithic Mass Graves at Tell Brak, Syria, and Violent Conflict during the Growth of Early City-States. *JFA* 36: 201–20.

Meiri, M.; Huchon, D.; Bar-Oz, G.; Boaretto, E.; Horwitz, L. K.; Maeir, A. M.; Sapir-Hen, L.; Larson, G.; Weiner, S.; and Finkelstein, I. 2013. Ancient DNA and Population Turnover in Southern Levantine Pigs – Signature of the Sea Peoples Migration? *Nature Science Reports* 3. www.nature.com/articles/srep03035 (accessed June 26, 2017).

Meyers, E. M.; Strange, J. F.; and Meyers, C. L. 1981. *Excavations at Ancient Meiron, Upper Galilee, Israel 1971–72, 1974–75, 1977.* Meiron Excavation Project 3. Cambridge, MA: ASOR.

Mogliazza, S. 2009. An Example of Cranial Trepanation Dating to the Middle Bronze Age from Ebla, Syria. *JAS* 87: 187–92.

Monson, J. M. 2005. Regional Settlement: Dothan in the Northern Arena. In *Dothan I: Remains from the Tell (1953–1964)*, ed. D. M. Master, J. M. Monson, E. H. E. Lass, and G. A. Pierce, 7–14. Excavations of Joseph P. Free at Dothan (1953–1964) 1. Winona Lake, IN: Eisenbrauns.

Murphy-O'Connor, J. 2008. *The Holy Land: An Oxford Archaeological Guide from the Earliest Times to 1700.* Oxford: Oxford University Press.

Olivieri, A.; Achilli, A.; Pala, M.; Battaglia, V.; Fornarino, S.; al-Zahery, N.; Scozzari, R.; Cruciani, F.; Behar, D. M.; Dugoujon, J. M.; Coudray, C.; Santachiara-Benerecetti, A. S.; Semino, O.; Bandelt, H. J.; and Torroni, A. 2006. The mtDNA Legacy of the Levantine Early Upper Palaeolithic in Africa. *Science* 314 (5806): 1767–70.

Ortner, D. J. 2012. Differential Diagnosis and Issues in Disease Classification. In *A Companion to Paleopathology*, ed. A. L. Grauer, 250–67. BCA 14. Malden, MA: Wiley-Blackwell.

Ortner, D. J., and Frohlich, B. 2008. *The Early Bronze Age I Tombs and Burials of Bâb edh-Dhrâ' Jordan.* REDSPJ 3. Lanham, MD: AltaMira.

Osterholtz, A. J., ed. 2016. *Theoretical Approaches to Analysis and Interpretation of Commingled Human Remains.* BST. Cham: Springer.

Osterholtz, A. J.; Baustian, K. M.; and Martin, D. L., eds. 2014. *Commingled and Disarticulated Human Remains: Working Toward Improved Theory, Method, and Data.* New York: Springer.

Panakhyo, M., and Jacobi, K. 2016. Limited Circumstances: Creating a Better Understanding of Prehistoric Peoples through the Reanalysis of Collections of Commingled Human Remains. In *Theoretical Approaches to Analysis and Interpretation of Commingled Human Remains*, ed. A. J. Osterholtz, 75–96. BST. Cham: Springer.

Parras, Z. 2004. *The Biological Affinities of the Eastern Mediterranean in the Chalcolithic and Bronze Age.* BAR International Series 1305. Oxford: BAR.

Perry, M. A. 2012. Paleopathology in Lebanon, Syria, and Jordan. In *The Global History of Paleopathology: Pioneers and Prospects*, ed. J. E. Buikstra and C. A. Roberts, 451–69. Oxford: Oxford University Press.

Perry, M. A., ed. 2012. *Bioarchaeology and Behavior: The People of the Ancient Near East.* BIHP. Gainesville: University Press of Florida.

Perry, M. A.; Coleman, D. S.; Dettman, D. L.; Grattan, J. P.; and al-Shiyab, A. H. 2011. Condemned to Metallum? The Origin and Role of 4th–6th Century AD Phaeno Minin Campresidents Using Multiple Chemical Techniques. *JAS* 38: 558–69.

Pilloud, M. A., and Larsen, C. S. 2011. "Official" and "Practical" Kin: Inferring Social and Community Structure from Dental Phenotype at Neolithic Çatalhöyük, Turkey. *AJPA* 145: 519–30.

Ponce, P. V. 2010. *A Comparative Study of Activity-Related Skeletal Changes in 3rd–2nd Millennium BC Coastal Fishers and 1st Millennium AD Inland Agriculturalists in Chile, South America.* PhD diss., University of Durham.

Porter, B. W., and Boutin, A. T., eds. 2014. *Remembering the Dead in the Ancient Near East: Recent Contributions from Bioarchaeology and Mortuary Archaeology.* Boulder: University of Colorado Press.

Price, R. M., trans. 1991. *Cyril of Scythopolis: The Lives of the Monks of Palestine.* Cistercian Studies Series 114. Kalamazoo, MI: Cistercian Press.

Pritchard, J. B. 1963. *The Bronze Age Cemetery at Gibeon.* UMM 25. Philadelphia: University Museum, University of Pennsylvania.

Rast, W. A., and Schaub, R. T. 2003. *Bab edh-Dhrâ': Excavations at the Town Site (1975–81).* REDSPJ 2. Winona Lake, IN: Eisenbrauns.

Riehl, S.; Bryson, R.; and Pustovoytov, K. 2008. Changing Growing Conditions for Crops during the Near Eastern Bronze Age (3000–1200 BC): The Stable Carbon Isotope Evidence. *JAS* 35: 1011–22.

Risdon, D. L. 1939. A Study of the Cranial and Other Human Remains from Palestine Excavated at Tell Duweir (Lachish) by the Wellcome-Marston Archaeological Research Expedition. *Biometrika* 31: 99–166.

Saller, S. J. 1966. Iron Age Tombs at Nebo, Jordan. *LibAnn* 16: 165–298.

Schmidt, C. W.; Remy, A.; Van Sessen, R.; Scott, R.; Mahoney, P.; Beach, J.; McKinley, J.; d'Anastasio, R.; Chiu, L. W.; Buzon, M.; de Gregory, R.; Sheridan, S. G.; Eng, J.; Watson, J.; Klaus, H.; Willman, J. C.; Da-Gloria, P.; Wilson, J.; Krueger, K.; Stone, A.; Sereno, P.; Droke, J. L.; Perash, R.; and Stojanowski, C. In press. Dental Microwear Texture Analysis of *Homo sapiens sapiens*: Foragers, Farmers, and Pastoralists. *AJPA*.

Schmidt, C. W., and Symes, S. A., eds. 2015. *The Analysis of Burned Human Remains.* Amsterdam: Elsevier/Academic.

Schrader, S. A. 2013. *Bioarchaeology of the Everyday: An Analysis of Activity Patterns and Diet in the Nile Valley.* PhD diss., Purdue University.

Seger, J. D. 1976. The MB II Fortifications at Schechem and Gezer: A Hyksos Retrospective. *ErIsr* 12: 34*–45*.

——— 1988. *Gezer V: The Field I Caves.* Annual of the Hebrew Union College/Nelson Glueck School of Biblical Archaeology 5. Jerusalem: Hebrew Union College/Nelson Glueck School of Biblical Archaeology.

Sessen, R. Van; Schmidt, C.; Sheridan, S. G.; Ullinger, J. M.; and Grohovsky, M. 2013. Dental Microwear Texture Analysis at Tell Dothan. *AJPA* 151: 276.

Sheridan, S. G. 1999. "New Life the Dead Receive": The Relationship between Human Remains and the Cultural Record for Byzantine St. Stephen's. *RB* 106: 574–611.

——— 2017. Bioarchaeology in the Ancient Near East: Challenges and Future Directions for the Southern Levant. *YPA* 162 (S63): 110–52.

Sheridan, S. G., and Gregoricka, L. A. 2015. Monks on the Move: Evaluating Pilgrimage to Byzantine St. Stephen's Monastery Using Strontium Isotopes. *AJPA* 158: 581–91.

Sheridan, S. G.; Ullinger, J. M.; Gregoricka, L. A., and Chesson, M. 0. 2014. Bioarchaeological Reconsideration of Group Identity at Early Bronze Age Bab edh-Dhra', Jordan. In *Remembering the Dead in the Ancient Near East: Recent Contributions from Bioarchaeology and Mortuary Archaeology*, ed. B. W. Porter and A. T. Boutin, 133–85. Boulder: University of Colorado Press.

Shormann, A. al-, and Khwaileh, A. 2011. Burial Practices in Jordan from the Natufians to the Persians. *EJA* 15: 88–108.

Sillen, A.; Hall, G.; Richardson, S.; and Armstrong, R. 1998. $^{87}Sr/^{86}Sr$ Ratios in Modern and Fossil Food-Webs of the Sterkfontein Valley: Implications for Early Hominid Habitat Preference. *Geochimica et Cosmochimica Acta* 62: 2463–73.

Smith, P.; Bar-Yosef, O.; and Sillen, A. 1984. Archaeological and Skeletal Evidence for Dietary Change during the Late Pleistocene/Early Holocene in the Levant. In *Paleopathology at the Origins of Agriculture*, ed. M. N. Cohen and G. J. Armelagos, 101–36. London: Academic.

Smith, P., and Kahila, G. 1992. Identification of Infanticide in Archaeological Sites: A Case Study from the Late Roman–Early Byzantine Periods at Ashkelon, Israel. *JAS* 19: 667–75.

Smith-Guzmán, N.; Rose, J.; and Kucken, K. 2016. Beyond the Differential Diagnosis: New Approaches to the Bioarchaeology of the Hittite Plague. In *New Directions in Biocultural Anthropology*, ed. M. K. Zuckerman and D. L. Martin, 295–316. Hoboken, NJ: Wiley.

Spronk, K. 1986. *Beatific Afterlife in Ancient Israel and in the Ancient Near East*. AOAT 219. Kevelaer: Butzon & Bercker; Neukirchen-Vluyn: Neukirchener Verlag.

Temple, D. H., and Goodman, A. H. 2014. Bioarchaeology Has a "Health" Problem: Conceptualizing "Stress" and "Health" in Bioarchaeological Research. *AJPA* 155: 186–91.

Thomas, A. 2014. Bioarchaeology of the Middle Neolithic: Evidence for Archery among Early European Farmers. *AJPA* 154: 279–90.

Thomas, R. M.; Ubelaker, D. H.; and Byrd, J. E. 2013. Tables for the Metric Evaluation of Pair-Matching of Human Skeletal Elements. *JFS* 58: 952–6.

Tilley, L. 2015. *Theory and Practice in the Bioarchaeology of Care*. BST. Cham: Springer.

Tilley, L., and Cameron, T. 2014. Introducing the Index of Care: A Web-Based Application Supporting Archaeological Research into Health-Related Care. *IJP* 6: 5–9.

Tilley, L., and Schrenck, A. A., eds. 2017. *New Developments in the Bioarchaeology of Care: Further Case Studies and Expanded Theory*. BST. New York: Springer.

Tufnell, O. 1958. *Lachish IV: The Bronze Age*. WMARENEP 4. London: Oxford University Press.

Tung, T. A. 2016. Commingled Bodies and Mixed and Communal Identities. In *Theoretical Approaches to Analysis and Interpretation of Commingled Human Remains*, ed. A. J. Osterholtz, 243–51. BST. Cham: Springer.

Ullinger, J. M. 2002. Early Christian Pilgrimage to a Byzantine Monastery in Jerusalem – A Dental Perspective. *Dental Anthropology* 16: 22–5.

———. 2010. *Skeletal Health Changes and Increasing Sedentism at Early Bronze Age Bab edh-Dhra', Jordan*. PhD diss., The Ohio State University–Columbus.

Ullinger, J. M., and Sheridan, S. G. 2015. Bone Color Changes in a Burned Burial Structure from Early Bronze Age Bab adh-Dhra', Jordan. In *The Analysis of Burned Human Remains*, Vol. 2, ed. C. W. Schmidt and S. A. Symes, 403–13. Amsterdam: Elsevier/Academic.

Ullinger, J. M.; Sheridan, S. G.; and Guatelli-Steinberg, D. 2015. Fruits of Their Labour: Urbanisation, Orchard Crops, and Dental Health in Early Bronze Age Jordan. *IJO* 25: 753–64.

Ullinger, J. M.; Sheridan, S. G.; Hawkey, D. E.; Turner, C. G., II; and Cooley, R. 2005. Bioarchaeological Analysis of Cultural Transition in the Southern Levant Using Dental Nonmetric Traits. *AJPA* 128: 466–76

Villotte, S. 2006. Connaissances médicales actuelles, cotation des enthésopathies: Nouvelle méthode. *Bulletins et mémoires de la Société d'Anthropologie de Paris* 18: 65–85.

Villotte, S.; Castex, D.; Couallier, V.; Dutour, O.; Knüsel, C. J.; and Henry-Gambier, D. 2010. Enthesopathies as Occupational Stress Markers: Evidence from the Upper Limb. *AJPA* 142: 224–34.

Villotte, S., and Knüsel, C. J. 2014. "I Sing of Arms and of a Man...": Medial Epicondylosis and the Sexual Division of Labour in Prehistoric Europe. *JAS* 43: 168–74.

Walker, P. L.; Byock, J.; Eng, J. T.; Erlandson, J. M.; Holck, P.; Prizer, K.; and Tveskov, M. A. 2004. Bioarchaeological Evidence for the Health Status of an Early Icelandic Population. *AJPA* 123 (S38): 204.

Wood, J. W.; Milner, G. R.; Harpending, H. C.; Weiss, K. M.; Cohen, M. N.; Eisenberg, L. E.; Hutchinson, D. L.; Jankauskas, R.; Česnys, G.; Katzenberg, M. A.; Lukacs, J. R.; McGrath, J. W.; Abella Roth, E.; Ubelaker, D. H.; and Wilkinson, R. G. 1992. The Osteological Paradox: Problems of Inferring Prehistoric Health from Skeletal Samples [and Comments and Reply]. *CA* 33: 343–70.

Yezerski, I. 1999. Burial-Cave Distribution and the Borders of the Kingdom of Judah toward the End of the Iron Age. *TA* 26: 253–70.

TWELVE

THE MIDDLE BRONZE AGE CANAANITE CITY AS A DOMESTICATING APPARATUS

ASSAF YASUR-LANDAU

WHAT IS A CANAANITE CITY?

Until the early 1990s, the term "urbanization" for the Middle Bronze Age in reference to the end of the long non-urban hiatus of the Intermediate Bronze Age was used simply to denote the existence of fortifications (Dever 1987: 154). Earthen ramparts became synonymous with urbanization in scholarship (Herzog 1997: 102) or, as put by Raphael Greenberg, "the ramparts were used by its builders to give concrete form to a pre-existing concept of 'city'; it was a conventional symbol of urbanism" (2002: 109). There was a vivid discussion, however, on the date of the first ramparts in relation to the renewed urbanization. Yigael Yadin weighed in with a notion that the Middle Bronze Age (MB) I was a pre-urban phase, while Moshe Kochavi, Ze'ev Herzog, and others presented the existence of MB I fortifications as proof of the existence of urban sites already in this phase (Herzog 1997: 102, with earlier references). As ramparts were perceived as sharing a common origin in Syria, the urbanization in the Middle Bronze Age southern Levant was frequently connected with northern influence. The rise of Canaanite cities was not considered to be a local evolutionary trajectory but was rather associated with a broader inter-regional narrative, in which these cities emerged as part of secondary state formation, exogenously inspired by earlier developments in Syria and Mesopotamia. As the region became a periphery of the Syro-Mesopotamian world and was incorporated into inter-regional trade networks, settlements in the southern Levant began indeed to display Syrian traits manifested in monumental architecture, in the form of fortifications, temples, and palaces (Greenberg 2002: 107).

Contrarily, William Dever (1993) argued that urbanization in the southern Levant must have been different from the Syro-Mesopotamia phenomenon because it developed in a profoundly different ecological environment: Mesopotamia enjoyed rich river plains, while Canaan's climate and landscape resulted in a lower carrying capacity. These environments were the outset of two different trajectories, leading, necessarily, to different outcomes. For a site to have the capacity to support its own inhabitants without provisions brought from the hinterland, it cannot exceed 6–8 ha in size and a population of 1,500–2,000 people. The first urban centers of Canaan include Tel Dan, Akko, Tel Kabri, Megiddo, Gezer, Aphek, Ashkelon, and Tell el-'Ajjul (Dever 1993). While Dever's scale may be exaggeratedly small, the approach that differentiates between the ancient Near Eastern and Mediterranean phenomena of urbanization on the basis of the difference in ecology may well be justified.

Steven Falconer and Stephen Savage (1995) also argued for different trajectories of development in Levantine and Mesopotamian cities, but they suggested that it stemmed from different forms of interactions between the cities and their hinterland. Perhaps the criteria for urbanism should be more flexible and based on the social and economic functions of a settlement rather than merely on its size. A convenient starting point may be Keith Branigan's definition of a city, which he presented at the beginning of a conference on urbanism in the Bronze Age Aegean: The city is "a relatively large, dense and permanent settlement of socially heterogeneous individuals, which performs specialist functions, of a non-agricultural type, in relationship to a broader hinterland" (2001: vii). Indeed, as Branigan duly noted, size is not everything in defining cities, but it is rather the social and economic services provided in them that are salient for this definition. Thus, for example, centers of great importance could be deceivingly small in size. Such is the maritime hub of Byblos, known for its elaborate contacts with Egypt; it was remarkably small in the days of the Old Kingdom: only 5 ha with a population of 1,000–2,000 people (Broodbank 2013: 302).

If so, is the Canaanite city of the Middle Bronze Age a peripheral offshoot of the Syro-Mesopotamian urban core, or does it reflect a local phenomenon that should be divorced from ancient Near Eastern (and other) concepts of urbanization? It will be argued here for a middle ground: The formation of the urban layout of Canaanite cities was a dialectical, highly local process. It entailed an uneasy discourse between the rulers' will to implement ambitious building plans inspired by Syro-Mesopotamian ideas of monumentality; the realities of the Mediterranean topography; and, just as importantly, the residents' will to keep their property safe from the expansion of public projects (Yasur-Landau 2011). At the same time, the intra-group tensions created by urbanization resulted in new adaptive methods of conflict resolution, as well as social control over the individuals in urban Canaanite society.

THE LAYOUT OF THE CITY

None of the cities in Canaan exhibits overall urban planning of the type seen in Middle Kingdom Egypt, such as the example seen in the layout of the town of Kahun, near the pyramid of Senusret II. Its residents lived in houses whose area, plan, and location had been predetermined in the foundation of the city. Ten elite mansions were located on both sides of the main east–west road in Kahun. A possible temple stood on the acropolis in the eastern part of the site. *Insulae* of small houses were located to its south. The western sector, separated by a wall from the rest of the town, consisted of long blocks of humble four- and five-room houses separated by east–west streets (Petrie 1891: 5–6, pl. XIV; Kemp 2006: 211–13). William Flinders Petrie suggested that these may have been the houses of the workmen and their families. The town was planned by a literate administration that used measured blueprints. An inscribed limestone tablet from Kahun reads: "A four house block – 30 × 20 cubits," most likely marking the place for four small houses to be built in a total area of 15 × 10 m (Kemp 2006: 195). Though southern Levantines must have visited similar planned settlements, such as the 12th Dynasty town at Tell el-Dab'a (Bietak 1996: 9; 2010: 17, fig. 11), they never implemented this idea in Canaan. The concept of dividing urban space by streets was not adopted in the southern Levant during the Middle and Late Bronze Age, as it was employed in Syria and even on Cyprus, as demonstrated by the orthogonal or semi-orthogonal plan of Tell Halawa on the Upper Euphrates during the MB II (Akkermans and Schwartz 2003: 307) and by thirteenth-century BCE Enkomi on Cyprus, where parallel east–west streets intersect with long north–south streets (Fisher 2014: 191–5).

As we will see below, the layouts of Canaanite cities were, to an extent, influenced by notions of monumentality emitting from Syria. There, the urban layout was determined largely by imposing massive building projects of fortifications, temples, and palaces on the urban landscapes – a concept that was inspired by Mesopotamia. The cases of Ebla and Qatna, both reflecting Middle Bronze Age planning, demonstrate this ideal well: Paolo Matthiae (2013: 265) regards the foundation of Ebla in the twentieth century BCE as *de novo*. The town was divided in two: the acropolis, surrounded by its own fortifications, and the lower town, which encircled the acropolis and was fortified by a huge earthen rampart. Rather than being centralized in one place, power was divided between palaces on the acropolis (the royal residence) and the lower town (Matthiae 2013: 274–5). This entire plan is probably the result of preplanning the locations of the main features at the site (Pinnock 2001: 22). The alteration of landscape by ramparts in the early Middle Bronze Age is manifested well in the huge rectangular plan of Qatna, probably devised during the MB I, with gates facing the four cardinal directions (Burke 2008: 213–17; Morandi Bonacossi 2014: 275).

As massive earthen ramparts represent an imported Syro-Mesopotamian feature found in most southern Levantine tells, it is important to examine their function in the urban landscape in order to see their impact on urban communities in Canaan. The ramparts were used for the defense of the urban population; their massive appearance alone may have deterred potential external threats (Burke 2008). This, however, is only a part of the story.

While enemies and competitors witnessed the might of the ramparts infrequently, those who lived in the cities experienced them daily: In imagination and perception, the imposing rampart settlement, emerging from amidst the flat plains of Syria and Mesopotamia, acted as a symbolic deterrent, a manifestation of strength, and a constant looming reminder to the inhabitants of the ruler's power. *The Epic of Gilgamesh* begins with an invitation to see the mighty walls of Uruk, built by the legendary king Gilgamesh: "see the upper wall, whose face gleams like copper. See its lower course, which nothing will equal!" (Foster 2001: 3). Warad-Sîn, who built the wall of Ur, aspired to achieve a similar psychological effect: "I made its height suppressing, had it release its terrifying aura" (E4.2.13.21 lines 80–95 [Frayne 1990: 243]). In the Mesopotamian experience, this imaginative aura was actually created by a heavy physical presence, blocking out the light: The city walls cast long shadows over the smaller houses below them. These shadows also extended outside the town: Adam Smith (2003: 216) described how, during the late third and early second millennia BCE, the imposing tell of Ur (currently 20 m higher than its surroundings) would have thrown a long shadow over the plain during sunset. The diminishing light was accompanied by the restriction of movement: Gates, cosmologically aligned with the cardinal directions, were not merely an element in the fortification system; they were used by rulers to regulate the entry into and exit from a city, controlling the access of residents to their homes in the city and their fields outside it (Stone 1995: 240; Smith 2003: 216).

While the gates were used to control access, the top of the wide ramparts was used, no doubt, for patrols that overlooked both the city and the land outside it. Thus, in a letter regarding the defense of the Yaminite town Mišlan, during the revolt against Zimri-lim, king of Mari, such patrols are mentioned: "Mišlan is well; your brother Yaggih-Addu is well ... We, your servants, are well. No one is neglecting the patrol of the rampart and the gates" (Fleming 2004: 74). We learn from this that the wide ramparts and gates were also areas in which troops patrolled.

Walls were not the only measure by which rulership manifested its power. Their construction was, at times, accompanied by the construction of monumental architecture within the city. For example, after the collapse of the Sargonid dynasty, King Ur-Nammu restored Ur's independence from Uruk by rebuilding the city wall and carrying out a vast building program within the city, focusing on cultic structures. He constructed the Ziggurat of Ur-Nammu and the great terrace (*temenos*) as well as refurbished the Temples of Nanna and Ningal (Smith 2003: 191).

TWO REGIONAL NARRATIVES OF CITIES: HAZOR AND MEGIDDO

It was argued above that the shape of Middle Bronze Age sites enclosed in ramparts, such as Hazor, Tel Dan, and Tel Kabri, indicates that the builders had an ideal plan in mind of a Syrian city, such as Ebla or Qatna, in which the site is given a regular plan, either oval or rectangular (Kempinski 1992a). However, the attempt to recreate a foreign political landscape met with the difficult reality of the Mediterranean landscape, bringing about tension between imagination and experience in the creation of a political landscape (cf. Smith 2003: 72–3, 202–20). The symmetrical shape of the site and the prerequisite that it be considerably higher than its surroundings (in order to emit the desired "fearful aura") can only be achieved in alluvial areas. These, however, are not common in the fragmented Mediterranean landscape, where some mountainous sites, such as Jerusalem, had to be located in a lower position than some hills surrounding them. The following examples of cities do not present an exhaustive catalog; instead, they illustrate the pronounced variety of city layouts in the formative era of the Middle Bronze Age, while continuing the regional narrative of the development of complexity, which began in the previous period.

Megiddo: From Village to City with Resisting Inhabitants

Large-scale construction projects were severely hindered in MB II Megiddo because of the considerable height of the Early Bronze Age tell and the existence of the large unfortified MB I settlement in Strata XIV and XIIIb, with the open-air cultic site taking up much of the central area of the tell (Loud 1948: 84; Kempinski 1989: 178). The transition from village to city at Megiddo was gradual and does not seem to reflect the implementation of a Syro-Mesopotamian building plan combining the elements of temples, a palace, and massive fortifications. There was never any attempt to alter the shape of the tell as there was at Hazor, Tel Kabri, Ashkelon, and Tel Dan by constructing a massive earthen rampart. Therefore, the site was never enlarged in a significant manner to accommodate both the building of the MB I fortifications and the natural development of domestic areas. This situation caused great friction and led to a power struggle between the ruling elite and the private householders throughout most of the Middle Bronze Age, especially in the area adjacent to the walls.

Stratum XIII in Area AA at Megiddo, dated to mid-MB I, is characterized by the appearance of a well-planned, elaborate fortification system (Loud 1948: 6–8, fig. 378; Burke 2008: 291–2) (Fig. 12.1). It includes a stepped approach, a

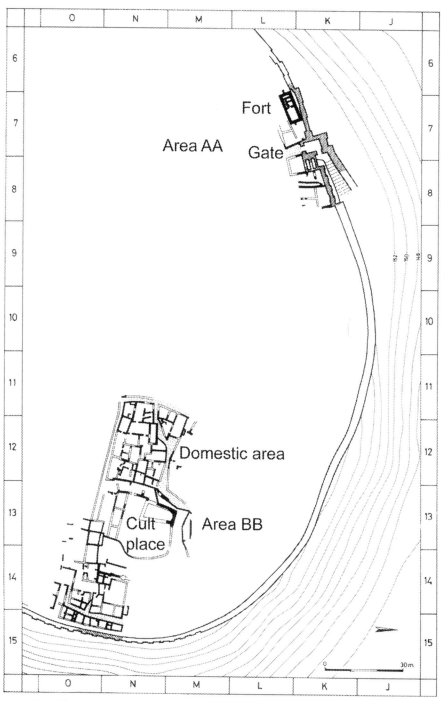

12.1. Megiddo Stratum XIII (from Herzog 1997: fig. 4.2). (Altered by A. Yasur-Landau. Courtesy of Z. Herzog, Tel Aviv University.)

gate, a brick city-wall, and an inner tower or small fort (L4014 [Loud 1948: fig. 378]) – a solid rectangular structure similar in shape to the one found by the south gate at Gezer (Herzog 1997: fig. 4.20). This development was not accompanied by the building of a palace or temples. Rather, the area next to the open-air cult precinct in Area BB was filled with densely packed domestic structures in Stratum XIIIb (Loud 1948: figs. 306, 307; Kempinski 1989: figs. 27, 28). Indeed, the transition to a city was probably gradual and included a phase featuring a large fortified village with narrow twisting alleys.

The first palace at Megiddo can be seen only in Stratum XII, Area BB (Loud 1948: fig. 308; Kempinski 1989: fig. 29; Herzog 1997: 104–7), built next to the sacred area (Fig. 12.2). This vast multi-room structure replaced the domestic structures preceding it. The evacuation of residents from Area BB was accompanied by the construction of dwellings at the expense of previous fortifications in Area AA. The gate to the town was presumably moved to the east, while the formal architecture of the Stratum XIII gate and tower in Area AA was replaced by at least three large courtyard houses (Loud 1948: figs. 23, 378). Their northern wall was adjacent to the city's fortification, and a street ran to their south. Burials were dug below the floors of these houses (T. 4094, 4099, 4107, 4108). Is it possible that these new houses were built to compensate the residents evicted from the area that had been reassigned for the construction of the new palace?

The pendulum swung again toward rulership initiatives in the days of Stratum XI, the transition between MB I and MB II (Loud 1948: fig. 379; Burke 2008: 292), when a new fortification program was implemented, including the addition of an eastern rampart, a glacis, and a gate (Fig. 12.3). The elaboration of the fortifications obliterated the Stratum XII courtyard houses. A new street separated the fortifications from a new group of houses built to the south, facilitating quick access to the wall, unhindered by private houses.

In a previous publication, I suggested that the resistance to public building projects by people whose houses these projects compromised was expressed in Stratum XI in a new venue of legitimizing private ownership: multiple burial tombs (Yasur-Landau 2011). These were found in Area AA (T. 4055 + 4056, 3175, 4099 [Loud 1948: figs. 29, 32]) and in Area BB (T. 3075, 3085 [Loud 1948: fig. 218]), and contained vast amounts of pottery and jewelry, representing multiple generations of burials. In constructing these tombs, the house became not only the residence of its current inhabitants but a manifestation of a lineage, which included both the living and their ancestors. These may be interpreted as reciprocal relations: the living honored the dead, perhaps also with offerings and feasts, and the dead, ever present in their own subterranean room of the house, gave historical depth and legitimacy to the claims of the living to their property.

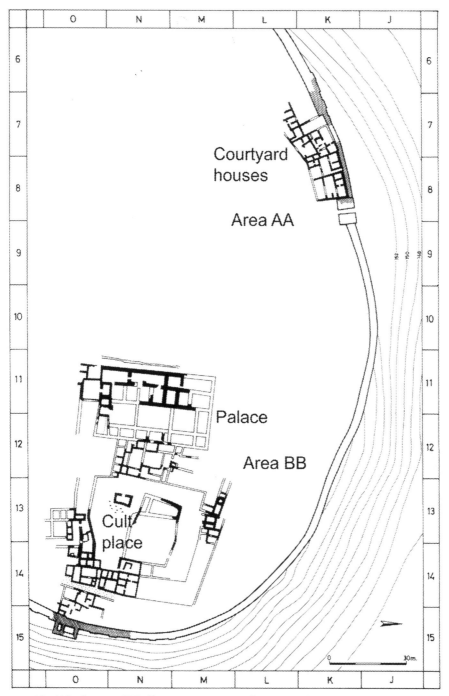

12.2. Megiddo Stratum XII (from Herzog 1997: fig. 4.3). (Altered by A. Yasur-Landau. Courtesy of Z. Herzog, Tel Aviv University.)

It seems that Syro-Mesopotamian ideas about monumentality and even Syrian-inspired architecture had little effect on the development of Megiddo as an urban center. As stated, a rampart was never constructed in order to reshape the site. The other two characteristics of Syrian architecture appear only in the late MB II Stratum X: the three-chamber Syrian gate in Area AA, and a Syrian-style *migdol* temple replacing the open-air cult area in Area BB (Kempinski 1989: fig. 34).

The Hula Valley: A Failed Attempt of Urbanization at Tel Dan and the Implementation of a Syrian Model at Hazor

The implementation at Tel Dan of a Syrian-inspired fortification system, including a rampart and a chambered gate, built over a preexisting, large unfortified settlement, did not result in the desired effect – that is, turning the site into a lasting urban center (Fig. 12.4). Dan was fortified during the latest part of the MB I or during the transition into the MB II (Biran 1994: 62; Ilan 1996: 164–5; Greenberg 2002: 35). The impressive fortification system included a rampart that had a stone core and encircled the entire tell, and a gate found in Area K. This massive, six-pier brick gate reflects imported Syrian architectural traditions. Surprisingly, this fortification system was used for only a brief period of time. It was built during Stratum XI, and the small pottery assemblage found on the gate's latest floor provides a *terminus ante quem* for its latest use (Biran 1994: 82, fig. 50), assigning it to the same stratum in which it was built, possibly the transitional MB I–MB II. Though an attempt was made to give the site a regular shape by the construction of the ramparts, the spring's location had to be considered and was probably the reason for positioning the gates off the cardinal directions, hindering a more ideal design (Kempinski 1992a).

Still, as may have been predicted, the construction of the ramparts brought about a dramatic change in the use of available space for habitation and fortification. In Area B, MB I domestic levels belonging to Stratum XII were buried under the rampart (Biran 1994: 51). The possible clash between ancestral rights over land and the ruling elites' will to construct monumental architecture, as seen at Megiddo, is evident also at Tel Dan in Area Y. Tombs 1025 and 902c, d, which were probably located originally below the floors of houses, were uncovered in this area, sealed by the rampart (Ilan 1996: 164, 202–8). The building of fortifications on top of domestic structures was no doubt an action dictated, in part, by the politics of inclusion and exclusion, which, in turn, led to social instability at the site. This may have played a role in the rapid decline of Tel Dan soon thereafter (Yasur-Landau 2011). During the MB II, Tel Dan's magnificent Syrian gate was blocked up, and finds from tombs at the site indicate that Tel Dan's links to trade and

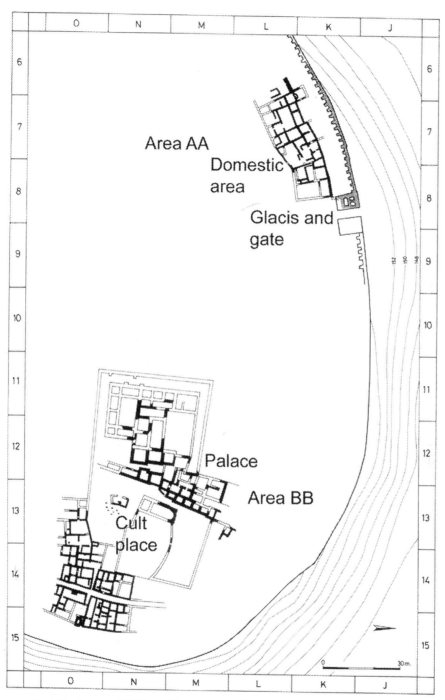

12.3. Megiddo Stratum XI (from Herzog 1997: fig. 4.17). (Altered by A. Yasur-Landau. Courtesy of Z. Herzog, Tel Aviv University.)

12.4. Plan and reconstruction of the Tel Dan gate (from Herzog 1997: fig. 4.7). (Courtesy of Z. Herzog, Tel Aviv University.)

influence from outside the region were almost completely severed. In fact, it is likely that the site, possibly with no functioning fortifications, became Hazor's subordinate shortly after its sudden rise in the MB II (Maeir 2000: 39).

In contrast to Megiddo, the evidence at Hazor suggests that the site was founded based on a preplanned Syrian model, with the location of the palace, temples, and fortifications determined from the outset (Fig. 12.5). The first settlement at the site was a small village built no earlier than the MB I–MB II transition, as indicated by tombs and scattered pottery on the upper tell. Immediately afterward, possibly in the earliest phase of the MB II, the site was fortified with an immense rampart, adding a huge lower town to the existing upper tell, which amounted to a total area of ca. 74 ha (Maeir 1997: 327; Ben-Tor 2004: 51; Burke 2008: 265–71).

The urban layout of Middle Bronze Age Hazor demonstrates the result of preplanning that took into account monumental architecture, while allowing some leeway for the internal development of domestic architecture (Kempinski 1992b: 125; for a discussion on the residential neighborhood in Area C, see below). The upper tell, Area A, was dedicated to temples and possibly also to a palace. A Middle Bronze Age temple excavated there presents a symmetrical Syrian plan (Zuckerman 2012: 110–12; Ben-Tor et al. 2017). The lower tell included formal structures of distinct Syrian style, such as the Orthostats Temple in Area H (Yadin 1972: 75–9; Ben-Tor 1989: plans XXXVII, XLI) and the three-chambered Middle Bronze Age gates in Areas

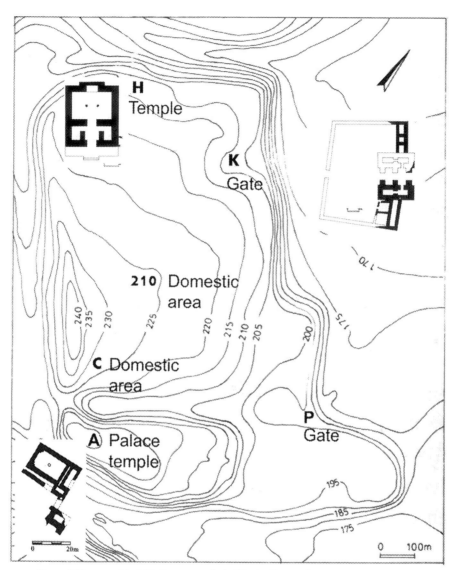

12.5. Plan of Hazor, with MB II symmetrical ("Syrian") temples in Areas A and H, and a "Syrian" gate in Area K (from Herzog 1997: fig. 4.8 A, C, D and after Zuckerman 2012: fig. 2). (Courtesy of Z. Herzog, Tel Aviv University.)

K and P (Yadin 1972: 58–65; Ben-Tor 1989: plan XLII; Mazar 1997: plan V.2, V.4). The dispersal of these monuments over the urban landscape in a manner reminiscent of Ebla's plan brought Ruhama Bonfil and Anabel Zarzecki-Peleg (2007: 27) to propose, tentatively, that Hazor, as suggested for Ebla, was divided into quarters; however, in the absence of a clear street system for Hazor, it is difficult to test this hypothesis.

The sudden massive construction project at Hazor during the MB II and the contemporary appearance of the many examples of Syrian-style architecture at the site were no coincidence. Middle Bronze Age cuneiform tablets from the site reveal its prominent position in the international economic and cultural networks of the Old Babylonian period. Hazor is not only a rare example of Middle Bronze Age Canaanite literacy, it is also the only site in the southern Levant mentioned in texts from the Mari archive (e.g., Malamat 1989: 52–69), and it was likely unique in the southern Levant in regards to implementing a literate administration using cuneiform script (Horowitz and Oshima 2006: 65–80). In fact, the appearance of the full Syrian, urban architecture package, complete with cuneiform script, in a place in which only a small village existed before, may indicate the direct involvement of powers from Syria in the foundation and construction of the city.

STABILITY AND CHANGE IN THE URBAN LAYOUT

Thus, flawed as it is, a city is born. As most cities in the Middle Bronze Age existed continuously from their founding, through the rest of this long period and well into the Late Bronze Age, it is important to present here several examples of continuity versus change in the urban layout.

During the Ur III and Old Babylonian periods in southern Mesopotamia, there were no strict rules about the location of palaces within a city. In some cities, they were built next to temples, such as the cases of Larsa, Eshnunna, and the Ehursag at Ur, where the palace was constructed adjacent to a temple complex (Smith 2003: 214). The location of palaces was dynamic also in Syrian cities. The Late Bronze Age royal palace of Qatna was built upon an earlier Middle Bronze Age cultic area, rather than over an earlier MB II palace (the "eastern palace"), which was located to the east of its successor. Other palaces were built at Hazor in the Late Bronze Age, in addition to the royal palace: to its south, the "southern palace" in Area C and to its north, the "lower city palace" in Area K (Morandi Bonacossi 2014).

At Megiddo, the location of the palace changed during the Middle Bronze Age, while the location of the central cult place did not. The sacred precinct of Megiddo enjoyed surprisingly uninterrupted longevity beginning as early as the Early Bronze Age, when it boasted a series of temples (Kempinski 1989: figs. 24–28). From the Intermediate Bronze Age well into MB II Stratum XI, this area was maintained as an open-air cult place, encircled by a *temenos* wall (Loud 1948: fig. 309; Kempinski 1989: 33). A Syrian-style *migdol* temple replaced the open-air cult area in Stratum X and maintained its position until the destruction of Megiddo at the end of the Late Bronze Age (Kempinski 1989: figs, 34, 42). The palace, however, changed locations. During Strata XII, XI, and X (Kempinski 1989: figs. 29, 33, 34; Herzog 1997: 104–7, 150–3), it stood in Area BB next to the sacred area, perhaps drawing legitimacy from it. In Stratum IX onward, following the gradual rise to power of a family residing in a house west of the city gate, the main palace of the city was relocated to Area AA, where it remained until the final destruction of the Late Bronze Age city in Stratum VII (Kempinski 1989: figs. 37, 38, 41; Herzog 1997: 165–9). The palace was replaced by the monumental "Nordburg" structure (perhaps non-palatial public structure), which existed in the Late Bronze Age (LB) II (Finkelstein, Ussishkin, and Halpern 2006: 847).

In sharp contrast to these examples of profound change, the city of Hazor with its pronounced Syrian connections displays impressive architectural continuity from the Middle to Late Bronze Age (Bonfil and Zarzecki-Peleg 2007: 26–7, fig. 1). During the LB II, the area of the acropolis was taken up by a large cultic complex (Area A), which included Building 7050 and two adjacent temples and a grand palace, still unexcavated (Area M and the areas between A and M [Zuckerman 2010; cf. Bonfil and Zarzecki-Peleg 2007, who view Building 7050 as a ceremonial palace]). The Area A complex stood on top of an earlier Middle Bronze Age complex of a temple (Zuckerman 2012: 100–12) and a palace; the latter is known from very few remains. In the lower town, a cult place existed in Area F from the MB II until the LB II (Yadin 1972: 42–6, 95–102). The structures in this area changed over time, but the area's function remained cultic. Similarly, the Area H Syrian-style *migdol* temple was in continuous use from the late MB II to the LB II (Yadin 1972: 75–95; Zuckerman 2012: 105–6). The location of the excavated gates in Areas K and P was maintained from the MB II to the LB II (Yadin 1972: 58–65). The minimal or absence of change in the areas designated at Hazor for fortification, the palace, and major cultic precincts may indicate that, similar to Ebla (see above), the major monumental or public features had been preplanned. The fact that the essence of this plan was maintained for centuries is a testimony to the strength of the rulership at Hazor.

A SERVICE APPROACH TO ACTIVITIES INSIDE THE CANAANITE CITY

The work of Benjamin Stanley and his colleagues (2016) on service access in premodern cities provides compelling evidence of inequality between elites and non-elites in access to religious services, assembly places, and market areas. However, access overall was better in small cities than in larger ones. This service approach allows for the examination of who benefitted from Middle Bronze Age urbanization. The level of services available to the residents of Canaanite cities during the Middle and Late Bronze Age appears to have been low.

In terms of sanitation, few non-palatial structures had access to built-in drains, in contrast to palatial structures. This is evident in residential Area C at Hazor, where few drains lead from houses (Yadin 1972: 28–38). At other sites where drains did exist, they diverted water from the main streets closest to the city wall into the gate area or under the wall itself (e.g., Tell Beit Mirsim, MB II Strata E and D [Herzog 1997: fig. 4.15, 16]; Hazor MB II, lower city, Strata 4 and 3 [Yadin 1972: 65–6]; Jericho MB II [Herzog 1997: fig. 4.12]; Megiddo, LB II Stratum VIII [Loud 1948: fig. 382]).

It is possible that at some sites water was provided to the inhabitants within the city, very likely for purposes of defense rather than simply to provide amenities for residents. Apparently, these sites each had a single water source that could be tightly controlled by the government. The springs of Tel Dan and Tel Kabri enabled year-round access to fresh water from within the city; the situation may have been similar in Jericho if indeed the spring was contained within the fortification line (Herzog 1997: fig. 4.11). There are indications that elaborate water systems were also constructed during the Middle Bronze Age; for example, a massive MB II fortification system in Jerusalem protected the Gihon Spring and the associated rock-cut water system (Maeir 2011: 176–7). Recent work at Gezer suggests that the rock-cut water management system there may also date to the Middle Bronze Age (Warner 2013). At Hazor, a large water reservoir dating to the late Middle Bronze Age or the Late Bronze Age, found on the upper tell, was very likely limited to the use of the palace (Yadin 1972: 127).

Assessing the accessibility of religious services to the townspeople is difficult. Formal direct access to temples and their courtyards were probably off limits to the majority of the populace, while open-air sanctuaries, as at Megiddo and Gezer, could offer a line of vision that would enable some form of wider public participation. At the same time, there is evidence – although more scarce – of more vernacular cult places that serviced the neighborhoods, such as the one in Area C at Hazor (Zukerman 2012: 102–3).

The largest open areas in these cities were the courtyards of the palaces and the temples. However, the winding, very narrow streets of most towns precluded the existence of large open-air markets in the cities and large assembly areas. Shops may have operated from the ground floors of domestic structures, as suggested for Jericho (Ziffer 1990: 17–18, fig. 11).

It would be perhaps overly optimistic to assume that the ramparts, walls, and gates were intended mainly for their value as protection of the citizens and rulers. Rather, beyond a deterrent of prospective enemies, they were a measure of population control. Entry to the city was limited to existing gates and their operating hours. As argued above, the shadow cast by the walls and ramparts was a constant reminder of their powers of restriction. The mere construction of the wall and rampart created an inherent crisis by limiting the available space for new private houses to be built and causing the phenomenon of densely built residential neighborhoods, which strived to use every square meter of available space.

CONCLUSIONS: THE CITY AS AN APPARATUS FOR DOMESTICATION

Was there a direct line of influence leading from Ebla and Qatna to the southern Levant, and was Canaanite urbanization a secondary or tertiary derivative of early second-millennium BCE Syrian urbanization? The distinctively different trajectories emerging from Megiddo, Tel Dan, and Hazor suggest that urbanization in the southern Levant during the Middle Bronze Age bore more resemblance to Italo Calvino's *Invisible Cities* (1974) then to V. Gordon Childe's model cities (1950). Each of the Canaanite sites had its own history, story, and formation process. A comparison between the first appearances of "Syrian"-style Middle Bronze Age city-gates, fortifications, temples, and palaces paints a considerably complex picture. Sites such as Megiddo and Aphek became cities during the MB I without adopting any visible Syrian trait, including the rampart (Yasur-Landau 2011). Ramparts first appeared in mid-MB I in southern coastal sites (Ashkelon, Yavneh-Yam) and in the north coast only late in the MB I (Akko, Tel Kabri). While ramparts differ significantly from one another in detail, architectural features with distinctive Syrian traits — gates and temples — only began to appear at urban sites in the transitional MB I–II (with the earliest being Tel Dan) but mainly in the MB II (at sites such as Ashkelon and Hazor). This chronological scheme advises against the approach that perceives a sudden transition from the initial pre-urban phase to the emergence of permanent fortified settlements, inspired by the Syro-Mesopotamian powers (Greenberg 2002: 106–7). This being said, the Hula Valley, much closer to Syria than to the Levantine coast, is likely an exception to the rule, with the massive and sudden implementation of a Syrian city layout in Hazor.

A portrait of the city as reflected through the social and economic services provided in it may cast a shadow over the joys of urbanization. The image of a city with crowded people within its walls, who have limited or no access to services provided by the public structures, does not reflect an effort of the ruling elite to bring the fruits and benefits of urbanization to most of the city's residents. Urbanization may actually be better portrayed as a deliberate domestication process aimed at controlling the populace. The houses buried underneath the fortifications at Tel Kabri and Tel Dan (Yasur-Landau 2011) and, no doubt, at other sites demonstrate the forcefulness of this process. The possible resistance of homeowners at Megiddo, building their houses over land formerly allotted to fortification, suggests that it took time for this domestication process to take effect.

Indeed, it seems that urbanization contributed to the taming of the Canaanite population at least in one aspect — a change in the persona of Canaanite males regarding engagement in single combat. Warrior tombs are a common trait of the MB I (Philip 1995; Cohen 2012). These are single interments with weapons, such as daggers, spearheads, and axes, all connected with hand-to-hand combat. They represent a pre-urban reality in which, as vividly depicted in the duel-to-the-death scene in the contemporary *Tale of*

Sinuhe, intergroup conflicts were resolved through socially accepted violence (Parkinson 1997; 32 B 100–106; Rainey and Notley 2006: 54).

To my mind, it is not accidental that warrior tombs become rarer toward the end of the MB I, as urban centers become common across Canaan. A recent study of lethal human violence, encompassing numerous past and present societies of various sociopolitical organizations, has pointed to a sharp decrease in the level of personal violence in states in comparison to chiefdoms, which is attributed to the monopolization of the legitimate use of violence by the state (Gómez et al. 2016). This may certainly explain partly the impact of urbanization on Canaanite society; that is, urbanization in Canaan created a balance between the warrior ideal that was still a celebrated notion, crucial for the protection of the city, and the state monopoly on violence – a balance that was reached in contemporary Amorite-dominated Mari (Bonneterre 1995).

The adoption of some elements of the Syro-Mesopotamian judiciary system by Hazor is reflected in an Akkadian tablet discussing a legal case brought before the king, regarding real estate in the territory of Hazor (Horowitz and Oshima 2006: 69–72). While we cannot be certain if this imported dispute-solving mechanism alleviated general tensions in the city, it doubtless strengthened the power of the ruler over the urban population.

At the same time, it is possible that the new living conditions of large communities, crowded in limited urban spaces, created additional adaptation mechanisms for solving internal strife in the urban neighborhoods of Canaanite cities. These mechanisms depended only on the power of the ruler, while working on multiple levels – from the household level to kinship group and from the neighborhood level to that of the city and the polity.

It is possible that mechanisms for preventing violent conflicts were similar to some systems of local leadership in Old Babylonian Amorite cities. There, neighborhoods (*babtū*) functioned as villages within cities and had their own local government system, including a mayor and elders (Potts 1997: 216–17; Schloen 2001: 287). Additional power for conflict resolution was held in the hands of elder assemblies (*puhrum*) and mayors (*rabiānū*) whose power was acknowledged by the king, the highest instance of law (Yoffee 2000: 55–8; Fleming 2004: 190–211).

With multiple tiers of enforcement and control over the individual, intragroup violence could be kept at bay even when the competition for living space within a city increased with population growth at the same time as a ruler sought to execute more ambitious building plans at the expense of private dwellings. Even in cases where there is evidence of high tension between residents and the ruling elite, such as at Megiddo, the urban nature of the site remained intact. Perhaps, somewhat pessimistically, the advent of the city should be regarded as a self-sharpening instrument of control, both decreasing internal strife and increasing the control of the ruling elite.

ACKNOWLEDGMENTS

I would like to thank Norman Yoffee and Guillermo Algaze for the most enlightening discussions on Near Eastern urbanization(s) and complex societies during the process of writing this chapter. This chapter is dedicated to Ze'ev Herzog, pioneer of the study of urban planning in ancient Israel.

REFERENCES

Akkermans, P. M. M. G., and Schwartz, G. M. 2003. *The Archaeology of Syria: From Complex Hunter-Gatherers to Early Urban Societies (c. 16,000–300 BC)*. CWA. Cambridge: Cambridge University Press.

Ben-Tor, A. 2004. Hazor and Chronology. *Egypt and the Levant* 14: 45–67.

Ben-Tor, A., ed. 1989. *Hazor III–IV: An Account of the Third and Fourth Seasons of Excavations, 1957–1958*, Vol. 2: *Text*. Jerusalem: IES; The Hebrew University of Jerusalem.

Ben-Tor, A.; Zuckerman, S.; Bechar, S.; and Sandhaus, D. 2017. *Hazor VII: The 1990–2012 Excavations; The Bronze Age*. Jerusalem; IES; The Institute of Archaeology, The Hebrew University of Jerusalem.

Bietak, M. 1996. *Avaris, the Capital of the Hyksos: Recent Excavations at Tell el-Dab'a; The First Raymond and Beverly Sackler Foundation Distinguished Lecture in Egyptology*. London: British Museum Press.

—— 2010. Houses, Palaces and Development of Social Structure in Avaris. In *Cities and Urbanism in Ancient Egypt: Papers from a Workshop in November 2006 at the Austrian Academy of Sciences*, ed. M. Bietak, E. Czerny, and I. Forstner-Müller, 11–68. DG 60; UZKOAI 35. Vienna: Austrian Academy of Sciences.

Biran, A. 1994. *Biblical Dan*. Jerusalem: IES; Hebrew Union College–Jewish Institute of Religion.

Bonfil, R., and Zarzecki-Peleg, A. 2007. The Palace in the Upper City of Hazor as an Expression of a Syrian Architectural Paradigm. *BASOR* 348: 25–47.

Bonneterre, D. 1995. The Structure of Violence in the Kingdom of Mari. *BCSMS* 30: 11–22.

Branigan, K. 2001. Preface. In *Urbanism in the Aegean Bronze Age*, ed. K. Branigan, vii–ix. SSAA. Sheffield: Sheffield Academic.

Broodbank, C. 2013. *The Making of the Middle Sea: A History of the Mediterranean from the Beginning to the Emergence of the Classical World*. London: Thames & Hudson.

Burke, A. A. 2008. *"Walled Up to Heaven": The Evolution of Middle Bronze Age Fortification Strategies in the Levant*. SAHL 4. Winona Lake, IN: Eisenbrauns.

Calvino, I. 1974. *Invisible Cities*. Trans. W. Weaver, from Italian. Orlando: Harcourt.

Childe, V. G. 1950. The Urban Revolution. *TPR* 21 (1): 3–17.

Cohen, S. L. 2012. Weaponry and Warrior Burials: Patterns of Disposal and Social Change in the Southern Levant. In *The 7th International Congress on the Archaeology of the Ancient Near East, 12 April–16 April 2010, the British Museum and UCL, London*, Vol. 1: *Mega-Cities & Mega-Sites – The Archaeology of Consumption & Disposal – Landscape, Transport & Communication*, ed. R. Matthews and J. Curtis, 307–19. Wiesbaden: Harrassowitz.

Dever, W. G. 1987. Archaeological Sources for the History of Palestine: The Middle Bronze Age; The Zenith of the Urban Canaanite Era. *BA* 50: 148–77.

1993. The Rise of Complexity in the Land of Israel in the Early Second Millennium B. C. E. In *Biblical Archaeology Today, 1990: Proceedings of the Second International Congress on Biblical Archaeology*, Supplement: Pre Congress Symposium: Population, Production and Power, ed. A. Biran and J. Aviram, 98–109. Jerusalem: IES.

Falconer, S. E., and Savage, S. H. 1995. Heartlands and Hinterlands: Alternative Trajectories of Early Urbanization in Mesopotamia and the Southern Levant. *AA* 60: 37–58.

Finkelstein, I.; Ussishkin, D.; and Halpern, B. 2006. Archaeological and Historical Conclusions. In *Megiddo IV: The 1998–2002 Seasons*, Vol. 2, ed. I. Finkelstein, D. Ussishkin, and B. Halpern, 843–59. MSSMNIA 24. Tel Aviv: Emery and Claire Yass Publications in Archaeology.

Fisher, K. D. 2014. Making the First Cities on Cyprus: Urbanism and Social Change in the Late Bronze Age. In *Making Ancient Cities: Space and Place in Early Urban Societies*, ed. A. T. Creekmore III and K. D. Fisher, 181–219. Cambridge: Cambridge University Press.

Fleming, D. E. 2004. *Democracy's Ancient Ancestors: Mari and Early Collective Governance.* Cambridge: Cambridge University Press.

Foster, B. R., ed. 2001. *The Epic of Gilgamesh: A New Translation, Analogues, Criticism.* Norton Critical Edition. New York: Norton.

Frayne, D. R. 1990. *The Royal Inscriptions of Mesopotamia: Early Periods*, Vol. 4: *Old Babylonian Period (2003–1595 BC)*. Toronto: University of Toronto Press.

Gómez, J. M.; Verdú, M.; González-Megías, A.; and Méndez, M. 2016. The Phylogenetic Roots of Human Lethal Violence. *Nature* 538: 233–7.

Greenberg, R. 2002. *Early Urbanizations in the Levant: A Regional Narrative.* NAAA. London: Leicester University Press.

Herzog, Z. 1997. *Archaeology of the City: Urban Planning in Ancient Israel and Its Social Implications.* MSSMNIA 13. Tel Aviv: Emery and Claire Yass Publications in Archaeology.

Horowitz, W., and Oshima, T. 2006. *Cuneiform in Canaan: Cuneiform Sources from the Land of Israel in Ancient Times.* Jerusalem: IES; The Hebrew University of Jerusalem.

Ilan, D. 1996. The Middle Bronze Age Tombs. In *Dan 1: A Chronicle of the Excavations, the Pottery Neolithic, the Early Bronze Age and the Middle Bronze Age Tombs*, ed. A. Biran, D. Ilan, and R. Greenberg, 163–267. ANGSBAJ. Jerusalem: Hebrew Union College–Jewish Institute of Religion.

Kemp, B. J. 2006. *Ancient Egypt: Anatomy of a Civilization.* 2nd ed. London: Routledge.

Kempinski, A. 1989. *Megiddo: A City-State and a Royal Centre in North Israel.* Materialien zur allgemeinen und vergleichenden Archäologie 40. Munich: Beck.

1992a. Dan and Kabri – A Note on the Planning of Two Cities. *ErIsr* 23: 76–81 (Hebrew).

1992b. Urbanization and Town Plans in the Middle Bronze Age II. In *The Architecture of Ancient Israel: From the Prehistoric to the Persian Period in Memory of Immanuel (Munya) Dunayevsky*, ed. A. Kempinski and R. Reich, 121–6. Jerusalem: IES.

Loud, G. 1948. *Megiddo II: Seasons of 1935–39.* OIP 62. Chicago: The University of Chicago Press.

Maeir, A. M. 1997. Tomb 1181: A Multiple-Internment Burial Cave of the Transitional Middle Bronze Age IIA–B. In *Hazor V: An Account of the Fifth Season of Excavation, 1968*, ed. A. Ben-Tor and R. Bonfil, 295–340. Jerusalem: IES; The Hebrew University of Jerusalem.

2000. The Political and Economic Status of MB II Hazor and MB II Trade: An Inter- and Intra-Regional View. *PEQ* 132: 37–58.

2011. The Archaeology of Early Jerusalem: From the Late Proto-Historic Periods (ca. 5th Millennium) to the End of the Late Bronze Age (ca. 1200 B.C.E.). In *Unearthing Jerusalem: 150 Years of Archaeological Research in the Holy City*, ed. K. Galor and G. Avni, 171–87. Winona Lake, IN: Eisenbrauns.

Malamat, A. 1989. *Mari and the Early Israelite Experience*. Schweich Lectures 1984. Oxford: Published for the British Academy by Oxford University Press.

Matthiae, P. 2013. *Studies on the Archaeology of Ebla, 1980–2010*. Wiesbaden: Harrassowitz.

Mazar, A. 1997. Area P. In *Hazor V: An Account of the Fifth Season of Excavation, 1968*, ed. A. Ben-Tor and R. Bonfil, 353–86. Jerusalem: IES; The Hebrew University of Jerusalem.

Morandi Bonacossi, D. 2014. Some Considerations on the Urban Layout of Second Millennium BC Qatna. In *Tell Tuqan Excavations and Regional Perspectives: Cultural Developments in Inner Syria from the Early Bronze Age to the Persian/Hellenistic Period; Proceedings of the International Conference, May 15th–17th, 2013, Lecce*, ed. F. Baffi, R. Fiorentino, and L. Peyronel, 275–96. Lecce: Congedo.

Parkinson, R. B. 1997. *The Tale of Sinuhe and Other Ancient Egyptian Poems, 1940–1640 BC*. Oxford: Clarendon.

Petrie, W. M. F. 1891. *Illahun, Kahun and Gurob, 1889–90*. London: Nutt.

Philip, G. 1995. Warrior Burials in the Ancient Near-Eastern Bronze Age: The Evidence from Mesopotamia, Western Iran and Syria-Palestine. In *The Archaeology of Death in the Ancient Near East*, ed. S. Campbell and A. Green, 140–54. Oxbow Monographs 51. Oxford: Oxbow.

Pinnock, F. 2001. The Urban Landscape of Old Syrian Ebla. *JCS* 53: 13–33.

Potts, D. T. 1997. *Mesopotamian Civilization: The Material Foundations*. Athlone Publications in Egyptology and Ancient Near Eastern Studies. London: Athlone.

Rainey, A. F., and Notley, R. S. 2006. *The Sacred Bridge: Carta's Atlas of the Biblical World*. Jerusalem: Carta.

Schloen, J. D. 2001. *The House of the Father as Fact and Symbol: Patrimonialism in Ugarit and the Ancient Near East*. SAHL 2. Winona Lake, IN: Eisenbrauns.

Smith, A. T. 2003. *The Political Landscape: Constellations of Authority in Early Complex Polities*. Berkeley: University of California Press.

Stanley, B. W.; Dennehy, T. J.; Smith, M. E.; Stark, B. L.; York, A. M.; Cowgill, G. L.; Novic, J.; and Ek, J. 2016. Service Access in Premodern Cities: An Exploratory Comparison of Spatial Equity. *Journal of Urban History* 42: 121–44.

Stone, E. C. 1995. The Development of Cities in Ancient Mesopotamia. *CANE* 1: 235–48.

Warner, D. 2013. Who Built the Water System at Gezer? A Preliminary Assessment of the Renewed Excavations. *ASOR Blog*. http://asorblog.org/2013/11/16/who-built-the-water-system-at-gezer-a-preliminary-assessment-of-the-renewed-excavations (accessed June 27, 2017).

Yadin, Y. 1972. *Hazor: The Head of All Those Kingdoms (Joshua 11:10)*. Schweich Lectures 1970. London: Published for the British Academy by Oxford University Press.

Yasur-Landau, A. 2011. "The Kingdom Is His Brick Mould and the Dynasty Is His Wall": The Impact of Urbanization on Middle Bronze Age Households in the Southern Levant. In *Household Archaeology in Ancient Israel and Beyond*, ed. A. Yasur-Landau, J. R. Ebeling, and L. B. Mazow, 55–84. CHANE 50. Leiden: Brill.

Yoffee, N. 2000. Law Courts and the Mediation of Social Conflict in Ancient Mesopotamia. In *Order, Legitimacy, and Wealth in Ancient States*, ed. J. Richards and M. Van Buren, 46–63. Cambridge: Cambridge University Press.

Ziffer, I. 1990. *At That Time the Canaanites Were in the Land: Daily Life in Canaan in the Middle Bronze Age 2 (2000–1550 B.C.E.)*. Tel Aviv: Eretz Israel Museum.

Zuckerman, S. 2010. "'The City, Its Gods Will Return There...': Toward an Alternative Interpretation of Hazor's Acropolis in the Late Bronze Age. *JNES* 69: 163–78.

——— 2012. The Temples of Canaanite Hazor. In *Temple Building and Temple Cult: Architecture and Cultic Paraphernalia of Temples in the Levant (2.–1. Mill. B.C.E.); Proceedings of a Conference on the Occasion of the 50th Anniversary of the Institute of Biblical Archaeology at the University of Tübingen (28–30 May 2010)*, ed. J. Kamlah, 99–125. ADPV 41. Wiesbaden: Harrassowitz.

THIRTEEN

CUNEIFORM WRITING IN BRONZE AGE CANAAN

YORAM COHEN

The purpose of this chapter is to discuss cuneiform writing as a reflection of literacy in Bronze Age Canaan.[1] It will show what cuneiform inscribed artifacts (mainly tablets and seals) can tell us about the way cuneiform literacy was achieved, and how, once achieved, writing was involved in the politics, economy, and social life in Canaan. The conclusion of the chapter will evaluate the spread of literacy and the scope of cuneiform writing in Canaan.

The materials presented here are finds recovered during archaeological excavations and those found by accident at or near archaeological sites. They comprise twenty-one letters, twenty-three administrative tablets, eight seals or votive objects, and fourteen school-related or scholarly materials.[2] In addition, the epistolary corpus found at Tell el-Amarna, which includes letters sent from cities throughout Canaan, will be considered: It amounts to approximately 100 letters that can be rather confidently associated with particular sites in Canaan (Moran 1992; Liverani 1998; Rainey and Schniedewind 2015).[3] The value of this corpus is that it shows the distribution of cuneiform in Canaan, as well as informs us of scribal proficiency, even if the evidence is not found on the soil of Canaan.

The geographical area under consideration is the south of Canaan (also called the southern Levant or Cisjordan). Without entering the complex and controversial question of what were the borders of Canaan during the Bronze Age, Hazor is considered as the northernmost city where cuneiform writing is attested. Hence, the Beqaʻa, the Bashan, and the Damascus area, as well as the

Phoenician coast, with Tyre, Sidon, Beirut, and Byblos, are left out in this survey. As far as the evidence of cuneiform writing goes, if the Tell el-Amarna correspondence is not taken into account, these locations, apart from Kamid el-Loz in the Beqa'a, which will be mentioned where due, have little to contribute to our understanding of the spread and use of cuneiform. Although a fair amount of letters from these sites were recovered from the Tell el-Amarna archive, they themselves are impoverished of finds discovered *in situ*.

AN HISTORICAL SKETCH OF CUNEIFORM WRITING IN CANAAN

During the Middle Bronze Age, Amorite kingdoms dominated all of the Levant from Aleppo to Ashkelon (Burke 2014). Textual production associated with the Amorite horizon in Syria and Canaan, as well as in Mesopotamia, is labeled as Old Babylonian, after the Akkadian dialect of Babylonia, which became the standard mode of expression in written communication. The textual remains in Canaan exhibit this Old Babylonian written dialect and make use of a variety of scribal conventions and habits typical of the period. Some of the materials recovered from Hazor can be tied to Old Babylonian scribal traditions and, in particular, to those common to the city of Mari (Demsky 1990: 158; Horowitz and Oshima 2006: 10–15).

Two events mark the transition from the Middle Bronze Age to the Late Bronze Age (from the end of the seventeenth century to the beginning of the sixteenth century BC). The first is the expulsion of the Hyksos from Egypt and the growing involvement and eventual rule of the 18th Dynasty kings over Canaan. The second event is the fall of the Amorite kingdoms in Syria and Babylonia in the wake of Hittite aggression. In the aftermath of Hittite involvement in Syria and Mesopotamia, the Mitanni state rose to prominence, and its influence radiated throughout the ancient Near East (Na'aman 1994). In Canaan, one can observe the proliferation of Hurrian and Indo-Aryan names in the textual documentation of the end of the fifteenth century to the early fourteenth century (at Ta'anach) and the Amarna period, during the second half of the fourteenth century. Hundreds of Mitanni-style seals recovered from Bronze Age Canaan sites also provide evidence of Mitannian influence in the region. Even if the seals may have been amuletic and not employed to seal documents, these objects are manifestations of the spread of Hurrian culture.

During Mitannian supremacy and even after the dismantlement of the Hurrian state by the Hittites, textual production in the ancient Near East witnessed some marked changes. There was a growing influence of Hurrian, as well as local Syrian dialects, on written Akkadian.[4] The Mitanni and later the Hittite Empire began experimenting in writing languages other than Akkadian (and Sumerian) through various textual genres, such as schooling texts, religious compositions, and historiography. These changes can also be detected in the materials from Canaan and throughout the el-Amarna letters corpus: written Akkadian becomes heavily influenced by local dialects, and, in particular circumstances, Canaanite was written in the cuneiform script (Demsky 1990: 158–9, *passim*; Moran 1992: xviii–xxi; Horowitz and Oshima 2006: 10–15; Vita 2015: 143–4).[5] Hence, although the type of textual materials (school texts, administrative documents, letters) is shared between the Middle Bronze Age and the Late Bronze Age, the later period exhibits scribal trends and fashions that have become widespread. In spite of the differences in textual production, we can treat the Middle Bronze Age and the Late Bronze Age as one in this survey. As much as it is realized today that we cannot speak of a clear break between the Middle Bronze Age and the Late Bronze Age in Canaan, so we must acknowledge some continuity in the use of cuneiform during the two phases. Although we lack the evidence, it is self-evident that cuneiform writing never fell out of use, because otherwise it would not have been employed by the Egyptian administration in Canaan during the Late Bronze Age.

In the first millennium, cuneiform writing was the outcome of the Neo-Assyrian, Neo-Babylonian, and Persian conquests and their subsequent occupation of the land and not so much the result of active local production of writing. The few cuneiform remains cannot stand in comparison to the alphabet in this period, which became the leading writing system throughout the eastern Mediterranean and beyond. They are evidence of foreign rule and not indicative of local literacy in the cuneiform writing system.

WRITING CUNEIFORM IN BRONZE AGE CANAAN

Cuneiform writing in Bronze Age Canaan was the result of an active study of the writing system and its implementation in the administration of various domains (e.g., economic, legal, diplomatic). We will first study the textual remains of ancient schooling and then review to what purposes writing was used in administrative spheres. Throughout we will examine the archival and archaeological contexts of the finds in order to discern their social meaning and historical reality (Fig. 13.1).

Even basic literacy in cuneiform could only have been achieved by a consciously driven learning process. Hence, in many places where cuneiform writing was discovered, teaching materials were also found. These constituted a specific curriculum whose origin was Babylonian and which was studied throughout the ancient Near East at a specific social institution – the scribal school, or *Edubba* (usually translated as "the tablet-house").

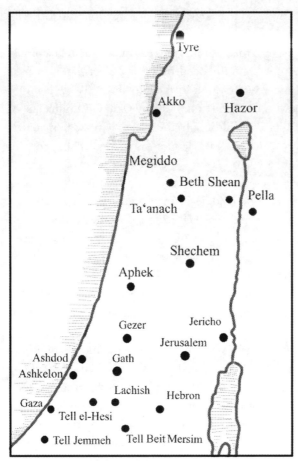

13.1. Sites associated with cuneiform writing in Canaan during the Bronze Age. (Map by Y. Cohen.)

The first set of learning aids were lexical lists (Veldhuis 2014). They gave students the knowledge of how to execute the cuneiform signs;[6] later, they acquainted the scribes with the logographic and syllabic values of the signs. Lexical lists are found throughout Late Bronze Age sites at Nuzi, Assur, Hattuša, Ekalte, Emar, Ugarit, and more. Lexical lists from Canaan are attested at three sites: Hazor, Ashkelon, and Aphek.

The Hazor and Ashkelon tablet fragments are exemplars of a well-known lexical list called Ura (or sometimes ḪAR-ra = ḫubullu). HAZOR 6 is an extract of the second tablet of the list; only its first column (in Sumerian) is preserved. ASHKELON 1 is identified as the first tablet of the list. Although it is broken, its format can be successfully reconstructed. The first column was Sumerian, followed by an Akkadian column; however, both are now lost. The third column of the list, partly preserved, contains Canaanite lexical entries (Huehnergard and van Soldt 1999 = Huehnergard and van Soldt 2008).

Such multi-lingual lexical lists, where the last column of the list is in the local language, are known from Hattuša and Ugarit. At these sites, it is rather obvious that such lists served in scribal education.[7]

The two fragmentary lexical lists from Aphek break away from the Babylonian lexical tradition and represent innovative entries. APHEK 3 is a three-column list that holds only five partly preserved lines: the first entry is in Sumerian, followed by Akkadian, and then Canaanite (Rainey 1976). It perhaps originally was contained on a prism, which was a tablet format typical of Old Babylonian schooling (see HAZOR 9 below). APHEK 1, barely preserved, was perhaps in the same format as APHEK 3 and, possibly, also copied out on a prism.

Related to this learning stage, although not within the genre of lexical lists, is a fragment of a four-sided prism – a mathematical table text found at Hazor (HAZOR 9). It was utilized to teach multiplication on the base of sixty; thus, it stands as a clear product of the Babylonian world of learning. Similar mathematical table texts are well known in Mesopotamia and beyond where they were used for schooling purposes, so there is no reason to assume any other role for HAZOR 9 (Horowitz 1997; Robson 2008: 154–5).

A more advanced stage of scribal education saw the introduction of Babylonian literature. In Canaan, Babylonian literature is represented by a single yet distinctive composition – *The Epic of Gilgamesh* from Megiddo. MEGIDDO 1, containing thirty-six lacunal lines, partly parallels the seventh tablet of the Standard Babylonian of *The Epic of Gilgamesh*, which relates the death of Enkidu (George 2003: 339–47). The Megiddo *Gilgamesh* joins other testaments of the hero's story at Late Bronze Age sites; the epic was known at Hattuša (in Akkadian, as well as in Hittite and Hurrian versions), Ugarit, and Emar (Beckman 2003; George 2003; 2007).

Clay liver models or clay models of other internal organs are widely spread artifacts. They are known from Babylonia, Syria (e.g., Mari, Ebla, Emar), Anatolia (Hattuša), and Canaan (Megiddo and Hazor [Meyer 1987; De Vos 2013; Cohen 2015]). The aim of these objects was to instruct diviners in the practice of extispicy. Although the models are not directly related to the school institution, their purpose is obviously academic. These objects imparted knowledge that was expressed through a highly technical language. The Megiddo liver models (though not inscribed) and the Hazor liver models (HAZOR 2, 3; HAZOR 17 [= Horowitz, Oshima, and Winitzer 2010]) stand witness to this rich Babylonian scholarly tradition.[8]

HAZOR 18 is a fragmentary tablet that contains a few sentences from what seems to be a law collection. Its reconstructed sections deal with compensation in case of physical damage done to a hired slave. Its subject matter is unique, but partial parallels were found in other ancient Near Eastern law codes (Vukosavović 2014). Thus, it may be considered a product of its times, like its more famous (and complete) Mesopotamian counterparts, the law codes of Ur-namma, Lipit-Ishtar, Eshnunna, and Hammurabi. It may also be viewed, however, as a scholarly composition, the product of the scribes of the court, which may have been transmitted to Hazor from elsewhere. Certainly in Mesopotamia, these ancient law codes were transmitted as academic compositions rather than practical law manuals.

While the intellectual pursuits of learning can be demonstrated, exercises meant to train future administrators are missing.[9] It can be assumed that although such tablets existed, they were quickly recycled, holding no value as archival materials in the school library.

The Babylonian schooling environment has been reconstructed by modern scholarship through the study of the archival and archaeological contexts at several key sites (e.g., Ur [Tell el-Muqayyar], Sippar-Amnanum [Tell ed-Der]).[10] Clear evidence of scribal schools in the western part of the cuneiform world can be found at Emar and Ugarit (Cohen 2009; 2012; van Soldt 2011).[11] At these two sites, we see that schooling was conducted in what can be broadly defined as domains of prominent individuals, who had strong ties with the city administration and royal or religious institutions. From a comparative perspective of places where teaching materials show up (Canaan included), we can consider the existence of institutions operating in similar social contexts, although it is obviously difficult to identify definite environments for schooling activities. In Canaan, one situation is certainly suggestive.[12] The lexical lists of Aphek, as well as the other cuneiform fragments from the site, were found together around the entrance of the Egyptian Governor's Residence (Gadot 2009: 583–6; Na'aman and Goren 2009: 460–71). This building, which probably played a role in Egyptian administration, also may have housed a school institution (Na'aman and Goren 2009: 468–9).

The find spots of other schooling materials are less informative. ASHKELON 1 was found in a disturbed area that was once part of a large courtyard building complex (dated to the thirteenth century) (Stager et al. 2008: 304–5). The mathematical prism fragment HAZOR 9 was recovered from a back room of the Monumental Building at Hazor.[13] It may have been deposited there either as a votive object (if the building is regarded as a temple) or as a luxury item (if we think of the complex as a palace).[14] The two uninscribed liver models from Megiddo were recovered from Temple 2048;[15] and the liver models HAZOR 2 and 3 come from a debris layer of possibly a Late Bronze Age temple in Area H.[16] This may suggest where extispicy was practiced and taught.

Of course, it is impossible to know how many scribal institutions existed in Canaan and whether each city where writing is attested held a scribal school. Apart from the most obvious candidate, Hazor, a close study of scribal traditions and scribal hands suggests at least several centers of learning (e.g., Megiddo, Ashkelon, Gezer), where the scribal trade was perhaps passed down generationally and training focused on students, who upon graduation traveled to be employed elsewhere (Izre'el 2012: 176; Vita 2015: 144–9).

How schooling materials reached the fringes of the cuneiform world is not something that can be easily traced or reconstructed. Some of the materials may have physically traveled from one site to the next.[17] Part of the knowledge, however, could have been actively transmitted by memory of one traveling scholar to the next. In Ugarit and Emar, circumstantial evidence can point to the employment of traveling teachers from either Babylonia or Assyria.[18] Two seals recovered at Canaan perhaps can indicate the activity of such peripatetic teachers. BETH SHEAN 1 is an Old Babylonian cylinder seal upon which is written, "Manum, the diviner, servant of Ea." When and under what circumstances it reached Beth Shean is not clear, although it was found in the Late Bronze Age Egyptian Garrison layer. Like other cylinder seals found in the city, although all anepigraphic, it may have been an import. Alternatively, the seal may have been in the possession of a professional diviner who arrived to teach or practice his trade at Beth Shean (Horowitz and Oshima 2006: 47). A similar scenario can be envisioned for the seal MEGIDDO 3, belonging to Izkur-Addu, who is titled as a dub.sar, "scribe." Perhaps, this scribe also acted as a teacher at Megiddo?

The above scenarios remain hypothetical because the social background of the scribes of Canaan is practically unknown.[19] It may be that they thought of themselves as part of a privileged community of scribes.[20] Regardless, from what is known elsewhere at this period, people who wrote cuneiform were definitely not one-dimensional. Scribes in the Bronze Age were high officials, diplomats, administrators, judges, traveling merchants, the priesthood, and even members of the royal family. Literacy was not limited to a single, well-defined professional class but rather could have been found among different members of the upper echelons of society (Charpin 2010).

Once a level of literacy was achieved through schooling, writing was put into use in administration. In Canaan, cuneiform writing for administrative purposes is represented by letters and economic documents of different types. The use of inscribed seals may also be indicative of the spread of literacy in administrative spheres.

Letter writing in Canaan, as elsewhere, was the result of scribal training and expertise. The study of the opening formulae and the epistolary etiquette of the el-Amarna corpus cannot but lead to the conclusion that these rested on age-old traditions (Mynářová 2007; Izre'el 2012: 182). In addition, we find in letters a display, at times, of scribal sophistication beyond basic writing skills. We can mention here in brief some of these features: the use of Canaanite glosses as an expression of scribal education, the use of rare or difficult logograms, and the employment of technical terms.[21] The introduction in letters of proverbs, poetic articulations, and imagery all point to high scribal literacy, although this is not to claim that these were necessarily learned in the school environment.[22] They could have been adopted in less formal settings.

Many sites from Canaan, some known only by their ancient names, sent missives to Tell el-Amarna.[23] Some were very prolific at letter sending; for example, Gezer, Gath, and Ashkelon have each sent over a dozen letters. Some sites are represented in the el-Amarna archive by six or seven letters (e.g., Jerusalem, Megiddo). Others are known by only two or three letters (e.g., Hazor, Lachish, Shechem). At a few sites in Canaan, letters were also found *in situ*, evidence that they were also sent to and between Canaanite cities: Beth Shean (BETH SHEAN 2), Ta'anach (TA'ANACH 1, 2, 5, 6, 8–11), Hazor (HAZOR 8, 10, 12), Shechem (SHECHEM 1), Aphek (APHEK 7), Jerusalem (JERUSALEM 1 = Mazar et al. 2010; JERUSALEM 2 = Mazar et al. 2014),[24] Gezer (GEZER 1, 2), and Tell el-Ḥesi (TELL EL-ḤESI 1 = EA 333) have together over 20 letters, but many are fragmentary.

In addition to prolific letter writing, the production of documents either for the palace, temple, or the citizens of the city can reveal to what degree writing was involved in the economy and daily life in Bronze Age Canaan. Although we have identified no more than twenty-three items of an administrative nature, their diversity can be quite informative.[25]

A number of documents are concerned with the herding and management of sheep. HEBRON 1 is a tabulated account of sheep: It exhibits the knowledge of drawing up ledger tables, the use of logographic writing for denoting livestock, and the employment of numerals in the conventional Mesopotamian numbering system. The repeated mention of a (or the) king suggests that the tablet was the product of the palace administration in Hebron.

MEGIDDO 6 is a document probably relating to sheep management: It is a list of men, perhaps herders, given sheep (Cogan 2013). Alternatively, it can be seen as a tally of sheep offered as sacrifice. Both possibilities speak of the document as being issued by a central authority rather than by an individual. Consider also GEZER 1 and 2, letter fragments that relate to sheep herding. A product of sheep, apart from meat and milk, is wool: Two docket-like tablets (HAZOR 14 and 16) list quantities of a certain type of cloth (Horowitz and Oshima 2010).

An economic document (HAZOR 7) gives a list of people who seem to have received some payment or reimbursement. The document was probably issued by the central authority. Of a somewhat similar nature is perhaps HAZOR 11, which deals with providing some commodity or payment (that remains unspecified) to individuals. Rosters of people, perhaps called to perform some service, are evident in six documents from Ta'anach (TA'ANACH 3, 4, 4a, 7, 12, 14).

HAZOR 5 shows us that writing was used at the court. This document is a summary of a case decided by the king that involved a dispute over privately held property. The legal formulation of the document follows Mesopotamian legal conventions. Of course, if Hazor 18 (see above) is considered a veritable law code and not simply an academic exercise, it should also be mentioned here. Shechem 2 contains only a partly preserved witness list, but it serves us well, demonstrating that tablets of a presumably private nature could be drawn by scribes. The document could have been, like Hazor 5, a court record or perhaps a sale transaction, loan, or testament involving the citizens of the city.[26]

Inscribed ceramic artifacts (a vessel [Hazor 1] and a jar stopper [Megiddo 5]) with private names may be considered as evidence of literacy in economic spheres.[27] Otherwise, cuneiform writing on objects is usually found on luxury items that were votive objects. One object is clearly such – Hazor 13 – a fragmentary stone bowl with a short dedicatory inscription. The inscription is so broken that it is difficult to say by whom it was commissioned or where it was manufactured. Its purpose as a votive object is suggested by its find spot.[28]

Seals are objects that provide clues to administrative practices and, especially when engraved, can point to literate administration; however, they can also be considered as miniature votive inscriptions. It is generally agreed that in Canaan, these objects may have had an apotropaic function (since many were found in tombs).[29] Therefore, in order to support the use of cylinder seals in administration, a clear economic or administrative context needs to be pointed out. The impressions of a stamp seal inscribed in cuneiform are found on a jug handle (Hazor 4): the sign LUGAL ("king") is discernible, but it is not clear if it is part of a private name or the royal title of a private name.[30] Tell Jemmeh 1, a clay cylinder seal inscribed with pseudo-cuneiform signs, was recovered at Tell Jemmeh (also known as Tel Gamma) from what looks like a storage room, suggested by the many jars in a Middle Bronze Age II layer (Ben-Shlomo 2014: 37–8).[31] Therefore, it is possible that this seal served in the administration. From the site of Beth Shean, which served as an Egyptian garrison, comes an Old Babylonian inscribed seal (Beth Shean 1), but it is not clear if it served the administration at the site.

Impressions of seals stamped or rolled across tablets are found only in specific cases: transactions involving witnesses and sometimes royal edicts or land donations. Such tablets are rare and very fragmentary in our corpus, hence the lack of a seal impression across any tablet.

Understanding how writing functioned in administration demands that the artifacts be placed in defined archival and archaeological contexts. For many of the finds from Canaan, such a context seems to be lacking. However, a closer look reveals that a large number of the finds, even if individual, come from telling contexts.

Evidence for archival storage of documents can be posited rather securely for three sites: Taʿanach, Aphek, and Hazor. At Taʿanach, the batch of letters and administrative documents were apparently stored in a clay chest, a practice attested also elsewhere. The archaeological context at Taʿanach remains unclear, but it is reasonable to suppose that the chest was laid in some structure (Sellin 1904: 41; Albright 1944; Glock 1993).[32] It can be assumed that the Egyptian Governor's Residence at Aphek functioned as an archive, simply due to the fact that all inscribed finds were recovered from the vicinity of one building.[33]

At Hazor, the Monumental Building and its surrounding can be considered as places of archival storage, if not perhaps where texts were actually produced (Ben-Tor 1996: 264).[34] The letters HAZOR 10 and 12, as well as the administrative document HAZOR 11 (and the mathematical prism HAZOR 9), were retrieved from the throne room and the adjacent rooms of the Monumental Building.[35] HAZOR 15 (an administrative document or a letter [Horowitz and Oshima 2007]) was found in Area A4, near the area of the Monumental Building. The two dockets, HAZOR 14 and 16, were found in Area A5, a mud-brick complex, of possible relation to the Monumental Building (Ben-Tor 2000: 248). The existence of an archive of the royal palace at Hazor can be contemplated, even if it has not yet been found: HAZOR 8 (a letter fragment) and HAZOR 5 (a court record) are possibly prosopographically related and hence chronologically linked (Horowitz and Oshima 2006: 78).[36] Although recovered separately, perhaps they were originally stored in the same place.

Other isolated finds come from archaeological contexts that may hint at the existence of archives or at the very least of the clear use of writing in administrative contexts. The letter from Tell el-Ḥesi was found in a Late Bronze Age layer near a large building with long storage rooms (Bliss 1894: 51–60; Albright 1942; Fargo 1993: 631). This building could have served the administration, perhaps housing within its walls an archive. The administrative document HEBRON 1 was found inside a Middle Bronze Age room, whose contents – bones of caprids and bovines, cooking vessels, and storage jars – suggests a cult complex (Ofer 1987–1988; 1993). JERICHO 1, a Late Bronze Age administrative tablet, was found on a debris pile outside of the Late Bronze Age monumental Middle Building.[37] A letter and an administrative document from Shechem can be associated with a large building that is probably to be dated to the Late Bronze Age (SHECHEM 1 and 2 [Sellin 1926: 317–19]). And finally, two tablet fragments from Pella were found in the pit of an administrative complex or the house of an official.[38] All these cases can be considered, with all due caution, as evidence of the use of writing by officials in administrative complexes throughout the urban centers of Middle–Late Bronze Age Canaan.

How many officials and bureaucrats possessed cuneiform literacy cannot be known. A study of individual scribal hands in the el-Amarna corpus suggests that for a period of between a generation and a generation and a half, a single scribe and up to as many as four scribes were active in letter writing per a particular city (Vita 2015). One can imagine that such scribes were also active in some form or another in local administration.

CONCLUSION

As demonstrated, cuneiform writing was widely distributed throughout Bronze Age Canaan. The sites where writing is represented, either directly or through the finds at Tell el-Amarna, include Akko, Hazor, Taʿanach, Megiddo, Pella, Beth Shean, Shechem, Jerusalem, Ashkelon, Gezer, Gath, Jericho, Hebron, Lachish, and Tell el-Ḥesi. It is inevitable that we ask now, however, in spite of this wide spread distribution, why is the number of finds from Canaan so low, barely 100 items (or over approximately 230 items with the el-Amarna corpus)? To begin answering this question, we need to ask whether we should expect a higher number of finds? The answer depends on our point of view. If the situation is compared with the quantity of finds from North Canaan, then one sees that, in fact, South Canaan is much better endowed with finds. Tyre, Sidon, Beirut, and Byblos were all important cities that sent correspondence to Tell el-Amarna and Ugarit. The cities of the Bashan area and the Beqaʿa are likewise represented in the el-Amarna archive. In spite of that, there is only one administrative tablet from Sidon, a lexical list from Byblos, two tablets from Tell Sakka (Damascus), and a few tablets from Kumidi in the Lebanese Beqaʿa.[39] Even further north, an important center such as Tell Nebi Mend (Qadesh) on the Orontes is relatively poor in finds.[40] Hence, the geographic spread *vis-à-vis* quantity demonstrates how much our assessment is based on the circumstances of discovery and our expectations.

This brings us to the second point: Canaan is often compared to sites in northern Syria and Anatolia that are rich in cuneiform documentation. Surely, some of these places, such as Ugarit and Hattuša, were large administrative or imperial centers; as a result, finding large quantities of written material is not surprising. However, we must remember that these sites, as well as smaller ones, such as Emar, fell at the end of the Late Bronze Age and were, archaeologically speaking, sealed. The fact that these sites were devoid of substantial, if any, habitation layers after the Bronze Age can explain the degree of preservation of large archives (and other material finds). Consider Karkemish, the Hittite imperial center in Syria: To date, not a single Late Bronze Age cuneiform document was recovered from the site, although its edicts and letters were found at Ugarit and Emar. This is not surprising, given the continuity of settlement into the Iron Age. The large Bronze Age sites in Canaan (northern and southern) were settled, if not continuously, in the Iron Age and, at times, beyond to the modern period. Hence, the chances of finding a Late Bronze Age archive intact are greatly reduced.

Finally, the larger sociopolitical situation should be taken into consideration. Since southern Canaan maintained close ties with Egypt, especially after the establishment of Egyptian rule during the 18th Dynasty, Egyptian administration may have been keen to use its own writing system in order to replace the use of cuneiform. It is not unreasonable to suppose that the alphabetic script toward the close of the Bronze Age also became more widespread. Because of the destruction visited upon Canaanite cities, obviously little is known; however, traces of evidence from the end of the Late Bronze Age and the beginning of the first millennium can allow us to postulate such processes were already set in motion (Millard 1999; Na'aman and Goren 2009: 469; Sanders 2009: 88–102).[41] After the settlement collapse of the Late Bronze Age, new writing systems found their foothold (mainly alphabetic but also others). In such a world, cuneiform was no longer needed, and hence all traces of scribal education in this script disappear. Observe that the finds from the first millennium do not include a single school or academic composition.[42] In light of our discussion about the scribal schools in the ancient Near East, it is clear that the lack of evidence can be considered as evidence in this case: School texts were not found because the schooling institution vanished from the western part of the ancient Near East.

It would be unwise to think that cuneiform writing in Canaan was as widespread as it was in contemporary Babylonia, Assyria, or Anatolia. However, we can conclude that during the second millennium, cuneiform writing undoubtedly reflects a social reality. Writing was an important component of life in Canaan. It was actively studied, pursued, and produced by individuals across many sites, ensuring Canaan a place in both local and international trade, diplomacy, and politics. It also was a component – at least to some extent – in the administration of the economy and social life.

NOTES

1 Previous studies of cuneiform in Canaan are Demsky 1990; Millard 1999; van der Toorn 2000; von Dassow 2004; Horowitz and Oshima 2006: 10–25; Sanders 2009: 76–102; and Izre'el 2012. Research for this chapter was supported by an Israel Science Foundation Grant (no. 241/15; "The Production and Dissemination of Scholarly and School Textual Materials during the Late Bronze Age: An Integrated Research Project"; together with Professor Yuval Goren, Ben-Gurion University of the Negev).
2 Materials found at controlled excavations or in accidental circumstances were collected and studied in Horowitz and Oshima 2006, which the reader is advised to consult for additional bibliography not produced here for the sake of brevity. Supplementary cuneiform artifacts found since are mentioned throughout the discussion. Note that the numbering of cuneiform artifacts follows the convention established in Horowitz and Oshima 2006.

3 There are about 125 letters in the Amarna archive from the area under investigation, but only about 100 can be historically associated with specific sites (Goren, Finkelstein, and Na'aman 2004; Mynářová 2007; Vita 2015).

4 For the use of Hurrian at Qatna, see Richter, Lange, and Pfälzner 2012: 29–42.

5 The complex question of how to interpret the mixed or hybrid (written) language of the Canaanite scribes will not be dealt with here (see von Dassow 2004; 2010; Rainey 2010; Izre'el 2012).

6 The execution of a single cuneiform sign, constituting of two, three, or many more strokes of the cuneiform stylus, was amazingly stable for thousands of years, regardless of where it was impressed on the clay – whether in Babylonia, Canaan, Syria, or Egypt (Taylor 2015).

7 ASHKELON 1 and HAZOR 6 come from the beginning of the list, i.e., they contain entries of the first and second tablets. This is typical of the distribution of lexical list tablets. The lower number tablets, with which schooling started, are abundant but the higher tablet numbers are rarer. The conclusion is that students, those of Hazor and Ashkelon included, copied the first tablets on the list, but many times did not finish copying all of it.

8 For the Megiddo models, see Meyer 1987: 29–32, pl. 26. Three uninscribed model fragments were also found at Hazor (Yadin 1961: pl. 316; Ben-Tor 1989: 223–9).

9 An example of an exercise tablet is perhaps APHEK 6. However, APHEK 7 ("The Governor's Letter") is a *bona fide* letter. Although its petrographic analysis reveals that the tablet was produced at the site, its historical content precludes it from being an exercise (*contra* Na'aman and Goren 2009: 463–5). It is probably a copy of the original letter sent to Egypt. It has been suggested that the cylinder seal letter (BETH SHEAN 2 [see below]) was meant to serve as a scribal aide-memoire for writing down epistolary introductory phrases (Rainey 1998: 240; von Dassow 2004: 672; Izre'el 2012: 176–7).

10 See the studies in Radner and Robson 2011.

11 The evidence for schooling is less clear at Hattuša (Weeden 2011; Gordin 2015) or at Amarna (Artzi 1992; Izre'el 1997), although their schooling materials are similar to what was found in Emar and Ugarit.

12 Four scholarly texts are without archaeological or archival context: MEGIDDO 1 (Gilgamesh) was found under accidental circumstances at the foot of the mound; HAZOR 6 (lexical list) was reportedly a surface find (Horowitz and Oshima 2006: 73); HAZOR 17 (liver model) was found in Area A2; and the fragments of HAZOR 18 (law code) were recovered from secondary contexts around Area M (Horowitz, Oshima, and Vukosavović 2012: 158, n. 3).

13 The tablet was found in the western room of the double-room recess of the Monumental Building (Ben-Tor 1996: 264). This double-room was exceptionally rich in unique finds, some votive (Ornan 2011; 2012). The function of the building is debated: it either served as a palace (Bonfil and Zarzecki-Peleg 2007; Ben-Tor 2016: 93–104) or as a temple (Zuckerman 2010).

14 For the suggestion that scholarly texts may have been deposited as votive objects, see Charpin 2010: 204–11.

15 One model was found on the floor of Temple 2048, the other outside the structure. The level is The University of Chicago's Stratum VIIB (or Late Bronze Age), but see Finkelstein 2013: 1335.

16 See n. 13 above.

17 Consider the conclusions of petrographic studies of schooling tablets: MEGIDDO 1 (Gilgamesh) was analyzed as produced of Gezer clay (Goren et al. 2009); the clay of ASHKELON 1 (lexical list) suggests the Lebanese littoral (Goren et al. 2009: 770–1); APHEK 1 and 3 (lexical lists) were identified as originating from either Shechem or Jerusalem (Na'aman and Goren 2009: 465). However, HAZOR 9 (mathematical table) is of local manufacture (Goren 2000: 34–5).
18 For Ugarit, see van Soldt 2012. For Emar, see Cohen 2004.
19 Aaron Demsky (1990, following Albright 1942) understood that SHECHEM 1 was a letter written by a teacher of the *Edubba* (see also Na'aman 2004). Wayne Horowitz and Takayoshi Oshima (2006: 121–3) offer a more neutral reading of the letter.
20 Oblique self-referential remarks issued by the Canaan scribes to their fellow scribes in Egypt can be found in some el-Amarna letters (e.g., EA 286) (Oppenheim 1965; Izre'el 1995a). This may indicate that, as elsewhere, the scribes were socially conscious. Scribes' personal "signatures" (or "colophons") have not survived.
21 For glosses, see Vita 2012 and Izre'el 2012: 182–3; 1995b. For logograms, see Moran 2003. For technical terms, see, e.g., Na'aman 1977.
22 For proverbs, see Cohen 2013: 224–31. For poetics, see, e.g., Izre'el 1995a: 2416–17 (EA 264). For imagery, see, e.g., Rainey 1999: 158* (TA'ANACH 2:6).
23 It was argued on various grounds that occasionally letters were sent from Beth Shean, Gaza, or Gezer, although their senders were identified as rulers of other cities (Goren, Finkelstein, and Na'aman 2004; Vita 2015). This may somewhat reduce the number of sites in which we think letters were written, but the common use of cuneiform to write letters is well demonstrated by finds recovered at actual sites throughout Canaan.
24 Both letters were recovered from the Ophel excavations. The clay analysis cautiously demonstrates that JERUSALEM 1 was produced from local clay, but JERUSALEM 2 perhaps in Egypt (Goren in Mazar et al. 2010; Goren in Mazar et al. 2014; see also Rollston 2010).
25 At Hattuša, no administrative records of private citizens have been recovered. In Emar, most of the documentation relates to the practices of private citizens (e.g., sale transactions, loans, testaments) and much less to the palace or the temple. In Ugarit, rich in diplomatic correspondence, the number of administrative documents is rather low, especially those relating to private citizens. The recovery of economic documents, in other words, depends on which archives were discovered, but it is also the outcome of the nature of this type of documentation which, on many occasions (apart from loans, sales transactions, or testaments), was ephemeral and hence not archived long term.
26 Fragmentary and uninformative administrative documents are APHEK 2 and 8, HAZOR 15, JERICHO 1, and two fragments from Pella (Black 1992; not found in Horowitz and Oshima 2006).
27 For HAZOR 1, see Yadin 1960: 81, 115–17, pl. 208. For MEGIDDO 5, a contextless find, see Lamon and Shipton 1939: 158, pl. 72.
28 The bowl was found in Area M in destruction debris, but it perhaps belongs to the Monumental Building (Ben-Tor 2000: 248–9; Zuckerman 2010: 165–72, esp. 171).
29 Inscribed seals found in tombs and unclear contexts are: ASHDOD 1, JERICHO 2 and 3, MEGIDDO 2 and 4, TA'ANACH 13, and TELL BETH MIRSIM 1 (pseudo-cuneiform).
30 It was found in the same heap as the liver models.
31 TELL JEMMEH 1 = Horowitz and Ornan 2014. Tell Jemmeh is identified with ancient Yurza (from where letters were sent to Tell el-Amarna) (Ben-Shlomo and van Beek 2014).

32 Taʿanach 14, discovered in 1968, comes from an unclear Late Bronze Age context (Glock 1971).
33 From the same context arrive two Egyptian inscribed objects (a plaque and a ring) and a Hittite bulla (Singer 1977 = Singer 2011: 561–72; Na'aman and Goren 2009: 465–6). Consider the Hieroglyphic Hittite seal found in a Late Bronze Age context at Megiddo (Singer 1992 = Singer 2011: 579–83). These artifacts are evidence of the Late Bronze Age (literate) world of diplomacy and international trade.
34 The dating of the building is Late Bronze Age, but some of its finds are older (see n. 13 above).
35 For Hazor 10, see Horowitz 2000: 16. For the petrographic analysis, see Goren, Finkelstein, and Na'aman 2004: 230. For Hazor 11, see Goren 2000: 38, 42.
36 Hazor 8 was discovered in a late secondary context (Ben-Tor 1992: 259). Hazor 5 was found on the mound (Hallo and Tadmor 1977: 2, n. 7).
37 The structure was dated to the Late Bronze Age (Garstang 1934: 116, 132; Bienkowski 1986: 112–18).
38 This is suggested by other finds in the pit: an impression of a stamp seal, a scarab seal, and Egyptian luxury items (Smith and Potts 1992: 51–65).
39 For Sidon, see Finkel 2006. For Byblos, see Cavigneaux 1983: 616, 618. For Tell Sakka, see Abdallah and Durand 2014. For Kumidi, see Hachmann 2012.
40 For Qadesh (four letters and one administrative text), see Millard 2010.
41 Consider in this respect the "cuneiform" alphabet items Beth-Shemesh 1, Taʿanach 15, and Tabor 1 (Sanders in Horowitz and Oshima 2006: 157–66).
42 The finds from the first millennium include royal inscriptions (Ashdod 2–4; Ben Shemen 1; Qaqun 1; Samaria 4; Sepphoris 1; Tell en-Naṣbeh 1), administrative documents (Gezer 3, 4; Tel Hadid 1, 2; Tell Keisan 1; Khirbet Kusiya 1; Mikhmoret 1; Samaria 1, 2; Sepphoris 2–4); and votive finds (e.g., Shephelah 1; a *Lamaštu* plaque) (Horowitz and Oshima 2006: 19–25).

REFERENCES

Abdallah, F., and Durand, J.-M. 2014. Deux documents cunéiformes retrouvés au Tell Sakka. In *Entre les fleuves,* Vol. 2: *D'Aššur à Mari et au-delà,* ed. N. Ziegler and E. Cancik-Kirschbaum, 233–48. Berliner Beiträge zum Vorderen Orient 24. Gladbeck: PeWe.

Albright, W. F. 1942. A Case of Lèse-Majesté in Pre-Israelite Lachish, with Some Remarks on the Israelite Conquest. *BASOR* 87: 32–8.

1944. A Prince of Taanach in the Fifteenth Century B.C. *BASOR* 94: 12–27.

Artzi, P. 1992. Nippur Elementary Schoolbooks in the "West." In *Nippur at the Centennial: Papers Read at the 35e Rencontre Assyriologique Internationale, Philadelphia, 1988,* ed. M. deJong Ellis, 1–5. Occasional Publications of the Samuel Noah Kramer Fund 14. Philadelphia: Samuel Noah Kramer Fund.

Beckman, G. 2003. Gilgamesh in Ḫatti. In *Hittite Studies in Honor of Harry A. Hoffner, Jr. on the Occasion of His 65th Birthday,* ed. G. M. Beckman, R. H. Beal, and G. McMahon, 37–57. Winona Lake, IN: Eisenbrauns.

Ben-Shlomo, D. 2014. Field III: The Southeastern Step Trench. In *The Smithsonian Institution Excavation at Tell Jemmeh, Israel, 1970–1990,* ed. D. Ben-Shlomo and G. W. Van Beek, 21–161. SCA 50. Washington, DC: Smithsonian Institution Scholarly Press.

Ben-Shlomo, D., and Van Beek, G. W. 2014. Introduction. In *The Smithsonian Institution Excavation at Tell Jemmeh, Israel, 1970–1990*, ed. D. Ben-Shlomo and G. W. Van Beek, 1–15. SCA 50. Washington, DC: Smithsonian Institution Scholarly Press.
Ben-Tor, A. 1992. Tel Hazor, 1992. *IEJ* 42: 254–60.
   1996. Excavations and Surveys: Tel Hazor, 1996. *IEJ* 46: 262–8.
   2000. Excavations and Surveys: Tel Hazor, 2000. *IEJ* 50: 243–9.
   2016. *Hazor: Cannanite Metropolis, Israelite City; "The Head of All Those Kingdoms" (Joshua 11:10)*. Jerusalem: IES.
Ben-Tor, A., ed. 1989. *Hazor III–IV: An Account of the Third and Fourth Seasons of Excavations, 1957–1958*, Vol. 2: *Text*. Jerusalem: IES; The Hebrew University of Jerusalem.
Bienkowski, P. 1986. *Jericho in the Late Bronze Age*. Warminster: Aris & Phillips.
Black, J. A. 1992. Two Cuneiform Tablets. In *Pella in Jordan 2: The Second Interim Report of the Joint University of Sydney and the College of Wooster Excavations at Pella, 1982–1985*, ed. A. W. McNicoll, P. C. Edwards, J. Hanbury-Tenison, J. B. Hennessy, T. F. Potts, R. H. Smith, A. Walmsley, and P. Watson, 299–301. MASup 2. Sydney: Meditarch.
Bliss, F. J. 1894. *A Mound of Many Cities, or, Tell el Hesy Excavated*. London: PEF.
Bonfil, R., and Zarzecki-Peleg, A. 2007. The Palace in the Upper City of Hazor as an Expression of a Syrian Architectural Paradigm. *BASOR* 348: 25–47.
Burke, A. A. 2014. Introduction to the Levant during the Middle Bronze Age. In *The Oxford Handbook of the Archaeology of the Levant, c. 8000–332 BCE*, ed. M. L. Steiner and A. E. Killebrew, 403–13. Oxford: Oxford University Press.
Cavigneaux, A. 1983. Lexikalische Listen. *RlA* 6: 609–41.
Charpin, D. 2010. *Reading and Writing in Babylon*. Cambridge, MA: Harvard University Press.
Cogan, M. 2013. A New Cuneiform Text from Megiddo. *IEJ* 63: 131–4.
Cohen, Y. 2004. Kidin-Gula – The Foreign Teacher at the Emar Scribal School. *RAAO* 98: 81–100.
   2009. *The Scribes and Scholars of the City of Emar in the Late Bronze Age*. HSS 59. Winona Lake, IN: Eisenbrauns.
   2012. The Historical and Social Background of the Scribal School at the City of Emar in the Late Bronze Age. In *Theory and Practice of Knowledge Transfer: Studies in School Education in the Ancient Near East and Beyond; Papers Read at a Symposium in Leiden, 17–19 December 2008*, ed. W. S. van Egmond and W. H. van Soldt, 115–27. NINEP 121. Leiden: The Netherlands Institute for the Near East.
   2013. *Wisdom from the Late Bronze Age*. WAW 29. Atlanta: SBL.
   2015. Review of Die Lebermodelle aus Boğazköy, by A. De Vos. *ZAVA* 105: 121–6.
Dassow, E. von. 2004. Canaanite in Cuneiform. *JAOS* 124: 641–74.
   2010. Peripheral Akkadian Dialects, or Akkadography of Local Languages. In *Language in the Ancient Near East: Proceedings of the 53e Rencontre Assyriologique Internationale*, Vol. 1, Part 2, ed. L. Kogan, S. Koslova, S. Loesov, and S. Tishchenko, 895–924. Babel und Bibel 4 (2); Orientalia et Classica 30 (2). Winona Lake, IN: Eisenbrauns.
De Vos, A. 2013. *Die Lebermodelle aus Boğazköy*. SBT 5. Wiesbaden: Harrassowitz.
Demsky, A. 1990. The Education of Canaanite Scribes in the Mesopotamian Cuneiform Tradition. In *Bar-Ilan Studies in Assyriology Dedicated to Pinḥas Artzi*, ed. J. Klein and A. J. Skaist, 157–70. Bar-Ilan Studies in Near Eastern Languages and Culture. Ramat-Gan: Bar-Ilan University Press.
Fargo, V. M. 1993. Ḥesi, Tell el-. *NEAEHL* 2: 630–4.

Finkel, I. L. 2006. Report on the Sidon Cuneiform Tablet. *AHL* 24: 114–20.
Finkelstein, I. 2013. Archaeological and Historical Conclusions. In *Megiddo V: The 2004–2008 Seasons*, Vol. 3, ed. I. Finkelstein, D. Ussishkin, and E. H. Cline, 1329–40. MSSMNIA 31. Winona Lake, IN: Eisenbrauns.
Gadot, Y. 2009. The Relative and Absolute Chronology of Late Bronze Age and Iron Age Tel Aphek. In *Aphek-Antipatris II: The Remains on the Acropolis; The Moshe Kochavi and Pirhiya Beck Excavations*, ed. Y. Gadot and E. Yadin, 581–91. MSSMNIA 27. Tel Aviv: Emery and Claire Yass Publications in Archaeology.
Garstang, J. 1934. Jericho: City and Necropolis, Fourth Report. *LAAA* 21: 99–136.
George, A. R. 2003. *The Babylonian Gilgamesh Epic: Introduction, Critical Edition and Cuneiform Texts*. Oxford: Oxford University Press.
   2007. The Gilgameš Epic at Ugarit. *Aula Orientalis* 25: 237–54.
Glock, A. E. 1971. A New Ta'annek Tablet. *BASOR* 204: 17–30.
   1993. Taanach. *NEAEHL* 4: 1428–33.
Gordin, S. 2015. *Hittite Scribal Circles: Scholarly Tradition and Writing Habits*. SBT 59. Wiesbaden: Harrassowitz.
Goren, Y. 2000. Provenance Study of the Cuneiform Texts from Hazor. *IEJ* 50: 29–42.
Goren, Y.; Finkelstein, I.; and Na'aman, N. 2004. *Inscribed in Clay: Provenance Study of the Amarna Tablets and Other Ancient Near Eastern Texts*. MSSMNIA 23. Tel Aviv: Emery and Claire Yass Publications in Archaeology.
Goren, Y.; Mommsen, H.; Finkelstein, I.; and Na'aman, N. 2009. A Provenance Study of the Gilgamesh Fragment from Megiddo. *Archaeometry* 51: 763–73.
Hachmann, R. 2012. *Die Keilschriftbriefe und der Horizont von el-Amarna*. Kāmid el-Lōz 20; Saarbrücker Beiträge zur Altertumskunde 87. Bonn: Habelt.
Hallo, W. W., and Tadmor, H. 1977. A Lawsuit from Hazor. *IEJ* 27: 1–11.
Horowitz, W. 1997. A Combined Multiplication Table on a Prism from Hazor. *IEJ* 47: 190–7.
   2000. Two Late Bronze Age Tablets from Hazor. *IEJ* 50: 16–28.
Horowitz, W., and Ornan, T. 2014. Cylinder Seals: A Clay Cylinder with Cuneiform Signs. In *The Smithsonian Institution Excavation at Tell Jemmeh, Israel, 1970–1990*, ed. D. Ben-Shlomo and G. W. Van Beek, 1017–19. SCA 50. Washington, DC: Smithsonian Institution Scholarly Press.
Horowitz, W., and Oshima, T. 2006. *Cuneiform in Canaan: Cuneiform Sources from the Land of Israel in Ancient Times*. Jerusalem: IES; The Hebrew University of Jerusalem.
   2007. Hazor 15: A Letter Fragment from Hazor. *IEJ* 57: 34–40.
   2010. Hazor 16: Another Administrative Docket from Hazor. *IEJ* 60: 129–32.
Horowitz, W.; Oshima, T.; and Vukosavović, F. 2012. Hazor 18: Fragments of a Cuneiform Law Collection from Hazor. *IEJ* 62: 158–76.
Horowitz, W.; Oshima, T.; and Winitzer, A. 2010. Hazor 17: Another Clay Liver Model. *IEJ* 60: 133–45.
Huehnergard, J., and van Soldt, W. H. 1999. A Cuneiform Lexical Text from Ashkelon with a Canaanite Column. *IEJ* 49: 184–92.
   2008. A Cuneiform Lexical Text with a Canaanite Column. In *Ashkelon 1: Introduction and Overview (1985–2006)*, ed. L. E. Stager, J. D. Schloen, and D. M. Master, 327–32. FRLLEA 1. Winona Lake, IN: Eisenbrauns.
Izre'el, S. 1995a. The Amarna Letters from Canaan. *CANE* 4: 2411–19.
   1995b. The Amarna Glosses: Who Wrote What for Whom? Some Sociolinguistic Considerations. *IOS* 15: 101–22.

1997. *The Amarna Scholarly Tablets.* Cuneiform Monographs 9. Groningen: Styx.

2012. Canaano-Akkadian: Linguistics and Sociolinguistics. In *Language and Nature: Papers Presented to John Huehnergard on the Occasion of His 60th Birthday*, ed. R. Hasselbach and N. Pat-El, 171–218. SAOC 67. Chicago: The Oriental Institute of The University of Chicago.

Lamon, R. S., and Shipton, G. M. 1939. *Megiddo I: Seasons of 1925–34, Strata I–V.* OIP 42. Chicago: The University of Chicago Press.

Liverani, M. 1998. *Le lettere di el-Amarna*, Vol. 1. Testi del Vicino Oriente antico 2; Letterature mesopotamiche 3. Brescia: Paideia.

Mazar, E.; Goren, Y.; Horowitz, W.; and Oshima, T. 2014. Jerusalem 2: A Fragment of a Cuneiform Tablet from the Ophel Excavations. *IEJ* 64: 129–39.

Mazar, E.; Horowitz, W.; Oshima, T.; and Goren, Y. 2010. A Cuneiform Tablet from the Ophel in Jerusalem. *IEJ* 60: 4–21.

Meyer, J.-W. 1987. *Untersuchungen zu den Tonlebermodellen aus dem Alten Orient.* AOAT 39. Kevelaer: Butzon & Bercker; Neukirchen-Vluyn: Neukirchener Verlag.

Millard, A. R. 1999. The Knowledge of Writing in Late Bronze Age Palestine. In *Languages and Cultures in Contact: At the Crossroads of Civilizations in the Syro-Mesopotamian Realm; Proceedings of the 42th Rencontre Assyriologique Internationale*, ed. K. Van Lerberghe and G. Voet, 317–26. OLA 96. Leuven: Peeters.

2010. The Cuneiform Tablets from Tell Nebi Mend. *Levant* 42: 226–36.

Moran, W. L. 1992. *The Amarna Letters.* Baltimore: The Johns Hopkins University Press.

2003. A Note on igi-kár, "Provisions, Supplies." In *Amarna Studies: Collected Writings*, ed. J. Huehnergard and S. Izre'el, 297–300. HSS 54. Winona Lake, IN: Eisenbrauns.

Mynářová, J. 2007. *Language of Amarna – Language of Diplomacy: Perspectives on the Amarna Letters.* Prague: Czech Institute of Egyptology.

Na'aman, N. 1977. ašītu (SG.) and ašâtu (PL.) – Straps and Reins. *JCS* 29: 237–9.

1994. The Hurrians and the End of the Middle Bronze Age in Palestine. *Levant* 26: 175–87.

2004. The ṣuḫāru in Second-Millennium BCE Letters from Canaan. *IEJ* 54: 92–9.

Na'aman, N., and Goren, Y. 2009. The Inscriptions from the Egyptian Residence: A Reassessment. In *Aphek-Antipatris II: The Remains on the Acropolis; The Moshe Kochavi and Pirhiya Beck Excavations*, ed. Y. Gadot and E. Yadin, 460–71. MSSMNIA 27. Tel Aviv: Emery and Claire Yass Publications in Archaeology.

Ofer, A. 1987–1988. Tell Rumeideh (Hebron) – 1986. *ESI* 6: 92–3.

1993. Hebron. *NEAEHL* 2: 606–9.

Oppenheim, A. L. 1965. A Note on the Scribes in Mesopotamia. In *Studies in Honor of Benno Landsberger on His Seventy-Fifth Birthday, April 21, 1965*, ed. H. G. Güterbock and T. Jacobsen, 253–6. Assyriological Studies 16. Chicago: The University of Chicago Press.

Ornan, T. 2011. "Let Ba'al Be Enthroned": The Date, Identification, and Function of a Bronze Statue from Hazor. *JNES* 70: 253–80.

2012. The Long Life of a Dead King: A Bronze Statue from Hazor in Its Ancient Near Eastern Context. *BASOR* 366: 1–24.

Radner, K., and Robson, E., eds. 2011. *The Oxford Handbook of Cuneiform Culture.* Oxford: Oxford University Press.

Rainey, A. F. 1976. A Tri-Lingual Cuneiform Fragment from Tel Aphek. *TA* 3: 137–9.

1998. Syntax, Hermeneutic and History. *IEJ* 48: 239–51.

1999. Taanach Letters. *ErIsr* 26: 153*–62*.

2010. The Hybrid Language Written by Canaanite Scribes in the 14th Century BCE. In *Language in the Ancient Near East: Proceedings of the 53e Rencontre Assyriologique*

Internationale, Vol. 1, Part 2, ed. L. Kogan, S. Koslova, S. Loesov, and S. Tishchenko, 851–61. Babel und Bibel 4 (2); Orientalia et Classica 30 (2). Winona Lake, IN: Eisenbrauns.

Rainey, A. F., and Schniedewind, W. M. 2015. *The El-Amarna Correspondence: A New Edition of the Cuneiform Letters from the Site of El-Amarna Based on Collations of All Extant Tablets*. 2 vols. Handbook of Oriental Studies 1, The Near and Middle East 110. Leiden: Brill.

Richter, T.; Lange, S.; and Pfälzner, P. 2012. *Das Archiv des Idadda: Die Keilschrifttexten aus den deutsch-syrischen Ausgrabungen 2001–2003 im Königspalast von Qatna*. Qatna Studien 3. Wiesbaden: Harrassowitz.

Robson, E. 2008. *Mathematics in Ancient Iraq: A Social History*. Princeton: Princeton University Press.

Rollston, C. A. 2010. A Fragmentary Cuneiform Tablet from the Ophel (Jerusalem): Methodological Musings about the Proposed Genre and *Sitz im Leben*. *Antiguo Oriente* 8: 11–21.

Sanders, S. L. 2009. *The Invention of Hebrew*. Traditions. Urbana: Univerity of Illinois Press.

Sellin, E. 1904. *Tell Ta'annek*. Denkschriften der Kaiserlichen Akademie der Wissenschaften, Philosophisch-Historische Klasse 50 (4). Vienna: Gerold.

1926. Die Ausgrabung von Sichem. *ZDPV* 49: 304–20.

Singer, I. 1977. A Hittite Hieroglyphic Seal Impression from Tel Aphek. *TA* 4: 178–90.

1992. A Hittite Seal from Megiddo. *BA* 58: 91–3.

2011. *The Calm before the Storm: Selected Writings of Itamar Singer on the Late Bronze Age in Anatolia and the Levant*. WAWSup 1. Leiden: Brill.

Smith, R. H., and Potts, T. 1992. The Middle and Late Bronze Ages. In *Pella in Jordan 2: The Second Interim Report of the Joint University of Sydney and the College of Wooster Excavations at Pella, 1982–1985*, ed. A. W. McNicoll, P. C. Edwards, J. Hanbury-Tenison, J. B. Hennessy, T. F. Potts, R. H. Smith, A. Walmsley, and P. Watson, 35–81. MASup 2. Sydney: Meditarch.

Soldt, W. H. van. 2011. The Role of Babylon in Western Peripheral Education. In *Babylon: Wissenskultur in Orient und Okzident*, ed. E. Cancik-Kirschbaum, M. van Ess, and J. Marzahn, 197–211. Topoi 1. Berlin: De Gruyter.

2012. The Palaeography of Two Ugarit Archives. In *Palaeography and Scribal Practices in Syro-Palestine and Anatolia in the Late Bronze Age: Papers Read at a Symposium in Leiden, 17–18 December 2009*, ed. E. Devecchi, 171–83. NINEP 119. Leiden: The Netherlands Institute for the Near East.

Stager, L. E.; Schloen, J. D.; Master, D. M.; Press, M. D.; and Aja, A. 2008. Part Four: Stratigraphic Overview. In *Ashkelon 1: Introduction and Overview (1985–2006)*, ed. L. E. Stager, J. D. Schloen, and D. M. Master, 215–323. FRLLEA 1. Winona Lake, IN: Eisenbrauns.

Taylor, J. 2015. Wedge Order in Cuneiform: A Preliminary Survey. In *Current Research in Cuneiform Palaeography: Proceedings of the Workshop Organised at the 60th Rencontre Assyriologique Internationale, Warsaw 2014*, ed. E. Devecchi, G. G. W. Müller, and J. Mynářová, 1–30. Gladbeck: PeWe.

Toorn, K., van der. 2000. Cuneiform Documents from Syria-Palestine: Texts, Scribes, and Schools. *ZDPV* 116: 97–113.

Veldhuis, N. 2014. *History of the Cuneiform Lexical Tradition*. Guides to the Mesopotamian Textual Record 6. Münster: Ugarit-Verlag.

Vita, J.-P. 2012. On the Lexical Background of the Amarna Glosses. *AF* 39: 278–86.

2015. *Canaanite Scribes in the Amarna Letters*. AOAT 406. Münster: Ugarit-Verlag.
Vukosavović, F. 2014. The Laws of Hazor and the ANE Parallels. *RAAO* 108: 41–4.
Weeden, M. 2011. *Hittite Logograms and Hittite Scholarship*. SBT 54. Wiesbaden: Harrassowitz.
Yadin, Y. 1960. *Hazor II: An Account of the Second Season of Excavations, 1956*. Jerusalem: Magnes Press, The Hebrew University of Jerusalem.
1961. *Hazor III–IV: An Account of the Third and Fourth Seasons of Excavations, 1957–1958*, Vol. 1: *Plates*. Jerusalem: Magnes Press, The Hebrew University of Jerusalem.
Zuckerman, S. 2010. "The City, Its Gods Will Return There...": Toward an Alternative Interpretation of Hazor's Acropolis in the Late Bronze Age. *JNES* 69: 163–78.

FOURTEEN

"CANAAN IS YOUR LAND AND ITS KINGS ARE YOUR SERVANTS"

Conceptualizing the Late Bronze Age Egyptian Government in the Southern Levant

SHLOMO BUNIMOVITZ

In a letter found in the Egyptian royal archive at Akhetaten (Tell el-Amarna) – the capital of the heretic pharaoh Akhenaten (Amenhotep IV) during the second half of the fourteenth century BCE – Burnaburiaš, king of Babylon, complains before his peer about a severe incident in which one of his trade caravans passing through Canaan was plundered by some local rulers, and the merchants were killed (EA 8; Moran 1992: 16–17; Rainey and Schniedewind 2015: 88–91). The angry Babylonian king demands justice from the pharaoh – quick investigation, compensation, and death sentences for the culprits – since "the Land of Canaan is your land and its kings are your servants." Indeed, the Late Bronze Age (ca. 1550–1150 BCE) in the southern Levant is characterized by Egypt's rule over the region. No wonder, then, that William F. Albright's dictum "during this whole period Palestine remained an integral part of the Egyptian Empire" (1960: 99) epitomized the long prevalent view in archaeology of Palestine regarding this period (Höflmayer 2015: 193, with references). It is mainly thanks to James Weinstein's ingenious reassessment of the "Egyptian Empire in Palestine" (1981) that we became aware of the changing nature of Egypt's political involvement in Canaan and the need to discern distinct phases along the continuum of this lengthy process.[1]

Inspired by these mind-provoking observations, I have attempted to explain changes in the social fabric of Late Bronze Age Canaan as an outcome of dialectical relations between Canaanite society and the Egyptian government (Bunimovitz 1995). In the twenty odd years that have passed since, not only has much relevant archaeological data been accumulated, but innovative anthropologically informed trials to define and understand the mechanism of the Egyptian governmental apparatus/apparatuses in Canaan were conducted (see below). In spite of these important developments, no consensus has been reached as yet regarding this issue. It should be realized that this is not a mere terminological question but a crucial matter relating to Canaanite reaction *vis-à-vis* Egyptian governmental policy. In light of this state-of-the-art, my intention in this chapter is to revisit the Late Bronze Age Egyptian rule in Canaan and its reciprocal relations with the local population and to offer some new insights concerning this subject.

BACKGROUND TO THE INQUIRY

Before reviewing the various models suggested for the Late Bronze Age Egyptian government in Canaan, a brief survey of the archaeological and documentary data at hand is instrumental as background to the discussion.

Late Bronze Age IA – The Early 18th Dynasty

The transition from the Middle to the Late Bronze Age in Canaan is marked by a long line of destructions and abandonments that laid waste to many sites. The attribution of this chaotic situation to a single agent – the early pharaohs of the 18th Dynasty, who supposedly campaigned time and again in Canaan following the expulsion of the Hyksos from Egypt – is emphatically refuted today.[2] Therefore, I see no reason to change my conclusions that destruction layers "were arbitrarily related to Ahmose or his successors, thus subjugating the archaeological facts to as yet vague historical data concerning Egyptian involvement in Palestine prior to Thothmes III's ... campaigns" (Bunimovitz 1995: 322), and the settlement crisis reflects a fateful combination of internal Canaanite instability and conflicts and a limited Egyptian military action. Notably, at this stage, no effort was taken by the Egyptians to establish a system of long-term governmental and/or administrative control in Canaan. The only site that reveals an Egyptian presence (mainly pottery) in the Late Bronze (LB) Age I is Tell el-'Ajjul (Sharuhen), presumably captured already by Ahmose (Kempinski 1974; Morris 2005: 60–7).

Late Bronze Age IB – From Thutmose III to the el-Amarna Period

Thutmose III's renowned campaign to Megiddo is often considered as a watershed delineating change in the policy of the early pharaohs of the 18th Dynasty toward Canaan and the starting point of an Egyptian Empire in the region. As part of this change, Thutmose III supposedly established military garrisons and governmental centers in key positions along the main roads of southern Canaan: Gaza, Jaffa, and Beth Shean (Weinstein 1981: 10–12;

14.1. Egyptian vessels from Jaffa. (Photo by A. A. Burke. Courtesy of The Jaffa Cultural Heritage Project.)

Hoffmeier 2004: 134–9; Morris 2005: 115–80; Höflmayer 2015). Since no systematic modern excavations have been conducted as yet at ancient Gaza, an archaeological profile of the Egyptian headquarters in Canaan is still wanting.

At Jaffa, excavations in the late 1950s exposed in Level VI *late* (LB IB) the remains of a kitchen with a rich assemblage of locally produced and imported Egyptian pottery associated with food storage, preparation, and consumption, especially of beer and bread – the two staples of Egyptian diet (Fig. 14.1). In close connection with the food preparation area, evidence for the production of the pottery used in the kitchen was exposed (Burke and Lords 2010; Burke et al. 2017: 93–8). While these finds attest to the earliest Egyptian presence at the site, no indication was found for protective fortifications around the Egyptian enclave. In light of Jaffa's mention in Thutmose III's list of conquered cities and the lack of LB IA destruction at the site, Aaron Burke and his colleagues (2017: 124–5) suggest that Jaffa came under Egyptian rule in the wake of the battle of Megiddo rather than because of a direct assault on the city. They consider the LB IB Egyptian pottery assemblage from Jaffa as contemporaneous with the pottery assemblage from Stratum R-1b at Beth Shean (see below).

In contrast to the seemingly nonviolent establishment of the first Egyptian "garrison" in Canaanite Jaffa, its end is marked by a heavy destruction. Immediately after this destruction – and probably as a lesson from it – the Egyptian base in Jaffa was fortified at the beginning of LB IIA as is apparent from the remains of an Egyptian-style massive mud-brick gate exposed in Phase RG-4b of the renewed excavations at the site. The gate functioned throughout the el-Amarna period (Burke et al. 2017: 105–7, 124–5).

The LB IA–II period at Beth Shean is represented by Stratum IX. It seems that the Egyptian presence at the site began in the LB IB (Stratum R-1b of Amihai Mazar's renewed excavations) but was quite restricted: The few architectural remains and the majority of the pottery were of Canaanite tradition, and only a limited number of locally manufactured Egyptian ceramics was found (Mazar and Mullins 2007: 18–21; Mazar 2011: 155–6). A small clay cylinder, which was discovered in the dump of the University of Pennsylvania excavations and bears a message from Tagi (the ruler of Ginti-kirmil? [see Goren, Finkelstein, and Na'aman 2004: 259]) to Lab'ayu, the ruler of Shechem (Horowitz and Oshima 2006: 48–9), is considered by Mazar (2011: 153–4) to support the idea (based on EA 289) that Beth Shean continued to serve as an Egyptian stronghold during the el-Amarna period.

The destruction inflicted on both early Egyptian garrisons in Jaffa and Beth Shean seems to attest to unsecured conditions in southern Canaan, presumably due to the minimal Egyptian presence in the region.

LB IIB – 19th–20th Dynasties

The rise of the 19th Dynasty to power marks a conspicuous change in the nature and extent of the Egyptian presence in southern Canaan. Egyptian sources and archaeological data alike suggest that the pharaohs of the 19th and 20th Dynasties took vigorous measures to increase their presence in southern Canaan and ensure their rule of the region (Weinstein 1981: 17–23; Singer 1988; Morris 2005: 343–611, 645–773).

First and foremost, the Egyptians invested in their existing bases at Jaffa and Beth Shean. The Jaffa garrison seems to have been renovated under Ramesses II, whose royal names were carved on a new gate established there. On top of the ruins of this gate, another one was rebuilt (Phases RG-4a and RG-3b [Burke et al. 2017: 107–14]) (Fig. 14.2). At Beth Shean, Strata VIII–VI present a new urban layout, which may have been established in the days of Seti I, with more governmental buildings being added later. These layers are also characterized by numerous steles and architectural monuments bearing inscriptions and the names of the pharaohs of the 19th and 20th Dynasties, as well as by anthropoid coffin burials, presumably of Egyptian personnel (Oren 1973; Mazar 2009: 3–23; 2011: 156–85) (Fig. 14.3).

In addition to reinforcing their presence in the few traditional strongholds, the Egyptians widened their hold in southern Canaan, mainly in the southern coastal plain and the Shephelah. In a process that took place especially under Ramesses II, Merenptah, and Ramesses III, these regions were subjected to direct Egyptian rule (Weinstein 1981: 17–22; Singer 1988). In many sites excavated in the area (e.g., Tell el-Farʿah South, Tel Seraʿ, Tell el-Ḥesi, Tell Jemmeh, Tel Mor, Gezer, Aphek), Egyptian-style fortified buildings containing both Egyptian and Canaanite material culture remains were found. Following William Flinders Petrie, these buildings are called "Governors' Residencies," supposedly having accommodated Egyptian governors/administrators (Oren 1984). Egyptian governmental buildings seem to have existed also in Ashkelon, Ashdod, and probably also at Tell eṣ-Ṣafi/Gath (Singer 1988; Stager 2008: 1580) and Qubur el-Walaydah (Lehmann 2011: 288). Egyptian offering bowls with hieratic inscriptions discovered at Tel Seraʿ and Lachish attest to the great amounts of grain tax collected by the Egyptians, presumably for the Temple of Amun in Gaza. Analysis of the processes that brought an

14.2. Ramesses II gate from Jaffa. (Courtesy of The Jaffa Cultural Heritage Project.)

end to the Egyptian Empire in Canaan is beyond the scope of the present chapter; suffice it to say that the last significant Egyptian presence in the region can be dated to the third quarter of the twelfth century BCE (Weinstein 1981: 22–3).

PREVIOUS ATTEMPTS TO CONCEPTUALIZE THE EGYPTIAN GOVERNMENT IN LATE BRONZE AGE CANAAN

As we have seen, early Syro-Palestinian archaeological scholarship referred to the Egyptian rule in southern Canaan simplistically as part of the New Kingdom's "empire." Egyptologists, however, were more observant, emphasizing conspicuous differences between the character of the Late Bronze Age

14.3. Lid of an anthropoid coffin from Beth Shean (Museum of Archaeology and Anthropology object no. 29–103–789). (Expedition to Beth Shean [Beisan]; C. Fisher, 1921–8. Courtesy of the University of Pennsylvania, Museum of Archaeology and Anthropology [image no. 150065].)

Egyptian "empire" in Nubia and Canaan; while the Egyptian policy in Nubia was described as colonization, in Canaan it was rather related to imperialism (e.g., Kemp 1978; Frandensen 1979; Redford 1992: 192–3; Hoffmeier 2004; see below). It is mainly the accumulation in recent years of new archaeological data concerning the last phase of Egyptian rule in Canaan (thirteenth–twelfth centuries BCE) that prompted attempts to conceptualize this rule. The following concise survey refers to the main suggestions.

Since throughout the Late Bronze Age, there is no evidence for a significant number of Egyptian settlers that "colonized" Canaan,[3] Ann Killebrew looked for a more nuanced definition of the imperialism practiced by the Egyptians in this region. Following Ronald Horvath's (1972) classificatory scheme of colonialism (and, for that sake, also of imperialism), she suggested that the Egyptian presence in Canaan during the New Kingdom period should be defined as "formal" or "administrative" imperialism, namely, "a form of intergroup domination in which formal (direct) controls over the affairs of the colony exist through a resident imperial administrative apparatus" (Killebrew 2005: 53; see also pp. 54–7).

Yet, another important category of imperialism is "informal" imperialism – "a type of intergroup domination in which formal administrative controls are absent and power is channeled through a local elite" (Horvath 1972: 49). This type of imperialism concurs with the model of "elite emulation" presented by Carolyn Higginbotham (1996; 2000; see also Koch 2014).

Criticizing the common view of Egyptian rule in Canaan as "direct rule," Higginbotham argues that save for the Egyptian presence at Deir el-Balaḥ, Gaza, Jaffa, and Beth Shean, the rest of Egyptian-style material remains uncovered in Canaan reflect elite emulation. This argument rests on insights gained by studies of core–periphery interaction showing that polities located at some distance from a prestigious culture tend to consider it as an important focus of civilization and power. By connecting themselves to such foci, the local rulers aggrandize their status and authority. Hence, local elites readily adapt cultural features of the "great civilization," such as language, dress, architectural and artistic styles, and especially symbols of power. Comprising "iconography of power," the adapted features transfer some of the prestige of the core to the peripheral rulers and support the legitimacy of their rule.[4] Yet, in order to fulfill this task, the adapted features must be understood by the target audience at the local level. Transformations in the borrowed features that enable their integration within the local culture are therefore a conspicuous marker of cultural emulation (see, e.g., Stockhammer 2012, with references).

Since the Canaanite elite depended on Egypt for their access to power, Higginbotham suggests that the high prestige of Egypt as a political power and cultural center motivated the local rulers to emulate Egyptian culture as a means of enhancing their stature. Close inspection of various aspects of Late Bronze Age material culture – the architecture of "Governors' Residencies" and other buildings; Egyptianized pottery and prestige items in domestic, funerary, and ritual contexts; and more – reveals, according to Higginbotham, a mixture of Egyptian and Canaanite features that is the result of cultural emulation and attests to voluntary Egyptianization of the Canaanite elite.

Higginbotham's interpretation of Egyptian rule in Canaan has been criticized and rejected by a number of scholars, yet accepted by others. Following his monumental research of Egyptian Late Bronze Age pottery in Canaan, Mario Martin (2004; 2011) contends that the large quantities of locally produced Egyptian-style pottery at many sites in Canaan, especially during the days of the 19th–20th Dynasties, should be regarded as tangible evidence for direct rule, namely, the physical presence of Egyptian administrative and/or military personnel. In his opinion, while Higginbotham's theory might explain the presence of goods of high prestige, such as jewelry, stone vessels, scarabs, and other objects that display the strong interaction between the Egyptian and Canaanite cultural spheres in the form of artistic eclecticism, hybridization, and syncretism and are likely to have been imitated, it cannot accommodate the mass-produced, low prestige, Egyptian-style household pottery that is not expected to be emulated by the Canaanite elites.

In her *opus magnum* about military bases and the evolution of foreign policy in Egypt's New Kingdom, Ellen Morris (2005: 8–17) points to three problematic facets of the elite emulation model. First, the unrealistic sharp dichotomy delineated by Higginbotham between direct rule and elite emulation. According to Morris, under many imperialistic regimes, the two phenomena are entangled. Second, the claim that should there have been direct Egyptian rule in Canaan one would expect to find imperial enclaves with pure Egyptian material culture fails to acknowledge the difference between Egyptian rule in Nubia and Canaan. Furthermore, it ignores the fact that indigenous material culture always existed side by side with Egyptian-style artifacts. Third, the methodology set up to test the elite emulation model privileges the study of individual categories of artifacts over the study of artifact assemblages. While elite emulation may indeed account for the occasional appearance of Egyptian or Egyptian-style prestige objects on Canaanite soil, it is seldom the only explanation for their presence. In the cosmopolitan atmosphere of the Late Bronze Age and the taste for luxury goods, the find of a foreign artifact within a tomb, for example, does not necessarily mean a desire by the deceased or his family to emulate aspects of the foreign culture. Furthermore, certain Egyptian prestige goods may have come to Canaan as gifts bestowed upon loyal local dignitaries by the Egyptian government.[5] Thus, Morris prefers the rule according to which the wider the range of Egyptian or Egyptian-style artifacts discovered at a Syro-Palestinian site, the greater the probability that Egyptians themselves had at one time been residents.

Aware of the harsh critique leveled at Higginbotham's model of elite emulation and the shortcomings of this model, Ido Koch (2014) has recently emphasized its importance as part of core–periphery theories that can explain the integration of local elite within an empire's system and the peripheral appearance of cultural traits that originated in its center. Relying on cross-cultural ethnographic research, he argues that this process was important for the construction of imperial power. The center has, in many cases, established administrative dominance in the governed peripheries, yet also embraced the local elite with its own symbols in order to implant ideological motives that justify its rule. As discussed by Koch, in the case of the Egyptian Empire in Canaan, there were many opportunities for the Canaanite elite to be exposed to Egyptian culture. Indeed, his article examines an assemblage of goose bones found in Late Bronze Age levels at Lachish, and he interprets it as attesting to the adoption of the Egyptian trait of goose keeping by the local elite that adapted it to their own needs of communal feasting – and thus presented themselves as Egyptian.

AN ALTERNATIVE INTERPRETATION: FROM EQUILIBRIUM IMPERIALISM TO THE "THIRD SPACE"

At this point of our inquiry, it becomes clear that neither the direct rule model (with its variants) nor the elite emulation model provides satisfactory conceptualization of all phases of the Late Bronze Age Egyptian government in Canaan. In fact, both models refer mainly to textual and archaeological data related to its last phase – the thirteenth–twelfth centuries BCE. Apparently, each phase of Egyptian rule in the southern Levant must be examined and interpreted on its own merits. Yet, one should not ignore a more general important insight gained from a comparison between Egyptian imperialism in Nubia and Canaan.

As already discussed by many Egyptologists, the Egyptians encountered a tribal sociopolitical structure and cultural traits in Nubia, which they considered inferior to theirs. This intercultural contact resulted in mass colonization and the transplantation of Egyptian administrative, economic, and religious institutions, as well as life ways on Nubian soil.[6] In contrast, the Egyptians met in Canaan a sophisticated and literate ancient civilization, politically developed and fully urbanized – just like Egypt itself. The pharaohs of the New Kingdom accepted, therefore, the Canaanite system as it was and did not try to change it. Moreover, as evident from both the textual and archaeological testimony discussed above, a permanent Egyptian administrative and military presence in Canaan during the LB IB–IIA seems to have been minimal, even in the Egyptian centers at Jaffa and Beth Shean. As Barry Kemp aptly observed almost four decades ago: "On many sites in Palestine…the purely archaeological record would not of itself incline one to the view that an Egyptian empire existed at all" (1978: 51).[7] Notably, the Egyptian garrisons and their installations (e.g., the granaries at Jaffa and the gates of Jaffa and Gaza) were guarded by local manpower recruited by the Canaanite rulers and not by Egyptian soldiers (EA 294, 296; see also Ta'anach letters 5, 6). Furthermore, the recurring requests of the local rulers to the pharaoh to send soldiers to save them from their enemies (e.g., EA 238, 244, 263, 286, 287) attest that these troops were not readily available in the nearby Egyptian centers. Apparently, Egyptian dominance in the Levant was based more on the obedience of local rulers and strict fulfillment of their obligations to the pharaoh than on direct rule. It seems, therefore, that from the days of Thutmose III to the end of the 18th Dynasty the Egyptian government in Canaan should be conceptualized as "equilibrium imperialism" characterized by indigenous self-maintenance with only a small imperial presence in certain enclaves (Bartel 1980: 17, fig. 1; 1985: 18–22; Smith 1991).

The model of "elite emulation" emphasizes the voluntary Egyptianization of the Canaanite elite as a unidirectional process in which a peripheral culture emulated a core "high" culture. In fact, the southern Levant in the Late Bronze Age saw the meeting of two "high" cultures – the Egyptian and the Canaanite. Though the carriers of the one were the rulers and the second were the ruled, the encounter led to mutual acculturation. Intriguing evidence for this process comes from the Egyptian strongholds in southern Canaan. For example, steles found in the temples of Beth Shean show Egyptians worshiping Canaanite gods (James and McGovern 1993: 240, 250, nos. 10, 11) (Fig. 14.4); anthropoid coffin burials from Deir el-Balaḥ are surrounded by local burial kits familiar to Canaanite burials along the coastal plain (Dothan 1979); and pottery assemblages from Beth Shean and Jaffa attest to mixed cultural traditions and foodways, hinting at intercultural marriages (see Mazar 2009: 17–23; Martin 2009: 465–7). These examples and others attest to the adoption of Canaanite cultural elements by Egyptian administrative and military personnel and to bi-directional emulation. It should be remembered that on the eve of the expulsion of the Hyksos from Egypt, Canaanite–Egyptian acculturation in the eastern Nile Delta reached its zenith, as evident from the Tell el-Dabʻa excavations. It is possible, therefore, that following the occupation of Canaan, Egyptian personnel within the newly established garrisons had Canaanite roots (cf. Morris 2005: 255, n. 157). On the other hand, one should not forget that in the Middle Bronze Age Egypt experienced Canaanite acculturation and prolonged service in Canaan also could have been fertile ground for absorption of Canaanite culture by Egyptian officials. Apparently, it is not easy to differentiate between the hybrids created in the Late Bronze Age: Canaanites that adopted Egyptian culture or Egyptians that adopted Canaanite culture (cf. Braunstein 2011). In the postcolonial discourse that recently has entered into archaeology, such cultural hybrids, which are the outcome of intercultural encounters in creative liminal spaces or "third space" (which displaces the certainties of either parental tradition), are considered as new entities that are more than the sum of their parts (Bhabha 1990; Papastergiadis 1997; Fahlander 2007).[8]

The majority of the Late Bronze Age Egyptian finds are dated to the LB IIB – the days of the 19th–20th Dynasties – and were discovered mainly in the southern coastal plain and at Beth Shean. Trying to explain these finds as reflecting "elite emulation" raises intriguing questions: Why was this process taking place

14.4. The Mekal Stele from Beth Shean. (Courtesy of Livius.org © 2018.)

especially at that time? Why was it limited to a specific region? It seems that the answers to these questions can be found in the historical context of the last phase of the Egyptian Empire in the southern Levant. In spite of the fact that at least part of the Canaanite inhabitants of this region, which presumably returned to Canaan in the wake of the fall of Avaris, were acculturated in the eastern Delta, and many Canaanite princes were indoctrinated in Egypt since the days of Thutmose III, there is no hint in the archaeological record from the early part of the Late Bronze Age of cultural emulation as a prevalent strategy among the Canaanite elite. Apparently, the nature of Egyptian governance at that time and the concentration of Egyptian activity in a few garrisons did not encourage widespread adoption of Egyptian cultural traits. Information about such a phenomenon is limited to these garrisons and rather reflects mutual Canaanite–Egyptian acculturation. Most probably the change in Egyptian governmental policy under the 19th–20th Dynasties, leading to the annexation of large parts of the southern coastal plain and the Shephelah, initiated a change in the survival strategy of the local rulers in these regions, and they adopted Egyptian symbols of power and cultural traits in order to survive. However, due to the difficulty of differentiating between the hybrids created by Egyptian–Canaanite intercultural encounters (see above), it is also possible that, as part of their new policy, the pharaohs installed in place of the local rulers Canaanite administrators who have been Egyptianized or Egyptian administrators who have been Canaanized.[9]

NOTES

1 The chronology and subdivisions of the Late Bronze Age used in this essay follow Panitz-Cohen 2014: table 36.1.
2 For recent summaries of Egyptian sources, archaeological data, and scholarly literature, see, e.g., Hoffmeier 2004: 121–33; Morris 2005: 35–41; and Höflmayer 2015.
3 For the terms "colony" and "colonialism," see Gosden 2004: 2–3.
4 In the context of the debate in Aegean archaeology about the sociopolitical and cultural meaning of the second millennium BCE "Minoan thalassocracy," Malcolm Wiener (1984) introduced into archaeological parlance the term "Versailles effect" to describe the impact of Minoan Crete on the culture of Mycenaean Greece. Looking at the French court as the prestigious source for emulation, the capitals of Europe in the eighteenth century CE began to take on many aspects of its life and culture with respect to art, architecture, furnishings, cloths, jewelry, tableware, gardens, etc. This process of elite emulation is very similar to the one delineated by Higginbotham (note, however, that there was no French conquest, economic domination, or colonization).
5 For a possible example, see Bunimovitz, Lederman, and Hatzaki 2013.
6 See, e.g., Kemp 1978; Frandensen 1979; Smith 1991; 2003; Redford 1992: 192–3; Hoffmeier 2004.
7 Morris's (2005: 141) suggestion that Egyptian garrison posts could remain archaeologically invisible since the Egyptians occupied Canaanite-built compounds and were provided with local supplies seems untenable.
8 Philipp Stockhammer (2012) suggested that the term "hybridity," which is loaded with biological and political connotations, should be replaced with the more neutral term "entanglement."
9 An enlightening example – apparently one of many – of an Asiatic-originated high-rank Egyptian official from the days of the 19th–20th Dynasties is the "royal butler" Ramessesemperre (Semitic name: Ben-azen of Ziri-Bashan) that led the Egyptian expedition to the copper mines at Timna' (Schulman 1976; 1988: 143–4).

REFERENCES

Albright, W. F. 1960. *The Archaeology of Palestine*. Rev. ed. Pelican Books A199. Harmondsworth: Penguin.

Bartel, B. 1980. Colonialism and Cultural Responses: Problems Related to Roman Provincial Analysis. *WA* 12: 11–26.

1985. Comparative Historical Archaeology and Archaeological Theory. In *Comparative Studies in the Archaeology of Colonialism*, ed. S. L. Dyson, 8–37. BAR International Series 233. Oxford: BAR.

Bhabha, H. 1990. The Third Space: Interview with Homi Bhabha. In *Identity: Community, Culture, Difference*, ed. J. Rutherford, 207–21. London: Lawrence & Wishart.

Braunstein, S. L. 2011. The Meaning of Egyptian-Style Objects in the Late Bronze Cemeteries of Tell el-Far'ah (South). *BASOR* 364: 1–36.

Bunimovitz, S. 1995. On the Edge of Empires – Late Bronze Age (1550–1200 BCE). In *The Archaeology of Society in the Holy Land*, ed. T. E. Levy, 320–31. NAAA. London: Leicester University Press.

Bunimovitz, S.; Lederman, Z.; and Hatzaki, E. 2013. Knossian Gifts? Two Late Minoan IIIA1 Cups from Tel Beth-Shemesh, Israel. *Annual of the British School at Athens* 108: 51–66.

Burke, A. A., and Lords, K. V. 2010. Egyptians in Jaffa: A Portrait of Egyptian Presence in Jaffa during the Late Bronze Age. *NEA* 73: 2–30.

Burke, A. A.; Peilstöcker, M.; Karoll, A.; Pierce, G. A.; Kowalski, K.; Ben-Marzouk, N.; Damm, J. C.; Danielson, A. J.; Fessler, H. D.; Kaufman, B.; Pierce, K.V.L.; Höflmayer, F.; Damiata, B. N.; and Dee, M. 2017. Excavations of the New Kingdom Fortress in Jaffa, 2011–2014: Traces of Resistance to Egyptian Rule in Canaan. *AJA* 121: 85–133.

Dothan, T. 1979. *Excavations at the Cemetery of Deir el-Balah*. Qedem 10. Jerusalem: The Institute of Archaeology, The Hebrew University of Jerusalem.

Fahlander, F. 2007. Third Space Encounters: Hybridity, Mimicry and Interstitial Practice. In *Encounters, Materialities, Confrontations: Archaeologies of Social Space and Interaction*, ed. P. Cornell and F. Fahlander, 15–41. Newcastle: Cambridge Scholars.

Frandensen, P. J. 1979. Egyptian Imperialism. In *Power and Propaganda: A Symposium on Ancient Empires [Held under the Auspices of the Institute of Assyriology at the University of Copenhagen, September 19th–21th, 1977]*, ed. M. T. Larsen, 167–90. Mesopotamia 7. Copenhagen: Akademisk.

Goren, Y.; Finkelstein, I.; and Na'aman, N. 2004. *Inscribed in Clay: Provenance Study of the Amarna Letters and Other Ancient Near Eastern Texts*. MSSMNIA 23. Tel Aviv: Emery and Claire Yass Publications in Archaeology.

Gosden, C. 2004. *Archaeology and Colonialism: Cultural Contact from 5000 BC to the Present*. Topics in Contemporary Archaeology. Cambridge: Cambridge University Press.

Higginbotham, C. R. 1996. Elite Emulation and Egyptian Governance in Ramesside Canaan. *TA* 23: 154–69.

2000. *Egyptianization and Elite Emulation in Ramesside Palestine: Governance and Accommodation on the Imperial Periphery*. CHANE 2. Leiden: Brill

Hoffmeier, J. K. 2004. Aspects of Egyptian Foreign Policy in the 18th Dynasty in Western Asia and Nubia. In *Egypt, Israel, and the Ancient Mediterranean World: Studies in Honor of Donald B. Redford*, ed. G. A. Knoppers and A. Hirsch, 121–42. PAe 20. Leiden: Brill.

Höflmayer, F. 2015. Egypt's "Empire" in the Southern Levant during the Early 18th Dynasty. In *Policies of Exchange: Political Systems and Modes of Interaction in the Aegean and the Near East in the 2nd Millennium B.C.E.; Proceedings of the International Symposium at the University of Freiburg Institute for Archaeological Studies, 30th May–2nd*

June 2012, ed. B. Eder and R. Pruzsinszky, 191–206. Oriental and European Archaeology 2. Vienna: Austrian Academy of Sciences.

Horowitz, W., and Oshima, T. 2006. *Cuneiform in Canaan: Cuneiform Sources from the Land of Israel in Ancient Times*. Jerusalem: IES; The Hebrew University of Jerusalem

Horvath, R. J. 1972. A Definition of Colonialism. *CA* 13: 45–57.

James, F. W., and McGovern, P. E. 1993. *The Late Bronze Egyptian Garrison at Beth Shan: A Study of Levels VII and VIII*. UMM 85. Philadelphia: University of Pennsylvania Museum of Archaeology Press.

Kemp, B. J. 1978. Imperialism and Empire in New Kingdom Egypt (c. 1575–1087 B.C.). In *Imperialism in the Ancient World*, ed. P. D. A. Garnsey and C. R. Whittaker, 7–57. Cambridge Classical Studies. Cambridge: Cambridge University Press.

Kempinski, A. 1974. Tell el-'Ajjul – Beth-Eglayim or Sharuhen? *IEJ* 24: 145–52.

Killebrew, A. E. 2005. *Biblical Peoples and Ethnicity: An Archaeological Study of Canaanites, Egyptians, Philistines, and Early Israel, 1300–1100 B.C.E.* ABS 9. Atlanta: SBL.

Koch, I. 2014. Goose Keeping, Elite Emulation and Egyptianized Feasting at Late Bronze Lachish. *TA* 41: 161–79.

Lehmann, G. 2011. Cooking Pots and Loomweights in a "Philistine" Village: Preliminary Report on the Excavations at Qubur el-Walaydah, Israel. In *On Cooking Pots, Drinking Cups, Loomweights and Ethnicity in Bronze Age Cyprus and Neighbouring Regions: An International Archaeological Symposium Held in Nicosia, November 6th–7th 2010*, ed. V. Karageorghis and O. Kouka, 287–314. Nicosia: A. G. Leventis Foundation.

Martin, M. A. S. 2004. Egyptian and Egyptianized Pottery in Late Bronze Age Canaan: Typology, Chronology, Ware Fabrics, and Manufacture Techniques; Pots and People? *Egypt and the Levant* 14: 265–84.

2009. The Egyptian Assemblage. In *Excavations at Tel Beth-Shean 1989–1996*, Vol. 3: *The 13th–11th Century BCE Strata in Areas N and S*, ed. N. Panitz-Cohen and A. Mazar, 434–77. BSVAP 3. Jerusalem: IES; The Institute of Archaeology, The Hebrew University of Jerusalem.

2011. *Egyptian-Type Pottery in the Late Bronze Age Southern Levant*. CCEM 29; DG 69. Vienna: Austrian Academy of Sciences.

Mazar, A. 2009. Introduction and Overview. In *Excavations at Tel Beth-Shean 1989–1996*, Vol. 3: *The 13th–11th Century BCE Strata in Areas N and S*, ed. N. Panitz-Cohen and A. Mazar, 1–32. BSVAP 3. Jerusalem: IES; The Institute of Archaeology, The Hebrew University of Jerusalem.

2011. The Egyptian Garrison Town at Beth-Shean. In *Egypt, Canaan and Israel: History, Imperialism, Ideology and Literature; Proceedings of a Conference at the University of Haifa, 3–7 May 2009*, ed. S. Bar, D. D. Kahn, and J. J. Shirley, 151–85. CHANE 52. Leiden: Brill.

Mazar, A., and Mullins, R. A. 2007. Introduction and Overview. In *Excavations at Tel Beth-Shean 1989–1996*, Vol. 2: *The Middle and Late Bronze Age Strata in Area R*, ed. A. Mazar and R. A. Mullins, 1–22. BSVAP 2. Jerusalem: IES; The Institute of Archaeology, The Hebrew University of Jerusalem.

Moran, W. L. 1992. *The Amarna Letters*. Baltimore: The Johns Hopkins University Press.

Morris, E. F. 2005. *The Architecture of Imperialism: Military Bases and the Evolution of Foreign Policy in Egypt's New Kingdom*. PAe 22. Leiden: Brill.

Oren, E. D. 1973. *The Northern Cemetery of Beth Shan*. UMM. Leiden: Brill.

1984. "Governors' Residencies" in Canaan under the New Kingdom: A Case Study of Egyptian Administration. *JSSEA* 14: 37–56.

Panitz-Cohen, N. 2014. The Southern Levant (Cisjordan) during the Late Bronze Age. In *The Oxford Handbook of the Archaeology of the Levant, c. 8000–332 BCE*, ed. M. L. Steiner and A. E. Killebrew, 541–60. Oxford: Oxford University Press.

Papastergiadis, N. 1997. Tracing Hybridity in Theory. In *Debating Cultural Hybridity: Multi-Cultural Identities and the Politics of Anti-Racism*, ed. P. Werbner and T. Modood, 257–81. Critique, Influence, Change 8. London: Zed Books.

Rainey, A. F., and Schniedewind, W. M. 2015. *The El-Amarna Correspondence: A New Edition of the Cuneiform Letters from the Site of El-Amarna Based on Collations of All Extant Tablets*. 2 vols. Handbook of Oriental Studies 1, The Near and Middle East 110. Leiden: Brill.

Redford, D. B. 1992. *Egypt, Canaan, and Israel in Ancient Times*. Princeton: Princeton University Press.

Schulman, A. R. 1976. The Royal Butler Ramessesmperrēʿ. *JARCE* 13: 117–30.

——— 1988. Catalogue of the Egyptian Finds. In *The Egyptian Mining Temple at Timna*, ed. B. Rothenberg, 114–47. Researches in the Arabah 1959–1984 1; Metal in History 2. London: Institute for Archaeo-Metallurgical Studies; Institute of Archaeology, University College London.

Singer, I. 1988. Merneptah's Campaign to Canaan and the Egyptian Occupation of the Southern Coastal Plain of Palestine in the Ramesside Period. *BASOR* 269: 1–10.

Smith, S. T. 1991. A Model for Egyptian Imperialism in Nubia. *Göttinger Miszellen* 122: 77–102.

——— 2003. *Wretched Kush: Ethnic Identities and Boundaries in Egypt's Nubian Empire*. London: Routledge.

Stager, L. E. 2008. Ashkelon, Tel. *NEAEHL* 5: 1578–86.

Stockhammer, P. W. 2012. Performing the Practice Turn in Archaeology. *Transcultural Studies* 1: 7–42.

Weinstein, J. M. 1981. The Egyptian Empire in Palestine: A Reassessment. *BASOR* 241: 1–28.

Wiener, M. H. 1984. Crete and the Cyclades in LM I: The Tale of the Conical Cups. In *The Minoan Thalassocracy: Myth and Reality; Proceedings of the Third International Symposium at the Swedish Institute in Athens, 31 May–5 June, 1982*, ed. R. Hägg and N. Marinatos, 17–26. Publications of the Swedish Institute at Athens 4, 32. Stockholm: Swedish Institute at Athens.

PART THREE

FIFTEEN

THE "CONQUEST" OF THE HIGHLANDS IN THE IRON AGE I

DAVID ILAN

At the end of the Late Bronze Age, in the late thirteenth or early twelfth century BCE, a number of small, unfortified settlements began to appear in the highlands of Canaan, on both sides of the Jordan River, where almost none had existed for perhaps 250 years, since the Middle Bronze Age. These new highland settlements are the crux of this chapter. Their appearance raises a number of questions: What instigated this surge of small settlements? What were the settlers' origins and cultural identities? How did they relate to the lowland peoples and their towns? How did the settlers' social and political organization and their alliances change over time? These questions have been discussed in other studies (e.g., Finkelstein 1988; 1995; Bloch-Smith and Alpert Nakhai 1999; Killebrew 2005; Faust 2006), and this one will incorporate some of their insights. Regarding origins, however, the conclusions offered here will be somewhat different.

The word "conquest," in quotation marks in the title of this chapter, is a reference to the title of Israel Finkelstein's 1995 synthetic treatment of the same topic. Both the term and the quotation marks remain relevant, as we shall see. Also, Finkelstein's collection, presentation, and analysis of data will remain a linchpin of any subsequent synthesis (see esp. Finkelstein 1988). The word "conquest" is also a reference to an ongoing core issue: The fact that the archaeology of the highlands of the southern Levant in the Iron Age I (ca. 1140–900 BCE) has always lived in the shadow of the biblical text. We cannot ignore the biblical text – it most likely contains echoes of historical *realia* – but we must be cognizant of its theological and political umbra.

As others have pointed out (e.g., Mazar 1992; Finkelstein 1995; Bloch-Smith and Alpert Nakhai 1999; Killebrew 2005; Faust 2006; Cline 2014), this was a critical juncture in time, when great empires were imploding, and new societies and political structures emerged out of the cultural detritus. Climate desiccation and changing weather patterns most likely contributed to this social upheaval (Kaniewski et al. 2013a; 2013b; Langgut, Finkelstein, and Litt 2013; Cline 2014; Langgut et al. 2015; Kaniewski, Guiot, and Van Campo 2015). Any analysis of highland settlement and culture must take into consideration the role of Egyptian hegemony in the southern Levant prior to its dissipation ca. 1140 BC and the social, political, and cultural responses to it.

CHRONOLOGY

Absolute chronology and relative chronology are separate but related issues. Relative chronology is determined by a set of typological traits (Fig. 15.1) that recur in a particular cultural horizon in the stratigraphies of archaeological sites, generally, though not always, in a geographically contiguous way. For the Iron Age I, perhaps the most widely referenced type is the cooking pot with an inwardly inclining upper wall and a rim that is folded out and down (see Mazar 2015) (see Fig. 15.1:5, 7). The lack of decoration on pottery, the paucity of certain types (alabastra, flasks, juglets), and the lack of imported pottery are other oft-cited features of Iron Age I highland material culture (see below). The collared-rim pithos (see Fig. 15.1:17) was once considered a chronological marker of the Iron Age I, but it is now clear that these vessels were introduced in the terminal Late Bronze Age (Killebrew 2001; 2005: 177, n. 74). In general though, Iron Age I material culture is very similar to Late Bronze Age material culture – the former is an outcome of the latter – and in practice the small fragmentary assemblages of the highlands are sometimes difficult to attribute to one or the other.

The absolute chronology of the Iron Age I horizon of material culture is still somewhat in flux. A slew of radiocarbon dates over the last two decades has clarified the dating of the lowland horizon to some degree, but the highland sites are still grossly underrepresented (Tables 15.1–15.3). Thus, we are forced to rely on relative chronology synchronisms for the highland sites. A few dated Egyptian objects from Mount Ebal and Lehun provide another peg, if a somewhat tenuous one (see below).

There is a growing consensus, based on a systematic sampling and evaluation of radiocarbon assays, that the Iron Age I ends and transitions to the Iron Age IIA around 900–880 BCE (Boaretto et al. 2005; Finkelstein and Piasetsky 2006; 2009; Sharon et al. 2007).[1] The beginning of the Iron Age I is more in doubt,

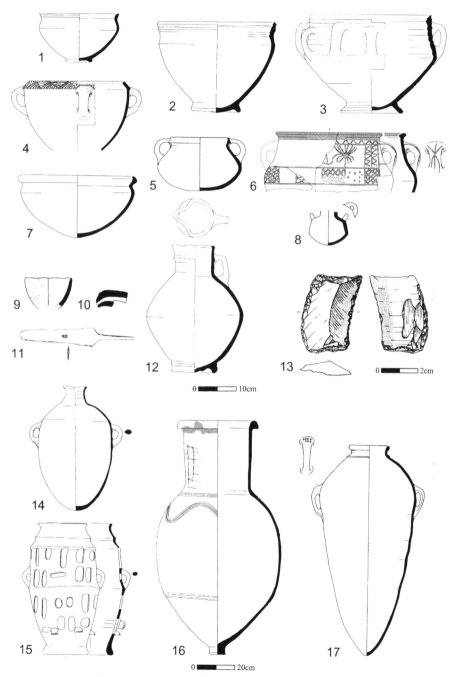

15.1. A selection of key Iron Age I highland material culture. (Drawings by N. Ze'evi and C. Herriott.)

especially for the highlands. For one thing, the ca. 1200 BC horizon is difficult to date due to the nature of the calibration curve's wiggle (Manning 2006–2007). For another, it depends on how one defines the material attributes of Iron Age I, and whether those of the highlands are synchronous with those of

TABLE 15.1. *Selected radiocarbon dates from terminal Late Bronze Age III/early Iron I contexts (compiled from Bruins et al. 2005; Sharon et al. 2007; Mazar and Bronk Ramsey 2008; Finkelstein and Piasetzky 2009; Asscher et al. 2015; and Burke et al. 2017).*

Site	Stratum, Context	Uncalibrated BP	Calibrated BCE (68%)	Material
Aphek	X12	2960 ± 25	1260–1120	Seeds
Jaffa	Transition RG-4A/3B	16 samples	1194–1125	Seeds and olive pits
Jaffa	Transition RG-3B/3A	5 samples	1156–1115	Seeds and olive pits
Jaffa	End RG-3A	5 samples	1151–1095	Wheat seeds
Zayit, Tel	–	3000 ± 40	1370–1130	Seeds
Megiddo	K6, destruction layer, floors, and olive press	2928 ± 11	1193–1113	Olive pits
Miqne-Ekron, Tel	VIIb	2907 ± 28	1190–1020	Seeds
Lachish	VI, destruction layer	2931 ± 21	1208–1110	
Qubur el-Walaydah	1–5d-1–6, DS-1, DS-5	9 samples	1270–1140	Barley seeds
Hevron, Tel	VII	2989 ± 34 2984 ± 18	1370–1040	Charcoal
Dothan, Tell	Tomb 1, Phases 1 and 4 (Late Bronze Age material culture)	2960–2900 ± 25	1261–1008	6 teeth
Rehov, Tel	D6	2950 ± 50 2935 ± 45 2920 ± 30 2880 ± 30	1130–1050	Olive pits
Keisan, Tell	13	2989 ± 17	1300–1130	Charcoal
Hazor	XII/XI	2996 ± 18	1390–1130	Olive pits
Dan, Tel	V	2930 ± 50	1192–1045	Olive pits

the lowlands. Finally, determining the starting date for the Iron Age I depends on how one correlates historical events to material culture.

Radiocarbon dates derived from short-lived samples dating to the end of the Late Bronze Age (LB III) and the transition to the Iron Age I are few in number. At the time of this writing, such dates come only from the lowland sites of Beth Shean, Megiddo, Lachish, and Qubur el-Walaydah (Finkelstein and Piasetsky 2009; Mazar 2009; Toffolo et al. 2014; Asscher et al. 2015). These would suggest a date of ca. 1140 BCE for the end of the Late Bronze Age and the beginning of the Iron Age I. This date also conforms to current thinking in regards to the end of Egyptian rule in Canaan, where the Iron Age is seen to begin once Egyptian suzerainty has ended in the middle of the 20th Dynasty (e.g., Ussishkin 1985; 1995; Ben-Dov 2011; Finkelstein and Piasetsky 2011).

TABLE 15.2. *Radiocarbon dates from middle Iron Age I contexts (compiled from Boaretto et al. 2005; Mazar et al. 2005; Ullinger et al. 2005; Finkelstein and Piasetzky 2006; 2009; Sharon et al. 2007; Mazar and Bronk Ramsey 2008; Toffolo et al. 2014; Asscher et al. 2015).*

Site	Stratum, Context	Uncalibrated BP	Calibrated BCE (68% range)	Material
el-Ahwat	–	2865–2815 ± 23	1120–925	Olive pits
Miqne-Ekron, Tel	VIB, destruction layer	2918 ± 26	1200–1040	Olive pits
Miqne-Ekron, Tel	VB	2832 ± 32	1025–925	Seeds
Qubur el-Walaydah	1–4 (a stratified pit)	14 samples	1140–1055	Barley seeds
Megiddo	K5, floor	2890 ± 20	1116–1040	Seeds
Shiloh	V, destruction layer	2873 ± 13	1050–1000	Seeds, raisins, fava beans
Dothan, Tell (TD-62)	Tomb 1, Phase 4	2870 ± 25	1121–973	1 tooth
Beth-Shemesh	6, destruction layer	2855 ± 29	1120–930	Olive pits
Beth-Shemesh	5, destruction layer	2811 ± 23	1040–895	Olive pits
Rehov, Tel	D4b-a	2878 ± 15	1130–1000	Olive pits
Dor, Tel	D2/13	2909 ± 24	1190–1040	Olive pits
Dor, Tel	D2/12	2857 ± 25	1060–940	Olive pits

TABLE 15.3. *Radiocarbon dates from late Iron Age I contexts (compiled from Ullinger et al. 2005; Sharon et al. 2007; Mazar and Bronk Ramsey 2008; Finkelstein and Piasetzky 2009).*

Site	Stratum, Context	Uncalibrated BP	Calibrated BCE (68% range)	Material
Keisan, Tell	9a, destruction layer	2855 ± 29	1190–930	Seeds, charcoal
Megiddo	K4, destruction layer	2851 ± 20	1047–996	Seeds
Qasile, Tell	X, destruction layer	2850 ± 24	1050–946	Seeds
Yoqne'am	XVII, destruction layer	2850 ± 23	1120–920	Olive pits, charcoal
Hadar	Destruction layer	2791 ± 52 2856 ± 13	1010–850; 1120–910	Seeds
Dor, Tel	D2/9–10	2798 ± 15	1000–900	Olive pits
Rehov, Tel	D3	2803 ± 19 2754 ± 24	980–840	Olive pits
Hammah	Destruction layer	2790 ± 23	974–915	Semolina
Dothan, Tell (TD-19)	Tomb 1, Phase 1	2750 ± 30	944–923	1 tooth, perhaps Iron Age IIA

However, the reader must be aware that some scholars begin the Iron Age I more or less with the 20th Dynasty (ca. 1200 BCE), calling this early phase "Iron Age IA," where the post-Egyptian withdrawal phase, starting in 1140 BCE, is termed the "Iron Age IB" (e.g., Mazar 1992; 2009).

To reiterate, there are almost no radiocarbon dates from highland assemblages (see Tables 15.1–15.3); the only ones at the time of this writing are from Shiloh Stratum V, Tel Hebron (assemblage still unpublished), and el-Ahwat, if one considers this a highland site (Sharon et al. 2007: 12). This makes Shiloh (with only one dated context) the type-site for tying in absolute and relative chronology via ceramic correlations in the central highlands west of the Jordan River (Finkelstein and Piasetsky 2006). It also leaves a critical but problematic role for material culture correlations with radiocarbon-dated lowland contexts. All this enhances the role of datable Egyptian objects found in Iron Age I material culture contexts, namely the Ramesside scarab seals from Mount Ebal, which Baruch Brandl (1986–7) has dated to the late thirteenth century BCE; 'Izbet Ṣarṭah (20th Dynasty [Giveon 1986]); and Lehun in Moab, dated to the 19th–20th Dynasties (Homès-Frederique 1997: 61; Eggler and Keel 2006: 182–3).

It is clear that small highland sites were first established on both sides of the Jordan River several generations before the Egyptian withdrawal, perhaps in the mid-thirteenth century (cf. Dever 1994: 215–16 and Faust 2006: 111, fig. 12:1, 2). For those who date the beginning of the Iron Age I to the end of Egyptian rule in 1140 BCE, this means that the wave of new settlements in the highlands began in the terminal Late Bronze Age (LB III) rather than in the Iron Age. For those who define the beginning of the Iron Age I as coeval with the expansion of new settlement in the highlands, the Iron Age I can be understood to have begun as early as 1250 BCE, in the 19th Dynasty. To this writer, it seems that the former option is more useful and convenient.

MATERIAL CULTURE

Pottery

A comprehensive account of Iron Age I pottery forms has been published by Amihai Mazar (2015). As noted above, many of the forms found in Iron Age I assemblages are identical to those of the Late Bronze Age IIB/III (Killebrew 2005: 177), while others show slight morphological changes that accrued over time. Late Iron Age I assemblages show more typological distance from the Late Bronze Age repertoire and more resemblance to the subsequent Iron Age IIA, as exemplified by the Khirbet Qeiyafa assemblage (Mazar 2015: 8; A. Faust, this volume).

Overall, the highland assemblage is utilitarian, with a limited repertoire and a dearth of decorated vessels and imported wares. Most common are cooking pots, followed by storage vessels (pithoi and storage jars), serving vessels (bowls and jugs), kraters, chalices, juglets, and lamps (see Fig. 15.1). All the highland ceramic forms are paralleled in the richer assemblages of the valleys and coastal plain, but a number of the lowland types and decorations are rare or absent from the highland corpus. Throughout the highlands of the southern Levant, ceramic assemblages are quite similar. In fact, the only real difference between the ceramic assemblages of the Galilee and those of the central and Jordanian highlands are to be found in pithos typology, with "wavy-band" and "Galilean" pithoi being present only in the Galilee (and the coastal plain).

Why are highland assemblages less varied and decorated, and more utilitarian than their lowland counterparts? The widely accepted explanation is that they represent less affluent, more isolated population groups. In Finkelstein's (1988: 270–5) view, they represent the expedient adoption of lowland ceramic forms by formerly nomadic highlanders with no ceramic tradition of their own. In Avraham Faust's (2006: 41–8) view, the modest repertoire was a conscious means of asserting egalitarianism and simplicity to distinguish highland group identity from that of the lowlands.

In Faust's view, too, the collared-rim pithos is a marker of highland – specifically "Israelite" – identity, even though the type occurs frequently in lowland assemblages as well. Ann Killebrew (2001; 2005: 177–81) rejects the idea of the collared-rim pithos as an ethnic marker but sees their distribution – weighted more toward the highlands – as indicating a "social boundary." This author would agree with David Wengrow (1996) and Avner Raban (2001) that the Egyptians introduced the collared-rim pithos as an administrative form with a standard volume (see below). Over time, with the collapse of Egyptian control, pithos form and volume lost consistency, though pithoi continued to be manufactured by specialists, at least into the eleventh century BCE and perhaps into the tenth. Highlanders probably did not view pithoi as emblematic of their cultural identity – the large vessels were a prosaic part of life from an emic point of view. But outsiders may have seen them as such (from the etic perspective), as many scholars do today.

Metals and Metallurgy

The copper mines of the Aravah Valley continued to be exploited in the Iron Age I (Yahalom-Mack 2009: 253–5). Here, copper ore was smelted and ingots produced. The Egyptians were involved heavily at Timnaʻ though there is some question as to whether they actually controlled production (Avner 2014). The mines of Feinan in modern-day Jordan appear to have replaced the Timnaʻ mines in the Iron Age IB into the Iron Age II. While Cyprus continued to produce copper in the thirteenth–twelfth centuries BCE, export transitioned to finished products, such as stands and bimetallic knives. It is clear that the source of most copper was Timnaʻ and then Feinan.

However, the dominant mode of metallurgical production was recycling, which would suggest metal shortages. At least 17 Iron Age I metal workshops have been found in the southern Levant, most of them are located in lowland sites. Such workshops housed furnaces, pits for charcoal storage, water containers for quenching, crucibles, blowpipe nozzles (see Fig. 15.1:9, 10), bellows pots, grinding and pounding stones, scrap metal, some slag, bone as a flux material, and sometimes finished artifacts. Molds are rare; they seem to have been one-off items that have not been preserved. Three workshops were identified in the highlands at the sites of Tel Harashim, Khirbet Raddana, and Jerusalem (Yahalom-Mack 2009: fig. II:41). Naama Yahalom-Mack has dated all three to the Iron Age IB (though this may be a case of fitting the evidence to the theory).

Metal artifacts are not rare finds in the highland sites of the Iron Age I. Yahalom-Mack (2009) has cataloged most of the metal objects, rostering lugged axes, knives, daggers (see Fig. 15.1:11), bangles, stick pins, spearheads, spear butts, arrowheads, tweezers, earrings, rings, and various points. As with pottery, the recovered metal artifacts are mainly utilitarian – even bangles, rings, and earrings had utility. They were a kind of portable wealth and a means of apotropaic protection, when earrings were cast in the form of the crescent moon, for example (Ilan 2016).

Most of the metal finds are of bronze – a copper-tin alloy. But iron begins to make an appearance, initially in the form of ornamental or prestige-imbued bangles and knives, then as other objects: chisels, daggers, sickles, tweezers, spearheads, spear butts, and needles (Yahalom-Mack and Eliyahu-Behar 2015). Iron becomes more normative in the late Iron Age I (cf. Ilan 2018c). The metal assemblages of the highlands are, proportionally, just as rich and varied as those of the lowlands, except for the fact that no metal vessels have been found in the highlands thus far.

Other Material Culture

Reports and discussions of ground stone, chipped stone, bone objects, loom weights, and balance weights are conspicuously absent from the publications of Iron Age I highland contexts; the few exceptions are rather poor and perhaps not representative (e.g., Finkelstein 1986: 93–4 ['Izbet Ṣarṭah]; Zertal 1986–1987: 148–50 [Mount Ebal]). Part of the explanation lays in the disturbed or meager contexts characteristic of highland assemblages. The other part lays in the lack of collection in early excavations, such as Beth-Zur, Tell el-Ful, and Bethel. The recent excavations at Tall al-'Umayri in Jordan uncovered three houses, in which a more comprehensive picture of material culture is evident (e.g., Herr and Clark 2009: 82–90).

Ground-stone assemblages include lower and upper millstones, thick-walled bowls, mortars, pestles, handstones, cuboids, and spheroids (e.g., Herr and Clark 2009: 88). The function of the last two is in question; they may be ballistae, and the cuboids may be abrasion tools. But they may well be balance weights, since they tend to have rather consistent masses in two groups: one of 300–400 grams and another around 500 grams (Ilan 2018a). This would indicate, not surprisingly, an organized system of exchange.

Judging from the few chipped-stone assemblages published (e.g., Mazar 1982: fig. 13 [Bull Site]; Friedman 1993 [Shiloh]), the technology and typology appear to follow the Bronze Age tradition, emphasizing the manufacture of trapezoidal sickle blades (see Fig. 15.1:13) and the utilization of ad hoc tools made on blades, flakes, burins, cores, and core trim elements (Rosen 1997).

Seals and impressions are present in a number of Iron Age I sites, and they are an important indicator of administration, religious belief, and cultural identity. These include Egyptian scarab seals of the 19th and 20th Dynasties (at Mount Ebal, Shiloh, 'Izbet Ṣarṭah, and Lehun) and various pyramidal, trapezoidal, and conical stamp seals bearing quadrupeds (Shiloh); a chariot scene (Shiloh); and geometric signs (Ebal, Tell en-Naṣbeh, and Tall al-'Umayri [Keel 1990; Eggler and Keel 2006]).

ARCHITECTURE AND VILLAGE LAYOUT

Very few highland settlements have been excavated to the extent that would allow a reliable analysis of their layouts. Finkelstein's (1988: 27–33) summary of highland settlement features is still the most convenient trait list. Some settlements were constructed over the remains of older Bronze Age towns (e.g., Shechem, Jerusalem, Shiloh, Hebron, Beth-Zur, Khirbet Rabud, Tall al-'Umayri). As a result, the architecture at these sites is oriented toward the circumference (best seen at Shiloh), where fortifications once existed. A few new settlements show an elliptical pattern, whereby household units were joined together to form a defensive circumvallation (Finkelstein 1988: 250–4). More new settlements, however, were small (0.5 ha or less), lack circumferential walls, and have an amorphous layout; they include no obvious public buildings. Those with longer histories (e.g., Ai, Khirbet Raddana, Beth-Zur) show organic growth – the filling in of open spaces, the subdivision of larger spaces into smaller ones, and the migration of doorways as family composition changed.

Some sites display more curvilinear architecture with larger open spaces, of which Giloh is the prime example. The Giloh configuration has been interpreted as being designed for animal husbandry, with corralling in mind, and perhaps protection (Mazar 1981). Toward the end of the Iron Age I, elliptical sites were being fortified (Khirbet ed-Dawwara, Khirbet Qeiyafa), perhaps an indication of alliance building and political consolidation leading up to the crystallization of territorial states in Israel, Judah, Moab, and Edom.

Houses are mostly rectilinear (see also A. Faust, this volume). In the Iron Age I, a standard type made it first appearance, having either a tripartite or quadripartite division with walls or rows of columns subdividing the whole. This is often called the "four-room" house or the "Israelite" house (e.g., Shiloh 1970; Stager 1985; Holladay 1992), though it is also found in coastal (Philistine) Tell Qasile and in the highlands of Jordan (Tall al-'Umayri, Lehun). Faust and Shlomo Bunimovitz (2003) have interpreted the layout of the quadripartite house as facilitating laws of purity and concepts of order, becoming, in the Iron Age II, a marker of Israelite identity.

What are the origins of the columned tripartite and quadripartite houses? One hypothesis is that its inspiration was the nomadic tent (Fritz 1977: 60–4; Kempinski 1978: 36). Another posits it as an evolutionary, practical outcome of the Canaanite agrarian lifestyle (Stager 1985: 17; Holladay 1992: 316). Manfred Bietak (1992) has pointed out a quadripartite house in the precinct of the Temple of Horemheb and Ay in western Thebes, Egypt, dating to the late Ramesside period (twelfth century BCE), suggesting that it is an "Israelite" house. But similar variants of this plan are common in Middle Kingdom Egypt, at Tell el-Dab'a in particular (Moeller 2016). Tripartite and quadripartite houses may be an Egyptian inspiration, initially adopted as part of the provincial administration. This is an idea that requires further investigation.

Another hallmark feature of Iron Age I settlement sites, and not only in the highlands, is the presence of numerous pits dug or hewn below household and outdoor surfaces, obscured from view. These were mainly, though not only, intended as grain silos (Finkelstein 1988: 264–9); however, they could also be used as sumps, latrines, and compost containers. They are much more frequent in the Iron Age I due to the danger of pillage that seems to have been particularly acute at this time (Ilan 2008).

SETTLEMENT PATTERNS

Highlands versus Lowlands, Northern Highlands versus Southern Highlands

In the Late Bronze Age, settlement was concentrated in the lowland valleys and coastal plain, with only a few towns and villages in the highlands (Bunimovitz 1995; this volume; Finkelstein 1995). Toward the later part of the Late Bronze Age, in the late thirteenth and twelfth centuries BCE, smaller settlements began to be constructed in the highlands at sites such as 'Izbet Ṣarṭah, Giloh, and Mount Ebal. The pre-existing Bronze Age towns – Jerusalem, Shechem, Dothan, Beth-Zur, Bethel, Hebron, and Khirbet Rabud in Israel and the West Bank; and Amman, Fuqhar, Irbid, and Sahab on the on the plateau of northern Jordan – show evidence for Iron Age I occupation, but this is always disturbed by subsequent occupation. Moreover, many of these sites were excavated in the first half of the twentieth century with deficient archaeological techniques, precluding any clear comprehension of stratigraphy or Iron Age I settlement characteristics.[2] Thus, it is not clear whether erstwhile highland centers continued as such in the Iron Age I.

In some parts of the country, the highland/lowland dichotomy is not clear. Do, for example, the larger Iron Age I sites of the Shephelah (the highland piedmont), such as Beth-Shemesh, Tel Eton, and Tell Beit Mirsim, or Tell Dothan in Samaria, belong to the highlands or the lowlands? Are they a category of their own (e.g., Faust and Katz 2011)? To some extent, then, the highland/lowland dichotomy is an artificial construct. Certainly, highland settlements coexisted and interacted with lowland settlements. The question is what was the nature of that interaction? We shall return to this in the concluding section.

Settlement density is greater in the northern highland territories and significantly lower in the south. In the hill country of Samaria, north of Jerusalem, up until the Jezreel Valley, density is at its highest (Finkelstein 1988: 119–204; Zertal 2004; 2007; Zertal and Mirkam 2016). In the challenging Galilee highlands, it is somewhat lower (Frankel 1994). South of Jerusalem, the territory of Judah shows significantly fewer settlements in the Iron Age I (Ofer 1994). The northern highlands of Jordan (biblical Gilead) show a dense settlement array that parallels that of Samaria (Mittman 1970; Ji 1995; Herr 2012), as does Amon. Moab, above the east bank of the Dead Sea, has somewhat fewer Iron Age I settlements (Miller 1989; 1991; 1992; Routledge 2004; Herr 2012; Porter 2013), and surveys of arid Edom, furthest south, show very few (Bienkowski 1992; Herr 2012).

Settlement Morphology

The Iron Age I settlements of the southern Levantine highlands are generally small, averaging about 5–6 dunams (Finkelstein 1988: 30). But they also display a measure of hierarchical organization. Finkelstein has identified three (1988–1989: 146–51) or four (1995) size categories. There are no cities or even towns *per se* (Herzog 1997: 195–99), but a few settlements reached sizes as large as 10–12 dunams (Shiloh, Ai, Tell en-Naṣbeh?). One defining feature of the larger settlements is the residential neighborhood with houses that share common walls (e.g., Ai, Khirbet Raddana, Shiloh, 'Izbet Ṣarṭah Stratum III, Lehun). Such settlements could be characterized as villages. In a few cases, tripartite or quadripartite houses could be adjoined with their back rooms forming a sort of casemate enclosure (e.g., 'Izbet Ṣarṭah Stratum III, Ai,

Lehun). In the later part of the Iron Age I – the Iron Age IB – true defensive walls were erected, for example at Khirbet ed-Dawwara (Finkelstein 1990: fig. 22).

More settlements could be characterized as hamlets or homesteads, with stone fences or corrals and one to five architectural units occupying perhaps a dunam or two (e.g., Giloh, the Bull Site). More diminutive still is what appear to be ephemeral campsites of seasonal agriculturalists or pastoralists. These often give up only a handful of chronologically diagnostic sherds, or none at all. Finally, we must recall the special sites that may be of a religious nature and may have serviced the highland peoples as either local shrines or regional cult centers. Here, the question of group identity comes into play (see below).

BURIAL PRACTICES AND BELIEFS ABOUT DEATH

The most striking thing about tombs and burials in the Iron Age I is how few of them there are (Kletter 2002; Faust 2004). The few tombs containing Iron Age I burial goods either contain Late Bronze Age artifacts as well or are located in a Late Bronze Age cemetery (Bloch-Smith 2004). At Tell Dothan Tomb 1, for example, the Late Bronze Age practice of multiple successive burials in the cave tomb continued from Late Bronze Age perhaps even into the tenth century BCE (Cooley and Pratico 1995; Gregoricka and Sheridan 2017). However, there are no burial grounds associated with the hundreds of small settlements in the highlands. Raz Kletter (2002) has suggested that the lack of Iron Age I burials is the outcome of highland society's poverty, lack of elite social groups, and the period's brevity. Faust (2004) has countered that the burial lacuna is more specifically related to an ideology of egalitarianism and simplicity, in contrast to Bronze Age practices. It is worth noting that the lack of burial is not only characteristic of the highlands; the early Iron Age Philistine heartland displays a dearth of burial remains as well, as do, to a lesser degree, the "Canaanite" lowland sites.

Gloria London (2011) has hypothesized that extensive faunal remains and ritual equipment – standing stones, an altar, and possibly ritual ceramics – in a Late Bronze Age/Iron Age I complex at Tall al-'Umayri in the highlands of Jordan provide a unique example of ancestor veneration and perhaps a *marzeah* ceremony, possibly in association with a nearby Early Bronze Age dolmen. This may hint at mortuary ritual that was widely practiced but undetected by archaeologists, something worth looking for in future prospecting.

RITUAL BEHAVIOR AND RELIGIOUS BELIEF

Evidence for ritual behavior and religious belief in the highlands of the Iron Age I is not abundant. Bronze Age–style temples are conspicuously absent; the great temple of Shechem seems to have been desacralized (Campbell 1993: 1384). Ritual activity can be identified in two types of contexts: isolated ritual places and household assemblages.

Ritual Space

A unique isolated compound was excavated by Adam Zertal (1986–1987) on Mount Ebal and interpreted by him and others as an Israelite cult complex, one mentioned in the Bible (Deut 27:1–9; Josh 8:30–35). The complex is delineated by stone fences (inner and outer "tememos walls"). An early (Late Bronze Age IIB/III) phase includes two separate structures (one resembling a quadripartite house), pits, and a large round stone installation containing large quantities of ash and animal bones. The later (Iron Age IA) phase consisted of a rectangular 9 by 14 m stone structure built over the earlier circular installation. It was fronted by two chambers divided by a sloping wall; possibly a ramp leading up to the constructed "altar." The inner matrix of this structure contained large quantities of ash and animal bones, and it was covered by a stone pavement. Zertal interpreted this as Joshua's altar. Opinion is divided as to this interpretation, with some scholars assigning the complex a more prosaic function (e.g., Kempinski 1986), and others suggesting that it is cultic but not Israelite (Coogan 1987). It was abandoned in the Iron Age IA and covered by a stone cairn. While most scholars do attribute a ritual function to the Mount Ebal complex, several important questions remain: For example, was this a regional ritual center or just a local one? Can it be assigned to a particular identity group with any confidence?

Another isolated site assigned a ritual role is the Bull Site in Samaria (Mazar 1982). Its architecture is fragmentary – what may be a small enclosure containing what looks like a standing stone (the biblical *maṣṣevah*) and perhaps the remains of a stone-built altar. The only real evocative find was an intact bronze bull figurine (Mazar 1982: figs. 2, 3), which could be associated with a number of male deities: for example, El, Yahweh, Hadad, or Ba'al.

Highland settlements and houses also included "cult rooms" containing ritual objects. Ziony Zevit (2001: 153–6) discusses one of these at Ai, Area D, Locus 65/68. This room contained benches, a fenestrated stand resting upon one of them (see below) and several distinctive vessels at the base of a bench. Larry Herr and Douglas Clark (2009) and London (2011: 220) have described the contents of another intermural ritual structure at Tall al-'Umayri that included a *maṣṣevah*, an altar, and what is interpreted as the remains of ritual feasting. One of the questions here is whether the identified ritual rooms were, in fact, parts of complete structures that were sacred in their entirety, despite the lack of ostensibly ritual items in other chambers.

Iconography

If there is anything that unites Iron Age I ritual contexts, it is the presence of standing stones (*maṣṣevot*). They have been found at the Bull Site (see above) and Tall al-'Umayri (London 2011: 220) and also at lowlands sites, such as Tel Dan (Ilan 2018b) and Hazor (Ben-Ami and Ben-Tor 2012: 7–17). Many others have probably fallen or been integrated into later architecture and gone unidentified. They are almost always unmodified natural stones selected for their oblong shape. None of them shows any sign of painting or engraving – they seem to have been aniconic by design. The function of *maṣṣevot* is still open to interpretation; it is likely that they had multiple functions – commemoration of ancestors, markers of covenants or territory, and, most likely, a means of communicating with deities whereby they would be imbued with the numinous (Graesser 1974).

Aside from the bronze bull from the Bull Site (see above), a number of ceramic vessels and stands bearing reliefs of animals have been recovered from hill country sites – mainly horned ruminants but also lions, a leopard, and a horse (Finkelstein 1988: 287–91) – at Khirbet Raddana, Tell en-Naṣbeh, Mount Ebal, Shiloh, Bethel, 'Izbet Ṣarṭah, and Tell Dothan in Samaria and at Tel Qishyon and Tel Kedesh in the Galilee. A zoomorphic vessel was found at Khirbet ed-Dawwara (Finkelstein 1990: figs. 20, 21). Faunal representations of this kind also occur in the lowlands. Finkelstein suggests that such vessels and stands had a ritual function, particularly since several of these sites are cult centers in the Bible: Bethel, Mount Ebal, and Shiloh (Finkelstein 1988: 291). The question here is what did the faunal imagery mean, or do, in the context of highland peoples' lives and beliefs? Perhaps they are the animal attributes of deities, meant to invoke those deities' protection or efficacy.

The human image is conspicuously rare. The only hill country exceptions are a face on a jug from Bethel (Kelso 1968: pl. 44) and a human figure riding a cart on a seal from Shiloh (Brandl 1993: fig. 8.16). Most intriguing are appendages on a stand from Ai (Marquet-Krause 1949: pl. 64) (see Fig. 15.1:15). They have been called claws (Finkelstein 1988: 291), but they look more like feet. Here, too, one is inclined toward a numinous interpretation.

Given the infrequency of imagery in the Iron Age I highlands, and human imagery in particular, it is worth raising the possibility that some kind of image ban was in force, at least among part of the highland population.

HIGHLAND SOCIETY: AN ARCHAEOLOGICAL INTERPRETATION

Social Organization

The highland settlement hierarchy is an expression of social structure, economic organization, and political control. The basic social unit was the extended household – the Hebrew *beth 'av* (Stager 1985; Lederman 1999:

146–9; A. Faust, this volume). These small settlements dotted the hilltops and slopes of the highlands, often having fenced compounds. Larger settlements, such as Ai and Shiloh, were certainly control centers, probably of clan-based intergroup collectivities ("tribes"), with "Big Man" leadership (Johnson and Earle 2000: 203–80). These included several extended households and probably single men from other households undergoing various modes and processes of affiliation.

At a later stage, after the dissipation of Egyptian hegemony, one or more simple chiefdoms may have emerged. M. B. Rowton's (e.g., 1973; 1977) concept of the "dimorphic chiefdom" – one characterized by distinct sedentary and nomadic populations living in symbiosis – has been suggested (Finkelstein 1993). While this is certainly possible, it was not the dominant sociopolitical dynamic. The emergence of chiefdoms (and later a territorial state) occurred as an outcome of internecine competition and conflict (over territory and property) and external threat – posed by the lowland Philistine and "Canaanite" polities (e.g., Faust 2006: 228–30).

The Question of Cultural Identity (Ethnicity)

Many, perhaps most, recent studies of social life and political organization in the early Iron Age southern Levant place group identity (i.e., ethnicity) as the central theme (e.g., Finkelstein 1996; 1997; Killebrew 2005; Faust 2006; 2016; Yasur-Landau 2010; Kletter 2014; Maier and Hitchcock 2017). Faust, in particular, views the collared-rim pithos, the quadripartite house, and the pork taboo as ethnic indicators of Israelite identity. This writer disagrees as far as the Iron Age I is concerned, though, in the Iron Age II, the quadripartite house and the pork taboo probably did become cultural markers.

All human societies organize in identity groups and identify other, contradistinctive groups. It has been suggested that such identification, and the social boundaries that accompany it, are a survival mechanism and a means of gaining access to resources (e.g., Barth 1969; McGuire 1982; Lucy 2005). But how is group identification expressed in material culture? To what degree is archaeology able to discern group identification by means of material culture remains? How is ethnicity manipulated in political relations between groups?

Virtually all researchers agree that multiple ethnicities inhabited the highlands as well as the lowlands (cf. Killebrew's [2005] "mixed multitudes"). It is also consensus that these competing groups formed alliances when expedient. What is much less clear is how the fortunes of these groups developed – how some groups may have been exterminated, and how new identity groups were formed as either the spin-offs of old ones or by the conjoining of preexisting groups, all of which must have occurred. Regarding the Philistines on the southern coast, recent scholarship has described processes of acculturation, hybridization, and cultural entanglement (Yasur-Landau 2012; Maeir, Hitchcock, and Horwitz 2013; Maier and Hitchock 2017);[3] culture formation and group identity is a complex, messy, shape-shifting affair. The formation of highland culture and group identity would have been the same. And again, we must always be cognizant of the influence of the Hebrew Bible on ethnic group identification by modern scholars; the Bible describes multiple identity groups, variously as bystanders, allies, but most often as enemies, in an ethnocentric account of Israel's history and theology.

By the ninth century BCE, the territorial states of Israel, Judah, Moab, and Edom were ensconced in the highlands and beyond. However, the mechanism of transition from identity group to territorial state is still debated (e.g., Faust 2006; 2016; Finkelstein and Lipschits 2011; Sapir-Hen, Meiri, and Finkelstein 2015).

Economy

Highland economies were clearly mixed and based primarily on field crops and pastoralism (e.g., Hopkins 1985; Rosen 1994). Different regions emphasized different branches depending on local conditions. Pastoralism was practiced everywhere, mainly in the form of transhumance, though nomadic pastoralism may have existed, especially if introduced from the more arid frontiers to the east and south (Alt 1966: 160–6; Zertal 1994: 66–9), but the evidence for this is rather weak.

The prevalence of sheep and goat in the faunal assemblages analyzed from sites, such as Sasa, Horvat Avot, Shiloh, and Tall al-'Umayri, suggests highly developed dairy, meat, and textile production (Hellwing and Adjeman 1986; Hellwing, Sade, and Kishon 1993; Horwitz 1996). Regarding textiles, it is odd that almost no loom weights have been documented from these or other highland sites. In discussing textile manufacture at Iron Age I Beth Shean, Assaf Yasur-Landau (2007) has raised the possibility that the flat Egyptian loom, anchored to the floor, was used because it required no loom weights. This explanation would also fit the situation in the highlands.

Bovids (cattle) are also indicated in highland faunal assemblages. While this speaks to dairy, meat, and hide production, it is equally important as an indication of plow agriculture. In western Asia, cows and oxen generally mean sedentary lifeways and long-term field cultivation. The fact that all the larger faunal samples include both large and small ruminants testifies to mixed husbandry, at least at all the larger sites. Many of the smaller fenced/corralled sites may represent short-range, short-term transhumance, emanating from villages.

Pork is virtually absent from the faunal collections of the highlands (as summarized in Faust 2006: 35 and Sapir-Hen et al. 2013: table 1), suggesting a pork taboo. The origins of this taboo are beyond the scope of this short synopsis, but suffice to say that several explanations for it have been offered. Pigs were never favored in western Asian husbandry – they were deemed more trouble than they were worth. While easy to raise and a good source of protein, they can quickly destroy field crops. Moreover, pigs provide only meat and no secondary products (Hesse and Wapnish 1997). Faust (2006: 35–40), among others, feels that the pork taboo was more of a way to assert group identity (read Israelites) against the Philistines, who favored pork (see A. M. Maeir, this volume). Both factors, in tandem, are probably valid.

The numerous silos in highland sites suggest that wheat and barley were the most important subsistence crops (Rosen 1994: 342–3). They would have been cultivated mainly in the valley bottoms and the eastern arid margins of the central highlands and those of central Jordan. No installations for the pressing of grapes and olives have been identified with certainty as dating to the Iron Age I. Moreover, there is very little evidence for large-scale terrace construction in the Iron Age I. Thus, horticulture does not seem to have been important yet (Finkelstein 1988–9: 149; Rosen 1994: 345–6). In fact, the large numbers of pithoi may be partly explained by the need to store oil and wine imported from the lowlands.

It is likely that subsistence and cash cropping strategies evolved in varying trajectories, among the different highland population groups, from the thirteenth through the tenth centuries BCE. Subsistence agriculture, pastoralism, and a domestic mode of production dominated at first. Over time, as settlement expanded and security increased, surpluses became possible and cash crop (olive, grape) cultivation ensued. Olive and grape cultivation requires a long-term investment of time and labor, and conditions of security. Security would have been optimally maintained by agreements and alliances between different settlements, clans, and tribes. As a byproduct, security pacts would have been accompanied by cooperative exchange agreements, strengthening alliances.

SUMMARY AND CONCLUSIONS

Here, we must address the questions posed at the beginning of the chapter: What initiated the surge of small settlements in the highlands? What were the settlers' origins and cultural identities? How did they relate to the lowland peoples and their towns? How did the settlers' social and political organization and their alliances change over time? A number of hypotheses have been put forth to explain the highland settlement phenomenon over the last century or so; these have been summarized in previous treatments (e.g., Finkelstein 1988: 293–319; Killebrew 2005: 181–5; Faust 2006: 170–87; Bloch-Smith and Alpert Nahkai 1999), and they will not be reexamined here, yet again. In this writer's view, Egyptian imperial strategy was the critical factor in the initial establishment of the settlement phenomenon. In any event, the evolution of highland settlement must be evaluated against the background of Egyptian collapse.

There is no doubt that the first settlements were established in the thirteenth or early twelfth century BCE when Egypt still maintained a network of garrisons and administrative centers in the lowlands. This is also when collared-rim pithoi first appear at a number of sites in the valleys, along the coast, and in the highlands (Artzy 1994; Raban 2001; Killebrew 2005: 177, n. 74).

It is quite clear that foreigners served the Egyptian crown, alongside Egyptians, in the empire's garrisons and administrative centers (Redford 1992: 207, 225–6). We also know, from the Harris Papyrus and other late Ramesside letters, that the Egyptians settled foreigners in "strongholds" in the twelfth century BCE (Redford 1992: 289, with references). It is likely that Egypt practiced a policy similar to that of Rome 1,000 years later – foreign soldiers and functionaries, by now married to local women with families, were encouraged at the end of their service to establish farmsteads in the problematic frontier zones. The purpose of this was twofold: (a) the settlers were to comprise a paramilitary presence and eyes and ears in a hostile environment; and (b) the settlers would develop this hinterland's agropastoral potential. One imagines that these settlers were also encouraged to foster good relations with local clans and tribes by using the carrot-and-stick approach. It was a risky enterprise, but the archaeological evidence suggests that, at least at first, it met with some success.

These settlers were given start-up assistance for the first few years. The collared-rim pithoi are one expression of this assistance and the settlements' connection to the Egyptian-controlled economy. As explicated above, collared-rim pithoi were introduced initially by the Egyptian administration in a standardized form having a fixed volume (Wengrow 1996; Raban 2001), perhaps based on Middle Bronze Age prototypes (Finkelstein 1988: 283–4). At first, they were multi-purpose containers for both provisions (water, wine, oil, seed grain) and agrarian production (grain); however, perhaps in the later Iron Age I, they began to be used systematically as containers for larger volumes of locally produced oil and wine.

In the mid-twelfth century BCE, during the 20th Dynasty, the Egyptian political system experienced a major upheaval, brought on by low Nile floods and political conflict between the entrenched and powerful Amun priesthood and the monarchy, and between rival heirs to Ramesses III, who was assassinated (Redford 2002). The Egyptians relinquished control of their province in Canaan at this time; the last royal inscription found in the southern Levant from the 20th Dynasty dates to Ramesses VI (Weinstein 1992). Local rebellion was probably part of the reason for the cessation of Egyptian rule. If Egypt could no longer offer protection or a secure market for agrarian produce, people would have had no reason to pay taxes, even those settlers whose parents or grandparents had served the Egyptian crown.

How did the Egyptian withdrawal affect local population groups? Probably in only negligible ways. Clans and tribal groups ("Big Man" collectivities) had already come to the conclusion that they had to make their own way by creating alliances. Exchange with neighboring collectivities and lowland polities continued and perhaps intensified with the Egyptians gone. But, the Egyptians' departure meant that localized conflict was more likely to flare up against the background of competition for resources and markets, especially at a time when the climate had become warmer, precipitation had declined (Langgut, Finkelstein, and Litt 2013; Kaniewski et al. 2013a; Kaniewski, Guiot, and Van Campo 2015), and immigration from foreign lands was a fact to be reckoned with (Yasur-Landau 2010; Cline 2014: 154–60), even in the highlands.

Out of this ongoing conflict emerged the territorial states of the Iron Age II – Aram, Edom, Israel, Judah, Moab, and others (see A. Faust, this volume; and D. M. Master, this volume). These were the solution to both localized confrontations, which would now be adjudicated by the central government, and external threats by belligerent states or tribes. Of course, territorial states ("kingdoms") came with problems of their own, but this is a topic beyond the purview of this chapter.

Iron Age I Settlement and the Hebrew Bible

One of the cardinal questions faced by researchers of the early Iron Age in the southern Levant is how to relate it to the Hebrew Bible; after all, more than 100 years of biblical and archaeological study emanated from questions raised by biblical studies. It has long been clear that the biblical text was a project intended to forward a theological and political agenda (initially that of the Davidic dynasty and the Jerusalem temple's priesthood), which was compiled and edited over hundreds of years, perhaps beginning in the eighth century BCE (e.g., Coogan 2014: 3–12, 178–85). The closer the events portrayed were to the date of the text's compilation, the more they tend to be confirmed by archaeological and extra-biblical sources (Grabbe 2007: 35–6). Events portrayed putatively dating to long before the actual compilation are much more problematic; they tend to have weak or little confirmation from outside sources. Given these caveats, does the biblical narrative have *anything* to say about the historical reality of the highlands in the Iron Age I?

While impossible to be certain, the books of Judges, Samuel, and, to a lesser extent, Joshua would seem to preserve memories of fragmented "Big Man" societies, shifting alliances, multiple group identities, and charismatic leadership.

Some biblical verses may preserve evidence of Egyptian rule; for example, the place called Me Nephtoach (Josh 15:9, 18:15) likely derives its name from the "Wells of Merenptah" (Merenptah being a 19th Dynasty pharaoh), located in the hill country and mentioned in the Papyrus Anastasi III (Aharoni 1979: 184; Rendsburg 1981). In Judg 6:9, just before Gideon is appointed to lead the Israelites against the Midianites, a prophet brings a reminder from God: "I delivered you out of the hand of the Egyptians, and out of the hand of all that oppressed you, and drove them out from before you, and gave you their land."

While these possible echoes are intriguing, in the final analysis, the biblical text – being a much later, tendentious composition – is of little use in reconstructing the historical *realia* of the Iron Age I southern Levant. If anything, it is the archaeology that informs and illuminates a deconstructive analysis of the text.

NOTES

1 For a somewhat earlier, mid-tenth-century BCE dating, see Mazar and Bronk Ramsey 2008.
2 For a roster of these, see Finkelstein 1988: 34–118.
3 For a similar scenario in the Beersheva Valley, see Herzog 1994: 146–8.

REFERENCES

Aharoni, Y. 1979. *The Land of the Bible: A Historical Geography*. 2nd rev. and enl. ed. Philadelphia: Westminster.
Alt, A. 1966. *Essays on Old Testament History and Religion*. Trans. R. A. Wilson, from German. Oxford: Blackwell.
Artzy, M. 1994. Incense Camels and Collared Rim Jars: Desert Trade Routes and Maritime Outlets in the Second Millennium. *OJA* 13: 121–47.
Asscher, Y.; Lehmann, G.; Rosen, S. A.; Weiner, S.; and Boaretto, E. 2015. Absolute Dating of the Late Bronze to Iron Age Transition and the Appearance of Philistine Culture in Qubur el-Waladayah, Southern Levant. *Radiocarbon* 57: 77–97.
Avner, U. 2014. Egyptian Timna – Reconsidered. In *Unearthing the Wilderness: Studies on the History and Archaeology of the Negev and Edom in the Iron Age*, ed. J. M. Tebes, 103–62. ANESSup 45. Leuven: Peeters.
Barth, F. 1969. Introduction. In *Ethnic Groups and Boundaries*, ed. F. Barth, 9–37. Boston: Little, Brown.
Ben-Ami, D., and Ben-Tor, A. 2012. The Iron Age I (Stratum "XII/XI"): Stratigraphy and Pottery. In *Hazor VI: The 1990–2009 Excavations; The Iron Age*, ed. A. Ben-Tor, D. Ben-Ami, and D. Sandhaus, 7–51. Jerusalem: IES.
Ben-Dov, R. 2011. *Dan III: Avraham Biran Excavations, 1966–1999; The Late Bronze Age Levels*. HUCA 9. Jerusalem: Hebrew Union College–Jewish Institute of Religion.
Bienkowski, P. 1992. *Early Edom and Moab: The Beginning of the Iron Age in Southern Jordan*. SAM 7. Sheffield: Collins.

Bietak, M. 1992. An Iron Age Four-Room House in Ramesside Egypt. *ErIsr* 23: 10*–12*.

Bloch-Smith, E. 2004. Resurrecting the Iron I Dead. *IEJ* 54: 77–91.

Bloch-Smith, E., and Alpert Nakhai, B. 1999. A Landscape Comes to Life: The Iron I Period. *NEA* 62: 62–92, 101–27.

Boaretto, E.; Jull, A. J. T.; Gilboa, A.; and Sharon, I. 2005. Dating the Iron Age I/II Transition in Israel: First Intercomparison Results. *Radiocarbon* 47: 39–55.

Brandl, B. 1986–7. Two Scarabs and a Trapezoidal Seal from Mount Ebal. *TA* 13–14: 166–72.

——— 1993. Scarabs and Other Glyptic Finds. In *Shiloh: The Archaeology of a Biblical Site*, ed. I. Finkelstein, S. Bunimovitz, and Z. Lederman, 203–22. MSSMNIA 10. Tel Aviv: Tel Aviv University.

Bruins, H. J.; van der Plicht, J.; Ilan, D.; and Werker, E. 2005. Iron-Age ^{14}C Dates from Tel Dan: A High Chronology. In *The Bible and Radiocarbon Dating: Archaeology, Text and Science*, ed. T. E. Levy and T. F. G. Higham, 323–36. London: Equinox.

Bunimovitz, S. 1995. On the Edge of Empires – Late Bronze Age (1500–1200 BCE). In *The Archaeology of Society of the Holy Land*, ed. T. E. Levy, 320–31. NAAA. London: Leicester University Press.

Burke, A. A.; Peilstöcker, M.; Karoll, A.; Pierce, G. A.; Kowalski, K.; Ben-Marzouk, N.; Damm, J. C.; Danielson, A. J.; Fessler, H. D.; Kaufman, B.; Pierce, K. V. L.; Höflmayer, F.; Damiata, B. N.; and Dee, M. 2017. Excavations of the New Kingdom Fortress in Jaffa, 2011–2014: Traces of Resistance to Egyptian Rule in Canaan. *AJA* 121: 85–133.

Campbell, E. F. 1993. Shechem. *NEAEHL* 4: 1345–54.

Cline, E. H. 2014. *1177 B.C.: The Year Civilization Collapsed*. TPAH. Princeton: Princeton University Press.

Coogan, M. D. 1987. Of Cults and Cultures: Reflections on the Interpretations of Archaeological Evidence. *PEQ* 119: 1–8.

——— 2014. *The Old Testament: A Historical and Literary Introduction to the Hebrew Scriptures*. 3rd ed. New York: Oxford University Press.

Cooley, R. E., and Pratico, G. D. 1995. Tell Dothan: The Western Cemetery, with Comments on Joseph Free's Excavations, 1953 to 1964. In *Preliminary Excavation Reports: Sardis, Bir Umm Fawakhir, Tell el-'Umeiri, the Combined Caesarea Expeditions, and Tell Dothan*, ed. W. G. Dever, 147–90. AASOR 52. Boston: ASOR.

Dever, W. G. 1994. From Tribe to Nation: State Formation Processes in Ancient Israel. In *Nuove fondazioni nel Vicino Oriente antico: Realtà e ideologia; Atti del colloquio 4–6 dicembre 1991, Dipartimento di Scienze Storiche del Mondo Antico, Sezione di Egittologia e Scienze Storiche del Vicino Oriente, Università degli Studi di Pisa*, ed. S. Mazzoni, 213–29. Seminari di orientalistica 4. Pisa: Giardini.

Eggler, J., and Keel, O. 2006. *Corpus der Siegel-Amulette aus Jordanien vom Neolithikum bis zur Perserzeit*. OBO 25. Fribourg: Academic; Göttingen: Vandenhoeck & Ruprecht.

Faust, A. 2004. "Mortuary Practices, Society and Ideology": The Lack of Iron Age I Burials in the Highlands in Context. *IEJ* 54: 174–90.

——— 2006. *Israel's Ethnogenesis: Settlement, Interaction, Expansion and Resistance*. AAA. London: Equinox.

——— 2016. The Emergence of Israel and Theories of Ethnogenesis. In *The Wiley Blackwell Companion to Ancient Israel*, ed. S. Niditch, 155–73. Chichester: Wiley Blackwell.

Faust, A., and Bunimovitz, S. 2003. The Four Room House: Embodying Iron Age Israelite Society. *NEA* 66: 22–31.

Faust, A., and Katz, H. 2011. Philistines, Israelites and Canaanites in the Southern Trough Valley during the Iron Age I. *Egypt and the Levant* 21: 231–47.

Finkelstein, I. 1986. *'Izbet Ṣarṭah: An Early Iron Age Site near Rosh Ha'ayin, Israel.* BAR International Series 299. Oxford: BAR.

1988. *The Archaeology of the Israelite Settlement.* Jerusalem: IES.

1988–1989. The Land of Ephraim Survey, 1980–1987: Preliminary Report. *TA* 15–16: 117–83.

1990. Excavations at Khirbet ed-Dawwara: An Iron Age Site Northeast of Jerusalem. *TA* 17: 163–208.

1993. The Sociopolitical Organization of the Central Hill Country in the Second Millennium B.C.E. In *Biblical Archaeology Today 1990: Proceedings of the Second International Congress on Biblical Archaeology, Supplement: Pre-Congress Symposium; Population, Production and Power, Jerusalem, June 1990*, ed. A. Biran and J. Aviram, 110–31. Jerusalem: IES.

1995. The Great Transformation: The "Conquest" of the Highlands Frontiers and the Rise of the Territorial States. In *The Archaeology of Society in the Holy Land*, ed. T. E. Levy, 349–65. NAAA. London: Leicester University Press.

1996. Ethnicity and the Origin of the Iron I Settlers in the Highlands of Canaan: Can the Real Israel Stand Up? *BA* 59: 198–212.

1997. Pots and People Revisited: Ethnic Boundaries in the Iron Age I. In *The Archaeology of Israel: Constructing the Past, Interpreting the Present*, ed. N. A. Silberman and D. Small, 216–37. JSOTSup 237. Sheffield: Sheffield Academic.

Finkelstein, I., and Lipschits, O. 2011. The Genesis of Moab: A Proposal. *Levant* 43: 139–52.

Finkelstein, I., and Piasetzky, E. 2006. The Iron I–IIA in the Highlands and Beyond: ^{14}C Anchors, Pottery Phases and the Shoshenq I Campaign. *Levant* 38: 45–61.

2009. Radiocarbon-Dated Destruction Layers: A Skeleton for Iron Age Chronology in the Levant. *OJA* 28: 255–74.

2011. The Iron Age Chronology Debate: Is the Gap Narrowing? *NEA* 74: 50–4.

Frankel, R. 1994. Upper Galilee in the Late Bronze–Iron I Transition. In *From Nomadism to Monarchy: Archaeological and Historical Aspects of Early Israel*, ed. I. Finkelstein and N. Na'aman, 18–34. Jerusalem: Yad Izhak Ben-Zvi; IES; Washington, DC: Biblical Archaeology Society.

Friedman, E. 1993. Flint Tools. In *Shiloh: The Archaeology of a Biblical Site*, ed. I. Finkelstein, S. Bunimovitz, and Z. Lederman, 197–202. MSSMNIA 10. Tel Aviv: Tel Aviv University.

Fritz, V. 1977. Bestimmung und Herkunft des Pfeilerhauses in Israel. *ZDPV* 93: 30–45.

Giveon, R. 1986. An Egyptian Scarab of the 20th Dynasty. In *'Izbet Ṣarṭah: An Early Iron Age Site near Rosh Ha'ayin, Israel*, ed. I. Finkelstein, 104–5. BAR International Series 299. Oxford: BAR.

Grabbe, L. L. 2007. *Ancient Israel: What Do We Know and How Do We Know It?* London: T & T Clark.

Graesser, C. F. 1974. Standing Stones in Ancient Palestine. *BA* 35: 34–65.

Gregoricka, L. A., and Sheridan, S. G. 2017. Continuity or Conquest? A Multi-Isotope Approach to Investigating Identity in the Early Iron Age of the Southern Levant. *AJPA* 162: 73–89.

Hellwing, S., and Adjeman, Y. 1986 Animal Bones. In *'Izbet Ṣarṭah: An Early Iron Age Site near Rosh Ha'ayin, Israel*, ed. I. Finkelstein, 141–52. BAR International Series 299. Oxford: BAR.

Hellwing, S.; Sade, M.; and Kishon, V. 1993. Faunal Remains. In *Shiloh: The Archaeology of a Biblical Site*, ed. I. Finkelstein, S. Bunimovitz, and Z. Lederman, 309–50. MSSMNIA 10. Tel Aviv: Tel Aviv University.

Herr, L. G. 2012. Jordan in the Iron I and IIA Periods. In *The Ancient Near East in the 12th–10th Centuries BCE: Culture and History; Proceedings of the International Conference Held at the University of Haifa, 2–5 May, 2010*, ed. G. Galil, A. Gilboa, A. M. Maeir, and D. Kahn, 207–20. AOAT 392. Münster: Ugarit-Verlag.

Herr, L. G., and Clark, D. R. 2009. From the Stone Age to the Middle Ages in Jordan: Digging up Tall al-'Umayri. *NEA* 72: 68–97.

Herzog, Z. 1994. From Nomadism to Monarchy in the Beer-Sheba Valley. In *From Nomadism to Monarchy: Archaeological and Historical Aspects of Early Israel*, ed. I. Finkelstein and N. Na'aman, 122–49. Jerusalem: Yad Izhak Ben-Zvi; IES; Washington, DC: Biblical Archaeology Society.

———. 1997. *The Archaeology of the City: Urban Planning in Ancient Israel and Its Social Implications*. MSSMNIA 13. Tel Aviv: Emery and Claire Yass Archaeology Press.

Hesse, B., and Wapnish, P. 1997. Can Pig Remains Be Used for Ethnic Diagnosis in the Ancient Near East? In *The Archaeology of Israel: Constructing the Past, Interpreting the Present*, ed. N. A. Silberman and D. Small, 238–70. JSOTSup 237. Sheffield: Sheffield Academic.

Holladay, J. S., Jr. 1992. House, Israelite. *ABD* 3: 308–18.

Homès-Frederique, D. 1997. *Découvrez Lehun et la Voie Royale: Les fouilles belges en Jordanie; À l'occasion d'une exposition organisée par la Comité Belge de Fouilles en Jordanie et les Musée Royaux d'Art et d'Histoire*. Brussels: Comité Belge de Fouilles en Jordanie.

Hopkins, D. C. 1985. *The Highlands of Canaan: Agricultural Life in the Early Iron Age*. Social World of Biblical Antiquity Series 3. Sheffield: Almond.

Horwitz, L. K. 1996. Fauna from Tel Sasa, 1980. *'Atiqot* 28: 59–62.

Ilan, D. 2008. The Socioeconomic Implications of Grain Storage in Early Iron Age Canaan: The Case of Tel Dan. In *Bene Israel: Studies in the Archaeology of Israel and the Levant during the Bronze and Iron Ages Offered in Honour of Israel Finkelstein*, ed. A. Fantalkin and A. Yasur-Landau, 87–104. CHANE 31. Leiden: Brill.

———. 2016. The Crescent-Lunate Motif in the Jewelry of the Bronze and Iron Ages in the Ancient Near East. In *Proceedings of the 9th International Congress of the Archaeology of the Ancient Near East (ICAANE), 9–13 June 2014, Basel*, Vol. 1: *Travelling Images – Transfer and Transformation of Visual Ideas*, ed. O. Kaelin, 137–50. Wiesbaden: Harrassowitz.

———. 2018a. The Scale Weights. In *Dan I: The Early Iron Age Levels*, ed. D. Ilan, 461–74. HUCA 11. Jerusalem: Hebrew Union College–Jewish Institute of Religion.

———. 2018b. The Stratigraphy and Architecture. In *Dan I: The Early Iron Age Levels*, ed. D. Ilan, 17–94. HUCA 11. Jerusalem: Hebrew Union College–Jewish Institute of Religion.

———. 2018c. The Metal Objects. In *Dan I: The Early Iron Age Levels*, ed. D. Ilan, 507–40. HUCA 11. Jerusalem: Hebrew Union College–Jewish Institute of Religion.

Ji, C.-H. C. 1995. Iron Age I in Central and Northern Transjordan: An Interim Summary of the Archaeological Data. *PEQ* 127: 122–40.

Johnson, A. W., and Earle, T. 2000. *The Evolution of Human Societies: From Foraging Group to Agrarian State*. 2nd ed. Stanford, CA: Stanford University Press.

Kaniewski, D.; Guiot, J.; and Van Campo, E. 2015. Drought and Societal Collapse 3200 Years Ago in the Eastern Mediterranean: A Review. *WIREs: Climate Change* 6: 369–82.

Kaniewski, D.; Van Campo, E.; Guiot, J.; Le Burel, S.; Otto, T.; and Baeteman, C. 2013a. Environmental Roots of the Late Bronze Age Crisis. *PLOS ONE* 8 (8): e71004. https://doi.org/10.1371/journal.pone.0071004 (accessed August 1, 2017).

Kaniewski, D.; Van Campo, E.; Morhange, C.; Guiot, J.; Zviely, D.; Shaked, I.; Otto, T.; and Artzy, M. 2013b. Early Urban Impact on Mediterranean Coastal Environments. *Scientific Reports* 3. www.nature.com/articles/srep03540 (accessed August 1, 2017).

Keel, O. 1990. Früheisenzeitliche Glyptik in Palästina/Israel. In *Studien zu den Stempelsiegeln aus Palästina/Israel*, Vol. 3: *Die frühe Eisenzeit*, ed. O. Keel, M. Shuval, and C. Uehlinger, 331–421. OBO 100. Fribourg: Universitäts-Verlag.

Kelso, J. L. 1968. *The Excavation of Bethel (1934–1960): (Joint Expedition of the Pittsburgh Theological Seminary and the American School of Oriental Research in Jerusalem)*. AASOR 39. Boston: ASOR.

Kempinski, A. 1978. Tel Masos: Its Importance in Relation to the Settlement of the Tribes of Israel in the Northern Negev. *Expedition* 20 (4): 29–37.

———. 1986. Joshua's Altar – An Iron Age I Watchtower. *BAR* 12 (1): 42.

Killebrew, A. E. 2001. The Collared Pithos in Context: A Typological, Technological, and Function Reassessment. In *Studies in the Archaeology of Israel and Neighboring Lands in Memory of Douglas L. Esse*, ed. S. R. Wolff, 377–98. SAOC 59; ASOR Books 5. Chicago: The Oriental Institute of The University of Chicago; Atlanta: ASOR.

———. 2005. *Biblical Peoples and Ethnicity: An Archaeological Study of Egyptians, Canaanites, Philistines, and Early Israel, 1300–1100 B.C.E*. ABS 9. Atlanta: SBL.

Kletter, R. 2002. People without Burials? The Lack of Iron I Burials in the Central Highlands of Palestine. *IEJ* 52: 28–48.

———. 2014. In the Footsteps of Bagira: Ethnicity, Archaeology, and "Iron Age I Ethnic Israel." *Approaching Religion* 4 (2): 2–15.

Langgut, D.; Finkelstein, I.; and Litt, T. 2013. Climate and the Late Bronze Collapse: New Evidence from the Southern Levant. *TA* 40: 149–75.

Langgut, D.; Finkelstein, I.; Litt, T.; Neumann, F. H.; and Stein, M. 2015. Vegetation and Climate Changes during the Bronze and Iron Ages (~3600–600 BCE) in the Southern Levant Based on Palynological Records. *Radiocarbon* 57: 217–35.

Lederman, Z. 1999. *An Early Iron Age Village at Khirbet Raddana: The Excavations of Joseph A. Callaway*. PhD diss., Harvard University.

London, G. 2011. A Ceremonial Center for the Living and the Dead. *NEA* 74: 216–25.

Lucy, S. 2005. Ethnic and Cultural Identities. In *The Archaeology of Identity: Approaches to Gender, Age, Status, Ethnicity and Religion*, ed. M. Diaz-Andreu, S. Lucy, S. Babić, and D. N. Edwards, 86–109. London: Routledge.

Maeir, A. M., and Hitchcock, L. A. 2017. The Appearance, Formation and Transformation of Philistine Culture: New Perspectives and New Finds. In *"Sea Peoples" Up-to-Date: New Research on Transformation in the Eastern Mediterranean in the 13th–11th Centuries BCE; Proceedings of the ESF-Workshop Held at the Austrian Academy of Sciences, Vienna, 3–4 November 2014*, ed. P. M. Fischer and T. Bürge, 149–62. DG 81; CCEM 35. Vienna: Austrian Academy of Sciences.

Maeir, A. M.; Hitchcock, L. A.; and Horwitz, L. K. 2013. On the Constitution and Transformation of Philistine Identity. *OJA* 32: 1–38.

Manning, S. W. 2006–7. Why Radiocarbon Dating 1200 BCE Is Difficult: A Sidelight on Dating the End of the Late Bronze Age and the Contrarian Contribution. *Scripta Mediterranea* 27–28: 53–80.

Marquet-Krause, J. 1949. *Les fouilles de 'Ay (et-Tell), 1933–1935: Entreprises par le Baron Edmond de Rothschild, membre de l'Institut; La résurrection d'une grand cité biblique.* BAH 45. Paris: Geuthner.

Mazar, A. 1981. Giloh: An Early Israelite Settlement Site near Jerusalem. *IEJ* 31: 1–36.

——— 1982. The "Bull Site" – An Iron Age I Open Cult Place. *BASOR* 247: 27–42.

——— 1992. The Iron Age I. In *The Archaeology of Israel*, ed. A. Ben-Tor, 258–301. New Haven, CT: Yale University Press; Tel Aviv: Open University of Israel.

——— 2009. Introduction and Overview. In *Excavations at Tel Beth-Shean, 1989–1996*, Vol. 3: *The 13th–11th Century BCE Strata in Areas N and S*, ed. N. Panitz-Cohen and A. Mazar, 1–32. BSVAP 3. Jerusalem: IES; The Institute of Archaeology, The Hebrew University of Jerusalem.

——— 2015. Iron Age I: Northern Coastal Plain, Galilee, Samaria, Jezreel Valley, Judah, and Negev. In *The Ancient Pottery of Israel and Its Neighbors from the Iron Age through the Hellenistic Period*, Vol. 1, ed. S. Gitin, 5–70. Jerusalem: IES.

Mazar, A., and Bronk Ramsey, C. 2008. ^{14}C Dates and the Iron Age Chronology of Israel: A Response. *Radiocarbon* 50: 159–80.

Mazar, A.; Bruins, H. J.; Panitz-Cohen, N.; and van der Plicht, J. 2005. Ladder of Time at Tel Reḥov: Stratigraphy, Archaeological Context, Pottery and Radiocarbon Dates. In *The Bible and Radiocarbon Dating: Archaeology, Text and Science*, ed. T. E. Levy and T. F. G. Higham, 193–255. London: Continuum.

McGuire, R. H. 1982. The Study of Ethnicity in Historical Archaeology. *JAA* 1: 159–78.

Miller, J. M. 1989. Moab and the Moabites. In *Studies in the Mesha Inscription and Moab*, ed. J. A. Dearman, 1–40. ABS 2. Atlanta: Scholars.

——— 1991. *Archaeological Survey of the Kerak Plateau: Conducted during 1978–1982 under the Direction of J. Maxwell Miller and Jack M. Pinkerton.* ASORAR 1. Atlanta: Scholars.

——— 1992. Early Monarchy in Moab? In *Early Edom and Moab: The Beginning of the Iron Age in Southern Jordan*, ed. P. Bienkowski, 77–92. SAM 7. Sheffield: Collins.

Mittman, S. 1970. *Beiträge zur Siedlungs- und Territorialgeschichte des nördlichen Ostjordanlandes.* ADPV 2. Wiesbaden: Harrassowitz.

Moeller, N. 2016. House Layouts in the Middle Kingdom. In *The Archaeology of Urbanism in Ancient Egypt from the Predynastic Period to the End of the Middle Kingdom*, ed. N. Moeller, 343–75. Cambridge: Cambridge University Press.

Ofer, A. 1994. "All the Hill Country of Judah": From Nomadism to Monarchy. In *From Nomadism to Monarchy: Archaeological and Historical Aspects of Early Israel*, ed. I. Finkelstein and N. Na'aman, 92–121. Jerusalem: Yad Izhak Ben-Zvi; IES; Washington, DC: Biblical Archaeology Society.

Porter, B. W. 2013. *Complex Communities: The Archaeology of Early Iron Age West–Central Jordan.* Tucson: The University of Arizona Press.

Raban, A. 2001. Standardized Collared-Rim Pithoi and Short-Lived Settlements. In *Studies in the Archaeology of Israel and Neighboring Lands in Memory of Douglas L. Esse*, ed. S. R. Wolff, 493–518. SAOC 59; ASOR Books 5. Chicago: The Oriental Institute of The University of Chicago; Atlanta: ASOR.

Redford, D. B. 1992. *Egypt, Canaan, and Israel in Ancient Times.* Princeton: Princeton University Press.

Redford, S. 2002. *The Harem Conspiracy: The Murder of Ramesses III.* DeKalb: Northern Illinois University Press.

Rendsburg, G. A. 1981. Merneptah in Canaan. *JSSEA* 11: 171–2.

Rosen, B. 1994. Subsistence Economy in the Iron Age I. In *From Nomadism to Monarchy: Archaeological and Historical Aspects of Early Israel*, ed. I. Finkelstein and N. Na'aman, 339–51. Jerusalem: Yad Izhak Ben-Zvi; IES; Washington, DC: Biblical Archaeology Society.

Rosen, S. A. 1997. *Lithics after the Stone Age: A Handbook of Stone Tools from the Levant*. Walnut Creek, CA: AltaMira.

Routledge, B. 2004. *Moab in the Iron Age: Hegemony, Polity, Archaeology*. Archaeology, Culture, and Society. Philadelphia: University of Pennsylvania Press.

Rowton, M. B. 1973. Autonomy and Nomadism in Western Asia. *Orientalia* 42: 247–58.

―― 1977. Dimorphic Structure and the Parasocial Element. *JNES* 36: 181–98.

Sapir-Hen, L.; Bar-Oz, G.; Gadot, Y.; and Finkelstein, I. 2013. Pig Husbandry in Iron Age Israel and Judah: New Insights Regarding the Origin of the "Taboo." *ZDPV* 129: 1–20.

Sapir-Hen, L.; Meiri, M.; and Finkelstein, I. 2015. Iron Age Pigs: New Evidence on Their Origin and Role in Forming Identity Boundaries. *Radiocarbon* 57: 307–15.

Sharon, I.; Gilboa, A.; Jull, A. J. T.; and Boaretto, E. 2007. Report on the First Stage of the Iron Age Dating Project in Israel: Supporting a Low Chronology. *Radiocarbon* 49: 1–46.

Shiloh, Y. 1970. The Four-Room House: Its Situation and Function in the Israelite City. *IEJ* 20: 180–90.

Stager, L. E. 1985. The Archaeology of the Family in Ancient Israel. *BASOR* 260: 1–35.

Toffolo, M. B.; Arie, E.; Martin, M. A. S.; Boaretto, E.; and Finkelstein, I. 2014. Absolute Chronology of Megiddo, Israel, in the Late Bronze and Iron Ages: High-Resolution Radiocarbon Dating. *Radiocarbon* 56: 221–44.

Ullinger, J. M.; Sheridan, S. G.; Hawkey, D. E.; Turner, C. G., II; and Cooley, R. 2005. Bioarchaeological Analysis of Cultural Transition in the Southern Levant Using Dental Nonmetric Traits. *AJPA* 128: 466–76.

Ussishkin, D. 1985. Level [sic] VII and VI at Tel Lachish and the End of the Late Bronze Age in Canaan. In *Palestine in the Bronze and Iron Ages: Papers in Honour of Olga Tufnell*, ed. J. N. Tubb, 213–30. London: Institute of Archaeology.

―― 1995. The Destruction of Megiddo at the End of the Late Bronze Age and Its Historical Significance. *TA* 22: 240–67.

Weinstein, J. M. 1992. The Collapse of the Egyptian Empire in the Southern Levant. In *The Crisis Years: The 12th Century B.C. from Beyond the Danube to the Tigris*, ed. W. A. Ward and M. S. Joukowsky, 142–50. Dubuque, IA: Kendall/Hunt.

Wengrow, D. 1996. Egyptian Taskmasters and Heavy Burdens: Highland Exploitation and the Collared-Rim Pithos of the Bronze/Iron Age Levant. *OJA* 15: 307–26.

Yahalom-Mack, N. 2009. *Bronze in the Beginning of the Iron Age in the Land of Israel: Production and Utilization in a Diverse Ethno-Political Setting*. PhD diss., The Hebrew University of Jerusalem.

Yahalom-Mack, N., and Eliyahu-Behar, A. 2015. The Transition from Bronze to Iron in Canaan. *Radiocarbon* 57: 285–305.

Yasur-Landau, A. 2007. A Note on the Late Bronze Age Textile Industry. In *Excavations at Tel Beth-Shean, 1989–1996*, Vol. 2: *The Middle and Late Bronze Age Strata in Area R*, ed. A. Mazar and R. A. Mullins, 669–71. Jerusalem: IES; The Institute of Archaeology, The Hebrew University of Jerusalem.

―― 2010. *The Philistines and Aegean Migration at the End of the Late Bronze Age*. Cambridge: Cambridge University Press.

2012. The Role of the Canaanite Population in the Aegean Migration to the Southern Levant in the Late Second Millennium BCE. In *Materiality and Social Practice: Transformative Capacities of Intercultural Encounters*, ed. J. Maran and P. W. Stockhammer, 191–7. Oxford: Oxbow.

Zertal, A. 1986–1987. An Early Age Cultic Site on Mount Ebal: Excavation Seasons 1982–1987. *TA* 13–14: 105–65.

1994. "To the Land of the Perizzites and the Giants": On the Israelite Settlement in the Hill-Country of Manasseh. In *From Nomadism to Monarchy: Archaeological and Historical Aspects of Early Israel*, ed. I. Finkelstein and N. Na'aman, 47–70. Jerusalem: Yad Izhak Ben-Zvi; IES; Washington, DC: Biblical Archaeology Society.

2004. *The Manasseh Hill Country Survey*, Vol. 1: *The Shechem Syncline*. CHANE 12 (1). Leiden: Brill.

2007. *The Manasseh Hill Country Survey*, Vol. 2: *The Eastern Valleys and the Fringes of the Desert*. CHANE 12 (2). Leiden: Brill.

Zertal, A., and Mirkam, N. 2016. *The Manasseh Hill Country Survey*, Vol. 3: *From Nahal 'Iron to Nahal Shechem*. CHANE 12 (3). Leiden: Brill.

Zevit, Z. 2001. *The Religions of Ancient Israel: A Synthesis of Parallactic Approaches*. London: Continuum.

SIXTEEN

IRON AGE I PHILISTINES
Entangled Identities in a Transformative Period

AREN M. MAEIR

The Philistines, one of the so-called Sea Peoples, are well known from the biblical narrative. In the last century or so, additional data have been provided about the Philistines and their culture, from the Egyptian inscriptions and reliefs (in particular, the Medinet Habu reliefs depicting battles between Ramesses III and the Sea Peoples), and especially from archaeological excavations in the southern Levant. For many years, based on somewhat simplistic readings of these data, a rather monolithic understanding of the underlying mechanisms and causes pertaining to the origins, appearance, constitution, transformation, and social structure of the Philistines and their culture has been espoused (e.g., Dothan 1982; 1989; Stager 1995; Barako 2000; Oren 2000; Killebrew 2005). For all intents and purposes, the appearance of the Philistines in Canaan was seen as a straightforward invasion of one of a group of peoples (the Philistines being one of the Sea Peoples) of a largely Aegean/Mycenaean origin, who destroyed and replaced the Canaanites in southwestern Canaan, bringing with them a foreign culture. At first, this culture seemed to dominate other cultures in the region. Later on, about two centuries after their arrival and settlement in Canaan, the Philistines supposedly went through a slow process of cultural assimilation, eventually losing their original foreign identity (e.g., Ehrlich 1996; Gitin 2004).

Recent research on the Philistines has challenged these long-held views and dramatically changed our understanding of the Philistines and their culture, particularly when the large amounts of archaeological data from Philistia (and especially from excavations in the last 20–30 years) was infused with fresh insights that utilized up-to-date social theory (e.g., Yasur-Landau 2010; Maeir and Hitchcock 2011; 2016; 2017; Hitchcock and Maeir 2013; 2014; Maeir, Hitchcock, and Horwitz 2013; Cline 2014; Middleton 2015). It is now clear that one can hardly see a monolithic process of invasion by a foreign entity. Rather, the Philistines should be seen as an entangled transcultural society, comprised of various groups deriving from the eastern and central Mediterranean, along with local Canaanites – all joining to form a unique culture. In addition, the multicultural character of the Philistines and their appearance at a time of sociopolitical disorder hints at the possibility that significant components of the Sea Peoples and the Philistines may, in fact, have had a pirate-like culture. The complex sociocultural background of the Philistines can be seen in the very diverse connections and subregional differentiation of the Philistine culture, indicating complex origins, relations, and developments. Finally, the transformation of Philistine culture is to be seen as a complex ongoing process, both during the Iron Age I and also into the later stages of the Iron Age.

BACKGROUND

From the late thirteenth through the mid-to-late twelfth centuries BCE, the political and socioeconomic structures and networks that existed in the central and eastern Mediterranean region during the Late Bronze Age (ca. 1500–1200 BCE) underwent major transformations (e.g., Cline 2014). Due to a complex set of underlying mechanisms, various political structures in the region changed substantially and, in some cases, collapsed and disappeared. The Egyptian Empire was substantially reduced in size, the Hittite Empire disintegrated, and the various Mycenaean palace kingdoms for all intents and purposes ceased to exist. As opposed to the intensive and extensive intercultural connections that existed during the Late Bronze Age, during this transition and the century or so afterward, there is a significant downgrading in the intensity of these connections. Simultaneously, newly defined (or, in some cases, redefined) cultures and groups begin to appear during this transition, including the Sea Peoples, Israelites, Arameans, and others. In Canaan – modern day Israel/Palestine, Jordan, Lebanon, and central and southern Syria – the transition between the Late Bronze Age and early Iron Age is very evident. Many of the Canaanite city states are either weakened or abandoned/destroyed, and the Egyptian Empire's hold on Canaan slowly recedes, finally ending sometime in the late twelfth century BCE.

During the latter part of the Late Bronze Age and the early Iron Age (late thirteenth–twelfth centuries BCE), various evidence, particularly from Egypt, informs us of various peoples and groups originating from the "Islands of the

Seas" – who are dubbed the "Sea Peoples" in modern research – appearing in various parts of the eastern Mediterranean (see chapters in Killebrew and Lehmann 2013). These "Sea Peoples" are identified by the Egyptians as being of different groups, including the Sherden, Sikila, Weshesh, and Peleset; it is the last group who are identified with the Philistines known from biblical and other texts, which will be expanded upon below. In the Egyptian documents, in particular, the reliefs from the Mortuary Temple of Ramesses III at Medinet Habu in Egypt, these groups supposedly attempt to invade areas under Egyptian control in the Levant.

Based on mentions of these groups in Egyptian documents and the appearance of the Philistines in biblical and other ancient texts, the scholarly consensus identifies a specific archaeological culture – the Philistine culture – which appears along the southern coastal plain of modern Israel/Palestine at this time. This culture and its social structure have unique and complex attributes – as will be discussed below.

Up until quite recently, the scholarly consensus was that Philistine culture derived from peoples of an Aegean origin (most likely related to the Mycenaean culture), who upon arriving in Canaan (ancient Palestine/Israel) captured and destroyed the local Canaanite cities in the southern coastal plain of Canaan (= Philistia), resettled these sites, and brought with them a unique Aegean-oriented culture. Over time, according to this paradigm, the culture slowly assimilated with the local Levantine cultures, until the Philistine culture eventually disappeared toward the end of the Iron Age (e.g., Dothan 1982; Stager 1995; Ehrlich 1996; Oren 2000).

Recent research has changed these views. Current evidence indicates that Philistine culture is not connected to a specific Aegean culture that conquered and destroyed the Canaanite culture in southern Canaan. Rather, one can see an amalgamation of various peoples of nonlocal origins (with Mycenaean, Minoan, Cypriot, Anatolian, and other connections) who settled in Canaan alongside the local Canaanites – with very little evidence of a destruction of the Canaanite sites in this region. It has been suggested that this culture should be seen as a unique "entangled" culture, developing from a diverse set of influences, which transforms into a new and definable cultural entity. In addition, recent research has suggested that the very background of the collapse of the Late Bronze Age sociopolitical structure may have led to the formation of pirate-like groups in the central and eastern Mediterranean, and it may very well be that significant portions of the peoples who make up the Philistine culture are in fact of pirate-like origins – perhaps even with charismatic pirate leaders (the so-called *seren* leaders of the biblical Philistines – whose name may be connected with the Luwian term *tarwanis* = "warlord").[1]

The developmental trajectory of Philistine material culture is quite well known following more than a century of intensive archaeological research in southern Palestine/Israel. Several important sites have been excavated, such as Ashdod, Ashkelon, Tel Miqne-Ekron, Tell eṣ-Ṣafi/Gath, and Tell Qasile, which have provided a rich archaeological sequence for the development of various manifestations of this culture, including its art and architecture. Philistine culture exists from ca. 1200 BCE until the late seventh century BCE, when the Babylonians destroy the last existing Philistine cities and exile all the remaining population to Mesopotamia (e.g., Stager 1996; Gitin 2004). During this ca. 600 year period, one can trace the development and change of Philistine culture.[2]

By its very nature, Philistine material culture was quite eclectic. Not only are the multiple origins of early Philistine culture influential, it was highly influenced by various surrounding cultures (e.g., Phoenician, Israelite, Judahite, Egyptian, Greek) throughout its existence to ca. 600 BCE.

ASPECTS OF PHILISTINE ARCHITECTURE AND ART

Architecture

Early Philistine culture exhibits various architectural features that point to non-Levantine components (e.g., Aja 2009; Hitchcock, Maeir, and Dagan 2016). This includes the appearance of prestige buildings (as at Tell eṣ-Ṣafi/Gath and Tell Qasile) containing axial pillars with a platform between them, similar to structures on Crete (such as at Sissi); a unique house type (the "linear house") seen in early Philistine domestic architecture, which supposedly has Aegean roots; bathtubs; and hearths (of at least three distinct types – square, rounded, and keyhole shaped). In addition, building methods and techniques that appear in the early Philistine culture (e.g., ashlar masonry, the use of columns rather than pillars, possible "megaron"-style buildings, specific brick architecture, "hydraulic plaster") may point to "western" influences in early Philistine architecture.

Cultic Buildings and Paraphernalia

Cultic Architecture. Philistine temples and cult-related buildings are known from the various stages of Philistine culture (e.g., Hitchcock, Maeir, and Dagan 2016). The architecture of the early Iron Age Philistine temples at Tell Qasile has been compared by some to temples in the Aegean region, such as at Phylakopi. The early Iron Age temples at Tel Miqne-Ekron display several Aegean-oriented features, such as non-axial columns (similar to, e.g., Tiryns and Midea), "megaron-like" entrances, and platforms between pillars. During the later stages of the Iron Age, temples at Tell eṣ-Ṣafi/Gath and Tel Miqne-Ekron seem to be quite similar to local Levantine architectural traditions but with hints of Aegean influences as well. Along with temples, cultic corners within domestic structures are known from various stages of the Iron Age in Philistia. Among the various objects found in these contexts are horned altars (mostly of stone, but one possibly made of plaster from early Iron Age Ashkelon), most with four horns, although one of them, from ninth-century BCE Tell eṣ-Ṣafi/Gath, has only two. It has been suggested that this two-horned altar harkens from a possible "western" tradition that is continued in Iron Age II Philistia, connected to the "horns of consecration" motif, and parallel to the two-horned altar from thirteenth-century BCE Myrtou-*Pyghades* in Cyprus.

Cultic Stands and Vessels. This includes cultic stands of various classes, primarily from the early Iron Age (e.g., Ben-Shlomo 2010). While most seem to be versions of well-known Levantine cult stands, commonly found in the region during the Bronze and Iron Ages, some of the stands from Philistia display unique shapes and features, which have led some to claim that they have Aegean connections. This is particularly so for the tenth-century BCE stands from Yavneh-Yam.

In addition to the cultic stands of various types, one can note, for example, "head cups," fruit-shaped vessels, trick vessels, phallic objects, miniature votive vessels, and decorated chalices.

Figurines. During the early Iron Age, Aegean influence can be seen in the figurines found in Philistia (e.g., Ben-Shlomo 2010). This includes local versions of Late Helladic (LH) IIIC "Psi" figurines, the so-called Ashdoda seated female figurine reminiscent of certain features of Aegean seated figurines (which is identified by some as a personification of the main Philistine deity), and some Aegean-inspired bovine figurines. With time, these Aegean-influenced figurines become less common, and local types, unique to Philistia, are seen. Both anthropomorphic and zoomorphic figurines are known, most rather small in size, except for a large female figurine/statue depicting a goddess from the late Iron Age temple at Tel Miqne-Ekron.

Cooking Traditions

The Philistine foodways have been shown to hint at nonlocal influences in Philistine culture. This includes food preferences (e.g., pork, dog, as well as new types of plant food) and new methods of cooking (as evidenced by the appearance of new cooking vessels, cooking jugs, and hearths). While in the past it was assumed that these hearths indicate connections with Mycenaean culture, in fact, the different types of hearths (rounded, pebble, and plastered keyhole) are indicative of the diverse (and non-Mycenaean) origin of these features with parallels from Cyprus and beyond (e.g., Ben-Shlomo et al. 2008; Gur-Arieh et al. 2012; Maeir and Hitchcock 2011; Frumin et al. 2015).

Burial

While in the early stages of research on the Philistines (e.g., Dothan 1982; Ben-Shlomo 2008), various types of burials were associated with early Philistine culture and thought to have various foreign connections (e.g., burials caves with a dromos thought to be connected to Cyprus; anthropomorphic coffins thought to be connected to Egypt; cremation urns thought to be connected with Anatolia). In fact, very few burials that can be clearly associated with early Philistine culture are able to be identified, and those that can (at, e.g., Azor, Tell eṣ-Ṣafi/Gath, Ashkelon) seem to represent mixed types of interments – making it difficult to point out any specific origins and influences in Philistine tomb architecture. This being said, future publication of DNA and isotopic studies (particularly from the large, Iron Age II Philistine cemetery at Ashkelon) may contribute to understanding the origins of the Philistines (see now Master and Aja 2017).

Pottery

Perhaps the most well-known material aspect of Philistine culture is their unique decorated pottery (e.g., Dothan 1982; Ben-Shlomo, Shai, and Maeir 2004; Maeir 2005; Ben-Shlomo 2006a). Following more than a century of research on Philistine pottery and, in particular, the decorated pottery, the following developmental framework can be established:

1. The earliest pottery associated with Philistine culture ("Philistine 1") can be defined as locally made Mycenaean/LH IIIC pottery with similarities and parallels in various Aegean, southern Anatolian, and Cypriot contexts, both in form and painted decoration. One cannot point to a singular origin and influence of this early pottery. While, for the most part, having linear and geometric decorations (usually monochrome), some figures and scenes are known with parallels from the Aegean. The Philistine 1 assemblage is mostly of various Late Helladic shapes, although it should be stressed that the complete repertoire of Late Helladic shapes in use in various LH IIIC contexts are not represented in Philistia. This pottery seems to appear in the late thirteenth century, continuing at most to the mid-twelfth century BCE. In addition, of no less importance, undecorated Aegean shapes appear at this stage (such as the cooking jug), along with various local Canaanite types, side by side with decorated Aegean-style pottery.

2. Sometime in the mid-/late twelfth century BCE, the second stage of Philistine pottery appears ("Philistine 2"). It is characterized by the continuation of some of the Late Helladic shapes but with a distinct change in decoration. A bichrome (usually red and black) decoration appears with linear, geometric, vegetal, and animals figures (including the iconic bird figure). This decoration is often painted on a thick, white slip background. While some of the decorative motifs continue Aegean styles, this phase seems to display a very eclectic collection of influences, both Levantine and foreign (Aegean, Egyptian, Cypriot), in decoration and shapes.
3. The third stage of development of Philistine pottery ("Philistine 3") appears sometime in the mid-to-late eleventh century BCE and is characterized as being a "degenerated" development of the earlier stages, meaning that while some of the earlier shapes and decorations of the second stage still continue, they have evolved and changed significantly over time, losing much of the original "flavor." Pottery decoration at this stage is primarily simple monochrome designs or, at times, a red slip. By and large, many aspects of the local Levantine pottery repertoire are incorporated into this assemblage
4. The fourth stage of development of decorated Philistine pottery (the so-called Late Philistine Decorated Ware) appears in the tenth century BCE. This group is limited to specific types of mainly closed vessels and is a combination of earlier Philistine motifs and shapes, along with Phoenician and other influences. At the same time, most of the pottery types in Philistia, from the tenth century BCE until the end of the Iron Age (ca. 600 BCE), are undecorated and are morphologically quite similar to other ceramic groups from the Levant.
5. By the late Iron Age, by and large, the Philistine ceramic repertoire can be seen as one of various regional Levantine ceramic assemblages, losing most of the nonlocally inspired characteristics seen in the early Iron Age assemblages (e.g., Gitin 2004). In general, toward end of the Iron Age, Philistine culture is highly influenced by connections with various parts of the ancient Mediterranean world, and various types of imported pottery are found in Philistia – particularly from the Aegean region (with a large sample found at late Iron Age Ashkelon).

Ivory

Ivory finds from Iron Age Philistia have decorative traditions, which seem to indicate both western influences (such as a pyxis lid from Tel Miqne-Ekron), along with types more at home in the Canaanite milieu (such as the decorated bowl from Tell eṣ-Ṣafi/Gath [see, e.g., Maeir et al. 2015]). It would appear that this diversity reflects the entangled nature of Philistine culture and the connections with neighboring cultures. During the early Iron Age, there are several examples of bimetallic knives with bone-shaped ivory handles. This object type is known from various early Iron Age contexts in the Levant and Cyprus, and seems to originate from southeastern Europe. A collection of ivories was found in the late Iron Age temple at Tel Miqne-Ekron, including various ivory objects of Egyptian origin, perhaps booty brought back by the Assyrians to the region following their conquest of Egypt in 671 BCE (e.g., Gitin 2004).

Glyptics

Seals and sealings from Iron Age Philistia, for the most part, are quite similar to local Levantine and, in some cases, Egyptian glyptics (Ben-Shlomo 2006b). This includes various types of stamp seals, with perhaps the only unique type typical of Iron Age I Philistia being the so-called anchor seals – termed thus due to their truncated pyramid shape, which is reminiscent of an ancient anchor. The motifs seen on the seals – whether geometric, figural, vegetal or, in some cases, writing – are quite similar to those seen in the glyptic repertoire of other Levantine Iron Age cultures (save, perhaps, for the depiction of a lyre player). It should be noted that suggestions to identify Aegean-style linear script on two early Iron Age seals from Ashdod have been shown to be incorrect.

Metal Objects

There is not a lot of evidence for metal objects from Iron Age Philistia. From the early Iron Age, a few objects are noteworthy, including an Aegean-style double axe from the Tell Qasile temples, two chariot linchpins (from Ashkelon and Tel Miqne-Ekron), possible fragments of a metal stand from Tel Miqne-Ekron (with Cypriot parallels), and bimetallic (iron blade and bronze rivet) knives. Somewhat surprisingly, despite the rather martial depiction of the Philistines, both in the Egyptian and biblical sources, almost no weapons have been found in Iron Age Philistia (Maeir and Hitchcock in press).

Recently, two small-scale metal workshops (in which both bronze and iron production can be seen) were discovered at Tell eṣ-Ṣafi/Gath (Eliyahu-Behar et al. 2012; Eliyahu-Behar, Workman, and Dagan in press), but with little evidence of the actual objects that had been produced. From the later Iron Age, evidence of bronze and iron implements (such as plows) have been found at Philistine sites.

Writing and Language

Very little is known about the languages and writing systems employed by the Philistines, particularly during the early Iron Age (e.g., Davis, Maeir, and

Hitchcock 2015; Maeir, Davis, and Hitchcock 2016). While in earlier research it was assumed that the Philistines in the early Iron Age spoke a language similar to Mycenaean Greek and most probably used a writing system similar to Aegean Bronze Age writing systems, after more than a century of research, this does not seem to be the case. Very few early Iron Age inscriptions have been found, and those that can be identified without a doubt as Philistine indicate that while some elements of the early Philistine language(s) may be Indo-European in origin, a distinct connection with Mycenaean Greek is untenable. Similarly, the lack of inscriptions with clear connections to Aegean writing systems seems to indicate that the Philistines did not use such a system during the early Iron Age. Not only might this be connected to the various non-Aegean components among the Philistines, but it may also be due to the fact that Aegean writing systems were based on the socioeconomic needs of a palace-based kingdom. Once the palace structures collapsed (and they were not copied in the Levant), the writing systems themselves did not survive, as they had no use.

DISCUSSION

Based on the evidence given above on the political and socioeconomic processes during the Late Bronze Age/Iron Age transition and the overview of Philistine material culture, a picture of Philistine society and culture can be drawn (see now Maeir and Hitchcock 2017).

During the early Iron Age, the Philistines were a group of very mixed origins (entangled), deriving from various regions and origins, including non-local and local Canaanite elements. A variety of evidence hints that substantial parts of the Philistine population may have derived from pirate-like groups that flourished during the breakup of Late Bronze Age Mediterranean societies in the late thirteenth and early twelfth centuries BCE. As such, when settling in Philistia, the culture that formed combined elements of various origins. The hierarchical structure of Philistine culture is hinted to by the later name of the Philistine leaders (*seren* [pl. *seranim*]), which may very likely originate from a Luwian title meaning "war leader." Thus, it would appear that early Philistine culture was not modeled on the Bronze Age Aegean palace structure but rather on that of a society led by a charismatic leader. This society was open to accepting peoples of different origins and traditions. The lack of destruction at early Iron Age Canaanite sites in Philistia indicates that not only were the Canaanites incorporated into Philistine culture, but, at most, nonlocal elements took over elite roles at these sites and did not supplant the entire socioeconomic structure.

Despite the change in leadership (*seren* instead of the Canaanite petty king known from the Late Bronze Age), the most important settlement form in early Philistine society remains urban entities – known from at least four of the five major Philistine cities (Ashkelon, Gaza, Tell eṣ-Ṣafi/Gath, Tel Miqne-Ekron).

The repertoire of Philistine material culture seems to indicate that while Aegean-oriented symbols and behaviors were of importance (and perhaps even dominated), other traditions existed, too. This may very well indicate that while this society was eclectic in nature, the cultural memory of this group, throughout the Iron Age, stressed the supposed Aegean origins of this group – perhaps due to the fact that the leadership strata was of nonlocal origin – and suppressed other origin components of this culture.

The importance of feasting and ritual drinking in Philistine culture is seen particularly in the earlier phases of the Iron Age (e.g., Hitchcock et al. 2015). It can be assumed that diacritical feasting played an important role in group cohesion – particularly in light of the entangled nature of the Philistine population. The fact that these feasts were not identical to feasting customs of cultures from which some of the Philistines derived also reflects this eclectic nature.

Despite it being suggested that the Philistines were of multiple origins and the nonlocals settled among local Canaanites, deep changes can be seen in a wide spectrum of behavioral indicators when one compares the Late Bronze and Iron Ages in Philistia. This is manifested in a broad range of elements, including diet, architecture, cult, burial, language, writing, etc. Thus, while one cannot accept the earlier suppositions of a monolithic migration as the explanation for the appearance of Philistine culture, nevertheless, migration and the arrival of substantial elements of the Philistine populace can be sustained.

As the Iron Age progressed, Philistine culture shed many of its foreign components; however, until the very end of the Iron Age, it retained some distinct nonlocal traditions (seen, e.g., in deity names, figurines, some dietary customs, etc.). Suggestions that by the tenth century BCE all the nonlocal elements were shed (due to external pressure by the Judahite kingdom) are simply incorrect.[3]

Based on Iron Age sources, it is clear that the Philistines defined themselves in relation to other groups and identities (not limited to ethnic) in the region. While in the early Iron Age this is easier to discern from an archaeological point of view, the clear distinctions of identity continue in the Iron Age II as well – both in the archaeological remains and, more explicitly, in the textual sources (biblical, Assyrian, Egyptian, etc.). This being said, attempts to clearly demarcate the borders between the Philistines and other groups during the Iron Age (e.g., Canaanites, Judahites, Israelites, etc.) may be more complex than is often assumed (Maeir and Hitchcock 2016). In particular, a very fluid and changing definition of the various identities within these groups must have existed in the transition zones between various areas of cultural influence, and the ability to shift allegiances and identities over time (and even simultaneously) makes a simplistic drawing of borderlines hard to accept.

The eclectic origins and nature of Philistine art and archaeology, definitely during the early Iron Age but continuing into the Iron Age II, can be seen as evidence of the "entangled" nature of Philistine culture. While strong "western" facets are observed, the notion in earlier research that this is evidence of a mass migration of peoples from the Mycenaean world is not sustained. Instead, it would appear that early Philistine culture is a mixture of peoples and influences of various origins and societal backgrounds, coming together during a period of immense changes. The Philistine society that formed during the early Iron Age can be seen as the direct result of both the continuity and breakdown of the Late Bronze Age world and how it played out during the Iron Age.

Sometime after the early Iron Age, the charismatic leader of the early Iron Age (*seren*) slowly took on more and more characteristics of the local Canaanite rulership traditions. Biblical and Assyrian texts indicate that by the Iron Age IIB, the leaders of the Philistines were seen as local kings, similar to the leaders of other small kingdoms in the southern Levant. It can be assumed that, by and large, other strata of Philistine society became more and more like the other Levantine societies in the region – "patronage kingdoms" composed of a petty king who had a web of connections with local leaders and, below that, a wide strata of urban and rural peasants (see Maeir and Shai 2016).

The end of Philistine culture is quite dramatic (e.g., Stone 1995; Stager 1996; Gitin 2004). In the late sixth century BCE, the remaining Philistine cities revolted against the Babylonian Empire. Subsequently, Nebuchadnezzar, king of Babylon, conducted a campaign to Philistia in 604 BCE and destroyed all of the Philistine cities. The inhabitants were either killed or exiled to Mesopotamia. While there, the exiled continued to identify themselves as the "men of Gaza" or of Ashkelon for another 150 years or so; the Philistines, as a specific cultural, political, and ethnic identity, disappeared. Soon afterward, during the Persian period, when Philistia was once again repopulated, the inhabitants were identified as Phoenicians – with little or no evidence for the continuity of earlier Iron Age traditions in this region.

The appearance, development, transformation, and eventual disappearance of Philistine society, relatively well documented in the archaeological record and in contemporaneous historical materials, provides us with an excellent example of the processes affecting a complex and entangled culture – as far as how it originally formed, but also how it interacted and changed over the course of ca. 600 years.

NOTES

1 For a recent general summary, see Maeir and Hitchcock 2017.
2 Recently, it has been suggested that another "Philistine related culture" may exist in northern Syria/southern Turkey, in the region of the Amuq Valley. Due to the fact that relations between the two cultures are still debated, we will not discuss this in detail in this study. For a recent critical view on these connections, see Younger 2016: 127–35.
3 For a detailed analysis, see Maeir and Hitchcock 2016; 2017.

REFERENCES

Aja, A. J. 2009. *Philistine Domestic Architecture in the Iron Age I*. PhD diss., Harvard University.
Barako, T. J. 2000. The Philistine Settlement as Mercantile Phenomenon? *AJA* 104: 513–30.
Ben-Shlomo, D. 2006a. *Decorated Philistine Pottery: An Archaeological and Archaeometric Study*. BAR International Series 1541. Oxford: Archaeopress.
    2006b. New Evidence of Seals and Sealings from Philistia. *TA* 33: 134–62.
    2008. The Cemetery of Azor and Early Iron Age Burial Practices. *Levant* 40: 29–54.
    2010. *Philistine Iconography: A Wealth of Style and Symbolism*. OBO 241. Fribourg: Academic.
Ben-Shlomo, D.; Shai, I.; and Maeir, A. M. 2004. Late Philistine Decorated Ware ("Ashdod Ware"): Typology, Chronology, and Production Centers. *BASOR* 335: 1–35.
Ben-Shlomo, D.; Shai, I.; Zukerman, A.; and Maeir, A. M. 2008. Cooking Identities: Aegean-Style and Philistine Cooking Jugs and Cultural Interaction in the Southern Levant during the Iron Age. *AJA* 112: 225–46.
Cline, E. H. 2014. *1177 B.C.: The Year Civilization Collapsed*. TPAH. Princeton: Princeton University Press.
Davis, B.; Maeir, A. M.; and Hitchcock, L. A. 2015. Disentangling Entangled Objects: Iron Age Inscriptions from Philistia as a Reflection of Cultural Processes. *IEJ* 65: 140–66.
Dothan, T. 1982. *The Philistines and Their Material Culture*. New Haven, CT: Yale University Press; Jerusalem: IES.
    1989. The Arrival of the Sea Peoples: Cultural Diversity in Early Iron Age Canaan. In *Recent Excavations in Israel: Studies in Iron Age Archaeology*, ed. S. Gitin and W. G. Dever, 1–21. AASOR 49. Winona Lake, IN: Published for ASOR by Eisenbrauns.
Ehrlich, C. S. 1996. *The Philistines in Transition: A History from ca. 1000–730 B.C.E.* SHCANE 10. Leiden: Brill.
Eliyahu-Behar, A.; Workman, V.; and Dagan, A. In press. Comparative Metallurgy in the Iron Age Levant: Early Philistine Iron Production at Tell es-Safi/Gath vs. Canaanite (Israelite?) Megiddo. In *Researches on Israel and Aram: Autonomy, Interdependence and Related Issues; Proceedings of the First Annual RIAB Center Conference, Leipzig, June 2016*, ed. A. Berlejung and A. M. Maeir. Researches on Israel and Aram in Biblical Times 1. Tübingen: Mohr Siebeck.
Eliyahu-Behar, A.; Yahalom-Mack, N.; Shilstein, S.; Zukerman, A.; Shafer-Elliott, C.; Maeir, A. M.; Boaretto, E.; Finkelstein, I.; and Weiner, S. 2012. Iron and Bronze Production in Iron Age IIA Philistia: New Evidence from Tell es-Safi/Gath, Israel. *JAS* 39: 255–67.
Frumin, S.; Maeir, A. M.; Horwitz, L. K.; and Weiss, E. 2015. Studying Ancient Anthropogenic Impacts on Current Floral Biodiversity in the Southern Levant as

Reflected by the Philistine Migration. *Scientific Reports* 5. www.nature.com/articles/srep13308 (accessed August 7, 2017).

Gitin, S. 2004. The Philistines: Neighbors of the Canaanites, Phoenicians and Israelites. In *100 Years of American Archaeology in the Middle East: Proceedings of the American Schools of Oriental Research Centennial Celebration, Washington, DC, April 2000*, ed. D. R. Clark and V. H. Matthews, 57–85. Boston: ASOR.

Gur-Arieh, S.; Boaretto, E.; Maeir, A. M.; and Shahack-Gross, R. 2012. Formation Processes in Philistine Hearths from Tell es-Safi/Gath (Israel): An Experimental Approach. *JFA* 37: 121–31.

Hitchcock, L. A.; Horwitz, L. K.; Boaretto, E.; and Maeir, A. M. 2015. One Philistine's Trash Is an Archaeologist's Treasure: Feasting at Iron Age I, Tell es-Safi/Gath. *NEA* 78: 12–25.

Hitchcock, L. A., and Maeir, A. M. 2013. Beyond Creolization and Hybridity: Entangled and Transcultural Identities in Philistia. *Archaeological Review from Cambridge* 28: 51–74.

―――. 2014. Yo-Ho, Yo-Ho, a *Seren*'s Life for Me! *WA* 46: 624–40.

―――. 2016. A Pirates' Life for Me: The Maritime Culture of the Sea People. *PEQ* 148: 245–64.

Hitchcock, L. A.; Maeir, A. M.; and Dagan, A. 2016. The Entanglement of Aegean Style Ritual Actions in Philistine Culture. In *METAPHYSIS: Ritual, Myth and Symbolism in the Aegean Bronze Age; Proceedings of the 15th International Aegean Conference, Vienna, Institute for Oriental and European Archaeology, Aegean and Anatolia Department, Austrian Academy of Sciences and Institute of Classical Archaeology, University of Vienna, 22–25 April 2014*, ed. E. Alram-Stern, F. Blakolmer, S. Deger-Jalkotzy, R. Laffineur, and J. Weilhartner, 519–26. Aegaeum 39. Leuven: Peeters.

Killebrew, A. E. 2005. *Biblical Peoples and Ethnicity: An Archaeological Study of Egyptians, Canaanites, Philistines, and Early Israel, 1300–1100 B.C.E.* ABS 19. Atlanta: SBL.

Killebrew, A. E., and Lehmann, G., eds. 2013. *The Philistines and Other "Sea Peoples" in Text and Archaeology*. ABS 15. Atlanta: SBL.

Maeir, A. M. 2005. Philister-Keramik. *RlA* 14: 528–36.

Maeir, A. M.; Davis, B.; and Hitchcock, L. A. 2016. Philistine Names and Terms Once Again: A Recent Perspective. *JEMAHS* 4: 321–40.

Maeir, A. M.; Davis, B.; Horwitz, L. K.; Asscher, Y.; and Hitchcock, L. A. 2015. An Ivory Bowl from Early Iron Age Tell es-Safi/Gath (Israel): Manufacture, Meaning and Memory. *WA* 47: 414–38.

Maeir, A. M., and Hitchcock, L. A. 2011. Absence Makes the Hearth Grow Fonder: Searching for the Origins of the Philistine Hearth. *ErIsr* 30: 46*–64*.

―――. 2016. "And the Canaanite Was Then in the Land"? A Critical View of the "Canaanite Enclave" in Iron I Southern Canaan. In *Alphabets, Texts and Artefacts in the Ancient Near East: Studies Presented to Benjamin Sass*, ed. I. Finkelstein, C. Robin, and T. Römer, 209–26. Paris: Van Dieren.

―――. 2017. The Appearance, Formation and Transformation of Philistine Culture: New Perspectives and New Finds. In *The "Sea Peoples" Up-to-Date: New Research on the Migration of Peoples in the 12th Century BCE*, ed. P. M. Fischer and T. Bürge, 149–62. DG 81; CCEM 35. Vienna: Austrian Academy of Sciences.

―――. In press. The Philistines Be upon Thee, Samson (Jud. 16:20): Reassessing the Martial Nature of the Philistines – Archaeological Evidence vs. Ideological Image? In *The Aegean and the Levant at the Turn of the Bronze Age and in the Early Iron Age*, ed. L. Niesiołowski-Spanò and M. Węcowski. Wiesbaden: Harrassowitz.

Maeir, A. M.; Hitchcock, L. A.; and Horwitz, L. K. 2013. On the Constitution and Transformation of Philistine Identity. *OJA* 32: 1–38.

Maeir, A. M., and Shai, I. 2016. Reassessing the Character of the Judahite Kingdom: Archaeological Evidence for Non-Centralized, Kinship-Based Components. In *From Sha'ar Hagolan to Shaaraim: Essays in Honor of Prof. Yosef Garfinkel*, ed. S. Ganor, I. Kreimerman, K. Streit, and M. Mumcuoglu, 323–40. Jerusalem: IES.

Master, D. M., and Aja, A. J. 2017. The Philistine Cemetery of Ashkelon. *BASOR* 377: 135–59.

Middleton, G. D. 2015. Telling Stories: The Mycenaean Origins of the Philistines. *OJA* 34: 45–65.

Oren, E. D., ed. 2000. *The Sea Peoples and Their World: A Reassessment*. UMM 108; University Museum Symposium Series 11. Philadelphia: University Museum, University of Pennsylvania.

Stager, L. E. 1995. The Impact of the Sea Peoples in Canaan (1185–1050 BCE). In *The Archaeology of Society in the Holy Land*, ed. T. E. Levy, 332–48. NAAA. London: Leicester University Press.

———. 1996. Ashkelon and the Archaeology of Destruction: Kislev 604 BCE. *ErIsr* 25: 61*–74*.

Stone, B. J. 1995. The Philistines and Acculturation: Culture Change and Ethnic Continuity in the Iron Age. *BASOR* 298: 7–32.

Yasur-Landau, A. 2010. *The Philistines and Aegean Migration at the End of the Late Bronze Age*. Cambridge: Cambridge University Press.

Younger, K. L., Jr. 2016. *A Political History of the Arameans: From Their Origins to the End of Their Polities*. ABS 13. Atlanta: SBL.

SEVENTEEN

MOVING BEYOND KING MESHA
A Social Archaeology of Iron Age Jordan

BENJAMIN W. PORTER

In 1868, members of the Bani Hamida tribe revealed an inscribed basalt stone resting on the surface of a ruined city named Dhiban to a passing Christian missionary. As epigraphers would determine soon after, this stone possessed a first-person account detailing the statecraft of Mesha, a ninth-century Moabite king (Fig. 17.1). The inscription described the king's wars against the Northern Kingdom of Israel, his subsequent actions to expand Moab's territory, and ambitious construction and irrigation projects. The inscription's decipherment led to great excitement throughout Europe because the text corroborated events described in the Hebrew Bible's 2 Kings 3. For scholars eager to find written sources to narrate the history of Jordan's Iron Age kingdoms, Mesha's inscription provided them with a reputedly factual description of Moab's ninth-century history.

Despite its valuable content, Mesha's inscription has been a poisoned chalice for archaeologists and historians of the Iron Age Levant. The inscription's decipherment inspired the exploration of ancient Jordan in the final decades of the nineteenth century. The twentieth century would see landscape surveys (e.g., Glueck 1940) and the excavation of major Iron Age settlements, such as the 'Amman Citadel, Busayra, Dhiban, Ḥesban, and many others.[1] This physical evidence, scholars believed, would hopefully fill in the remaining gaps in the historical sequence culled from the Hebrew Bible, the "Moabite Bible" that was the Mesha Inscription, and other chance epigraphic finds. Beginning in the 1980s, the Mesha Inscription took on a renewed purpose as

SOCIAL ARCHAEOLOGY OF IRON AGE JORDAN

17.1. The Mesha Stele (Louvre, AP 5066). The light gray stone is the original portions, while the black stone is a cast reconstructed from a frieze of now-missing portions. (Photo by Mbzt. Courtesy of Wikimedia Commons [CC BY-SA 3.0 (http://creativecommons.org/licenses/by-sa/3.0)].)

historians and archaeologists turned to writing social histories, using the text to issue general statements about the political and social structure of Jordan's Iron Age societies (LaBianca and Younker 1995). Mesha's characterization of Moabite society as one that consisted of distinct familial identities fixed to territories resonated with evolutionary typologies, such as "tribes," "chiefdoms," and segmentary lineage systems that were discussed throughout twentieth-century political anthropology. Believing they had discovered parity between an ancient "emic" worldview and a scholarly "etic" typology, scholars used trait lists built on ethnographic observations of, for instance, tribal societies with pastoralist economies, to reconstruct Iron Age society. One outcome of this line of reasoning has been that politics is the singular lens through which the investigation of Iron Age society is understood. Iron Age persons, their identities and motivations, and their relationships with each other are reduced to static categories, such as "pastoralist," "tribe," or "king." Confusion often ensues when archaeological evidence does not easily fit within such predefined categories or is absent altogether.

The archaeology of Jordan's Iron Age societies presently appears at an impasse, unable to resolve the rigid scholarly ontologies with the thin and difficult to interpret archaeological record. One productive direction is to recognize that Mesha's (or his scribe's) goal was not merely to chronicle events but rather, prescribe a vision for how his expanded kingdom should be understood. Mesha casts west-central Jordan as a space consisting of distinct identities fixed to territories, using phrases, such as "Land of 'Atarot" and "Land of Madaba," to which groups such as the "Men of Gad" and "Men of Sharon" were assigned. Mesha's goal in his narrative was to integrate disparate segments within a single territorial and symbolic rubric of "Moab" under the sponsorship of the god Kemosh (Routledge 2004: 133–53). Hence, the Mesha Inscription deploys a hegemonic vision of Moab, one that seeks to naturalize the expanded Moabite territory – and Mesha's legitimacy to rule it – by drawing on broadly recognized frameworks of "tradition" that were likely recognized by the stele's audience.

Therefore, by questioning the structuralist ontology that has dominated scholarship on Iron Age Jordan for the past twenty-five years, it is possible to create opportunities to discover the myriad ways that the material world of Iron Age Jordan mediated real and ideal identities and relationships. Scholars may observe how groups assembled themselves in dynamic networks of political, economic, and social relationships that often obscure predefined categories. Given the brevity of space, three episodes are queried in this chapter to understand the diversity and complexity of social life at different moments in Iron Age history. This ambitious mission, it must be said from the onset, falls short of its goals due to the quality and abundance of available evidence. More research is needed if scholars desire to move beyond Mesha's rhetoric to understand the everyday social worlds of Jordan's Iron Age peoples.

COMPLEX COMMUNITIES ACROSS THE IRON AGE I

During and following the demise of the Canaanite polities that canvassed the Levant in the late thirteenth and twelfth centuries, a patchwork of diffuse

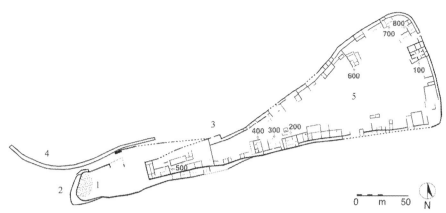

17.2. Map of Khirbat al-Mudayna denoting Buildings 100 through 800: (1) a tower, (2) a moat, (3) a possible gate, (4) a paved pathway, and (5) a courtyard. (Drawing by B. W. Porter.)

settlement systems emerged in venues throughout Jordan. Archaeological investigations determined that each system contained multiple small 1–2 ha settlements that were relatively equal in size and, often, architectural design. The conspicuous absence of rank-size settlement hierarchies within systems suggests that villages were relatively autonomous entities. Yet, the similarities in building design and material culture across settlements indicate communities were aware of each other and likely collaborated when advantageous.

While Iron Age I settlement systems are visible throughout western Jordan (Ji 1995), two systems are particularly well documented. One system is located along the Wadi al-Mujib watershed that drains north and then west into the Jordan Valley (Porter 2013). At least seven settlements emerged and declined between the twelfth and mid-tenth centuries BCE. These settlements positioned themselves on the edges of steep canyons at the bottom of which were thin riparian zones with key resources for subsistence, including water, soils, and wild animals. Excavations have determined that these settlements consisted of domestic residences encircling large empty courtyards. Substantial fortification systems made up of walls, moats, and towers protected these residences (Fig. 17.2). The predominance of domestic residences indicates that households were a basic unit of Jordan's Iron Age I societies, a pattern found throughout the Iron Age Levant. An intra-site comparison of domestic residences, however, reveals that they differed slightly in size and structure. Such patterns indicate a limited degree of inequality in wealth and authority that were likely exacerbated during periods of scarcity, when those households that had limited food reserves grew dependent on other households with more abundant resources (Porter 2013: 104–32).

A second Iron Age I settlement system, quite different in design from the Wadi al-Mujib system, emerged in southwestern Jordan between the twelfth and mid-tenth centuries BCE (Levy, Najjar, and Ben-Yosef 2014). These settlements were strategically located adjacent to outcrops of copper ores located in the seasonal tributaries that drained into the Wadi Aravah. The best documented settlements were studied in and around the Wadi Feinan. Khirbat en-Nahas, for instance, was a mining community whose domestic residences were surrounded by slag heaps, the residue of an intensive copper mining and smelting industry that was a major supplier for the Levant and possibly Egypt.

Archaeologist have interpreted western Jordan's settlements as those belonging to kingdoms that were mentioned in the Hebrew Bible (e.g., Glueck 1940). Biblical passages present Iron Age I Jordan's societies as politically integrated within bounded territories under the rule of kings, such as Eglon (Judges 3). These passages, most likely written several centuries after the events they purport to describe, overstated Jordan's Iron Age I political organization in order to contrast the representation of ancient Israel as a confederacy of tribes. When this skeptical interpretation of the biblical evidence is considered in tandem with a clear-eyed understanding of settlement systems like those found in the Wadi al-Mujib and Wadi Feinan, it becomes clear that Iron Age I society did not require the guiding hand of a supra-regional political organization to take the forms that it did (*contra* Finkelstein and Lipschits 2011). Rather, these settlement systems are best understood as emergent networks of communities that were based on relationships between households. The fact that households gathered themselves in nucleated settings rather than segment themselves in individual units across the landscape reveals a tacit strategy to create purposeful communities. The short duration of these communities suggests that these arrangements were temporary solutions to mitigate anxieties over food scarcity and household security, or, in the case of Feinan, pool labor resources to maximize copper production.

STATECRAFT, RITUAL, AND MORTUARY PRACTICES IN THE IRON AGE II

Current evidence suggests that most Iron Age I settlements of western Jordan dissipated during the mid-tenth century. An unfortunate gap exists in the archaeological record from this time until the ninth century, a gap that will hopefully be remedied in future research. Whatever developments occurred during this century-long lacuna laid the groundwork for the emergence of ethno-political territorial polities that first come into view during the mid-ninth century BCE. Written sources describing the emergence of the kingdoms of Gilead, Ammon, Moab, and Edom include only a small amount of epigraphic sources (e.g., the Mesha Stele; the Siran bottle; the Qos Gabr seal) and passages in the Hebrew Bible that describe ancient Israel's relationships with its neighbors (2 Kings 3). This thin historical record has driven scholars to

17.3. Iron Age II fortifications on Dhiban's southeast corner. Ashlars dating to the Iron Age II are the lowest set; Nabataean and Byzantine fortifications rest on top. (Photo by B. W. Porter.)

investigate their capital administrative settlements. Limited ninth–seventh-century BCE archaeological deposits at administrative settlements, such as the 'Amman Citadel, Dhiban, and Busayra, contain evidence for monumental buildings, gates, and fortification systems. These features simultaneously played practical roles in the kingdom's governance while also standing as powerful symbols of the state's efficacy.

The ancient Moabite capital Dibon (modern Dhiban) stands as one of the most intensively studied and published of the Iron Age capitals. Excavations have yielded evidence of monumental architecture and elite material cultural assemblages that help archaeologists understand the political and economic role these buildings played. Research at Dhiban has determined that the settlement was substantially transformed during the ninth and eighth centuries BCE, conspicuously in the decades following the events described in the Mesha Inscription.[2] The northern tell was artificially enlarged at least 0.75 ha and then encircled with fortification walls and towers (Fig. 17.3). A monumental building at least 20 m wide and perhaps as much as 43 m long was constructed at the tell's highest point. Recent excavations have identified large reservoirs on the northern tell's western edge that may date to the Iron Age. An extramural necropolis with several chambers built into the bedrock was also used in the Iron Age II and III. Current evidence suggests that settlement activity declined in the seventh century.

Despite the kingdoms' outward presentation of themselves as socially and territorially cohesive, hidden transcripts in the Mesha Inscription suggest these kingdoms were anything but integrated. Laid bare in Mesha's language is his challenge of imposing a new territorial ideal – "Moab" – upon a social landscape characterized by preexisting segmentary lineages residing in already defined territories. Having left no texts behind for scholars to understand their reception of Mesha's and other Iron Age kings' activities, these groups can only be understood through their material remains that have been identified in surveys and excavations. Domestic residences and other buildings have been identified at partially excavated settlements, such as Khirbat al-Mudayna on the Wadi ath-Thamad, Tall as-Sa'idiyeh, and Tall al-'Umayri.[3] The recovered evidence indicates that Iron Age II communities organized their social networks and subsistence practices at the household and community levels, much like the Iron Age I societies described above.

Similar to their southern Levantine neighbors, Jordan's Iron Age kingdoms were each affiliated with a patron deity. *Kemosh* and *Qws* were affiliated with Moab and Edom, respectively, while *Milkom* was likely affiliated with Ammon. The popularity of these patron deities is evident in the onomastic evidence of Iron Age personal names that have been documented in epigraphic sources. Parents would embed theophoric elements consisting of gods' names or nicknames in children's personal names, signaling the family's devotion to the deity. The frequent use of the Edomite deity *Qws*, for instance, in names documented in epigraphic sources found in southwest Jordan and southern Israel attests to the god's prominence in the Iron Age II and III (Porter 2004: tables 1, 2). The evidence suggests that people from all economic and social sectors implemented these naming practices, from ordinary people to the kings and their royal courts.

The worship of these patron deities as well as other deities took place in a variety of contexts dating to the Iron Age II and III. A multi-room temple complex was recently identified at 'Ataruz with several altars, vessels, and figurines, pointing to intense ritual activity within its rooms (Ji 2012). Scholars strongly suspect that a large monumental building (Building A) at Busayra was dedicated to ritual practice based on multiple conspicuous features, most notably a likely shrine room located off of a courtyard on the building's northern half (Bienkowski 2002) (see Fig. 17.4 below). At Khirbat al-Mudayna on the Wadi ath-Thamad, a small enclosed room contained incense altars and figurines that point to ritual activities (Temple 149 [Daviau 2012: 437–8]). A roadside station (WT-13) indicates that ritual was an important element of travel across the landscape (Daviau 2012: 443–6). A *temenos* wall surrounded a one-room building that contained a significant number of vessels and figurines. Large amounts of discarded faunal remains that were discovered at the station point to the practice of animal sacrifice. Small corners in domestic residences contained figurines, small altars, and dedicated vessels that were used in daily ritual activities.

Similar to the popularity of personal names bearing theophoric elements, the diversity of ritual spaces in monumental buildings, domestic spaces, and even roadside stations attest to the fact that a broad swath of society could participate in the national cult.

Mortuary practices are another important window into the social world of Jordan's Iron Age II societies. Chamber tombs designed for a small number of persons have been identified in extramural necropoleis adjacent to settlements (e.g., Dhiban [Winnett and Reed 1964]). These chamber tombs were carved into the sides of cliffs and usually contained a wide bench for laying out the deceased's body and associated objects assumed to be needed in the afterlife. This mortuary practice may have been reserved for prominent families due to the limited number of tombs discovered thus far. A more common mortuary venue during the Iron Age I and II was the large tomb chambers modified from caves and sinkholes in the karst landscape (e.g., Umm Dimis [Worschech 2003]). Multiple individuals were buried in these chambers; their remains, however, were commingled, making it difficult to distinguish individuals from each other. Similar to the chamber tombs, jewelry, weapons, and metal and ceramic vessels for holding food were interred with the deceased. These tombs likely contained members of extended lineage groups that held ancestral rights to the territory in which the chamber resided. A subtle gesture of ancestor veneration can be detected in an Iron Age I chamber (Cave A4) in the Baqa'a Valley (McGovern 1986) where multiple crania were singled out from other skeletal elements and lined up along the room's perimeter.

THE IMPOSITION OF EMPIRE IN THE IRON AGE III

Jordan's Iron Age kingdoms were not immune to the aggressive policies of Mesopotamian empires that began in the eighth century and continued for the rest of the first millennium. Similar to their Levantine counterparts, the first experience of Jordan's Iron Age societies with empire was through the threat of violence that often saw settlements destroyed and populations deported. Of the four Iron Age kingdoms, Gilead likely had the earliest and most violent encounters with the Assyrians. Written sources and limited archaeological evidence suggest the Assyrian army campaigned in northwestern Jordan in the latter half of the eighth century. Assyrian court documents indicate that Ammon, Moab, and Edom's kings mitigated Assyria's threats of violence with the payment of tribute, taxes, and expressions of loyalty to the Assyrian kings (Weippert 1987). These interactions with the empires influenced Jordan's ruling elites who simultaneously represented themselves as loyal imperial subjects and yet powerful rulers of their kingdoms (Porter 2004). This influence is visible in the monumental building program at Bozrah (modern

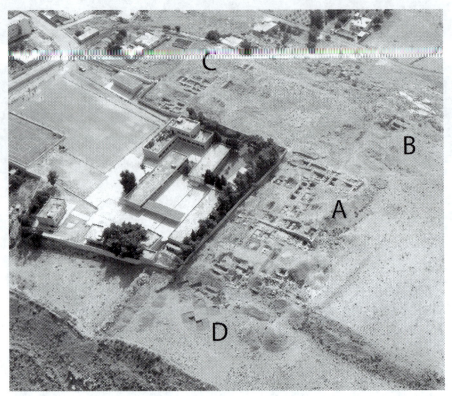

17.4. Busayra (ancient Bozrah), the Edomite administrative capital, looking south over the acropolis. Features include: (a) monumental building (Field A); (b) postern gate and domestic residences (Field B); (c) monumental building (Field C); and (d) domestic residences (Field D). (Photo by D. L. Kennedy. Courtesy of the Aerial Photographic Archive for Archaeology in the Middle East [APAAME]. Modified from APAAME_20141019_DLK-0287.jpg. [CC BY-NC-ND 2.0 (https://creativecommons.org/licenses/by-nc-nd/2.0/)].)

Busayra), the administrative capital of Edom (Bienkowski 2002). An acropolis encircled by a fortification system sits atop a well-defended spur with canyons on either side. Excavations identified two monumental buildings (Buildings A and C) with interior courtyards that resemble larger administrative buildings in Assyrian capitals in northern Iraq such as Kalhu (modern Nimrud) (Fig. 17.4). Recent geophysical research by this author and his colleagues has identified additional subsurface features associated with these monumental buildings that await study (Brown et al. 2016).

The economic stability of the so-called *pax Assyriaca* that lasted much of the seventh century saw the development of international markets that crossed the Levant, linking the Mediterranean Basin with Mesopotamia. Jordan's agropastoralist and craft economies participated in these networks. Many areas saw the expansion of small settlements across the landscape and, at times, into semiarid environmental zones that were less ideal for agricultural production (Routledge 2004: 192–201). The presence of loom weights in settlements such as Mudeibi (Wade and Mattingly 2003) and Jawa (Daviau 2002: 180–201) attest to the presence of, and possibly increase in, weaving activities and the production of finished textiles from readily available animal wool. Much sought-after prestige goods, such as incense, passed through Jordan on its way from southwestern Arabia to emporia on the Mediterranean coast, such as Gaza. Tridacna shells harvested from the Red Sea were likely carved in southern Jordan into elaborate designs and then traded throughout eastern Mediterranean markets (Bienkowski 2002: 454–8). All evidence suggests that the *pax Assyriaca* opened eastern Mediterranean and Mesopotamian markets to Jordan's Iron Age producers. Such markets also brought ceramic and metal prestige objects to western Jordan. Demand for these objects was apparently so great that local imitations mimicking the originals were produced using more common materials (Routledge 1997).

The demise of the Assyrian Empire and the rise of its Neo-Babylonian successors brought a period of destruction and administrative neglect throughout the Levant during the sixth century BCE. Jordan's Iron Age societies were somewhat more resilient compared to their neighbors to the west, who saw their major cities destroyed and populations deported to southern Mesopotamia. Written sources are conflicted on whether or not Ammon, Moab, and Edom were annexed into the Babylonian Empire's administrative system. Excavations at Tall al-'Umayri indicate that the settlement continued well past the decades when other cities (e.g., Jerusalem) and towns had been destroyed. In southwest Jordan, the monumental buildings at Busayra (described above) were destroyed at some point in the sixth century, possibly during the Babylonian king Nabonidus's 553 BCE campaign (Bienkowski 2002: 477–78). The town, however, was resettled soon after these events, likely before the end of the century, and was used into the fifth century BCE.

Compared to the Babylonians, the Achaemenid Persian Empire took a greater interest in administering the Levant upon establishing their rule in 539 BCE. Nevertheless, whatever political and economic infrastructure remained from the Iron Age II kingdoms declined during the sixth and into the fifth and fourth centuries BCE. Jordan would not see a resurgence in population levels until the development of the Nabataean kingdom beginning in the first century BCE. On the plateau, many settlements show evidence for limited occupation activity, with small amounts of ceramic vessels and coins found in thin deposits (see Bienkowski 2008). Archaeological surveys also report limited numbers of fifth–fourth-century settlements on the plateau (Miller 1991). Although the thinness of the evidence makes interpretations difficult, all clues indicate that the region's industries continued to produce raw and finished products for broader markets, although not at such intensive levels seen, for instance, during Assyrian rule.

The situation in the Jordan Valley, however, is more visible due to a greater amount of evidence. Settlement activity was more intense in areas north of the Dead Sea, likely a result of the region's agricultural potential and strategic position on a north–south highway. Excavations at Tell Deir 'Alla, Tell al-Mazar, Tall as-Sa'idiyeh, and other settlements have detected buildings, agricultural pits, and cemeteries dating to the fifth and fourth centuries. The Jordan Valley likely played the role of a bread basket for the emporia that developed along the Mediterranean coast. Cemetery A at Tell el-Mazar provides a glimpse into the fifth-century societies that lived and worked in the Jordan Valley (Yassine 1984). At least 85 graves were excavated with single-individual interments, ranging from infants to the elderly. Biological males and females were differentiated in mortuary commemoration practices. Males were interred in an extended position on their back, usually with metal weapons. Females were interred in a flexed leg position on their side with modest amounts of jewelry and tools needed for domestic production. Some individuals were buried with luxury items that are attested in other Levantine settlements, indicating that the Tell al-Mazar community had access to broader prestige good markets.

CONCLUSION

So much of the past century of archaeological research on the societies of Iron Age Jordan has understandably aimed to reconstruct the political and historical development of the four major kingdoms. Thanks to this research, archaeologists and historians have a good understanding of architectural features and material cultural assemblages. An understanding of Iron Age social life remains limited, however. Scholars still lack an understanding of how, for instance, Iron Age persons crafted identities that may have complimented or contradicted broader collective identities (e.g., "Moabite"). How did social life, especially during the Iron Age II and III, unfold within the backdrop of western Jordan's environment that was an often-unreliable partner in terms of natural resources?

The reason these and other questions have not yet been answered is partly a paradigmatic issue. Scholars have only engaged superficially with the large body of archaeological theory – household archaeology, gender archaeology, the archaeology of ritual and religion, to name only a few – that sets out tools and perspectives for understanding social life in past societies. But even with these intellectual frameworks in place, scholars must develop research designs that draw on rigorous sampling methods that will test their ideas. The past century of field research in Jordan has, after all, shown that the necessary evidence is not easily recovered through traditional excavation methods. With more careful spadework, analysis, and publication in the coming decades, Iron Age social life in ancient Jordan will reveal itself.

NOTES

1 For a review, see Herr and Najjar 2008.
2 For a summary and bibliography, see Porter et al. 2007.
3 For a list of settlement names, see Herr and Najjar 2008: table 10.3, 4.

REFERENCES

Aerial Photographic Archive for Archaeology in the Middle East (APAAME). www.apaame.org/.

Bienkowski, P. 2002. *Busayra: Excavations by Crystal-M. Bennett, 1971–1980*. British Academy Monographs in Archaeology 13. Oxford: Published for the CBRL by Oxford University Press.

——— 2008. The Persian Period. In *Jordan: An Archaeological Reader*, ed. R. B. Adams, 335–52. London: Equinox.

Brown, S. H.; Porter, B. W.; Simon, K.; Markussen, C.; and Wilson, A. T. 2016. Newly Documented Domestic Architecture at Iron Age Busayra (Jordan): Preliminary Results from a Geophysical Survey. *Antiquity Project Gallery*. http://antiquity.ac.uk/projgall/brown350 (accessed August 1, 2018).

Daviau, P. M. M. 2002. *Excavations at Tall Jawa, Jordan*, Vol. 2: *The Iron Age Artefacts*. CHANE 11 (2). Leiden: Brill.

——— 2012. Diversity in the Cultic Setting: Temples and Shrines in Central Jordan and the Negev. In *Temple Building and Temple Cult: Architecture and Cultic Paraphernalia of Temples in the Levant (2.–1. Mill. B.C.E.); Proceedings of a Conference on the Occasion of the 50th Anniversary of the Institute of Biblical Archaeology at the University of Tübingen (28–30 May 2010)*, ed. J. Kamlah in cooperation with H. Michelau, 435–58. ADPV 41. Wiesbaden: Harrassowitz.

Finkelstein, I., and Lipschits, O. 2011. The Genesis of Moab: A Proposal. *Levant* 43: 139–52.

Glueck, N. 1940. *The Other Side of the Jordan*. New Haven, CT: ASOR.

Herr, L. G., and Najjar, M. 2008. The Iron Age. In *Jordan: An Archaeological Reader*, ed. R. B. Adams, 311–34. London: Equinox.

Ji, C.-H. C. 1995. Iron Age I in Central and Northern Transjordan: An Interim Summary of Archaeological Data. *PEQ* 127: 122–40.

——— 2012. The Early Iron Age II Temple at Ḥirbet ʿAṭārūs and Its Architecture and Selected Cultic Objects. In *Temple Building and Temple Cult: Architecture and Cultic Paraphernalia of Temples in the Levant (2.–1. Mill. B.C.E.); Proceedings of a Conference on the Occasion of the 50th Anniversary of the Institute of Biblical Archaeology at the University of Tübingen (28–30 May 2010)*, ed. J. Kamlah in cooperation with H. Michelau, 203–21. Wiesbaden: Harrassowitz.

LaBianca, Ø. 1990. *Sedentarization and Nomadization: Food System Cycles at Hesban and Vicinity in Transjordan*. Hesban 1. Berrien Springs, MI: Andrews University Press in cooperation with the Institute of Archaeology, Andrews University.

LaBianca, Ø. S., and Younker, R. W. 1995. The Kingdoms of Ammon, Moab, and Edom: The Archaeology of Society in Late Bronze/Iron Age Transjordan (ca. 1400–500 BCE). In *The Archaeology of Society in the Holy Land*, ed. T. E. Levy, 399–415. NAAA. London: Leicester University Press.

Levy, T. E.; Najjar, M.; and Ben-Yosef, E., eds. 2014. *New Insights into the Iron Age Archaeology of Edom, Southern Jordan: Surveys, Excavations and Research from the University* of California, San Diego – Department of Antiquities of Jordan, Edom Lowlands Regional Archaeology Project (ELRAP). 2 vols. MonArch 35. Los Angeles: The Cotsen Institute of Archaeology Press.

McGovern, P. E. 1986. *The Late Bronze and Early Iron Ages of Central Transjordan: The Baq'ah Valley Project, 1977–1981*. UMM 65. Philadelphia: University Museum of Archaeology and Anthropology.

Miller, J. M. 1991. *Archaeological Survey of the Kerak Plateau*. ASORAR 1. Atlanta: Scholars.

Porter, B. W. 2004. Authority, Polity, and Tenuous Elites in Iron Age Edom (Jordan). *OJA* 23: 373–95.

——— 2013. *Complex Communities: The Archaeology of Early Iron Age West-Central Jordan*. Tucson: The University of Arizona Press.

Porter, B. W.; Routledge, B.; Steen, D.; and al-Kawamlha, F. 2007. The Power of Place: The Dhiban Community through the Ages. In *Crossing Jordan: North American Contributions to the Archaeology of Jordan*, ed. T. E. Levy, P. M. M. Daviau, R. W. Younker, and M. Shaer, 315–22. London: Equinox.

Routledge, B. 1997. Mesopotamian "Influence" in Iron Age Jordan: Issues of Power, Identity and Value. *BCSMS* 32: 33–41.

——— 2004. *Moab in the Iron Age: Hegemony, Polity, Archaeology*. Archaeology, Culture, and Society. Philadelphia: University of Pennsylvania Press.

Wade, J. M., and Mattingly, G. L. 2003. Ancient Weavers at Iron Age Mudaybi'. *NEA* 66: 73–5.

Weippert, M. 1987. The Relations of the States East of the Jordan with the Mesopotamian Powers during the First Millennium BC. *SHAJ* 3: 97–106.

Winnett, F. V., and Reed, W. L. 1964. *The Excavations at Dibon (Dhiban) in Moab*. 2 vols. AASOR 36–7. New Haven, CT: ASOR.

Worschech, U. 2003. *A Burial Cave at Umm Dimis North of el-Balu*. Beiträge zur Erforschung der antiken Moabitis (Ard el-Kerak) 3. Frankfort: Lang.

Yassine, K. 1984. *Tell el Mazar I: Cemetery A*. Amman: University of Jordan.

EIGHTEEN

A SOCIAL ARCHAEOLOGY OF THE KINGDOM OF JUDAH

Tenth–Sixth Centuries BCE

AVRAHAM FAUST

A DISCLAIMER

We must note that the available data is not even, and there are regions and periods that, due to geopolitical circumstances or archaeological formation processes, are better known than others. Thus, due to geopolitical reasons (including security problems, relative remoteness, and unclear and changing political status), the heartland of the kingdom of Judah – the highlands from Bethlehem just south of Jerusalem to the southern tip of the Hebron hill country – is far less known archaeologically than any other region west of the Jordan River. Relatively few excavations took place in this region, and even surveys were partial. The disparity in knowledge is striking when compared with the Shephelah to its west, which is studied extensively: The area was systematically surveyed, and dozens of scientific excavations took place there (Faust 2014a). Additionally, the Assyrian campaigns of the late eighth century BCE, concentrated in the Shephelah, and the Babylonian offensives of the early sixth century BCE, covering the entire area, resulted in massive destruction layers. These strata have yielded a wealth of detailed information, leading to the late Iron Age being far better known than the earlier part of the Iron Age II, from which only bits and pieces are known (Faust and Sapir 2018). As a consequence of the Assyrian campaign in 701 BCE being focused on the Shephelah, the highlands are far less known – even in this period – thus creating another imbalance in our information regarding the different parts of Judah.

These gaps and imbalances must be taken into account when reconstructing the social history of Judah, otherwise a skewed picture will emerge.

IRON AGE I: SETTING THE SCENE

In order to appreciate the processes that accompanied the development of social complexity in the Iron Age II, we must first set the scene and briefly present the preceding Iron Age I settlements. Population centers in the highlands reached a peak at this time, and, despite only partial research, it is clear that the area was filled with many settlements, albeit small, including the excavated sites of Jerusalem (fairly large), Khirbat Za'akuka, Giloh, Khirbet Umm et-Tala, Beth-Zur, Allon Shevut, and Hebron, among others (Faust 2014a, with references). It appears that most of the settlers in this region – if not all – were Israelites (Faust 2006, with references). The Judean Desert to the east was practically uninhabited at the time, and settlement in the Beersheva Valley was sparse, including Tel Masos, Nahal Yatir, and Beersheva. The ethnic identity of the settlers is not clear; it is possible that some of them were Israelites, while others were not (e.g., Herzog 1994; Finkelstein 1995), especially given the fluid nature of identity in such settings. The Shephelah, which used to be a population hub in the preceding Late Bronze Age, was almost devoid of habitation in the Iron Age I. Most of the Late Bronze Age settlements were destroyed or abandoned, and only a few continued to exist. Those were comprised of a small string of settlements in the eastern Shephelah, including Tell Beth Mirsim, Tel Eton, Tel Yarmouth, and Beth-Shemesh, representing a small Canaanite enclave between the Israelites in the highlands and the Philistines in the coastal plain (Bunimovitz and Lederman 2011; Faust and Katz 2011). Clearly, the highlands during the Iron Age I were the main settlement center in Judah.

IRON IIA: THE FORMATION OF STATEHOOD

The circumstances surrounding the transition to the Iron Age II have been hotly debated in recent years (Finkelstein and Mazar 2007, with references). While some scholars accept the historicity of the core narratives about the kingdom of David and Solomon in the tenth century BCE, others challenge them altogether; in addition, another group doubts many aspects of the biblical story but maintains that there was a monarchy at the time, centered around Jerusalem. As we will see below, this is supported by an updated examination of the archaeological data.

The transition from the Iron Age I to the Iron Age II[1] in Judah was accompanied by many changes, and most small settlements in the highlands were abandoned (e.g., Khirbat Za'akuka, Giloh, Khirbet Umm et-Tala, Beth-Zur,

Allon Shevut [Faust 2015]). People apparently concentrated at some sites that consequently became larger (e.g., Tell en-Naṣbeh, Hebron, Jerusalem). Jerusalem in the Iron Age IIA was a relatively large settlement, and remains were found on the eastern slopes of the City of David toward the Kidron Valley, at the Giv'ati Parking Lot to the west, and even at the Ophel excavations to the north (Faust 2017). The Shephelah was gradually resettled in a process that lasted almost 200 years. The earliest excavated new site in the Shephelah is Khirbet Qeiyafa, and we accept the excavators' basic interpretation of the site as connected to the emerging highlands polity (Garfinkel, Ganor, and Hasel 2010; see also Finkelstein and Fantalkin 2012; and Faust 2013). Other settlements followed, and by the end of the Iron Age IIA (second half of the ninth century BCE) the area was dotted with many new settlements, such as Lachish, 'Azekah, Tel Burna, Tel Zayit, and others, that joined the existing cities of Tell Beit Mirsim, Tel Eton, and Beth-Shemesh. Although the issue is debated, it appears that the new settlers in the Shephelah were Israelites from the highlands, and the region was gradually colonized by Judah (Faust 2013). Evidence also suggests that the existing Canaanite population of the eastern Shephelah gradually assimilated, and, at least by the eighth century BCE, it became Israelite.

The settlement in the Beersheva and Arad Valleys also changed its character during this time. Some sites, such as Tel Masos and Nahal Yatir, which were probably inhabited by non-Israelites, were abandoned, while settlements, such as Beersheva, which were most likely settled by Israelites or affiliated groups, changed their character and eventually became fortified (cf. Herzog 1994 and Finkelstein 1995). This is also the likely background for the establishment of the Negev fortresses, probably with strong connection to the polity in the north (which we identify as the United Monarchy) (Cohen 2004), and the mining operations at Timna' (Ben-Yosef, Langgut, and Sapir-Hen 2017) and Feinan (Levy, Najjar, and Ben-Yosef 2014), which both show clear connections with the north at this phase (e.g., the existence of four-room houses at Khirbat en-Nahas (see below), the faunal remains at Timna').

Gradually, over the course of the Iron Age IIA, settlements became larger and more complex (e.g., Lachish, Beth-Shemesh, Tell Beit Mirsim). Society was still kinship based (Master 2001; Stager 2003; Faust 2012a) – despite the changes, this was true of society in Judah until the fall of the kingdom – but it became more complex, and changes were inevitable. Additional types of affiliation were beginning to emerge, mainly in parallel with the existing kinship structure but, in the long run, also at its expense. It appears that the growing social complexity and changing social discourse were also expressed in changes in material culture. Thus, the disappearance of the collared rim jars (west of the Jordan) might be connected with changes in kinship structure that accompanied the abandonment of the countryside, and these prominent objects lost their symbolic function in the new environment, whereas the surge in the popularity of slip and burnish symbolized the new society that emerged and new social relations within a more hierarchical society (Faust 2002, 2006).

Still, due to the abovementioned biases in data (little information on the highlands and lack of destruction layers in the Iron Age IIA), we know relatively little about the Iron Age IIA.

IRON AGE IIB: GROWING COMPLEXITY

More settlements are known from this period than from any preceding era. Settlements were also larger than before, leading scholars to suggest that this was a settlement peak.[2] Judah in the Iron Age IIB had a complex network of settlements with Jerusalem at its center as a primate city, reaching some 650 dunams and enclosed within the period's new city walls (Fig. 18.1). The

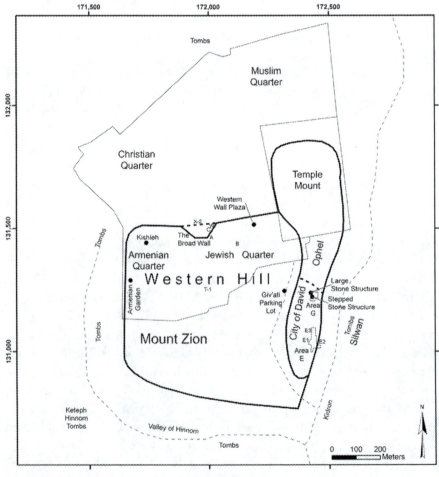

18.1. Jerusalem in the late Iron Age. (Map by A. Faust.)

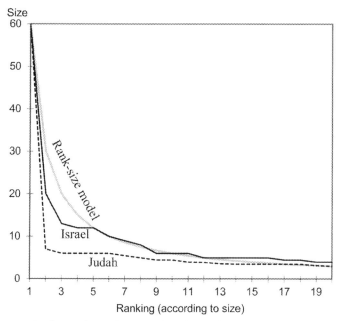

18.2. Settlement hierarchy in the kingdoms of Judah and Israel. (Graph by A. Faust.)

second largest city (Lachish) was some seventy dunams. Additional towns dotted the landscape of Judah (e.g., Tel Eton, Beth-Shemesh, Tell Beit Mirsim, Tel Halif, Beersheva). Between them, mainly in the highlands, one can identify villages, hamlets, and farmsteads. Years ago, Gabriel Barkay correctly noted that Jerusalem was a primate city (1989, following Jefferson 1939), being about ten times larger than the second largest settlement. The kingdom of Israel, by contrast, followed the rank-size model quite nicely, revealing differences in settlement hierarchy between the two kingdoms (Fig. 18.2) with Israel having a more developed settlement hierarchy and more urbanization (Faust 2012a: 198–206).

Evidence suggests that society in Judah was stratified at the time, especially in the cities (Dever 1995; 2017; Faust 2012a). This can be seen in the dwellings, as well as in the new Judahite tombs, which became popular at the time (see below). The typical dwelling of this era is the famous four-room house, and most families in Judah lived in it or one of its variants (see below). In the cities, small, low-quality three-room houses (usually 30–70 m^2) were dominant; the three main rooms were usually not further subdivided. One can also identify a small group of nicely built, urban, large four-room houses, usually 120–240 m^2 (Fig. 18.3); many of the rooms in those houses were further subdivided. While the size of the houses, the quality of their construction, the use of common walls between houses, and their location testify to the status of their owner, the size of the houses and their inner subdivision suggest that the large houses accommodated large extended families – the biblical *beth 'av* – whereas the smaller

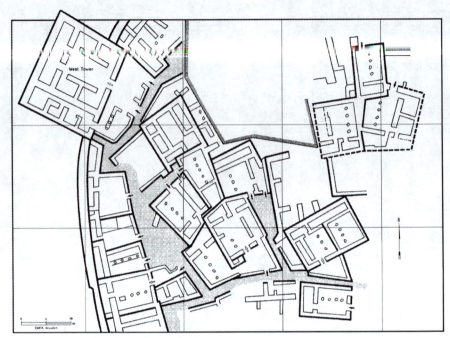

18.3. Plan of the northwestern quarter at Tell Beit Mirsim, exposing an elite dwelling superseding all other houses (from Shiloh 1970: 187). (Courtesy of the IES.)

houses contained nuclear families.[3] Interestingly, the reality in the countryside was somewhat different, and the typical rural house was a large four-room building that was apparently used by extended families. It appears that both landed peasantry (the main segment of the population in the highlands) and the urban elite maintained large kinship units, whereas the poorer segments of the population in the cities who gradually became densely settled lived in nuclear families (Faust 2012a: 159–77, with references). The size of the agricultural production installations identified in association with these houses support their identification with small nuclear families (Faust 2012a). An examination of the many urban houses unearthed reveals, therefore, that the majority belonged to small nuclear families, while a small minority belonged to the elite. Almost completely absent is evidence for something like a "middle class" between the two groups (Fig. 18.4). This picture of a large lower class and small upper class in the towns is typical of what is sometimes called "less-developed state societies" (Nolan and Lenski 2009: 145–6). In the kingdom of Israel, by contrast, one can observe a broader social spectrum including a large number of midsized and mid-quality structures, which are typical of more developed agrarian states (Faust 2012a: 196–8).

The burial practices of the eighth century also expose sharp socioeconomic differences. While the tombs of the kings, representing the uppermost segment of society are not yet identified, the existing spectrum includes impressive single or double burial caves found in the Siloam cemetery opposite the City

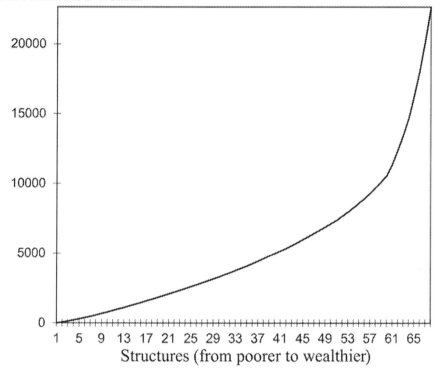

18.4. The kingdom of Judah: differences in the quality of buildings. (Graph by A. Faust.)

of David, in which leading individuals were interred; through large and elaborate multi-family tombs in the Jerusalem area, such as the ones at Keteph Hinnom and Saint Etienne, in which elite lineages buried their dead over generations; large and elaborate family tombs found throughout Judah; simple family tombs unearthed at many sites; simpler burials unearthed near Jerusalem; and even simple inhumations in the ground, representing large segments of the poorer population (Dever 1995; Barkay 1999; Faust 2012a).

It is quite clear that the kingdom of Judah's economy was gradually incorporated within the international system that encompassed the entire region (Faust and Weiss 2011).[4] While some advances were no doubt the result of a long and gradual internal process, others reflect direct and indirect influences from nearby regions. Thus, the growth of the late eighth-century olive oil industry in the Shephelah (e.g., at Tell Beit Mirsim and Beth-Shemesh) might result from interaction with the northern kingdom of Israel, which had a more sophisticated olive oil industry (Eitam 1979). The growth of this industry in general probably resulted from the incorporation of Judah within the growing economic world system of the Mediterranean, powered to a large extent by the Phoenicians (Aubet 2001; see below), most likely through the mediation of the kingdom of Israel and also Philistia. The growth of international

(Phoenician and, to some extent, Arabian) trade also greatly influenced some segments of Judahite society, especially the upper classes, and possibly accelerated some other socioeconomic changes within the society.

Some innovations might be attributed to refugees from the kingdom of Israel (destroyed in 722/720 BCE), although there is, in my view, some exaggeration on this matter, especially regarding the number of refugees (see also Faust 2014b and Na'aman 2014). Still, while the number might not have been very large, one can assume that qualitatively there were influences that go beyond the actual number of refugees (e.g., Israelite influences on religion in Judah).

The pressure exerted by Assyria in the last third of the eighth century required internal changes in the economy of Judah in order to collect the required tribute. The connections with Assyria gradually led to cultural influences, at least as far as the elite are concerned. Thus, we can see how biblical authors, for example, negotiated Assyrian ideology in direct and indirect manners (e.g., Machinist 1983; Aster 2007). The dark shadow cast by Assyria over the entire region during the second half of the eighth century BCE (e.g., Kuhrt 1995: 458–72) increased the feelings of insecurity, contributing to the disintegration of social cohesion, especially in the later part of the eighth century. Once Assyrian campaigns in western Asia began, people must have felt that things could not be taken for granted anymore (see Byrne 2004: 145–8; see below).

Assyria's pressure reached its zenith in the late eighth century. Following the death of Sargon II in 705 BCE, large parts of the empire revolted. In 701 BCE, Sennacherib arrived in the west and reestablished Assyrian domination there. An examination of the archaeological record and the textual sources available (both biblical and Assyrian) indicate that Sennacherib devastated the Shephelah, but destruction in the highlands was partial. It appears that Hezekiah capitulated during the campaign, the Assyrians accepted his surrender, and large parts of the highlands were spared. Jerusalem was also spared, and Hezekiah remained king (e.g., Faust 2008). This, however, had profound influence on the history of Judah, and although much of the ceramic repertoire probably continued for some time after 701, this year usually marks the end of the Iron Age IIB in Judah.

The above processes led to further changes within Judahite society and the development of new forms of organization, partially, at least, at the expense of traditional structures (cf. Halpern 1996). Socioeconomic differences deepened, some segments of society were more influenced by "foreign" traits, state administration increased, and production became more industrialized, as can be seen, for example, in pottery production that can now be called "mass produced." Society gradually became more segmented, objects became less personal, and material culture was, to some extent, alienated (Faust and

Bunimovitz 2008: 157; cf. Gosden 2004: 36–9). Urbanization and hired labor led to the weakening and perhaps even the disintegration of a number of large kinship units in some cities (Faust 2012a: 110–15, 264–6).

IRON AGE IIC: FLOURISHING ECONOMY

The above-discussed changes, both social and political, led to a somewhat different reality in the seventh century BCE. As a consequence of Sennacherib's campaign, the Shephelah was not only devastated, but parts of it were also torn from Judah. Most other parts of Judah, however, flourished during the seventh century, reaching an unparalleled peak (Finkelstein 1994; Faust 2008). Jerusalem, the capital, incorporated many extramural neighborhoods and was most likely larger than before. Jerusalem's countryside, which began developing in the eighth century BCE, reached an unparalleled peak in the seventh century, with hundreds of farmsteads, towns, and royal estates dotting the region. The area of Benjamin, as well as the Judean highlands, the Judean Desert, and even the Beersheva–Arad Valleys, also reached peak settlement at this time. This expansion is in line with the development of the economy.

In the seventh century – although one can debate the exact date within this century – Judah was incorporated within the flourishing Mediterranean economic world that was created mainly by Phoenician activity and that now incorporated the Philistine cities and perhaps even Edom. In contrast to the Neo-Assyrian provinces in the north, the south flourished and appears to have been part of a single economic unit, at the fringe of the Mediterranean world (Faust and Weiss 2011, with many references). The continued growth of Arabian trade contributed to the prosperity, as its products crossed the Negev on the way to Mediterranean ports. Assyria greatly benefitted from its vassals' prosperity and the tribute it subsequently extracted, which stands in stark contrast to the economic reality in its own provinces in the former kingdom of Israel's territories.

These changes, along with the abovementioned changes of the late eighth century, led to a weakening of all the traditional social frameworks and the total disintegration of some, especially in the larger and more central settlements, where most families in the eighth–seventh centuries were nuclear. Thus, the nuclear family and even the individual became prominent at the expense of the extended family or the *beth 'av*. The transformation can also be seen in the biblical texts (Halpern 1996), where there is a change from the more traditional idea of collective punishment to one of personal responsibility. Collective responsibility (e.g., the punishment of sons for the sins of their fathers [e.g., Exod 20:4, 34:7; Num 14:18; Deut 5:8]) reflects a traditional society, where three or four generations lived together or in close proximity. Other verses, however, place responsibility only upon the relevant individuals, for example, "In those days they shall say no more, 'Parents have eaten sour grapes, and the children's teeth are blunted.' But every one shall die for his own sins; whosoever eats the sour grapes, his teeth shall be blunted" (Jer 31:29–30; see also Ezek 18:2–4). Baruch Halpern anchors this development chronologically, relying on the fact that Jeremiah and Ezekiel (of the late Iron Age) express the idea of personal responsibility and oppose collective responsibility.[5] Those verses echo the archaeologically observed changes and the prominent position of small houses with small installations in late eighth–seventh-century BCE Judahite towns. It is likely that this is also the background of the religious reforms of the seventh century; however, this is beyond the scope of the present chapter.

While the seventh century was mostly a period of stability in Judah, the decline of the Assyrian Empire and the rise of the Babylonians was a period of turmoil. The last great king of the seventh century, Josiah, estimated that the Babylonians would win the war against the Assyrians and the Egyptians, so he came to their aid but died in an attempt to stop the king of Egypt on his way to the battlefield. This started a period of instability, in which Judah was subordinate to Egypt and then Babylonia, and was involved in a series of revolts, which ended in 586 BCE, when the kingdom was crushed by Nebuchadnezzar II, and its capital, along with the temple, was destroyed.

IRON AGE IID: THE CONSEQUENCES OF DESTRUCTION

The Babylonian destructions of the early sixth century had drastic effects. Practically all Iron Age sites in Judah, both rural and urban, were destroyed or abandoned, and the vast majority of them were not resettled in the Persian period. This was, inevitably, accompanied by the death of a significant percentage of the population and the exile of the remaining elite. Although thousands remained, we witness a demographic catastrophe that resulted in the drastic transformation of life in Judah, paving the way for new developments (Faust 2012b, with references).

Such demographic and settlement devastations inevitably led to social changes. In this case, the evidence shows that it resulted in social disintegration. In addition to the great settlement and demographic decline, this is exemplified also by the disappearance of both the four-room house and the Judahite tomb. The four-room house is the embodiment of Israelite society and values (see below), and the Judahite tomb became an emblem of the traditional *beth 'av* in Judah (see below). The material traits that accompanied the Judahite individual from birth to death and dominated the built landscape of Judah in the eighth and seventh centuries went out of use over the course of the sixth century BCE, and while a few were still used, none was built/hewn at the time. This means that the most salient symbols of Iron Age

SOCIAL ARCHAEOLOGY OF THE KINGDOM OF JUDAH

society became meaningless in the aftermath of the Babylonian destructions. The social implications of the destruction were therefore severe. Judah in subsequent centuries should be viewed as a post-collapse society (Tainter 1999; Faust 2012b).

The Four-Room House and Israelite Society

The term "four-room house" is generic, referring to a new type of dwelling that became extremely popular and dominant during the Iron Age (Shiloh 1970; 1973; Netzer 1992; Holladay 1997; Faust and Bunimovitz 2003; 2014, with many references). The "ideal type" of this structure is a long house with

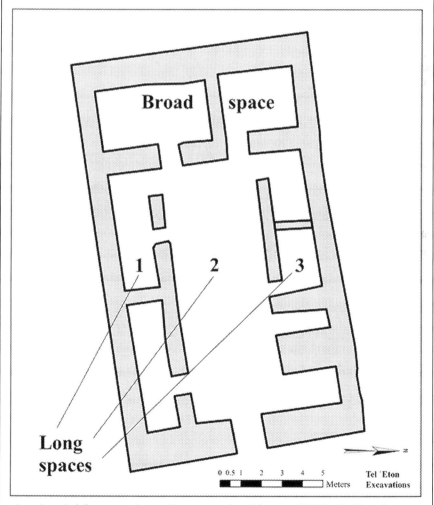

18.5. A typical four-room house (the governor's residency at Tel Eton). Note that most spaces are further subdivided into a number of rooms. (Courtesy of the Tel 'Eton Expedition.)

four main spaces or areas (Fig. 18.5): a broad space at the back, and three long spaces stemming forward from it, sometimes separated by a combination of stone pillars and walls. The entrance was usually located in the central (long) room. Not all houses, however, precisely follow this ideal plan, and there is some variation, mainly in the number of long spaces (see also Fig. 18.3). One can therefore refer to three-, four-, and five-room houses, although all subtypes are usually referred to by the name "four-room house." Additionally, many of the main areas were further subdivided, and hence the term "four-room" is misleading, and "four spaces/areas" would be more accurate. The variation in form of the inner division of the main spaces into smaller units probably resulted from the life cycle of the family. Still, the basic plan is quite rigid and easy to identify. Various studies have attempted to reconstruct the typical activities that took place in the different spaces, attributing certain rooms to storage, others to sleeping and production, while designating some of the side rooms as stables. The finds within the various houses, however, show that despite the rigid planning, the various spaces were not used uniformly.

Prototypes of this house can be seen as early as the late thirteenth–twelfth centuries BCE in some villages in the highlands, and the ideal plan of the four-room house crystallized during the eleventh and mainly tenth centuries. From this time until the sixth century BCE, this is the most prevalent type of house at most Iron Age sites in Israel and Judah; large four-room houses are prevalent in the rural sector whereas smaller three-room houses are more abundant in urban settings, where larger four-room houses are relatively rare. These differences are most likely the result of differing family structure and wealth, whereas large houses were used by rich and large extended families, and smaller (three-room) houses were used by poorer, urban nuclear families.[6]

Most scholars tend to attribute this house to the Israelites, mainly due to its spatial and temporal distribution that seem to correspond with Israelite settlement. Though criticized, this opinion is still the most prevalent, since these houses dominated the built landscape of Israelite settlements, where almost all houses were built in this manner, and are rare outside Israelite settlements. The house's distribution in time and space, and the extremely dominant position it had cannot be explained merely by its functionality; it must have had some social and/or ideological meaning. This is further supported by the disappearance of this house form after the Assyrian and Babylonian destructions of Israel and Judah, when the respective societies collapsed, and their social structure completely disintegrated. No changes in peasant life and no architectural or agricultural inventions took place at the time; therefore, it is clear that the house's demise is connected with the collapse of Israelite society.

It has been suggested that some of the house's architectural characteristics (a few of them revealed by access analysis) mirror Israelite values and ethnic behavior, for example, egalitarian ethos, purity, privacy, and cosmology. These are reflected in the spatial syntax of the house, as well as in the biblical text. Moreover, because the Israelites were preoccupied with order (Douglas 1966), once this kind of house became typical, it eventually became the appropriate and "right" one. The house, therefore, was suitable for the Israelite way of life (or, more likely, had an important role in shaping this way of life) and was used in urban and rural settings by both the rich and poor. Variations between the houses denoted social differences within society, but the fact that all members of society used this house transmitted a clear message of social belonging. The importance of this house to the Israelites is strengthened by the fact that this unique plan or template influenced public construction, and it appears that the typical Judahite tombs of the late Iron Age are also a reflection of this basic plan (see below). The house can therefore be viewed as a microcosmos of the Israelite world, reflecting the Israelite perception of space and embodying Israelite society and its values.[7]

In summary, while formed in the Iron Age I probably to meet the functional needs of hill-country settlers, the four-room house took shape during the process of ethnic negotiation and boundary construction that accompanied Israelite ethnogenesis. Some of its architectural characteristics reflect Israelite values and ethnic behavior, related to privacy, purity, and cosmology. It is thus the amalgamation of function, process, and mind that created the "Israelite house," which, once crystallized, lived for hundreds of years and disappeared following the destruction of Israel and Judah, when its creators and maintainers lost coherence and were dispersed (Faust and Bunimovitz 2003; 2014).

The Judahite Tombs as Reflecting Social Changes

No Iron Age I and IIA burials are known from the core of Judah, and it appears that most of the population prior to the eighth century buried its dead in simple inhumations in the ground (just like in the kingdom of Israel) (Kletter 2002; Faust 2004). The causes for this are probably related to the Israelite egalitarian ethos, which is also reflected in many other material traits and in the Bible (Faust 2006, with references). Only some of the people in the Canaanite enclave in the Shephelah – mainly its elite – interred their dead in burial caves (e.g., Katz and Faust 2014). This changed in the eighth century when a new type of burial – the Judahite tomb – was adopted *en masse* in Judah.

The typical Judahite tomb was a hewn cave, shaped like a ת, with a corridor in the middle and three benches on the sides of the corridor (Fig. 18.6). The dead were left on the benches to decompose, and the bones were then transferred to a repository that was hewn below one of the benches or at the corner. Hundreds of such caves (including some variants) were identified over the years, reflecting, as we have seen, much of the socioeconomic spectrum of Judah.

It is likely that the idea of using tombs was adopted from the Shephelah, where burial caves were utilized (even if on a small scale) during the Iron Age I–IIA. However, why did the people in Judah change their tradition of using simple inhumations? It has been suggested that the adoption of the Judahite tomb was the extended families' response to the social changes of the eighth century (Faust and

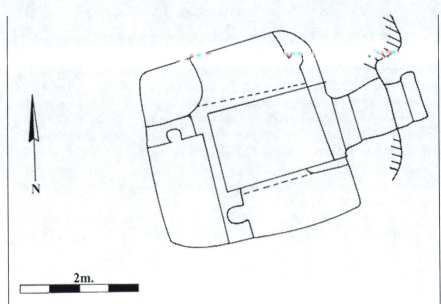

18.6. A typical Judahite tomb from Gibeon (from Eshel 1987: fig. 9). (Courtesy of the IES.)

Bunimovitz 2008).[8] As the processes of population growth, urbanization, mass production, insecurity, and alienation intensified, the traditional families felt threatened and needed to "protect" themselves. One of the main messages transmitted by the Judahite tomb, which was used by extended families over generations, can probably be summarized as "we are a big, strong, and coherent family. The generations continue and the family will persist forever." During earlier eras, when extended families were the norm, "exposed" transmission of such messages was not needed. Yet, when the status of the extended families weakened, there was an urgent need to stress *continuity* and *permanency*. It was essential to tie the family together and strengthen the individual's sense of belonging, so that the family would not disintegrate. The response to the continued crises and insecurity was an attempt to immortalize the family in stone. When other families disintegrated, those that survived stressed their continuity, both to themselves and others. Thus, the new form of burial became an important component of life in Judah.

When Judah was destroyed in 586 BCE, however, and its social structure disintegrated, the large families disappeared, and there was no more need for this tomb. Some of the survivors continued to use their family tombs for some time; however, their progeny did not live in traditional extended families anymore and did not continue to use the tombs. The tradition gradually died away.

NOTES

1 We follow Amihai Mazar's (e.g., 2011) modified conventional chronology and date the Iron Age I–II transition to the first half of the tenth century BCE, perhaps to around 970 BCE.

2 Population estimates are very problematic on various grounds and cannot be trusted. We will therefore not attempt to count the number of inhabitants in eighth-century Judah.
3 The small houses were typically not organized as compounds that can be associated with large units.
4 For the economy, see Katz 2008.
5 The dating of the passages is debated, but this is beyond the scope of this chapter.
6 Rich families were usually larger, and there is much overlap between the groups.
7 For an extensive discussion and references, see Faust and Bunimovitz 2003; 2014.
8 The tomb was not only adopted but also adapted. The typical Judahite tombs followed the basic spatial configuration of the four-room house (see above), further strengthening the importance of the latter. For an extended survey of tombs, see Bloch-Smith 1992 and Yezerski 2013.

REFERENCES

Aster, S. Z. 2007. Transmission of Neo-Assyrian Claims of Empire to Judah in the Late Eighth Century B.C.E. *HUCA* 78: 1–44.

Aubet, M. E. 2001. *The Phoenicians and the West: Politics, Colonies and Trade*. 2nd edn. and exp. ed. Cambridge: Cambridge University Press.

Barkay, G. 1989. Jerusalem as a Primate City. In *Settlements, Population and Economy in the Land of Israel*, ed. S. Bunimovitz, M. Kochavi, and A. Kasher, 24–5. Tel Aviv: Tel Aviv University (Hebrew).

 1999. Burial Caves and Dwellings in Judah during Iron Age II: Sociological Aspects. In *Material Culture, Society and Ideology: New Directions in the Archaeology of the Land of Israel*, ed. A. Faust and A. M. Maeir, 96–102. Ramat-Gan: Bar-Ilan University (Hebrew).

Ben-Yosef, E.; Langgut, D.; and Sapir-Hen, L. 2017. Beyond Smelting: New Insights on Iron Age (10th c. BCE) Metalworkers Community from Excavations at a Gatehouse and Associated Livestock Pens in Timna, Israel. *JAS: Reports* 11: 411–26.

Bloch-Smith, E. 1992. *Judahite Burial Practices and Beliefs about the Dead*. Sheffield: Sheffield Academic.

Bunimovitz, S., and Lederman, Z. 2011. Canaanite Resistance: The Philistines and Beth-Shemesh – A Case Study from Iron Age I. *BASOR* 364: 37–51.

Byrne, R. 2004. Lie Back and Think of Judah: The Reproductive Politics of Pillar Figurines. *NEA* 67: 137–51.

Cohen, R. 2004. *Ancient Settlements of the Negev Highlands,* Vol. 2: *The Iron Age and the Persian Period*. IAA Reports 20. Jerusalem: IAA.

Dever, W. G. 1995. Social Structure in Palestine in the Iron II Period on the Eve of Destruction. In *The Archaeology of Society in the Holy Land*, ed. T. E. Levy, 416–31. NAAA. London: Leicester University Press.

 2017. *Beyond the Texts: An Archaeological Portrait of Ancient Israel and Judah*. Atlanta: SBL.

Douglas, M. 1966. *Purity and Danger: An Analysis of the Concept of Pollution and Taboo*. Harmondsworth: Penguin.

Eitam, D. 1979. Olive Presses of the Israelite Period. *TA* 6: 146–55.

Eshel, H. 1987. The Late Iron Age Cemetery of Gibeon. *IEJ* 37: 1–17.

Faust, A. 2002. Burnished Pottery and Gender Hierarchy in Iron Age Israelite Society. *JMA* 15: 53–73.

 2004. "Mortuary Practices, Society and Ideology": The Lack of Iron Age I Burials in the Highlands in Context. *IEJ* 54: 174–90.

2006. *Israel's Ethnogenesis: Settlement, Interaction, Expansion and Resistance.* AAA. London: Equinox.

2008. Settlement and Demography in Seventh-Century Judah and the Extent and Intensity of Sennacherib's Campaign. *PEQ* 140: 168–94.

2012a. *The Archaeology of Israelite Society in Iron Age II.* Winona Lake, IN: Eisenbrauns.

2012b. *Judah in the Neo-Babylonian Period: The Archaeology of Desolation.* ABS 18. Atlanta: SBL.

2013. The Shephelah in the Iron Age: A New Look on the Settlement of Judah. *PEQ* 145: 203–19.

2014a. Highlands or Lowlands? Reexamining Demographic Processes in Iron Age Judah. *UF* 45: 111–42.

2014b. On Jerusalem's Expansion during the Iron Age II. In *Exploring the Narrative: Jerusalem and Jordan in the Bronze and Iron Ages*, ed. E. van der Steen, J. Boertien, and N. Mulder-Hymans, 256–85. London: Bloomsbury.

2015. Chronological and Spatial Changes in the Rural Settlement Sector of Ancient Israel during the Iron Age: An Overview. *RB* 122: 247–67.

2017. Jebus, the City of David and Jerusalem: Jerusalem from the Period of the Settlement to the Period of Neo-Babylonian Rule. In *Jerusalem: Five-Thousand Years of History*, ed. A. Faust, J. Schwartz, and E. Baruch, 35–72. Ramat-Gan: The Ingeborg Renner Center for Jerusalem Studies (Hebrew).

Faust, A., and Bunimovitz, S. 2003. The Four Room House: Embodying Iron Age Israelite Society. *NEA* 66: 22–31.

2008. The Judahite Rock-Cut Tomb: Family Response at a Time of Change. *IEJ* 58: 150–70.

2014. The House and the World: The Israelite House as a Microcosm. In *Family and Household Religion: Toward a Synthesis of Old Testament Studies, Archaeology, Epigraphy, and Cultural Studies*, ed. R. Albertz, B. Alpert Nakhai, S. M. Olyan, and R. Schmitt, 143–64. Winona Lake, IN: Eisenbrauns.

Faust, A., and Katz, H. 2011. Philistines, Israelites and Canaanites in the Southern Trough Valley during the Iron Age I. *Egypt and the Levant* 21: 231–47.

Faust, A., and Sapir, Y. 2018. The "Governor's Residency" at Tel 'Eton, the United Monarchy, and the Impact of the Old-House Effect on Large-Scale Archaeological Reconstructions. *Radiocarbon* 60: 801–20.

Faust, A., and Weiss, E. 2011. Between Assyria and the Mediterranean World: The Prosperity of Judah and Philistia in the Seventh Century BCE in Context. In *Interweaving Worlds: Systemic Interaction in Eurasia, 7th to 1st Millennia BC*, ed. T. C. Wilkinson, S. Sherratt, and J. Bennet, 189–204. Oxford: Oxbow.

Finkelstein, I. 1994. The Archaeology of the Days of Manasseh. In *Scripture and Other Artifacts: Essays on the Bible and Archaeology in Honor of Philip J. King*, ed. M. D. Coogan, J. C. Exum, and L. E. Stager, 169–87. Louisville, KY: Westminster John Knox.

1995. *Living on the Fringe: The Archaeology and History of the Negev, Sinai and Neighbouring Regions in the Bronze and Iron Ages.* MMA 6. Sheffield: Sheffield Academic.

Finkelstein, I., and Fantalkin, A. 2012. Khirbet Qeiyafa: An Unsensational Archaeological and Historical Interpretation. *TA* 39: 38–63.

Finkelstein, I., and Mazar, A. 2007. *The Quest for Historical Israel: Debating Archaeology and the History of Early Israel.* ABS 17. Atlanta: SBL.

Garfinkel, Y.; Ganor, S.; and Hasel, M. 2010. The Contribution of Khirbet Qeiyafa to Our Understanding of the Iron Age Period. *Strata* 28: 39–54.

Gosden, C. 2004. *Archaeology and Colonialism: Cultural Contact from 5000 BC to the Present.* Topics in Contemporary Archaeology. Cambridge: Cambridge University Press.

Halpern, B. 1996. Sybil, or the Two Nations? Archaism, Kinship, Alienation and the Elite Redefinition of Traditional Culture in Judah in the 8th–7th Centuries B.C.E. In *The Study of the Ancient Near East in the Twenty-First Century*, ed. J. S. Cooper and G. M. Schwartz, 291–338. Winona Lake, IN: Eisenbrauns.

Herzog, Z. 1994. The Beer-Sheba Valley: From Nomadism to Monarchy. In *From Nomadism to Monarchy: Archaeological and Historical Aspects of Early Israel*, ed. I. Finkelstein and N. Na'aman, 122–49. Jerusalem: Yad Izhak Ben-Zvi; IES; Washington, DC: Biblical Archaeology Society.

Holladay, J. S. 1997. Four-Room House. *OEANE* 2: 337–41.

Jefferson, M. 1939. The Law of the Primate City. *Geographical Review* 29: 226–32.

Katz, H. 2008. "*A Land of Grain and Wine . . . a Land of Oil and Honey*": *The Economy of the Kingdom of Judah.* Jerusalem: Yad Izhak Ben-Zvi (Hebrew).

Katz, H., and Faust, A. 2014. The Chronology of the Iron Age IIA in Judah in the Light of Tel 'Eton Tomb C3 and Other Assemblages. *BASOR* 371: 103–27.

Kletter, R. 2002. People without Burials? The Lack of Iron I Burials in the Central Highlands of Palestine. *IEJ* 52: 28–48.

Kuhrt, A. 1995. *The Ancient Near East, c. 3000–330 BC*, Vol. 1. Routledge History of the Ancient World. London: Routledge.

Levy, T. E.; Najjar, M.; and Ben-Yosef, E., eds. 2014. *New Insights into the Iron Age Archaeology of Edom, Southern Jordan.* Los Angeles: The Cotsen Institute of Archaeology Press.

Machinist, P. 1983. Assyria and Its Image in the First Isaiah. *JAOS* 103: 719–37.

Master, D. M. 2001. State Formation Theory and the Kingdom of Ancient Israel. *JNES* 60: 117–31.

Mazar, A. 2011. The Iron Age Chronology Debate: Is the Gap Narrowing? Another Viewpoint. *NEA* 74: 105–11.

Na'aman, N. 2014. Dismissing the Myth of a Flood of Israelite Refugees in the Late Eighth Century BCE. *ZAW* 126: 1–14.

Netzer, E. 1992. Domestic Architecture in the Iron Age. In *The Architecture of Ancient Israel from the Prehistoric to the Persian Period in Memory of Immanuel (Munya) Dunayevsky*, ed. A. Kempinski and R. Reich, 193–201. Jerusalem: IES.

Nolan, P., and Lenski, G. 2009. *Human Societies: An Introduction to Macrosociology.* 11th rev. and upd. ed. Boulder, CO: Paradigm.

Shiloh, Y. 1970. The Four Room House: Its Situation and Function in the Israelite City. *IEJ* 20:180–90.

―――. 1973. The Four Room House – The Israelite Type-House? *ErIsr* 11: 277–85 (Hebrew).

Stager, L. E. 2003. The Patrimonial Kingdom of Solomon. In *Symbiosis, Symbolism, and the Power of the Past: Canaan, Ancient Israel, and Their Neighbors from the Late Bronze Age through Roman Palaestina; Proceedings of the Centennial Symposium, W. F. Albright Institute of Archaeological Research and the American Schools of Oriental Research, Jerusalem, May 29–31, 2000*, ed. W. G. Dever and S. Gitin, 63–74. Winona Lake, IN: Eisenbrauns.

Tainter, J. A. 1999. Post-Collapse Societies. In *Companion Encyclopedia of Archaeology*, Vol. 2, ed. G. Barker, 988–1039. London: Routledge.

Yezerski, I. 2013. Typology and Chronology of the Iron Age II–III Judahite Rock-Cut Tombs. *IEJ* 63: 50–77.

NINETEEN

PHASES IN THE HISTORY OF THE KINGDOM OF ISRAEL

DANIEL M. MASTER

According to the Hebrew Bible, the kingdom of Israel was unstable. The tribes of Israel shifted their allegiance from the house of Saul in Gibeah to the house of David in Jerusalem; following this, they declared loyalty to the house of Jeroboam in Shechem, followed by the house of Baasha in Tirzah, and the house of Omri (and others) in Samaria. The kingdom was destroyed in the late eighth century by the Assyrians and was never reconstituted except in the memories of the house of David who hoped for a future day in which all Israel would once again be ruled from Jerusalem.

Such an outline of fluctuating loyalties is relatively unremarkable among the Levantine kingdoms in the Iron Age. It rests on the interplay between two widely attested Near Eastern political forms: the tribal collective and the monarchy. But in this case, since the political history of the kingdom of Israel is recorded in the Hebrew Bible, questions have been raised among biblical scholars about its reliability. Archaeology has been called in to adjudicate, but it rarely provides a definitive evaluation. As a result, the critical evaluation of the Hebrew Bible and the syntheses of archaeology exist side by side, each with their own uncertainties and each in need of the other for the best picture of Iron Age history.

The Hebrew Bible, whatever its weaknesses, remains the most important source that we have for detailing the politics of the Iron Age, while archaeology provides an overarching geographic, economic, and social picture (Hawkes 1954). As scholars progressively uncover more of the ancient world through archaeology and the recovery of contemporary texts, the possibilities for understanding the kingdom of Israel become progressively richer. The following summary attempts to sketch out some recent developments in both fields which gesture toward a framework for a general history of the kingdom.

ISRAEL AS A POLITICAL COLLECTIVE AND ETHNIC GROUP

The use of "Israel" to describe a collective is the first item of interest. This entity has long been understood to be a tribal confederacy representing a stage in the hierarchy of a typical patrimonial society (Stager 1985; 1998). While such political confederacies were common in the ancient Near East, the structures which bound them together were varied. As Daniel Fleming describes, the tribal collectives of the Simal and Yamina of the Bronze Age Mari texts encompassed multiple constituent kin groups and practiced a variety of subsistence strategies (2012: 210–15; Miglio 2014: 76). Despite a host of differences, they could mobilize together to achieve political goals (Fleming 2004: 230). Brandon Benz extended these observations into the Late Bronze Age Tell el-Amarna corpus, pointing to a variety of political entities that had dynamic existences within the international world of the Late Bronze Age (Benz 2013: 278–93). Both Fleming and Benz struggle to apply these observations as a model for ancient Israel, primarily because tribal collectives were so diverse. Tribal collectives such as Israel could have been organized in the highlands or lowlands; could have been centralized or decentralized; need not have occupied contiguous territories; could have coalesced around a shared religious, geographic, or economic interest; and could have engaged in all varieties of agriculture or pastoralism. The examples from the ancient Near East open an array of idiosyncratic possibilities. Still, all agree that it was typical for tribal groups such as an "Israel" to form durative political bonds using kin-based language. When Merenptah refers for the first time to a group called "Israel," the historian is not surprised (Hasel 1998: 195–204). New groups appeared on the scene all the time.

Though the term "Israel" existed from the thirteenth century, this does not mean that the name denoted precisely the same groups or geographic location through the centuries. Once formed, Near Eastern groups continued to develop. Bryan Stone (1995) and Seymour Gitin (1998) envision the Philistines, contemporaries of Israel, as an enduring ethnic group[1] with dramatically shifting cultural manifestations. Their suggestion, however, is equally true for a people such as Israel, who appear with the same appellation in texts separated by centuries.[2] Indeed, the meaning of "Israel" as a religious, political, or ethnic collective has not ceased to evolve over the last 3,000 years.

ISRAEL AS A KINGDOM AND STATE

At some point, however, this entity called "Israel" adopted kingship as a form of political expression. This is also not remarkable. For patrimonial societies, kingship was the most common form of consolidated political action in the region (King and Stager 2001: 201–58; Master 2001; Schloen 2001). Recent work has also highlighted that the tribe and kingdom were not mutually exclusive. As Anne Porter (2010) has argued, a variety of structures allowed for the maintenance of large-scale polities (kingdoms) *within* the context of ongoing kin-based organizations (tribes). A monarch could be king of Israel; yet, if Israel functioned in a fashion typical of most Near Eastern societies, the tribes retained underlying decision-making structures which could be mobilized for or against a monarch.

More controversially, the kingdom of Israel has been described as an ancient "state," a term fraught with disagreement (e.g., Smith 2003). Generally speaking, "state" has very specific connotations related to internal authority which have been common since, at least, Thomas Hobbes (1651). Hobbes's concept of a state (or commonwealth) comprised the sole legitimate source of authority in a given territory. This centralized concept of the European state, combined with the post-Westphalian idea of geographic borders, became the model for anthropologists who sought to define the rise of complex societies (Weber 1946: 82). In this sense, the kingdom of Israel was never a state and is better referred to as a tribal kingdom (Master 2001).

But, even in the modern world, this Hobbesian perspective does not work well. For example, in modern parlance, China, Ghana, France, Liechtenstein, and Syria are named as sovereign states. Their internal cohesion, degree of bureaucracy, and level of internal control are radically different. These political entities are connected primarily by their recognition as independent international actors by some great powers.[3]

If one isolates just this single commonality – international recognition – it is clear that ancient groups also sought and received acknowledgment from great powers (e.g., Egypt, Assyria) as independent international actors and, having achieved it, practiced a kind of statecraft.[4] The ancient Near East had its own standards to support claims to statehood; victories on the battlefield or economic attainments were instantiated in a capital city and its palace. In some cases, the status of the city outside traditional power structures was critical (as with Aziru at Sumur [Benz 2013: 291] or at Samaria). In other cases, the antiquity of the city brought new avenues for legitimacy (as with the adoption of the *sakkanakum* tradition by the kings of Mari [Miglio 2014: 57–61] or as at Jerusalem). In this sense, Israel did function as a state at several points, and its kings practiced statecraft when they had attained the requisite international status. It is this narrow concept of the state and statecraft that we will explore in the following paragraphs.

BEFORE THE ISRAELITE STATE

The world of diplomacy and reputation is very difficult to map across the archaeological landscape,[5] much more so when the political entities are small and fleeting. Israel first appears in the late thirteenth-century Merenptah Stele as a people without reference to an urban center. Many would argue that this can be paired with the Song of Deborah in Judges 5, which pictures a set of highland tribes with a relationship framed in terms of a common allegiance to the god Yahweh.[6] In this text, some of the tribes, those in the hills of the northern West Bank, southern Galilee, and the western fringe of the Transjordan were under some sort of stress imposed by a coalition of lowland Canaanite kings (Schloen 1993). From a political standpoint, this text points to a world of uncertain connections between discontiguous highland enclaves simply trying to survive; it is a picture of a weak Israel (Fig. 19.1). From the text, it is not clear who else lived in these highlands, nor did these spaces necessarily represent the whole of those who expressed allegiance to the god Yahweh. But, if we accept that the Hebrew Bible authentically communicates this Israel as primarily living in the highlands in the Iron 1, then the uniform archaeological patterns of those highland sites reveals a likely context for early Israelite life.

Iron 1 highland villages (e.g., 'Izbet Ṣarṭah [Finkelstein 1986], Tell al-'Umayri [Herr 1998], Shiloh [Finkelstein, Bunimovitz, and Lederman 1993], the Lower Galilee [Gal 1992]) show pillared houses containing families engaged in agriculture, pastoralism, food storage, and small crafts (Stager 1985). In this moment, terracing transformed the productivity of the highlands, particularly in terms of olive oil production (Stager 1985: 6–9). In the midst of these villages, several highland cities preserved the legacy of Bronze Age governance and internationalism. Shechem maintained a raised acropolis crowned by a substantial tower temple, which was architecturally undiminished as a place of refuge from the time of its building until sometime in the late twelfth century (Stager 2003). As such, it represents an important locus of physical continuity for the political traditions of the Bronze Age into the early Iron Age.

Farther to the south, Jerusalem also remained surrounded by huge Bronze Age fortifications (Reich and Shukron 2008: 1801–3)[7] and possessed a tradition of international recognition and kingship dating back to the Egyptian Execration Texts. As in the Bronze Age (Alt 1925), so in the early Iron Age, Jerusalem and Shechem had the strongest international claims to authority.

By the eleventh century, the village culture of the highlands was also present at several lowland cities, showing an expansion of highland cultural ways, and, perhaps by implication, highlanders themselves. Tel Dan (Stratum IV) had many affinities with Iron 1 settlements of the highlands to the south, including similar cooking pots, storage vessels, and faunal patterns (Ilan 1999: 132–3, 204–7). Similarly, at Hazor, the post-Bronze Age village (Strata XII–XI)

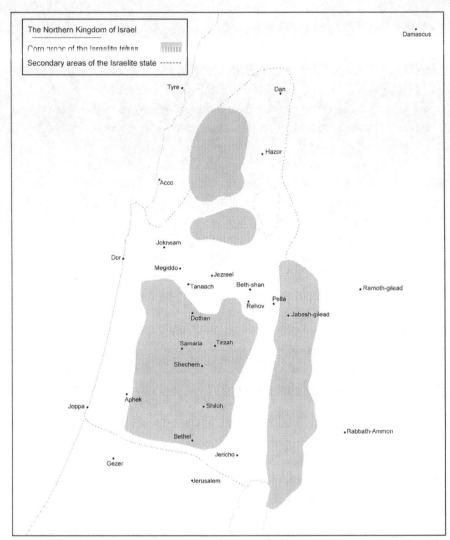

19.1. Key excavations in the Northern Kingdom of Israel. (Prepared by D. M. Master. Base map courtesy of J. Monson and Biblical Backgrounds.)

showed similar patterns (Ben-Ami and Ben-Tor 2012: 25–6). None of these movements is necessarily Israelite, but, at the very least, the Iron 1 highland cultural affinities provide a backdrop for these cities to be part of later Iron 2 kingdoms based in the hills.

Still, the regions of Iron 1 highland culture were split by the main transit corridor of the north – the valley system linking the Jezreel, 'Ein Harod, and Jordan Valleys.[8] In the Iron 1, the cities in these valleys maintained Bronze Age cultural patterns (Finkelstein 2003; Münger 2013). The Hebrew Bible recalls this cultural distinction in an odd record of Israelite failure: the list of cities which the Israelite tribes did not conquer (Josh 15:63, 16:10, 17:11–13; Judg 1:27–36).

Some have argued that these references represent a later monarchic apology for the taking of these cities from the tribes for the purposes of the central government (Kallai 1998: 139–43; Rainey and Notley 2006: 134); but behind this tendentious purpose, the list corresponds to the important Bronze Age cities in the lowlands with cultural continuity into the Iron 1 (Levin 2012).[9]

ROAD TO STATEHOOD – THE GEOGRAPHIC IMPERATIVE

Faust argues that between the Iron 1 and early Iron 2, settlement in the highlands underwent a marked shift as people left rural villages for larger cities (2015). Once in the cities, they lived in the same types of pillared houses that had dominated the rural landscape in the eleventh century, and the rest of their lives seem to be in continuity with what came before. It was not a wholesale change in all aspects of material culture, but rather a reconfiguration of settlement patterns in response, according to Faust, to security concerns. If Stager is correct that the Iron 1 period saw a substantive increase in terracing for olive groves (1985), this would have allowed centralization to take place without seeing a diminution of production, as olive groves need not have been directly adjacent to the new urban centers. This physical transformation could have created the need for more robust structures of social cohesion or provided opportunities for enhanced collective action; however, even a dramatic shift in highlands settlement does not clearly point the way forward to a powerful kingdom of Israel.[10]

In order to achieve international significance, the highlanders would have had to win control of lowland cities in order to unite the scattered highland enclaves and to control key trade routes.[11] In the Iron Age, this expansion of highland power into the lowlands probably took place in the Iron 2a, and the touchstone for this transition is Stratum V at Megiddo.[12] Yigael Yadin contended that there was a tenth-century stratum made up of monumental buildings and fortifications (Stratum VA–IVB), which stratigraphically predated the major ninth-century Iron Age fortification wall (Stratum IVA, Wall 325). According to Yadin, this was the beginning of highland power in the valleys. Yadin (1960) located a casemate wall, the original use of a six-chambered gate, and at least two palaces (6000, 1723) in this earlier phase. The gate has parallels to several other cities with highland affinities, and Palace 6000 is the first example of what would become the major type of administrative building in the kingdom of Israel (Lehmann and Killebrew 2010). Yadin, and many since, have been explicit about linking this beginning with King Solomon's rule over Israel from a capital in Jerusalem (1 Kgs 9:15). While every aspect of Yadin's synthesis has been hotly disputed, it is still probably the case that this stratum, whatever the details, represents a decisive victory of highland culture, not only expressing power in the lowlands but displaying that power in monumental architecture.

More recent excavations by Tel Aviv University have attempted to reassess the date of this transition; however, several ambiguities have hindered a conclusive resolution. First, as seen by the excavations at Tel Jezreel (Finkelstein 1999) and Tel Rehov, the Iron IIA ceramic sequence is not distinctive enough to clearly distinguish between tenth–early ninth-century ceramics (Mazar 2005: 20). This ceramic conclusion, first noticed by Yohanan Aharoni and Ruth Amiran, has hindered the precise phasing of loci in the new excavations at Megiddo, which are not physically connected to previously excavated material (Ben-Tor and Zarzecki-Peleg 2015: 135–6; *contra* Herzog and Singer-Avitz 2006). Additionally, radiocarbon dating – for years thought to hold the key to precise determination of tenth and ninth-century strata – has been indecisive at Megiddo for the key strata (Toffolo et al. 2014). Finally, stratigraphic correlations between The University of Chicago and Tel Aviv University expeditions have proven difficult since the areas excavated by modern methods are far more complex than those described by The University of Chicago team.[13]

Highland control over these lowlands, at whatever moment, remains the key indicator that a highland alliance had the strength to play an international role; it is the difference between weak insular tribes and an international state.

In typical Near Eastern fashion, the tribes of the kingdom of Israel would also have needed a capital city with a palace in order to be "like the nations" (1 Sam 8:5). The biblical text recognizes an initial achievement of these ends through the conquest of Jerusalem and an enhancement of its existing palace complex. While the specific historical weight of these texts is debated, the Deuteronomist has the geopolitics right. Jerusalem, with its Bronze Age royal history, would have been the best option for an early tenth-century highland group seeking to attract international attention.

Any group uniting the highlands and the lowland valleys, and occupying a known Bronze Age capital would quickly have come to the attention of other great powers. In the late tenth century, Pharaoh Shishak campaigned into the Negev, into the central highlands, and through the Jordan and Jezreel Valleys (Rainey and Notley 2006: 85–9). This was a novel path of conquest compared to earlier Bronze Age Egyptian campaigns. Mario Liverani argues that these paths of destruction represent the interstices between a nascent kingdom of Israel in the northern hills and a small kingdom of Jerusalem in the southern hills (2005: 101–3). It is even more likely that this represents the Egyptian intention to push upstart highland powers away from lowland expansion (e.g., Megiddo Stratum VA–IVB, Rehov Stratum V, Ta'anach Stratum IIB, Yoqne'am Stratum XIV). In either case, the outcome was surely the same: The lowlands were defeated while Galilee, the northern highlands, and the western slopes of Transjordan were unscathed. Tribal kingdoms may have still crowned monarchs at this point, but the path to international recognition would have been forced to begin again.

THE OMRIDE STATE

According to the Hebrew Bible, the rejection of the house of David left the northern tribes with internal control over tribal Israel but without a good option for an internationally recognized capital. In the biblical recollection, the new rulers of the Israelite collective attempted to establish their legitimacy by co-option of the old Bronze Age capital of Shechem. Shechem was a center of highland politics in the Bronze Age memory, but, by this point, it would have been a meager village, unable to sustain northern statecraft (Campbell 2002: 8–9). For renewed international legitimacy, the kingdom of Israel would wait for the house of Omri.

As Ron Tappy (1992) has detailed, the house of Omri constructed a huge acropolis enclosure with a massive casemate wall in the early ninth century (Building Period 2, Pottery Period 3 early). This new city, the largest in the Northern Kingdom, gave the house of Omri precisely the type of international credibility it desired. Indeed, even after the dynasty had been replaced, the great power of Assyria still referred to this kingdom of Israel as the *bīt-Ḫumrî* (Younger 2003). The power of this dynasty was also displayed in its comprehensive control over the lowlands.[14] Megiddo (Stratum IVA) saw substantial fortification. Tel Rehov shows its highland connections (Stratum IV) through at least two references to a Nimshi, a name that also appears in the patronymic of the Israelite king, Jehu, alongside a tantalizing reference to an "[E]lisha'" (Aḥituv and Mazar 2014). Jonathan Greer argues that not only was Tel Dan an Israelite center in this period (2013: 46, n. 11; see also Biran 1994 and Bruins et al. 2005; *contra* Arie 2008), but the types and ages of the sacrificial animals in the precinct match what would be expected by a group following religious strictures, such as those in the Hebrew Bible. He further notes that the polemics of the Hebrew Bible against the Dan high place never accuse those officiating of worshiping a god other than the Israelite national god Yahweh (Greer 2013: 125–6). Hazor (Stratum VIII) also seems connected to the Israelite kingdom with an impressive fortress following an established pattern for the north (Lehmann and Killebrew 2010) and domestic architecture emphasizing the pillared houses of the type that had been typical in the highlands since the Iron 1. At Tel Jezreel, a fortified enclosure with fortified towers in the typical Israelite pattern marks another capital. According to the excavators, this city laid claim to the lowland passes on behalf of the highland kingdom (Ussishkin 2007).

If these lowland areas were secondary to the highland cores of the Israelite polity, their cultural trajectories may have followed different paths as well. A longitudinal study of pig DNA pointed to the introduction of new genetic strains of European pig into the Jezreel Valley (at Megiddo, Tel Jezreel, and Beth Shean) during the ninth century (see tables in Meiri et al. 2013; *contra* the discussion in Meiri et al. 2013). These new strains appear to have come from elsewhere in the Mediterranean and show that western (likely Tyrian) influence changed the practices of animal husbandry even for areas within the control of the Israelite kingdom. However, these new influences seem confined to the Jezreel and Jordan Valleys and the coastal plain, areas peripheral to the highland core of Israel. One could attempt to extrapolate from the lowlands to the kingdom of Israel as a whole (see Sapir-Hen et al. 2013), but this is problematic. At Tel Dan and Hazor, which seem to have had highland affinities from the earlier Iron 1, pig is extremely rare (Wapnish and Hesse 1991: 18; Sapir-Hen et al. 2013).[15]

It is reasonable to suggest that at this moment in the ninth century, the kingdom of Israel's power expanded to fill the gaps between its scattered highland heartlands. Combined with the capital at Samaria, the kingdom had all the elements necessary for international relevance. It was able to dominate neighboring kingdoms, such as Geshur, Moab (Mesha Stele), and Jerusalem, and it could project power internationally. This statecraft is most clearly illustrated in the kingdom's substantive participation with the Levantine alliance in the battle of Qarqar against Shalmaneser III (Kurkh Monolith).

But such statecraft had its dangers. In the late ninth century, the Hebrew Bible records the campaigns of Hazael, king of Aram-Damascus, campaigning as far south as Gath (Tell eṣ-Ṣafi). Though the historical usefulness of the sections of the Hebrew Bible that deal with the Aramaean wars of the late ninth century is debated (see Halpern and Lemaire 2010: 135–50), the recent excavations of Hazael's siege at Gath (Tell eṣ-Ṣafi) fit with the geopolitical picture described in the texts (Maier 2012: 34–48). For a king of Damascus to extend power to Philistia necessitated control over routes through the northern lowlands, and this route is illustrated by a cumulative path of destruction through the Huleh Basin (Tel Dan Inscription, destruction of Hazor Stratum VII), the Jordan Valley (destruction of Tel Rehov Stratum IV), the western entrance to the Jezreel Valley (destruction of the Jezreel Enclosure), and the southernmost pass through the Carmel ridge (destruction of Tell Dothan). The most direct way to curtail the power of the kingdom of Israel was to diminish highland control over the lowlands. Hazael need not have inflicted any substantial damage to the highland enclaves that represented the heartland of tribal Israel. He merely left the kingdom divided, contained, and internationally irrelevant.

AN EIGHTH-CENTURY STATE

Following Adad-nirari's campaign against Damascus, the pressure on the Northern Kingdom was relieved (Calah Orthostat Slab), and the kingdom was once again able to expand into the lowlands and beyond. Because the stratigraphy of Samaria is so problematic (Tappy 2001), it is difficult to chart the ebbs and flows of the kingdom from this site alone. The Samaria Ivories, which surely show an international focus (Suter 2011), cannot be dated on archaeological grounds but likely relate to this eighth-century *floruit* (Tappy 2001: 444–95). The same is true of the substantive quantities of the imported Phoenician red-slipped and polished platters and bowls frequently called "Samaria Ware" (Aznar 2005: 171–6). Even though the kingdom of Israel may have been politically resurgent, it remained just another polity on the periphery of a Mediterranean market managed by Phoenician merchants (Broodbank 2013: 499–500). Even the typical "torpedo jar" found at so many Israelite cities in the eighth century seems to have thoroughly Phoenician origins (Aznar 2005: 157–8)

The Samaria Ostraca are more closely dated to the early eighth century on paleographic grounds, and they show a robust palace economy (Master 2014: 83–5); however, their focus is so provincial that they cannot give a sense of the kingdom's expansion into the lowlands. At Beth Shean, Amihai Mazar notes the use of the four-room house syntax in larger administrative buildings, as well as ostraca, which closely parallel those at Samaria. According to Mazar, all of this points to a site under Israelite control (Beth Shean Stratum P-7 [Mazar 2006: 33]). Jar handles made in Samaria with the administrative stamp of a certain *zkryw* are found at Tel Dan and et-Tell (Bethsaida), linking them to highland administration (Brandl 2009).[16] To the south, epigraphic discoveries at Kuntillet Ajrud show some expansion of early eighth-century power deep into the Negev. The direct reference to Yahweh of Samaria and the use of certain northern spellings argue that the *Sar 'Ir* (commandant of the fortress) answered to the king of Israel (Meshel 2012: xxi–xxii).

By the late eighth century, it was Assyria's turn to diminish the reach of the Israelite kingdom. Tiglath-pileser III campaigned into the northern valleys (2 Kgs 15:29), moving all the way to Ashkelon (annals and summary inscriptions translated by Hayim Tadmor [1994: 83, 171]). The precise chronology of these moves is less important in this context than their geopolitical significance. By breaking highland control over the coastal plain and Jezreel Valley, Assyria again isolated the kingdom of Israel. At Megiddo, a new city (Stratum III) was built according to Assyrian design concepts, pointing to permanent Assyrian control. In their earlier conquests in the northern Levant, Assyria incorporated new territories into their empire and even sought to develop them (Fales 2008; Herrmann 2011). The south was a different story (Faust 2011; *contra* Younger 2015). From 735 to 721 BC, Assyria completely dismembered the kingdom of Israel. Samaria limped along in some form as a provincial capital (Tappy 2001), and new farmsteads sprang up on the fringes of the highlands (Master et al. 2005: 129; Mazar and Ahituv 2011; Faust 2015); but, by any comparative measure, Assyria left a devastated land.[17] The final decline and fall of the kingdom of Israel can be attributed to one overwhelming factor: the crushing might of the expanding Assyrian Empire.

Israel, both as a ritual collective and as a kingdom, was destroyed by the end of the eighth century, but the house of David in Jerusalem successfully appropriated Israel's heritage in the years that followed. Whether one agrees that they had some historical claim or not, their adoption enshrined the kingdom of Israel in the biblical text and created an interest in this petty Levantine kingdom that has far outstripped its original geopolitical significance.

NOTES

1 Fleming (2012: 252–4) argues that studies of ethnicity are an unhelpful rubric for studying ancient Israel, but his implication that these might be "monolithic" or "territorially based" is out of step with the best in the study of ethnicity (since Barth 1969). Fleming's substitute of "peoples" "that name themselves" merely sublimates the theoretical issues. Comparative studies of ethnogenesis, boundary maintenance, and even assimilation remain helpful comparative data sets for the study of ancient Israel.
2 Despite the caveats above, the compilation of Iron 2 houses by Avi Faust (2006; 2012) represents an important benchmark for evaluating Israel over time. Faust demonstrates that the dominant house form of the Iron 2 "kingdom of Israel" is in unbroken cultural continuity with the house forms of the earlier Iron 1 period, virtually back to the time of Merenptah's "Israel." This does not *prove* that the inhabitants of the earlier Iron 1 houses had the same political allegiance or ethnic self-identification as the Iron 2 inhabitants; however, using the direct-historical approach, it is sympathetic to that historical reconstruction.
3 International recognition is not given in a vacuum, so attention is paid to historically specific, internal factors which support statehood claims, but, in the end, international recognition is the *sine qua non* of statehood.
4 For this aspirational sense, see Richardson 2012: 4.
5 The reconstruction of the physical boundaries of the kingdom of Israel is fraught with difficulties for precisely this reason. By the eighth century (see below), the increase in epigraphic finds provides a greater degree of confidence in political arrangements. Before this, one can point to general patterns in material culture affinities. In some cases, the reliance on material patterns to show political control fails completely. Often these material culture patterns have more do with economy than with political or ethnic similarity. For instance, eleventh-century Tel Dor is argued, from later Egyptian sources, to be a city ruled by a branch of the Sea Peoples, but one would never know this from its pervasive Canaanite/Phoenician material culture (Gilboa and Sharon 2008). Similarly, 1 Kings 4 argues that Tel Dor was, at least for a moment, politically subject to the kingdom of Israel in the tenth century, but the material culture provides no hint that this could be the case (Gilboa, Sharon, and Bloch-Smith 2015: 72). Both examples highlight the potential differences between political control and material culture affinities.
6 The dating and coherence of this text is disputed (for summary and recent discussion, see Knohl 2016). We continue to find Lawrence Stager's 1986 discussion of this text most compelling. In any case, even if the text is dated later, it does not change our evaluation that it describes a weak, discontiguous highland network.

7 New results complicate this synthesis by arguing that some portion (at least) of these fortifications should be dated to the Iron Age IIB, see Regev et al. 2017.
8 The situation in the Beth Netofa Valley is less well known. Tell el-Wawiyat seems to show Late Bronze Age continuity (Stratum III) until at least the eleventh century (Stratum II) when the site shows affinities with the small villages of the highlands (Alpert Nakhai, Dessel, and Wisthoff 1993: 1500–1).
9 Israel Finkelstein (2003: 75) argues that these narratives are of no historical value for this period. He further argues that without such texts, it is problematic to discuss the political orientation of any city. He is willing to overlook his self-imposed evidentiary lacunae in order to argue, *sans* epigraphic evidence, that these cities represent a political "New Canaan" (2003: 77). Coincidentally, Finkelstein's final conclusions closely match the portrayal in the biblical texts (2003: 77–8).
10 The only substantive archaeological distinction between settlement patterns are patterns of urban dominance (e.g., Early Bronze 2–3, Middle Bronze 2, Iron 2) and those of rural dominance (e.g. Early Bronze 1, Iron 1, Persian). In both situations, absent textual witness, one cannot be certain whether the cities or villages are individually governed or united in some sort of regional affiliation.
11 For a similar general model applied to southwestern Iran, see Alizadeh 2010: 360.
12 Many see the highland expansion beginning as early as Megiddo Stratum VB (Finkelstein 2013: 32). If this cultural interpretation is accepted, it also serves to mark emerging highland power. Megiddo Stratum VA–IVB, however, pairs the highland affinities with substantive monumental construction.
13 Area H of the Tel Aviv University excavations, which has produced the best ceramic corpus, highlights this difficulty. The University of Chicago Stratum VA–IVB has been linked to Tel Aviv University Levels H-7, H-6, and H-5 by various recent excavators (Finkelstein and Ussishkin 2006; Knauf 2006; Arie 2013b). This ambiguity reflects no deficiency on the part of the archaeologists; the material is that unclear. Stratum IVA, Wall 325, the wall which ringed the city in the ninth century, remains the linchpin for linking new excavations to The University of Chicago stratigraphy, but none of the material from the Tel Aviv University excavations has a direct relationship to Wall 325; all connections are cut by a later trench. The closest anyone has come to making the link is via a distinctive plaster floor in Area H, which is equivalent to a plaster floor in the adjacent University of Chicago excavations. The floor was drawn by The University of Chicago team as touching Wall 325 (Loud 1948: fig. 389 [not fig. 380 as cited in Arie 2013a: 271]) and labeled as belonging to Stratum IVA. If this join between Wall 325 and the plaster floor is correct, it would connect Level H-5 to Megiddo Stratum IVA (pottery is Iron Age IIA late [ninth century]), and Level H-6 or H-7 to Megiddo Stratum VA–IVB (pottery is Iron Age IIA early [tenth century]). This would support a traditional placement of Megiddo Stratum VA–IVB in the tenth century. However, the most recent publication of the Tel Aviv University team argues that The University of Chicago team falsified their plans at this key point (Arie 2013a: 271). Sadly, if The University of Chicago excavators faked the connection between this floor and Wall 325, one is left adrift. Level H5 is no more likely than Level H6 or H7 to be connected to Stratum VA–IVB. None can be connected to Wall 325, and hence, nothing can be definitively linked to The University of Chicago stratification. In my own view, no good reason exists to impugn The University of Chicago team to this degree. Later building along the interior of Wall 325 need not have severed all earlier connections. The most recent publication speculated that Level H-5 should be

connected to Megiddo Stratum VA–IVB (Iron Age IIA late [ninth century]), but this is because this phasing is most convenient for the excavator's preferred historical reconstruction (Arie 2013b: 741).

14 As a further caution, not all lowland–highland connections can be framed in terms of political control. As Mordechai Kislev has shown, the grain of Beth Shean was imported from the highlands in many periods within a variety of political configurations (Simchoni and Kislev 2006: 681).
15 We are not proposing the pig is an ethnic marker but rather an indication of variant economic/cultural trajectories.
16 See also the local seal of *l'mdyw*.
17 The eponyms for rulers of Samaria (690) and Megiddo (679) in Millard 1994: 50–1 and a few fragmentary administrative texts notwithstanding.

REFERENCES

Ahituv, S., and Mazar, A. 2014. The Inscriptions from Tel Reḥov and Their Contribution to the Study of Script and Writing during the Iron Age IIA. In *"See, I Will Bring a Scroll Recounting What Befell Me" (Ps 40:8): Epigraphy and Daily Life from the Bible to the Talmud; Dedicated to the Memory of Professor Hanan Eshel*, ed. E. Eshel and Y. Levin, 39–68, 189–203. JAJSup 12. Göttingen: Vandenhoeck & Ruprecht.

Alizadeh, A. 2010. The Rise of the Highland Elamite State in Southwestern Iran. *CA* 51: 353–83.

Alpert-Nakhai, B.; Dessel, J. P.; and Wisthoff, B. L. 1993. Wawiyat, Tell el-. *NEAEHL* 4: 1500–1.

Alt, A. 1925. *Die Landnahme der Israeliten in Palästina: Territorialgeschichtliche Studien*. Leipzig: Druckerei der Werkgemeinschaft.

Arie, E. 2008. Reconsidering the Iron Age II Strata at Tel Dan: Archaeological and Historical Implications. *TA* 35: 6–64.

——— 2013a. Area H: Levels H-9 to H-5. In *Megiddo V: The 2004–2008 Seasons*, Vol. 1, ed. I. Finkelstein, D. Ussishkin, and E. H. Cline, 247–74. MSSMNIA 31. Winona Lake, IN: Eisenbrauns.

——— 2013b. The Iron IIA Pottery. In *Megiddo V: The 2004–2008 Seasons*, Vol. 2, ed. I. Finkelstein, D. Ussishkin, and E. H. Cline, 668–728. MSSMNIA 31. Winona Lake, IN: Eisenbrauns.

Aznar, C. A. 2005. *Exchange Networks in the Southern Levant during the Iron Age II: A Study of Pottery Origin and Distribution*. PhD diss., Harvard University.

Barth, F. 1969. Introduction. In *Ethnic Groups and Boundaries: The Social Organization of Cultural Difference*, 9–37. Boston: Little, Brown.

Ben-Ami, D., and Ben-Tor, A. 2012. The Iron Age I (Stratum "XII/XI"): Stratigraphy and Pottery. In *Hazor VI: The 1990–2009 Excavations; The Iron Age*, ed. A. Ben-Tor, D. Ben-Ami, and D. Sandhaus, 7–51. Jerusalem: IES; The Institute of Archaeology, The Hebrew University of Jerusalem.

Ben-Tor, A., and Zarzecki-Peleg, A. 2015. Iron Age IIA–B: Northern Valleys and Upper Galilee. In *The Ancient Pottery of Israel and Its Neighbors from the Iron Age through the Hellenistic Period*, Vol. 1, ed. S. Gitin, 135–88. Jerusalem: IES.

Benz, B. C. 2013. *The Varieties of Sociopolitical Experience in the Late Bronze Age Levant and the Rise of Early Israel*. PhD diss., New York University.

Biran, A. 1994. *Biblical Dan*. Jerusalem: IES; Hebrew Union College–Jewish Institute of Religion.

Brandl, B. 2009. An Israelite Administrative Jar Handle Impression from Bethsaida (et-Tell). In *Bethsaida: A City by the North Shore of the Sea of Galilee*, Vol. 4, by R. Arav, 136–46. Kirksville, MO: Truman State University Press.

Broodbank, C. 2013. *The Making of the Middle Sea: A History of the Mediterranean from the Beginning to the Emergence of the Classical World*. Oxford: Oxford University Press.

Bruins, H. J.; van der Plicht, J.; Ilan, D.; and Werker, E. 2005. Iron-Age 14C Dates from Tel Dan: A High Chronology. In *The Bible and Radiocarbon Dating: Archaeology, Text and Science*, ed. T. E. Levy and T. F. G. Higham, 323–36. London: Equinox.

Campbell, E. F., ed. 2002. *Shechem III: The Stratigraphy and Architecture of Shechem/Tell Balâṭah*. ASORAR 6. Boston: ASOR.

Fales, M. 2008. On *Pax Assyriaca* in the Eighth–Seventh Centuries BCE and Its Implications. In *Isaiah's Vision of Peace in Biblical and Modern International Relations: Swords into Plowshares*, ed. R. Cohen and R. Westbrook, 17–35. Culture and Religion in International Relations. New York: Palgrave Macmillan.

Faust, A. 2006. *Israel's Ethnogenesis: Settlement, Interaction, Expansion and Resistance*. AAA. London: Equinox.

——— 2011. The Interests of the Assyrian Empire in the West: Olive Oil Production as a Test-Case. *Journal of the Economic and Social History of the Orient* 54: 62–86.

——— 2012. *The Archaeology of Israelite Society in Iron Age II*. Winona Lake, IN: Eisenbrauns.

——— 2015. Settlement, Economy, and Demography under Assyrian Rule in the West: The Territories of the Former Kingdom of Israel as a Test Case. *JAOS* 135: 765–89.

Finkelstein, I. 1986. *'Izbet Ṣarṭah: An Early Iron Age Site near Rosh Ha'ayin, Israel*. BAR International Series 299. Oxford: BAR.

——— 2003. City-States to States: Polity Dynamics in the 10th–9th Centuries B.C.E. In *Symbiosis, Symbolism, and the Power of the Past: Canaan, Ancient Israel, and Their Neighbors from the Late Bronze Age through Roman Palaestina; Proceedings of the Centennial Symposium William F. Albright Institute of Archaeological Research and American Schools of Oriental Research, Jerusalem, May 29–May 31, 2000*, ed. W. G. Dever and S. Gitin, 75–83. Winona Lake, IN: Eisenbrauns.

——— 2013. *The Forgotten Kingdom: The Archaeology and History of Northern Israel*. Ancient Near East Monographs 5. Atlanta: SBL.

Finkelstein, I.; Bunimovitz, S.; and Lederman, Z. 1993. *Shiloh: The Archaeology of a Biblical Site*. MSSMNIA 10. Tel Aviv: Institute of Archaeology of Tel Aviv University.

Finkelstein, I., and Ussishkin, D. 2006. A Different Interpretation of the 2000 Season Stratigraphy (Levels H-6 and H-5). In *Megiddo IV: The 1998–2002 Seasons*, Vol. 1, ed. I. Finkelstein, D. Ussishkin, and B. Halpern, 143–8. MSSMNIA 24 (1). Tel Aviv: Emery and Claire Yass Publications in Archaeology.

Fleming, D. E. 2004. *Democracy's Ancient Ancestors: Mari and Early Collective Governance*. Cambridge: Cambridge University Press.

——— 2012. *The Legacy of Israel in Judah's Bible: History, Politics, and the Reinscribing of Tradition*. New York: Cambridge University Press.

Gal, Z. 1992. *Lower Galilee during the Iron Age*. ASORDS 8. Winona Lake, IN: Eisenbrauns.

Gilboa, A., and Sharon, I., with contributions from N. Raban-Gerstel, R. Shahack-Gross, A. Karasik, U. Smilansky, and A. Eliyahu Behar 2008. Between the Carmel and the Sea: Tel Dor's Iron Age Reconsidered. *NEA* 71: 146–70.

Gilboa, A.; Sharon, I.; and Bloch-Smith, E. 2015. Capital of Solomon's Fourth District? Israelite Dor. *Levant* 47: 51–74.

Gitin, S. 1998. Philistia in Transition: The Tenth Century BCE and Beyond. In *Mediterranean Peoples in Transition: Thirteenth to Early Tenth Centuries BCE in Honor of Professor Trude Dothan*, ed. S. Gitin, A. Mazar, and E. Stern, 162–83. Jerusalem: IES.

Greer, J. S. 2013. *Dinner at Dan: Biblical and Archaeological Evidence for Sacred Feasts at Iron Age II Tel Dan and Their Significance*. CHANE 66. Leiden: Brill.

Halpern, B., and Lemaire, A. 2010. The Composition of Kings. In *The Books of Kings: Sources, Composition, Historiography and Reception*, ed. A. Lemaire and B. Halpern, 123–53. Leiden: Brill.

Hasel, M. G. 1998. *Domination and Resistance: Egyptian Military Activity in the Southern Levant, ca. 1300–1185 B.C.* Leiden: Brill.

Hawkes, C. 1954. Archeological Theory and Method: Some Suggestions from the Old World. *American Anthropologist* 56: 155–68.

Herr, L. G. 1998. Tell El-Umayri and the Madaba Plains Region during the Late Bronze–Iron Age I Transition. In *Mediterranean Peoples in Transition: Thirteenth to Early Tenth Centuries BCE in Honor of Professor Trude Dothan*, ed. S. Gitin, A. Mazar, and E. Stern, 251–64. Jerusalem: IES.

Herrmann, V. H. R. 2011. *Society and Economy under Empire at Iron Age Sam'al (Zincirli Hoyuk, Turkey)*. PhD diss., The University of Chicago.

Herzog, Z., and Singer-Avitz, L. 2006. Sub-Dividing the Iron Age IIA in Northern Israel: A Suggested Solution to the Chronological Debate. *TA* 33: 163–95.

Hobbes, T. 1651. *Leviathan, or, The Matter, Forme, & Power of a Common-Wealth, Ecclesiasticall and Civill*. London: Andrew Crooke.

Ilan, D. 1999. *Northeastern Israel in the Iron Age I: Cultural, Socioeconomic and Political Perspectives*. PhD diss., Tel Aviv University.

Kallai, Z. 1998. The United Monarchy of Israel – A Focal Point in Israelite Historiography. In *Biblical Historiography and Historical Geography: Collection of Studies*, 139–43. Beiträge zur Erforschung des Alten Testaments und des antiken Judentums 44. Frankfurt am Main: Lang.

King, P. J., and Stager, L. E. 2001. *Life in Biblical Israel*. Library of Ancient Israel. Louisville, KY: Westminster John Knox.

Knauf, A. E. 2006. The 2000 Season (Levels H-7, H-6 and H-5). In *Megiddo IV: The 1998–2002 Seasons*, Vol. 1, ed. I. Finkelstein, D. Ussishkin, and B. Halpern, 137–42. MSSMNIA 24. Tel Aviv: Emery and Claire Yass Publications in Archaeology.

Knohl, I. 2016. The Original Version of Deborah's Song, and Its Numerical Structure. *VT* 66: 45–65.

Lehmann, G., and Killebrew, A. E. 2010. Palace 6000 at Megiddo in Context: Iron Age Central Hall Tetra-Partite Residencies and the *Bīt-Ḥilāni* Building Tradition in the Levant. *BASOR* 359: 13–33.

Levin, Y. 2012. Conquered and Unconquered: Reality and Historiography in the Geography of Joshua. In *The Book of Joshua*, ed. E. Noort, 361–70. Bibliotheca Ephemeridum Theologicarum Lovaniensium 250. Leuven: Peeters.

Liverani, M. 2005. *Israel's History and the History of Israel*. Trans. C. Peri and P. R. Davies, from Italian. Bible World. London: Equinox.

Loud, G. 1948. *Megiddo II: Seasons of 1935–39*. OIP 62. Chicago: The University of Chicago Press.

Maeir, A. M. 2012. The Tell es-Safi/Gath Archaeological Project 1996–2010: Introduction, Overview and Synopsis of Results. In *Tell es-Safi/Gath I: The 1996–2005 Seasons*,

Vol. 1: *Text*, ed. A. M. Maeir, 1–88. Ägypten und Altes Testament 69. Wiesbaden: Harrassowitz.

Master, D. M. 2001. State Formation Theory and the Kingdom of Ancient Israel. *JNES* 60: 117–31.

——— 2014. Economy and Exchange in the Iron Age Kingdoms of the Southern Levant. *BASOR* 372: 81–97.

Master, D. M.; Monson, J. M.; Lass, E. H. E.; and Pierce, G. A., eds. 2005. *Dothan*, Vol. 1: *Remains from the Tell (1953–1964)*. Winona Lake, IN: Eisenbrauns.

Mazar, A. 2005. The Debate over the Chronology of the Iron Age in the Southern Levant: Its History, the Current Situation, and a Suggested Resolution. In *The Bible and Radiocarbon Dating: Archaeology, Text and Science*, ed. T. E. Levy and T. F. G. Higham, 15–30. London: Equinox.

——— 2006. *Excavations at Tel Beth-Shean, 1989–1996*, Vol. 1: *From the Late Bronze Age IIB to the Medieval Period*. BSVAP 1. Jerusalem: IES.

Mazar, A., and Aḥituv, S. 2011. Tel Reḥov in the Assyrian Period: Squatters, Burials, and a Hebrew Seal. In *The Fire Signals of Lachish: Studies in the Archaeology and History of Israel in the Late Bronze Age, Iron Age, and Persian Period in Honor of David Ussishkin*, ed. I. Finkelstein and N. Na'aman, 265–80. Winona Lake, IN: Eisenbrauns.

Meiri, M.; Huchon, D.; Bar-Oz, G.; Boaretto, E.; Horwitz, L. K.; Maeir, A. M.; Sapir-Hen, L.; Larson, G.; Weiner, S.; and Finkelstein, I. 2013. Ancient DNA and Population Turnover in Southern Levantine Pigs – Signature of the Sea Peoples Migration? *Scientific Reports* 3. www.nature.com/articles/srep03035 (accessed October 11, 2017).

Meshel, Z. 2012. Summary. In *Kuntillet 'Ajrud (Ḥorvat Teman): An Iron Age II Religious Site on the Judah-Sinai Border*, xxi–xxii. Jerusalem: IES.

Miglio, A. 2014. *Tribe and State: The Dynamics of International Politics and the Reign of Zimri-Lim*. Gorgias Studies in the Ancient Near East 8. Piscataway, NJ: Gorgias.

Millard, A. R. 1994. *The Eponyms of the Assyrian Empire, 910–612 BC*. State Archives of Assyria Studies 2. Helsinki: Neo-Assyrian Text Corpus Project.

Münger, S. 2013. Early Iron Age Kinneret – Early Aramaean or Just Late Canaanite? Remarks on the Material Culture of a Border Site in Northern Palestine at the Turn of an Era. In *Arameans, Chaldeans, and Arabs in Babylonia and Palestine in the First Millennium B.C.*, ed. A. Berlejung and M. P. Streck, 149–82. Leipziger altorientalistische Studien 3. Wiesbaden: Harrassowitz.

Porter, A. 2010. From Kin to Class – and Back Again! Changing Paradigms of the Early Polity. In *The Development of Pre-State Communities in the Ancient Near East: Studies in Honour of Edgar Peltenburg*, ed. D. Bolger and L. C. Maguire, 72–8. Themes from the Ancient Near East BANEA Publication Series 2. Oxford: Oxbow.

Rainey, A. F., and Notley, R. S. 2006. *The Sacred Bridge: Carta's Atlas of the Biblical World*. Jerusalem: Carta.

Regev, J.; Uziel, J.; Szanton, N.; and Boaretto, E. 2017. Absolute Dating of the Gihon Spring Fortifications, Jerusalem. *Radiocarbon* 59: 1171–93.

Reich, R., and Shukron, E. 2008. Jerusalem – An Update to Vol. 2. *NEAEHL* 5: 1801–3.

Richardson, S. 2012. Early Mesopotamia: The Presumptive State. *Past & Present* 215: 3–49.

Sapir-Hen, L.; Bar-Oz, G.; Gadot, Y.; and Finkelstein, I. 2013. Pig Husbandry in Iron Age Israel and Judah: New Insights Regarding the Origin of the "Taboo." *ZDPV* 129: 1–20.

Schloen, J. D. 1993. Caravans, Kenites, and *Casus Belli*: Enmity and Alliance in the Song of Deborah. *Catholic Biblical Quarterly* 55: 18–38.

2001. *The House of the Father as Fact and Symbol: Patrimonialism in Ugarit and the Ancient Near East.* Winona Lake, IN: Eisenbrauns.

Simchoni, O., and Kislev, M. E. 2006. Charred Remains of Products of Olive-Oil Production in the Iron Age. In *Excavations at Tel Beth-Shean, 1989–1996,* Vol. 1: *From the Late Bronze Age IIB to the Medieval Period,* ed. A. Mazar, 679–86. BSVAP 1. Jerusalem: IES.

Smith, A. T. 2003. *The Political Landscape: Constellations of Authority in Early Complex Polities.* Berkeley: University of California Press.

Stager, L. E. 1985. The Archaeology of the Family in Ancient Israel. *BASOR* 260: 1–35.

——— 1986. Archaeology, Ecology, and Social History: Background Themes to the Song of Deborah. *Congress Volume: Jerusalem, 1986,* by J. A. Emerton, 221–34. VTSup 40. Leiden: Brill.

——— 1998. Forging an Identity: The Emergence of Ancient Israel. In *The Oxford History of the Biblical World,* ed. M. D. Coogan, 123–75. New York: Oxford University Press.

——— 2003. The Shechem Temple where Abimelech Massacred a Thousand. *BAR* 29 (4): 26–35, 66–9.

Stone, B. J. 1995. The Philistines and Acculturation: Culture Change and Ethnic Continuity in the Iron Age. *BASOR* 298: 7–32.

Suter, C. E. 2011. Images, Tradition, and Meaning: The Samaria and Other Levantine Ivories of the Iron Age. In *A Common Cultural Heritage: Studies on Mesopotamia and the Biblical World in Honor of Barry L. Eichler,* ed. G. Frame, E. Leichty, K. Sonik, J. Tigay, and S. Tinney, 219–41. Bethesda, MD: CDL.

Tadmor, H. 1994. *The Inscriptions of Tiglath-pileser III, King of Assyria: Critical Edition, with Introductions, Translations, and Commentary.* Jerusalem: The Israel Academy of Sciences and Humanities.

Tappy, R. E. 1992. *The Archaeology of Israelite Samaria,* Vol. 1: *Early Iron Age through the Ninth Century BCE.* Atlanta: Scholars.

——— 2001. *The Archaeology of Israelite Samaria,* Vol. 2: *The Eighth Century BCE.* Winona Lake, IN: Eisenbrauns.

Toffolo, M. B.; Arie, E.; Martin, M. A. S.; Boaretto, E.; and Finkelstein, I. 2014. Absolute Chronology of Megiddo, Israel, in the Late Bronze and Iron Ages: High-Resolution Radiocarbon Dating. *Radiocarbon* 56: 221–44.

Ussishkin, D. 2007. Samaria, Jezreel and Megiddo: Royal Centres of Omri and Ahab. In *Ahab Agonistes: The Rise and Fall of the Omri Dynasty,* ed. L. L. Grabbe, 293–309. Library of Hebrew Bible/Old Testament Studies 421; European Seminar in Historical Methodology 6. London: T & T Clark.

Wapnish, P., and Hesse, B. 1991. Faunal Remains from Tel Dan: Perspectives on Animal Production at a Village, Urban and Ritual Center. *ArchaeoZoologia* 4 (2): 9–86.

Weber, M. 1946. *From Max Weber: Essays in Sociology.* Trans. and ed. H. Gerth and C. W. Mills, from German. New York: Oxford University Press.

Yadin, Y. 1960. New Light on Solomon's Megiddo. *BA* 23: 62–8.

Younger, K. L., Jr. 2003. Black Obelisk. In *The Context of Scripture,* Vol. 2: *Monumental Inscriptions from the Biblical World,* ed. W. W. Hallo and K. L. Younger Jr., 269–70. Leiden: Brill.

——— 2015. The Assyrian Economic Impact on the Southern Levant in the Light of Recent Study. *IEJ* 65: 179–204.

Zimhoni, O. 1997. *Studies in the Iron Age Pottery of Israel: Typological, Archaeological, and Chronological Aspects.* Tel Aviv Occasional Publications 2. Tel Aviv: Institute of Archaeology, Tel Aviv University.

TWENTY

THE ALPHABET COMES OF AGE
The Social Context of Alphabetic Writing in the First Millennium BCE

CHRISTOPHER A. ROLLSTON

This chapter focuses on epigraphic *realia*, that is, a selection of actual alphabetic inscriptions, written in a number of languages, from various archaeological sites (thus, literary works such as those of the Hebrew Bible, the Old Testament Apocrypha and Pseudepigrapha, Plato, Xenophon, Cicero, and Virgil are not included here). Moreover, numismatic evidence, a world unto itself, will also not be treated in this article, nor will the vast textual material from the Dead Sea Scrolls (see Tov 2004 and the literature cited therein). Rather, within this article, there will be a selection of epigraphic texts from archaeological sites, especially those from the Levantine world, with the intent of highlighting some of the rich diversity of the epigraphic material in alphabetic languages.

In terms of the *Sitz im Leben* of ancient inscriptions from the ancient Near Eastern world, I would emphasize that most epigraphic texts hail from elite circles, the majority of which are associated with some sort of governmental aegis. I think the evidence demonstrates that this is the case not just for the nonalphabetic writing systems of Mesopotamia and Egypt, but also for the ancient alphabetic writing systems (Rollston 2010: 85–90). Thus, writing was not a non-elite venture; moreover, literacy rates would have been very low. After all, learning an alphabetic writing system may not have been as difficult as learning a nonalphabetic writing system, but learning to write and read well was not something that could be accomplished in a brief period of days, weeks, or even months (Rollston 2010: 91–135). Nevertheless, some scholars in the modern field wish to posit high levels of literacy for antiquity. Part of the difficulty in the modern period is that some scholars have presupposed that the presence of an alphabetic writing system rapidly results in high rates of literacy. But the low levels of literacy during the Middle Ages should remind us that the presence of an alphabetic writing system and high levels of literacy are not absolute correlatives. Moreover, I would contend that the reason for high levels of literacy in much of the modern world is not primarily the result of an alphabetic writing system, but rather primarily a result of the governmentally mandated education of the masses in the modern period. An alphabetic writing system may raise the percentages some, but in and of itself, it does not necessarily result in high percentages of literacy among non-elites.

In terms of order and sequence of the discussion about inscriptions in this chapter, there will be an initial brief discussion of the origins of the alphabet, then a considerable focus on the development and use of the Phoenician script and language, the rise of Aramaic and Hebrew (script and language), as well as the origins, early attestations, and subsequent usage of the Greek alphabet and the Latin alphabet. Naturally, there will be some reference to and discussion of the basic content of various inscriptions, so as to assist in describing the social context of writing in the first millennium BCE. Because of the constraints of space and time, a number of important alphabetic scripts and languages (e.g., Lihyanite, Thamudic, Etruscan, Ethiopic, Palmyrene, Nabataean) will be referenced but will not be discussed in any detail.

THE ORIGINS OF WRITING, THE ORIGINS OF THE ALPHABET, AND THE NATURE OF ALPHABETIC WRITING

Writing is first attested during the late fourth millennium BCE in the great cultural centers of the ancient Near Eastern world: Mesopotamia and Egypt. With the invention of this technology (and writing certainly is a technology), we can begin to speak of "history" in the technical sense. Moreover, because writing in Mesopotamia arguably antedated writing in Egypt, Samuel Kramer's volume is rightfully entitled *History Begins at Sumer* (1981), with "Sumer" the early term for southern Mesopotamia. The writing systems that were invented in Mesopotamia and Egypt, however, were not alphabetic. Rather, the writing systems of these regions were nonalphabetic.

Before briefly describing the nonalphabetic writing systems of Mesopotamia and Egypt, it is useful first to define (as a means of forming a contrast) the technical term "alphabet." In essence, the "alphabet" can be used of a writing system in which each grapheme ("letter") of a writing system is intended to signify a single phoneme ("phoneme" can be defined as the smallest meaningful unit of sound). Alphabetic writing systems normally have a rather small number of graphemes, usually in the range of twenty to forty.

In contrast, the writing systems of ancient Mesopotamia and Egypt were nonalphabetic.[1] The "signs" used for the writing systems of Mesopotamia and Egypt were nonalphabetic in the sense that a "sign" (e.g., a cuneiform wedge or an Egyptian hieroglyph) could signify an entire word (for which the term "logogram" is used) or an entire syllable (for which the term "syllabogram" is used), or could signify a "determinative." The terms "logogram" and "syllabogram" are not difficult to understand, but the term "determinative" may require some explanation. Namely, a determinative is a sign that was used either before or after a noun or nominal in order to signify something about the nature of the noun or nominal that it was modifying. For example, a scribe writing the term "spear" could use the determinative for "metal" before or after the word for "spear" (e.g., if the spear was made of bronze). Similarly, before the personal name of a god or a goddess, a scribe might use a determinative for "deity" (e.g., in Mesopotamian cuneiform, the "dingir" sign). Or again, a scribe referring to a "boat" might use the determinative for "wood" before or after the term for "boat." A trained scribe would be capable of using (at any given time) a few hundred signs. Naturally, therefore, because of the nature of the nonalphabetic writing systems of ancient Mesopotamia and Egypt, scribal education was a long and arduous process. Literacy rates in these regions were arguably quite low, probably in the range of 2 to 6–8 percent. After all, learning to write and read well required years, and, of course, most vocations (e.g., pastoralism, agriculture, pottery production, metallurgy) in society did not require the ability to write and read.

The origins of alphabetic writing are not in the late fourth millennium BCE (as with the nonalphabetic writing systems of Mesopotamia and Egypt) but rather in the early second millennium around 1800 BCE. That is, alphabetic writing is first attested some 1,400 or 1,500 years after nonalphabetic writing. The preferable term for this first alphabetic writing is "Early Alphabetic." But sometimes the terms "Proto-Canaanite," "Canaanite," and "Proto-Sinaitic" are used. The language of the Early Alphabetic inscriptions is a dialect (or various dialects) of Northwest Semitic, but the shapes of the signs used are normally modeled on some of the signs of the Egyptian writing system (e.g., Hieroglyphic and Hieratic). For this reason, it is reasonable to contend that the inventors of Early Alphabetic were Semites from the Levant who were familiar with the Egyptian writing system (because of the frequent travel that Levantine populations made into and out of Egypt, as well as the frequent hegemonic presence of Egypt in the Levant). The earliest of the Early Alphabetic inscriptions were found at Serabit el-Khadem and Wadi el-Hol, both of which are sites in Egypt (Darnell et al. 2005: 63–124).

The Early Alphabet was quite pictographic (it would gradually become more linear but would always retain something of its pictographic origins). That is, the shapes of the Early Alphabetic letters are essentially drawings of things, especially the sorts of things that would be part of the ordinary life of ancient peoples: a house, an ox, a person's head, a person's hand, a fish, a mace, a snake, and a bow. But the pictures of these sorts of things are not intended to signify the object. That is, the drawing of a "house" was not supposed to signify a house, but rather it was to signify the phoneme "b," since the first sound of the Semitic word for "house" (*bayit*) is "b." Similarly, the drawing of a "snake" was not intended to signify a "snake," but rather the sound "n," as the Semitic word for "snake" is *naḥash*. Or, again, the drawing of the palm of the "hand" was not intended to signify the word "palm," but rather the sound "k," as the Semitic word for "palm of the hand" is *kap*. That is, the drawing was intended to signify the first sound of the object that was drawn. There is a technical term for this, namely, the acrophonic principle.

Naturally, once the first alphabetic writing system had been invented, it had the potential to transform rapidly the technology of writing, displacing nonalphabetic writing systems such as those of Mesopotamia and Egypt. After all, alphabetic writing is not as complicated as nonalphabetic writing (e.g., the number of graphemes is just under 30 for Early Alphabetic). Therefore, someone might presuppose that the usage of alphabetic writing would have soon displaced nonalphabetic writing as the writing technology of choice; but it did not. In many respects, this is not surprising. After all, change takes time. And scribal education in ancient Mesopotamia and Egypt was a conservative tradition, preserving texts, copying again and again the great literature of the early period, and even attempting to retain the vocabulary and linguistic features of bygone eras. In many respects, the situation in ancient Mesopotamia and Egypt is not all that different from the way in which the Latin language continued to be the language of scholars and the religious tradition long after the vernacular dialects had developed and displaced Latin among much of the rest of the population.

During the lion's share of the early, middle, and late horizons of the second millennium BCE, linear alphabetic writing is attested at a small number of sites in the Levantine world (e.g., Lachish, Qubur al-Walaydah, Gezer). Predictably, however, alphabetic writing did not displace nonalphabetic writing. There is a partial exception to this, but *only* partial: Ugaritic (Segert 1984). The script of Ugaritic inscriptions is alphabetic (and the language itself is a dialect of Northwest Semitic). The Ugaritic alphabet originally consisted of twenty-seven letters, but three additional letters were ultimately added. Significantly, however, it is cuneiform in shape (rather than pictographic or linear). That is, the script of Ugaritic is "wedge-shaped." This is quite an innovation, as it was arguably an attempt to preserve the general appearance of Mesopotamian cuneiform (although the signs are entirely different, of course, as Mesopotamian cuneiform is nonalphabetic, and the Ugaritic script is alphabetic), while also embracing the putative elegance and utilitarianism of the alphabetic writing system. Much of the textual material written in the Ugaritic language is literary in nature, texts such as the great epics known as Aqhat, Kirta, and Ba'al. In addition, though, there are some epistolary texts (i.e., "letters"), as well as some incantations, some ritual texts, some legal texts (including treaty materials and some contracts), a number of administrative texts, some scientific texts (e.g., Hippiatric Prescriptions), and some abecedaries (Bordreuil and Pardee 2009). Most of these texts date to the thirteenth century, and the overwhelming majority were found at the ancient Syrian sites of Ugarit, with a small number found at nearby Ras Ibn Hani, but some Ugaritic texts have been found at sites such as Kedesh, Cyprus (e.g., Hala Sultan Tekke), Lebanon (e.g., Kamid el-Loz and Sarepta), and Palestine (e.g., Ta'anach, Beth-Shemesh). Of importance to mention is that there is a longer and a shorter form of the Ugaritic alphabet (the shorter predominates outside of Ugarit and Ras Ibn Hani), and there are also two different attested orders of the alphabet in Ugaritic: the Abgad and the Halḥam (something that can be discerned on the basis of the orders attested in Ugaritic abecedaries). Nevertheless, the alphabetic script of Ugarit (i.e., Ugaritic cuneiform) never gained a foothold as the putative official script of any (other) Levantine polity. It is noteworthy in this connection that even the el-Amarna letters from Canaan were written in (Peripheral) Akkadian, not some local dialect (Moran 1992), but this is arguably a result of the status of Akkadian as the *lingua franca* of the era. Yet, as William Moran (2003) demonstrated, there is some language interference from Canaanite in the Levantine Akkadian of the el-Amarna letters, something that linguists customarily refer to as "L-1 Transfer," and there are also some Canaanite glosses in these letters as well; however, the fact remains that the language of these letters is still Akkadian. In any case, even at the site of Ugarit, it was Akkadian (written in the Mesopotamian cuneiform script) that was used most heavily, not the Ugaritic script and language. Nevertheless, the Early Alphabetic script had much influence, and it is even from the Early Alphabetic script that the Proto-Arabic script derived (cf. South Arabian and even Ethiopic, as well as scripts such as Thamudic and Liyanite).

THE PHOENICIAN STANDARDIZATION OF THE ALPHABET AND SELECT FIRST-MILLENNIUM PHOENICIAN INSCRIPTIONS

During the final century or two of the second millennium BCE, alphabetic writing ultimately began to dislodge the hegemony that nonalphabetic writing had long held. And it is most reasonable to contend that it was the Phoenicians who galvanized this movement; after all, the first of these inscriptions is written in the Phoenician language, and the script used for these inscriptions is different from Early Alphabetic writing in three major ways: the number of graphemes is fixed at twenty-two (which corresponds with the number of consonantal graphemes in Phoenician), the direction of writing is consistently sinistrograde (i.e., right to left), and the stance of the letters is substantially fixed (previously, alphabetic writing had as many as twenty-seven or twenty-eight letters; it could be written sinistrograde, dextrograde, boustrophedon, or columnar; and the stance exhibited enormous variation). It is worth emphasizing at this point that it is often said that "the Phoenicians invented the alphabet." Technically speaking, this is not the case. Rather, the Phoenicians can be credited with standardizing the alphabet (with regard to the number of letters, the direction of writing, and the stance of the letters).

The earliest of the Phoenician inscriptions dates to around the eleventh century or the very early tenth century BCE, with the Azarba'al Inscription, a marvelous inscription written in the Phoenician script and the Phoenician language (Rollston 2010: 20). This inscription is incised into bronze and contains six lines of text, none of which is necessarily complete. It hails from and was excavated at the Phoenician port city of Byblos. Although the precise nature of this inscription is not normally considered certain, the content revolves around the inheritance of ancestral land (*nḥl*) and money (Phoenician *ksp*, "silver").

Also hailing from Byblos of the tenth century are a series of additional royal inscriptions, all chiseled into stone. The Ahiram Inscription is written on a large sarcophagus, and, of course, it is a burial inscription, replete with the standard ancient caveats about not disturbing the dead. Here is my translation of this inscription: "The sarcophagus that 'Ethba'al, son of Ahiram, king of Byblos, made for Ahiram, his father, when he placed him in his eternity. And if a king among kings, or a governor among governors, or a commander of an army should come to Byblos, and uncover this sarcophagus, may the scepter of his rule be ripped away, may the throne of his kingdom be overturned, and may rest flee from Byblos. And as for him, may his royal records be effaced from before Byb[los]."

Another from Byblos is the Yehimilk Inscription. This is a dedicatory inscription, written in the Phoenician language and script, and can be read as follows: "The temple [literally: "house"] that Yehimilk, king of Byblos, built. He restored all the fall temples. May Ba'al-Shamen and Ba'alat Byblos and the Assembly of the Holy Gods of Byblos lengthen the days of Yehimilk and his years over Byblos because the righteous and just king before the Holy Gods of Byblos is he." This inscription has been chiseled into a dressed stone, and the letters of this inscription are hung from a ceiling line (standard procedure for many inscriptions).

The Abiba'al and Eliba'al Inscriptions are also from the tenth century and are written in the Phoenician language and script. However, these two inscriptions are written on royal Egyptian statuary. Namely, the Abiba'al Inscription is inscribed on a statute of Pharaoh Sheshonq I (reigned ca. 945–924 BCE) and the Eliba'al Inscription was inscribed on a bust of Pharaoh Osorkon I (reigned ca. 924–889 BCE). This is a reflection, of course, of the very close relations that the Phoenicians had with the Egyptians throughout most of Phoenician history.[2] Although brief, the content of these inscriptions is of substantial importance, as cumulatively they reveal the names of a number of Byblian kings, aspects of the Phoenician religion (including the names of some of the Phoenician gods), and funerary practices, as well as aspects of trade and diplomacy. Most of the Phoenician inscriptions would have been written on papyrus and so did not survive the ravages of time, but these on stone (and others on pottery) are especially useful in understanding aspects of the social world of Phoenicia at the beginning of the first millennium BCE. Of course, their content and media (writing surface) demonstrates that these inscriptions are elite governmental inscriptions, not the product of the general populace.

The Phoenicians were, of course, often traversing land and sea. Therefore, it is not at all surprising that Phoenician inscriptions have been found at archaeological sites throughout much of the ancient Mediterranean world. For example, at the site of Kefar Veradim (Israel), a stunning bronze bowl was found in a tomb. It dates to the late eleventh century or early tenth century BCE and is written in the Phoenician script and also (arguably) the Phoenician language. It reads: "The cup of Pesaḥ, son of Shema." It may very well have been an heirloom piece, handed down for a few decades prior to being deposited with a deceased member of the family (Rollston 2010: 27–8). The Gezer Calendar is an agricultural calendar, inscribed on a small piece of limestone. It refers to seasons of the agricultural year and the harvesting of various agricultural commodities. It is written in the Phoenician script (Rollston 2010: 29–33) and (arguably) also in the Phoenician language. Moreover, from Nora (on the south coast of Sardinia) comes a Phoenician inscription of the ninth century BCE, dated to the ninth century BCE. This inscription is among the most fascinating inscriptions, with content arguably reflecting maritime themes: "He was driven from Tarshish. He found in Sardinia, as did his forces. Milkuton, son of Shubon, the commander of (King) Pummay."[3] Similarly, from Kition on Cyprus comes a broken but important pottery bowl (fired in antiquity) and incised into it are some six lines of text, written in the Phoenician language and cursive script of the eighth century BCE (Rollston 2010: 35, 37). Or again, the Karatepe Inscription (from ancient Anatolia) is written in the Phoenician language and script, and it dates to the eighth century BCE as well. This inscription is particularly long, and it is a dedicatory inscription of sorts. It includes reference to a certain "Azitiwada, servant of Baʻal" who had been elevated to a position of high power by "Awarku, king of the Danunians." He claims to have brought order to the land, engaged in public works, restored the temple, and engaged in diplomatic measures far and wide (Rollston 2010: 40–1). In short, the Phoenician script and language spread far and wide during the early centuries of the first millennium BCE. Moreover, the *Sitz im Leben* for the use of the alphabet was elite circles, especially royal circles (as is clear from the content and media of the inscriptions above). Furthermore, it should be emphasized that the script and orthography of these inscriptions is consistently that of a trained scribe (or trained scribal stonemason) with substantial formal training. That is, the high caliber of these inscriptions, as well as the content, demonstrates that these texts were the product of the scribal establishment.

Of significance is the fact that there were also a number of inscriptions written in the Phoenician script that were found at Kuntillet Ajrud (Aḥituv, Eshel, and Meshel 2012). One of these is written in black ink on plaster, but with reference to Yahweh, the national god of Israel (Inscription 4.1.1). In addition, there is another inscription in the Phoenician script on plaster that is poetic in nature and refers to "Ba'al on a day of war" and also to the god 'El (Inscription 4.2). Of course, both of these divine names can be used for Yahweh (especially in the early eighth century), but it may be most reasonable to contend that this inscription was a reflection of Phoenician religious practices not Israelite (although the word "Yahweh" is restored in this inscription by the editors, its presence is far from certain). In any case, these inscriptions in the Phoenician script from Kuntillet Ajrud are nicely done (though fragmentary now) and reflect some very impressive scribal training.

During the second half of the first millennium BCE, Phoenician inscriptions continued to be produced. The Eshmunazar Sarcophagus Inscription (from Sidon) is very long (second only to the Karatepe Inscription in length for a Phoenician inscription) and constitutes a paradigmatic example of the continuation of the great Phoenician scribal tradition. This inscription can be dated to sometime around the fifth century BCE. This text is written in the first person (though the deceased is speaking from the grave, as it were) and states "I have been taken before my time, the son of brief days, smitten, an orphan, the son of a widow, and I am lying in this box, and in this grave, in a place which I built." After this mournful incipit, the inscription (continuing with the first person) utters curses upon any who might desecrate Eshmunazar's resting place. He also refers to his mother, Am'ashtart, priestess of Astarte (*KAI* 14). From about the same period, or perhaps a century earlier, are some temple tariffs found on Cyprus just north of Kition. These tariffs are present on a limestone table, with the letters painted in black on both sides in a beautiful cursive script. These inscriptions are fascinating because they refer to expenses paid to artisans and workers, such as masons, those conducting the sacrifices, stone carvers, and scribes (*KAI* 37). During the succeeding centuries, Phoenician inscriptions continue to be attested in the Phoenician homeland, with many ostraca also being attested for centuries, from the Phoenician homeland to the island of Cyprus and beyond. Moreover, in addition to this, as the centuries passed, the old Phoenician colonies continued to produce inscriptions as well. These are often referred to as Punic (e.g., Carthage), and those that postdate the Roman conquest of Carthage (ca. 146 BCE) are often referred to as Late Punic (Jongeling and Kerr 2005).

THE USE OF THE ALPHABET FOR ARAMAIC AND HEBREW INSCRIPTIONS DURING THE FIRST MILLENNIUM BCE

One of the most important inscriptions from the ninth century BCE is that of the Tell Fakhariyeh Bilingual Statue Inscription: The Akkadian text is on the front of the full-sized statue, and the Aramaic text is on the back. The Aramaic portion of this inscription is written in the Phoenician script (but in the Aramaic language). The fact that the Aramaic portion uses the Phoenician script is important and demonstrates that script and language are two different things, independent variables (we should know this intuitively, as the Latin script is used to write a variety of languages, including English, French, German, Spanish, etc.). In the case of the Tell Fakhariyeh Inscription, it, too, is a royal inscription, commissioned by a king of the region of Gozan named Had-Yithi. Within this inscription, he mentions his patron deity, the god Hadad-Sikanu. Moreover, Had-Yithi emphasizes the importance of his many public works. Among the most interesting aspects of this inscription are the "curse and blessing" sections, condemning anyone who might deface or destroy the statue and its inscriptions (Rollston 2010: 58–9).

Also hailing from the ninth century is the Tel Dan Stele. The inscription is chiseled into stone. Written in the Phoenician script and the Aramaic language, it was probably commissioned by the Aramaean (Syrian) king Hazael of Damascus. The initial portion of this inscription is broken, but the content dovetails quite nicely with the things known about Hazael from Neo-Assyrian texts and the Hebrew Bible, so it is a reasonable assumption that Hazael commissioned this inscription. It was placed at the site of Tel Dan as a "victory stele" after King Hazael had killed (probably with the assistance of Jehu of Israel) "King Jehoram of Israel" and "King Ahaziah of Judah." Within this inscription, Hazael contends that "Hadad made me king" and "Hadad went before me" (in battle). In short, this is a paradigmatic victory stele, intended to memorialize the victory of Hazael and the defeat of King Jehoram and King Ahaziah (Rollston 2010: 51–2). It is worth emphasizing that the script of the Tel Dan Stele is rather flawless, with the letters carefully chiseled in straight lines upon a dressed stone. In addition, the language and the orthography are well done. And, of course, the content is royal in nature. This is the work of a master scribe (or master stonemason), working at the behest of the Syrian monarch.

During the eighth century, Aramaic was rapidly becoming the *lingua franca* of the ancient Near Eastern world. The Sefire Treaty texts (consisting of three steles) date to the eighth century BCE and are seminal diplomatic documents, recording a treaty between Mati'el of Arpad (the vassal) and Bar-Ga'yah, king of Ktk (the hegemon). This treaty-text contains an introduction, stipulations, a list of gods (as witnesses to the treaty), and curses against Mati'el for any violation of the treaty (Fitzmyer 1995).

In addition to the floruit of the Aramaic language, the Aramaic script also becomes a distinctive script during the eighth century BCE. Lion weights from Nineveh and the Nimrud Ostracon date to the eighth century and are written in the distinctive Aramaic script (Naveh 1970). Furthermore, this continues during the seventh century with the Assur Clay Tablets, as well as the famed Assur Ostracon from an official known as Bel-Etir, who makes historical references to (among others) Tiglath-pileser III (745–727 BCE) and Sennacherib (705–681 BCE).

During the second half of the first millennium BCE, major works in Aramaic continue to be written and copied. One of the most important of such texts is that of the Aramaic version of the Besitun (Behistun) Inscription. Of course, the version of this inscription that is best known is the monumental version (McCarter 1996: 6–7). This version had been chiseled into the rock face of a cliff in ancient Persia, commissioned by the Persian king, Darius I (reigned 522–486 BCE), to commemorate his rise to the throne after the death of Cambyses (reigned 530–522 BCE) and his rapid subjugation of the usurper Gaumata. The monumental version is a trilingual: Akkadian, Old Persian, and Elamite. It was on the basis of the monumental version that Henry Rawlinson was able to decipher Akkadian during the middle of the nineteenth century (on the basis of the Old Persian). The Aramaic version of the Besitun Inscription had been discovered on the island of Elephantine, the location of a Jewish military colony near the first cataract of the Nile (near Aswan). It was written on papyrus in a semiformal cursive Aramaic script. It can be dated to the fifth century BCE (Naveh 1970: 35), thus not more than a century after the monumental version had been produced (Greenfield and Porten 1982). It hails from official military circles at Elephantine.

Also from Elephantine and reflective of the diverse nature of Aramaic inscriptions is the Passover Letter. There was a Jewish temple on the island of Elephantine for the worship of *Yhw* (i.e., Yahweh). As for this letter, it was sent by Hananiah (cf. Neh 1:1–3) to a certain Yedaniah (the Jewish commander of the fortress on Elephantine). The letter is dated to the fifth year of Darius II (419 BCE) and notified the Jews of Elephantine that the Passover was to be observed and that this had the support of the Persian crown. Within the Elephantine correspondence is also a subsequent letter from Yedaniah to Bagoas, the governor of Judah. In it, he requests the support of Bagoas in the rebuilding of the Jewish temple on Elephantine. He notes that the Jewish temple had been built long ago, but that it had been destroyed (in ca. 410 BCE) by the priests of the god Khnum (who also had a temple on the island).

Of course, the totality of the Elephantine materials in Aramaic is quite vast and includes not only many papyri but also ostraca. In addition to the epistolary materials at Elephantine, there are a number of texts with legal formulary as well. In essence, then, the contents of the Elephantine epigraphic texts are useful in providing a window into religion, political events, and legal matters – a treasure trove of data about elite activities in the fifth century BCE (Lindenberger 2003: 41–79; Azzoni 2013).

Some important Aramaic papyri dating to the fourth century BCE were found at Wadi ed-Daliyeh (Gropp 2001). These papyri are all fragmentary, with the most fully preserved papyrus actually only about half complete. These papyri were found in a cave, along with the remains of a number of people. All of the papyri are legal in nature. Many of the documents revolve around slave sales, and at least one is about the sale of a house. The documents are also important in that they contain (when it is preserved) a date formula, referencing the Persian king on the throne at the time (e.g., Artaxerxes II, Artaxerxes III, Darius III). It has been suggested that the family owning the archive had hidden in the cave in the wake of Alexander the Great's conquest of the region. In any case, this is an elite family's archive, something demonstrated by the ownership of slaves, as well as by the fact that all of these property transfers (i.e., slaves and house) were recorded by a professional scribe. Thus, these are not the documents of a family of modest means.

Among the Aramaic ostraca of the second half of the first millennium BCE are some 100 from Tel Arad (Aharoni 1981: 153–76 [translation by Joseph Naveh]). Some forty of these ostraca are legible or partially so. These ostraca are administrative in nature and refer often to food commodities and to animals (e.g., horses, donkeys). Many of the names in these ostraca are Hebrew. Among the most interesting facets of these texts (aside from their importance as reflections of the administrative apparatus in Judah during the Persian period) are the fact that the divine name *Qos* occurs a number of times, suggesting that there was an Edomite presence at the site as well. In any case, the main point is that these, too, are products of a governmental administration, not that of common folk.

Although most of these inscriptions are late (often hailing from the early decades and centuries of the Common Era), it is worth noting that Palmyrene and Nabataean are Aramaic dialects, and the script of these inscriptions derives from the Aramaic script of the preceding centuries, much as the script of the Punic and Neo-Punic inscriptions derives from the earlier Phoenician script.

The Old Hebrew script developed from the Phoenician script (as did Aramaic). Aramaic became a distinct national script in the eighth century BCE, but Hebrew became a distinct national script during the ninth century BCE. The earliest evidence for Hebrew as a distinct national script in the ninth century comes from the sites of Tel Rehov, Tel Arad, and the Mesha Stele.[4]

It is in the late ninth century and the early eighth century that the Old Hebrew script really comes to be used widely in Israel and Judah. Among the most important of the early Old Hebrew Inscriptions are those from Kuntillet Ajrud (Aḥituv, Eshel, and Meshel 2012). The Old Hebrew inscriptions from this site are all reflective of high-caliber scribal workmanship, with the morphology and stance of the script nicely executed. Most of these inscriptions are ink on pottery (e.g., pithoi). Among the most important content of these inscriptions, and that which has garnered the most interest, are the inscriptions that are to be read: "Message of ..., I bless you [pl.] by Yahweh of Samaria and his Asherah"(Inscription 3.1) and "Message of 'Amaryaw, 'Say to my lord, are you well? I bless you (ms) by Yahweh of Teman and his Asherah" (Inscription 3.6). Structured with aspects of standard letter formulary, these inscriptions are particularly important for understanding aspects of the religion of ancient Israel and Judah, as they refer to the national god of Israel as having a consort, namely, Asherah (cf. also the tomb inscription from Khirbet el-Qom with a similar reference to Yahweh and Asherah). In addition, these inscriptions also convey the sense that some believed there were local manifestations of Yahweh (i.e., DN of GN), something that is attested widely in the ancient Near Eastern world (McCarter 1987).

From the site of Israelite Samaria come some 100 Old Hebrew ostraca (Reisner, Fisher, and Lyon 1924). They date to the reign of Jeroboam II (early eighth century BCE) and refer to the receipt or shipment of commodities, such as wine and oil. These inscriptions often contain a date formula (arguably to be linked to the reign of Jeroboam II) and often a personal name. Although these ostraca are brief, and many are faded (some to the point of not being legible), they do testify to the administrative apparatus that was present in the late Omride period in the Northern Kingdom of ancient Israel. Also of importance is the fact that the script of these inscriptions is very well done, the orthography is consistent, and Hieratic numerals are used frequently (demonstrative of the mathematical training in which an Old Hebrew scribe would have engaged). These inscriptions are the products of Israelites scribes trained in a formal fashion (Rollston 2006).

The Siloam Tunnel Inscription is an Old Hebrew inscription, and it dates to the late eighth century, arguably to the reign of Hezekiah of Judah (reigned 715–687 BCE). This inscription is chiseled into stone and is six lines long. The script is superb, the orthography is the standard for Old Hebrew of this period, and the content is important. In essence, this inscription notes that the water tunnel (in which it was found) was ca. 1,200 cubits long (1,800 ft), and the workers began at opposite ends and then met in the middle. It also mentions that as the two teams of workers neared each other that they could hear one another (perhaps the sound of the pick axes being used). Although this inscription does not reference Hezekiah, the paleographic date of the inscription, the nature of the water tunnel (diverting water from a spring outside the city underground and then brining it through the tunnel to a place inside the city), and the various literary references to Hezekiah having built the tunnel (e.g., 2 Kgs 20:20; 2 Chr 32:30; Sir 48:17–18) strongly argue for Hezekiah as the commissioner of the tunnel and inscriptions. It seems convincing to contend that Hezekiah had this water tunnel built after he rebelled against the Neo-Assyrian king, Sennacherib (reigned 705–681 BCE), in anticipation of his punitive campaign to the region (cf. Sennacherib Prism). In short, this inscription is a reflection of a royal project, commissioned by Hezekiah in the late eighth century; thus, it is a product of officialdom.

From the Judean sites of Lachish (Torczyner 1938) and Tel Arad (Aharoni 1981) come some of the largest numbers of legible Old Hebrew inscriptions. Many of these are letters (i.e., epistolary documents), attesting to the formal epistolary training that was part of the curriculum of scribes in Israel and Judah (Rollston 2006: 67). Among the most important aspects of these inscriptions is that a fair number are military correspondence between high military officials. Again, the point is that these inscriptions are not some sort of mundane document connected with the everyday life of ordinary people; these are aspects of formal correspondence between Judean military officials.

Hebrew continued to be used at times during the period after the fall of Jerusalem in 586 BCE to Nebuchadnezzar II of Babylon, but the numbers are small in comparison with Aramaic inscriptions. Part of the reason for this is that it was predominantly the elites of Judah who were exiled in 597 and 586 BCE, and during the exile, the language and script of the *lingua franca*, that is, Aramaic, gained hegemony even among the Judahite exiles (who returned from Babylon to Judah after the victory of Cyrus the Great over Babylon in 539 BCE). The fact that large blocks of the biblical books of Daniel and Ezra are written in Aramaic is a reflection of this, as is the usage of Aramaic (e.g., Targums) during the late Second Temple period and the early post-biblical period (i.e., after the fall of Jerusalem to the Romans in 70 CE). Nevertheless, Hebrew continued to be used in Judah at times, something that seems to be demonstrated rather nicely by some of the burial inscriptions on ossuaries in Jerusalem from the late first century BCE and early first century CE.

DISCUSSION OF THE ORIGINS OF THE GREEK SCRIPT

The Greeks borrowed the Phoenician alphabet and used it to write Greek inscriptions. There are various lines of evidence that demonstrate this. First and foremost is the fact that the shapes of the letters themselves are those of the Phoenician alphabet. In addition, the names of the letters of the Greek alphabet are Semitic in origin, not Greek. For example, the Greek letter-name *alpha* has no etymology in Greek. Similarly, the Greek letter-name *bēta* has no etymology in Greek. Or, again, the Greek letter-name *kappa* has no etymology in Greek. Or, yet again, the Greek letter-name *rhō* has no etymology in Greek. However, there are good etymologies for all of these letter-names in Semitic. Thus, the Greek letter-name *alpha* derives from the Semitic word *aleph*, which means "ox." Similarly, the Greek letter-name *bēta* derives from the Semitic word *bayit* (*bet*), which means "house." Or, again, the Greek letter-name *kappa* derives from the Semitic word *kap(p)*, which means "palm of the hand." Or, yet again, the Greek letter-name *rhō* derives from the Semitic word *rosh*, means "a (human's) head." Furthermore, the order of the letters of the Greek alphabet essentially follows that of the Semitic alphabet (Abgad order, not Halḥam order).

Among the Greek authors commenting on the Phoenicians and the origins of the alphabet is Herodotus (ca. 484–425 BCE). Among his most important references to the origins of the Greek alphabet are those in connection with Cadmus (whom Herodotus believed to be a historical personage). He states that some Phoenicians came with Cadmus to the country called Boeotia, and that "among many other kings of learning, they brought into Hellas the alphabet, which had hitherto been unknown, as I think, to the Greeks." Significantly, he goes on to state:

> And presently as time went on, the sound and the form of the letters were changed. At this time the Greeks that dwelt round them for the most part were Ionians; who having been taught the letters by the Phoenicians, used them with some few changes of form, and in so doing gave to these characters (as indeed was but just, seeing that the Phoenicians had brought them into Hellas) the name of Phoenician.
>
> (*Hist.* 5.57–8; translation by A. D. Godley [1975: 3])

Diodorus Siculus (fl. 60–30 BCE) also made some reference to the origins of the alphabet. Namely, he cites a certain Dionysius as follows:

> Among the Greeks, Linus was the first to discover the different rhythms and song, and when Cadmus brought from Phoenicia the letters, as they are called, Linus was again the first to transfer them into the Greek language, to give a name to each character, and to fix its shape. Now the letters, as a group, are called "Phoenician" because they were brought to the Greeks from the Phoenicians.
>
> (*Bibl. hist.* 3.67.1; translation by C. H. Oldfather [1967: 307])

Even more revealing are some of the additional details that Diodorus references. Namely, the Phoenicians did not invent the alphabet, but rather they learned them from the Syrians. Here are his precise words:

> And in reply to those who say that the Syrians are the discovers of the letters, the Phoenicians having learned them from the Syrians and then passed them on to the Greeks, and that these Phoenicians are those who

> sailed to Europe together with Cadmus and this is the reason why the Greeks call the letters "Phoenician," they tell us, on the other hand, that the Phoenicians were not the first to make this discovery, but that they did no more than to change the forms of the letters, whereupon the majority of humankind made use of the way of writing them as the Phoenicians devised it, and so the letters received the designation we have mentioned above.
>
> (*Bibl. hist.* 5.74.1; translation by Oldfather [1970: 295, 297])

Although Diodorus wrote a number of centuries after the development of the Greek alphabet, the fact remains that his basic synopsis does correspond with epigraphic *realia*, namely, the Phoenicians did not invent the alphabet but rather adapted the alphabet that had been developed by Levantine peoples during the preceding centuries.

The date for the Greek adoption of the Semitic alphabet is a matter of much debate. The two basic proposals are enshrined in the writings of P. Kyle McCarter Jr. and Joseph Naveh. Namely, McCarter has argued that the origins of the Greek alphabet "may be traced to the reign of Pygmalion of Tyre," that is, the late ninth and early eighth centuries BCE (1975: 123–6). However, in order to account for the fact that Greek is written dextrograde (i.e., left to right), McCarter contends that there may very well have been some earlier experimentation with the alphabet by the Greeks (because the Phoenician alphabet was being written consistently sinistrograde already by the eleventh century BCE). However, Naveh contends that the date for the borrowing of the alphabet by the Greeks must have been sometime during the late twelfth century BCE or the first half of the eleventh century BCE, "just before right-to-left writing became the standard practice, around 1050 B.C." (1987: 178). It is worth emphasizing in this connection that some of the most recent epigraphic finds (e.g., those of Khirbet Qeiyafa and Tell eṣ-Ṣafi/Gath) demonstrate that the Early Alphabetic script persisted (in certain peripheral regions outside of Phoenicia proper) for some 50 to 100 years, that is, down into the tenth century BCE. Thus, it may very well be that a date for the origins of the Greek alphabet is later than Naveh had posited, but earlier than McCarter had suggested. In any case, the things that can be stated with more confidence are that: (a) the earliest Greek inscriptions date to the eighth century BCE, and (b) the Greeks borrowed the twenty-two consonantal letters of the Phoenician alphabet (some of which the Greeks used as vowel letters [e.g., *alpha*, *ēta*]) but also gradually introduced five additional letters (namely, *upsilon, phi, xi, psi,* and *ōmega*).

Although the earliest of the Greek inscriptions are dated to the eighth century BCE, the majority of extant Greek inscriptions of the first millennium BCE are from the second half of the millennium. In terms of genres, some of these inscriptions are monumental in nature, some are religious (e.g., from temples), some are political, and a fair number are funerary (McLean 2002). Many Greek inscriptions were found in Greece itself, of course, but because of Hellenization (beginning in earnest with Alexander the Great), Greek inscriptions are found throughout much of the ancient world. Among the most interesting of the Greek inscriptions from the Levant is the Balustrade Inscription (attested in two fragmentary copies, the first found in 1871 by Charles Clermont-Ganneau), an inscription that would have once been part of the balustrade of the Jewish Second Temple in Jerusalem (McCarter 1996: 129–30). The contents of this inscription are striking because, in essence, the inscription proclaims that gentiles must be careful not to enter the inner courts of the temple. And the inscription states that if a gentile enters into one of the inner courts, he himself will be responsible for his own death (by capital punishment). Another particularly interesting Greek inscription also hails from the city of Jerusalem. It is a synagogue inscription and arguably dates to the first century CE. Its Greek text reads as follows: "Theodotus, son of Vettenos, priest and ruler of the synagogue, son of the ruler of the synagogue, grandson of the ruler of the synagogue, built the synagogue for the reading of the Law and the Teaching of the Commandments, and (he built) the hostelry, and the house-top rooms, and the bathrooms, for the lodging of those who have need from abroad, which his forefathers and the elders and Simonides had established."

Moving now to the language of Egypt during the beginning of the Common Era, it is worth noting that the Greek script is that which was used to write Coptic (an Egyptian language). To be precise, the Coptic alphabet consists of the Greek alphabet, with the addition of six letters borrowed from the Demotic (Egyptian) script. This is an important component of the later history and usage of the Greek alphabet, and a testimony to the hegemony the Greek alphabet came to have even in Egypt.

THE ORIGINS AND USAGE OF THE LATIN ALPHABET: A SELECTION

The Latin alphabet is modeled on the Greek alphabet, with some influence from the Etruscan alphabet (and the Etruscan alphabet derived from the Greek alphabet, which, of course, derived from the Phoenician).[5] The earliest of the Latin inscriptions hails from around the sixth or seventh century BCE. Of course, it is with the rise of the Roman Republic and especially the Roman Empire that there was a dramatic proliferation of Latin inscriptions.[6] Just as with the corpus of Alphabetic Semitic and Greek inscriptions, so also with Latin inscriptions – the majority are official in nature, texts connected with a governmental hierarchy or of wealthy elites outside of government. To be sure, there are some graffiti, just as there are with Greek and Semitic, and some of this material can arguably be associated with the populace (and it is normally painfully obvious that those penning graffiti were not formally trained in writing). Nonetheless, writing and reading were largely an elite venture for Latin inscriptions, just as with writing in antiquity in general.

In sum, the history of alphabetic writing in the first millennium is absolutely stunning. Most of the epigraphic texts that we have are those of elites, that is, those with substantial financial resources or those connected in some fashion with governmental apparatuses. In essence, writing and reading were not normally practices connected with non-elites. To be sure, there are some inscriptions that fall into that category, but it is normally very painfully obvious, because of the low caliber of the script and orthography. Some of the ossuary inscriptions in Jerusalem hail from these sorts of non-elite contexts. In any case, in terms of the *Sitz im Leben* of alphabetic writing, the evidence is quite decisive in revealing that it is elites, not non-elites, who are writing and reading. And, of course, this fact reminds us that in our attempts to write a social history the epigraphic material can only be part of the equation, as the majority of writers and readers of inscriptions (and literary texts) come from a segment of society (i.e., elite society), not from society as a whole.

NOTES

1 For a discussion, see Houston 2004.
2 For a discussion and references, see Rollston 2016: 284–9.
3 For a discussion, see Cross 1972.
4 The Mesha Stele is written in the Moabite language but in the Old Hebrew script, as Moab had been under Moabite hegemony for several decades during the ninth century BCE (see B. W. Porter, this volume).
5 Note that Etruscan is usually written sinistrograde, not dextrograde. Moreover, Etruscan inscriptions were normally written *scriptio continua*, that is, without word dividers.
6 See, e.g., the selection in Gordon 1983: 69–72.

REFERENCES

Aharoni, Y., in cooperation with J. Naveh. 1981. *Arad Inscriptions*. JDS. Jerusalem: IES.
Aḥituv, S.; Eshel, E.; and Meshel, Z. 2012. The Inscriptions. In *Kuntillet ʿAjrud (Ḥorvat Teman): An Iron Age II Religious Site on the Judah-Sinai Border*, by Z. Meshel, 73–142. Jerusalem: IES.
Azzoni, A. 2013. *The Private Lives of Women in Persian Egypt*. Winona Lake, IN: Eisenbrauns.
Bordreuil, P., and Pardee, D. 2009. *A Manual of Ugaritic*. Linguistic Studies in Ancient West Semitic 3. Winona Lake, IN: Eisenbrauns.
Cross, F. M. 1972. An Interpretation of the Nora Stone. *BASOR* 208: 13–19.
Darnell, J. C.; Dobbs-Allsopp, F. W.; Lundberg, M. J.; McCarter, P. K.; and Zuckerman, B. 2005. *Two Early Alphabetic Inscriptions from the Wadi el-Ḥôl: New Evidence for the Origin of the Alphabet from the Western Desert of Egypt*. AASOR 59. Boston: ASOR.

Fitzmyer, J. A. 1995. *The Aramaic Inscriptions of Sefire*. 2nd rev. ed. Biblica et Orientalia 19. Rome: Pontifical Biblical Institute.

Godley, A. D., trans. 1975. *Herodotus*, Vol. 1. LCL 117. Cambridge: Harvard University Press.

Gordon, A. E. 1983. *Illustrated Introduction to Latin Epigraphy*. Classics. Berkeley: University of California Press.

Greenfield, J. C., and Porten, B. 1982. *The Bisitun Inscription of Darius the Great: Aramaic Version*. Corpus Inscriptionum Iranicarum, Inscriptions of Ancient Iran 5, The Aramaic Versions of the Achaemenian inscriptions, etc., Texts 1. London: Lund Humphries.

Gropp, D. M. 2001. *Wadi Daliyeh II: The Samaria Papyri from Wadi Daliyeh*. DJD 28. Oxford: Clarendon.

Houston, S. D. 2004. *The First Writing: Script Invention as History and Process*. Cambridge: Cambridge University Press.

Jongeling, K., and Kerr, R. M. 2005. *Late Punic Epigraphy: An Introduction to the Study of Neo-Punic and Latino-Punic Inscriptions*. Tübingen: Mohr Siebeck.

Kramer, S. N. 1981. *History Begins at Sumer: Thirty-Nine Firsts in Man's Recorded History*. 3rd rev. ed. Philadelphia: University of Pennsylvania Press.

Lindenberger, J. M. 2003. *Ancient Aramaic and Hebrew Letters*. 2nd ed. WAW 14. Atlanta: SBL.

McCarter, P. K., Jr. 1975. *The Antiquity of the Greek Alphabet and the Early Phoenician Scripts*. HSM 9. Missoula, MT: Published by Scholars Press for Harvard Semitic Museum.

1987. Aspects of the Religion of the Israelite Monarchy: Biblical and Epigraphic Data. In *Ancient Israelite Religion: Essays in Honor of Frank Moore Cross*, ed. P. D. Miller Jr., P. D. Hanson, and S. D. McBride, 137–55. Philadelphia: Fortress.

1996. *Ancient Inscriptions: Voices from the Biblical World*. Washington, DC: Biblical Archaeology Society.

McLean, B. H. 2002. *An Introduction to Greek Epigraphy of the Hellenistic and Roman Periods from Alexander the Great down to the Reign of Constantine (323 B.C.–A.D. 337)*. Ann Arbor: University of Michigan Press.

Moran, W. L. 1992. *The Amarna Letters*. Baltimore: The Johns Hopkins University Press.

2003. *Amarna Studies: Collected Writings*. HSS 54. Winona Lake, IN: Eisenbrauns.

Naveh, J. 1970. *The Development of the Aramaic Script*. Proceedings of The Israel Academy of Sciences and Humanities 5 (1). Jerusalem: The Israel Academy of Sciences and Humanities.

1987. *Early History of the Alphabet: An Introduction to West Semitic Epigraphy and Palaeography*. 2nd rev. ed. Jerusalem: Magnes.

Oldfather, C. H., trans. 1967. *Diodorus of Sicily*, Vol. 2. LCL 303. Cambridge, MA: Harvard University Press.

1970. *Diodorus of Sicily*, Vol. 3. LCL 340. Cambridge, MA: Harvard University Press.

Reisner, G. A.; Fisher, C. S.; and Lyon, D. G. 1924. *Harvard Excavations at Samaria: 1908–1910*. 2 vols. Cambridge, MA: Harvard University Press.

Rollston, C. A. 2006. Scribal Education in Ancient Israel: The Old Hebrew Epigraphic Evidence. *BASOR* 344: 47–74.

2010. *Writing and Literacy in the World of Ancient Israel: Epigraphic Evidence from the Iron Age*. ABS 11. Leiden: Brill.

2016. Phoenicia and the Phoenicians. In *The World around the Old Testament: The People and Places of the Ancient Near East*, ed. B. T. Arnold and B. A. Strawn, 267–308. Grand Rapids, MI: Baker Academic.

Segert, S. 1984. *A Basic Grammar of the Ugaritic Language with Selected Texts and Glossary*. Berkeley: University of California Press.

Tov, E. 2004. *Scribal Practices and Approaches Reflected in the Texts Found in the Judean Desert*. STDJ 54. Leiden: Brill.

Torczyner, H. 1938. *Lachish (Tell ed Duwier) I: The Lachish Letters*. WMARENEP 1. London: Oxford University Press.

PART FOUR

TWENTY ONE

PEOPLE, MATERIAL CULTURE, AND ETHNO-RELIGIOUS REGIONS IN ACHAEMENID PALESTINE

OREN TAL

Geographically, Persian-period Palestine seems to have been divided into several ethno-religious regions: Philistia and Edom on the south; Phoenicia along the central and northern coastal plain; and Judah and Samaria on the central mountain ridge. Still, the ethnicity and/or religion of other regions, such as the Carmel Mountain ridge, the Lower and Upper Galilee, and the rift valley, are somewhat unclear and may have been inhabited by several ethnic and/or religious elements.

Ethnically, the nucleus of the Iron Age populations – the Philistines, Edomites, Israelites, and Judahites' descendants – were to some extent already being mixed with the neighboring Semitic elements (among which Mesopotamian deportees) and Egyptians prior to the Achaemenid rule over Philistia. Phoenicians (from Phoenicia proper) also must have been a significant component in the population of the Palestinian lowlands, especially after the division of the Palestinian coastal plain (and its immediate lowlands) among Sidon and Tyre under the Achaemenids. 'Eshmon'azor II, king of Sidon, was granted the Sharon Plain (*KAI* §14.1.1.9; *ANET* 662) in the last third of the sixth century BCE (Elayi 2006), most probably as tribute given for the participation of the Sidonian fleet during Cambyses' and/or Darius I's successful campaigns to Egypt (ca. 525 and 517 BCE). It may also be assumed that on the same occasion Tyre was granted the lands of the Plain of Akko and Philistia (quite similarly to the treaty from the 670s BCE between Asarhaddon and Ba'al of Tyre [Borger 1956: 108, lines 18–20]). While later (i.e., Hellenistic) archaeological findings show hegemony of the city of Tyre over centers in the Plain of Akko (cf., e.g., Naveh 1997; Ariel and Naveh 2003), an important historical testimony regarding Sidonian and Tyrian Palestinian land division and political affiliation is known from an account dated to the end of the Persian period, the *Periplus* of Pseudo-Scylax, recently assigned to the year 338/337 BCE (Shipley 2012: 122–3).

We have only indirect historical accounts on the crystallization of Samaritans and Edomites in Persian-period Palestine. These are the Edicts of Cyrus (2 Chron 36:22–23; Ezra 1:1–4, 6:1–12), which provide us with an historical context on Jews for the period. While these edicts suggest the renaissance of Jewish life in Judah, and especially Jerusalem, in the early stages of Achaemenid rule over Palestine, their historicity is still debated, and the archaeological evidence clearly favors a lengthier process of return over decades if not centuries (cf., e.g., De Groot 2001; Finkelstein 2009).

The ethno-religious regions of Achaemenid Palestine seem to have been administrated differently; while Judah had Jerusalem as its religious capital, Samaria's religious center at Mount Gerizim did not hold the status of a capital, as it was was located in the city of Samaria (שמרין בירתא) (Gropp 2001; Dušek 2007). Edom's Ptolemaic-period administration had two centers of the hyparchy, Marisa on the west and Adora on the east (Diod. Sic. 19.95.2, 19.98.1; see also Durand 1997: 216–23, *passim* [P. Cairo Zen. 1.59015 verso]), and it may project a similar status in the Late Persian period. The newly annexed regions of the Phoenician entities of Sidon and Tyre were probably subject to their mother cities, which were, in fact, the center of their principalities.

Seeking the contrasts of these ethno-religious regions in material culture is not an easy task; more often than not, the archaeological evidence provides us with similarities or complexities rather than with defined markers of identities. One such aspect relates to burial practices; the plethora of excavated burial sites in Palestine and the neighboring regions show similarities in many customs: inhumation (rather than cremation), repeated position and orientation of the deceased, restricted number of tomb types, a high occurrence of single burials, and a high occurrence for the presence of grave goods (Wolff 2002). Moreover, tracing unique mortuary practices within a certain ethno-religious region seems impossible. On the other hand, the numismatic evidence of the period – although more apparent in the fourth century BCE – does provide us with defined markers of identity. Sidonian and Tyrian coins, as well as indigenous coinages of what can be defined as southern Palestinian issues (of Philistia, Samaria, Judah, and possibly Edom), are found frequently in their respected area of political affinity. It is no exaggeration to state that the indigenous coins of Palestine dated to the second half of the fifth and mostly fourth centuries BCE in many cases represent the main – if not the sole – artistic and possibly religious material evidence related with certainty to the populations of this region, as will be shown below.

It seems that the identity markers of the people of Persian-period Palestine are easier to track in the domain of direct (and indirect) religious, ritual, or cultic-related material evidence. For this purpose, we will survey the suggested borders for the ethno-religious regions of these peoples and the finds that are often associated with their presence.

PHOENICIA

Tracing the borders of Phoenicia in Palestine under Achaemenid rule raises difficulties. The hinterland borders of Sidon's newly annexed centers (*d'r wypy 'rṣt dgn h'drt 'š bšd šrn*, "Dor and Joppa the mighty lands of grain in the Sharon Plain" [*KAI* §14.1.1.9; *ANET* 662]) are not entirely clear. The southern borders of the Sharon are debated. While a minimalist view would favor Joppa (Jaffa) and its southern hinterland, a maximalist view would prefer the Lod/Ono Valley. A later 163 BCE inscription suggests that Sidonian control was as far south as Yavneh-Yam in Hellenistic times (if not earlier) (*SEG* 41: no. 1556; Isaac 1991).

Tyrian control over Palestine is similarly unclear; epigraphic finds (such as inscribed storage jars and ostraca) with the regnal years of the Tyrian kings from the second half of the fourth century BCE were found in Shiqmona and farther to the south in the Edom and Gaza region (Lemaire 1991; 2006: 423), while later Hellenistic bullae and stamp impressions from Tel Kedesh (Upper Galilee) (Ariel and Naveh 2003) and the Plain of Akko show the use of Tyrian civic count (Naveh 1997). Moreover, while the Palestinian coast and its immediate lowlands were clearly under Phoenician (Sidonian and Tyrian) control up to Gaza at the time, the eastern frontiers of Phoenician control and/or hegemony are even more difficult to follow; to what extent were the Samarian foothills Phoenician and, for that matter, the Carmel Mountain ridge (see Dar 2014: 283, 289–90)?

Archaeologically, excavations carried out in the region's major and secondary urban centers, as well as in the rural and military settlements, show the predominance of a few types of finds. In the epigraphic domain, the prevalence of Phoenician-script inscriptions, whether secular or cult-oriented, is well attested (cf., e.g., Delavault and Lemaire 1979; see also Deutsch and Heltzer 1994).

Another type of find is figurines especially made of clay but also out of stone and metal. Recent developments in the study of terra-cottas have shown trends of regionalism among the people of the Levant (with the exceptions of Judah and Samaria, where figurines are almost entirely absent from Persian-period contexts), hence a Phoenician group is noticeable where three categories are apparent: human (men, women, children) representations, riders (on horses), and masks (which are remarkably Phoenician in the Levantine milieu) (cf., e.g., Stern 2010). While in many cases human figurines are considered dedicatory due to the fact that several came from *favissae* (repository pits)

(Lipiński 2003: 300–5), their exclusive role in Phoenician cult might be unbalanced because of their presence in a variety of contexts.

With the deciphering of the erased text known as the Customs Account, dated to year 11 of either Xerxes I (475 BCE) or Artaxerxes I (454 BCE), we became familiar firsthand with the kinds of goods Phoenician (and Greek) ships traded during one ten-month sailing season (approximately from March to December) (Yardeni 1994). While Phoenician trade ships are mostly associated with the transport of wine, metals (iron, bronze, tin), wood (for various uses), wool, and clay (*tyn šmwš*, probably of Samian origin) (see Tal 2009: 7–8, n. 38), it is likely that some of these goods were monopolized in Phoenician hands. Still, with the exception of Phoenician wine and its assumed predominance at Phoenician sites (based on the prevalence of Phoenician carinated shoulder jars [cf. Bettles 2003]), other goods are hardly detectable in archaeological terms. In addition, the frequent appearance of certain types of Attic Black Plain Wares at Phoenician coastal sites (namely, vessels that were imported for their own sake and not for their contents [Tal 2003]) may provide further evidence of Phoenician trade and be an ethno-religious marker. In this context, one may also add additional vessel forms that are notably Phoenician, among them certain types of dipper and perfume juglets, amphoriskoi, and anthropomorphic vessels (cf. Stern 2015), the last of which may also be used in trade due to their (pharmaceutical or cosmetic?) contents.

Another aspect of Phoenician culture is coinage. Phoenician coins appeared at least a century and a half after the first Greek (Lydian) coins, which were regularly imported to the region as evidenced by hoards and single finds. Official coin minting has always been a monopoly of the ruling authority, which was also the case in Achaemenid Phoenicia, where autonomous coin minting was exercised by the four city-states of Arwad, Byblos, Sidon, and Tyre under permission granted by the Achaemenid administration. Suggestions have also been made regarding the possible existence of small Persian-period mints in Tripoli, Beirut, and Tel Dor, of which the interpretation remains highly questionable, as it is normally based on a single coin-type found at the site (cf. Elayi and Elayi 2014: 9 [Tripoli] and Qedar 2000–2002 [Tel Dor]). Whether Persian authorities responded to a specific local request, it was a systematic endorsement, if explicit approval was needed, or the right to mint coins was implicit in the autonomous status are still debated, as there are no explicit sources on Phoenician official authorization for coin minting.[1] Phoenician city-states were autonomous and separate entities with independent economic activities and social histories. Several common features bind the phenomenon together and justify the term "Phoenician numismatics." First, the four city-states had a common interest in maritime trade and warfare owing to their strategic location on the Levantine coast, a fact evidenced by maritime-related iconography and symbolism. Second, the coins of all four

21.1. Selection of Phoenician coins: (top) Tyrian and (bottom) Sidonian. (Courtesy of Classic Numismatic Group, Inc. [www.cngcoins.com].)

Phoenician city-states were minted mainly in silver with bronze coins being introduced in the fourth century BCE, but with no gold coin minting. Third, Phoenician weight standards, different to the Attic and Persic standards, was used by three of the four cities during most of their minting stages and points to political-economic alliances, strong economic ties, and continuous intra-regional trade. In terms of iconography, Phoenician coins, as Phoenician art in general, display a mixture of influences, including Egyptian, Greek, Mesopotamian, and Anatolian motifs executed in a local fashion.

The control of the city-states of Sidon and Tyre over the northern and central coastal plain of Achaemenid Palestine is well attested in numismatic finds, where the prevalence of Tyrian coins is in Tyrian-controlled areas (especially in the northern coastal plain), and the prevalence of Sidonian coins is in Sidonian-controlled areas (especially in the central coastal plain/Sharon Plain) (Elayi and Elayi 2004; 2009) (Fig. 21.1).

The southern coastal plain exhibits an entirely different picture; the division of the Palestinian coastal plain (and its immediate lowlands) among Sidon and Tyre under the Achaemenids has been discussed at some length elsewhere (Gitler and Tal 2006a: 44–6). As stated above, an important historical testimony regarding Sidonian and Tyrian Palestinian land division and political affiliation is known from an account dated to the end of the Persian period: the *Periplus* of Pseudo-Scylax (Shipley 2012: 122–3). The paragraph that relates to Coele-Syria describes the area between the Sharon Plain and Philistia as follows:

> Δῶρος πολίς Σιδωνίων· [Ἰόππη πολίς ἐκτε-]θῆναί φασιν ἐνθῦατα τὴν Ἀνδρομ[έδαν τῷ] κήτει· Ἀσκά]λων πολίς Τυρίων καὶ βασίλεα. Ἐν[θαῦθα ὅρος ἐστὶ τῆς Κοίλης] Συρίας.
>
> "Doros a city of Sidonians, [city of Joppa] where it is said Andromeda was exposed [to the monster, Asca]lon a city of Tyrians and a Palace. Here [it is the boundary of Coele-]Syria."
>
> (104.3; translation by O. Tal)

While Ashdod (Azotos) is absent from Pseudo-Scylax's listings, and Ashkelon (Ascalon) seems to mark Coele-Syria's southernmost border, it is likely that the three minting authorities of Philistia – Ashdod, Ashkelon, and Gaza – were under Tyrian suzerainty due to the fact that they possibly employed a central collective mint, given the existence of die links between their coins (Gitler and Tal 2009). The coinage of Philistia (the so-called Philisto-Arabian coins), namely the "civic" issues of the cities of Ashdod, Ashkelon, and Gaza, emerged in the second half of the fifth century and continued to be minted in the fourth century BCE up to the end of Achaemenid rule (Gitler and Tal 2006a). In fact, the coinage of Philistia represents the earliest and most significant phase in the early monetary development of Palestine, as the region of Philistia is the first to witness the transition from a bullion-based to a coin-based economy (that was partial in its emergence and probably encompassed the higher levels of society) (Fig. 21.2). It is thus in Persian-period Philistia where the development of the metal economy of Palestine from *Hacksilber* to coins (Archaic and Athenian) and a proper local monetary economy began. Philistia's early coinage was probably confined to the "large" silver (and some silver-plated) *sheqel* denomination (customarily, yet erroneously, referred to as a "tetradrachm"). By the fourth century BCE, a proper monetary economy is evident in Philistian coinage; each coin type is normally produced in three different denominations: the quarter-*sheqel* (*rb' šql* or simply *rb'* (one-quarter of a Philistian *šql*), customarily referred to as a "drachm," the *m'h* (1/24 of Philistian *šql*), customarily referred to as an "obol," and the half *m'h* (1/48

21.2. Philistian coins from: (top) Ashdod, (center) Ashkelon, and (bottom) Gaza. (Courtesy of The Israel Museum, Jerusalem.)

of Philistian *šql*), customarily referred to as "hemiobol" (cf. Tal 2007: 21–2) (Fig. 21.3).

To date, some 400 Philistian coin types are known, that is, coins bearing different motifs regardless of their denomination. The coins' motifs reflect contemporary fashions, foreign influences, and broad local imagery. Philistian coins show the name of the minting authorities, that is, Ashdod (*šdd* – with ' as a pictograph of a bull's head, or in abbreviated forms '*d*, '*š*, and *šd*) written in Aramaic script; Ashkelon ('*n* or ' alone) written in Phoenician script; and Gaza ('*zh*, or in abbreviated forms '*z*, *z*', or ' alone, and *m* (denoting Marnas – Gaza's primary deity) all are normally written in lapidary Aramaic script, but most depictions of the letter ' (as a full circle) are actually Phoenician script. There are also coins with isolated or two–three (Aramaic) letters whose meaning is uncertain, but one should bear in mind that most of the Philistian coins do not carry inscriptions or dates (Fig. 21.4). They are defined as Philistian on the basis of circulation, fabric, metrology, and especially iconography. The iconography of the Philistian coinage was influenced by Western (Greek, eastern Greek, and southern Anatolian), Eastern (Phoenician

21.3. Philistian denominations as demonstrated by a coin type from Ashdod: (top) *rb' šql*, (center) *m'h*, and (bottom) half *m'h*. (Courtesy of The Israel Museum, Jerusalem.)

21.4. Selection of Philistian coins. (Courtesy of The Israel Museum, Jerusalem.)

and Achaemenid in the broad sense of the terms), and Egyptian sources. In fact, Philistian coinage is one of the most variable artistic forms in numismatic evidence known from Palestine (and beyond). However, the most striking influence on the Philistian coinage is notably Athenian. The people of Philistia observed these foreign motifs and frequently adopted and adapted them to local use.

SAMARIA

The assumed satrapy of Late Persian- (and Early Hellenistic-) period Samaria seems to be confined to the Samarian highlands. While the region's administrative capital was in the city of Samaria (שמרין בירתא), the region's religious center was at Mount Gerizim.

Archaeologically, excavations carried out in the region's major centers of Samaria, Shechem, and Mount Gerizim, as well as other settlements of the period, do not exhibit exclusive finds that can be defined as Samaritan in their nature, with the exception of Samarian coins. This coinage is merely known from the last two generations and isolated coin finds in the antiquities black market. It is worthy to note the existence of two hoards of Samarian coins: the "Samaria Hoard" (Meadows and Wartenberg 2002: 9.413 – "Samaria, before 1990"; see Meshorer and Qedar 1991) and the "Nablus Hoard" (Thompson, Mørkholm, and Kraay 1973: 1504; see Gitler and Tal 2017). A significant number of Samarian coins also came from the controlled archaeological excavations at Mount Gerizim, which may suggest their use as temple payments, as previously suggested by Persian-period coinage from Judah (Ronen 2003–2006: 29–30). Ya'akov Meshorer and Shraga Qedar were the first to study these coins systematically. They termed coins of the same type but of different denomination "types"; as a result, a corpus of 224 Samarian coins was published (1999; see also 1991), largely based on the 182 coins attributed to the "Samaria Hoard." Since 1999, approximately 60 new coins have appeared on the antiquities black market (Gitler and Tal 2006b; Ronen 2007; and others yet unpublished, including the "Nablus Hoard") and in excavations (cf. Ariel 2016).

To date, some 200 coin types are known, that is, coins bearing different motifs regardless of their denomination. Samaria struck silver (and some silver-plated) coins erroneously, yet customarily, referred to them as "drachms," "obols," "hemiobols," and smaller fractions (cf. Tal 2007: 20), rather than the *rb' šqln* (or simply *rb'*), *m'n*, and half *m'n* discussed above (Fig. 21.5). The most common denominations in the Samarian coinage are the *m'n* and half *m'n*. A single dated coin type is subjectively dated to around 372 BCE; however, minting probably started earlier (in the late fifth or early fourth century BCE) based on the eye design (Gitler and Tal 2014: 24), and

21.5. Selection of anepigraphic Samarian coins. (Courtesy of The Israel Museum, Jerusalem.)

21.6. Samarian denominations: (top) *rbʿ šql*, (center) *mʿh*, and (bottom) half *mʿh*. (Courtesy of The Israel Museum, Jerusalem.)

minting continued – albeit intermittently – until the Macedonian conquest (Meshorer and Qedar 1999: 71). Several Samarian coins show the geographical name of the province, that is, *šmryn* in full or abbreviated as *šmry*, *šmrn*, *šmr*, *šm*, *šn*, or just as *š*, written in Aramaic script. Samarian coins show also a variety of private names (sometimes together with the abbreviated name of the province); these probably refer to Samarian officials (priests?) (Dušek 2012: 152–5) (Fig. 21.6). The main artistic influence of Samarian coinage is categorically Achaemenid (or Phoenician with its roots in Achaemenid art). Like Philistian coins, most of the Samarian coins do not carry inscriptions or dates. They are defined as Samarian on the basis of circulation, fabric, metrology, and especially iconography (Fig. 21.7).

21.7. Selection of epigraphic Samarian coins: (top) *šmryn*, (center) *bdyḥbl*, and (bottom) *wny*. (Courtesy of The Israel Museum, Jerusalem.)

In addition, an analysis of Samarian epigraphic material (papyri, coins, literary sources, ostraca) in order to identify the theophorics used by different ethno-religious groups suggests a preference of over 50 percent for Israelite names followed by Aramaic, and somewhat equally diverse Akkadian, Iranian, Phoenician, and Edomite (Zadok 1998: 783–4).

JUDAH

The assumed satrapy of Late Persian- (and Early Hellenistic-) period Judah differs geographically from its late Iron Age territory. The region, according to the consensual view, is bordered by 'Ein Gedi on the south, the Ellah Valley on the west, the assumed Judah/Samaria border just north to Bethel, and the hamlets on the northwestern shores of the Dead Sea to the east. In terms of settlement archaeology, the region's major border sites are Beth-Zur and 'Ein Gedi on the south, 'Azekah to the west, and Bethel to the north. The region's administrative and religious capital was Jerusalem.

Archaeologically, the Judahite material culture of the period is distinguished by some distinctive pottery types, among which bowls, bottles, and storage jars, all of which are not necessarily restricted to Judah but rather to Judah and Samaria or the Palestinian central mountains (Stern 2015). One exception is the *yhd/yh* seal impressions on stamped jar handles (and their Persian-period predecessors [cf. Lipschits and Vanderhooft 2011]). The almost total absence of anthropomorphic images as seen, for example, in contemporaneous figurines and statuettes is also worth noting (which is also true for Samaria).

The coinage of Judah is restricted at present to less than twenty Persian-period *yhd* coin types (as reference for coins of the same type but not of the same denomination). The abbreviated toponym *yhd* was used to identify both the province (*medinta*) of Judah and the city of Jerusalem as its capital (*birta*). The total number of coin types is relatively small when compared to the contemporary coinages of Philistia and Samaria. Jerusalem struck (in the main) small silver coins bearing the abbreviated geographical name of the province *yhd* (and less frequently in full *yhwd*) but sometimes bearing the legends of personal names and titles (*yḥzqyh*, *yḥzqyh hpḥh*, *ywḥnn hkwhn*, *yhwdh*) in Persian (and early Hellenistic/Greco-Macedonian) times.

21.8. Selection of Judahite coins. (Courtesy of J.-P. Fontanille and The Israel Numismatic Society [http://www.menorahcoinproject.org (YHD-07, YHD-09, YHD-13, YHD-16)].)

Most of these coins (with a few exceptions) have two weight groupings, with average weights of 0.48 g and 0.26 g. The coins of these groupings are erroneously, yet customarily, referred to as "obols" and "hemiobols," rather than *grh*, that is, 1/24 of Judahite *šql* of 11.4 g and one half *grh*, that is, 1/48 Judahite *šql* (see Ronen 2003–2006; Tal 2007: 19–20). There are also smaller fractions.

Stylistically, the coins can be identified as Athenian-styled and Judahite-styled issues. Athenian-styled issues normally bear a depiction of the head of Athena appears on the obverse and an owl with an olive spray, together with the paleo-Hebrew (or Aramaic) legend *yhd* (or *yhwd*) on the reverse (see Meshorer 2001: nos. 2–14, 20–3). Judahite-styled issues were more varied, featuring divinities, humans, animals, and floral motifs (see Meshorer 2001: nos. 15–19, 24–8) (Fig. 21.8). These coins have been extensively studied ever since they were first defined as Jewish coins by E. L. Sukenik (1934). The chronology of the *yhd* coins is debated; the Persian-period coinage of Judah is the subject of numerous studies. There is a consensus that minting began in Judah sometime in the fourth century BCE; however, there is also a debate over the chronological development of the coins, that is, with regard to the date of each type,[2] and those bearing personal names and titles which can hardly be attributed to known historical figures.

EDOM

The assumed satrapy of the Late Persian (and Early Hellenistic) period in Idumea differs geographically from the territory of Edom in the late Iron Age. Although the name "Edom" is normally reserved for the older, Transjordanian abode of the Edomites, a distinction was made in the scientific literature, and the Greek place-name *Idoumaía* – or more frequently the Roman *Idum(a)ea* – became the preferred toponym of the region that is generally located in the interior of southern Palestine. The region, according to a consensus of scholars, is bordered by the Negebite desert to the south, Philistia to the west, Judah to the north, and the Dead Sea and the Transjordanian mountain ridge on the east. In terms of settlement archaeology, the region's major border sites are Beth-Zur and Hebron on the north; Beersheva, Tel 'Ira, Aroer, and Arad on the south; Tell Jemmeh, and Tell el-Far'ah South on the west; and the hamlets of the southern Dead Sea to the east.

Archaeologically, Edomite culture is largely attested in two cultic art forms that are not exclusive to Edom: figurines and cube-shaped incense burners normally made of stone. The common use of figurines suggests a variety of roles in public and private cults and everyday life. Figurines from this period were found at a number of Edomite sites, mainly Maresha, Lachish, and Beersheva. The iconographic style is varied, and they are considered among a number of Persian and Hellenistic types that are not unique to Palestine but are rather typical of the entire Levant, as well as the western parts of the East. The provenance of these anthropomorphic and zoomorphic (normally clay) figurines attests to their use in public and/or popular practice as apotropaic items of worship (items that can ward off evil) or as votive offerings. Those to which a religious-cultic significance can be ascribed reflect the popular faith of the people of the period. They represent local and foreign deities (who were obviously viewed as local but in foreign trappings) that can be identified by iconographic elements (known attributes and/or compositions) and were accepted in the Persian (and Hellenistic) East due to their "abilities" – salvation, healing, fertility, guidance, etc. The figurines and statuettes found in cult assemblages certainly served as votive offerings, and those found in domestic assemblages may have had apotropaic or royal significance.

Cube-shaped limestone altars were found in many Persian-period sites at Edom and in greater numbers in Lachish and Beersheva (cf. Stern 1982: 183–95). These items, which apparently were used for the burning of incense, are known from a number of sites in assemblages dated mainly to the sixth, fifth, and fourth centuries BCE. The altars normally have a depression for the incense at the top and a four-legged or flat-worked base. They were often decorated with shallow reliefs on the front in geometric or zoological patterns and rarely bear inscriptions. They are divided typologically into shallow altars and high altars. Their discovery in the Solar Shrine at Lachish and the Hellenistic temple at Beersheva indicates their use in public cult, but they are also known from domestic assemblages attesting to their use in private (household) cults. It should be borne in mind that both figurines and cube-shaped altars are almost entirely absent from the tombs of this period, and it appears that the cult connected with them served mainly the world of the living.

The ethno-religious character of the people of Edom may be largely exhibited in the frequent appearance of names in the Idumean (or Edomite) ostraca that have been published thus far (numbering some 1,100 of about 1,750), it seems that the region had a mixed population, as was the case in contemporaneous neighboring Philistia (Yardeni 2016: 660–723; see also Porten and Yardeni 2014; 2016). An attempt to dissect ethno-religious groups by identifiable theophorics would suggest a somewhat equal division of Edomite and Arab names (ca. 30% each), followed by Western Semitic (ca. 25%), Judahite (ca. 10%), and Phoenician names (ca. 5%), whereas the remaining smaller ethno-religious groups were underrepresented (Tal 2016: ix–x; see also Zadok 1998: 788–822). Even if we take a name as a reference to ethnicity, it still will not clarify the nature of places of origin or even ethno-religious relations between groups. For example, it is unclear whether Edomite names relate to descendants of the biblical Edomites (Transjordanians and Negebites) (Qedarites?). Another open issue is to what extent can we differentiate Arabs from Edomites in the Late Persian (and Early Hellenistic) periods in terms of material culture? The considerable number of publications dealing with the finds from Hellenistic Marisa, the major administrative center of Idumaea's western toparchy, among which distinct artificial subterranean complexes of diverse functions: *columbaria/dovecotes*, olive presses, baths, quarries, cisterns, stables, ritual caves, storage chambers, and *loculi*-type burial caves, as well as distinguishable small finds, such as (circumcised) phalli, *kernoi*, and holed (that is punctured after firing) pottery vessels, may provide valuable directions. However, one must remember that by the Hellenistic period, the site's ethnicity (and religion) was most probably more varied.

The coinage of Edom refers to a recently identified group of peculiar Athenian-styled Palestinian coins (Gitler, Tal, and van Alfen 2007). These coins – mainly *rbʿ šqln* ("drachms" [one-quarter of an Edomite *šql*]) and also *mʿn* ("obols") – were struck from worn obverse dies (i.e., dies damaged by prolonged use), which were then recut and repolished. As a result, the coins' obverses in many cases are simply dome shaped, with no traces of Athena's head or helmet being recognizable, whereas the reverse normally shows the owl, olive spray (and crescent), and legend AΘE in fair condition (Fig. 21.9). The distribution of these coins suggests that they circulated in the boundaries of what we define as Edom in the later part of the Persian period (fourth century BCE) and might well have been the silver money mentioned in several Edomite ostraca (cf. Tal 2007: 17–19).

EPILOGUE

In this chapter, we have suggested ethno-religious regions and inspected material culture of the four major ethno-religious groups of Persian-period Palestine: the Phoenicians, the Samaritans, the Jews, and the Edomites. We gave emphasis to coinages, as one of the few true material markers of Achaemenid Palestine ethno-religious regions. The minting of coins shares social, political, and economic aspects. From a social point of view, local coin

21.9. Edomite rbʿ šqln. (Courtesy of The Israel Museum, Jerusalem.)

minting was, to some extent, a token of collective definition and a shared visual art that established a connection between function and image. From a political point of view, it emphasized the relative autonomy of Achaemenid Palestine ethno-religious regions (and capitals), vouched for their status under Achaemenid rule, and was a means of control of the local population. Economically, monetizing the local economy granted the ruling authorities a fixed income from each series of coins they produced. Coined money, which is legal tender, is by virtue more valuable than uncoined metal. Numismatics, still viewed as a specialized discipline separate from archaeology and history, offers important insights into culture studies. The numismatic picture dominated by autonomous coin minting in southern Palestine (and Phoenicia) during the Persian period reveals a reality where the Persian administration did not intervene in the economic life of the Phoenician city-states who were left to decide most — if not all — aspects of their monetary operations. It seems that, in their case, the only economic preoccupation of the Persian kings was the regular payment of tributes and taxes by the local rulers.

NOTES

1 Research into Phoenician (and southern Palestinian [see below]) numismatics has seen a shift in recent decades; the study has become an independent branch, separate from Greek numismatics, to which it has traditionally belonged.
2 For the latest attempt to define the relative typological chronology, see www.menorahcoinproject.org.

REFERENCES

Ariel, D. T. 2016. Circulation of Locally Minted Persian-Period Coins in the Southern Levant. *Notae Numismaticae* 11: 13–62.

Ariel, D. T., and Naveh, J. 2003. Selected Inscribed Sealings from Kedesh in the Upper Galilee. *BASOR* 329: 61–80.

Bettles, E. A. 2003. *Phoenician Amphora Production and Distribution in the Southern Levant: A Multi-Disciplinary Investigation into Carinated-Shoulder Amphorae of the Persian Period (539–332 BC)*. BAR International Series 1183. Oxford: Archaeopress.

Borger, R. 1956. *Die Inschriften Asarhaddons, Königs von Assyrien*. AO 9. Graz: s.n.

Dar, S. 2014. Samaritan Communities on Mt. Carmel and Ramot Menashe. In *Knowledge and Wisdom: Archaeological and Historical Essays in Honour of Leah Di Segni*, ed. G. C. Bottini, L. D. Chrupcała, and J. Patrich, 283–91. Publications of the Studium Biblicum Franciscanum 54. Milan: Terra Santa.

De Groot, A. 2001. Jerusalem during the Persian Period. *New Studies on Jerusalem* 7: 77–81. (Hebrew; English abstract on p. 9*).

Delavault, B., and Lemaire, A. 1979. Les inscriptions phéniciennes de Palestine. *Rivista di Studi Fenici* 7: 1–39.

Deutsch, R., and Heltzer, M. 1994. *Forty New Ancient West Semitic Inscriptions*. Tel Aviv: Archaeological Center Publication.

Durand, X. 1997. *Des grecs en Palestine au IIIe siècle avant Jésus-Christ: Le dossier syrien des archives de Zénon de Caunos, 261–252*. Cahiers de la Revue biblique 38. Paris: Gabalda.

Dušek, J. 2007. *Les manuscrits araméens du Wadi Daliyeh et la Samarie vers 450–332 av. J.-C.* CHANE 30. Leiden: Brill.

——— 2012. Again on Samarian Governors and Coins in the Persian Period: A Rejoinder to Edward Lipiński and Michał Marciak. In *The Samaritans and the Bible: Historical and Literary Interactions between Biblical and Samaritan Traditions*, ed. J. Frey, U. Schattner-Rieser, and K. Schmid, 119–55. Studia Judaica 70; Studia Samaritana 7. Berlin: de Gruyter.

Elayi, J. 2006. An Updated Chronology of the Reigns of Phoenician Kings during the Persian Period (539–333 BCE). *Transeuphratène* 32: 11–43.

Elayi, J., and Elayi, A. G. 2004. *Le monnayage de la cité phénicienne de Sidon à l'époque perse (Ve–IVe s. av. J.-C.)*. Supplements to Transeuphratène 11. Paris: Gabalda.

——— 2009. *The Coinage of the Phoenician City of Tyre in the Persian Period (5th–4th Cent. BCE)*. OLA 188; Studia Phoenicia 20. Leuven: Peeters.

——— 2014. Context of Phoenician Coin Production in the Persian Empire. *Annali dell'Istituto Italiano di Numismatica* 60: 9–18.

Finkelstein, I. 2009. Persian Period Jerusalem and Yehud: A Rejoinder. *The Journal of Hebrew Scriptures* 9. www.jhsonline.org/Articles/article_126.pdf (accessed July 24, 2017).

Gitler, H., and Tal, O. 2006a. *The Coinage of Philistia of the Fifth and Fourth Centuries BC: A Study of the Earliest Coins of Palestine*. Collezioni numismatiche 6. Milan: Ennerre.

2006b. Coins with the Aramaic Legend ŠHRW and Other Unrecorded Samarian Issues. *Schweizerische Numismatische Rundschau* 85: 47–68.

2009. More Evidence on the Collective Mint of Philistia. *INR* 4: 21–37.

2014. More Than Meets the Eye: Athenian Owls and the Chronology of Southern Palestinian Coinages of the Persian Period. *INR* 9: 15–27.

2017. A Preliminary Report on the Nablus 1968 Hoard of the Fourth Century BC. In *Proceedings of the XV International Numismatic Congress, Taormina, September 21–25, 2015*, Vol. 2, ed. M. Caccamo Caltabiano, B. Carroccio, D. Castrizio, M. Puglisi, and G. Salamone, 604–8. Rome: Arbor Sapientiae.

Gitler, H.; Tal, O.; and van Alfen, P. 2007. Silver Dome-Shaped Coins from Persian-Period Southern Palestine. *INR* 2: 47–62.

Gropp, D. M. 2001. *Wadi Daliyeh II: The Samaria Papyri from Wadi Daliyeh*. DJD 28. Oxford: Clarendon.

Isaac, B. 1991. A Seleucid Inscription from Jamnia-on-the-Sea: Antiochus V Eupator and the Sidonians. *IEJ* 41: 132–44.

Lemaire, A. 1991. Le royaume de Tyr dans la seconde moitié du IVe siècle av. J.-C. In *Atti del II Congresso Internazionale di Studi Fenici e Punici, Roma, 9–14 novembre 1987*, Vol. 1, ed. E. Acquaro, 131–50. Collezione di studi fenici 30. Rome: Consiglio Nazionale delle Ricerche.

2006. La Transeuphratène en transition (c. 350–300). *Persika* 9: 405–41.

Lipiński, E. 2003. Phoenician Cult Expressions in the Persian Period. In *Symbiosis, Symbolism, and the Power of the Past: Canaan, Ancient Israel, and Their Neighbors from the Late Bronze Age through Roman Palestina; Proceedings of the Centennial Symposium W. F. Albright Institute of Archaeological Research and American Schools of Oriental Research, Jerusalem, May 29–31, 2000*, ed. W. G. Dever and S. Gitin, 297–308. Winona Lake, IN: Eisenbrauns.

Lipschits, O., and Vanderhooft, P. 2011. *The Yehud Stamp Impressions: A Corpus of Inscribed Impressions from the Persian and Hellenistic Periods in Judah*. Winona Lake, IN: Eisenbrauns.

Meadows, A., and Wartenberg, U., eds. 2002. *Coin Hoards 9: Greek Hoards*. Royal Numismatic Society Special Publication 35. London: Royal Numismatic Society.

Meshorer, Y. 2001. *A Treasury of Jewish Coins: From the Persian Period to Bar Kokhba*. Jerusalem: Yad Izhak Ben-Zvi; New York: Amphora.

Meshorer, Y., and Qedar, S. 1991. *Coinage of Samaria in the Fourth Century BCE*. Los Angeles: Numismatic Fine Arts International.

1999. *Samarian Coinage*. Numismatic Studies and Researches 9. Jerusalem: The Israel Numismatic Society.

Naveh, J. 1997. Excavations of the Courthouse Site at 'Akko: Phoenician Seal Impressions. *'Atiqot* 31: 115–19.

Porten, B., and Yardeni, A. 2014. *Textbook of Aramaic Ostraca from Idumea*, Vol. 1: *Dossiers 1–10; 401 Commodity Chits*. Winona Lake, IN: Eisenbrauns.

2016. *Textbook of Aramaic Ostraca from Idumea*, Vol. 2: *Dossiers 11–50; 263 Commodity Chits*. Winona Lake, IN: Eisenbrauns.

Qedar, S. 2000–2002. Tissaphernes at Dor? *INJ* 14: 9–14.

Ronen, Y. 2003–2006. Some Observations on the Coinage of Yehud. *INJ* 15: 28–31.

2007. Twenty Unrecorded Samarian Coins. *INR* 2: 29–34.

Shipley, D. G. J. 2012. Pseudo-Skylax and the Natural Philosophers. *JHS* 132: 121–38.

Stern, E. 1982. *Material Culture of the Land of the Bible in the Persian Period, 538–332 B.C.* Warminster: Aris & Phillips.

2010. Figurines and Cult Objects of the Iron Age and Persian Period. In *Excavations at Dor: Figurines, Cult Objects and Amulets, 1980–2000 Seasons*, 3–113. Jerusalem: IES; The Institute of Archaeology, The Hebrew University of Jerusalem.

2015. Persian Period. In *The Ancient Pottery of Israel and Its Neighbors from the Iron Age through the Hellenistic Period*, Vol. 2, ed. S. Gitin, 565–617. Jerusalem: IES.

Sukenik, E. L. 1934. Paralipomena Palaestinensia: The Oldest Coins of Judaea. *Journal of the Palestine Oriental Society* 14: 178–84.

Tal, O. 2003. Some Cultural Trends in Plain Black Attic Imports Found in the Coastal Plain of Palestine. In *Griechische Keramik im kulturellen Kontext: Akten des Internationalen Vasen-Symposions in Kiel vom 24. bis 28.9.2001 veranstaltet durch das Archäologische Institut der Christian-Albrechts-Universität zu Kiel*, ed. B. Schmaltz and M. Söldner, 271–3. Münster: Scriptorium.

2007. Coin Denominations and Weight Standards in Fourth-Century BCE Palestine. *INR* 2: 17–28.

2009. On the Identification of the Ships of *kzd/ry* in the Erased Customs Account from Elephantine. *JNES* 68: 1–8.

2016. Idumea (Edom) in the Fourth Century BCE: Historical and Archaeological Introduction. In *The Jeselsohn Collection of Aramaic Ostraca from Idumea*, by A. Yardeni, ix–xix. Jerusalem: Yad Izhak Ben-Zvi.

Thompson, M.; Mørkholm, O.; and Kraay, C. M., eds. 1973. *An Inventory of Greek Coin Hoards*. New York: Published for the International Numismatic Commission by the American Numismatic Society.

Wolff, S. R. 2002. Mortuary Practices in the Persian Period of the Levant. *NEA* 65: 131–7.

Yardeni, A. 1994. Maritime Trade and Royal Accountancy in an Erased Customs Account from 475 B.C.E. on the Aḥiqar Scroll from Elephantine. *BASOR* 293: 67–78.

2016. *The Jeselsohn Collection of Aramaic Ostraca from Idumea*. Jerusalem: Yad Izhak Ben-Zvi.

Zadok, R. 1998. A Prosopography of Samaria and Edom/Idumea. *UF* 30: 781–828.

TWENTY TWO

LAND/HOMELAND, STORY/HISTORY
The Social Landscapes of the Southern Levant from Alexander to Augustus

ANDREA M. BERLIN

THE NET OF HISTORY ENSNARES TWO MEN

On March 18, 335 BCE, a man named Yehohanan was sold as a slave. The seller, Hananiah, received 35 silver shekels from Yehonur, the buyer (Samaria Papyrus 1: Cross 1963: 113; Gropp 2001: 33–44). A scribe in Samaria recorded the sale on a sheet of papyrus retained by Yehonur, proof of ownership in the event that Yehohanan challenged his status or tried to escape.

Just three years after Yehonur bought Yehohanan, the long-time political status quo dissolved. In the space of seventeen months, the young Macedonian Alexander twice defeated the Achaemenid king, Darius III, and advanced into the southern Levant. Various local elites were suddenly obliged to make a hard political choice (Kasher 2011: 138–53, esp. 152–3).[1] Some from Samaria, including Yehonur, chose Persia. They seized the newly appointed Macedonian governor, Andromachus, and burned him alive – but then were forced to flee when Alexander, already in Egypt, sent a Macedonian force to track them down. The soldiers discovered 200 people hiding in a cave within the Wadi ed-Daliyeh, a jagged complex of cliffs and ravines 14 km north of Jericho. They set a fire at the cave's mouth, which asphyxiated everybody inside, including Yehonur and, presumably, the enslaved Yehohanan (Curt., *Hist. Alex.* 4.8.9–10; Lapp and Lapp 1974).

Yehonur's and Yehohanan's lives and deaths were bound by two forces: political power from above and a fixed social order that determined their options from birth (Friedman 1990; Sivertsev 2005: 12–20; Honigman 2011: 121). In the middle centuries of the first millennium BCE, these forces controlled Levantine lives, whether by offering opportunities or curtailing horizons. In the course of the three centuries that comprise the Hellenistic period, material remains reflect the appearance of other forces – individual agency, widespread literacy, social mobility, and a measure of civic autonomy – along with the fundamental shift they propelled, from a world in which people were largely acted upon to one in which more individuals could and did exercise choice in how to define themselves and conduct their lives.[2]

That world did not appear overnight. In the third century BCE, there were only glimmers. Upon the death of Alexander in 323 BCE, Ptolemy I claimed Egypt and then, after two decades of fighting and negotiating, in 301 came to an agreement with Seleucus I, making the Litani River just north of Tyre the border between their new kingdoms. Ptolemy moved quickly to turn high-level political settlement into ground-level reality. He deployed three components: territory, administration, and new imperially sanctioned cults.

LAND BECOMES TERRITORY

Territory is space that has been purposefully bounded: appropriated, measured, and marked. The political geographer Stuart Elden calls territory a "political technology," a geographic manifestation of authority (2013: 322–4). The practice is a particular necessity for new imperial states, now ruling over various peoples who have been long situated in places newly claimed. Rulers must make a persuasive geographic argument, establish compelling boundaries, and thereby transform space into territory.[3]

Material evidence reflects Ptolemy I's understanding of this imperative. Early in his rule, he installed sanctuaries on the perimeters of his territory. Two were to the Greek nature deity Pan, long associated with the Macedonian royal house. One Pan shrine was in the Wadi Hammamat of Egypt's eastern desert (Bard 1999: 870). The second was in the northeastern corner of the Hula Valley, in a wild spot above a rushing spring, at the foot of Mount Hermon (Ma'oz 1993; 1995; 1996; Berlin 1999) (Fig. 22.1).

The Ptolemaic-era remains from the Mount Hermon Paneion are strictly ceramic: fragments of cooking pots, most with signs of use, and small saucers and bowls (Berlin 1999: 29–31). Almost all were made of Hula Valley spatter-painted ware, a gritty local product. These pieces, few and poor, suggest that the shrine's visitors were mostly, if not wholly, locals, who brought food in part as dedication to the deity and in part to enjoy *al fresco*.

The Mount Hermon Paneion was one-half of the imperial territory-making project here. The other half lay some 30 km southwest, across the Hula Valley and on the edge of the Upper Galilee plateau, on the mound of Kedesh. Here,

22.1. The Sanctuary of Pan (Banias) at Mount Hermon. (Photo by A. M. Berlin.)

some 200 years earlier, the Tyrian royal house had built a huge compound, about 2,400 m² (Berlin and Herbert 2013: 374–6; 2015: 422–3) (Fig. 22.2). Under Ptolemy I, the building was reclaimed for the collection of agricultural produce, likely grain and wine. Several rooms held heavy plastered bins to measure commodities as they were brought in. Others held enormous storage jars, which analysis has shown held bread wheat (*Triticum aestivum*) (Berlin et al. 2003). The wheat was both tax revenue and imperial supply; a papyrus dating to 259 BCE records that a Ptolemaic official named Zenon stopped at Kedesh and received two artabas of flour (αλεύρων) for the final leg of his trip (P. Cairo Zen. 59004).

22.2. Administrative Building at Kedesh. (Photo by SkyView Ltd. Courtesy of the Tel Kedesh Excavations.)

Together, the compound at Kedesh and the Mount Hermon Paneion transformed a sparsely populated rural area into bounded imperial, and specifically, Ptolemaic territory. A visit here was physical acknowledgment of a new political status quo.

ADMINISTRATION AND ITS HUMAN EFFECTS

On the papyrus recording his visit to Kedesh, Zenon carefully noted the amount of flour received at each stop, along with an explanation of the unit of collection. Initially, this was an artaba of thirty choinikes, or about twenty-four liters; but midway through, this was replaced by an artaba of forty choinikes. The difference in quantity is approximately the amount necessary for a single loaf of bread. Such attention to detail is typical of the new administrative system under which people now lived. Consider, for example, two subsections of a single fiat pertaining to Coele-Syria, issued by Ptolemy II in his twenty-fourth year (260 BCE):[4]

> Those holding the tax contracts for the villages ... shall register at the same time the taxable and tax-free livestock in the villages, and their owners with fathers' names and place of origin, and by whom the livestock are managed. Likewise they shall declare whatever unregistered livestock they see up to Dystros of the 25th year in statements on royal oath. (col. 1, lines 17–21)

By order of the king: If anyone in Syria and Phoenicia has bought a free native person or has seized and held one or acquired one in any other manner – to the *oikonómos* in charge in each hyparchy within 20 days from the day of the proclamation of the ordinance. If anyone does not register or present him he shall be deprived of the slave and there shall in addition be exacted for the crown 6000 drachmas per head ... As for those persons purchased in royal auctions, even if one of them claims to be free, the sales shall be valid for the purchasers

(col. 1, line 33–col. 2 = right col., line 11)

The human effects of these and other policies are made clear by Lester Grabbe: "bureaucracy was extended down to the lowest level, the village ... All property was noted and records kept for tax purposes; ... [and] the practice of enslaving free individuals [was widespread]" (2008: 21). The Ptolemies treated their new territory as a personal bank, either cultivated by individuals and then taxed or managed directly by royal agents. Periodic visits by imperial envoys stitched it together, as seen by Zenon's route: Strato's Tower, inland to Jerusalem and Jericho, across the Jordan to the estate of Tobiah outside Philadelphia (Amman), north into Gaulanitis, west to Beth Anath and Kedesh, and, finally, Akko-Ptolemais, and home.

The evidence from the rural interior suggests a sharply bifurcated social order. In the Hula Valley, near the Paneion and the compound at Kedesh, a number of settlements appear in the third century. Typical is Tel Anafa. On this small mound, there were a few houses of two and three rooms, untrimmed boulder walls, pebble floors, and courtyards with tamped earth surfaces. Inhabitants partially subsisted on wild pig and deer, and, as suggested by fifteen loom weights found against a wall, made their clothes (Herbert 1994: 13–14; Redding 1994: 265–78; Berlin 1997a: 18–19). Their possessions were strictly utilitarian: small bowls and saucers, cooking pots, grinding bowls, and water pitchers – all made of spatter-painted ware (Berlin 1997b: 7–9). The only imported items were about twenty small perfume bottles from the area around Tyre – this despite proximity to Kedesh, whose new administrators used various types of cooking and table vessels acquired from coastal suppliers (Stone 2013: 296–7). The connection between the two sites was likely extractive: Tel Anafa's inhabitants were probably tenant farmers, growing and delivering grain to the administrators at Kedesh.

A similar pattern appears in the central hills. At Samaria, there are coastal and Mediterranean imports and various forms of cooking vessels. At Shechem, residents had only basic household items, locally made, and only one form of cooking pot in the kitchen (Stone 2013: 297). In the countryside, surveyors have identified field towers and over 600 plots of arable land, vineyards, and olive groves; cultivation began in the third century (Dar 1986: 88–109; Mattila 2015a). The plots are irregularly arranged and vary greatly in size, with the largest over 100 times the size of the smallest. Such a pattern could reflect "multiple private owners ... engaged in small-scale commodity production" (Mattila 2014: 312; see also Mattila 2015b); however, the marked disparities may instead reflect large estates claimed and managed for the crown and smallholders, whether tenants or slaves, working marginal lands (see Kloppenborg 2006: 289–90). In either interpretation, the pattern reinforces a crisply delineated social order of "haves" and "have-nots" (Tscherikower 1937: 21–4, 56–7).[5]

Ptolemaic rule not only reified long-existing social inequities, it also provided additional customers. On May 13, 257 BCE, Tobiah, a wealthy scion of an elite Judean family living on the outskirts of Philadelphia (Amman), sent two letters to Apollonius, the finance minister of Ptolemy II. The first detailed an array of animals for the king. The second detailed human gifts: four young boys – Haemos, Atikos, Audomos, and Okaemos – all "alert and of good breeding," and their minder, Aeneas, all for Apollonius himself (P. Cairo Zen. 1.59075; Bagnall and Derow 1981: 113–14, no. 257; Durand 1997: 179–84; Krautbauer, Llewelyn, and Wassell 2014). Seventy-five years after Hananiah purchased Yehohanan, Ptolemaic policies continued to reify older social arrangements in the rural interior.

It was different on the coast, where revenue came from skimming a financial share from the activities of maritime entrepreneurs. Material remains indicate that commerce was able to satisfy imperial collectors as well as raise local living standards. At every coastal city and town – Tyre, Akko-Ptolemais, Dor, Jaffa, Ashdod, and Ashkelon – third-century household goods included Aegean wine; fine table wares from Cyprus, Cilicia, and Asia Minor; specialty kitchen equipment, such as Aegean baking pans; and imported perfumes carried in glass bottles (Arbel 2011: 192; Nitschke, Martin, and Shalev 2011; Berlin and Stone 2016) (Fig. 22.3). None of these goods was a luxury item. They were middle-class comforts – domestic niceties to be had with a bit of extra money and ready access.

CULTS AND LITERACY: NEW ROUTES TO SOCIAL ADVANCEMENT

Territory can impress, administration can control – but neither can build personal connections or political loyalty. To affect this, Ptolemy I and his successors introduced new deities. Most significant was Serapis, whose cult Ptolemy I enlarged with the construction in Alexandria of an enormous Serapeion and whose worship was spread as a matter of imperial policy.[6] There were cults at Jaffa (Kaplan and Kaplan 1989) and Samaria, the latter known from an impressive slab of black limestone inscribed with names of

22.3. Third-century BCE imported household goods from Tel Dor. (Courtesy of E. Stern and the Tel Dor Excavations.)

Hegesander; his wife, Xenarchis; and their children as dedicators, and of Serapis and Isis as dedicatees (Crowfoot, Crowfoot, and Kenyon 1957: 37, no. 13; Magness 2001).

Serapis was a stand-in for the king, while Isis was conflated with the Ptolemaic queens – the joint cult marketed via faience jugs with relief images of the queen carrying a cornucopia and making a libation (Thompson 1973; Plantzos 2011; Landvatter 2012). On the Samaria inscription, it is notable that Xenarchis is also named and Isis honored. Hegesander and Xenarchis present themselves as a couple, directly linked via the terse ritual formulary to Serapis and Isis, who in turn would have been understood as cosmic stand-ins for the

Ptolemaic king and queen. The inscription provides material acceptance of one family's political loyalty to and affiliation with the Ptolemaic royal house, personal reinforcement of the imperial project.

The Ptolemies also encouraged a cult in which they *themselves* were deified. This royal cult was – or was arranged to appear as – a creation from below, a voluntary expression of honor promulgated by priests and local elites (Pfeiffer 2010).[7] A small stele found at Jaffa, with seven lines inscribed in Greek, dedicated by one Anaxikles, shows this practice in action (SEG 10.467; Lupu 2003):

> The Great King Ptolemy
> the Father-loving God, the son of King
> Ptolemy and queen
> Berenike, the Benefactor [Gods],
> [and grandson] of Ptolemy, king
> [Philadelphos, is honored by] Anaxikles
> [..., p]riest of the king.[8]

Who was Anaxikles?[9] A "priest of the king;" but, without an ethnikon, he was likely a local elite with a Greek name. This accords with the way in which Anaxikles describes Ptolemy's lineage: three generations of parentage, which is standard Semitic practice but unusual for Greek or Ptolemaic identifications. Since the slab is too small to have supported a dedicatory statue (Lupu 2003: 195), it seems to have been a simple marker, conceived by a loyalist acting on his own. Like the faience jugs, this is a material totem of political loyalty.

The inscriptions of Hegesander and Anaxikles, Tobiah's personal letters and much other individual documentation from the third century Levant were written in Greek. Under the Ptolemies, Greek became the language of records, official correspondence, and commercial matters – equally a tool of and a proxy for the imperial presence. In the glittering new capital cities and commercial centers of the Hellenistic world – Pergamon, Ephesus, Antioch, and Alexandria – kings and elites sponsored libraries, museums, and academies. For those living in the provincial outskirts, Greek literacy gave entry into a Mediterranean-wide knowledge network (Stremlin 2008: 984). It provided a ticket of admission into a social milieu beyond the political confines of territory and the social confines of birth. The Ptolemaic system encouraged those who could to learn Greek; one result was that when the political baton passed to the Seleucids, some of those Greek speakers were poised and eager to become more integrated into the language's deeper cultural ambit.

CONTINUITIES AND TRANSITIONS

Anaxikles' stele commemorated Ptolemy IV's stopgap victory over Antiochus III on July 22, 217, at Raphia, the southernmost point of Ptolemaic territory in the Levant.[10] The Seleucid contender had already claimed Tyre, Akko-Ptolemais, the Galilee, Transjordan, and Samaria, aided by multiple defections of key commanders.[11] What Antiochus III failed to achieve at Raphia, he successfully effected twenty years later. In 197 BCE, he defeated the army of Ptolemy V at the Mount Hermon Paneion, and the entirety of the southern Levant passed into Seleucid control.

The high-level transfer of territory was accompanied, for a time, by a ground-level continuation of administration. In the war's aftermath, the two monarchs crafted an agreement that freed both to deal with other pressing needs and plans. In that agreement, the daughter of Antiochus, Cleopatra I, was married to Ptolemy, with the tax revenues of Coele-Syria as her dowry (Kaye and Amitay 2015: 142–3). The system lasted for about two decades; but in 178 BCE, financial pressures led Seleucus IV to rescind the agreement, impose a new fiscal system, and create a new position of supervisor of the temples of Coele-Syria and Phoenicia. The new supervisor was Olympiodoros, whose appointment the king considered sufficiently weighty that it was announced via permanent public stone inscriptions; fragments have been found at Tyre and Marisa in Idumea (Cotton and Wörrle 2007; Gera 2009; Hacham 2012: 176–7; Honigman 2014: 297–404; Cotton-Paltiel, Ecker, and Gera 2017).

The broad oversight afforded Olympiodoros went hand-in-hand with another aspect of Seleucid administration: the empowerment of local communities. There are various material reflections of this from both local and imperial vantage points. One comes from the administrative compound at Kedesh, now in Seleucid hands. In the early second century BCE, the building was again refurbished: new reception rooms, additional facilities for the collection of agricultural produce, and most notably an archive (Berlin and Herbert 2013: 377; 2015: 426–7). Over 2,000 clay sealings date from the era of Seleucid control, but only a few come from Antioch. Instead, the archive primarily held documents sealed by the rings of private individuals, with an additional small number from nearby civic entities, Sidon, Tyre, and Kedesh itself, represented by a seal bearing a shaft of wheat, a cluster of grapes, and the city's name written in Greek (Ariel and Naveh 2003: 64–9, 72–4, 75–7) (Fig. 22.4).

A second widespread set of remains are civic weights with the name of the market inspector (*agoranomos*) and a date according to the Seleucid era (Finkielsztejn 2010; 2014; Korzakova 2010; Kushnir-Stein 2011). The weights appear, suddenly, in 173 BCE (on present evidence). While by far the greatest number come from Marisa in Idumea (thanks to that site's long and careful excavation), examples from almost every Levantine coastal city from Antioch to Gaza, as well as inland cities such as Gerasa and Scythopolis, attest to the breadth of the system. Unlike the Ptolemies, under whom money was collected by well-connected elites who had personal agreements with the king, or

22.4. Civic sealings from the archive of the Administrative Building at Kedesh: (left) a sealing "Of the Sidonians" (K00 BL0086); (center) a double-dated bilingual sealing from the *koinon* of Tyre (165 BCE) (K00 BL0462); and (right) a sealing of Kedasa (Kedesh) (K00 BL00463). (Courtesy of the Tel Kedesh Excavations.)

by inspectors sent from Alexandria, the weights attest to a new professional class of annually appointed magistrates working within the Seleucid system but also empowered locally (Finkielsztejn 2014: 177).[12]

The weights transmit two messages. The first is one of imperial oversight, communicated both by the common mode of dating according to the Seleucid era and a single metrological standard (Finkielsztejn 2007: 55; 2014: 177; Kushnir-Stein 2011). The second message is one of local autonomy and identity. In addition to year and *agoranomos* name, weights carried the city's name and specific images that acted as identifying logos, at least for the cities of northern and central Phoenicia: an anchor for Antioch; an elephant for Seleucia; scales for Marathos; paired cornucopias with an Isis crown for Byblos; a dolphin or a trident for Berytus; a galley for Sidon; a Tanit or palm tree for Tyre (Finkielsztejn 2014).

That Phoenician cities asserted particular identities is not new. Under the Achaemenids and continuing under the Ptolemies, inhabitants of these cities revealed themselves via an array of specific material markers – coins, seals, and amulets – as well as by particular details of writing and personal names with theophoric components (Peckham 2014: 370–475, with abundant references). What is different now, however, is a subtle but powerful change in the intersection of economic empowerment and cultural identity. This change can be discerned by consideration of remains specific to Sidonians and Tyrians.

In the second century, Sidonian communities are attested in three towns in the southern Levant: Marisa, Shechem, and Yavneh-Yam. At Marisa, they owned a large tomb complex, in which their leader, Apollophanes, son of Sesmaios, was buried in 196 BCE (Peters and Thiersch 1905: 36–7; Jacobson 2007). From his inscription, we know that Apollophanes and his fellow Sidonians arrived at Marisa around 230 BCE, when the city still lay within the Ptolemaic orbit. The Sidonian community at Shechem is known from a report preserved by Josephus, in which they make a request to Antiochus IV (176–164

22.5. A Tanit sealing (one of nine identical sealings) from the archive of the Administrative Building at Kedesh. (Courtesy of the Tel Kedesh Excavations.)

BCE) that they "not be treated like Judeans, because they are Sidonians by origin and have different customs" (*Ant.* 12.5.5 § 258–64; Isaac 1991: 136–7, 142–3). Finally, from Yavneh-Yam, a harbor settlement on the southern coast, the Sidonian community is attested in an inscription that records a letter from Antiochus V (164–162 BCE), granting them immunity from some form of taxation (Isaac 1991). All three communities identify themselves as distinct, respectively as Sidonians "in Marisa," "the Port of Jamnia," and "in Shechem." But only under the Seleucids do they expect and receive separate economic and/or legal status.

Tyrians felt and received the same. Tyrian civic weights were especially assertive: Some were written only in Phoenician and dated to "the era of the people of Tyre" (which began in 275 BCE). Others were bilingual and also dated to the Seleucid era. All carried one of several specific civic symbols: a schematic rendition of the lunar deity Tanit, a palm tree, a caduceus, and/or a mask of Herakles-Melqart (Finkielsztejn 2014: 172–3). The sense of a separate Tyrian status is reinforced by a group of nine identical sealings from the Kedesh archive that display Tanit above an inscription in Phoenician script that reads "He who is over the land" (Ariel and Naveh 2003: 62–4) (Fig. 22.5). The phrase, logo, and find spot suggest that under the Seleucids, the Tyrians enjoyed some measure of economic autonomy.

TERRITORY BECOMES HOMELAND

Under Seleucid rule, new freedoms intersected with a sense of release from the suffocations of Ptolemaic administrators. Disentangling cause and effect is impossible; probably both are responsible for one broad trend: the evocation of heritage, an identity based on one's past. For peoples living in lands remade as imperial territories, a particular past is self-validating. It turns current rulers into political ephemera, recently arrived on the scene and, hopefully, soon to depart. Such a sensibility had already appeared in the mid-late fourth century among Judeans, at least members of the administrative and literary classes, in the use of a paleo-Hebrew script, both on coins and also stamped on the handles of jars used to collect agricultural commodities (Cross 1961: 3; Lipschits and Vanderhooft

2011: type 13). In contrast to common Aramaic (script and language), paleo-Hebrew was a deliberate signifier; it imbued Judean writers and their words with ancient authority.[13] By the early second century, the Judeans were not alone in seeking such legitimation and emotional reassurance.

In 176 BCE, a scribe in Marisa drafted a marriage agreement in Aramaic on a piece of broken pottery. QWSRM hoped to marry a young lady named Arsinoë, for which purpose his father, QWSYD, was in negotiation with Arsinoë's father, also named QWSYD (Eshel and Kloner 1996). The repetition of the ancient Edomite theophoric QWS is striking – although since QWS appears in 20% of all personal names at Marisa, it might be coincidence (Eshel and Kloner 1996: 6, n. 12; Eshel, Puech, and Kloner 2007: 59).[14] But then in line 5, it is written that the arrangement be done "according to the *nomos* of the daughters of [Edom?]." *Nomos*, a Greek word written here in Aramaic, can mean custom or tradition, or something more formal. Esther Eshel and Amos Kloner opt for "custom" (1996: 11–12), but it may be that young QWSRM and his father intended something more assertive than that. Under the Seleucids, they were free to deploy their own *nomoi*, similar to the Sidonians of Shechem. The phrase, along with their names, suggests a purposefully Edomite consciousness.

In the third century, contemporary with the new cult to Serapis and Isis at Samaria, a Samaritan community had established itself on Mount Gerizim (Fig. 22.6).[15] It was, initially, small and physically modest, but that changed in the first half of the second century BCE, when there appear some 395 inscriptions in Aramaic, Hebrew, and also paleo-Hebrew (Magen,

22.6. Aerial view of the Hellenistic sanctuary and fortified enclosure on Mount Gerizim, looking south. (Courtesy of Y. Hofman.)

Misgav, and Tsfania 2004; Dušek 2012; Kartveit 2014). Many are carved on large architectural stones, such as columns or lintels, so that they would have been originally parts of structures (Kartveit 2014: 456). One typical (except for the fact that it is fully preserved) inscription reads:

> This is [the stone] that Delayah, son of Shim'on, dedicated for himself and his children/sons, [this] ston[e for] good remembrance before God in this place. (Kartveit 2014: 452)

Delayah stretched his inscription over the stone's full 2 m length, ending with "in this place," a phrase common to many of these dedications, as well as unique to Mount Gerizim (Kartveit 2014: 451, 456, 465). Also common in these inscriptions is that people regularly named their home villages, which are mostly around Mount Gerizim. The geographic designations have power: They insist on *this* specific spot and unify *this* community of worshippers (Kartveit 2014: 466).[16] Delayah and his fellow Samaritans confronted the practice of imperial territory-making head on. With words, they redrew the imperial map to make a geography of their own.

At the northern edge of the Hula Valley, on the summit of the ancient city of Dan, stood the remains of a long deserted biblical sanctuary, which, in the third century BCE, petitioners began again to visit. Their offerings were simple and poor, similar to those up the road at the Paneion: a few lamps, perfume bottles, and small bowls and saucers – all made of poor local clay (Biran 1994: 214–17). Then, in the second century, a man named Zoilus left an offering of quite a different sort: a slab of limestone, inscribed in Greek and Aramaic, "To the god among the Danites, Zoilus made a vow" (Biran 1981; Tzaferis 1992). The use of Greek indicates Zoilus's desire to make his vow for the unnamable god of a biblical people widely understood. As on Mount Gerizim, he defied current political claims by evoking the aura and protection of the past.

JUDEANS AND OTHERS

The appointment of Olympiodoros in 178 BCE was the first in a series of Seleucid actions that culminated in the 160s in an uprising in Judea, led by Judah Maccabee, a member of the ambitious Hasmonean family from rural Modi'in (Schwartz 1993; Nongbri 2005: 99–105). In the late 140s, there were substantive shifts in the region's political force field, a result of armed infighting between multiple contenders for the Seleucid throne. Several sites were destroyed or abandoned: Mazor in Judea, Khirbet el-Eika in the Lower Galilee, and Kedesh and Khirbet esh-Shuhara in the Upper Galilee (Aviam and Avitai 2002; Syon 2002; Berlin and Herbert 2013: 379; 2015: 428–30; U. Leibner, pers. comm., 2016). Judah's brother, Simon, took control of Jerusalem by force (1 Macc 13:49–52). Within the next generation, the

22.7. Household pottery from late second-century BCE Jerusalem. (Courtesy of the IES.)

Seleucids lost their grip; in the 120s, many places asserted political autonomy, including the Phoenician coastal cities of Sidon, Tyre, and Akko-Ptolemais and also Jerusalem, which at this time was under the control of Simon's son, John Hyrcanus.

Jerusalem was a temple-city, the only sizable settlement in otherwise rural Judea (Berlin 1997a: 15–16; 2013a: 154–6). It was readily accessed from the coast: In 259 BCE, Zenon came here directly after disembarking at Strato's Tower, and, in the years of Ptolemaic and early Seleucid rule, residents had Mediterranean goods, such as imported table vessels and Rhodian wine (Hayes 1985: 183; Tushingham 1985: 37, 41; Ariel 1990: 12–25; Rosenthal-Heginbottom 2003: 206–8; Berlin 2013a: 157). In the second half of the second century BCE, when the city came under Hasmonean control, the lives of its residents changed. A new fortification wall extended from the citadel to the City of David, people moved to the Western Hill – and almost all imported goods disappeared (Geva 2003: 148–50; Berlin 2013a: 153–4). Household items now comprised only essentials: small dishes, cooking pots, juglets, water pitchers, large jars, a few saucer lamps, and perfume bottles – all locally made (Fig. 22.7).

Meanwhile, the Hasmoneans themselves adopted several aspects of Hellenistic display culture. In Modi'in, Simon expanded the family tomb with seven pyramids, evoking the Mausoluseum at Halicarnassus. Jerusalem's elites soon followed suit, building display tombs with pyramids, exterior columns, and decorated facades (Rahmani 1967; 1982; Berlin 2002).[17] In the oasis of Jericho, Hyrcanus built an estate that his successors enhanced with pools, pavilions, and reception rooms with Hellenistic-style painted walls (Netzer 2001: 40–67). Hyrcanus also issued coins carrying Greek-style victory wreaths and cornucopias, the

Mediterranean symbol for abundance (Noy 2012). His sons continued the practice, issuing coins with wreaths, diadems, and the (Seleucid) anchor.

The lives of non-elite Judeans must have been simple by choice, because, in the later second century BCE, domestic comforts abounded throughout this region: interior décor, glass and fine red-slipped ceramic table wares, imported perfumes, and colorful personal accessories (Slane 1997: 272; Rozenberg 2008: 283–424; Nitschke, Martin, and Shalev 2011: 143; Grose 2012: 1–11). At Tel Anafa in the Hula Valley, a Tyrian built a villa with a private bath and a second-story dining room adorned with multi-colored painted panels and gilded Corinthian pilasters (Herbert 1994: 14; Kidd 2015) (Fig. 22.8). A house at Dor

22.8. A reconstruction of the painted plastered wall in the dining room from the villa at Tel Anafa (ca. 100 BCE). (Courtesy of the Tel Anafa Excavations.)

was decorated with an *opus vermiculatum* mosaic depicting theater masks, equal in quality to the floors in the Attalid palaces in Pergamon (Stewart and Martin 2003). One Dor entrepreneur even manufactured jars stamped in the Aegean mode, advertising local goods (Ariel et al. 1985). At Marisa, houses had Ionic pilasters and painted walls. Aegean wine was everywhere, at coastal settlements – Akko-Ptolemais, Dor, Strato's Tower, Ashdod, and Ashkelon – and inland ones – Tel Anafa, Scythopolis, Samaria, and Marisa (Berlin 1997a: 22–3).

In the last decade of the second century, with the Seleucid king Antiochus IX in control of little more than the city of Damascus and its environs, John Hyrcanus dismantled this bustling, Mediterranean-inflected world and remade the political landscape via force. He attacked and partially destroyed Marisa, Mount Gerizim, Samaria, and Scythopolis (Josephus, *Ant.* 13.254–58, 275–79; Berlin 1997a: 30–1). Along the coast, Dor, Strato's Tower, Jaffa, and Yavneh-Yam were abandoned or diminished. Autonomous civic authorities disappeared; the last known *agoranomos* weight dates to 108 BCE (Finkielsztejn 1998; 2014: 178). By 100 BCE, Alexander Jannaeus, younger son of John Hyrcanus, ruled a Hasmonean state.[18]

New small settlements appeared across the Jordan, in the Samaritan countryside, and in the Lower Galilee (Alexandre 2008; 2013: 6–8, 19; Cohen, Avshalom-Gorni, and Porat 2013). Everybody used the coins of Jannaeus, minted in Jerusalem, demonstrating regular contact with the capital (Syon 2015: 57–61, 155–64). No matter where they lived, Judeans (we may now begin calling them Jews) continued to use simple household goods – locally made dishes, cooking vessels, pitchers, and storage jars – although those living in larger towns in the north, such as Sepphoris and Gamla also used glass and red-slipped table vessels, indicating continued contacts with coastal suppliers.

Political unity jostled up against social factions: temple priests, apocalyptic groups, members of the Qumran sect, and many others. Members of these groups were literate, therefore educated, elites; for them, writing itself was a conduit to relevance and significance.[19] The Dead Sea Scrolls – their words and also their physicality – provide evidence that this community was large: In the roughly 930 manuscripts from the Judean caves, more than 500 scribal hands can be identified, and the quantity and variations in details (e.g., different preparations of skins and inks) suggest that many scrolls were brought from elsewhere (Wise 2015: 32–3). Words had power, which many chose to deploy: No two of the Dead Sea Scrolls manuscripts share an immediate prototype, meaning that variants were in use simultaneously: Copiers regularly introduced new information, and writers reframed older material to make it speak to present circumstances (Wise 2015: 32; Jokiranta et al. 2016: 11–17). There was no canon, no authorized group of texts; literate Jews held a diverse array of ideas, beliefs, and points of view (Najman 2012). From one angle, the manuscripts testify to cultural dynamism; from another, they illuminate deeply founded disagreements.

In the first century BCE, some Jews adopted the ritual of purifying immersion in small stepped plastered pools (*miqva'ot*). The practice was new and outside the strictures of temple practice. Their distribution suggests that the Hasmoneans may have introduced the idea; *miqva'ot* appear in the palaces at Jericho; a few private houses in the Upper City of Jerusalem; Gezer, which Simon is said to have captured (1 Macc 14:7); and Umm el-'Umdan, which is ancient Modi'in, and Gamla in the southern Golan, a conquest of Alexander Jannaeus, where one private *miqveh* and one neighborhood *miqveh* were built in a new neighborhood of the early first century BCE (Berlin 2014a). These last two were short-lived; by the mid-first century BCE, one was built over, and the other turned into a storage bin (Amit 2010: 193–4; Goren 2010: 138, 146).

STORY BECOMES HISTORY, HOMELAND (AGAIN) BECOMES TERRITORY

Of all the uses to which writing can be put, one of most powerful is history. History is a strategy, a tool for confronting and reframing one's world and experiences. History elevates events beyond themselves, inoculates against unwelcome renditions, and eases the offensiveness of social marginalization.[20] Toward the end of the second century, as Hyrcanus was remaking portions of the southern Levant, one Judean composed the narrative we know today as 1 Maccabees. Writing in Hebrew for his own people to read and remember, he recounted how arrogant imperial outsiders spawned a culture war that turned into a real battle, led and won by the Hasmoneans, who fought for ancestral territory and "the covenant of the fathers."[21] 1 Maccabees and other contemporary and competing renditions are what the sociologist Eviatar Zerubavel calls "time maps," accounts that explain a people's journey from the past to the present moment (2003; cf. Goodman 1994: 171 and Nongbri 2005: 87, n. 11).

1 Maccabees made a narrative case for an independent Judean state. Politics intervened. In 38 BCE, on the outskirts of Jerusalem, Herod, a scion of a well-connected Idumean family, defeated the Hasmonean prince, Mattathias Antigonus. Seven years later, after the battle of Actium, the Roman general, Octavian, made Herod a client-king in control of Galilee, Samaria, Perea, Judea, and Idumea. As had Ptolemy I, Herod moved quickly to mark his territory, building temples to Augustus and Roma at Samaria, the Mount Hermon Paneion, and his new city at Caesarea (Berlin 2015). In 2 BCE, Herod's son, Herod Philip, built a fourth such edifice at the southern end of his new capital of Caesarea Philippi, on the hill of Horvat Omrit, overlooking the Hula Valley (Overman and Schowalter 2011; Berlin 2013b).

Thus, at the turn of the eras, the peoples of the southern Levant found themselves once more living within physically bounded imperial territory, now effectively Roman. In many places, previous patterns returned. In

Idumea and along the coast, population revived, as did comfortable middle-class lifestyles, seen in the appearance of Aegean and Italian wines and dishes, and houses with interior wall paintings and mosaics. Most Jews opted out of this culture, however. They used only basic household items, augmented by a distinctive array of simple white chalk vessels and plain oil lamps (Magen 2002; Berlin 2005: 429–37; 2014a). *Miqva'ot* became more common and in more settings: in houses and neighborhoods, by oil presses, and at the entrances to village synagogues (Berlin 2005: 453; Reich 2013). This placement evoked Herod's magnificent new temple in Jerusalem, where large purification pools lay in front of the entrance areas. There was now among Jews an increasing class divide, as Jerusalem's elites lived in large, beautifully decorated homes amid Mediterranean luxuries (Avigad 1989: 10; Berlin 2005: 442–51; 2014a; 2014b; Talgam and Peleg 2008).

Over the three centuries of the Hellenistic period, political forces first subsumed and then empowered the peoples living in this region. QWSRM, Delayah, Zoilus, and many anonymous Jewish writers and scribes – they and others asserted ownership over specific places, pasts, and traditions. This raised consciousness was a two-sided legacy. It could enhance feelings of legitimacy despite external circumstances; however, it could also lead to feeling trapped between circumstance and destiny, stuck on the wrong side of history.

How to live in a world so wrongly arranged? At the turn of the eras, this was a challenge for many – and many solutions arose. Apocalyptic writers imagined a fiery end for the wicked (Collins 1983). Some Galilean Jews formulated a utopian dream, a kingdom of God on earth (Bazzana 2010). In the year 6 CE, at least one revolutionary sought to remake a more tangible kingdom, in the mode of 1 Maccabees: "a certain Judas, a Gaulanite from a city named Gamala [*sic*] threw himself into the cause of rebellion ... and appealed to the nation to make a bid for independence" (Jospehus, *Ant.* 18.4).

The Romans took over a landscape mined with other peoples' visions. What they saw as territory had been made homeland; what they might have regarded as story had been made history. In the short term, as is often the case, political will and military might prevailed. But in the long term, the view afforded us by the passage of time, it is the visions that have proven to be the more durable. Like history, they have a habit of returning.

NOTES

1 Archaeological evidence shows that at this time Tyrians abandon their compound at Kedesh. Supplies were laid in at Nahal Tut and Ramat ha-Nadiv, probably collected to feed the troops engaged in the siege of Tyre (Alexandre 2006; Peleg-Barkat and Tepper 2014). Sha'ar ha-Amakim may be part of this defensive line as well (Segal, Młynarczyk, and Burdajewicz 2014).

2 This approach is analogous to Keith Hopkins's definition of structural differentiation, which he defines as "the process by which an undifferentiated institution (for example, a family group charged with multiple functions) becomes divided into separate institutions (such as schools for education, factories for production), each charged with a single main function" (1978: 89). I thank Sylvie Honigman for this reference.

3 Gilles de Rapper calls shrines "places where the social production of the border takes place" (2010: 259). Paul Kosmin (2014) treats this practice, writ large, as carried out by Seleucus I and his successors.

4 This is the Rainer Papyrus (now SB 8008) on which, see Lenger 1964: 21–2; Bagnall and Derow 1981: 95–6; and Grabbe 2001: 135–6 (from which this translation comes).

5 Peter Schäfer gives a succinct synopsis: "Whereas the upper classes in particular were active participants in and beneficiaries of the new economic order, the simple rural population were exploited even more intensively than before" (1995: 17). For the longer-term effects, see Kloppenborg 2006: 284–90, 359–64, 367–76.

6 According to later authors, a temple to Serapis existed in Egypt already in 323 BCE (Plut., *Alex.* 76; Arr., *Anab.* 7.26.2).

7 Stefan Pfeiffer notes that as a cult to a living king, the Ptolemaic royal cult was a creation of the priests, an innovation that grafted the notion of Greek dynastic rule onto traditional Egyptian practice.

8 Translation of Pfeiffer, from an unpublished paper "Great King Ptolemy – the Victorious King in the Light of a Greek Inscription from Jaffa (SEG 10.467)," presented at the conference, "Judaea in the Long Third Century BCE: The Transition between the Persian and Hellenistic Periods," Tel Aviv University, June 2, 2014.

9 In what follows, I am indebted to Pfeiffer and his work cited above in n. 8.

10 Decree of Raphia, 18 sq.; Gera 1998: 12. We know of three other inscriptions such as that of Anaxikles – one from Tyre (*SEG* 7.326; Notley 2011: fig. 8.3) and two from Marisa (Clermont-Ganneau 1900: 536–8).

11 In 219 BCE, the Ptolemaic governor Theodotus the Aetolian defected to Antiochus, handing over Tyre and Akko-Ptolemais (Polyb. 4.37.5, 5.40.103, 5.61.3–5–5.62.3). In the course of this same conflict, Ptolemy, son of Thraseus, defected, an event best known from the Hefzibah Inscription (see Landau 1966; Fischer 1979; Bertrand 1982; and Piejko 1991).

12 In time, these and other local officials became "des instruments de l'autonomie de mouvement dans le domaine commercial" (Finkielsztejn 2015: 178). When central power faded, this autonomy was transformed into political autonomy, notable especially in the evidence of independent eras beginning in 126 BCE.

13 For a socio-linguistic analysis, see Schwartz 1995. For a clear unraveling of the development and terminology associated with paleo-Hebrew, I am grateful to David Vanderhooft's paper, "Aramaic, Paleo-Hebrew, and 'Jewish' Scripts in the Ptolemaic Period," given at the conference, "Judaea in the Long Third Century B.C.E.: The Transition between the Persian and Hellenistic Periods," Tel Aviv University, June 2, 2014.

14 QWS names do not suddenly appear in the Hellenistic period; they are also attested on Persian-period ostraca from Beersheva and Khirbet el-Qom (Geraty 1975; Naveh 1979).

15 Their presence is attested both by archaeological remains (Magen 2008) and also by at least one third-century Qumran scroll classified as pre-Samaritan (4QExod-Lev^f [Zahn 2015: 309]). Yitzhak Magen, Haggai Misgav, and Levana Tsfania (2004: 19) understand this development as being in specific and direct opposition to the Judean position. It

may be, however, that *both* the Judean *and* the Samaritan developments were reactions to an inhospitable, even suffocating, imperial ideology and authority.

16 Two inscriptions from the Aegean island of Delos complement the large corpus from Mount Gerizim (Bruneau 1982). Both praise benefactors for their support of "Israelites who send their temple tax to Argarizein." On the basis of the Delos inscriptions, we may say that this community sees themselves as "Israelites," a designation that separates them from Jerusalem. Magnar Kartveit sees in all this a newly formulated "Samaritan self-consciousness" (2014: 451).

17 The most succinct evaluation remains Elias Bickerman's: "the Maccabees eradicated one kind of Hellenism only to facilitate the growth of another kind" (1962: 178).

18 Any reconstruction of Judean/Jewish settlement outside of Judea rests on a vast literature that itself rests, first of all, on a comparative philology of the two primary ancient accounts: 1 Maccabees and Josephus's *Antiquities*. For an elegant treatment of the discrepancies between these two texts, see Schwartz 1989 along with its considerable references. The ancient sources are opaque witnesses to what must have been multiple on-the-ground realities; using them to explain patchy archaeological remains runs the risk of creating the very story that the ancient authors hoped to establish. For a sober use of coins as evidence for the expansion of Judean settlement beyond Judea before 100 BCE, see Syon 2006; 2015: 142–50.

19 The linked issues of texts, manuscripts, writing, and education are fundamental to any social reconstruction, and beyond the limits of this chapter. For a comprehensive and clear overview of the literature, see Sivertsev 2005: 4–20.

20 In the later Hellenistic and early Roman era, history became a competitive genre (Baumgarten 1981: 265–8; Himmelfarb 2005: 125), with many entrants: Manetho; Berossos; Josephus; and Philo of Byblos, whom, Baumgarten says, retold Phoenician myths so as to make "anything important … done first by the Phoenicians" (1981: 32–5).

21 The classic formulation is Bickerman's: "the Maccabean documents were produced in order to make history, not report it" (1979: 4). On the author's literary milieu and influences, see Weitzman 2004. One example of manufacturing history via story is the fictional relationship with Sparta (1 Macc 12:2, 5–23; 14:16–23), on which see Eilers 2013: 158. Much recent scholarship has focused on the author of 1 Maccabees rhetorical use of scripture as justification (Nongbri 2005; van der Kooij 2012; Elgvin 2016). The transformative practice is not confined to the author of 1 Maccabees; see, e.g., the varying treatments by the authors of 2 and 3 Maccabees of the episode of Olympiodoros, Heliodoros, Onias III, and the Jerusalem temple (2 Macc 3; 3 Macc 1–2) (Hacham 2012). Sylvie Honigman calls both 1 and 2 Maccabees "narrative as message" (2014: 24–5).

REFERENCES

Alexandre, Y. 2006. Nahal Tut (Site VIII): A Fortified Storage Depot from the Late Fourth Century BCE. *'Atiqot* 52: 131–89.
  2008. Karm er-Ras (Areas C, D). *HA–ESI* 120. www.hadashot-esi.org.il/report_detail_eng.aspx?id=602&mag_id=114 (accessed August 20, 2016).
  2013. Kafr Kanna (Jebel Khuwweikha): Iron II, Late Hellenistic and Roman Remains. *HA–ESI* 125. www.hadashot-esi.org.il/images//Kafr-Kanna-En-new4934.pdf (accessed July 26, 2017).

Amit, D. 2010. The Miqva'ot. In *Gamla II: The Architecture; The Shmarya Gutmann Excavations, 1976–1988*, ed. D. Syon and Z. Yavor, 193–5. IAA Reports 44. Jerusalem: IAA.

Arbel, Y. 2011. The Hasmonean Conquest of Jaffa: Chronology and New Background Evidence. In *The History and Archaeology of Jaffa*, Vol. 1, ed. M. Peilstöcker and A. Burke, 187–96. JCHPS 1; MonArch 26. Los Angeles: The Cotsen Institute of Archaeology Press.

Ariel, D. T. 1990. *Excavations at the City of David, 1978–1985: Directed by Yigal Shiloh*, Vol. 2: *Imported Stamped Amphora Handles, Coins, Worked Bone and Ivory, and Glass*. Qedem 30. Jerusalem: The Institute of Archaeology, The Hebrew University of Jerusalem.

Ariel, D. T., and Naveh, J. 2003. Selected Inscribed Sealings from Kedesh in the Upper Galilee. *BASOR* 329: 61–80.

Ariel, D. T.; Sharon, I.; Gunneweg, J.; and Perlman, I. 1985. A Group of Stamped Hellenistic Storage-Jar Handles from Dor. *IEJ* 35: 135–52.

Aviam, M., and Avitai, A. 2002. Khirbet esh-Shuhara. In *Eretz Zafon: Studies in Galilean Archaeology*, ed. Z. Gal, 119–34. Jerusalem: IAA.

Avigad, N. 1989. *The Herodian Quarter in Jerusalem: Wohl Archaeological Museum*. Jerusalem: Keter.

Bagnall, R. S., and Derow, P., eds. 1981. *Greek Historical Documents: The Hellenistic Period*. Sources for Biblical Study 16. Chico, CA: Published by Scholars Press for the SBL.

Bard, K. A., ed. 1999. *Encyclopedia of the Archaeology of Ancient Egypt*. New York: Routledge.

Baumgarten, A. 1981. *The Phoenician History of Philo of Byblos: A Commentary*. Études préliminaires aux religions orientales dans l'Empire romain 89. Leiden: Brill.

Bazzana, G. B. 2010. *BASILEIA* – The Q Concept of Kingship in Light of Documentary Papyri. In *Light from the East: Papyrologische Kommentare zum Neuen Testament; Akten des internationalen Symposions vom 3.–4. Dezember 2009 am Fachbereich Bibelwissenschaft und Kirchengeschichte der Universität Salzburg*, ed. P. Artz-Grabner and C. M. Kreinecker, 153–68. Philippika 39. Wiesbaden: Harrassowitz.

Berlin, A. M. 1997a. Between Large Forces: Palestine in the Hellenistic Period. *BA* 60: 2–51.

———. 1997b. The Plain Wares. In *Tel Anafa II*, Part 1: *The Hellenistic and Roman Pottery*, ed. S. C. Herbert, 1–244. JRASup 10 (2) 1; KMFS. Ann Arbor: Kelsey Museum of the University of Michigan.

———. 1999. The Archaeology of Ritual: The Sanctuary of Pan at Banias/Caesarea Philippi. *BASOR* 315: 27–45.

———. 2002. Power and Its Afterlife: Tombs in Hellenistic Palestine. *NEA* 65: 138–48.

———. 2005. Jewish Life before the Revolt: The Archaeological Evidence. *JSJ* 36: 417–70.

———. 2013a. Manifest Identity: From *Ioudaios* to Jew; Household Judaism as Anti-Hellenization in the Late Hasmonean Era. In *Between Cooperation and Hostility: Multiple Identities in Ancient Judaism and the Interaction with Foreign Powers*, ed. R. Albertz and J. Wöhrle, 151–75. JAJSup 11. Göttingen: Vandenhoeck & Ruprecht.

———. 2013b. Review of *The Roman Temple Complex at Horvat Omrit: An Interim Report*, ed. J. A. Overman and D. N. Schowalter. BASOR 369: 244–7.

———. 2014a. Herod the Tastemaker. *NEA* 77: 108–19.

———. 2014b. Household Judaism. In *Galilee in the Late Second Temple and Mishnaic Periods*, Vol. 1: *Life, Culture, and Society*, ed. D. A. Fiensy and J. R. Strange, 208–15. Minneapolis: Fortress.

2015. Herod, Augustus, and the Augusteum at the Paneion. *ErIsr* 31: 1*–11*.

Berlin, A. M.; Ball, T.; Thompson, R.; and Herbert, S. C. 2003. Ptolemaic Agriculture, "Syrian Wheat," and *Triticum aestivum. JAS* 30: 115–21.

Berlin, A. M., and Herbert, S. C. 2013. Tel Kedesh. In *The Oxford Encyclopedia of the Bible and Archaeology*, Vol. 2, ed. D. M. Master, 373–81. New York: Oxford.

2015. Kedesh of the Upper Galilee. In *Galilee in the Late Second Temple and Mishnaic Periods*, Vol. 2: *The Archaeological Record of Galilean Cities, Towns, and Villages*, ed. D. A. Fiensy and J. R. Strange, 419–36. Minneapolis: Fortress.

Berlin, A. M., and Stone, P. J. 2016. The Hellenistic and Early Roman Pottery. In *'Akko II: The 1991–1998 Excavations; The Early Periods*, ed. M. Hartal, D. Syon, E. Stern, and A. Tatcher, 133–202. IAA Reports 60. Jerusalem: IAA.

Bertrand, J. M. 1982. Sur l'inscription d'Hefzibah. *ZPE* 46: 167–74.

Bickerman, E. 1962. *From Ezra to the Last of the Maccabees: Foundations of Post-Biblical Judaism.* Schocken Paperbacks SB36. New York: Schocken Books.

1979. *The God of the Maccabees: Studies on the Meaning and Origin of the Maccabean Revolt.* Trans. H. R. Moehring, from German. Studies in Judaism in Late Antiquity 32. Leiden: Brill.

Biran, A. 1981. To the God Who Is in Dan. In *Temples and High Places in Biblical Times: Proceedings of the Colloquium in Honor of the Centennial of Hebrew Union College–Jewish Institute of Religion, Jerusalem, 14–16 March 1977*, ed. A. Biran, 142–51. Jerusalem: Nelson Glueck School of Biblical Archaeology of Hebrew Union College–Jewish Institute of Religion.

1994. *Biblical Dan*. Jerusalem: IES; Hebrew Union College–Jewish Institute of Religion.

Bruneau, P. 1982. "Les Israélites de Délos" et la juiverie délienne. *BCH* 106: 465–504.

Clermont-Ganneau, C. 1900. Inscriptions grecques d'Éleuthéropolis (Palestine). *CRSAIBL* 44: 536–41.

Cohen, M.; Avshalom-Gorni, D.; and Porat, L. 2013. Khirbat el-Mizrath: A Farmhouse-Fortress from the Late Hellenistic and Early Roman Periods. *HA–ESI* 125 (Hebrew). www.hadashot-esi.org.il/images//mizrat-he.pdf (accessed July 26, 2017).

Collins, J. J. 1983. The Genre Apocalypse in Hellenistic Judaism. In *Apocalypticism in the Mediterranean World and the Near East: Proceedings of the International Colloquium on Apocalypticism, Uppsala, August 12–17, 1979*, ed. D. Helholm, 531–48. Tübingen: Mohr.

Cotton, H. M., and Wörrle, M. 2007. Seleukos IV to Heliodoros: A New Dossier of Royal Correspondence from Israel. *ZPE* 159: 191–205.

Cotton-Paltiel, H. M.; Ecker, A.; and Gera, D. 2017. Juxtaposing Literary and Documentary Evidence: A New Copy of the So-Called Heliodoros Stele and the *Corpus Inscriptionum Iudaeae/Palaestinae* (*CIIP*). *BICS* 60: 1–15.

Cross, F. M., Jr. 1961. The Development of the Jewish Scripts. In *The Bible and the Ancient Near East: Essays in Honor of William Foxwell Albright*, ed. G. E. Wright, 133–202. London: Routledge; Kegan & Paul.

1963. The Discovery of the Samaria Papyri. *BA* 26: 110–21.

Crowfoot, J. W.; Crowfoot, G. M.; and Kenyon, K. M. 1957. *Samaria-Sebaste: Reports of the Work of the Joint Expedition in 1931–1933 and of the British Expedition in 1935*, Vol. 3: *The Objects from Samaria*. London: PEF.

Dar, S. 1986. *Landscape and Pattern: An Archaeological Survey of Samaria 800 B.C.E.–636 C.E.* BAR International Series 308. Oxford: BAR.

Durand, X. 1997. *Des grecs en Palestine au IIIe siècle avant Jésus-Christ: Le dossier syrien des archives de Zénon de Caunos, 261–252*. Cahiers de la Revue biblique 38. Paris: Gabalda.

Dušek, J. 2012. *Aramaic and Hebrew Inscriptions from Mt. Gerizim and Samaria between Antiochus III and Antiochus IV Epiphanes*. CHANE 54. Leiden: Brill.

Eilers, C. 2013. Diplomacy and the Integration of the Hasmonean State. In *Belonging and Isolation in the Hellenistic World*, ed. S. L. Ager and R. A. Faber, 155–65. Phoenix Supplements 51. Toronto: University of Toronto Press.

Elden, S. 2013. *The Birth of Territory*. Chicago: The University of Chicago Press.

Elgvin, T. 2016. Violence, Apologetics, and Resistance: Hasmonaean Ideology and *Yaḥad* Texts in Dialogue. In *The War Scroll, Violence, War and Peace in the Dead Sea Scrolls and Related Literature: Essays in Honour of Martin G. Abegg on the Occasion of His 65th Birthday*, ed. K. Davis, K. S. Baek, P. W. Flint, and D. M. Peters, 317–40. STDJ 115. Leiden: Brill.

Eshel, E., and Kloner, A. 1996. An Aramaic Ostracon of an Edomite Marriage Contract from Maresha, Dated 176 B.C.E. *IEJ* 46: 1–22.

Eshel, E.; Puech, E.; and Kloner, A. 2007. Aramaic Scribal Exercises of the Hellenistic Period from Maresha: Bowls A and B. *BASOR* 345: 39–62.

Finkielsztejn, G. 1998. More Evidence on John Hyrcanus I's Conquests: Lead Weights and Rhodian Amphora Stamps. *Bulletin of the Anglo-Israel Archaeological Society* 16: 33–63.

——— 2007. Poids de plomb inscrits du Levant: Une réforme d'Antiochos IV? *Topoi* suppl. 8: 35–60.

——— 2010. The Maresha Scale Weights: Metrology, Administration and History. In *Maresha Excavations Final Report III: Epigraphic Finds from the 1989–2000 Seasons*, ed. A. Kloner, E. Eshel, H. B. Korzakova, and G. Finkielsztejn, 175–92. IAA Reports 45. Jerusalem: IAA.

——— 2014. Poids et étalons au Levant à l'époque hellénistique. *Dialogues d'histoire ancienne* suppl. 12: 163–82.

Fischer, T. 1979. Zur Seleukideninschrift von Hefzibah. *ZPE* 33: 131–8.

Friedman, J. 1990. Notes on Culture and Identity in Imperial Worlds. In *Religion and Religious Practice in the Seleucid Kingdom*, ed. P. Bilde, T. Engberg-Pedersen, L. Hannestad, and J. Zahle, 14–39. Studies in Hellenistic Civilization 1. Aarhus: Aarhus University Press.

Gera, D. 1998. *Judaea and Mediterranean Politics, 219 to 161 B.C.E.* Brill's Series in Jewish Studies 8. Leiden: Brill.

——— 2009. Olympiodoros, Heliodoros and the Temples of Koile Syria and Phoinike. *ZPE* 169: 125–55.

Geraty, L. T. 1975. The Khirbet el-Kôm Bilingual Ostracon. *BASOR* 220: 55–61.

Geva, H. 2003. Hellenistic Pottery from Areas W and X-2. In *Jewish Quarter Excavations in the Old City of Jerusalem*, Vol. 2: *The Finds from Areas A, W and X-2; Final Report*, ed. H. Geva, 113–75. Jerusalem: IES.

Goodman, M. 1994. Jewish Attitudes to Greek Culture in the Period of the Second Temple. In *Jewish Education and Learning: Published in Honour of Dr. David Patterson on the Occasion of His Seventieth Birthday*, ed. G. Abramson and T. Parfitt, 167–74. Chur: Harwood Academic.

Goren, D. 2010. The Architecture and Stratigraphy of the Hasmonean Quarter (Areas D and B) and Area B77. In *Gamla II: The Architecture; The Shmarya Gutman Excavations, 1976–1988*, ed. D. Syon and Z. Yavor, 113–52. IAA Reports 44. Jerusalem: IAA.

Grabbe, L. L. 2001. Jewish Historiography and Scripture in the Hellenistic Period. In *Did Moses Speak Attic? Jewish Historiography and Scripture in the Hellenistic Period*, ed.

L. L. Grabbe, 129–55. JSOTSup 317; European Seminar in Historical Methodology 3. Sheffield: Sheffield Academic.

2008. *A History of the Jews and Judaism in the Second Temple Period,* Vol. 2: *The Coming of the Greeks; The Early Hellenistic Period (335–175 BCE).* London: T & T Clark.

Gropp, D. M. 2001. *Wadi Daliyeh II: The Samaria Papyri from Wadi Daliyeh.* DJD 28. Oxford: Clarendon.

Grose, D. 2012. The Glass Vessels. In *Tel Anafa II,* Part 2: *Glass Vessels, Lamps, Objects of Metal, and Groundstone and Other Stone Tools and Vessels,* ed. A. M. Berlin and S. C. Herbert, 1–98. JRASup 10 (2) 2; KMFS. Ann Arbor: Kelsey Museum of the University of Michigan.

Hacham, N. 2012. Sanctity and the Attitude towards the Temple in Hellenistic Judaism. In *Was 70 CE a Watershed in Jewish History? On Jews and Judaism before and after the Destruction of the Second Temple,* ed. D. R. Schwartz and Z. Weiss in collaboration with R. A. Clements, 155–79. Ancient Judaism and Early Christianity 78. Leiden: Brill.

Hayes, J. W. 1985. Hellenistic to Byzantine Fine Wares and Derivatives in the Jerusalem Corpus. In *Excavations in Jerusalem, 1961–1967,* Vol. 1, ed. A. D. Tushingham, 181–96. Toronto: Royal Ontario Museum.

Herbert, S. C. 1994. *Tel Anafa I: Final Report on Ten Years of Excavation at a Hellenistic and Roman Settlement in Northern Israel.* 2 vols. JRASup 10 (1); KMFS. Ann Arbor: Kelsey Museum of the University of Michigan.

Himmelfarb, M. 2005. The Torah between Athens and Jerusalem: Jewish Difference in Antiquity. In *Ancient Judaism in Its Hellenistic Context,* ed. C. Bakhos, 113–29. JSJSup 95. Leiden: Brill.

Honigman, S. 2011. King and Temple in *2 Maccabees*: The Case for Continuity. In *Judah between East and West: The Transition from Persian to Greek Rule (ca. 400–200 BCE); A Conference Held at Tel Aviv University, 17–19 April 2007,* ed. L. L. Grabbe and O. Lipschits, 91–130. LSTS 75. London: T & T Clark.

2014. *Tales of High Priests and Taxes: The Books of the Maccabees and the Judean Rebellion against Antiochos IV.* Berkeley: University of California Press.

Hopkins, K. 1978. *Conquerors and Slaves.* Sociological Studies in Roman History 1. Cambridge: Cambridge University Press.

Isaac, B. 1991. A Seleucid Inscription from Jamnia-on-the-Sea: Antiochus V Eupator and the Sidonians. *IEJ* 41: 132–44.

Jacobson, D. M. 2007. *The Hellenistic Paintings of Marisa.* PEFA 7. Leeds: Maney.

Jokiranta, J. M.; Antin, K. M.; Bonnie, R. G. L. M.; Hakola, R. T.; Tervanotko, H. K.; Uusimäki, E. K.; and Yli-Karjanmaa, S. P. 2016. Changes in Research of Late Second Temple Period Judaism: An Invitation to Interdisciplinarity. Presented at the annual meeting of Changes in Sacred Texts and Traditions at the University of Helsinki's Center of Excellence.

Kaplan J., and Kaplan H. 1989. Remains of a Serapis Cult in Tel Aviv. *ErIsr* 20: 352–9. (Hebrew)

Kartveit, M. 2014. Samaritan Self-Consciousness in the First Half of the Second Century B.C.E. in Light of the Inscriptions from Mount Gerizim and Delos. *JSJ* 45: 449–70.

Kasher, A. 2011. Further Revised Thoughts on Josephus' Report of Alexander's Campaign to Palestine (*Ant.* 11.304–347). In *Judah between East and West: The Transition from Persian to Greek Rule (ca. 400–200 BCE); A Conference Held at Tel Aviv University, 17–19 April 2007,* ed. L. L. Grabbe and O. Lipschits, 131–57. LSTS 75. London: T & T Clark.

Kaye, N., and Amitay, O. 2015. Kleopatra's Dowry: Taxation and Sovereignty between Hellenistic Kingdoms. *Historia* 64: 131–55.

Kidd, B. 2015. Masonry Style in Phoenicia. Reconstructing Sumptuous Mural Decoration from the "Late Hellenistic Stuccoed Building" at Tel Anafa. In *Beyond Iconography: Materials, Methods, and Meaning in Ancient Surface Decoration*, ed. S. Lepinski and S. McFadden, 77–95. Selected Papers on Ancient Art and Architecture 1. Boston: AIA.

Kloppenborg, J. S. 2006. *The Tenants in the Vineyard: Ideology, Economics, and Agrarian Conflict in Jewish Palestine*. Wissenschaftliche Untersuchungen zum Neuen Testament 195. Tübingen: Mohr Siebeck.

Kooij, A. van der. 2012. The Claim of Maccabean Leadership and the Use of Scripture. In *Jewish Identity and Politics between the Maccabees and Bar Kokhba: Groups, Normativity, and Rituals*, ed. B. Eckhardt, 29–49. JSJSup 155. Leiden: Brill.

Korzakova, H. B. 2010. Lead Weights. In *Maresha Excavations Final Report III: Epigraphic Finds from the 1989–2000 Seasons*, ed. A. Kloner, E. Eshel, H. B. Korzakova, and G. Finkielsztejn, 159–73. IAA Reports 45. Jerusalem: IAA.

Kosmin, P. J. 2014. *The Land of the Elephant Kings: Space, Territory, and Ideology in the Seleucid Empire*. Cambridge, MA: Harvard University Press.

Krautbauer, A.; Llewelyn, S.; and Wassell, B. 2014. A Gift of One Eunuch and Four Slave Boys: P.Cair.Zen. I 59076 and Historical Construction. *JSJ* 45: 305–25.

Kushnir-Stein, A. 2011. Inscribed Hellenistic Weights of Palestine. *INR* 6: 35–60.

Landau, Y. H. 1966. A Greek Inscription Found near Hefzibah. *IEJ* 16: 54–70.

Landvatter, T. 2012. The Serapis and Isis Coinage of Ptolemy IV. *American Journal of Numismatics* 24: 61–90.

Lapp, P. W., and Lapp, N. L. 1974. *Discoveries in the Wâdī ed-Dâliyeh*. AASOR 41. Cambridge, MA: ASOR.

Lenger, M.-T. 1964. *Corpus des ordonnances des Ptolémées (C. Ord. Ptol.)*. Mémoires de la Classe des lettres 57 (1). Brussels: Académie Royale de Belgique.

Lipschits, O., and Vanderhooft, D. S. 2011. *The Yehud Stamp Impressions: A Corpus of Inscribed Impressions from the Persian and Hellenistic Periods in Judah*. Winona Lake IN: Eisenbrauns.

Lupu, E. 2003. A New Look at Three Inscriptions from Jaffa, Jerusalem, and Gaza. *Scripta Classical Israelica* 22: 193–202.

Magen, Y. 2002. *The Stone Vessel Industry in the Second Temple Period: Excavations at Hizma and the Jerusalem Temple Mount*. JSP 1. Jerusalem: IES.

―― 2008. *Mount Gerizim Excavations*, Vol. 2: *A Temple City*. JSP 8. Jerusalem: Staff Officer of Archaeology, Civil Administration of Judea and Samaria; IAA.

Magen, Y.; Misgav, H.; and Tsfania, L. 2004. *Mount Gerizim Excavations*, Vol. 1: *The Aramaic, Hebrew and Samaritan Inscriptions*. JSP 2. Jerusalem: Staff Officer of Archaeology, Civil Administration of Judea and Samaria; IAA.

Magness, J. 2001. The Cults of Isis and Kore at Samaria-Sebaste in the Hellenistic and Roman Periods. *HTR* 94: 157–77.

Ma'oz, Z. 1993. Banias. *NEAEHL* 1: 136–43.

―― 1995. Banias, Temple of Pan – 1991/1992. *ESI* 13: 2–7.

―― 1996. Banias, Temple of Pan – 1993. *ESI* 15: 1–5.

Mattila, S. L. 2014. Inner Village Life in Galilee: A Diverse and Complex Phenomenon. In *Galilee in the Late Second Temple and Mishnaic Periods*, ed. D. A. Fiensy and J. R. Strange, 312–45. Minneapolis: Fortress.

2015a. The Distribution of Land among Villagers in Greco-Roman Palestine: An Unpublished Land Survey and the Comparative Data from Egypt. Presented at the annual meeting of ASOR.

2015b. They Were Not Mainly "Peasants": Towards an Alternative View of Village Life in Greco-Roman Palestine and Egypt. *ASOR Blog*. http://asorblog.org/2015/08/25/they-were-not-mainly-peasants/ (accessed February 4, 2016).

Najman, H. 2012. The Vitality of Scripture within and beyond the "Canon." *JSJ* 43: 497–518.

Naveh, J. 1979. The Aramaic Ostraca from Tel Beer-Sheba (Seasons 1971–1976). *TA* 6: 182–98.

Netzer, E. 2001. *The Palaces of the Hasmoneans and Herod the Great*. Jerusalem: Yad Izhak Ben-Zvi; IES.

Nitschke, J. L.; Martin, S. R.; and Shalev, Y. 2011. Between Carmel and the Sea: Tel Dor; The Late Periods. *NEA* 74: 132–54.

Nongbri, B. 2005. The Motivations of the Maccabees and Judean Rhetoric of Ancestral Tradition. In *Ancient Judaism in Its Hellenistic Context*, ed. C. Bakhos, 85–111. JSJSup 95. Leiden: Brill.

Notley, R. S. 2011. Greco-Roman Jaffa and Its Historical Background. In *The History and Archaeology of Jaffa*, Vol. 1, ed. M. Peilstöcker and A. A. Burke, 95–107. JCHPS 1; MonArch 26. Los Angeles: The Cotsen Institute of Archaeology Press.

Noy, I. 2012. The Victory Wreath of Hyrcanus I. *INR* 7: 31–42.

Overman, J. A., and Schowalter, D. N., eds. 2011. *The Roman Temple Complex at Horvat Omrit: An Interim Report*. BAR International Series 2205. Oxford: Archaeopress.

Peckham, J. B. 2014. *Phoenicia: Episodes and Anecdotes from the Ancient Mediterranean*. Winona Lake, IN: Eisenbrauns.

Peleg-Barkat, O., and Tepper, Y. 2014. Between Phoenicia and Judaea: Preliminary Results of the 2007–2010 Excavation Seasons at Horvat 'Eleq, Ramat HaNadiv, Israel. *Strata* 32: 49–80.

Peters, J. P., and Thiersch, H. 1905. *Painted Tombs in the Necropolis of Marissa (Marêshah)*. London: PEF.

Pfeiffer, S. 2010. Das Dekret von Rosette: Die ägyptischen Priester und der Herrscherkult. In *Alexandreia und das ptolemäishe Ägypten: Kulturbegegnungen in hellenistischer Zeit*, ed. G. Weber, 84–108. Berlin: Antike.

Piejko, F. 1991. Antiochus III and Ptolemy Son of Thraseas: The Inscription of Hefzibah Reconsidered. *L'antiquité classique* 60: 245–59.

Plantzos, D. 2011. The Iconography of Assimilation: Isis and Royal Imagery on Ptolemaic Seal Impressions. In *More Than Men, Less Than Gods: Studies on Royal Cult and Imperial Worship; Proceedings of the International Colloquium Organized by the Belgian School at Athens (November 1–2, 2007)*, ed. P. P. Iossif, A. S. Chankowski, and C. C. Lorber, 389–416. Leuven: Peeters.

Rahmani, L. Y. 1967. Jason's Tomb. *IEJ* 17: 61–100.

1982. Ancient Jerusalem's Funerary Customs and Tombs, Part Three. *BA* 45: 43–53.

Rapper, G. de 2010. Religion on the Border: Sanctuaries and Festivals in Post-Communist Albania. In *Religion and Boundaries: Studies from the Balkans, Eastern Europe and Turkey*, ed. G. I. Valtchinova, 247–65. Istanbul: Isis.

Redding, R. W. 1994. The Vertebrate Fauna. In *Tel Anafa I: Final Report on Ten Years of Excavation at a Hellenistic and Roman Settlement in Northern Israel*, Vol. 1, by S. C. Herbert, 279–322. JRASup 10 (1) 1; KMFS. Ann Arbor: Kelsey Museum of the University of Michigan.

Reich, R. 2013. *Miqwa'ot (Jewish Ritual Baths) in the Second Temple, Mishnaic, and Talmudic Periods.* Jerusalem: Yad Izhaq Ben-Zvi; IES (Hebrew).

Rosenthal-Heginbottom, R. 2003. Hellenistic and Early Roman Fine Wares and Lamps from Area A. In *Jewish Quarter Excavations in the Old City of Jerusalem, Conducted by Nahman Avigad, 1969–1982, Vol. 2: The Finds from Areas A, W and X-2; Final Report,* by H. Geva, 192–223. Jerusalem: IES.

Rozenberg, S. 2008. *Hasmonean and Herodian Palaces at Jericho: Final Reports of the 1973–1987 Excavations, Vol. 4: The Decoration of Herod's Third Palace at Jericho.* Jerusalem: IES.

Schäfer, P. 1995. *The History of the Jews in Antiquity: The Jews of Palestine from Alexander the Great to the Arab Conquest.* Oxford: Routledge.

Schwartz, S. 1989. The "Judaism" of Samaria and Galilee in Josephus's Version of the Letter of Demetrius I to Jonathan (*Antiquities* 13.48–57). *HTR* 82: 377–91.

———. 1993. A Note on the Social Type and Political Ideology of the Hasmonean Family. *JBL* 112: 305–9.

———. 1995. Language, Power and Identity in Ancient Palestine. *Past & Present* 148: 3–47.

Segal, A.; Młynarczyk, J.; and Burdajewicz, M. 2014. *Excavations of the Hellenistic Site in Kibbutz Sha'ar-Ha'Amakim (Gaba), 1984–1998: Final Report.* 2nd rev. ed. Haifa: The Zinman Institute of Archaeology, University of Haifa.

Sivertsev, A. M. 2005. *Households, Sects, and the Origins of Rabbinic Judaism.* JSJSup 102. Leiden: Brill.

Slane, K. W. 1997. The Fine Wares. In *Tel Anafa II,* Part 1: *The Hellenistic and Roman Pottery,* ed. S. C. Herbert, 247–406. JRASup 10 (2) 1; KMFS. Ann Arbor: Kelsey Museum of the University of Michigan.

Stewart, A., and Martin, S. R. 2003. Hellenistic Discoveries at Tel Dor, Israel. *Hesperia* 72: 121–45.

Stremlin, B. 2008. The Iron Age World-System. *History Compass* 6: 969–99.

Stone, P. 2013. Hidden in PLAIN Sight: Ceramic Assemblages and Daily Life in the Ptolemaic Southern Levant. In *Networks in the Hellenistic World: According to the Pottery in the Eastern Mediterranean and Beyond,* ed. N. Fenn and C. Römer-Strehl, 293–9. BAR International Series 2539. Oxford: Archaeopress.

Syon, D. 2002. Coins from the Excavations at Khirbet esh-Shuhara. In *Eretz Zafon: Studies in Galilean Archaeology,* ed. Z. Gal, *123–*34. Jerusalem: IAA.

———. 2006. Numismatic Evidence of Jewish Presence in Galilee before the Hasmonean Annexation? *INR* 1: 21–4.

———. 2015. *Small Change in Hellenistic-Roman Galilee: The Evidence from Numismatic Site Finds as a Tool for Historical Reconstruction.* Numismatic Studies and Researches 11. Jerusalem: The Israel Numismatic Society.

Talgam, R., and Peleg, O. 2008. Mosaic Pavements in Herod's Day. [Rev.] paperback ed. In *The Architecture of Herod, the Great Builder,* ed. E. Netzer, 377–83. Grand Rapids, MI: Baker Academic.

Thompson, D. B. 1973. *Ptolemaic Oinochoai and Portraits in Faience: Aspects of the Ruler-Cult.* Oxford Monographs on Classical Archaeology. Oxford: Clarendon.

Tscherikower, V. 1937. Palestine under the Ptolemies: A Contribution to the Study of the Zenon Papyri. *Mizraim* 4–5: 9–90.

Tushingham, A. D. 1985. Excavations in the Armenian Garden on the Western Hill. In *Excavations in Jerusalem 1961–1967,* Vol. 1, 1–175. Toronto: Royal Ontario Museum.

Tzaferis, V. 1992. The "God Who Is in Dan" and the Cult of Pan at Banias in the Hellenistic and Roman Periods. *ErIsr* 23: 128*–35*.

Weitzman, S. 2004. Plotting Antiochus's Persecution. *JBL* 123: 219–34.
Wise, M. O. 2015. *Language and Literacy in Roman Judaea: A Study of the Bar Kokhba Documents*. Anchor Yale Bible Reference Library. New Haven, CT: Yale University Press.
Zahn, M. M. 2015. The Samaritan Pentateuch and the Scribal Culture of Second Temple Judaism. *JSJ* 46: 285–313.
Zerubavel, E. 2003. *Time Maps: Collective Memory and the Social Shape of the Past*. Chicago: The University of Chicago Press.

TWENTY THREE

THE EFFECTS OF EMPIRE ON DAILY LIFE IN THE PROVINCIAL EAST (37 BCE–313 CE)

ALEXANDRA L. RATZLAFF

The reign of Herod as *rex socius et amicus populi romani*, begins a more outwardly Roman administration of what would eventually become the Roman province of Judaea and later Syria-Palaestina. This transition was only a step further in the gradual process of Roman cultural influence, some aspects of which were imposed and others reflected the preferences of the region's population and even the individual. It is important to keep in mind that there is no standard "Roman civilization" against which to gauge provincial culture. Roman influence and acculturation was experienced differently across the empire – even the city of Rome underwent continuous changes with the various cultural influences constantly flooding the city. Each province also started at a different baseline of interaction and familiarity with the Roman sphere of material culture and traditions. Cultural change is a slow process that involves more than simply adopting a predetermined set of preferences and practices. In addition, the resistance to adopt the "Roman package" of style and material culture does not translate into opposition to the colonialism of Rome (Laurence 1998: 2).

In Judaea, the population was a civilized amalgamation of cultural influences, with the coastal Mediterranean societies, hellenized and Jewish populations, and other small enclaves of various other cultural groups. Rome had encountered highly complex societies before, particularly in the East (Egypt, Pontus, etc.); however, Judaea distinguished itself by having such varied cultural groups within a single region. Many of the aspects that characterize

Roman lifeways were already in place in Judaea due to its hellenized background in the preceding centuries. The Jewish community in Judaea had an identity that was able to withstand drastic political changes and rulership for centuries as a result of having what other groups did not, a written codified text – the Jewish Bible, their source for theological belief and rules of moral and social conduct, as well as a national history (Millar 1993: 338). This enabled them to absorb aspects of Roman life while maintaining their own social identity.

The archaeological record provides us with examples of how the provincial population chose to express itself in public and private. In aspects of the household, customs of life and entertainment, and even in death, individuals chose the facets of society to which they felt compelled to align themselves. This chapter will show, through an examination of material culture, how daily life was influenced by the Roman presence in the region and what aspects continued to prevail in the face of new ideas.

THE HOUSEHOLD: DOMESTIC ARCHITECTURE

Roman influence in its newly acquired province of Judaea may be most outwardly recognized through the examples of public buildings and monuments erected under the guise of the region's new administration. However, domestic architecture reflects the experience of the masses; it was rarely imposed and shows a preference of the individual(s) who lived there. The architecture, organization, and functionality of private dwellings during the first–third centuries CE reflects a set of mitigating factors, such as geography, urban verses rural locations, and social class. The shear diversity of the Roman Empire and the cultural influence that flowed into it prevented the model of the Roman house from ever being fixed through time or geography. Aspects of change and the introduction of new features in domestic architecture may be better indicators of Rome's influence in the domestic sphere.

There is consistency in the Hellenistic/Judaean tradition of rural manor–building that remained only marginally affected by the transition to Roman rule. In this respect, the influence of Rome on the architecture of domestic building was that it coalesced very well with the pre-existing regional traditions. In Yizhar Hirschfeld's survey of domestic architecture of Roman and Byzantine Palaestine, he identifies three main types of houses with the primary differentiation between them being the location of the courtyard, whether it was enclosed as an interior space surrounded by rooms (courtyard-style house) or adjacent to the house externally but still connected (simple and complex houses) (Hirschfeld 1995: 21). These range from single room or complex (multiple wings) houses, with attached courtyards, to a central courtyard house. While the courtyard house closely resembles a traditional Roman peristyle house, it lacks the colonnade surrounding the courtyard (Ward-Perkins 1974: 38–41; Hirschfeld 1995: 290). In fact, the courtyard-style house has a long history in the eastern Mediterranean. Adoption of the "traditional Roman" atrium house or central-courtyard house did not immediately accompany Judaea becoming a Roman province.

The countryside continued the regional tradition of building variations of courtyard-adjacent homes, while new architectural forms and styles with Roman influence emerged in cities. The large urban villa at Sepphoris, famous for its Dionysiac mosaic built at the beginning of the third century (Fig. 23.1), is an example of a departure from Hellenistic or Judaean urban building design,

23.1. The "Mona Lisa of the Galilee" (possibly Venus), part of the Dionysus mosaic floor in Sepphoris. (Photo by C. Raddato. Courtesy of Wikimedia Commons [https://creativecommons.org/licenses/by-sa/2.0/deed.en].)

embracing a more traditionally Roman architectural layout. It featured a peristyle courtyard in the center of a two-story building and a large *triclinium* (dining hall) to its north, both of which were surrounded by bedrooms, living rooms, and service rooms accessed by narrow corridors (Netzer and Weiss 1994: 29). Other examples of atrium houses have been discovered at Jerusalem, Aphek, and Samaria-Sebaste, in which there is a noticeable transition in the courtyard from adjacent to the house to the center, and evidence of a colonnade can be found surrounding the central courtyard. At Samaria-Sebaste, the house was constructed near the Temple to Augustus at the highest area of the site and may have been the residence of the temple's priest (Reisner, Fisher, and Lyon 1924: 180–5). A less common example of an Early Roman or late Herodian (first BCE–first CE) rural atrium house comes from Tell el-Judeideh, where there was a single-story complex with two separate wings and a central atrium – an architectural plan indicative of the local landowner's exposure and preference for the Roman style (Hirschfeld 1995: 87). The contemporary wealthy estate "Hilkiya Palace" at Khirbet el-Muraq has a similar peristyle-courtyard architectural plan on a larger scale, where a central courtyard is decorated with a mosaic floor, surrounded by columns and flanked on two sides by *triclinia* (Damati 1972: 173). Perhaps not surprisingly, examples of Roman influence in domestic architecture are found in areas where Roman cultural traditions prevailed in other spheres of life, such as religion, entertainment, and social organization.

While the use of mosaics as architectural ornamentation was initially introduced by the Greeks, the expansion of the empire led to the establishment of regional workshops to support the demand for the art form. Provincial elites chose to display their personal wealth and sense of Roman identity in private. Mosaics in Roman households provided visual cues for the function of space along with the use of specific themes to interact with the viewer in a deliberate way. Artistically, there continued to be a preference in the Greek-speaking portion of the empire for the Hellenistic style of central panels of figures framed with a design motif. Hellenistic themes and décor in mosaics came to be closely linked with pagan cult – images associated with Dionysus were among the most popular. Roman stylistic traditions and imagery were not encountered with trepidation, as Hellenism had introduced many of these ideas and helped to break down prohibitions regarding representations of human and animal figures in décor. Some of the earliest examples in the Holy Land come from Beth Shean in the early first century CE, where a geometric pattern of hexagons surrounds a black dolphin, similar to mosaics found at Pompeii (Domus P. Papui Proculi) (Talgam 2014: 20). In the following century, mythological scenes and naturalistically rendered figures were still in line with Hellenistic traditions but gained their own stylistic and technical qualities (Talgam 2014: 27). By the third century, the *triclinium* in the House of Dionysus at Sepphoris provides one of the best examples of Roman art, depicting the myth cycle of Dionysus and his cult in 15 panels. Decorating the *triclinium* is a mosaic floor with 15 panels depicting the life of the Greek god Dionysus, framed by 22 medallions with hunting scenes, and an outer U-shaped frame depicting a rural procession. Many of the other rooms also have floors decorated with colorful geometric patterns and walls with evidence of frescoes in bright colors in geometric and floral designs. Mosaics allowed Jewish, pagan, and Christian cultural elements to intermingle without losing their own identities. Dionysus and his attributes, in particular, had affinities that were embraced by both the Jewish and pagan populations. It is unclear if the house belonged to one of the city's pagan citizens, who may have held a government position, or a member of the Jewish elite trying to garner favor with the Roman administration through the outwardly Roman nature of the building.

FUNERARY PRACTICES

The Roman presence in the region not only impacted the ways people lived, but also how they were memorialized in death. Funerary practices in Judaea had already incorporated Greek and Hellenistic customs and designs into their traditional rock-cut tombs. Examples of this influence can be seen first in the family tomb of Simon the Hasmonean in Modi'in then by Jerusalem's elite, with examples including the tomb of Queen Helena of Adiabene (the Tomb of Kings), the tomb of Bene Hezir, and Jason's tomb (Magness 2013: 230–5). Funerary customs, in general, experienced a transition at the beginning of the first century BCE, in which rock-cut family tombs introduced *loculi* instead of benches where the deceased were laid out. During the reign of Herod, ossuaries replaced pits and repositories for secondary inhumations, some containing multiple individuals (Fig. 23.2). As opposed to sarcophagi, ossuaries simply needed to be as large as the longest bone of the body (the femur) with the bones deposited in them only after the flesh had been removed over time.

Contemporaneously, the Roman mode of disposing of the dead had been cremation. Ashes were deposited in *cineraria* (cinerary urns), small casket-shaped containers with gabled lids and sometimes with carved decorations and/or inscriptions. These urns were found throughout the empire, including western-central Anatolia (Afyon), where stone cinerary urns are strikingly similar in size, shape, and their lids to plain Jerusalem ossuaries but contain cremations rather than secondary burials of bones (Magness 2013: 242). Outwardly, the adoption of *cineraria* in the form of ossuaries allowed those in Judaea trying to emulate Roman customs to embrace this funerary practice without having to actually cremate the dead and break Jewish law. In Hebrew or Aramaic, the term *gluskoma* (from the Greek *glōssokomon*, "casket") is often used to refer to Judaean ossuaries; on one ossuary, the

23.2. First-century CE Jewish ossuaries at the Dominus Flevit church on the Mount of Olives. (Photo by I. Scott. Courtesy of Wikimedia Commons [https://creativecommons.org/licenses/by-sa/2.0/deed.en].)

word *kayka* is inscribed in Palmyrene script meaning "amphora" in reference to a funerary urn, indicating that Roman *cineraria* were the inspiration for Judaean ossuaries (Magness 2011: 153). Burial in ossuaries not only reflected Roman influence on the Jewish population but allowed for increased individualization in a more monumentalized form of burial for elites trying to improve their social and political status in the community (Fine 2010: 447). Just as the adoption of ossuaries was tied to Jerusalem's elites, the use of ossuaries after 70 CE disappears from the city with the departure or death of the elites who had built the rock-cut tombs (Magness 2013: 242). As Jewish populations dispersed to the Galilee and southern Judaea following the First Jewish Revolt, varying forms of ossuaries are found in these regions; however, by the late third century CE, ossuaries fall out of use entirely. The use of rock-cut tombs in which ossuaries were placed is a phenomenon of the upper classes of society, and only represents a small portion of how the general population treated the dead. A large portion of the population, including the poor, criminals, and slaves, would have treated their dead in ways less recognizable in the archaeological record, using public funerary pyres (*ustrinae*) or potters' fields. Roman customs eventually returned to a preference for inhumation by the end of the second–mid-third century CE, depositing their dead in sarcophagi, often elaborately carved with decorations.

CERAMICS

Ceramic vessels were a ubiquitous product found in every household in antiquity. Regionalization in form and fabric characterizes the consumption of pottery in the Holy Land during the first three centuries CE. The cultural communities and sociopolitical circumstances that define the period, particularly the First and Second Jewish Revolts, had a major impact on the production, importation, and preference of pottery. An early shift in ceramics is found in the Galilee at various sites (e.g., Shiqmona, Tel Anafa, Pella); with gentile and mixed (gentile and Jewish) populations, there was consistency from the first century BCE–first century CE in the use of red-slipped bowls and plates. However, in Jewish communities within the region (at Yodefat, Capernum, and Gamla), the use of red-slipped tablewares ends, and such wares are replaced with locally produced bowls and saucers, as well as chalk vessels (Berlin 2002: 58–9). In Early Roman Galilee, the most common type of storage jar was Shikhin Ware, produced in the central Galilee near Sepphoris.

Just outside of Jerusalem, during the late first–mid-second centuries CE, the transfer of the Legio X *Fretensis* to a permanent base necessitated the production of ceramics and foodstuffs for the army. Excavation at Binyanei Ha'uma yielded fine table wares, cooking wares, and kitchen wares, all produced at the site. The red-slip forms from Binyanei Ha'uma are local imitations of Western Sigillata (Samian Ware), originating in Italy, Gaul, and Spain from the first century BCE until the early third century CE, with very few examples of vessels decorated in relief scenes (Magness 2002: 193). Thin-walled drinking vessels decorated in relief accompanied the red-slip tableware as copies of metal and glass vessels produced in the Western Empire. Of the decorated table wares, Dionysaic motifs are the most common and reflect the popularity of the cult among the soldiers occupying Aelia Capitolina (Magness 2002: 200). Similar vessel types were found in excavations of Jerusalem's Jewish Quarter, where, during the Early Roman period, Eastern Sigillata A and its imitations were the dominant tableware for residents of the upper city but not among Jewish households (Rosenthal-Heginbottom 2014: 387). Here, too, thin-walled vessels were a fashionable copy of glass and metal drinking cups popular in the West. Along the coast, particularly at Caesarea, imported fine wares were a common phenomenon from the first century BCE to the fourth century CE. Forms from Italy and Gaul included Western Sigillata and Pompeian Red Ware during the first century BCE through first century CE. Eastern Sigillata D from Cyprus and Eastern Sigillata A from Asia Minor were found in the greatest abundance. During the first century CE, while Eastern Sigillata A was popular at Caesarea, the type disappeared almost entirely from Galilean settlements. Other imported forms from around the Mediterranean were found at the port city alongside locally produced fine wares and cooking vessels, such as Kefar Hananyah Ware. Pottery characteristic of the region of Judah, including spherical juglets, incurved bowls, Judean bag-shaped jars, and Herodian cooking pots, penetrates southern coastal sites, such as Jaffa, but not the northern coast or the Galilee (Tsuf 2011: 272–3). Fluctuations in the importation of tablewares or affinities for locally produced vessels can be tied in many cases to maintaining a sense of group identity when confronted with an opposing faction. Here, the choice of local Judean wares was a statement by the local Jewish communities that they were reaffirming their cultural ties as opposed to buying Mediterranean imports.

The variety of storage jars used for the trade of goods over long and short distances peaked at the end of the first century BCE/beginning of the first century CE. This period represents the height of economic activity. By the beginning of the third century CE, there was a dramatic drop in the different types of vessels. Commodities transported in amphorae were overwhelmingly wine and olive oil produced in numerous centers across the Mediterranean. However, other items, such as dried goods and fish products (i.e., garum), were also transported in storage jars. Archaeologically, amphorae appear in domestic contexts, such as at villas and houses in urban centers, as well as in public buildings, including warehouses, religious complexes (temples, synagogues, churches), and, of course, in shipwrecks when they were being transported. At the transition from the first century BCE to first century CE, some of the most dominant forms were variants of the Dressel (productions sites range across the Mediterranean) and Rhodian amphorae (produced at sites in the Aegean and Asia Minor). Beginning in the late first century CE, two new forms appear in Palestine, the Palestinian Bag Jar and Gaza Jar (Fig. 23.3). These vessel types

23.3. Palestinian Bag Jar and Gaza Jar, currently housed in the Classical Artifact Research Collection at Brandeis University. (Photo by H. Wong.)

are found in great quantities at sites throughout the province for the next several centuries. They represent the predominant vessel for commodities exported from Palestine and found as far afield as Spain and Wales, in addition to their use in intra-regional trade.

Lamps

The use of lamps was a practical necessity across all classes of society; they provided a cheap and easy means of illumination. Hellenistic lamps spread the mold-made tradition, and by the first century BCE, they were as common as the previous wheel-thrown lamps throughout the Mediterranean world. Easily mass produced by carving a stone mold or covering a sample lamp in clay or plaster to create a new mold, the lamps were able to be made cheaply in huge quantities, although with less decoration. From the first century BCE to the first century CE, mold-made factory lamps were produced in many large cities of the ancient world. In Judaea, Herodian lamps were a mix of wheelmade and handmade construction, but essentially plain lamps, or those with only minimal floral or geometric designs became popular as a new alternative within the market. Their popularity likely did not begin until just after the reign of Herod (37–4 BCE) until the end of the Second Jewish Revolt (132–135 CE). Sweeping changes under Hadrian brought a pronounced Roman character to the region, particularly those imposed at Aelia Capitolina (Jerusalem). Among the items manufactured at the Legio X *Fretensis*'s pottery workshop at Binyanei Ha'uma near its base was a new style of round lamp with a decorated discus at its center (Fig. 23.4).

23.4. Mold-made discus lamp with a goat and a tree from Israel, currently housed in the Classical Artifact Research Collection at Brandeis University. (Photo by H. Wong.)

These were also adorned with geometric designs, flora, and fauna, as well as considerably more pagan iconography, featuring human faces, deities, and mythological figures (Wexler and Gilboa 1996: 115–21). In providing room for images, the discus lamps had small holes for filling with oil, breaking Jewish purity laws in some instances for both their decoration and not having a filling hole large enough for a coin to pass through, a feature maintained by the previous Herodian lamps (Gardner 2014: 286). Discus lamps found in excavations throughout the Holy Land provide examples of the center disc missing, which could have been deliberately broken for ritual purification or is often missing due to it being the thinnest and most susceptible area to breakage during use or post-depositionally (Wexler and Gilboa 1996: 127). Archaeological excavations have shown that most lamps found in Syria-Palaestina are products of local industries creating imitations of lamps originating in urban Roman centers. While heavily influenced by the art of lamps made in Rome, the local industries in Syria-Palaestina demonstrated a wealth of variety in their choice of decoration; the "double-axe"-and-volute motif was the region's preeminent form (Wexler and Gilboa 1996: 130). Lamps were not only a functional part of everyday life but were imbued with religious, social, and political themes that appealed to their owners.

Roman Army

The Roman Army's presence in Judaea during the first through third centuries CE is largely optimized by their role in the two Jewish wars. For a small province, Judaea's tumultuous cultural and sociopolitical environment would eventually draw nearly one-quarter of all the Roman legions to its borders. The eight camps, siege ramp, and circumvallation at the base of Masada are visual reminders of the force necessary to seize the remaining Jewish Zealots in Herod's former palace (Fig. 23.5). Veterans of the First Jewish Revolt were likely settled at the newly established *colonia* at Caesarea, where tax exemptions and a highly Romanized environment would have appealed to the former soldiers (Pliny, *Nat.* 5.14.69). According to Josephus, 800 more veterans were settled at Emmaus (B.J. 7.6.6.216–17). As a consequence of the revolt, the Legio X *Fretensis* was left there as the province's occupying force along with several cavalry *alae* and infantry *cohorts* (Josephus, B.J. 7.1.2.5).

In the period leading up to the Bar Kokhba Revolt, Hadrian transformed Judaea from a one-legion province (Legio X *Fretensis*), under a legatus of ex-praetor status, to a two-legion province (initially Legio II *Trainana* then Legio VI *Ferrata*), ruled by an ex-consul (Millar 1993: 107). The second revolt also required a major investment in force by the Roman army, utilizing four legions plus a significant auxiliary force. Following the revolt, Hadrian removed Judaea from the map entirely and reorganized the region as Syria-Palaestina with two permanent legions (plus additional numerous auxiliaries) and two *colonia* (Caesarea, Jerusalem).

23.5. Camp F at Masada, looking northwest. (Photo by Mars Infomage. Courtesy of Wikimedia Commons [https://creativecommons .org/licenses/by/2.0/deed.en].)

The immediate impact of the large number of forces in the region would have first and foremost been the physical presence of the soldiers, being housed in cities, and the construction of new legionary bases. Unlike the Western Empire, the East was highly urbanized for troops to be billeted in cities, including Nicopolis, Hebron, Neapolis, Emmaus, Samaria-Sebaste, and Eleutheropolis (Isaac 1990: 115–16). At Aelia Capitolina, veterans of the Legio X *Fretensis* were settled in the *colonia* alongside the same legion who now maintained the legionary base there (Isaac 1990: 323–4). Prior to the onset of the Second Jewish Revolt, the Legio VI *Ferrata* was established at a new legionary base built in the Jezreel Valley (at Caparcotna) and remained there until their transfer to Udruh in the early fourth century CE. The legionary presence in peace-time contributed to the overall maintenance of the provincial infrastructure, as well as providing security, which was the primary mechanism by which Roman imperialism prospered. The cultural transformation of a population was a long, and often, piece-meal process; what held the empire together was maintaining security for its masses, coupled with an administration and infrastructure of public amenities that people would chose to utilize. The social impact of the army's presence in the long term would have been the cultural influence and, presumably, the positive Roman sentiment they brought to these communities. Evidence found at production centers, such as the Legio X *Fretensis*'s pottery kilns at Binyanei Ha'uma, show a certain level of self-sufficiency by the legionary bases to produce their own goods in the form of stamped pottery, roof tiles, and stamps to mark bread (Magness 2005). However,

> the army was also a consumer, and settled veterans often resulted in new trade networks and products. Literacy was also high within the army, increasing Greek and Latin usage in the communities where they were settled.

ENTERTAINMENT AND OTHER PUBLIC BUILDINGS

Among Herod's initiatives to adopt Roman practices, he promoted public spectacles and competitions as new entertainment for the provincial population.[1] While the underpinnings of Roman entertainment may have been accelerated under Herod, Greek theaters in the East had existed for centuries. By the mid-first century CE and continuing through the next two centuries, Roman theaters, circuses, and amphitheaters for athletic competitions, circus races, and theatrical and amphitheatrical performances were constructed throughout the province, providing the inhabitants, who came from a veritable range of cultural backgrounds, with various sources of entertainment.[2] During the time of Herod the Great and his successors, very few cities had theaters, hippodromes, or amphitheaters; however, by the end of the first century CE and even more so during the second and third centuries CE, Roman Judaea/Palaestina had many buildings constructed for entertainment (Weiss 2010: 623).

The Hellenistic influence of theaters and their appeal to a broad range of cultural groups led to their construction within the urban layout of many cities, while hippodromes and amphitheaters were later constructions added outside the city, usually in close proximity to roads (Weiss 1999: 23–5). In total, there were an estimated 30 theaters in Judaea/Palaestina during the second through third centuries, while there were only approximately eight hippodromes and five amphitheaters, including those built by Herod at Caesarea, Jerusalem, and Jericho (Humphrey 1996; Weiss 2010: 625).

In Judaea/Palaestina, the hippodrome was used for chariot races and athletic competitions, including gladiatorial and animal games. This made it more interchangeable with the functions often associated with amphitheaters in other parts of the province, which is possibly the reason why so few actual amphitheaters have been identified here (Humphrey 1996: 535–9).

By the first century CE, these entertainment buildings had conformed to a more monumental form compared to their Near Eastern predecessors. Herod's hippodromes at Caesarea, Jericho, and Jerusalem are some of the earliest examples in the province; however, in the case of Caesarea, it was designed according to the Roman model, while most others were a new hybrid plan that combined elements of the hippodrome and amphitheater models (Humphrey 1996: 125–7).

The construction of amphitheaters in the second–third centuries CE suggests a shift in the popularity of certain types of entertainment, particularly from chariot racing to gladiatorial combats (*munera gladiatorum*) and animal baiting, along with a move away from more traditionally Greek games to Roman traditions. Elliptical Roman-style amphitheaters were either renovated from disused hippodromes, such as at Neapolis and Scythopolis, or built as new constructions, as in the case in Eleuthropolis (Weiss 2010: 633).

The theater, hippodrome, and amphitheater were popular institutions among the gentile population prior to and following the region's incorporation into the empire. During the time of Herod and through the first century CE, Jews considered attending the entertainment events at these venues a pagan practice, many of which were held in honor of the emperor and the very buildings themselves decorated with idols (Goodman 1983: 81–3). However, by the second and third centuries CE, many Jews watched and even participated in these entertainment events despite earlier rabbinic objections. An example in the change in rhetoric toward games and spectacles comes from the third-century *amora* Rabbi Shimon ben Pazi: "Happy is the man that has not gone to theaters and circuses of idolaters and has not stood in the way of sinners, [happy is] he who does not attend contests of wild beasts" (b. 'Abod. Zar. 18b, as translated in Weiss 2010: 635–6). There is no prohibition of going to the events or denouncing those who do, but rather he applauds the man who chooses not to take part.

The construction of formal venues for public entertainment and the type of spectacles and games held in them reflect a conscious move toward adopting aspects Roman urban life. While theatrical and athletic performances had been introduced during the Hellenistic period, gladiatorial games and wild beast spectacles were uniquely Roman phenomena. By the third century CE, the Jewish and Gentile communities were brought together to enjoy this Roman tradition. The initial push toward the adoption of Roman forms of entertainment and permanent structures to house them came under Herod; however, their incorporation into the lifeways of the provincial population were the result of the long process of Roman acculturation.

INFRASTRUCTURE

The primary function of roads was the movement of the Roman army and supplies within and through the province. Unlike some of the western provinces, Judaea and the East had a system of roads established as early as the Bronze and Iron Ages, long before Alexander the Great or Pompey marched through the region. Beyond the necessity for troop movement, the road network helped form an integral part of the provincial infrastructure. In addition to building new roads, particularly over difficult terrain, Roman engineering was also used to improve existing roads: bringing the network into the imperial organization with milestones, *caravanserai*, and other facilities that would support military and commercial traffic as well as imperial communications (*cursus publicus*) (Isaac 1990: 109).[3]

Four north–south arteries and a series of connected east–west routes formed the backbone of the Judaea/Palaestina road system, linking the main military and government nodes at Caesarea, Jerusalem, the legionary base at Legio, and the veteran colony at Ptolemais-Acco with other towns, including Scythopolis (army winter quarters), Neapolis, Tiberias, Diospolis, Nicopolis, Eleutheropolis, Caesarea Philippi, Ashkelon, Jaffa, Apollonia, Jericho, and Hebron, leading to neighboring provinces (Isaac 2010: 148).

Much of what is known about this intricate network has come from the numerous inscribed milestones found at intervals all along the roads. Evidence for Rome's increased activity in the province during the second century CE comes from an extensive series of milestones dated to the reign of Hadrian (ca. 120 and 129/130 CE), also a time when the provincial military garrison was doubled and the Roman colony established at Aelia Capitolina in Jerusalem (Isaac 2010: 150). Given the relatively small size of the area, the number of milestones from the first and second centuries is actually quite large, reflecting the significant military forces in the region (Isaac 1990: 108). Following the First Jewish War and continuing through the second century, the army was responsible for monitoring and policing the roads to suppress banditry (*stationarii*) (Fuhrmann 2012: 250).

The functionality of the road network unquestionably benefitted the Roman administration, but it also has a substantial impact on trade and communications across the province and access to the networks beyond it, connecting to larger imperial highways and ports. Prices were intimately tied to the difficultly of moving goods; better roads ultimately led to the ability to transport goods more efficiently, offering consumers greater variety and better market value. The improved and expanded road network also increased the mobility of people, allowing them to interact with other communities, as well as buy and trade products in regional markets.

The road network was only one part of the infrastructure in which the Romans invested; new aqueducts were built and older Herodian and Hellenistic constructions were further maintained due to the expansion of towns, often at the junctures of these roads, and the growing military presence. Of the 28 Greco-Roman water systems, eleven supply urban centers were responsible for their maintenance (Amit, Patrich, and Hirschfeld 2002). Just as the military had been employed in the construction of the roads, they were often the force behind the erection of aqueducts. Epigraphic evidence from the high-level aqueduct at Caesarea refers to detachments of the Roman army (from the Legio X *Fretensis*, Legio VI *Ferrata*, and Legio II *Traiana*) having built

23.6. The remnants of the Roman aqueduct at Caesarea Maritima. (Photo by Mark87. Courtesy of Wikimedia Commons.)

it under the Emperor Hadrian (Lehmann and Holum 2000: 71–7) (Fig. 23.6). Roman aqueducts supplied towns and cities with water for public baths, fountains, and latrines, as well as private households. Often accompanying the construction of aqueducts were sewage systems to carry waste away from urban centers.

BATHS

The use of water in the ancient Mediterranean world was often dictated by what people could store in cisterns from rain, the access to natural springs and rivers, and the building of wells. Generally, water was a valuable commodity used for drinking, while bathing was a distant priority.[4] Baths were an intersection of cultures and social classes, where, in most cases, both sexes used the facilities together. The introduction of Greco-Roman bathhouses in the mid-second century BCE coincides with the appearance of the earliest examples of *miqva'ot* (Reich 1990: 8–9). Use of the baths by the hellenized and gentile population would have been a natural progression from the small baths already in use in the East. Rabbinic sources and archaeological finds refer to Jewish *miqva'ot* within a public bathhouse (Grossberg 2001: 171). Pre-Hellenistic bathing involved a fixed installation (a bathing tub [*loutron*]) within a home; however, Roman baths were a much more public experience (Hoss 2005: 90). This transition from the private to public sphere may have contributed to the adoption of Roman-style baths later in Palestine than in other parts of the Mediterranean. Not only was there a possible reluctance to be naked in public by the inhabitants of Palestine, but, at least among the Jewish population, bathing was a purification process while Roman bathing practices were primarily a daily social event at a public place (Hoss 2005: 91). Those who did partake would have been exposed to a deluge of propaganda through the décor. The imperial cult and the medicinal practices of Asclepius often mingled at the bath complexes, where they were, at times, built in association with local temples, such as at Hammat Gader (Tiberias).

Objections to the use of this Roman institution by the Jewish population range from usage on the Sabbath and the need to continuously fuel the furnaces, to their decoration incorporating sculptures and mosaics of the Roman gods, emperors, and benefactors, providing an outwardly pagan theme – all of this in addition to the obvious salaciousness of the sexes intermingling naked and dressed. However, as Yaron Eliav (2010: 611) points out, Jews on the whole had little opposition to Roman-style bath-houses as an institution; rather, they were a legitimate component of Jewish life. Of course, there were exceptions to this, and questions on an individual basis were raised concerning the impurity of the baths and the idolatry of the décor; however, these objections seem to reflect exceptions to the prevailing acceptance of the practice. We should also acknowledge the unique circumstances of Palestine's absorption into the empire as a heavily hellenized region that may have been more selective in their reception to Roman influence.

Roman technology and engineering allowed for the regular supply of water by way of aqueducts and systems of water transportation developed with the use of Roman concrete, cement, and the arch (Eliav 2010: 606). Early eastern examples of Roman bath complexes can be found at the Herodian palaces of Jericho, Masada (Fig. 23.7), Machaerus, and Herodium (Netzer 2006). Herod's incorporation of Roman-style bathing in his fortified palaces aligns with his overall adoption of many Roman customs and propaganda aimed at winning imperial favor. Beyond Herod's influence, a semi-public Early Roman bath in a large Jewish estate has been identified at Horvat 'Aqav, adjacent to Ramat ha-Nadiv (Hirschfeld 2000: 311–29; Eliav 2010: 609). Early Roman baths of the first century CE have been found just south of Jerusalem in the village of Artas and in the Upper Galilee at Rama (Tzaferis 1980: 66). Over the course of the next two centuries (second–third centuries CE) bathhouses could be found at cities, such as Caesarea Maritima, Tiberias, Sepphoris, and Scythopolis.

23.7. The hypocausts under the floor of the Herodian-period bath at Masada. (Photo by A. Teicher. Courtesy of Wikimedia Commons [https://creativecommons.org/licenses/by/2.5/deed.en].)

CONCLUSIONS

The transition to Roman control of Judaea/Palaestina was felt most in the administrative changes that came with a new imperial government. Cultural changes gradually occurred over time, but many ethnic and societal boundaries remained in place. While material culture is helpful in identifying trends in consumption and transformation of the cultural landscape, its presence does not always directly reflect a specific cultural identity. In the Holy Land, the transition of powers was often just that; while those in power may have changed, the myriad of cultural groups found ways to maintain their distinct lifeways. In many cases, forms of material culture can represent a hybrid of both symbolic and functional value. Certain objects were chosen based on their economic or technical benefits, not necessarily because of the social or cultural implications of their use. Ultimately, preferences in material culture should be viewed as choices made in a local context rather than sweeping provincial-wide changes (Berlin 2002: 57–8).

Roman control over the Holy Land was imposed through the government and army, but the dissemination of Roman lifeways was a gradual process with its roots in the hellenized population. Gentile populations essentially remained culturally Greek and Semitic while embracing "Romanized" lifeways. Similarly, the Jewish population retained its cultural identity despite two wars and an imposed Roman administration. Ultimately, the adoption and rejection of the material culture, beliefs, and activities that characterized Roman life occurred on the level of the individual and community and not under the guise of the broad label "*provincia.*"

NOTES

1 Under Herod, quinquennial games in honor of Augustus were instituted at Jerusalem and Caesarea. Resembling the Olympic Games, they included a range of athletics, horse and chariot races, and musical performances (Josephus, *A.J.* 15.270, 16.136–8).
2 The Roman victory in the First Jewish War led to the introduction of new forms of entertainment. The distinctively Roman gladiatorial combat and wild beast shows were held in the region's northeastern cities, celebrating Titus's victory (Millar 1993: 78). These were a foreign element to even the Hellenistic populations who often found affinities with Roman customs.
3 Road construction was typically a function of the army, carried out in times of peace or immediately following conflicts, sometimes utilizing local labor.
4 Bathing facilities had existed in Judaea/Palaestina prior to the arrival of the Romans. Hybrid Hellenisitic baths were smaller versions that developed out of the Greek gymnasium complex (Fagan 1999: 6).

REFERENCES

Amit, D.; Patrich, J.; and Hirschfeld, Y. 2002. *The Aqueducts of Israel*. JRASup 46. Portsmouth, RI: JRA.

Berlin, A. M. 2002. Romanization and Anti-Romanization in Pre-Revolt Galilee. In *The First Jewish Revolt: Archaeology, History, and Ideology*, ed. A. M. Berlin and J. A. Overman, 57–73. London: Routledge.

Damati, E. 1972. Khirbet el-Muraq. *IEJ* 22: 173.

Eliav, Y. Z. 2010. Bathhouses as Places of Social and Cultural Interaction. In *The Oxford Handbook of Jewish Daily Life in Roman Palestine*, ed. C. Hezser, 605–22. Oxford: Oxford University Press.

Fagan, G. G. 1999. *Bathing in Public in the Roman World*. Ann Arbor: University of Michigan Press.

Fine, S. 2010. Death, Burial, and Afterlife. In *The Oxford Handbook of Jewish Daily Life in Roman Palestine*, ed. C. Hezser, 440–62. Oxford: Oxford University Press.

Fuhrmann, C. J. 2012. *Policing the Roman Empire: Soldiers, Administration, and Public Order*. Oxford: Oxford University Press.

Gardner, G. E. 2014. City of Lights: The Lamps of Roman and Byzantine Jerusalem. *NEA* 77: 284–90.

Goodman, M. 1983. *State and Society in Roman Galilee, A.D. 132–212*. Oxford Centre for Postgraduate Hebrew Studies Series. Totowa, NJ: Rowman & Allanheld.

Grossberg, A. 2001. A Mikveh in the Bathhouse. *Cathedra* 99: 171–84.

Hirschfeld, Y. 1995. *The Palestinian Dwelling in the Roman–Byzantine Period*. SBFCMi 34. Jerusalem: Franciscan Printing Press; IES.

Hirschfeld, Y., ed. 2000. *Ramat Hanadiv Excavations: Final Report of the 1984–1998 Seasons.* Jerusalem: IES.

Hoss, S. 2005. *Baths and Bathing: The Culture of Bathing and Baths and Thermae in Palestine from the Hasmoneans to the Moslem Conquest with an Appendix on Jewish Ritual Baths (Miqva'ot).* Oxford: Archaeopress.

Humphrey, J. H. 1996. Amphitheatrical "Hippo-Stadia." In *Caesarea Maritima: A Retrospective after Two Millennia*, ed. A. Raban and K. G. Holum, 121–9. Documenta et Monumenta Orientis Antiqui 21. Leiden: Brill.

Isaac, B. 1990. *The Limits of Empire: The Roman Army in the East.* Oxford: Clarendon.

——— 2010. Infrastructure. In *The Oxford Handbook of Jewish Daily Life in Roman Palestine*, ed. C. Hezser, 145–64. Oxford: Oxford University Press.

Laurence, R. 1998. Introduction. In *Cultural Identity in the Roman Empire*, ed. R. Laurence and J. Berry, 1–9. London: Routledge.

Lehmann, C. M., and Holum, K. G. 2000. *The Greek and Latin Inscriptions of Caesarea Maritima.* The Joint Expedition to Caesarea Maritima Excavation Reports 5. Boston: ASOR.

Magness, J. 2002. In the Footsteps of the Tenth Roman Legion in Judea. In *The First Jewish Revolt: Archaeology, History, and Ideology*, ed. A. M. Berlin and J. A. Overman, 189–212. London: Routledge.

——— 2005. The Roman Legionary Pottery. In *Excavations on the Site of the Jerusalem International Convention Center (Binyanei Ha'uma): A Settlement of the Late First to Second Temple Period, the Tenth Legion's Kilnworks, and a Byzantine Monastic Complex; The Pottery and Other Small Finds*, ed. B. Arubas and H. Goldfus, 69–191. JRASup 60. Portsmouth, RI: JRA.

——— 2011. *Stone and Dung, Oil and Spit: Jewish Daily Life in the Time of Jesus.* Grand Rapids, MI: Eerdmans.

——— 2013. *The Archaeology of the Holy Land from the Destruction of Solomon's Temple to the Muslim Conquest.* Corr. ed. New York: Cambridge University Press.

Millar, F. 1993. *The Roman Near East, 31 BC–AD 337.* Cambridge, MA: Harvard University Press.

Netzer, E. 2006. *The Architecture of Herod, the Great Builder.* Texte und Studien zum antiken Judentum 117. Tübingen: Mohr Siebeck.

Netzer, E., and Weiss, Z. 1994. *Zippori.* Jerusalem: IES.

Reich, R. 1990. *Miqwa'ot (Jewish Ritual Baths) in Eretz-Israel, in Second Temple, Mishnah and Talmud Periods*, PhD diss., The Hebrew University of Jerusalem.

Reisner, G. A.; Fisher, C. S.; and Lyon D. G. 1924. *Harvard Excavations at Samaria 1908–1910*, Vol. 1. HSS 1. Cambridge, MA: Harvard University Press.

Rosenthal-Heginbottom, R. 2014. Imported Hellenistic and Early Roman Pottery – An Overview of the Finds from the Jewish Quarter Excavations. In *Jewish Quarter Excavations in the Old City of Jerusalem, Conducted by Nahman Avigad, 1969–1982*, Vol. 6: *Areas J, N, Z and Other Studies; Final Report*, ed. H. Geva, 377–413. Jerusalem: IES; The Institute of Archaeology, The Hebrew University of Jerusalem.

Talgam, R. 2014. *Mosaics of Faith: Floors of Pagans, Jews, Samaritans, Christians, and Muslims in the Holy Land.* Jerusalem: Yad Izhak Ben-Zvi; State College, PA: The Pennsylvania State University Press.

Tsuf, O. 2011. The Jaffa-Jerusalem Relationship during the Early Roman Period in Light of Jewish-Judean Pottery at Jaffa. In *The History and Archaeology of Jaffa*, Vol. 1, ed. M. Peilstöcker and A. A. Burke, 271–90. JCHPS 1; MonArch 26. Los Angeles: The Cotsen Institute of Archaeology Press.

Tzaferis, V. 1980. A Roman Bath at Rama. *'Atiqot* 14: 66–75.
Ward-Perkins, J. B. 1974. *Roman Imperial Architecture*. History of World Architecture. New York: Abrams.
Weiss, Z. 1999. Adopting a Novelty: The Jews and the Roman Games in Palestine. In *The Roman and Byzantine Near East,* Vol. 2: *Some Recent Archaeological Research*, ed. J. H. Humphrey, 23–49. JRASup 31. Portsmouth, RI: JRA.
   2010. Theatres, Hippodromes, Amphitheatres, and Performances. In *The Oxford Handbook of Jewish Daily Life in Roman Palestine*, ed. C. Hezser, 623–40. Oxford: Oxford University Press.
Wexler, L., and Gilboa, G. 1996. Oil Lamps of the Roman Period from Apollonia-Arsuf. *TA* 23: 115–31.

TWENTY FOUR

THE SOCIAL ARCHAEOLOGY OF THE SOUTHERN LEVANT IN THE BYZANTINE PERIOD

Rethinking the Material Evidence

ITAMAR TAXEL

The southern Levant, and more specifically the area of historical Palestine and part of modern Jordan, was one of the most pivotal territories of the early Byzantine Empire. The administrative division of the region, which can also be viewed as the greater Holy Land, was crystallized around 400 CE[1] and includes the provinces of Palaestine (divided in its turn to Prima, Secunda, and Tertia), the western part of Arabia, and the southern part of Phoenice. Since Constantine the Great became sole emperor of the Christianized Roman Empire in 324 CE and until the accomplishment of the region's conquest by the Arab Muslims in 640 CE, the Christian Byzantine regime has left a unique imprint on the local landscape and population, first and foremost through Christianity and its many physical and ideological expressions. Yet, the religious and ethnic makeup of the discussed region was far more complex; despite the empire's formal Christianization, the population of Palaestina, Arabia, and Phoenice remained predominantly polytheist well into the fifth century CE (if not until the sixth century in some areas), while prominent minorities of Jews and Samaritans resided mainly in Palaestina and certain locations in Arabia and Phoenice. This population, which by ca. 600 CE numbered, at least in Palestine proper, some one million people (its peak in antiquity), lived in a few dozen urban and semi-urban centers, and mostly in hundreds – if not thousands – of villages, hamlets, farms, and monasteries of various types and standings. It should be, therefore, no surprise that this three century-long process of settlement and population growth and economic prosperity[2] has resulted in a plethora of contemporaneous literary sources and especially numerous archaeological remains, which have been documented in virtually every part of the region.[3]

Indeed, the exploration of sites and remains dated to the Byzantine – or late antique (roughly fourth to eighth centuries CE) – era occupies a substantial share of the highly intensive archaeological activity carried out throughout the southern Levant, especially in modern Israel, since the early twentieth century (see Taxel 2013). Various historical and archaeological aspects of the Byzantine/late antique period in the southern Levant have been studied in recent decades, while contributing to our understanding of the region's urban and rural society, economy, and material culture. Nevertheless, many issues still await more serious scholarly treatment. Recently, Luke Lavan (2013: 53–5) determined what he believes are "four strands of thought which suggest a distinctive archaeology of Late Antiquity," namely: (1) "the opportunities afforded by exceptional preservation;" (2) "the analysis of the newly built architecture and newly made material culture of the period;" (3) "the study of the archaeology of reoccupation and reuse in a civilization which had inherited venerable buildings and objects from a very old cultural tradition;" and (4) "the development of thematic research strategies adapted to key questions we pose of Late Antiquity (both culturally specific and generic but neglected subject areas)." Regarding the final point, Lavan mentioned various themes – associated with either architectural or artifactual remains – "in which we happen to have Late Antique gaps." In his article, Lavan concentrated on the third research subject, which he described as "the archaeology of use/reuse and occupation/reoccupation – with a focus of pre-existing classical buildings." In my view, though, the concepts of use and reuse, or – in other words – the use-life of man-made products (which forms part of their more extended life cycle), should include not only the architectural/monumental medium but also smaller artifacts preserved in archaeological context.

In what follows, I would like to shed light on selected thematic issues, which partially depart from Lavan's third and fourth "strands" as I interpret them, that, as many other themes, have barely been studied in relation to the Byzantine period in our region (regardless of the question whether they are unique to this period). In these case studies, I primarily use excavated material culture evidence – both structures and objects – while reevaluating these finds in order to better understand specific aspects of Byzantine-period social life and daily behavior. Obviously, the limited scope of the present contribution allows for only snapshots of these issues; each holds the potential of being fully developed in future scholarly work.

OBJECTS' BIOGRAPHY, PEOPLE'S BIOGRAPHY: THE CERAMIC EVIDENCE

Recent decades have seen a dramatic increase in studies dedicated to a variety of subjects related to the broader discipline of behavioral archaeology. Much of this research has tackled the complicated issue of the biography, or life cycle, of man-produced landscapes and elements, notably portable artifacts, while being based on pioneering anthropological, ethno-archaeological, and sociological works on the subject, such as those of Igor Kopytoff (1986) and Michael Brian Schiffer (1995; 1996). The basic premise behind these studies is that objects change and accumulate histories through their existence; hence, it should be possible to reveal relationships between people and objects by unraveling object histories. Pottery vessels constitute one of the most intensively studied classes of artifacts in this respect, since ceramics have played a major role in almost every aspect of daily life in antiquity and among many present-day societies alike (e.g., Skibo 1992; 2013). This was, of course, also true for the ancient Mediterranean, especially during the Roman period and late antiquity, when numerous production centers mass-produced a variety of ceramic forms that were often traded across substantial distances either for their own value or the commodities they contained. The most comprehensive recent study on this subject (Peña 2007) has inspired several other works, which focus from various perspectives on pottery life cycle and disposal practices in the Greek, Roman, and late antique world (e.g., Lawall and Lund 2011). However, the eastern Mediterranean and the Levant in particular have rarely been discussed in this respect; yet, this lacuna is intended to be overcome by thorough research carried out on the life cycle of ceramics in Palestine during late antiquity and the Early Middle Ages (i.e., the end of the Roman, Byzantine, and Early Islamic periods), based on archaeological and literary evidence (Taxel in press a).

One of the behavioral practices within the life cycle of ceramics, which is clearly discernible archaeologically (and, at times, textually), can testify to the mental, social, and economic circumstances that lay at its basis: reuse. It is determined as the transformation of vessels from one state to another in the systemic context (namely, in a human behavioral system), while the utilized vessel may have been reused for a purpose similar to or different from its original use, in the latter case, either without being modified or after some physical modification (J. Theodore Peña's Types A, B, and C reuse, respectively [2007: 10]). A reused ceramic item can be represented by a complete or near-complete vessel, a vessel with detached part(s), a holed or pieced vessel, or by a detached/cut/broken vessel part.

Of all the ceramic classes documented in the archaeological record of these periods in Palestine (and elsewhere), transport amphorae and storage jars – first and foremost the locally produced bag-shaped jars and so-called Gaza amphorae – present the highest ratios and most varied practices of reuse. The reuse of other ceramic classes, namely table, cooking, and utilitarian[4] wares and lamps, as well as architectural ceramics (roof tiles and flat bricks), was much more peripheral and inconsistent. In my study, I have thus far identified twenty-five major reuse practices related to these vessel classes and architectural ceramics, as summarized in Table 24.1.

TABLE 24.1. *Summary of ceramics' reuse practices in Late Roman, Byzantine, and Early Islamic Palestine.*

Reuse Practice	Vessel/Artifact Class	Notes
Packaging container	Transport/storage wares	
Storage container	Transport/storage wares; closed tablewares; open and closed cooking wares; closed utilitarian wares; lamps	The storing or hoarding of coins and other valuables was especially common using small- or medium-sized closed vessel forms other than transport/storage wares.
Water drawing vessel	Transport/storage wares; closed tablewares; closed utilitarian wares	
Settling vat/sump	Transport/storage wares; open tablewares; open utilitarian wares	
Pipe	Transport/storage wares; closed utilitarian wares	
Bellows	Transport/storage wares	
Architectural element	Transport/storage wares	
Fish nest	Transport/storage wares	
Oven/hearth or brazier	Transport/storage wares; open utilitarian wares	
Bowl/basin or trough	Transport/storage wares; closed utilitarian wares	
Stand or prop	Transport/storage wares	
Obstruction/regulation (?) device	Transport/storage wares	
Dovecote	Transport/storage wares	
Strainer	Transport/storage wares; closed utilitarian wares	
Funnel	Transport/storage wares; closed utilitarian wares	
Libation conduit	Transport/storage wares	
Burial container	Transport/storage wares	
Grave marker	Transport/storage wares	
Grinding, polishing, or scooping implement	Transport/storage wares; open tablewares	
Body hygiene implement	Transport/storage wares	
Stopper, gaming piece/token, spindle whorl, or toy	Transport/storage wares; tablewares; cooking wares; utilitarian wares	This category is usually represented by plain or pierced sherd disks, the great majority of which were made of transport/storage ware fragments.

(cont.)

TABLE 24.1. *(cont.)*

Reuse Practice	Vessel/Artifact Class	Notes
Epigraphic media	Thinspun/ground mirror; closed utilitarian wares	
Foundation or termination offering	Open tablewares (?); closed cooking wares	
Paving tile	Architectural ceramics (roof tiles)	
Baking tray, grinding palette (?), or lid/stopper	Architectural ceramics (roof tiles and flat bricks)	

Indeed, the reuse of pottery vessels and vessel parts, including many of the abovementioned practices, is archaeologically attested in the southern Levant in earlier and later periods as well. However, virtually every archaeologist working in the region is well acquainted with the enormous quantities of potsherds associated with almost every excavated or surveyed Byzantine/late antique-period context. This outstanding ubiquity is the result of the intensity of contemporaneous settlement and human activity, and the mass production and mass consumption of ceramics and/or the foodstuffs marketed in them (in the case of amphorae and certain storage jars), which specifically characterized the time period of the fourth to seventh centuries CE. Thus, the ratio – and variety – of the behavioral practices of ceramics' reuse are understandably higher in the archaeological record of the Byzantine southern Levant, which likely reflects actual past reality.

Nevertheless, it seems that yet another agent has contributed to the increasing reuse of pottery vessels by the local population. A prominent characteristic of the region's Byzantine material culture – and hence of the mentality of the population who produced, used, and maintained it – is a tendency toward pragmatism, if not, at times, economic frugality. This down-to-earth attitude is best reflected by the contemporaneous architecture in town and country, with the triumph of a new functional, haphazard, private-oriented building tradition that served economic and individual interests, and the widespread use of *spolia* in both public and private buildings (see Taxel 2010: 84–5; in press b). Thus, similar to the reuse of spoliated architectural elements, the reuse of pottery was naturally embedded in the daily behavior of people everywhere across the Byzantine southern Levant (and beyond), a tendency which continued into the following centuries. This was despite, if not because of, the low economic value of pottery vessels (including those which were considered luxurious), certainly in the atmosphere of mass production and consumption typical to the Byzantine southern Levant.

According to Peña, this behavior in the greater Roman world:

> involved the casual, adventitious use of vessels and vessel parts that happened to be at hand ..., whereas in others it involved the careful

modification of vessels or vessel parts to render these suitable for some specific purpose ... In some cases vessels and/or vessel parts were systematically and intensively reused for an application different from that for which they had been manufactured/acquired ..., and in some cases practices of this sort were so widespread they may have satisfied a significant portion of the demand for objects intended to fulfill that particular function ..., reducing or eliminating altogether the need to manufacture objects specifically for that purpose. (2007: 320–1)

With respect to the reuse practices described in Table 24.1, the modification of vessels or vessel parts is illustrated, for instance, by finds from seventh-century contexts at the harbor town of Yavneh-Yam.[5] These include the reuse of three vessels (an amphora and a storage jar with detached upper sections and a complete cooking pot) as sunken storage facilities in a room's floor (Fig. 24.1), the reuse of amphora bases as stoppers (Fig. 24.2:1, 2), and the reuse of a jar's detached upper section as a funnel (Fig. 24.2:3). As to more casual or spontaneous behaviors of reuse, noteworthy is an anecdotal testimony given by the late sixth–early seventh-century CE monk John Moschos in one of the supplementary tales to his *Pratum spirituale*. In that story about a certain Palestinian communal monastery, Moschos tells that one of the monks stole the shawl of another monk and hid it inside a *Gazition* (Gaza amphora), which was in his cell (Nissen 1938: suppl. tale 9). Regardless of whether this tale is fiction or based on a true event, it contains a few important details about daily life in Byzantine Palestine – in monastic and non-monastic communities alike. First, it is evident that empty transport amphorae were often kept after being emptied of their original contents in order to be reused for various purposes; in Moschos's tale, this was a Gaza amphora, which was likely empty and apparently washed when it was reused as a hiding place for the stolen shawl. Second, some of these reuse practices could have been ad hoc solutions for urgent needs, as indicated by the aforementioned story.

LIVING IN THE FIELD: THE MULTIFACETED MEANING OF ARTIFACTS IN AGRICULTURAL CONTEXTS

When one thinks about a domestic context in antiquity, one would usually imagine typical residential spaces in which people lived and acted, usually on a permanent scale throughout the day, first and foremost dwellings. The most typical activities associated with domestic contexts are food preparation and consumption, habitation/sleeping, production of various commodities (usually for self-consumption, such as textiles), personal hygiene, and small- to medium-scale storage (notably of foodstuff). However, this category also includes other types of residence-related spheres, where activity has taken place during parts of the day or at specific times of the year and was often characterized by only part of the abovementioned activities.

A good example for such a seasonal/temporal form of occupation is agricultural watchtowers/booths. Such features are well known in certain regions of Palestine, especially in parts of the Negev and the central hill country, where they were usually dated to the Byzantine period and documented as isolated structures in the rural landscape (usually within the area of terraced or fenced fields), sometimes with an apparent spatial/functional relation to other elements, such as winepresses. These watchtowers/booths are small, usually single-roomed, square/rectangular (seldom round) structures whose inner dimensions are rarely larger than ca. 3 × 3 m. Elements of this kind – though usually somewhat larger in size – have formed part of the traditional Palestinian agricultural landscape well into the twentieth century. Local ethnographic evidence from the nineteenth and twentieth centuries has shown that each of these structures was owned by a given peasant family, and the entire family often lived in its watchtower/booth during part or all of the summer and early autumn seasons (the main harvest time) in order to save the time needed to move from the permanent residence in the village/farmstead and back and to prevent thieves and unwanted strangers from stealing the crop. At the same time, the structures were also used for the storage of harvested fruits, products processed from them, tools, and other needed equipment. During the rest of the year, the watchtowers/booths usually remained unused (Ron 1977: 25–60).

Based on these parallels, scholars today agree that watchtowers/booths in antiquity basically fulfilled the same purposes (e.g., Decker 2006: 501–3). However, contra to what is known about modern structures of this kind, it was claimed that the ancient structures "lack the space to be full-time residences" (Decker 2006: 516). Still, this claim has yet to be examined against the artifactual evidence. Indeed, a review of the ceramics and other finds retrieved from excavated watchtowers/booths of the Byzantine and beginning of the Early Islamic periods clearly shows that certain daytime and/or nighttime domestic activities – notably food preparation and consumption – did occur in these spaces during at least several days or weeks of the year. The ceramic assemblages associated with these structures are usually modest and – judging by their predominantly fragmentary state – apparently reflect objects discarded at their locations of use or left behind after an activity area has been cleaned up. The pottery represented in these assemblages is a microcosm of the often more varied ceramic finds known from full-scale, contemporaneous, residential contexts – namely, it includes a limited variety of table, cooking, utilitarian, and storage wares. Some watchtowers/booths also yielded modest quantities of glass fragments, stone and metal artifacts, and coins. Notable examples include

24.1. At Yavneh-Yam, an amphora, storage jar, and cooking pot reused as sunken storage facilities in a room's floor. (The clay oven in front of the first two vessels in the upper image is from an earlier phase.) (© M. Fischer and I. Taxel)

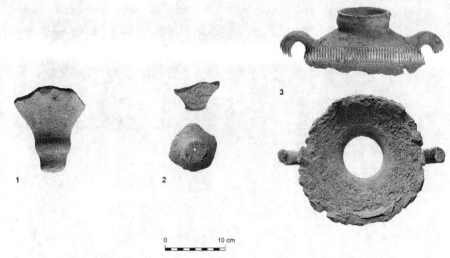

24.2. At Yavneh-Yam, (1, 2) amphora bases, one with a drilled hole, reused as stoppers; and (3) an upper section of a storage jar, reused as a funnel (note the incrustation of a semifluid substance, probably mortar/plaster mixture, on the interior). (© M. Fischer and I. Taxel)

Beersheva (Sontag 2000), Nahal Yattir (Haiman 2008) (Fig. 24.3), Qedumim (Maharian 2000), and the environs of Ḥorbat Anusha and Ḥorbat Leved (Sion et al. 2007: 123–5, 127–9).

A noteworthy detail common to all of these and other published assemblages is the total absence of lamps. This is not to say that lamps were never used in watchtowers/booths; it can only be speculated that their remains were not found by archaeologists, or the occupants took the lamps with them when departing the structures while leaving behind only broken or otherwise unusable vessels. On the other hand, one would suggest that people's presence and activity in and around the isolated watchtowers/booths was largely confined to daylight hours,[6] which may support Michael Decker's abovementioned claim, rejecting their use as full-time residences. Also, the apparent lack of large, heavy grinding and milling stone implements from these structures indicates that the processing of raw foodstuffs was rarely carried out there; the people who used these spaces likely brought with them ready-made food and/or ingredients from their permanent residences that did not necessitate intensive processing before eating/cooking.

Another type of architecturally or spatially independent agricultural context relevant to the present discussion is winepresses, which existed separately from settlements, namely in the agricultural landscape that surrounded them. Indeed, such elements usually yield very limited and/or fragmentary/worn artifactual assemblages, which more often than not represent later activities within the winepress or in its immediate vicinity (in this case, the material could be either contemporaneous with or later than the winepress). Still, the possibility that some of the ceramics and other objects deposited inside and

SOCIAL ARCHAEOLOGY IN THE BYZANTINE PERIOD

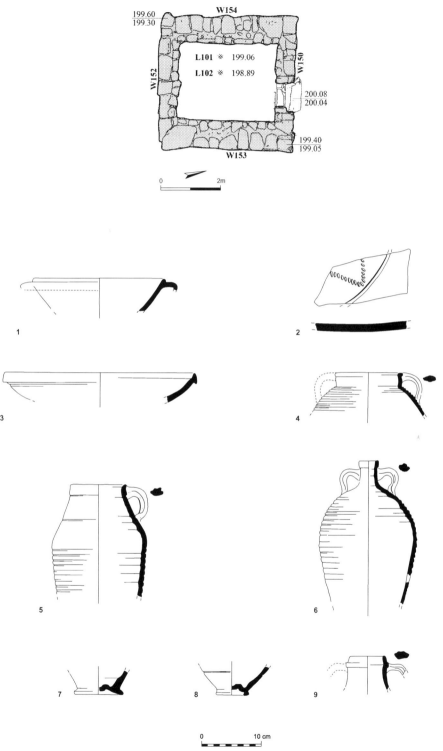

24.3. A plan of the watchtower/booth and selected ceramic finds from Nahal Yattir (after Haiman 2008: figs. 1, 2). (Courtesy of the IAA.)

around such features (regardless of the cause of deposition) represents domestic activities contemporaneous with and related to their original use should not be ruled out. The most obvious domestic activity of this kind is the preparation and consumption of food by the laborers who operated the installations or worked in the surrounding lands (as demonstrated also by ethnographic parallels from nineteenth- and twentieth-century Palestine and Transjordan). Thus, Byzantine-period table, cooking, storage, and/or utilitarian wares and lamps, and sometimes other artifact classes which are found – albeit as secondary refuse assemblages – dumped into contemporaneous Palestinian winepresses, may, in part, represent such an activity. This is demonstrated by the finds from Tirat Karmel (Segal 2007) (Fig. 24.4) and Ḥorbat Bustan (Talmi and Katsnelson 2015) on Mount Carmel, and Ḥorbat Kosit in the central coastal plain (Masarwa 2004).

Possible artistic illustrations of the presence (and use) of pottery vessels in agricultural landscapes are provided by mosaic floors from two Byzantine-period Palestinian churches. At Be'er Shema‘ in the northwestern Negev, an amphora or large double-handled jug is shown hanging by a rope from a vine beside a man playing a flute. At Jabaliyah near Gaza, two amphorae are depicted hanging by a rope from fruit trees as part of pastoral scenes (see Talgam 2014: 104, 110, figs. 144, 156). These depictions are likely based on actual daily scenes, with the abovementioned ceramic containers apparently holding wine or drinking water consumed by agricultural laborers.[7]

TRACING WOMEN AND MEN IN THE PRIVATE SPHERE

The study of gender has become in recent decades a legitimate discipline in archaeological research, while encompassing a steadily increasing number of theoretical and material-based works.[8] This is also true for the Greco-Roman world, especially in the central Mediterranean and Europe (e.g., Allison 2013; 2015; Foxhall 2013), though a few recent studies discuss gender-related issues in the eastern Roman provinces and the Byzantine world as well (e.g., Cassis 2008; see below). With respect to these periods and regions, the rich literary and epigraphic record comes to our aid in order to better identify and understand the presence of women, men, and sometimes children in various archaeologically documented contexts, notably typical private domestic spaces but also in military, public, and funerary ones; these attempts have usually been made by analyzing both the architectural/spatial spaces and the artifacts they contained. Yet, very few of those studies have been dedicated to the southern Levant during the Roman and Byzantine periods, despite the abundance of excavated archaeological remains and the plethora of textual sources. Below, I refer to these works while briefly touching on some relevant themes in the archaeology of the Byzantine southern Levant.

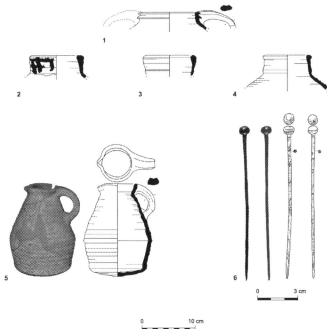

24.4. A general view of the winepress and selected ceramic and metal finds at Tirat Karmel (after Segal 2007: figs. 2, 4). (Courtesy of the IAA.)

In accordance with the growing acknowledgment that dwellings in antiquity (the Byzantine period included) were more often than not multi-functional dynamic entities which housed a variety of activities carried out by different people – men, women, and children of different ages and statuses –

within the course of different temporal units (parts of the day or year), scholars also agree that "it is not easy or probably appropriate to think of houses as either being exclusively gendered spaces or having specifically prominent spaces" (Foxhall 2013: 115–25; cf., specifically for Roman Dura-Europos and Roman-Byzantine Galilee, Meyers 2007: 116–23 and Baird 2014: 211–15). Still, certain material culture media can be attributed to daily roles fulfilled predominantly by women (regardless of their social status) in most households, notably certain grinding and milling implements, food preparation devices (ovens and the like, and cooking vessels), and loom weights/spindle whorls, thus – especially when found *in situ* – allowing for the identification of specific spaces within domiciles where activities were taken care of by women during at least part of the day; similarly, jewelry, especially bracelets and earrings, are usually considered as feminine characteristics.[9] On the contrary, artifacts associated with personal hygiene and health, such as spatulas and glass unguentaria/tubes, are more ambiguous in this respect and could have been equally used by women and men, albeit apparently more frequently by the former. Needles, too, are less gender-specific objects, even if in practice they were used mostly by women for both cloth working and hair arranging (O'Hea 2000; Allison 2013: 79–82, 93–8, 100–3; 2015: 110–15).

Turning to the archaeological remains of dwelling complexes in the Byzantine southern Levant, it would be obvious, therefore, to claim that regular civic settlement and habitation forms (namely, urban centers, villages, and farms) were inhabited by both men and women, and the past presence of both sexes in a given domestic sphere can be deduced in almost every case. Thus, village dwellings, such as those excavated at 'Ein Gedi (on the western Dead Sea shore) exhibit a variety of spaces that were either mono- or multifunctional but, at any rate, were likely used – simultaneously and/or during different times – by both men and women. In addition, these structures normally yielded stationary cooking/baking devices (Hirschfeld 2007: 50–93, *passim*) and a variety of grinding and milling implements (Sidi 2007: 546–55, pls. 3–11) that can at least partially be associated with female labor. Here, it is worth mentioning the suggestion by Carol Meyers (2008: 70) that certain types of grinding/milling implements in Roman–Byzantine Galilee (and presumably the entire southern Levantine territory) were used by women, while others were operated by men, as they required a more "professional" manpower, which, in her view, was associated with commercialized flour production. To the first category, Meyers attributed the simple grinding bowls/mortars, the saddle quern, and the rotary quern; to the last category, she ascribed the frame or so-called Olynthus mill and the donkey or Pompeian mill. Although in reality this division was probably less clear-cut, it suggests that domestic complexes in which grinding and milling implements of both categories (though mostly of the former) are found – such as in the case of 'Ein Gedi – both men but usually women were engaged in flour production for the households' daily needs.

But what about other settlement forms, to which one, usually less automatically, assigns a feminine presence? Penelope Allison (2013) has already shown – based on textual and material evidence – that Roman military bases, especially the largest ones, were typically inhabited not only by masculine military troops but also by a certain number of women (and sometimes children) that represented the former's family members and apparently some hired civilian personnel. This was also true for at least some of the Late Roman and Byzantine fortresses documented in the Levant's southern fringe zones. For instance, the large legionary fort of el-Lejjūn on the Kerak Plateau (early fourth to mid-sixth century CE) had an extramural *vicus*, namely a complex of various buildings that *inter alia* housed the civilian population – family members included – annexed to the army units. This *vicus* was abandoned in the late fourth century, and its inhabitants probably moved into the fortress, which, by that time, was occupied by fewer soldiers. In the excavations of part of the *vicus* and especially of the fortress' barracks was retrieved a large variety of small artifacts associated with women and children – bone hairpins, jewelry (including earrings and bracelets) made of various materials, and spindle whorls, which were interpreted as reflecting the soldiers' families (McDaniel 2006: 299–310, figs. 2, 3, 5, 6, 8, 10, 14, 19, 20, *passim*; Parker 2006: 561). In smaller contemporaneous fortresses excavated in the region the question of feminine presence seems to be somewhat more ambiguous. In the sixth–seventh-century fortress of 'En Boqeq on the western Dead Sea shore, no spindle whorls and almost no typical female jewelry (with the exception of one glass bracelet [Gichon 1993: 434–6, pl. 60:36]) were found. However, the excavations yielded some rotary millstones (Gichon 1993: 437–8, pl. 59:3–6) and a 0.75-meter-long wooden object that was identified as a weaving sword, an implement commonly used in ancient cloth making (Sheffer and Tidhar 1991: 29, fig. 30). The rotary querns, despite their initial identification with women's labor (cf. Meyers' view [see above]), could of course be operated by men, so also for the weaving sword and the other loom equipment originally associated with it. As noted by Allison (2013: 93–4), the literary evidence from the Roman period indicates that men were sometimes engaged in weaving, and this task may have taken place in military contexts. Yet, the single glass bracelet may indicate that women were occasionally present in the fortress, though the nature of these individuals is unknown. At the fourth-century fortress of Yotvata in the Aravah Valley, no jewelry (glass or otherwise) was found at all, which Carolyn Swan tends to attribute to the "absence of a civilian population in or around the fort" (2015: 160). The lack of clear evidence of female presence in the fortress was also

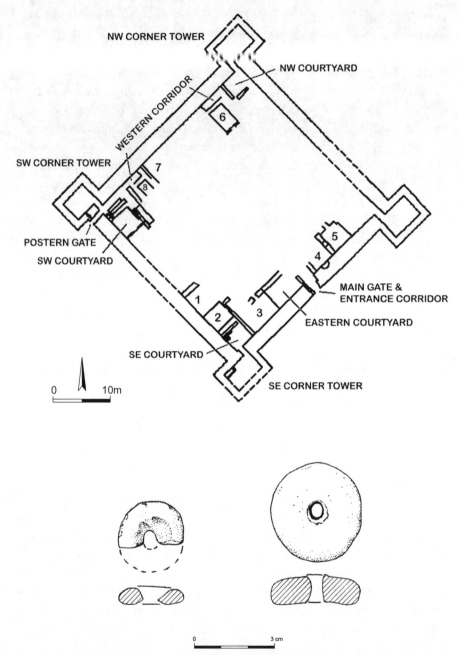

24.5. A plan of the fort and two spindle whorls found in it at Yotvata (after Davies and Magness 2015: fig. 7 and Ratzlaff 2015: fig. 5.8: 31, 32). (Courtesy of J. Magness, G. Davies, and Eisenbrauns.)

expressed by one of the site's excavators (J. Magness, pers. comm., 2015), though at least two spindle whorls were reported by Alexandra Ratzlaff (2015: 201, 211, fig. 5.8: 31, 32) (Fig. 24.5) as recovered in contexts belonging to the fortress phase (the site also had post-fortress phases). Although meager, the spindle whorls' evidence is, in my opinion, firmer than, say, glass bracelets, to suggest that the population of the Yotvata fortress included a certain female component during at least part of its existence.[10]

SUMMARY

In her article on women in the Byzantine archaeological record, Marica Cassis (2008: 153) claimed that "[g]endered archaeology is not about attempting to locate particular women, but rather about attempting to place women into the picture of the past and to understand the creation of sites within the context of a complete society. In order to do so, it is necessary to ask different questions of the excavated material." Here, I have attempted to demonstrate a few of those different questions that – after about a century of archaeological investigation of Byzantine remains in the southern Levant – should be asked of the highly rich material evidence that constantly comes to light in local excavations and surveys. The three case studies presented above – ceramics' life cycle, off-site agricultural structures, and the tracing of women and men in domestic contexts and the like – and the specific questions I presently asked of them display in a nutshell the scholarly potential of these and many other themes of the archaeology of the Byzantine period. The society – the people behind the objects and structures – of the Byzantine southern Levant, their daily behavior, mentality, movement between locations, and social affiliations can be further unveiled by tackling new or lesser-studied research fields and gleaning from them the answers to our questions.

NOTES

1 I wish to thank Yulia Gotlieb (Institute of Archaeology, Tel Aviv University) for her assistance in preparing the illustrations for this article.
2 Albeit not necessarily geographically and temporally uniform (see Taxel in press b, with references).
3 For general reviews on Byzantine Palestine and Jordan, see Tsafrir, Di Segni, and Green 1994; Patrich 1995; Parker 1999; and Watson 2001. For the region's population, settlement patterns and economy, see more specifically Dauphin 1998; Bar 2008; Decker 2009; and Taxel in press b.
4 This functional class is represented by a variety of small- to medium-sized open and closed vessels that were employed for the preparation, processing and/or short- and long-term storage of food and other substances, as well as for a variety of specialized purposes. Such vessels include basins, *mortaria*, jugs, juglets, small jars, flasks, water-wheel jars, funnels, chamber pots, incense burners, etc. Needless to mention, some of these forms could fulfill a multifunctional designation, usually as tablewares.
5 The Yavneh-Yam excavations were directed by Moshe Fischer in 1992–2011 (since 2005, under the codirection of Fischer and myself) on behalf of Tel Aviv University. The final report is in preparation.

6 Lamps are often found in an intact or near-complete state in various archaeological contexts, which indicates their relative durability to post-depositional agents compared to most other vessel forms and possibly their higher resistance rate within activity contexts in antiquity as well. Still, lamps – as other small, closed vessels – were broken from time to time, and if lamps were regularly used in small agricultural watchtowers/booths, we would expect to find at least a few lamp fragments in some of the excavated structures.

7 These mosaic scenes may support Tim Ingold's (1993: 167–8) claim that certain trees constitute features or particular places by themselves in agricultural "taskscapes," as they are bound up in the lives of the people who work around them and use them for their needs. Interestingly, the painting Ingold (1993: 164–71) used to illustrate his ideas – *The Harvesters*, by Pieter Bruegel the Elder (from 1565) – shows ceramic vessels as components of various pastoral activities. Despite the temporal and cultural differences between the scenes shown in the Byzantine-period Palestinian mosaics and the Dutch Renaissance painting, they have much in common, both in their contents and their importance as illustrations of activities – and their associated artifacts – which are nearly invisible in the archaeological record.

8 So is the field of childhood archaeology, which is often naturally linked to gendered archaeology (see Lillehammer 2010 and – more specifically for the Byzantine world – Pitarakis 2009).

9 See Cassis 2008: 152; Meyers 2008; Allison 2013: 94–5; Foxhall 2013: 121; and Baird 2014: 220–3, 229. For gendered objects in Byzantine-period funerary assemblages, see Tal and Taxel 2015: 105, 197–8.

10 Still, one presumably should not automatically expect to find spindle whorls in every context known as having been inhabited – even predominantly – by women. This is indicated by the excavations of the Byzantine and Early Islamic monastery at Ḥorvat Ḥani, which, according to one of its mosaic inscriptions, functioned as a nunnery. Nonetheless, not even one spindle whorl was found at the site (U. Dahari, pers. comm., 2015), though this absence may be related to the general paucity of finds in the excavations (Dahari and Zelinger 2014: 191).

REFERENCES

Allison, P. M. 2013. *People and Spaces in Roman Military Bases*. Cambridge: Cambridge University Press.

2015. Characterizing Roman Artifacts to Investigate Gendered Practices in Contexts without Sexed Bodies. *AJA* 119: 103–23.

Baird, J. A. 2014. *The Inner Lives of Ancient Houses: An Archaeology of Dura-Europos*. Oxford: Oxford University Press.

Bar, D. 2008. *"Fill the Earth": Settlement in Palestine during the Late Roman and Byzantine Periods, 135–640 C.E.* Jerusalem: Yad Izhak Ben-Zvi (Hebrew).

Cassis, M. C. 2008. A Restless Silence: Women in the Byzantine Archaeological Record. In *The World of Women in the Ancient and Classical Near East*, ed. B. Alpert Nakhai, 139–54. Newcastle upon Tyne: Cambridge Scholars.

Dahari, U., and Zelinger, Y. 2014. The Excavation at Ḥorvat Ḥani – Final Report and a Survey on Nuns and Nunneries in Israel. In *Knowledge and Wisdom: Archaeological and Historical Essays in Honour of Leah Di Segni*, ed. G. C. Bottini, L. D. Chrupcała, and J. Patrich, 179–203. SBFCMa 54. Milan: Terra Santa.

Dauphin, C. 1998. *La Palestine byzantine: Peuplement et populations*. BAR International Series 726. Oxford: Archaeopress.
Davies, G., and Magness, J. 2015. The 2003–2007 Excavations: Architecture and Stratigraphy. In *The 2003–2007 Excavations in the Late Roman Fort at Yotvata*, ed. G. Davies and J. Magness, 1–68. Winona Lake, IN: Eisenbrauns.
Decker, M. 2006. Towers, Refuges, and Fortified Farms in the Late Roman East. *LibAnn* 56: 499–520.
2009. *Tilling the Hateful Earth: Agricultural Production and Trade in the Late Antique East*. Oxford Studies in Byzantium. Oxford: Oxford University Press.
Foxhall, L. 2013. *Studying Gender in Classical Antiquity*. Key Themes in Ancient History. Cambridge: Cambridge University Press.
Gichon, M. 1993. *En Boqeq: Ausgrabungen in einer Oase am Toten Meer*, Vol. 1: *Geographie und Geschichte der Oase; Das spätrömanisch-byzantinische Kastell*. Mainz am Rhein: Zabern.
Haiman, M. 2008. Nahal Yattir. *HA–ESI* 120. www.hadashot-esi.org.il/Report_Detail_Eng.aspx?id=740&mag_id=114 (accessed August 3, 2017).
Hirschfeld, Y. 2007. Architecture and Stratigraphy. In *En-Gedi Excavations II: Final Report (1996–2002)*, ed. Y. Hirschfeld, 23–156. Jerusalem: IES; The Institute of Archaeology, The Hebrew University of Jerusalem.
Ingold, T. 1993. The Temporality of the Landscape. *WA* 25: 152–74.
Kopytoff, I. 1986. The Cultural Biography of Things: Commoditization as Process. In *The Social Life of Things: Commodities in Cultural Perspective*, ed. A. Appadurai, 64–92. Cambridge: Cambridge University Press.
Lavan, L. A. 2013. Distinctive Field Methods for Late Antiquity: Some Suggestions. In *Field Methods and Post-Excavation Techniques in Late Antique Archaeology*, ed. L. A. Lavan and M. Mulryan, 51–90. LAA 9. Leiden: Brill.
Lawall, M. L., and Lund, J., eds. 2011. *Pottery in the Archaeological Record: Greece and Beyond; Acts of the International Colloquium Held at the Danish and Canadian Institutes in Athens, June 20–22, 2008*. Gösta Enbom Monographs 1. Aarhus: Aarhus University Press.
Lillehammer, G. 2010. Archaeology of Children. *Complutum* 21 (2): 15–45.
Maharian, E. 2000. Qedumim, Bar-On Industrial Zone. *HA–ESI* 112: 50*–52*.
Masarwa, A. 2004. Ḥorbat Kosit. *HA–ESI* 116: 70*.
McDaniel, J. 2006. The Small Finds. In *The Roman Frontier in Central Jordan: Final Report on the Limes Arabicus Project, 1980–1989*, Vol. 2, ed. S. T. Parker, 293–327. Washington, DC: Dumbarton Oaks Research Library and Collection.
Meyers, C. L. 2008. Grinding to a Halt: Gender and the Changing Technology of Flour Production in Roman Galilee. In *Engendering Social Dynamics: The Archaeology of Maintenance Activities*, ed. S. Montón-Subías and M. Sánchez-Romero, 65–74. BAR International Series 1862. Oxford: Archaeopress.
Meyers, E. M. 2007. The Problems of Gendered Space in Syro-Palestinian Domestic Architecture: The Case of Roman-Period Galilee. In *From Antioch to Alexandria: Recent Studies in Domestic Architecture*, ed. K. Galor and T. Waliszewski, 107–24. Warsaw: Institute of Archaeology, University of Warsaw.
Nissen, T., ed. 1938. Unbekannte Erzählungen aus dem Pratum Spirituale. *Byzantinische Zeitschrift* 38: 351–76.
O'Hea, M. 2000. Make-Up, Mirrors, and Men: Some Early Byzantine Glass from Syro-Palestine. In *Annales du 14e Congrès de l'Association Internationale pour l'Histoire du Verre, Italia/Venezia–Milano 1998*, 219–22. Lochem: Association Internationale pour l'Histoire du Verre.

Parker, S. T. 1999. An Empire's New Holy Land: The Byzantine Period. *NEA* 62: 134–80.
———. 2006. History of the Roman Frontier East of the Dead Sea. In *The Roman Frontier in Central Jordan: Final Report on the Limes Arabicus Project, 1980–1989*, Vol. 2, ed. S. T. Parker, 517–75. Washington, DC: Dumbarton Oaks Research Library and Collection.
Patrich, J. 1995. Church, State and the Transformation of Palestine: The Byzantine Period (324–640 CE). In *The Archaeology of Society in the Holy Land*, ed. T. E. Levy, 470–87. NAAA. London: Leicester University Press.
Peña, J. T. 2007. *Roman Pottery in the Archaeological Record*. Cambridge: Cambridge University Press.
Pitarakis, B. 2009. The Material Culture of Childhood in Byzantium. In *Becoming Byzantine: Children and Childhood in Byzantium*, ed. A. Papaconstantinou and A.-M. Talbot, 167–251. Washington, DC: Dumbarton Oaks Research Library and Collection.
Ratzlaff, A. 2015. The Militaria and Small Finds. In *The 2003–2007 Excavations in the Late Roman Fort at Yotvata*, by G. Davies and J. Magness, 201–19. Winona Lake, IN: Eisenbrauns.
Ron, Z. Y. D. 1977. *Stone Huts as an Expression of Terrace Agriculture in the Judean and Samarian Hills*. PhD diss., Tel Aviv University (Hebrew).
Schiffer, M. B. 1995. *Behavioral Archaeology: First Principles*. Foundations of Archaeological Inquiry. Salt Lake City: University of Utah Press.
———. 1996. *Formation Processes of the Archaeological Record*. Salt Lake City: University of Utah Press.
Segal, O. 2007. Tirat Karmel. *HA–ESI* 119. www.hadashot-esi.org.il/Report_Detail_Eng.aspx?id=586&mag_id=112 (accessed August 3, 2017).
Sheffer, A., and Tidhar, A. 1991. The Textiles from the 'En-Boqeq Excavation in Israel. *Textile History* 22: 3–46.
Sidi, N. 2007. Stone Utensils. In *En-Gedi Excavations II: Final Report (1996–2002)*, ed. Y. Hirschfeld, 544–73. Jerusalem: IES; The Institute of Archaeology, The Hebrew University of Jerusalem.
Sion, O.; 'Ad, U.; Haiman, M.; and Parnos, G. 2007. Excavations and Surveys at Ḥorbat Anusha and Ḥorbat Leved in the Samarian Shephelah. *'Atiqot* 55: 109–59 (Hebrew).
Skibo, J. M. 1992. *Pottery Function: A Use-Alteration Perspective*. ICA. New York: Plenum.
———. 2013. *Understanding Pottery Function*. Manuals in Archaeological Method, Theory and Technique. New York: Springer.
Sontag, F. 2000. Be'er Sheva', Ramot. *HA–ESI* 111: 91*–92*.
Swan, C. 2015. The Glass. In *The 2003–2007 Excavations in the Late Roman Fort at Yotvata*, ed. G. Davies and J. Magness, 142–71. Winona Lake, IN: Eisenbrauns.
Tal, O., and Taxel, I. 2015. *Samaritan Cemeteries and Tombs in the Central Coastal Plain: Archaeology and History of the Samaritan Settlement outside Samaria (ca. 300–700 CE)*. Ägypten und Altes Testament 82. Münster: Ugarit-Verlag.
Talgam, R. 2014. *Mosaics of Faith: Floors of Pagans, Jews, Samaritans, Christians, and Muslims in the Holy Land*. Treasures of the Past. Jerusalem: Yad Izhak Ben-Zvi; University Park, PA: The Pennsylvania State University Press.
Talmi, L., and Katsnelson, N. 2015. Ḥorbat Bustan. *HA–ESI* 127. www.hadashot-esi.org.il/Report_Detail_Eng.aspx?id=20773&mag_id=122 (accessed August 3, 2017).
Taxel, I. 2010. *Aspects of the Material Culture of the Rural Settlement in the Province of Palaestina Prima in the Fifth–Seventh Centuries CE*. PhD diss., Tel Aviv University (Hebrew).

2013. Late Antique Archaeology in the Holy Land: Evolution, Fieldwork Methods and Post-Excavation Analyses. In *Field Methods and Post-Excavation Techniques in Late Antique Archaeology*, ed. L. A. Lavan and M. Mulryan, 157–86. LAA 9. Leiden: Brill.

In press a. *Fragile Biography: The Life Cycle of Ceramics and Refuse Disposal Patterns in Late Antique and Early Medieval Palestine.* BABESCH Supplements 35. Leuven: Peeters.

In press b. The Southern Levant in the Byzantine Period (324–640): Old and New Debates in Light of Archaeological Contributions. In *The Cambridge Companion to Byzantine Archaeology*, ed. M. J. Decker. Cambridge: Cambridge University Press.

Tsafrir, Y.; Di Segni, L.; and Green, J. 1994. *Tabula Imperii Romani: Iudaea Palaestina; Eretz Israel in the Hellenistic, Roman and Byzantine Periods.* Jerusalem: The Israel Academy of Sciences and Humanities.

Watson, P. 2001. The Byzantine Period. In *The Archaeology of Jordan*, ed. B. MacDonald, R. Adams, and P. Bienkowski, 461–502. LA 1. Sheffield: Sheffield Academic.

TWENTY FIVE

RURAL COMMUNITIES AND LABOR IN THE MIDDLE ISLAMIC-PERIOD SOUTHERN LEVANT

IAN W. N. JONES

In this chapter, I am concerned primarily with the ways labor, production, and consumption shaped village life in the southern Levant (Fig. 25.1) during the Middle Islamic period, or the years AD 1000–1400.[1] These issues are not unique to the Middle Islamic period, and, where useful, I trace certain continuities or changes between the Early, Middle, and Late Islamic periods. Archaeological interest in the Middle Islamic period in general has expanded substantially in the last two decades, however, and with it the amount of available data on Middle Islamic-period villages. One need only compare Donald Whitcomb's (1997) summary of the state of the field, which covers the Levant in five pages, to Bethany Walker's (2010) nearly fifty-page overview of Middle Islamic archaeology in the southern Levant, and then consider that over half a decade has passed since the publication of that article to gain a sense of the scale of current work. Because of this, we now have an excellent picture of how southern Levantine villages fit into the broader political and economic systems of the Levant and Egypt. While issues of daily life and the organization of villages themselves have not been neglected, they are also not as well understood. I focus on several of these here: the types and division of rural labor, local involvement in cash cropping, and the socioeconomic aspects of a common pottery style, Handmade Geometrically Painted Ware, but begin by addressing the urban–rural divide in the Middle Islamic period.

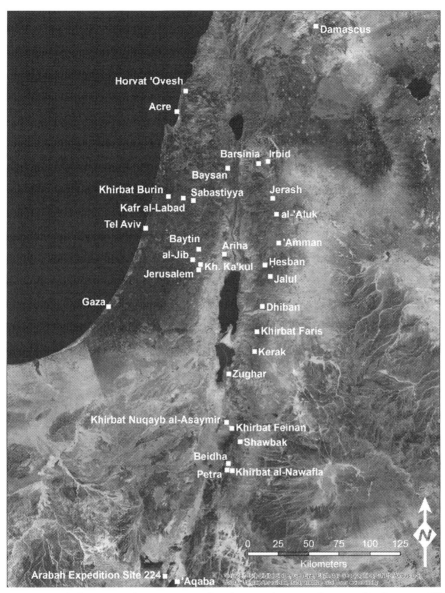

25.1. Map of Islamic-period sites mentioned in the text. (Basemap © Esri and its licensors. All rights reserved. Altered by I. W. N. Jones.)

URBAN AND RURAL SOURCES

Historical sources have allowed for a detailed reconstruction of the organization of urban crafts and their place within communities. The Cairo Geniza documents, dating primarily to the tenth–thirteenth centuries, contain references to "about 265 manual occupations" (Goitein 1967: 99), and based on a wider sample of documents, Maya Shatzmiller (1994: 200) has identified nearly 600 "unique occupations in the Manufacturing sector" for the eighth–fifteenth centuries. Certain sections of Fustat (Old Cairo) were named after specific crafts, demonstrating that concentrations of workshops and markets could shape the social space of the city, but the Geniza documents also demonstrate that specific crafts and commercial enterprises were not strictly limited to specific quarters, and craft and residential quarters could be mixed (Goitein 1967: 83–4, 193; 1983: 15). This is particularly true when considering the work of craftswomen in textile production, which more often than not took place in their homes (Shatzmiller 1994: 358–9; Rapoport 2007: 22–6). In addition to the socio-spatial aspects of crafts, the Geniza documents also provide information about aspects of labor that cannot be determined archaeologically, for example, vocational training (Goitein 1971: 191–2), the concentration of certain occupations within certain religious groups (Goitein 1967: 100–1), and the nature of craft and commercial partnerships (Goitein 1967: 164–83), including those between members of different religions (Goitein 1971: 293–8).

While Fustat is the easiest example to discuss, as the Geniza documents are a uniquely rich source of information, crafts and industry occupied a similar space in the cities of the Levant during the Middle Islamic period. In the Jerusalem Haram documents, mostly dating to the late fourteenth century, Huda Lutfi (1985: 242–3, 297–304) has identified thirty-one distinct terms referring to craftspeople, in addition to others referring to various traders, and ten quarters of the city named after professions. As in Fustat, crafts were not segregated to specific sections of Jerusalem, nor were craft/industrial spaces strictly separated from residential space (Luz 2014: 98–101). As an archaeological example, Kay Prag (2017: 268) reinterprets the Middle Islamic-period structure in the Armenian Garden – originally identified as a *khan* by A. D. Tushingham (1985: 108) – as a mixed industrial space, with evidence of both metal smithing and pottery production. This, along with evidence of blacksmithing at Sites R.I and S.II to the southeast of the Old City, demonstrates the presence of craft/industrial quarters near or in residential areas of Jerusalem during both the Middle and Late Islamic periods (Prag 2017: 85, 128–31, 263).

By contrast, no source like the Cairo Geniza or the Jerusalem Haram documents exists for the countryside, a lacuna that archaeology can address – although several caveats must be addressed here. First, this is not to suggest a clean division between urban and rural. Certainly, the Cairo Geniza and Jerusalem Haram documents describe economic and social connections between city and countryside. Likewise, particularly in Jordan, these categories are somewhat difficult to define, and some places are referred to interchangeably, even in the same source, as both cities and villages (Walker 2011: 39). The richly detailed picture of community and daily life in the city painted by the Cairo Geniza – each of these topics is given a full volume in Shlomo Goitein's (1971; 1983) study – is unparalleled for the countryside, but is likewise unparalleled for "urban" sites such as Kerak.

Second, this is not to suggest that historical sources are of no use in studying rural life. Walker's work, in particular, demonstrates that this is not the case, and economic and legal documents, as well as chronicles, contain a wealth of information about the countryside (see especially Walker 2011). The information these contain is, perhaps unsurprisingly, primarily political and economic. They are quite useful in addressing questions concerning, for example, land tenure, relationships between local people and the state, and agricultural policy. If we are instead interested in the quotidian aspects of village life, however, we are much more reliant on archaeology.

A third caveat that should be kept in mind is variation within regions, as well as regionalism within the southern Levant as a whole. As an example, excavations at the Mamluk-period village of Khirbat Burin in the eastern Sharon produced a ceramic assemblage that included, in addition to a wide variety of local wares, imports from Cyprus, Syria, Italy, and China (Kletter and Stern 2006: 192–7). Walker rightly argues that these "speak against rural isolation, at least in this part of the Levant" (2013: 319). Within the region, however, Italian imports are more common at villages close to Acre, a center of Venetian trade in this period (see below), and less common at villages farther inland (Kletter and Stern 2006: 208). On the Kerak Plateau in central Jordan, a similar pattern is evident. Although few sites have been excavated, imported glazed wares are virtually unknown except at the town of Kerak itself, and even locally produced glazed wares are uncommon at villages farther than 11 km from Kerak (Brown 2000: 86–8). While villages were generally not isolated, the degree to which they were integrated into regional and international trade systems varied considerably within regions, particularly on the basis of distance from regional centers. Likewise, the networks to which regional centers belonged varied. This variation extends to many other aspects of village life, not all of which can be fully discussed here.

RURAL LIFE AND THE DIVISION OF LABOR

Most labor in the countryside was agricultural, domestic, or pastoral. This broad characterization, however, masks considerable variation in economic strategies and community organization over the course of the Middle Islamic period. At Khirbat Faris, a fairly typical farming village on the Kerak Plateau, twelfth-century settlement is characterized by seasonal occupation in "Transverse Arch" houses with grain storage installations, which are associated with a semisedentary, mixed agropastoral economy (McQuitty 2007b: 51). In the fourteenth through sixteenth centuries, this shifted to sedentary settlement in barrel-vaulted houses without spaces for grain storage, indicating more intensive agricultural production, as well as, potentially, control or direct taxation of surpluses by the Mamluk state (McQuitty 2007a: 163–4; 2007b: 52).

This was certainly a regionalized phenomenon, and these shifts played out differently in other parts of the southern Levant. The key point is that even in a single village, the ratio of pastoral to agricultural labor could vary substantially over the course of several centuries.

A strictly gendered division between agricultural/pastoral and domestic labor should also not be assumed. While this is difficult to reconstruct both archaeologically and historically, Shatzmiller argues that rural "women, in addition to their domestic tasks, were involved in a very similar spectrum of agricultural tasks to that of men" (1994: 348–9). Given the amount of labor required, both men and women would certainly have participated in harvesting. This was the case, for example, in the twentieth-century Palestinian village of Baytin, where harvests also served as mixed-gender social events (Lutfiyya 1966: 31). On a daily level, labor was likely less mixed, but both women and men probably performed a range of agricultural, pastoral, and domestic tasks.

In addition to agricultural, domestic, and pastoral labor, some craft specialists were also present in many village communities. Blacksmiths must have been among these, as iron agricultural tools would certainly have required repair, and may have been produced locally. While iron tools themselves are commonly found in Middle Islamic villages, published evidence for blacksmithing is fairly rare. At Khirbat al-Nawafla in Wadi Musa, both agricultural tools and blacksmithing slag were found ('Amr et al. 2000: 246), but most other examples known are either in urban or specialized contexts, for example, Arabah Expedition Site 224, a blacksmith's workshop associated with fourteenth-century repairs to the Egyptian *hajj* route (Rothenberg 1972: 226–8). Nonetheless, evidence from earlier and later periods – including a Late Byzantine blacksmith's workshop at Horvat 'Ovesh in Upper Galilee (Aviam and Getzov 1998), fourth–eighth-century smithing at Barsinia in northern Jordan (Bani-Hani, Abd-Allah, and el-Khouri 2012), and Guy Le Strange's (1886: 299) brief description of a workshop operating at al-'Aluk, near Jerash, in the late nineteenth century – indicates that these would have been a common feature of village life. Certain villagers may also have been part-time craft specialists, including specialist producers of *tawabin* (bread ovens). In twentieth-century Baytin, women from one family produced stoves, *tawabin*, and beehives (Lutfiyya 1966: 119); however, this is not universal, and in other villages, *tawabin* were not specialist products (Ebeling and Rogel 2015: 332).

Spinning and weaving tools have been found at many excavated Middle Islamic-period village sites, including Khirbat Ka'kul (Seligman 2006: 46), Jalul (al-Shqour 2009: 42; Gane, Younker, and Ray 2010: 220), Dhiban (Porter et al. 2005: 207), and Beidha (Sinibaldi and Tuttle 2011: 445), and at smaller "urban" sites such as Ḥesban (Platt and Ray 2009). Based on the prevalence of spinning in cities – Lutfi (1985: 298) calculates that at least 31 percent of the women who appear in the Jerusalem Haram documents were spinners, for example – cloth produced in villages was primarily for domestic consumption. There may be some exceptions to this, however. Carpets from Shawbak are mentioned in the Jerusalem Haram documents (Lutfi 1985: 295), but the lack of evidence for spinning at the site raises the question of whether villages in the region may have supplied spun rather than raw fibers – primarily wool (see Vannini, Marcotulli, and Ruschi 2013: 373, n. 30) – for this production. Indeed, considering that a Mamluk "dye workshop" at the site thought to be evidence for carpet production is more likely a soap workshop (Vannini, Marcotulli, and Ruschi 2013: 375–7), it is possible that the carpets themselves were produced in villages in the region of Shawbak rather than at the castle. Regardless, the villages would have been of critical importance in supplying the raw materials for the urban textile industry. In addition to wool, this also included cotton, which was grown in the Jordan Valley and regions farther to the north; by the end of the fourteenth century, it was also being exported in large quantities to Europe, primarily by Italian traders in Acre (Ashtor 1983: 24, 43, 174, 201, 253–4; Amar 1998: 115). The degree to which rural cloth production was gendered along the same lines as in cities, with women doing most of the spinning and men most of the weaving (Lutfi 1985: 298), would be an interesting subject for further investigation. Based on ethnographic evidence, however, this cannot necessarily be assumed. In twentieth-century Baytin, sewing was generally done by women, but men did most of the spinning (Lutfiyya 1966: 117–18).

CASH CROPS AND RELATED INDUSTRIES

During the Early Islamic period, agricultural products of the higher plateau regions, for example, the Balqa' in central Jordan and the regions of Jibal and Sharah in the south, included grains, fruit, olives, vines, honey, sheep, and goats, while dates, rice, bananas, and indigo could be grown in the Jordan Valley and the lowlands surrounding the Dead Sea (al-Muqaddasi 1896: 69–72; Walmsley 2001: 634). Indigo, as a primary cash crop of the Early and earlier Middle Islamic periods, is perhaps the most relevant here, as its production linked rural communities that grew it to specialized – primarily male and probably primarily Jewish (Balfour-Paul 1997: 75–8) – indigo dyers based in cities and towns in the lowlands: Ariha (Jericho), Baysan (Beth Shean), and Zughar (Ghawr al-Safi) (al-Muqaddasi 1896: 69). By the late twelfth century, however, sugar had replaced indigo as the region's primary cash crop. The Crusaders, Ayyubids, and Mamluks encouraged, and often mandated, its cultivation in the Dead Sea lowlands, Jordan Valley, Galilee, and Hula Valley (Abu Dalu 1995; Stern 1999; Burke 2004; Walker 2010: 145–9; Politis

2013). Because of the specific requirements of growing sugar, traditional cropping cycles were disrupted on land that became part of "sugar estates" (Walker 2008: 82, 84). While these estates could cause conflict between villagers and local officials, particularly when officials abused their power, this was generally not the case (Walker 2009: 60). The intensification of sugar production and expansion of cereal agriculture into more marginal areas may have had longer-term environmental impacts that affected villagers, as argued by Sofia Laparidou and Arlene Rosen (2015), although Bernhard Lucke and his colleagues argue, based on work in northern Jordan, that "land degradation seems merely a modern problem" (2012: 124). Nonetheless, it is clear that villagers preferred to grow other cash crops, and during the Ottoman period, sugar was replaced in these regions by cotton, sesame, and indigo (Balfour-Paul 1997: 59–61; Walker 2011: 85).

In its earlier phase – beginning in the later twelfth century in the southern Levant – the sugar industry would also have required a fairly substantial amount of copper to make the large cauldrons in which cane juice was boiled, known in Arabic as *dusut* (see Sato 2015: 42–3). During the Ayyubid period, this copper was obtained primarily from the mines in the Feinan region of southern Jordan.[2] Earlier structures were repurposed for copper smelting at Khirbat Feinan, and a new village was established ca. 7 km to the northwest at Khirbat Nuqayb al-Asaymir. The spatial layout of the industry, with smelting concentrated at only two sites, indicates that this was a centralized initiative, and the artifacts found at Khirbat Nuqayb al-Asaymir, including both common handmade ceramics and luxury tablewares imported from Damascus, demonstrate that miners, metallurgists, and Ayyubid administrators all lived together at the site (Jones, Levy, and Najjar 2012: 89–90). The presence of (currently unpublished) gaming pieces at Khirbat Nuqayb al-Asaymir suggests that its residents' leisure activities may not have been all that different from those documented in urban settings (see, e.g., Little 1975: 107). This picture stands in contrast to the copper industry in southern Aravah during the Early Islamic period, characterized instead by a system of more dispersed smelting camps. This production was less centralized, and the nature of nearby settlements suggests the possibility that this work was undertaken by semisedentary Bedouin (Avner and Magness 1998; Nol 2015; Jones et al. 2017), with little suggestion of the presence of government administrators.

HANDMADE GEOMETRICALLY PAINTED WARES (HMGPW)

Many of the most vexing problems in the archaeology of the Middle Islamic southern Levant concern the nearly ubiquitous handmade ceramics of the period, in particular, HMGPW (Fig. 25.2). A key problem has been dating, which will not be discussed in this chapter except to note that it is commonly

25.2. HMGPW jug from Khirbat Nuqayb al-Asaymir. (Photo by L. Trujillo. Courtesy of T. E. Levy and the University of California, San Diego, Levantine and Cyber-Archaeology Lab.)

accepted that HMGPW emerged during the twelfth century and continued to be produced at least into the sixteenth century (Walker 2010: 123–4). More relevant here are lingering questions of production, distribution, and consumption.

Although found in urban contexts, HMGPW generally makes up a much higher proportion of pottery assemblages in villages (Johns 1998: 69) and has been called village pottery "par excellence" (François 2002: 162). This has led some archaeologists to assume that HMGPW was produced at the village or even household level by nonspecialist potters. This view, based primarily on ethnographic descriptions of modern village pottery production in Palestine and Jordan (e.g., Einsler 1914; Crowfoot 1932, Meishen 1985, see also Brown 2000: 91–2), was challenged 20 years ago by Jeremy Johns (1998: 70–1) and Eveline van der Steen (1997–1998: 124–5). Both point to the homogeneity of decorative motifs and forms over HGMPW's wide geographical distribution as evidence of craft specialization, arguing that it was traded from a relatively small number of production centers, or, as Johns (1998: 71) suggests, made by "itinerant" potters. In a recent petrographic study of vessels from northern Israel, Jerusalem, and Ḥesban, R. Smadar Gabrieli, David Ben-Shlomo, and Walker (2014) suggest a more complicated scenario involving both centers of specialist production and local producers. At most sites, HMGPW from several production centers was present, but in the northern Upper Galilee, only local HMGPW was found (Gabrieli, Ben-Shlomo, and Walker 2014: 213–14, 217). This could reflect household-based production in certain regions (e.g., the Upper Galilee) but may also indicate that certain villages, towns, and regions were integrated into a wider range of networks than others, which relied primarily on local production centers.

Specialization does not rule out village-level production. In his study of Gamo potters in southern Ethiopia, John Arthur (2014) documents full-time specialists in villages producing ceramics both for local consumption and sale at regional markets. Likewise, the production documented by Grace Crowfoot (1932: 182) was concentrated in specific villages; pots used in Sabastiyya were made at Kafr al-Labad, and pots used in Jerusalem at al-Jib. It should not, therefore, be assumed that specialized production – even full-time specialization – was urban.

The social aspects of the consumption of HMGPW are, likewise, not yet well understood. Robin Brown (2000: 93–4) pointed out that HMGPW forms tend to be restricted to serving vessels, which are socially visible, while handmade "utilitarian" wares are generally simply decorated, if at all. The decoration reflects, then, the social interactions during which this pottery would have been used. Economic explanations for the popularity of the ware, whether framed as an inability of villagers to afford presumably more expensive wheelmade ceramics or to access these wares to begin with (Johns 1998: 80–2; Brown 2000: 92), do not hold up when considering excavated sites. As an example, sixty-five percent of the sherds from a Mamluk-period cistern fill at Khirbat Faris were wheelmade, indicating that villagers clearly had access to these wares (McQuitty et al. 1997: 189, 207, fig. 10). In a study of a different group of handmade pottery from northeastern Syria, Raffaella Pappalardo (2014: 27) suggests that, rather than reflecting economic decline, handmade ceramics were a "convenient choice made by consumers" for wares that would have seen daily use. This is a refreshing perspective, as consumer choice has often been neglected in discussions of HMGPW. This particular argument does not, however, explain why the geometric motifs on HMGPW vessels remained essentially the same for four centuries, if not longer. Likewise, it does not explain the very wide distribution of HMGPW within the Levant (Johns 1998: 68), or the fact, noted by Whitcomb (1997: 103, n. 28) and Johns (1998: 73) but rarely addressed, that similar but clearly distinguishable ceramics emerge at around the same time in North Africa and much of West and Central Asia. Whitcomb (1997: 103) suggested, based on its distribution, that HMGPW was, initially, "possibly a reaction to [Crusader] occupation" in the Levant "which continued as a popular symbol through the Mamluk period." While this does not entirely explain the patterns described above, it is very likely that HMGPW, rather than simply being a cheap replacement for higher-quality glazed wares, is an expression of a specific, perhaps primarily rural, identity.

CONCLUSION

As archaeological interest in the Middle Islamic period has grown, so has our knowledge of the ways villages were integrated into political and economic networks in the southern Levant. Many aspects of daily life in these villages remain, unfortunately, less clear. Social perspectives have not been neglected, but considering the inadequacy of purely economic perspectives in explaining the distribution and longevity of HMGPW, greater consideration of the effects of villagers' agency and preferences on archaeologically observable patterns is required. The examples discussed in this chapter certainly suggest that there is reason to hope this will be the case moving forward.

ACKNOWLEDGMENTS

This chapter was written while I was a Council of American Overseas Research Centers fellow at ACOR in 'Amman, Jordan, and I owe enormous thanks to the ACOR staff – in particular, Barbara Porter, Glenn Corbett, and Jack Green – for supporting my work. I must also thank Thomas E. Levy and Mohammad Najjar for generously allowing me to discuss unpublished material from of our work in Feinan. While writing this chapter, I had productive discussions about HMGPW and related ceramics with Piotr Makowski, Stephen McPhillips, Elisa Pruno, Raffaele Ranieri, Micaela Sinibaldi, Eveline van der Steen, and Aleksandra Węgrzynek. Kathleen Bennallack provided comments on an earlier draft that greatly improved the final product. All errors are, of course, my own.

NOTES

1 This "archaeological periodization" was first proposed by Whitcomb (1992: 386). See also the visions in Walker and LaBianca 2003: 448, table 1; and Jones, Najjar, and Levy 2014: 175, fig. 12:69.
2 For the political aspects of this industry, see Jones, Najjar, and Levy 2014: 188–95.

REFERENCES

Abu Dalu, R. A. 1995. Taqniyyat Ma'āṣir al-Sukkar fī Wādī al-Urdunn Khilāl al-Fitrāt al-Islāmiyya [The Technology of Sugar Mills in the Jordan Valley during the Islamic Periods]. *SHAJ* 5: 37–48 (Arabic).

Amar, Z. 1998. Written Sources Regarding the Jazirat Fara'un (Coral Island) Textiles. *'Atiqot* 36: 114–19.

'Amr, K.; al-Momani, A.; al-Nawafleh, N.; and al-Nawafleh, S. 2000. Summary Results of the Archaeological Project at Khirbat an-Nawāfla/Wādī Mūsā. *ADAJ* 44: 231–55.

Arthur, J. W. 2014. Pottery Uniformity in a Stratified Society: An Ethnoarchaeological Perspective from the Gamo of Southwest Ethiopia. *JAA* 35: 106–16.

Ashtor, E. 1983. *Levant Trade in the Later Middle Ages*. Princeton: Princeton University Press.

Aviam, M., and Getzov, N. 1998. A Byzantine Smithy at Ḥorvat 'Ovesh, Upper Galilee. *'Atiqot* 34: 63–83. (Hebrew; English summary on pp. 6*–7*).

Avner, U., and Magness, J. 1998. Early Islamic Settlement in the Southern Negev. *BASOR* 310: 39–57.

Balfour-Paul, J. 1997. *Indigo in the Arab World*. London: Routledge.

Bani-Hani, M.; Abd-Allah, R.; and el-Khouri, L. 2012. Archaeometallurgical Finds from Barsinia, Northern Jordan: Microstructural Characterization and Conservation Treatment. *Journal of Cultural Heritage* 13: 314–25.

Brown, R. M. 2000. The Distribution of Thirteenth- to Fifteenth-Century Glazed Wares in Transjordan: A Case Study from the Kerak Plateau. In *The Archaeology of Jordan and Beyond: Essays in Honor of James A. Sauer*, ed. L. E. Stager, J. A. Greene, and M. D. Coogan, 84–99. HSMP; SAHL 1. Winona Lake, IN: Eisenbrauns.

Burke, K. S. 2004. A Note on Archaeological Evidence for Sugar Production in the Middle Islamic Periods in Bilād al-Shām. *MSR* 8 (2): 109–18.

Crowfoot, G. M. 1932. Pots, Ancient and Modern. *PEQ* 65: 179–87.

Ebeling, J., and Rogel, M. 2015. The *tabun* and Its Misidentification in the Archaeological Record. *Levant* 47: 328–49.

Einsler, L. 1914. Das Töpferhandwerk bei den Bauernfrauen von Ramallah und Umgegend. *ZDPV* 37: 249–60.

François, V. 2002. Production et consommation de vaisselle à Damas, à l'époque ottomane. *BEO* 53–54 (suppl.): 157–70.

Gabrieli, R. S.; Ben-Shlomo, D.; and Walker, B. J. 2014. Production and Distribution of Hand-Made Geometrical-Painted (HMGP) and Plain Hand-Made Wares of the Mamluk Period: A Case Study from Northern Israel, Jerusalem and Tall Hisban. *Journal of Islamic Archaeology* 1: 193–229.

Gane, C. E.; Younker, R. W.; and Ray, P. 2010. Madaba Plains Project: Tall Jalul 2009. *Andrews University Seminary Studies* 48: 165–223.

Goitein, S. D. 1967. *A Mediterranean Society: The Jewish Communities of the Arab World as Portrayed in the Documents of the Cairo Geniza,* Vol. 1: *Economic Foundations.* Berkeley: University of California Press.

———. 1971. *A Mediterranean Society: The Jewish Communities of the Arab World as Portrayed in the Documents of the Cairo Geniza,* Vol. 2: *The Community.* Berkeley: University of California Press.

———. 1983. *A Mediterranean Society: The Jewish Communities of the Arab World as Portrayed in the Documents of the Cairo Geniza,* Vol. 4: *Daily Life.* Berkeley: University of California Press.

Johns, J. 1998. The Rise of Middle Islamic Hand-Made Geometrically-Painted Ware in Bilād al-Shām (11th–13th Centuries A.D.). In *Colloque International d'Archéologie Islamique, IFAO, Le Caire, 3–7 février 1993,* ed. R.-P. Gayraud, 65–93. Textes arabes et études islamiques 36. Cairo: Institut Français d'Archéologie Orientale.

Jones, I. W. N.; Ben-Yosef, E.; Lorentzen, B.; Najjar, M.; and Levy, T. E. 2017. Khirbat al-Manaʿiyya: An Early Islamic-Period Copper-Smelting Site in the South-Eastern Wadi ʿAraba, Jordan. *Arabian Archaeology and Epigraphy* 28: 297–314.

Jones, I. W. N.; Levy, T. E.; and Najjar, M. 2012. Khirbat Nuqayb al-Asaymir and Middle Islamic Metallurgy in Faynan: Surveys of Wadi al-Ghuwayb and Wadi al-Jariya in Faynan, Southern Jordan. *BASOR* 368: 67–102.

Jones, I. W. N.; Najjar, M.; and Levy, T. E. 2014. "Not Found in the Order of History": Toward a "Medieval" Archaeology of Southern Jordan. In *From West to East: Current Approaches to Medieval Archaeology,* ed. S. D. Stull, 171–96. Newcastle-upon-Tyne: Cambridge Scholars.

Kletter, R., and Stern, E. J. 2006. A Mamluk-Period Site at Khirbat Burin in the Eastern Sharon. *ʿAtiqot* 51: 173–214.

Laparidou, S., and Rosen, A. M. 2015. Intensification of Production in Medieval Islamic Jordan and Its Ecological Impact: Towns of the Anthropocene. *The Holocene* 25: 1685–97.

Le Strange, G. 1886. A Ride through ʿAjlûn and the Belkâ during the Autumn of 1884. In *Across the Jordan: Being an Exploration and Survey of Part of Hauran and Jaulan,* ed. G. Schumacher, 268–323. London: Bentley.

Little, D. P. 1975. Did Ibn Taymiyya Have a Screw Loose? *Studia Islamica* 41: 93–111.

Lucke, B.; Shunnaq, M.; Walker, B. J.; Shiyab, A.; al-Muheisen, Z.; al-Sababha, H.; Bäumler, R.; and Schmidt, M. 2012. Questioning Transjordan's Historic Desertification: A Critical Review of the Paradigm of "Empty Lands." *Levant* 44: 101–26.

Lutfi, H. 1985. *Al-Quds al-Mamlûkiyya: A History of Mamlûk Jerusalem Based on the Ḥaram Documents.* Islamkundliche Untersuchungen 113. Berlin: Schwarz.

Lutfiyya, A. M. 1966. *Baytîn, a Jordanian Village: A Study of Social Institutions and Social Change in a Folk Community.* The Hague: Mouton.

Luz, N. 2014. *The Mamluk City in the Middle East: History, Culture, and the Urban Landscape.* Cambridge Studies in Islamic Civilization. New York: Cambridge University Press.

McQuitty, A. M. 2007a. Khirbat Fāris: Vernacular Architecture on the Karak Plateau, Jordan. *MSR* 11 (1): 157–71.

———. 2007b. Rural Settlement on the Karak Plateau: Khirbat Fāris. *SHAJ* 9: 49–52.

McQuitty, A. M.; Sarley-Pontin, M. A.; Khoury, M.; Hope, C.; and Hope, C. F. 1997. Mamluk Khirbat Faris. *ARAM* 9: 181–226.

Mershen, B. 1985. Recent Hand-Made Pottery from Northern Jordan. *Berytus* 33: 75–87.

al-Muqaddasi, M. A. 1896. *Description of Syria, including Palestine.* Trans. G. Le Strange, from Arabic. Library of the Palestine Pilgrims' Text Society 3. London: Palestine Pilgrims' Text Society.

Nol, H. 2015. The Fertile Desert: Agriculture and Copper Industry in Early Islamic Arava (Arabah). *PEQ* 147: 49–68.

Pappalardo, R. 2014. "Wheel-Free": The Islamic Handmade Pottery from Tell Barri (Syria). In *Proceedings of the 8th International Congress on the Archaeology of the Ancient Near East, 30 April–4 May 2012, University of Warsaw,* Vol. 3: *Archaeology of Fire – Conservation, Preservation and Site Management – Bioarchaeology in the Ancient Near East – Islamic Session – Selected Papers from Workshop Sessions,* ed. P. Bieliński, M. Gawlikowski, R. Koliński, D. Ławecka, A. Sołtysiak, and Z. Wygnańska, 419–38. Wiesbaden: Harrassowitz.

Platt, E. E., and Ray, P. J., Jr. 2009. The Textile Tools from Tell Hesban and Vicinity. In *Small Finds: Studies of Bone, Iron, Glass, Figurines, and Stone Objects from Tell Hesban and Vicinity,* by P. J. Ray Jr., 163–96. Hesban 12. Berrien Springs, MI: Andrews University Press.

Politis, K. D. 2013. The Sugar Industry in the Ghawr aṣ-Ṣāfī, Jordan. *SHAJ* 11: 467–80.

Porter, B. W.; Routledge, B.; Steen, D.; Parlsow, C.; Jong, L. de; and Zimmerle, W. 2005. Tall Dhībān 2004 Pilot Season: Prospection, Preservation, and Planning. *ADAJ* 49: 201–16.

Prag, K. 2017. *Excavations by K.M. Kenyon in Jerusalem 1961–1967,* Vol. 6: *Sites on the Edge of the Ophel.* LSS 18. Oxford: Oxbow.

Rapoport, Y. 2007. Women and Gender in Mamluk Society: An Overview. *MSR* 11 (2): 1–47.

Rothenberg, B. 1972. *Were These King Solomon's Mines? Excavations in the Timna Valley.* New Aspects of Archaeology. New York: Stein & Day.

Sato, T. 2015. *Sugar in the Social Life of Medieval Islam.* Islamic Area Studies 1. Leiden: Brill.

Seligman, J. 2006. Jerusalem, Khirbat Ka'kul (Pisgat Ze'ev H): Early Roman Farmsteads and a Medieval Village. *'Atiqot* 54: 1–73.

Shatzmiller, M. 1994. *Labour in the Medieval Islamic World.* Islamic History and Civilization 4. Leiden: Brill.

Shqour, R. al-. 2009. 2008 Excavations at the Islamic Village at Tall Jalūl. *ADAJ* 53: 35–43.

Sinibaldi, M., and Tuttle, C. A. 2011. The Brown University Petra Archaeological Project: 2010 Excavations at Islamic Bayḍā. *ADAJ* 55: 431–50.

Steen, Eveline J. van der. 1997–1998. What Happened to Arabic Geometric Pottery in Beirut? *ARAM* 9–10: 121–7.

Stern, E. J. 1999. *The Sugar Industry in Palestine during the Crusader, Ayyubid and Mamluk Periods in Light of the Archeological Finds.* MA thesis, The Hebrew University of Jerusalem (Hebrew, with English summary).

Tushingham, A. D. 1985. *Excavations in Jerusalem 1961–1967,* Vol. 1: *Excavations in the Armenian Garden on the Western Hill.* Toronto: Royal Ontario Museum.

Vannini, G.; Marcotulli, C.; and Ruschi, P. 2013. Crusader, Ayyubid and Early Mamluk Shawbak and the History of Medieval South Jordan: The Archaeology and Restoration of the Mamluk Workshop. *SHAJ* 11: 359–80.

Walker, B. J. 2008. The Role of Agriculture in Mamluk-Jordanian Power Relations. *BEO* 57 (suppl.): 79–99.

―――. 2009. Popular Responses to Mamluk Fiscal Reforms in Syria. *BEO* 58: 51–68.

2010. From Ceramics to Social Theory: Reflections on Mamluk Archaeology Today. *MSR* 14: 109–57.

2011. *Jordan in the Late Middle Ages: Transformation of the Mamluk Frontier*. Chicago Studies on the Middle East 8. Chicago: Middle East Documentation Center.

2013. What Can Archaeology Contribute to the New Mamlukology? Where Culture Studies and Social Theory Meet. In *Ubi Sumus? Quo Vademus? Mamluk Studies – State of the Art*, ed. S. Conermann, 311–35. Mamluk Studies 3. Bonn: V&R Unipress; Bonn University Press.

Walker, B. J., and LaBianca, Ø. S. 2003. The Islamic Quṣūr of Tall Ḥisbān: Preliminary Report on the 1998 and 2001 Seasons. *ADAJ* 47: 443–71.

Walmsley, A. 2001. Restoration or Revolution? Jordan between the Islamic Conquest and the Crusades: Impressions of Twenty-Five Years of Archaeological Research. *SHAJ* 7: 633–40.

Whitcomb, D. S. 1992. Reassessing the Archaeology of Jordan of the Abbasid Period. *SHAJ* 4: 385–90.

1997. Mamluk Archaeological Studies: A Review. *MSR* 1: 97–106.

TWENTY SIX

SOCIETY IN THE FRANKISH PERIOD

RABEI G. KHAMISY

Frankish-period society, with its rich variety of ethnic and religious groups, has attracted the interest of scholars since the 1860s. Studies have often aimed to show whether the Franks inhabited rural settlements; from the outset, both written sources and archaeological remains have been taken into account. However, conclusions have fallen into one of two different categories: The earlier studies claimed that the Franks had integrated extensively in rural settlements, while the later work rejected this idea. In the 1990s, Ronnie Ellenblum adopted the earlier point of view, supporting it with additional historical and archaeological evidence. The current chapter will examine a selection of Frankish-period archaeological remains in an attempt to reach a better understanding of society at that time.

PREVIOUS STUDIES

The French scholar Emmanuel Rey (1866: 17–19) stated that Franks and indigenous people lived together in almost all types of settlements, including rural communities, in the Latin East. Rey set the standard that was followed by scholars until the 1930s;[1] however, in the 1950s, a different suggestion was posited, claiming that the Franks had mainly settled in large cities and fortresses (Cahen 1950–1951: 286; Smail 1956: 57–63; Prawer 1980: 102–42).[2] R. C. Smail, for example, presented a long list of things that the Franks adapted from Eastern cultures, including food and architectural styles, but he did not consider these to be proof that the Franks had integrated with the locals in rural settlements (Smail 1956: 40, 43, 62–3).

The same matter was raised again in the 1990s by Ellenblum (1998), whose conclusion supported the earlier suggestion but with further details. According to him, many rural settlements were inhabited by Franks, sometimes alongside indigenous Christians. He added that the Frankish settlements were developed only in regions containing well-established local Christian communities (Ellenblum 1998: 213–87). This led him to suggest that the Frankish settlements in Galilee did not extend east of an imaginary line connecting the region of Fassūṭa (map ref. 1792.2728) in the north, with al-Baina (map ref. 1755.2595) and Nazareth (map ref. 1780.2340) in the south (Ellenblum 1998: 258, map 5). However, this view was criticized by Denys Pringle, who claimed that several of Ellenblum's suggestions, although based on archaeological remains and contemporary documents, are not strikingly unidirectional and could be explained differently (2003: 169, n. 26, 173–8).

The limited length of the current chapter prevents a full overview of historical discussions dealing with Frankish-period society; thus, the focus will be on the most recent archaeological studies. However, a short historical background of the Franks' arrival in the Levant will present a useful context to better understand the field under discussion.

THE ARRIVAL OF THE CRUSADERS

On their way to Jerusalem, the first Crusaders passed through the Byzantine Empire, met its people, and were exposed to their lifestyles. In addition, they reached the walls and great fortifications of many diverse places, such as Constantinople and Antioch. In fact, a considerable number of Crusaders, the peasants in particular, had never come across such a different culture. When they reached Mar'ash, the Franks went in two directions. Some of the troops continued eastward and reached Edessa, gaining control over the city at the beginning of 1098. From there, they established their role in the city and its county. This region had been under Christian rule before the Franks arrived but paid taxes to the neighboring Muslims rulers (Prawer 1969–1970 1: 208). A few months later, on June 3, 1098, after a siege of more than seven months, the main Crusader contingents succeeded in taking Antioch – one of the most important cities in the eastern Mediterranean – and a new principality was born there.[3]

The Franks' endeavors to occupy Latakia, Tripoli, and other places in between failed, and, as a result, they were unable to establish a new principality south of Antioch. At this stage, they decided to move rapidly toward Jerusalem (Prawer 1969–1970 1: 217–18), leaving Latakia's occupation to the coming years (Mayer 1988: 65).[4] In 1109, the county of Tripoli was established north of the kingdom of Jerusalem.

Even though the Frankish counties of Edessa, Antioch, and Tripoli occupied an area much larger than the kingdom of Jerusalem,[5] and their strategic importance had greatly contributed to the existence of the kingdom of Jerusalem,[6] they will not be part of the current discussion.

On July 15, 1099, Jerusalem fell to the Franks and the First Crusader kingdom was established (Prawer 1969–1970 1: 230; Mayer 1988: 55–6). However, apart from Jaffa, none of the coastal cities had been captured at the time.[7] In order to expand the kingdom's area and connect it with the previously occupied North Syrian regions, the Franks set off on a series of invasions, probably starting with Tiberias. The city fell to Godfrey of Bouillon, probably in September 1099 (see Pringle 1993–2009 2: 351). A few months later, the Franks turned their attention to the coastal region. After capturing Haifa in 1100, they started targeting other cities from south to north. Arsuf and Caesarea fell in April and May 1101, respectively, and Acre was gained in 1104 (Pringle 1993–2009 1: 59, 166, 222; 4: 5). Tyre, the last Muslim locality north of Jerusalem, fell in 1124 after resisting several Frankish attacks (Pringle 1993–2009 4: 177, with references). In the meantime, the Franks occupied Tripoli, Beirut, and Sidon in 1109 and 1110,[8] this time from north to south. Ascalon, the last Fatimid city along the coast, was captured in 1153 (Pringle 1993–2009 1: 61).

URBAN SOCIETY

The Frankish occupation of the cities in the Latin East had naturally created a drastic demographic change, mainly by increasing the Christian population and decreasing the number of Muslims. Jerusalem, being the most important city for Christians, seems to have been treated in a very special way by the Franks. After its occupation in 1099, non-Christians were expelled, and Jerusalem became an entirely Christian city. However, a few historical accounts provide evidence for the existence of some Muslims and Jews in the city before it fell to Saladin in 1187, after which the new rulers opened the doors for these communities to return. But in 1229, the Franks received the city back and once again expelled the Jewish community. In 1244, the city was taken by the Khawarizmians and handed to the Ayyubids, who accepted the Jewish community again (Boas 2001: 39–40). This situation seems to have been exceptional compared to other major cities (Kedar 1990: 147–8).[9] Unlike non-Christians, Eastern Christian communities had been treated differently. In Jerusalem, almost all Eastern sects had existed there and generally lived in their own quarters (Kedar 1990: 37–9). It should be added that the population was divided into several classes – that is, nobles and burgesses – while these two had their own further subdivisions (see Kedar 1990: 36–7).

Jerusalem included many essential structures for day-to-day life. Its churches, markets, learning institutions, fortifications, hospitals, bathhouses, stables, and so forth are conclusive proof of the diversity of the social activities in the city (see Pringle 1993–2009 vol. 3 and Boas 2001). In fact, the Frankish remains in the city offer the clearest evidence for some of the social activities at the time. The Church of the Holy Sepulchre, which is regarded to be one of the greatest building projects carried out by the Franks in the East, is the only church in the kingdom designed to welcome different groups of pilgrims at the same time.[10] This in itself indicates the number of different ethnic and religious groups who frequently entered the city, met its inhabitants, and left their mark on the local society. Jerusalem contained 75 churches in the twelfth century and 34 in the thirteenth (Pringle 2003: 176, table 3, 177). The remains of many of them are still visible, shedding light on the large number of different societies that inhabited the city during that time.[11]

The other important feature that was impressively preserved in Jerusalem is the markets, which were the optimal meeting place between visitors and the city's inhabitants. Residents had the opportunity to work in different commercial and industrial fields. Among the items sold in Jerusalem's markets were meat, cheese, chickens, eggs, birds, herbs, fruits, spices, cookery, and fish, but also clothes, fur, and probably gold works and wax candles, which are mentioned as being worked by Syrians in one of the markets (Boas 2001: 191–8, esp. 144–5, 147, 149, 153, 155).[12] In addition, Pringle identified a market specializing in saddles and horse equipment that was mentioned in a twelfth-century Hospitaller document (2014: 185–6, n. 17). Adrian Boas noted that with the growth of pilgrimage in the twelfth century, more shops of cooked food were needed (2001: 149). This shows that there was a symbiosis between the number of pilgrims and the development of marketing. It might be suggested that the growing number of pilgrims led to the establishment of other types of shops – less common and important than the above mentioned – that may have provided the pilgrims with additional objects from the Holy Land. Presumably, artists and writers could also sell their souvenir artworks, such as metalwork, drawings, stone works, books, and guide books. This might find support in the accounts that mention gold workers and wax candles.[13] In addition, Peter Edbury (pers. comm., 2017) suggests that in the late thirteenth century, manuscripts of the Old French text of William of Tyre may have been copied in Acre and sold to pilgrims "off the shelf" – the point being that, given the time a pilgrim would normally spend in the East, there would be no time for the purchaser to commission a copy.

In Tiberias, the major Crusader city in the eastern Galilee and the center of the important principality of Galilee (Kedar 1990: 144), the social situation was rather different. Here, Muslims and Jews lived together with the different Christian sects (Pringle 1993–2009 2: 351, 352).[14] By establishing Frankish rule over the city, Godfrey of Bouillon and Tancred, prince of Galilee, encouraged the re-establishment of churches in the city and its vicinity, particularly on Mount Tabor and in Nazareth (Huygens 1986: 438; Mayer 2010 1: 124–5, no. 20). Historical evidence from both Frankish and Eastern writers sheds light on the development of the region under Frankish control, showing the re-establishment of villages that had been dismantled a few years earlier, probably by the Seljuks. Presumably, many of these villages were settled by Franks and/or indigenous Christians from neighboring Muslim villages that survived the Seljuk invasions. It appears that during the Frankish rule over this region, many villages were built, and different ethnic and religious groups lived inside its borders, mainly involved in agriculture.[15]

Following the battle of Ḥaṭṭīn and the fall of the kingdom in 1187, the Franks succeeded in recovering some lands; after the Third Crusade, Acre, the principal maritime city, became the most important Frankish location in what is sometimes termed "the second kingdom of the Franks." At present, Acre still has many valuable Frankish-period remains that shed light on the different societies and their activities in the city. In addition to the archaeological remains, Acre received the attention of many contemporary and later travelers and historians, whose descriptions have contributed greatly to our understanding of the city's layout, its development, and its population. Ibn Jubayr, an Andalusian Muslim pilgrim, visited Acre in 1184 and described many features and elements, including the harbor and the streets. He also recorded that the Muslims were using a small building at the location of the pre-Frankish-period main mosque of the city, which had become the Latin cathedral (Ibn Jubayr 2008: 318). Twelfth- and thirteenth-century charters occasionally give detailed information about particular properties, and persons from different ethnic and religious groups are mentioned (see Pringle 1993–2009 4: 3–175, *passim*).

The final urban center to be discussed here is Tyre, in which, as witnessed by Muslim historians, Muslims continued to live throughout the Frankish period. Ibn Qalānisī (1908: 211) records that after the fall of the city in 1124, many Muslims left, but others did not. Ibn Jubayr (2008: 321) added that after the peace conditions were confirmed, some Muslims decided to return to the city. This on its own is very different from what occurred in Jerusalem, Acre, and many other cities (Kedar 1990: 133–6). Letting Muslims stay in their houses is understandable, if remarkable, when compared with the events in other major cities except Sidon; however, to allow them to return after leaving is a very puzzling act by the Franks and perhaps sheds light on the changes to Frankish views regarding Muslims during the first two decades of establishing the kingdom. It seems likely that living with Muslims became more acceptable as time passed. Or, maybe, Ibn Jubayr, writing 60 years after the events, was not precise in his description.

SOCIETY IN THE FRANKISH PERIOD

The destruction of Tyre by al-Ashraf Khalīl in 1291 seems to have left the city with only a few notable remains, such as the cathedral, and two towers: Burj ʿAyn Ḥīrām and Burj al-Maghāriba.[16] The magnificence of the cathedral and the construction style of the other buildings allow us to draw conclusions about the wealthier inhabitants and communities within the city. Additionally, the Muslims seem to have retained some properties and mosques, at least until 1187 (Ibn Jubayr 2008: 321).

An important point that sheds light on urban society, especially in the major cities such as Acre, Tyre, and Jerusalem, is the division of these cities into different quarters, each belonging to a different group, such as the military orders and the Italian communities.[17] For example, the city of Tyre contained, *inter alia*, Venetian, Genoese, and Pisan Quarters. The Hospitallers and Templars possessed properties in the city and its vicinity.[18]

RURAL SETTLEMENTS

As already explained above, it is now generally accepted that Franks settled many villages in the countryside. As with the urban centers, this chapter will only consider some of the most important and relevant finds, especially those unearthed in extensive excavations.

Few villages from the Frankish period have been excavated. However, the remains in many sites may be identified with specific ethnic and/or religious groups. The village of al-Qubayba belonged to the Church of the Holy Sepulchre and was clearly laid out as a "street village,"[19] a plan whereby the houses are built along a road, with the doors facing the road and the gardens located on the other side of the house. This design did not exist in rural settlements within the Levant prior to the Franks' arrival. In fact, all planned villages seem to have been settled by the Franks as early as the beginning of the twelfth century.

In addition to the architectural aspects that differ between cities and villages, there was a difference in the ethnicity and religions of the inhabitants. It is true that in both settlement types, Franks, different sects of local Christians, Muslims, and Jews had settled, but the Druze, for example, were only mentioned in connection with the mountainous region east of Sidon. In his account written at the end of the 1160s, Benjamin of Tudela tells, for the first time, about this group and its beliefs (Asher 1907: 61–2; Prawer 1988: 199).[20]

By studying historical events and the development of castles and settlements in the twelfth century, Boas (2007) found a correlation between the security conditions and the development and use of castles, and suggested that rural settlements were established and developed around fortified centers, mainly during safe periods.[21] This is clear evidence about the immediate influence of safe conditions on the behavior of people. However, archaeological remains can clarify additional social activities, which will be discussed below.

CRUSADER SOCIETY THROUGH ARCHAEOLOGY

Here, we will examine three material culture remains – all essential to the study of societies. The first is the architectural styles of houses in the Frankish period; an important social aspect in the development of the Frankish house relates to the possible influence of Eastern architecture on Frankish domestic buildings. The second is the ceramic material from different urban and rural settlements, which sheds light on trade at the time and the socioeconomic status of the people using the vessels. Another field is numismatics; the value and design of coins can contribute to the identification of the local groups using them and help in understanding their beliefs.[22]

In general, different societies were involved in industry, such as sugar production, milling, and producing ceramics and metals.[23] They also dealt with agriculture, which is reflected in the hundreds of charters and contemporary descriptions of orchards, vineyards, and many other crops[24] but are also reflected in numerous archaeological remains, such as winepresses, water mills, and other installations that have been preserved at several Frankish-period sites.[25]

Domestic Architecture during the Frankish Period

Although different styles of houses had existed in the East, both in urban and rural settlements,[26] in general, the Eastern house, especially the Muslim one, was designed to keep the inner rooms, particularly the bedrooms, out of view. It seems likely that the entrance was planned to give indirect access to the courtyard, which was surrounded or partly surrounded by different rooms for all the functions needed in the house. In addition, the windows, if they existed, were usually narrow and located high in the walls to prevent a clear view from neighboring houses and the streets (Boas 2010: 18–31).

In opposition, the western houses, especially in the early years of the kingdom, were clearly influenced by the common architectural styles in the countries of origin of the Latin settlers, that is, from the regions of France, Italy, England, Spain, Hungary, and so forth (Boas 2010: 13–14). Boas, indeed, listed many housing styles, of which examples survive in archaeological remains in settlements that belonged to the kingdom of Jerusalem, especially in Acre.[27] However, it seems likely that the Franks adapted several of the Eastern elements that they had met in their day-to-day life, a fact that is reflected in the architectural design of several preserved houses. One of the main elements of these is the indirect entrance, which does not appear to have been typical of Western house design.[28]

In his classification of the houses' types, Boas divided them into two major groups: town houses and village houses. The town houses included, according to him, six styles, while the village houses were less complicated and generally similar to each other. The town houses mentioned by Boas (2010: 249–57) are the courtyard house, the palace, the tower house, the merchant house with ground-floor shops, the house built on burgage plots, and the hovels. The current study will not discuss these types in detail but will present some archaeological evidences that help in understanding the society in a few towns, such as Acre.

For example, a few houses of the palace style were found in Acre. This style was common in Italy and the building included, *inter alia*, shops and apartments. The archaeological remains prove that the palaces were large buildings and may indeed include the abovementioned elements, as told in contemporary documents.[29] It is clear that these buildings were used for particular communities, especially the Italians.

The Use of Ceramics in the Frankish Period

Studies on Crusader ceramics have developed greatly during the last three decades, a matter that has contributed to several wider aspects, such as production technologies, production sites, trade, and function (see, e.g., Avissar and Stern 2005 and Stern 2012; 2016). However, some scholars have studied other aspects and from the basis of the different ceramic types, together with other historical and archaeological evidence, have attempted to distinguish between the different ethnic groups settling in the urban centers and their hinterlands. An important study in this field dealing with the kingdom of Jerusalem with particular focus on Acre and six rural sites in its region was recently published by Edna Stern (2015). She analyzed the different types of ceramics from these places and categorized them according to different features. In addition to the identification of handmade ceramics, which are technologically the simplest type, the main divisions are between imported and local ceramics, and glazed and unglazed ones. According to the proportion of the different types at each site and between the different sites, Stern tried to identify or confirm previous identifications of the inhabitants. The places with a high proportion of handmade ceramics were noted as being inhabited by local people. The glazed pottery, especially the imported ones, shed light on trade routes but also suggest that the standard of living was high in places with a high proportion of these ceramics, and Stern suggested that these places were inhabited by Franks.[30]

Whatever the case, ceramics are regarded among the most important material remains contributing to identifying differences between various classes of inhabitants and settlements. Indeed, they might be very indicative in classifying settlements and their inhabitants regardless of their ethnic belonging.

Coins of the Frankish Period

As with ceramics, coins are also indicative for studying societies. Robert Kool (2007) suggested, on the basis of historical and archaeological remains, that the inhabitants of both al-Qubayba and Bayt Jubrīn, as well as other settlements, circulated both Frankish and Muslim coins, such as the Zengid *fulus*, with some coins being of gold. The acceptance and circulation of money belonging to a different community might be a clear indication of the good integration of these societies, but the circulation on its own also shows the extent to which rural communities were monetized.

The Franks occasionally referred to the Fatimid gold dinars in their documents, and thus they certainly used the term in their transactions (Khamisy 2012: 136). In addition, preserved Crusader coins prove that the Franks used the designs of previously existing Muslim coins extensively in order to mint new types, carrying both Muslim and Christian features on the same coin (see Bates and Metcalf 1989: esp. 439–73). In fact, Muslim inscriptions on Frankish bezants (gold coins) and drachms (silver coins) were changed to Christian Arabic inscriptions only in 1251 following the order of Pope Innocent IV, who received information about the Muslim inscriptions only in 1250 (Bates and Metcalf 1989). However, keeping the coins with Arabic inscription sheds light on the relations between the Frankish and Muslim cultures. Perhaps, it reflects a strong influence on Frankish society, but also such coins could be used easily when dealing with commerce.

CONCLUSIONS

The Frankish conquest of the eastern Mediterranean brought several new cultures to the region that influenced and changed many previously existing customs and cultures. However, the new settlers were also greatly influenced by the existing local cultures – a fact that left its mark on many of the Franks' day-to-day functions that can be observed through archaeological and historical investigations, examining vessels, coins, architecture, and other material finds. The Franks arrived in stages, as both pilgrims and crusaders, and it seems likely that the newcomers inevitably found that the earlier arrivals had already been influenced by the Eastern cultures and changed their habits, thoughts, and mental attitudes. The battle of Ḥaṭṭīn, in which thousands of Franks were killed and expelled, can be regarded as a new starting point, similar to the First Crusade, and it may be that the majority of the Frankish inhabitants after the Third Crusade and the recovery of part of the kingdom were newcomers that had no acquaintance with the lifestyle in the Latin East. Nevertheless, as happened with the first Franks from the first kingdom, the new arrivals also started to influence and be influenced in their new lands.

While societies in the Frankish period can be studied through historical events, the archaeological remains are always essential for understanding many social aspects and the elements of day-to-day life that are missing from historical texts. Inhabitants of many religions, sects, ethnic groups, and different classes lived in both urban and rural settlements, and, in many cases, neighbored each other. They were involved in industry, agriculture, medicine, and other practices that are not discussed here.

On the basis of the three important archaeological remains discussed within this chapter – architecture, ceramics, and coins – I have tried to present the mutual influence of the Frankish and Eastern societies on each other, and the multiplicity within Frankish-period society in terms of ethnicity, religion, and class. A better understanding of the societies during the Frankish period, especially the rural societies, must involve additional archaeological excavation in the different regions they controlled.[31]

ACKNOWLEDGMENTS

I would like to thank Professor Peter Edbury for reading and commenting on the chapter and for sharing a new suggestion before its publication. My profound thanks are also extended to Professor Adrian Boas and Professor Denys Pringle for their comments.

NOTES

1 For additional references, see Ellenblum 1998: 3, n. 3.
2 For additional references, see Ellenblum 1998: 3, n. 1.
3 For the boundaries of the principality, see Riley-Smith 1990: 35.
4 Latakia was captured in 1103.
5 For a map of the five Frankish major regions, see Riley-Smith 1990: 35.
6 The county of Edessa, the earlier and larger between them, had served as an obstacle for the Muslims during the first half of the twelfth century, preventing them from attacking the other principalities. For this role, see Prawer 1969–1970 1: 209.
7 For the occupations until 1100, see Riley-Smith 1990: 35.
8 For Beirut and Sidon, see Pringle 1993–2009 1: 111; 2: 317. For Tripoli, see Prawer 1969–1970 1: 284–5 and Mayer 1988: 68.
9 In fact, Benjamin Kedar's chapter deals in detail with many aspects concerning the Muslims' situation under Frankish rule and their relations with them.
10 For all Jerusalem's churches, see Pringle 1993–2009 vol. 3. For the church of the Holy Sepulchre, see Pringle 1993–2009 3: 6–72. For the design and its specialty, see Boas 1999: 124–5. For the different Christian groups of Jerusalem, see Hamilton 1979; 1980; 1996.
11 For details about these churches and other ecclesiastical buildings in Jerusalem, see Pringle 1993–2009 vol. 3.
12 For the Furriers' market, see Pringle 2014: 184–5.
13 For these, see Boas 2001: 155

14 For the city of Tiberias, see Pringle 1993–2009 2: 351–66. For the principality, see the references in Pringle 1993–2009 2: 351.
15 For details on the Mount Tabor region, see Khamisy 2016. The author is now carrying out a detailed study of the activities in the principality of Galilee during the Frankish period.
16 For remaining Frankish-period buildings in Tyre, see Antaki-Masson 2013–2014: 281–91. For the cathedral, see Pringle 1993–2009 4: 182–204. For other churches, see Pringle 1993–2009 4: 204–30.
17 For Acre, see Pringle 1993–2009 4: 11–17. For Tyre, see Ibn Jubayr 2008: 321. For Jerusalem, see Boas 1999: 14, fig. 2.1; 2001: xvi, map; and Pringle 1993–2009 3: 478–81.
18 Both Merav Mack (2007) and Pringle (1993–2009 4: 212, fig. 16) attempted to draw part of Tyre's map according to the contemporary documents.
19 For details and other villages, see Boas 1999: 63–70; 2001: 98–9.
20 Joshua Prawer (1975: 65) raised the possibility that the *shuyūkh* (sg. *shaykh*) mentioned by the Franks in Wādī al-Taym were indeed Druze.
21 Boas (2007) was able to recognize three stages in the development of rural settlements.
22 There are other important fields beyond the scope of this chapter reflecting social behavior, such as music, arts, law (see the chapters in Edbury 2014), and other aspects dealing with languages, literature, and intellectual activities (Folda 1995; 2005).
In addition, a great deal of information about hospitals is given in historical accounts, and it is hoped that their remains will be uncovered in the future. Unfortunately, no excavation of a Frankish-period hospital is currently being carried out.
23 For sugar production, see, e.g., Peled 2009. For ceramics and references to previous studies, see Stern 2015. For metalwork, see, e.g., Boas 1999: 155–64, 170–9.
24 See, e.g., the vineyards and orchards mentioned in Strehlke 1869: esp. 120–8, no. 120; see also Marsilio Zorzi's account regarding the Tyre hinterland (Berggötz 1991: 149–68) and Burchard of Mount Sion's (Sandoli 1984: 206–7) description of the different kinds of agriculture in the last years of the kingdom at 1283 (Laurent 1864: 86–8; for an English translation, see Stewart 1896: 99–102).
25 For different kinds of industries, see Boas 2010: 152–9. For Crusader winepresses, see Frankel 2017.
26 In his recent research, Boas (2010) presented the different styles of houses that were common at the time, and he discussed the possible influence of Eastern style on the Western in the kingdom of Jerusalem.
27 The main styles discussed by Boas are the houses on the burgage plots, the merchant palaces, the tower house, the courtyard house, the hall house, and the village house.
28 For details, see Boas 2010: *passim* but mainly at pp. 14–17, 249–360 (appendixes 1, 2). For adapting the entrance style, see Boas 2010: 273.
29 For examples and discussion, see Boas 2010: 252–4, 263, 267–8, 275, 279.
30 Another reading of the historical accounts and the archaeological remains of Khirbat Zuwanītā and Kisrā, which she suggested had been settled by indigenous people, leads me to suggest with high degree of certainty that the former village was inhabited by Franks, while the latter was possibly inhabited by Franks but almost certainly by Christians. This study is now being edited and will be published soon. However, in the meantime, see Khamisy 2012: 23–8, 139–44.
31 The author had already excavated in a Frankish village located 800 m to the southeast of Montfort Castle and in Castellum Regis. These excavations are the beginning of a series of excavations in rural settlements in the Galilee.

REFERENCES

Antaki-Masson, P. 2013–2014. Inventaire des marques lapidaires médiévales du Liban. *Mélanges de l'Université Saint-Joseph* 65: 229–95.

Asher, A., trans. and ed. 1907. *The Itinerary of Rabbi Benjamin of Tudela*, Vol. 1: *Text, Bibliography, and Translation*. New York: Hakesheth.

Avissar, M., and Stern, E. J. 2005. *Pottery of the Crusader and Mamluk Periods in Israel*. IAA Reports 26. Jerusalem: IAA.

Bates, M. L., and Metcalf, D. M. 1989. Crusader Coinage with Arabic Inscriptions. In *A History of the Crusades*, Vol. 6: *The Impact of the Crusades on Europe*, ed. H. W. Hazard and N. P. Zacour, 421–82. Madison: The University of Wisconsin Press.

Berggötz, O. 1991. *Der Bericht des Marsilio Zorzi: Codex Querini-Stampalia IV3 (1064)*. Kieler Werkstücke C, Beiträge zur europäischen Geschichte des frühen und hohen Mittelalters 2. Frankfurt am Main: Lang.

Boas, A. J. 1999. *Crusader Archaeology: The Material Culture of the Latin East*. London: Routledge.

2001. *Jerusalem in the Time of the Crusades: Society, Landscape and Art in the Holy City under Frankish Rule*. London: Routledge.

2007. Three Stages in the Evolution of Rural Settlement in the Kingdom of Jerusalem during the Twelfth Century. In *In Laudem Hierosolymitani: Studies in Crusades and Medieval Culture in Honour of Benjamin Z. Kedar*, ed. I. Shagrir, R. Ellenblum, and J. Riley-Smith, 77–92. Crusades, Subsidia 1. Aldershot: Ashgate.

2010. *Domestic Settings: Sources on Domestic Architecture and Day-to-Day Activities in the Crusader States*. Medieval Mediterranean 84. Leiden: Brill.

Cahen, C. 1950–1951. Notes sur l'histoire des croisades et de l'Orient latin, II: Le régime rural syrien au temps de la domination franque. *Bulletin de la Faculté des Lettres de l'Université de Strasbourg* 29: 286–310.

Edbury, P. W. 2014. *Law and History in the Latin East*. Collected Studies 1048. Surrey: Ashgate Vaiorum.

Ellenblum, R. 1998. *Frankish Rural Settlement in the Latin Kingdom of Jerusalem*. Cambridge: Cambridge University Press.

Folda, J. 1995. *The Art of the Crusaders in the Holy Land, 1098–1187*. Cambridge: Cambridge University Press.

2005. *The Art of the Crusaders in the Holy Land, 1187–1291*. Cambridge: Cambridge University Press.

Frankel, R. 2017. The Winepress at Montfort. In *Montfort: History, Early Research and Recent Studies*, ed. A. J. Boas and R. G. Khamisy. Leiden: Brill.

Hamilton, B. 1979. A Medieval Urban Church: The Case of the Crusader States. *Studies in Church History* 16: 159–70.

1980. *The Latin Church in the Crusader States: The Secular Church*. London: Variorum.

1996. The Latin Church and the Crusader States. In *East and West in the Crusader States*, Vol. 1: *Acta of the Congress Held at Hernen Castle in May 1993*, ed. K. Ciggaar, A. Davids, and H. Teule, 1–20. OLA 75. Leuven: Peeters.

Huygens, R. B. C., ed. 1986. *Willelmi Tyrensis Archiepiscopi Chronicon*. Corpus Christianorum, Continuatio Mediaevalis 63. Turnholt: Brepols.

Ibn Jubayr. 2008. *The Travels of Ibn Jubayr*. Trans. R. J. C. Broadhurst, from Arabic. New Delhi: Goodword Books.

Ibn Qalānisī. 1908. *Dhayl taʾrīkh dimashq*. Beirut: s.n.

Kedar, B. Z. 1990. The Subjected Muslims of the Frankish Levant. In *Muslims under Latin Rule, 1100–1300*, ed. J. M. Powell, 135–74. Princeton Legacy Library. Princeton: Princeton University Press.

Khamisy, R. G. 2012. *Political, Social and Economic Activities of the Franks in the Western Galilee, 1104–1291*. PhD diss., University of Haifa (Hebrew).

—— 2016. The Mount Tabor Territory under Frankish Control. In *Crusader Landscapes in the Medieval Levant: The Archaeology and History of the Latin East*, ed. M. Sinibaldi, K. J. Lewis, B. Major, and J. A. Thompson, 39–53. Cardiff: University of Wales Press.

Kool, R. 2007. Coin Circulation in the *Villeneuves* of the Latin Kingdom of Jerusalem: The Cases of Parva Mahumeria and Bethgibelin. In *Archaeology and the Crusades: Proceedings of the Round Table, Nicosia, 1 February 2005*, ed. P. W. Edbury and S. Kalopissi-Verti, 133–56. Athens: Pierides Foundation.

Laurent, J. K. M., ed. 1864. *Peregrinatores medii aevi quatuor*. Leipzig: Hinrichs.

Mack, M. 2007. The Italian Quarters of Frankish Tyre: Mapping a Medieval City. *Journal of Medieval History* 33: 147–65.

Mayer, H. E. 1988. *The Crusades*. 2nd ed. Oxford: Oxford University Press.

Mayer, H. E., ed. 2010. *Die Urkunden der lateinischen Könige von Jerusalem*. 4 vols. Hannover: Hahnsche Buchhandlung.

Peled, A. 2009. *Sugar in the Kingdom of Jerusalem: A Crusader Technology between East and West*. Jerusalem: Yad Izhak Ben-Zvi (Hebrew).

Prawer, J. 1969–1970. *Histoire du Royaume latin de Jérusalem*. 2nd ed. 2 vols. Paris: CNRS.

—— 1975. *The Crusaders: A Colonial Society*. Jerusalem: Bialik Institute (Hebrew).

—— 1980. *Crusader Institution*. Oxford: Oxford University Press.

—— 1988. *The History of the Jews in the Latin Kingdom of Jerusalem*. Oxford: Clarendon.

Pringle, D. 1993–2009. *The Churches of the Crusader Kingdom of Jerusalem: A Corpus*. 4 vols. Cambridge: Cambridge University Press.

—— 2003. Churches and Settlement in Crusader Palestine. In *The Experience of Crusading*, Vol. 2: *Defining the Crusader Kingdom*, ed. P. W. Edbury and J. Phillips, 161–78. Cambridge: Cambridge University Press.

—— 2014. A Rental of Hospitaller Properties in Twelfth-Century Jerusalem. In *Deeds Done beyond the Sea: Essays on William of Tyre, Cyprus and the Military Orders Presented to Peter Edbury*, ed. S. B. Edgington and H. J. Nicholson, 181–96. Crusades, Subsidia 6. London: Routledge.

Rey, E. G. 1866. *Essai sur la domination française en Syrie durant le Moyen Âge*. Paris: Thunot.

Riley-Smith, J., ed. 1990. *The Atlas of the Crusades*. London: Times Books.

Sandoli, S. de, ed. 1984. *Itinera Hierosolymitana Crucesigantorum (saec. XII–XIII)*, Vol. 4: *Tempore Regni Latini Extremo (1245–1291)*. SBFCMa 24. Jerusalem: Franciscan Printing Press.

Smail, R. C. 1956. *Crusading Warfare (1097–1193)*. Cambridge Studies in Medieval Life and Thought 3. Cambridge: Cambridge University Press.

Stern, E. J. 2012. Mi'ilya: Evidence of an Early Crusader Settlement. *'Atiqot* 70: 63*–76*.

—— 2015. Pottery and Identity in the Latin Kingdom of Jerusalem: A Case Study of Acre and Western Galilee. In *Medieval and Post-Medieval Ceramics in the Eastern Mediterranean – Fact and Fiction: Proceedings of the First International Conference on Byzantine and Ottoman Archaeology, Amsterdam, 21–32 October 2011*, ed. J. Vroom, 287–315. Medieval and Post-Medieval Mediterranean Archaeology Series 1. Turnhout: Brepols.

2016. Maritime Commerce in the Latin East as Reflected in the Import of Ceramics. In *The Crusader World*, ed. A. J. Boas, 519–43. Routledge Worlds. London: Routledge.

Stewart, A., trans. 1896. *Burchard of Mount Sion, A.D. 1280*. Palestine Pilgrims' Text Society 12. London: Palestine Pilgrims' Text Society.

Strehlke, E. 1869. *Tabulae Ordinis Theutonici: Ex Tabularii Regii Berolinensis Codice Potissimum*. Berlin: Weidmann.

PART FIVE

TWENTY SEVEN

THEMES AND PATTERNS IN HUMAN–ANIMAL INTERACTIONS

Hunting, Domestication, and Livestock Husbandry

NIMROD MAROM

Animals have played a major role in economic, ecological, and symbolic systems since the dawn of humanity (Russell 2012). The history of interaction between humans, animals, and the environment is a major objective of zooarchaeological research, which is concerned with the analysis and interpretation of faunal remains from archaeological sites (Hesse and Wapnish 1985; Davis 1987; O'Connor 2000; Sykes 2014). In the last decades, animal bone archaeology has expanded due to both growing awareness of its utility in studying the past and the availability of new technologies, such as stable isotope analyses (Makarewicz and Sealy 2015) and ancient DNA studies (Larson and Burger 2013; Meiri et al. 2013; Hagelberg, Hofreiter, and Keyser 2015). This resulted in a plethora of new knowledge and has thoroughly reworked our approach to faunal analysis and its role in understanding human societies.

This chapter seeks to survey major themes in zooarchaeological research as viewed from a southern Levantine perspective (Grigson 1995). Hunting, domestication, and livestock economy will be presented as long-term interactions developing through time between people and animals. These interactions were not mutually exclusive: Hunting did not cease when livestock herding began, but it did change its function (Russell 2012). In a similar way, animal domestication was an ongoing process that lasted well into the first millennium BCE, long after its formative Neolithic beginning (Larson and Fuller 2014; Perry-Gal et al. 2015). The interweaving of hunting, ongoing domestication, and livestock husbandry relates to an explanatory space in which social complexity is a major vector of variability. This viewpoint provides a raster to articulate the human/animal/environment interactions studied in zooarchaeology with other branches of archaeological and historical knowledge.

THEMES AND PATTERNS IN HUMAN–ANIMAL INTERACTIONS

Hunting

Obtaining meat by hunting or scavenging is an activity carried out by all members of the genus *Homo* who have lived in the region from the Lower Paleolithic (Goren-Inbar et al. 1994; Gaudzinski 2004) to the present day (Mendelssohn and Yom-Tov 1999). The subsistence value, mode of procurement, and social significance of hunting underwent at least four distinctive stages that can be observed in the zooarchaeological record. The first stage is that of Pleistocene hunter-gatherers, who roamed across relatively large territories in the fluctuating climate of the ice ages. Hunter-gatherers assumed from a very early date a uniquely human hunting pattern of prime-age males (Stiner 1994; Yeshurun, Bar-Oz, and Weinstein-Evron 2007; Rabinovich, Gaudzinski-Windheuser, and Goren-Inbar 2008), with the favorite prey species being mountain gazelles and fallow deer (Bar-Oz 2004; Yeshurun 2016). This pattern is unique in that it targets the most difficult demographic component to bring down among ungulates and is distinct from other mammalian carnivores who hunt indiscriminately for males and females, aiming for the young and the infirm. The meat from the kills was shared (Stiner, Barkai, and Gopher 2009). In addition to gazelles and fallow deer that comprised the mainstay of Paleolithic diet, wild cattle, boar, and red and roe deer constitute a typical list of the large prey taxa brought down by earlier hunter-gatherers. It appears that the composition of Pleistocene faunal assemblages is predicated on the availability of terrestrial mammals around the site, which, in turn, was a function of the proximity of suitable habitats (Lyman 1986).

The second stage of hunting followed the wake of early Holocene climatic amelioration. Increasing habitat productivity in the Mediterranean climatic zone triggered hunter-gatherer sedentarization, demographic growth, and intensification of resource extraction in the quintessential complex hunter-gatherer Natufian culture (Bar-Yosef 1998). Growing pressure on game resources resulted in the depletion of larger game animals, which have low reproduction rates (Stiner et al. 1999). Hunting shifted toward the utilization of a broader spectrum of game (Stiner, Munro, and Surovell 2000; Munro 2004; Weissbrod et al. 2012). The role of wild cattle, boar, and larger deer was marginal in the Natufian economy, with gazelles dominating the faunal assemblages along with small (tortoises, mole rats) or small and hard to capture (partridges, hares) game (Yeshurun, Bar-Oz, and Weinstein-Evron 2014). Foxes drawn to scavenging opportunities around human hamlets were also caught and perhaps eaten (Yeshurun, Bar-Oz, and Weinstein-Evron 2009). It may be that the first domestic dogs in the region (Davis and Valla 1978) were employed by humans in hunting.

The third stage of hunting history characterized the first farming societies. The domestication of founder crops (wheat, barley, lentils, chickpeas, vicia [Zohary, Hopf, and Weiss 2012]) was optimally practiced in alluvial valleys and near water sources (Kuijt and Goring-Morris 2002). The territorial farming existence put humans in constant friction with other denizens of these water-rich habitats: wild cattle and boar. Indeed, wild cattle and boar figure more prominently in the faunal assemblages from the Early Neolithic (Marom and Bar-Oz 2009). Their hunting provided large amounts of shareable meat, got rid of dangerous agricultural pests, and, in the case of wild cattle, appears to have assumed deep symbolic meanings (Cauvin 2000; Horwitz and Goring-Morris 2004). By the late seventh millennium BCE, both wild cattle and boar show marked signs of overhunting, followed by the appearance of domesticated cattle and pigs (Marom and Bar-Oz 2013). Hunting continued to supplement human agropastoral production until the modern period.

The final stage of the regional hunting history is typical of complex hierarchical societies. Subsistence hunting, no doubt, continued to play part in the periphery (Lev-Tov, Porter, and Routledge 2011), but – perhaps echoing an earlier Neolithic tradition – hunting reverted to an elite occupation that propagated a "macho" identity and helped maintain exclusive cliques among the ruling elites (Allsen 2006). Hunting in an increasingly populated landscape has resulted in the local extinction of larger game animals from the southern Levant: The aurochs, hartebeest, red deer, and behemoth were all gone by the end of the Iron Age. The final blow to the fallow deer, wild ass, leopard, bear, and roe deer commenced with the introduction of firearms to the region in the nineteenth and twentieth centuries, which has endowed prestige hunters with too lethal capabilities (Tsahar et al. 2009).

Domestication

A second theme of human/animal/environment interactions is domestication, here defined as a process in which human selective pressure subsumes a larger role in determining the biological and social characteristics of domesticated species (Hemmer 1990), accompanied by a cultural transformation that viewed animals as capital and property (Bökönyi 1989). Domesticated animals are smaller than their wild progenitors, their bodily (and especially cranial) proportions change, and they reproduce earlier and at a quicker rate. These and related changes are triggered by adaptation to higher stress levels induced by crowding with conspecifics and by interactions with humans and are mediated by a complex hormonal mechanism (Hemmer 1990).

The first farming societies can be thought of as a community of symbiotic species in which humans formed the definitive hub. Domesticated plants and animals were propagated by humans and became a very efficient resource extraction mechanism, binding together alluvial landscape for plant, cattle, and pig husbandry, and bordering hilly regions for sheep and goat grazing. This adaptive species' syndicate was extremely successful demographically and, when coupled with sedentism and territorialism, led by necessity to rapid geographical expansion.

The question of the exact timing, as well as the multi- or single origin of the "agricultural package," is important but beyond our present scope (Horwitz et al. 1999; Lev-Yadun, Gopher, and Abbo 2000). From a southern Levantine perspective, it appears as though founder crops and domesticated sheep and goats were introduced from the northern Levant during the ninth century BCE. The appearance in the region of domesticated cattle and pigs was staggered: The earliest evidence for these occur in the central-northern Jordan Valley at the very end of the Early Neolithic (early sixth millennium BCE [Marom and Bar-Oz 2013]), but, tellingly, other sites — sometimes only tens of kilometers away — do not keep domesticated pigs until a thousand years later (Haber, Dayan, and Getzov 2005; Davis 2012). This puzzling pattern may have to do with difficulty in re-articulating an already complex subsistence system, regulated by ritual, to major innovation. It may also be that communities were already using differences in the utilization of cattle and pigs as wild or domesticated animals to set each other apart.

Be that as it may, by the end of the Late Neolithic the agricultural package consisting of goats, sheep, cattle, and pigs was firmly in place throughout the southern Levant (Horwitz et al. 1999). In addition to the Neolithic date of their binding to the "human species' syndicate," these first domesticated animals have three things in common. First, they were all major hunter-gatherer prey taxa of the Pleistocene Middle East, domesticated through the "prey pathway" by non-directed and gradual intensification of game management (Zeder 2012). Second, these animals were bound to and owned by a specific human community, tying together different proximate landscapes (hilly forests, water-rich valleys) to its economic system by converting plant material to human consumables. Third, the domestication of these livestock taxa happened in a Fertile Crescent epicenter, from which they rapidly spread westward along with the human communities with which they were associated (Bökönyi 1974; Conolly et al. 2011).

These characteristics of the first wave of animal domesticates contrast what we may dub "second-wave" domesticates (Fig. 27.1). In the southern Levant, these consist mainly of the donkey, horse, camel, and chicken that are

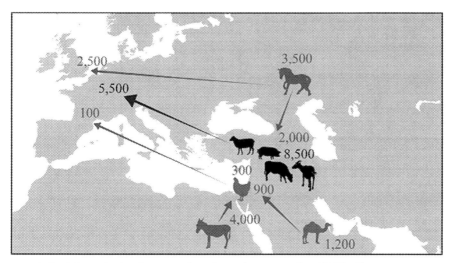

27.1. Animal domestication from a southern Levantine perspective. Middle silhouettes represent "first-stage" animals domesticated in a cultural center and spreading along with humans; top and bottom silhouettes represent "second-stage" animals, which were domesticated in a cultural-economic periphery and spread quickly along trade and exchange networks. Dates are approximate and BCE. (Drawing by A. Regev-Gisis.)

distinguished by undergoing a two-phase process of binding and propagation into human communities. All of these animals were domesticated off-center in relation to the core area of the first wave of domestication: the donkey in Northeast Africa (Rossel et al. 2008), the horse in the Eurasian steppes (Orlando 2015), and the camel in the Arabian Peninsula (Uerpmann and Uerpmann 2002; Almathen et al. 2016). This off-center domestication was followed by a second-phase, rapid expansion across Eurasia and North Africa (within climate tolerance limits for camels) that was, importantly, detached from the human/landscape/livestock complex. In other words, these animals did not necessarily follow the human communities of which they were part but spread along trading routes and exchange networks in a very rapid way.

Donkeys, horses, and camels were transport animals employed for short (horse: military), medium (donkeys: intra- and inter-settlement), and long (camel) ranges (Clutton-Brock 1999). It appears that their adoption by human communities had to do with cultural and historical changes in connectivity and political organization: The donkey was quickly adopted in the region while it supported short-distance overland connections (Bar-Oz et al. 2013), but the camel was only adopted much later when long-distance, desert-crossing overland trade became common (Sapir-Hen and Ben-Yosef 2013). Similarly, the horse spread quickly in the Near East with the advent of a political organization able to support its standard deployment in battle by the large city-states of the second millennium BCE (Yadin 1963). The timing and mode of propagation of second-wave domesticates as opposed to their Neolithic antecedents illustrates the dynamic and long-term nature of this slow revolution binding animal and human communities together through history.

Livestock Management

In a similar way to hunting and domestication, livestock management systems also evolved through time and in relation to the growing complexity of human social and economic systems (Table 27.1). As described above, the basic production unit in the southern Levant consists of a community utilizing proximal fields for agriculture and a distal hinterland for sheep and goat grazing. By the fifth millennium BCE, cattle and pigs comprised part of the near-settlement economic system in the Mediterranean climatic zone by providing, respectively, traction to significantly augment agricultural productivity (Halstead 1995) and a handy means to efficiently recycle garbage to animal fat and protein (Zeder 1998). Short-range transhumance was probably practiced to keep grazing livestock away from the fields during the growing season and fertilize them with dung after the harvest (Borowski 1998). With some changes, such as the replacement of pigs by chickens as a garbage-to-food converter in the late first millennium (Perry-Gal et al. 2015; Redding 2015), this basic arrangement of production lasted until modern times.

Maintaining a herd of sheep and goats provides one important resource that can be easily disembedded: male animals that are not required for breeding. Since the sex ratio at birth among sheep and goats is approximately even, and only one male in five to ten is typically kept to service the females, a great number of animals can be redistributed (Zeder 1991; 1994). In a stand-alone community, redistribution of spare livestock would be an internal affair, mediated by social obligation and ritual; however, once part of a hierarchical and complex economic system, male livestock would become a prime target for taxing. This can be seen in numerous examples of the presence of mainly young male animals in the faunal remains from towns and cities, as opposed to female and very young animals recovered from the remains of villages (Hesse and Wapnish 1985; Marom et al. 2009).

Truly large economies exerted a strong enough market pull to not only redirect extra male animals to them but also shift the livestock system in their hinterlands toward producing more sheep (Marom et al. 2014). While sheep have fatter meat and milk, and also tradable wool – all of which are desirable from a consumer perspective – keeping them is inherently risky because they are more susceptible to disease, and they reproduce slowly in comparison to goats (Redding 1984). Also, unlike goats, sheep are mainly grazers. The similar food preferences to cattle would force spatial segregation and more specialized

TABLE 27.1. *A schematic summary showing the evolution of domestication, livestock husbandry, and hunting over time.*

Period\Activity	Paleolithic	Epipaleolithic	Neolithic	Chalcolithic	Bronze–Iron	Hellenistic–Roman
Hunting	Subsistence hunting, large game	Subsistence hunting, intensification	Supplementary hunting, pest control, ritual	Supplementary, ritual (?)	Status symbol	Status symbol
Domestication		Commensal pathway	Prey pathway	Prey pathway + directed	Prey pathway + directed	Directed
Livestock			Autarkic economies	Autarkic economies	Some intensification for exchange	Differentiated specialized economy

and long-distance transhumance to grass-rich regions, either in marginal areas at the edge of the "sawn" or in nearby hills modified by fire and woodcutting to promote herbaceous growth.

Within the boundaries of larger towns and cities, two notable patterns appear to hold true across most periods in the zooarchaeological record of Israel. First, pigs are very uncommon, typically comprising less than 10% of the animals represented in the faunal remains (Zeder 1998). Given the very high reproductive rate of pigs (Redding 2015), this low frequency attests to the presence of a very small number of suids in towns. Beginning in the Iron Age, this was justified by religious taboo; however, the number of pigs is also relatively low in many Canaanite, later Philistine, Hellenistic, Roman, and Byzantine cities (Hesse 1990; Lev-Tov 1999; Sapir-Hen, Meiri, and Finkelstein 2015). This suggests that pigs, which cannot be easily transported on the hoof, were not redistributed from the hinterland for logistical reasons (Redding 2015).

Second, cities and towns show spatial patterning of animal consumption activities. Certain species and body parts are discarded in specific areas but not in others, reflecting social inequality (Crabtree 1990; Davis 2008; deFrance 2009; Greer 2013; Arbuckle and McCarty 2014) or specialized butchery areas (Hesse and Wapnish 1996), in which slaughter offal is discarded, and consumption areas, in which dressed portions were eaten. Differences in the quality of meat cuts and the presence of exotic/imported animals and wild game are often held to reflect status differences within a settlement (Ervynck et al. 2003; Marom et al. 2009; Sapir-Hen, Gadot, and Finkelstein 2016); from the Bronze Age onward, fish and mollusks remains provide powerful indices to status in inland sites through their connection to trade networks (e.g., Lernau 1986).

CONCLUSIONS

This chapter offers a summary of three themes in the history of human–animal interactions from a local perspective, emphasizing the key role of economic complexity in that history and the interconnectedness of hunting, domestication, and livestock management. Hunting changed from a means of living to a prestige-enhancing pursuit by livestock domestication, which was an ongoing process re-oriented by the rise of economic networks, fueled — to a great extent — by agropastoral surplus production and redistribution, using animal transportation. Conceiving, refining, and testing formal models integrating ancient DNA and stable isotope studies in the exploration of the interaction between humans and animals, beyond the level of a single archaeological period, culture, and monocausal explanations of change, is a challenge facing the archaeology of the region in years to come.

ACKNOWLEDGMENTS

I wish to thank Asaf Yasur-Landau, Eric Cline, and Yorke Rowan for inviting me to contribute to this volume, and Guy Bar-Oz for offering comments on the manuscript.

REFERENCES

Allsen, T. T. 2006. *The Royal Hunt in Eurasian History*. Encounters with Asia. Philadelphia: University of Pennsylvania Press.

Almathen, F.; Charruau, P.; Mohandesan, E.; Mwacharo, J. M.; Orozco-terWengel, P.; Pitt, D.; Abdussamad, A. M.; Uerpmann, M.; Uerpmann, H.-P.; De Cupere, B.; Magee, P.; Alnaqeeb, M. A.; Salim, B.; Raziq, A.; Dessie, T.; Abdelhadi, O. M.; Banabazi, M. H.; al-Eknah, M.; Walzer, C.; Faye, B.; Hofreiter, M.; Peters, J.; Hanotte, O.; and Burger, P. A. 2016. Ancient and Modern DNA Reveal Dynamics of Domestication and Cross-Continental Dispersal of the Dromedary. *PNAS* 13: 6707–12.

Arbuckle, B. S., and McCarty, S. A. 2014. *Animals and Inequality in the Ancient World*. Boulder: University of Colorado Press.

Bar-Oz, G. 2004. *Epipaleolithic Subsistence Strategies in the Levant: A Zooarchaeological Perspective*. ASPRMS. Boston: Brill Academic.

Bar-Oz, G.; Nahshoni, P.; Motro, H.; and Oren, E. D. 2013. Symbolic Metal Bit and Saddlebag Fastenings in a Middle Bronze Age Donkey Burial. *PLOS ONE* 8 (3): e58648. https://doi.org/10.1371/journal.pone.0058648 (accessed August 14, 2017).

Bar-Yosef, O. 1998. The Natufian Culture in the Levant, Threshold to the Origins of Agriculture. *EA* 6 (5): 159–77.

Bökönyi, S. 1974. *History of Domestic Mammals in Central and Eastern Europe*. Budapest: Akadémiai Kiadó.

———. 1989. Definition of Animal Domestication. In *The Walking Larder: Patterns of Domestication, Pastoralism, and Predation*, ed. J. Clutton-Brock, 22–7. London: Unwin Hyman.

Borowski, O. 1998. *Every Living Thing: Daily Use of Animals in Ancient Israel*. Walnut Creek, CA: AltaMira.

Cauvin, J. 2000. *The Birth of the Gods and the Origins of Agriculture*. New Studies in Archaeology. Cambridge: Cambridge University Press.

Clutton-Brock, J. 1999. *A Natural History of Domesticated Mammals*. 2nd ed. Cambridge: Cambridge University Press.

Conolly, J.; Colledge, S.; Dobney, K.; Vigne, J-.D.; Peters, J.; Stopp, B.; Manning, K.; and Shennan, S. 2011. Meta-Analysis of Zooarchaeological Data from SW Asia and SE Europe Provides Insight into the Origins and Spread of Animal Husbandry. *JAS* 38: 538–45.

Crabtree, P. J. 1990. Zooarchaeology and Complex Societies: Some Uses of Faunal Analysis for the Study of Trade, Social Status, and Ethnicity. *Archaeological Method and Theory* 2: 155–205.

Davis, S. J. M. 1987. *The Archaeology of Animals*. New Haven, CT: Yale University Press.

———. 2008. "Thou Shalt Take of the Ram . . . the Right Thigh; for It Is a Ram of Consecration . . .": Some Zoo-Archaeological Examples of Body-Part Preferences. In *Uomini, piante e animali nella dimensione del sacro*, ed. F. d'Andria, J. de Grossi Mazzorin, and G. Fiorentino, 63–70. Beni archeologici, Conoscenza e tecnologie 6. Bari: Edipuglia.

2012. Animal Bones at the Naḥal Zehora Sites. In *Village Communities of the Pottery Neolithic Period in the Menashe Hills, Israel. Archaeological Investigations at the Sites of Naḥal Zehora*, Vol. 3, ed. A. Gopher, 1258–320. MSSMNIA 29. Tel Aviv: Emery and Claire Yass Publications in Archaeology, Institute of Archaeology, Tel Aviv University.

Davis, S. J. M., and Valla, F. R. 1978. Evidence for Domestication of the Dog 12,000 Years Ago in the Natufian of Israel. *Nature* 276: 608–10.

deFrance, S. 2009. Zooarchaeology in Complex Societies: Political Economy, Status, and Ideology. *JAR* 17: 105–68.

Ervynck, A.; van Neer, W.; Hüster-Plogmann, H.; and Schibler, J. 2003. Beyond Affluence: The Zooarchaeology of Luxury. *WA* 34: 428–41.

Gaudzinski, S. 2004. Subsistence Patterns of Early Pleistocene Hominids in the Levant – Taphonomic Evidence from the 'Ubeidiya Formation (Israel). *JAS* 31: 65–75.

Goren-Inbar, N.; Lister, A.; Werker, E.; and Chech, M. 1994. A Butchered Elephant Skull and Associated Artifacts from the Acheulian Site of Gesher Benot Ya'aqov, Israel. *Paléorient* 20 (1): 99–112.

Greer, J. S. 2013. *Dinner at Dan: Biblical and Archaeological Evidence for Sacred Feasts at Iron Age II Tel Dan and Their Significance*. CHANE 66. Leiden: Brill.

Grigson, C. 1995. Plough and Pasture in the Early Economy of the Southern Levant. In *The Archaeology of Society in the Holy Land*, ed. T. E. Levy, 245–68. NAAA. London: Leicester University Press.

Haber, A.; Dayan, T.; and Getzov, N. 2005. Pig Exploitation at Hagoshrim: A Prehistoric Site in the Southern Levant. In *First Steps of Animal Domestication: New Archaeozoological Approaches*, ed. J.-D. Vigne, J. Peters, and D. Helmer, 80–5. Oxford: Oxbow.

Hagelberg, E.; Hofreiter, M.; and Keyser, C. 2015. Ancient DNA: The First Three Decades. *Philosophical Transactions of the Royal Society* B370. http://rstb.royalsocietypublishing.org/content/370/1660/20130371 (accessed August 15, 2017).

Halstead, P. 1995. Plough and Power: The Economic and Social Significance of Cultivation with the Ox-Drawn Ard in the Mediterranean. *BSA* 8: 11–22.

Hemmer, H. 1990. *Domestication: The Decline of Environmental Appreciation*. Cambridge: Cambridge University Press.

Hesse, B. 1990. Pig Lovers and Pig Haters: Patterns of Palestinian Pork Production. *JoE* 10: 195–225.

Hesse, B., and Wapnish, P. 1985. *Animal Bone Archeology: From Objectives to Analysis*. Manuals on Archeology 5. Washington, DC: Taraxacum.

1996. Pigs' Feet, Cattle Bones and Birds' Wings. *BAR* 22 (1): 62.

Horwitz, L. K., and Goring-Morris, A. N. 2004. Animals and Ritual during the Levantine PPNB: A Case Study from the Site of Kfar Hahoresh, Israel. *Anthropozoologica* 39: 165–78.

Horwitz, L. K.; Tchernov, E.; Ducos, P.; Becker, C.; von den Driesch, A.; Martin, L. A.; and Garrard, A. 1999. Animal Domestication in the Southern Levant. *Paléorient* 25 (2): 63–80.

Kuijt, I., and Goring-Morris, A. N. 2002. Foraging, Farming and Social Complexity in the Pre-Pottery Neolithic of the South-Central Levant: A Review and Synthesis. *JWP* 16: 361–440.

Larson, G., and Burger, J. 2013. A Population Genetics View of Animal Domestication. *Trends in Genetics* 29: 197–205.

Larson, G., and Fuller, D. Q. 2014. The Evolution of Animal Domestication. *Annual Review of Ecology, Evolution, and Systematics* 45: 115–36.

Lernau, H. 1986. Fish Bones Excavated in Two Late Roman–Byzantine *Castellae* in the Southern Desert of Israel. In *Fish and Archaeology: Studies in Osteometry, Taphonomy, Seasonality and Fishing Methods*, ed. D. C. Brinkuizen and A. T. Clason, 85–102. BAR International Series 294. Oxford: BAR.

Lev-Tov, J. S. E. 1999. The Social Implications of Subsistence: Analysis of Faunal Remains from Tel Miqne-Ekron. *ASOR Newsletter* 49: 13–15.

Lev-Tov, J. S. E.; Porter, B. W.; and Routledge, B. E. 2011. Measuring Local Diversity in Early Iron Age Animal Economies: A View from Khirbat al-Mudayna al-'Aliya (Jordan). *BASOR* 361: 67–93.

Lev-Yadun, S.; Gopher, A.; and Abbo, S. 2000. The Cradle of Agriculture. *Science* 288: 1602–3.

Lyman, R. L. 1986. On the Analysis and Interpretation of Species List Data in Zooarchaeology. *JoE* 6: 67–81.

Makarewicz, C. A., and Sealy, J. 2015. Dietary Reconstruction, Mobility, and the Analysis of Ancient Skeletal Tissues: Expanding the Prospects of Stable Isotope Research in Archaeology. *JAS* 56: 146–58.

Marom, N., and Bar-Oz, G. 2009. "Man-Made Oases": Neolithic Patterns of Wild Ungulate Exploitation & Their Consequences for the Domestication of Pigs & Cattle. *Before Farming* 2009 (1). www.academia.edu/581281/Marom_N._and_Bar-Oz_G._2009._Man-Made_Oases_Neolithic_patterns_of_wild_ungulate_exploitation_and_their_consequences_for_the_domestication_of_pigs_and_cattle_._Before_Farming_2009_1_article_2 (accessed August 15, 2017).

2013. The Prey Pathway: A Regional History of Cattle (*Bos taurus*) and Pig (*Sus scrofa*) Domestication in the Northern Jordan Valley, Israel. *PLOS ONE* 8 (2): e55958. https://doi.org/10.1371/journal.pone.0055958 (accessed August 15, 2017).

Marom, N.; Raban-Gerstel, N.; Mazar, A.; and Bar-Oz, G. 2009. Backbone of Society: Evidence for Social and Economic Status of the Iron Age Population of Tel Reḥov, Beth Shean Valley, Israel. *BASOR* 354: 55–75.

Marom, N.; Yasur-Landau, A.; Zuckerman, S.; Cline, E. H.; Ben-Tor, A.; and Bar-Oz, G. 2014. Shepherd Kings? A Zooarchaeological Investigation of Elite Precincts in Middle Bronze Age Tel Hazor and Tel Kabri. *BASOR* 371: 59–82.

Meiri, M.; Huchon, D.; Bar-Oz, G.; Boaretto, E.; Horwitz, L. K.; Maeir, A. M.; Sapir-Hen, L.; Larson, G.; Weiner, S.; and Finkelstein, I. 2013. Ancient DNA and Population Turnover in Southern Levantine Pigs – Signature of the Sea Peoples Migration? *Scientific Reports* 3. www.nature.com/articles/srep03035 (accessed August 15, 2017).

Mendelssohn, H., and Yom-Tov, Y. 1999. *Mammalia of Israel*. Fauna Palaestina. Jerusalem: The Israel Academy of Sciences and Humanities.

Munro, N. D. 2004. Zooarchaeological Measures of Hunting Pressure and Occupation Intensity in the Natufian: Implications for Agricultural Origins. *CA* 45 (suppl. 4): S5–34.

O'Connor, T. 2000. *The Archaeology of Animal Bones*. Stroud: Sutton.

Orlando, L. 2015. Equids. *Current Biology* 25: R973–8.

Perry-Gal, L.; Erlich, A.; Gilboa, A.; and Bar-Oz, G. 2015. Earliest Economic Exploitation of Chicken outside East Asia: Evidence from the Hellenistic Southern Levant. *PNAS* 112: 9849–54.

Rabinovich, R.; Gaudzinski-Windheuser, S.; and Goren-Inbar, N. 2008. Systematic Butchering of Fallow Deer (*Dama*) at the Early Middle Pleistocene Acheulian Site of Gesher Benot Ya'aqov (Israel). *JHE* 54: 134–49.

Redding, R. W. 1984. Theoretical Determinants of a Herder's Decisions: Modeling Variations in the Sheep/Goat Ratio. In *Animals in Archaeology, Vol. 3: Early Herders and Their Flocks*, ed. J. Clutton-Brock and C. Grigson, 223–41. BAR International Series 202. Oxford: BAR.

———. 2015. The Pig and the Chicken in the Middle East: Modeling Human Subsistence Behavior in the Archaeological Record Using Historical and Animal Husbandry Data. *JAR* 23: 325–68.

Rossel, S.; Marshall, F.; Peters, J.; Pilgram, T.; Adams, M. D.; and O'Connor, D. 2008. Domestication of the Donkey: Timing, Processes, and Indicators. *PNAS* 105: 3715–20.

Russell, N. 2012. *Social Zooarchaeology: Humans and Animals in Prehistory*. Cambridge: Cambridge University Press.

Sapir-Hen, L., and Ben-Yosef, E. 2013. The Introduction of Domestic Camels to the Southern Levant: Evidence from the Aravah Valley. *TA* 40: 277–85.

Sapir-Hen, L.; Gadot, Y.; and Finkelstein, I. 2016. Animal Economy in a Temple City and Its Countryside: Iron Age Jerusalem as a Case Study. *BASOR* 375: 103–18.

Sapir-Hen, L.; Meiri, M.; and Finkelstein, I. 2015. Iron Age Pigs: New Evidence on Their Origin and Role in Forming Identity Boundaries. *Radiocarbon* 57: 307–15.

Stiner, M. C. 1994. *Honor among Thieves: A Zooarchaeological Study of Neandertal Ecology*. Princeton: Princeton University Press.

Stiner, M. C.; Barkai, R.; and Gopher, A. 2009. Cooperative Hunting and Meat Sharing 400–200 kya at Qesem Cave, Israel. *PNAS* 106: 13207–12.

Stiner, M. C.; Munro, N. D.; and Surovell, T. A. 2000. The Tortoise and the Hare: Small Game Use, the Broad-Spectrum Revolution, and Paleolithic Demography. *CA* 41: 39–73.

Stiner, M. C.; Munro, N. D.; Surovell, T. A.; Tchernov, E.; and Bar-Yosef, O. 1999. Paleolithic Population Growth Pulses Evidenced by Small Animal Exploitation. *Science* 283: 190–4.

Sykes, N. J. 2014. *Beastly Questions: Animal Answers to Archaeological Issues*. London: Bloomsbury Academic.

Tsahar, E.; Izhaki, I.; Lev-Yadun, S.; and Bar-Oz, G. 2009. Distribution and Extinction of Ungulates during the Holocene of the Southern Levant. *PLOS ONE* 4: e5316. https://doi.org/10.1371/journal.pone.0005316 (accessed August 15, 2017).

Uerpmann, H.-P., and Uerpmann, M. 2002. The Appearance of the Domestic Camel in South-East Arabia. *Journal of Oman Studies* 12: 235–60.

Weissbrod, L.; Bar-Oz, G.; Yeshurun, R.; and Weinstein-Evron, M. 2012. Beyond Fast and Slow: The Mole Rat *Spalax ehrenbergi* (Order Rodentia) as a Test Case for Subsistence Intensification of Complex Natufian Foragers in Southwest Asia. *QI* 264: 4–16.

Yadin, Y. 1963. *The Art of Warfare in Biblical Lands in the Light of Archaeological Discovery*. London: Weidenfeld & Nicolson.

Yeshurun, R. 2016. Paleolithic Animal Remains in the Mount Carmel Caves: A Review of the Historical and Modern Research. In *Bones and Identity: Zooarchaeological Approaches to Reconstructing Social and Cultural Landscapes in Southwest Asia*, ed. N. Marom, R. Yeshurun, L. Weissbrod, and G. Bar-Oz, 1–24. Oxford: Oxbow.

Yeshurun, R.; Bar-Oz, G.; and Weinstein-Evron, M. 2007. Modern Hunting Behavior in the Early Middle Paleolithic: Faunal Remains from Misliya Cave, Mount Carmel, Israel. *JHE* 53: 656–77.

———. 2009. The Role of Foxes in the Natufian Economy: A View from Mount Carmel, Israel. *Before Farming* 2009 (1). www.academia.edu/384726/The_Role_of_Foxes_In_the_Natufian_Economy_a_View_From_Mount_Carmel_Israel (accessed August 15, 2017).

———. 2014. Intensification and Sedentism in the Terminal Pleistocene Natufian Sequence of el-Wad Terrace (Israel). *JHE* 70: 16–35.

Zeder, M. A. 1991. *Feeding Cities: Specialized Animal Economy in the Ancient Near East*. SSAI. Washington, DC: Smithsonian Institution Press.

———. 1994. Of Kings and Shepherds: Specialized Animal Economy in Ur III Mesopotamia. In *Chiefdoms and Early States in the Near East: The Organizational Dynamics of Complexity*, ed. G. Stein and M. S. Rothman, 175–91. MWA 18. Madison, WI: Prehistory.

———. 1998. Pigs and Emergent Complexity in the Ancient Near East. In *Ancestors for the Pigs: Pigs in Prehistory*, ed. S. M. Nelson, 109–22. MASCA Research Papers in Science and Archaeology 15. Philadelphia: MASCA, University Museum of Archaeology and Anthropology, University of Pennsylvania.

———. 2012. Pathways to Animal Domestication. In *Biodiversity in Agriculture: Domestication, Evolution, and Sustainability*, ed. P. Gepts, T. R. Famula, R. L. Bettinger, S. B. Brush, A. B. Damania, P. E. McGuire, and C. O. Qualset, 227–59. Cambridge: Cambridge University Press.

Zohary, D.; Hopf, M.; and Weiss, E. 2012. *Domestication of Plants in the Old World: The Origin and Spread of Domesticated Plants in South-West Asia, Europe, and the Mediterranean Basin*. 4th ed. Oxford: Oxford University Press.

TWENTY EIGHT

FINDING A WORLD OF WOMEN

An Introduction to Women's Studies and Gender Theory in Biblical Archaeology

STEPHANIE L. BUDIN

A WORLD OF THEORY

Since the 1960s and 1970s, there has been an effort on the part of feminist scholars in the humanities and social sciences to integrate women into the studies of their fields of inquiry. In the field of classics, for example, Sarah Pomeroy's 1975 publication of *Goddesses, Whores, Wives, and Slaves: Women in Classical Antiquity* inaugurated a new era of women's studies and feminist scholarship in the analysis of Greco-Roman historiography and literature. Just over a decade later, *Discovering Eve: Ancient Israelite Women in Context* (1988), by Carol Meyers, was at the forefront of a new wave of biblical scholarship focused on the role of the female in biblical texts and archaeology. In the three decades since that latter work appeared, the field of feminist scholarship in biblical studies has grown considerably. As Meyers noted in the updated edition of her work, "[b]efore, I struggled to find worthwhile scholarly resources; here I struggled to judiciously represent or incorporate scholarly trends without overwhelming the reader with references to every pertinent study" (2013: x).

This modern history of incorporating women into the archaeological and historiographic records is traditionally divided into three "waves." The "first wave" of the mid-twentieth century sought to *find* women in the ancient records, to document the existence of a full half of the human species that was responsible for the rise and fall of villages, empires, and religions in antiquity.[1]

Concomitant with this aim to include the female sex in the study of the ancient world was a desire to bring attention to and, if possible, correct the androcentric biases that dominated the study of the ancient world. Such an endeavor included not only shifting the focus of studies away from such traditional emphases as wars and politics onto more "basic" topics as the structure of the family, but also an inquiry into *who* was doing the scholarship – that is, were women being left out of historical investigation because the scholars in charge of those investigations were, for the most part, if not exclusively, male?

"Second-wave" feminism emerged in the 1970s and was primarily concerned with the historical (and not so historical) *oppression* of women. Michelle Zimbalist Rosaldo and Louise Lamphere's *Woman, Culture & Society* (1974) was a watershed in the application of second-wave feminist studies to a broad range of historical and contemporary issues pertaining to the universal subjugation of the female of the species. Here, anthropologists, psychologists, and sociologists, such as Sherry Ortner and Nancy Chodorow, delved into questions concerning the development of patriarchal tendencies in the familial context; the relationship between women, nature, and culture in structuralist ideologies; and the historicity (or not) of tales of ancient matriarchies.[2]

The academic results of these first two waves were clearly positive, leading to the rise of "women's studies" in universities in the Americas and Europe. Greater focus was paid to the role of women in ancient (and modern) societies, apparent in the articles and monographs dedicated to the female sex (such as those of Pomeroy and Meyers) in disciplines ranging from classical literature to the rise of farming in Neolithic communities.

However, weaknesses were also evident. As noted by Ruth Whitehouse:

> First, [women's studies] tends simply to substitute a new female bias for the previous male one. Second, it can lead to what is sometimes called "pseudo-inclusion," in which the study of women is recognized as valid, but becomes a specialism, comparable in archaeology to something like the study of lithics, which any individual archaeologist may choose to concentrate on or not. Further, it is studied mostly by women, becoming effectively ghettoized and marginal to mainstream studies within the discipline. (2007: 28)

In short, the "add women and stir" approach (Tringham 1991: 95) allowed women to be a focus of study but did not challenge or otherwise change the relevant disciplines to be more gender-inclusive.

Enter "third-wave" feminism. Strongly influenced by the works of Michel Foucault (1978–1986) and Judith Butler (1990; 2006), third-wave feminist studies in the 1990s branched into the four related disciplines of women's studies, feminist studies, gender studies, and queer theory. Women's studies continued the ideals of the first wave, finding and focusing on women (and eventually girls [Kieburg and Moraw 2014]) in the humanities and social sciences. Feminist studies continued the second wave, exploring and exposing the oppression of women, both in areas of academic study (the ancient world, village culture) and within academia itself. In this latter regard, for example, scholars, such as Diane Bolger (2008) and Beth Alpert Nakhai (2014), have reported on the number of female scholars who are tenured in university faculties, are accepted for publications in academic journals, or are invited onto panels at conferences. The ratio of female to male in these contexts strongly determines the extent to which "women's concerns" appear on course schedules and in indices.

Gender studies examine the *social construction* of both femininity *and* masculinity, looking at how different societies and cultures determine appropriate behaviors and ideologies for biological females and males. Originally, following on the heels of Simone de Beauvoir, it was understood that sex was a biological phenomenon, and gender – the cultural attributes associated with the sexes ("feminine" or "masculine") – was culturally constructed and thus relative (Gatens 1996: chapter one, with references). Or, to put it another way, gender was not physiologically determined, and biology was not destiny.

> Originally intended to dispute the biology-as-destiny formulation, the distinction between sex and gender serves the argument that whatever biological intractability sex appears to have, gender is culturally constructed: hence, gender is neither the causal result of sex nor as seemingly fixed as sex ... Taken to its logical limit, the sex/gender distinction suggests a radical discontinuity between sexed bodies and culturally constructed genders. (Butler 2006: 8–9)

At the vanguard of the new discipline of gender archaeology was *Engendering Archaeology: Women in Prehistory*, edited by Joan Gero and Margaret Conkey (1991). Although several of its chapters continued to focus on women specifically (such as Gero's "Genderlithics: Women's Roles in Stone Tool Production," which rather calls to mind Whitehouse's reference to lithics and ghettoism above), many chapters consider the role of gender *per se* in contexts such as household archaeology and food acquisition strategies.

Following on the heels of gender theory is queer theory. Based on the works of Jacques Lacan and Foucault, philosophers such as Butler and Monique Wittig have argued that because "biological" sex is a "fact" established by those who already embrace notions of binary (and oppositional) genders, the concept of binary sex (man : woman) is *also* an artificial, culturally constructed notion (Wittig 1993: 103, Butler 2006: 148–50). In short, there is no more reality behind the idea of two sexes than there is of two genders. Thus, Butler argues:

> If the immutable character of sex is contested, perhaps this construct called "sex" is as culturally constructed as gender; indeed, perhaps it was always already gender, with the consequence that the distinction between sex and gender turns out to be no distinction at all. ... As a result, gender is not to culture as sex is to nature; gender is also the discursive/cultural means by which "sexed nature" or "a natural sex" is produced and established as "prediscursive," prior to culture, a politically neutral surface *on which* culture acts. (2006: 9–10 [emphasis original])

Queer theory, then, posits the existence of both multiple genders *and* multiple sexes. Third and fourth gender individuals might manifest as biological hermaphrodites, castrated males, homosexual males and females, or individuals who adopt the gender aspects of an alternate sex for personal or professional reasons (e.g., cult functionaries who practice ritual transvestitism).

Queer theory can go to extremes, occasionally even denying the ontological category of "body" (Alberti 2013: 96). Fortunately, such radical notions have had little part to play in archaeological discourse, where the received wisdom continues to be that "all known human groups appear to have some form of gender division which relates in some way to the two main sexes" (Hamilton 2000: 22; see also Mina 2007: 264). Rather than challenging the notion of biological sex, more practical queer theory focuses on the possible multiplicity of genders functioning within society (much as gender theory), as well as the multiplicity of sexualities, eschewing heteronormativity for all different categories of sexual "normal."

WOMEN'S STUDIES IN BIBLICAL ARCHAEOLOGY

So, what has Butler to do with Beersheva? The significance of women's studies in the realm of biblical archaeology and the concomitant greater light shed on ancient women can be easily seen in a simple case study involving the study of Israelite households. In 1985, Lawrence Stager published an article on Iron Age Israelite domestic architecture, entitled "The Archaeology of the Family in Ancient Israel." Admirably examining the archaeology of "daily life" rather than the palaces and fortresses – and stables – of earlier generations of archaeologists, Stager's aim was to determine the standard layout of the Israelite home and what it told us about family structure, population, and social customs. The extensive archaeological data derived from throughout the hill country were augmented with evidence from the Bible and ethnographic parallels from the contemporary Middle East. However, Stager paid minimal attention to such matters as pottery distribution throughout the domiciles under discussion – and thus the cooking and storage patterns typically associated with women's labor — while devoting several pages to the location of animals (presumably belonging to men) within the standard "four-room house." When considering family dynamics (purportedly the topic of his article, per the title), he referred exclusively to male-focused biblical texts and the ethnographic parallels mentioned previously. He concluded:

> From ethnography we have noted the intricate web of marriage customs, patterns of inheritance and land ownership, and labor organization that was spun about the joint family in rural communities in the Middle East. The biblical *bêt 'āb* was enmeshed in a similar web of social and economic relationships. (Stager 1985: 22)

Women are nowhere to be found in the article. Their roles as cooks, weavers, potters, and mothers are rendered null and void, as Stager focuses on notions of animal husbandry and the composition and preservation of the "father's house," both in biblical times and the contemporary world that furnished his evidence for what probably took place *vis-à-vis* such matters as marriage and labor organization. So much for the archaeology of the "family."

Jump ahead to 2003. In her essay "Material Remains and Social Relations: Women's Culture in Agrarian Households of the Iron Age," Meyers takes the same point of departure as Stager – the Iron Age Israelite household. Here, however, Meyers focuses on the implements of daily living historically and ethnographically associated with women – cooking wares and textile tools. Concerning the former, although not recorded *in situ*, Meyers notes the presence of multiple grain-grinding stones in the homes of eleventh–tenth-century 'Izbet Ṣarṭah, as well as the proximity of ovens, grinding stones, and cooking vessels in House 75 of Beersheva (2003: 430–1, with references). The presence of multiple grinding stones within individual household units strongly suggests that several females worked together at the task, "in which women of one household and even of neighboring households gather together to grind, knead, and bake" (Meyers 2003: 431). Meyers' hypothesis is strengthened by the data in Aubrey Baadsgaard's 2008 essay "A Taste of Women's Sociality: Cooking as Cooperative Labor in Iron Age Syro-Palestine," in which Baadsgaard documents the location and size of *tannur* and *tabun* ovens within Iron Age domestic units. Although the majority (55 percent) of such ovens were found inside houses, another 21 percent were located in outer courtyards, 13 percent were in open areas, and 5 percent were in public buildings.

> The existence of cooking facilities both inside and outside of houses fits well with the expectation that ovens should be found in multiple enclosed and open locations in order to accommodate seasonal changes and patterns of smoke dispersal, as well as the sharing of cooking facilities by women from multiple households. Ovens from open and public areas have a larger average diameter than those from domestic structures, further evidence that these larger facilities were shared across the community. (Baadsgaard 2008: 28–9)

Looking further into the domestic archaeological data, it appears that such food preparation tasks went hand-in-hand with another traditional female industry: textiles. Examining the object clusters from three domestic units (B 743, F607, F608) from early sixth-century Timna' (Tel Batash), Deborah Cassuto in her 2008 essay "Bringing the Artifacts Home: A Social Interpretation of Loom Weights in Context" noted the proximity of textile implements (primarily loom weights and spindle whorls) to cooking objects, such as grinding stones, mortars, pestles, ovens, and cooking pots – all located within the central ground-floor long-room of the four-room house. That is, they came to light in the main activity room of the house with direct access to the household exterior (Cassuto 2008: 76). Such data not only reinforce the communal nature of women's tasks, as seen with the cooking apparatus (the cooks now joined by the spinners and weavers), but also give evidence for the extra-domestic sociability of women at work: Just as the bakers might meet up at communal ovens, so, too, "housewives" had direct access to the area beyond the house and external social networks.

Altogether, the group nature of female tasks provided a distinctly feminine social network, both within and external to the so-called *beth 'av*, and provided the means of transmission of such knowledge. As concluded by Meyers:

> The presence of female work groups, whether for food-processing or crafts production, signals the existence of women's networks. Gendered household activity areas were thus social spaces, in which women shared with each other certain kinds of knowledge and experienced certain kinds of interaction ... That women gathered, however sporadically, to engage in the serial or simultaneous operations of cloth and clothing manufacture meant that those experienced in the craft passed on their skills and knowledge to younger artisans ... Whether kneading dough together in a communal trough of working side-by-side with differing foodstuffs, women sharing productive social space meant that they had access to social knowledge as well as technical knowledge. They knew each other and thus each other's families; and this sphere of relationships ... meant that women had information otherwise unavailable to men that was critical for forging political connections, solving economic problems..., and assisting with difficulties such as illness or death in individual households. (2003: 435–6, excerpted)

Such data provide a far clearer picture of the household and family and its dynamics not only within itself but also with the surrounding community.

GENDER THEORY IN BIBLICAL ARCHAEOLOGY

One of the primary concerns in gender theory is the identification and dismantling of *gender essentialism*. In contrast to gender theory's core notion that gender is socially constructed, gender essentialism posits that certain traits are innate to either females or males, blurring the lines between the biological and the social. To quote Whitehouse, "[g]ender essentialism can be described as the assumption of a universal binary dichotomy between women and men and corresponding notions of universal features of femininity and masculinity" (2007: 29). For example, the idea that men are innately prone to violence, and women are innately social. Such concepts not only run contrary to the socially ascribed nature of gender, but, following queer theory, they also reinforce the notion of two sexes, disregarding both the volatile continuum between them, as well as all other possible axes of analysis and interpretation.

Perhaps no greater tendency toward gender essentialism exists than the idea that women are innately maternal, and that maternity is a universal and highly public concern for females. So much would appear to be present in the Bible, where women, barred from access to the religious and political apparatus except through male family, are overwhelmingly presented as concerned with aspects of maternity, including such "subcategories" as infertility, childbearing, matters of sons' inheritance, and Levirate marriage.

This tendency in the wholly male-authored biblical texts, combined with the gender essentialist idea that women are primarily maternal beings, has colored the interpretation of all female figurines to emerge from the Levant, both in Bronze and Iron Ages, all of which, without fail, have been, and often continue to be, identified as "fertility figurines."[3]

For these reasons, the remarkably *rare* presence of maternal iconography from the Levant has been wholly overlooked. The pregnant female – the so-called *dea gravida* ("pregnant goddess") – appears only for about a century in Iron Age Phoenicia, barely influencing the iconographies to the north or south. Images of parturition – prevalent in contemporary Iron Age Cyprus and Greece (Vandervondelen 2002) – are not to be found. Only about a dozen images depicting a female with child – the kourotrophos – exist, and in both Syria and Israel/Palestine, these images, either shown holding a child upon the lap or to the side, are direct importations or adaptations of Egyptian prototypes (Budin 2011: 149–72). In Syria, the Egyptian motif of the divine wet nurse was adopted, showing a version of Horus/pharaoh as an infant upon the lap of a goddess or queen. To the south, in Israel/Palestine, the Egyptian potency figurine appeared, in which an image of a nude female on a bed, occasionally accompanied by an infant, was used to raise potency in magical endeavors. Based on the idea that fertility comes from the male who himself must be stimulated by feminine eroticism:

> [I]t might be better to focus less on notions of female fertility when thinking of the figurines and to focus instead on their eroticism and what was probably more important for the Egyptians themselves: the resultant potency that led to fertility. This being the case, let us consider the

> possibility that notions of potency might be applicable outside the narrow fields of fertility and reproduction. If potency might be understood, quite simply, as the power to accomplish an intended aim, then any object that stimulates potency might assist in the accomplishment of that aim, whatever it might be. The female figurines, then, might serve as (magical, ritual) items which enhance the efficacy of any potential intention. (Budin 2011: 134)

The only iconography that depicts maternity in the land of the Bible, then, is a direct Egyptian import, and one only tangentially associated with fertility or reproduction.

So, too, are the items that might truly be associated with women's concerns for pregnancy and parturition in ancient Israel: images of Bes, the dwarf who protected women and children in Egyptian iconography. Images of Bes appear throughout Israel beginning in the Iron Age II period, as do names containing the "bes" element.[4] Bes molds have come to light in Israel, indicating that the images was not only imported but adopted and adapted into the Levantine religion (Meyers 2005: 32, with references).

Nevertheless, one must note that the only iconography from ancient Israel that in any way indicates an interest in or concern with maternity comes from Egypt.[5] Furthermore, all data from the societies surrounding the Bronze and Iron Age Levant – Canaanite Ugarit, Mesopotamia, Mitanni, and Egypt – indicate that fertility was seen to be a *male* attribute, not female as in the modern West (Budin 2015: *passim*). In these same societies, the iconographic and documentary evidence left *by females* reveal that these women, when speaking in their own voices, did not derive status from their role as mother. To the contrary, the women who appear in early art portrayed themselves in positions of status that derived either from family or profession. Queens, princesses, and nobility portrayed status *vis-à-vis* their fathers and husbands. Priestesses did the same with their cultic positions. Servants who had any status acquired it through their more noble connections, and these connections were emphasized in the inscriptions and iconography. As Julia Asher-Greve has noted:

> [I]ndependent women worked for queens or other court women, some were priestesses, or daughters of priestesses. Apart from marriage, court and temple offered positions that apparently gave women at least some independence as well as the means to donate votive gifts or acquire high quality seals of expensive materials. Imagery rarely shows women with husband or children but primarily in religious, ceremonial and/or public contexts. (2006: 74)

It is only in the Bible that the emphasis is placed on maternity. Here, the biblical matriarchs – denied any access to the religious or political hierarchy available to women in other ancient Near Eastern societies – wielded power and status *exclusively* through their male offspring, offspring pointedly given by a male deity and recorded in a text voiced and penned exclusively by males (Budin 2015: 47).

In the end, the emphasis on women and maternity in ancient Israel has been unduly exaggerated, especially when attempting to consider the views and concerns of actual women rather than palatial scribes. The lack of maternal iconography has been overshadowed by the essentializing idea that women are naturally maternal and the founts of human (and other) fertility. Yet, the physical remains speak differently.

Application of women's studies and gender theory is now offering a remedy for such essentializing assumptions. In addition to correcting the "female = fertility" paradigm, alternate, less gender-biased roles for women are coming to the fore for early Israelite women. For example, in contrast to the paucity of kourotrophic figurines, there are numerous depictions of females playing drums, a practice associated in the Bible with military victory (Paz 2007: 83–5, with biblical references). Based on such finds, it would appear that the women of ancient Israel were more closely associated with the celebration of successful warfare and the preservation of the state than motherhood.

NOT SO THEORETICAL PITFALLS

> *There is nothing distinctively "female" about the way that women are portrayed in the Bible.* (Frymer-Kensky 1992: 120)

As noted at the beginning of this chapter, the various categories of women's/feminist/gender/queer theories came later to biblical studies than to other fields, such as classics.[6] Part of this is because the Bible represents several still-extant religions, and inevitably people become more emotionally involved in the technicalities of what comes from the texts or grounds of the "Holy Land" than they do about, say, the homeland of Odysseus.

Even more problematic is the masculine emphasis of the Bible, both Hebrew and Christian. Basically, those studying the patriarchal, wholly male-centric texts serving as the foundation of Judaism, Christianity, and Islam have trouble establishing any kind of feminist agenda. As a result, while biblical archaeology is making headway in the realms of gender studies, textual biblical studies still manifest certain theoretical problems when it comes to feminist analyses. The gravest of these is apologetics.

"Apologetics" refers to those scholars who attempt to show that the Bible is actually female-positive, and that a monotheistic religion based on an exclusive male deity is just as beneficial to women as men and equally advantageous as a religion featuring a feminine divine. No scholar has dedicated more energy to this than Tikva Frymer-Kensky, especially in her 1992 book *In the Wake of the*

Goddesses: Women, Culture and the Biblical Transformation of Pagan Myth. In this work, Frymer-Kensky attempts to show that not only is the Bible not inherently sexist, but that there is little gender distinction within the text at all. Although admitting that certain traditions do appear to favor males over females – such as the complete male control of female sexuality and the ability to punish infractions in that category with death (Frymer-Kensky 1992: 119) – ultimately, according to the author, biblical females have all the same concerns, priorities, strategies, and tactics as males, or at least reasonably unempowered males (Frymer-Kensky 1992: 125).

Such an argument, however, involves considerable contortion of the evidence and not a little denial: The evidence does not support the hypothesis. When presenting the agendas of the women of the Bible, Frymer-Kensky notes their concerns with motherhood, being wives, and being mothers (1992: 121–7 – yes, that redundancy is present in the text). Absent are the "male" concerns with politics and military conquest, economic acquisition, and sibling rivalries. The author's statements that, "[t]he public arenas of palace, temple, and law court were normally male preserves, and women, by and large, operated in the domestic sphere" (Frymer-Kensky 1992: 120), comes strongly to the fore here (although that statement is less accurate for the polytheistic goddess-worshipping societies of the ancient Near East than in monotheistic Israel). When biblical females do engage in such masculine pursuits, as was the case with Jezebel and Athalia in the book of Kings, they are portrayed as evil and killed.

Frymer-Kensky argues that the Bible presents no distinctively female way of accomplishing tasks, even while noting that women are far more likely to have to act *through* males due to the lack of female authority. Yet, her three examples of women's apostatic practices are weaving for Asherah, weeping for Tammuz, and baking cakes for the Queen of Heaven – all specifically female actions (weaving, lamenting, baking) (Frymer-Kensky 1992: 127). Likewise, she claims that no biblical female uses sex to achieve an objective (Frymer-Kensky 1992: 130), overlooking Tamar, Delilah, Ruth, Esther, Judith, and possibly even Abigail. In an attempt to deny an engendered, specifically female community – and in stark contrast to tales of *male* bonding in the Bible, as with Joseph and Benjamin or David and Jonathan – Frymer-Kensky notes the absence of strong female bonds/relationships in the Bible (excluding the example of Naomi and Ruth). Instead, she writes:

> [T]he biblical stories also do not indicate "sisterly solidarity." Women do not band together to promote women's causes, they do not go out of their way to help each other, and they do not show the consciousness of similar goals or shared experiences that would allow them to understand each other. The co-wives, Rachel and Leah (actual sisters) and Penina and Hannah are rivals ... So too, in Deborah's victory song, the mothers have no sympathy for other women. (Frymer-Kensky 1992: 127)

Frymer-Kensky sees this as a *good* thing, a sign of gender-neutrality in the Bible. She does not consider that, rather than showing gender neutrality, the tendency to isolate women from support groups, including other females, is now a commonly recognized aspect of domestic abuse, a sign of female disempowerment. Nor does she consider the contrary evidence of the archaeological data: As discussed above, the placement of cooking and weaving implements in Israelite domestic architecture confirms the presence of women's communities. And she does not consider the voice or concerns of the biblical authors themselves. The notions of "sisterhood" or "woman power" were apparently not a high priority for the elite male scribes composing the Bible in the seventh century. Quite simply, the Bible presents a biased lie, one strongly engendered and based on an exclusively male voice.

In the end, Frymer-Kensky does admit that "[t]he Bible's gender-free concept of humanity contrasted sharply with Israelite reality" (1992: 143). But the idea that biblical archaeology's foundational text is somehow "gender-free" is untenable. In an attempt to put a more "female friendly" face upon the religions of the book, Frymer-Kensky has contorted the evidence beyond recognition. A far more balanced approach is necessary, with less of a "feminist" agenda and more grounding in the textual and archaeological data.[7] Women's studies need not, and sometimes should not, be feminist.

CONCLUSION

Finding and exploring a world of women in a discipline dominated by a staunchly patriarchal text has been a challenge. Slowly but surely, and quickly gaining pace, women's studies and gender theory are taking hold in biblical studies, both in archaeology and textual analyses. Scholars, such as Meyers, Phyllis Bird, Peggy Day, Alpert Nakhai, and Susan Ackerman among many others, are contributing to bringing ancient Israelite women out from the shadows of the patriarchs and the shadows of their homes. It will not ever be possible to put a feminist face onto the texts of the Bible, but more careful analysis of the pages and the stones will allow for a much greater understanding of the women of ancient Israel/Palestine, their social roles, their communities, their sources of power, and all the other things the biblical authors and contemporary (male) scholars did not find conducive to their own agendas.

NOTES

1 It is important to note that this "First Wave" refers to academics, not to the first wave of modern feminism that emerged in the late nineteenth century and focused on living women's political rights and the suffragette movement. Meyers (2005) does note, though,

that even in the nineteenth century, feminist approaches were being taken to the Bible, specifically Elizabeth Cady Stanton's *The Woman's Bible* (1885–98) (Meyers 2005: 2).

2 The mirage of matriarchy was heavily predicated upon the nineteenth-century works of J. J. Bachofen (1861), Friedrich Engels (1884), and L. H. Morgan (1877), stoked by Marxists ideologies into the twentieth century. Although this myth of ancient matriarchy has been mostly laid to rest in academia (see esp. Eller 2000), it remains passionately espoused in more radical feminist circles – notably those influenced by the late Marija Gimbutas.

3 That the female sex is responsible for fertility is yet another gender essentialist notion influencing the interpretation of ancient religion and art.

4 On the iconography, see Keel and Uehlinger 1998: 217–23. On the onomastics, see Meyers 2005: 32, with references.

5 *Contra* Keel and Uehlinger 1998: 84, where the authors claim that "[t]he Canaanite nursing goddess is an indigenous form, not just a local adaptation of an Egyptian theme."

6 To date, queer theory has hardly been touched in biblical studies. One might look in Nissinen 1998 for some initial work.

7 Bringing us, once again, back to the works of Meyers.

REFERENCES

Alberti, B. 2013. Queer Prehistory: Bodies, Performativity, and Matter. In *A Companion to Gender Prehistory*, ed. D. R. Bolger, 86–107. BCA 21. Chichester: Wiley-Blackwell.

Alpert Nakhai, B. 2014. Reconstructing Women's Lives in Iron Age Israel: The Complex Interplay between Text and Archaeology. Presented at the Gender, Methodology and the Ancient Near East Workshop, University of Helsinki.

Asher-Greve, J. 2006. "Golden Age" of Women? Status and Gender in Third Millennium Sumerian and Akkadian Art. In *Images and Gender: Contributions to the Hermeneutics of Reading Ancient Art*, ed. S. Schroer, 41–81. OBO 220. Fribourg: Academic; Göttingen: Vandenhoeck & Ruprecht.

Baadsgaard, A. 2008. A Taste of Women's Sociality: Cooking as Cooperative Labor in Iron Age Syro-Palestine. In *The World of Women in the Ancient and Classical Near East*, ed. B. Alpert Nakhai, 13–44. Newcastle upon Tyne: Cambridge Scholars.

Bachofen, J. J. 1861. *Das Mutterrecht: Eine Untersuchung über die Gynaikokratie der alten Welt nach ihrer religiosen und rechtlichen Natur*. S.l.: Krais & Hoffmann.

Bolger, D. R. 2008. Gendered Fields in Near Eastern Archaeology: Past, Present, Future. In *Gender through Time in the Ancient Near East*, ed. D. R. Bolger, 335–59. GA. Lanham, MD: AltaMira.

Budin, S. L. 2011. *Images of Woman and Child from the Bronze Age: Reconsidering Fertility, Maternity, and Gender in the Ancient World*. Cambridge: Cambridge University Press.

2015. Fertility and Gender in the Ancient Near East and Egypt. In *Sex in Antiquity: Exploring Gender and Sexuality in the Ancient World*, ed. M. Masterson, N. Sorkin Rabinowitz, and J. Robson, 30–49. London: Routledge.

Butler, J. 1990. *Gender Trouble: Feminism and the Subversion of Identity*. Thinking Gender. New York: Routledge.

2006. *Gender Trouble: Feminism and the Subversion of Identity*. 2nd ed. Routledge Classics. New York: Routledge.

Cassuto, D. 2008. Bringing the Artifacts Home: A Social Interpretation of Loom Weights in Context. In *The World of Women in the Ancient and Classical Near East*, ed. B. Alpert Nakhai, 63–77. Newcastle upon Tyne: Cambridge Scholars.

Eller, C. 2000. *The Myth of Matriarchal Prehistory: Why an Invented Past Won't Give Women a Future*. Boston: Beacon.

Engels, F. 1884. *Der Ursprung der Familie, des Privateigenthums und des Staats*. Hottingen-Zürich: Schweizerische Genossenschaftsbuchdruckerei.

Foucault, M. 1978–1986. *The History of Sexuality*. 3 vols. Harmondsworth: Penguin.

Frymer-Kensky, T. 1992. *In the Wake of the Goddesses: Women, Culture, and the Biblical Transformation of Pagan Myth*. New York: Fawcett Columbine.

Gatens, M. 1996. *Imaginary Bodies: Ethic, Power, and Corporeality*. New York: Routledge.

Gero, J. M. 1991. Genderlithics: Women's Roles in Stone Tool Production. In *Engendering Archaeology: Women and Prehistory*, ed. J. M. Gero and M. W. Conkey, 163–93. SA. Oxford: Blackwell.

Gero, J. M., and Conkey, M. W., eds. 1991. *Engendering Archaeology: Women and Prehistory*. SA. Oxford: Blackwell.

Hamilton, N. 2000. Ungendering Archaeology: Concepts of Sex and Gender in Figurine Studies in Prehistory. In *Representations of Gender from Prehistory to the Present*, ed. M. Donald and L. Hurcombe, 17–30. Studies in Gender and Material Culture. New York: St. Martin's; Basingstoke: Macmillan.

Keel, O., and Uehlinger, C. 1998. *Gods, Goddesses, and Images of God in Ancient Israel*. Minneapolis: Fortress.

Kieburg, A., and Moraw, S., eds. 2014. *Mädchen im Altertum [Girls in Antiquity]*. Frauen – Forschung – Archäologie 11. Münster: Waxmann.

Meyers, C. L. 1988. *Discovering Eve: Ancient Israelite Women in Context*. Oxford: Oxford University Press.

2003. Material Remains and Social Relations: Women's Culture in Agrarian Households of the Iron Age. In *Symbiosis, Symbolism, and the Power of the Past: Canaan, Ancient Israel, and Their Neighbors from the Late Bronze Age through Roman Palaestina; Proceedings of the Centennial Symposium, W. F. Albright Institute of Archaeological Research and American Schools of Oriental Research, Jerusalem, May 29–31 2000*, ed. W. G. Dever and S. Gitin, 425–44. Winona Lake, IN: Eisenbrauns.

2005. *Households and Holiness: The Religious Culture of Israelite Women*. Facets. Minneapolis: Fortress.

2013. *Rediscovering Eve: Ancient Israelite Women in Context*. Oxford: Oxford University Press.

Mina, M. K. 2007. Figurines without Sex; People without Gender? In *Archaeology and Women: Ancient and Modern Issues*, ed. S. Hamilton, R. D. Whitehouse, and K. I. Wright, 263–82. Publications of the Institute of Archaeology, University College London. Walnut Creek, CA: Left Coast.

Morgan, L. H. 1877. *Ancient Society, or, Researches in the Lines of Human Progress from Savagery... to Civilization*. London: Macmillan.

Nissinen, M. 1998. *Homoeroticism in the Biblical World: A Historical Perspective*. Minneapolis: Fortress.

Paz, S. 2007. *Drums, Women, and Goddesses: Drumming and Gender in Iron Age II Israel*. OBO 232. Fribourg: Academic; Göttingen: Vandenhoeck & Ruprecht.

Pomeroy, S. B. 1975. *Goddesses, Whores, Wives, and Slaves: Women in Classical Antiquity*. New York: Schocken.

Rosaldo, M. Z., and Lamphere, L. 1974. *Woman, Culture & Society*. Stanford: Stanford University Press.

Stager, L. E. 1985. The Archaeology of the Family in Ancient Israel. *BASOR* 260: 1–35.

Stanton, E. C. 1895–98. *The Woman's Bible*. 2 vols. New York: European Publishing.

Tringham, R. E. 1991. Households with Faces: The Challenge of Gender in Prehistoric Architectural Remains. In *Engendering Archaeology: Women and Prehistory*, ed. J. M. Gero and M. W. Conkey, 93–131. SA. Oxford: Blackwell.

Vandervondelen, M. 2002. Child Birth in Iron Age Cyprus: A Case Study. In *Engendering Aphrodite: Women and Society in Ancient Cyprus*, ed. D. R. Bolger and N. J. Serwint, 143–56. ASORAR 7; CAARI Monographs 3. Boston: ASOR.

Whitehouse, R. D. 2007. Gender Archaeology and Archaeology of Women: Do We Need Both? In *Archaeology and Women: Ancient and Modern Issues*, ed. S. Hamilton, R. D. Whitehouse, and K. I. Wright, 27–40. Publications of the Institute of Archaeology, University College London. Walnut Creek, CA: Left Coast.

Wittig, M. 1993. One Is Not Born a Woman. In *The Lesbian and Gay Studies Reader*, ed. H. Abelove, M. A. Barale, and D. M. Halperin, 103–9. New York: Routledge.

TWENTY NINE

SOCIAL ARCHAEOLOGY IN THE LEVANT THROUGH THE LENS OF ARCHAEOMETALLURGY

EREZ BEN-YOSEF AND SARIEL SHALEV

The southern Levant is one of the regions around which the research discipline of *archaeometallurgy* – the study of ancient metals, their manufacturing techniques, and their role in ancient societies – has evolved. The pioneering work of Beno Rothenberg in the ancient copper ore district of Timna' (e.g., Rothenberg [ed.] 1990) is considered by many to be the keystone in what is now a flourishing and well-recognized research field, with fundamental contributions to the study of ancient societies (Pigott 1999; Roberts and Thornton 2014). Rothenberg's project was one of the earliest to recognize the importance of integrating various research avenues in order to achieve a comprehensive understanding of metallurgical practices and their meaning within their social context, including, for example, field archaeology, geology, experimental archaeology, ethno-archaeology, geochemistry, mineralogy, and other laboratory techniques ("archaeometry"). Indeed, archaeometallurgy is one of the most interdisciplinary practices in archaeology, involving expertise and techniques from earth and material sciences, in addition to common archaeological methods (Killick and Fenn 2012).

Rothenberg's research focused predominantly on extractive metallurgy, namely the production of metals from ore (in this case, copper). This particular aspect of archaeometallurgical research has thrived in the southern Levant ever since (Veldhuijzen 2006; Hauptmann 2007; Ben-Yosef 2010), resulting in an unparalleled contribution to the archaeometallurgy of copper production (cf. Tylecote 1992 and Craddock 1995). Conversely, archaeometallurgy of metal artifacts was introduced relatively late to the archaeology of the southern Levant, with studies beyond typology starting systematically only with the chemical analyses of the objects from the Late Chalcolithic hoard of the Cave of the Treasure (Key 1980; for a short overview of this aspect of archaeometallurgy in Israel, see Shalev 2008). The study of metal artifacts is focused on questions such as manufacturing techniques (e.g., Scott 2010) and provenance (e.g., Gale and Stos-Gale 2000), adding to our understanding of past social realities based on assessments of artisanship and rareness (e.g., specialization and social stratification), reconstructions of trade systems, and more. Another component of archaeometallurgical research concerns the study of metallurgical workshops (smithy, forge, and the like). These workshops were usually located within settlements and dedicated to secondary metallurgical processes, such as alloying, recycling, mending, and the production of final tools and other items. Contrary to the focal role they had in any society that engaged with metals, very few metallurgical workshops were reported in the southern Levant until recently. These were mostly identified by particular objects, such as crucibles or pot-bellows; as these objects are rare, and their identification is easily confused – most workshops were probably missed in past excavations. However, with greater awareness to the type of evidence left by alloying, recycling, casting, annealing, and other activities (e.g., Veldhuijzen 2009), more workshops are being identified and studied (e.g., Eliyahu-Behar et al. 2012).

In the following, we review some of the topics that are at the core of archaeometallurgical research in the southern Levant, with emphasis on the contribution of the study of ancient metals and metallurgical technologies to social archaeology.

METALS AND PERIODIZATION: STONE – COPPER – BRONZE – IRON?

Metals and alloys (a mix of two or more metals) have unique qualities that made them attractive as raw material in past (and present) human societies. Qualities such as bright shiny colors and luster, malleability and durability, together with being rare, made metals, such as gold and silver, perfect for the production of ornaments, and prestige and cult items, as well as – later on in the history of humankind – coinage. Strength (without brittleness), a quality introduced with the discovery of alloys, made materials such as bronze optimal for the production of agricultural tools and weapons. Excluding gold, all metals in antiquity had to be produced from minerals by pyrotechnological processes (except in rare cases [see overview in Craddock 1995]). Thus, the advancement of metals in societies depended on technological inventions and innovations, and consequently different metals and alloys were introduced at different times with considerable regional variations across the globe.

Two major metallurgical advancements were considered early on as fundamental shifts in the materiality of humankind: the introduction of bronze and iron. Together with stone, these two materials were part of the three-age system that C. J. Thomsen introduced already in the early nineteenth century as a chronological tool (see overview in Trigger 2006: 121–65) and later discussed by Marxist archaeologists (most notably, V. Gordon Childe [1944, e.g., 1944]) and others as dictating core aspects of social mechanisms. While the introduction of "true" bronze (an alloy of copper and tin in a typical ratio of 1:9, respectively) revolutionized social processes by dramatically improving the quality of tools, the introduction of iron triggered social processes by making metal available to all, as it was an abundant and rather inexpensive material (see below).

An elaborated and more nuanced version of the three-age system is, in fact, still in use today for pre- and proto-historic periods. For the southern Levant, the nomenclature was fixed in the early stages of research (cf. Albright 1949), and as the definition of each period is predominantly based on ceramic typologies, the terminology is often confusing in regard to the history of metallurgy in the region. For example, except one rare find, the first appearance of metal objects in the region did not occur in the beginning of the Chalcolithic period (Greek: χαλκός = "copper," λίθος = "stone") but only in the *Late* Chalcolithic (following the system introduced in Garfinkel 1999). "True" bronze appears only in the Early Bronze Age IV (late third millennium BCE), and iron becomes a dominant metal at least two centuries after the beginning of the Iron Age (Gottlieb 2010; Yahalom-Mack and Eliyahu-Behar 2015).

All of the common metals and alloys known in antiquity were found in the archaeological record of the southern Levant, including copper and its alloys (bronze, brass, variants of arsenic/antimony/nickel bronzes), iron, gold, silver, lead, and tin. However, only iron and copper were produced locally (see below) with some evidence hinting at the possible production of gold in the Aravah Valley during the Byzantine and Early Islamic periods (Gilat et al. 1993; Meshel 2006).

ORE EXTRACTION

> A land whose stones are iron, and out of whose hills you can dig copper. (Deut 8:9 [English Standard Version])

Metaphorically intended or not, Deut 8:9 reflects the geological reality of the land. Iron ore is abundant and can be found all over the southern Levant in various geological formations, similar to other places around the world. This quality made iron relatively cheap, hence Childe's (1942) epithet "the democratic metal." Iron ore has been mined mostly from surface outcrops near settlements; as a result, iron mines are rarely recognized in the archaeological record. In the southern Levant, only the site of Mugharat al-Warda in northern Jordan has been identified as a substantial iron ore mine, and recent investigation demonstrates that it was used for millennia (al-Amri 2008). Smaller mines of iron minerals, such as the Roman-era pyrite/limonite mine near 'Ein Gedi (Hadas 2004), might indicate a deliberate effort to obtain pigments (ocher), rather than minerals for smelting (cf. the lead [galena] mines in Mount Hermon [Dar 1994: 255–60]).

Copper ore, on the other hand, is relatively rare and is concentrated in regions of specific geological settings. Consequently, ancient copper mines are more readily identified; however, many of the ancient copper ore districts, including the important mines of Cyprus and Ergani (in eastern Anatolia), were severely damaged by early modern exploitation that left very little with which archaeologists could work. The copper ore districts of the southern Levant (Fig. 29.1) were saved from such a fate and are considered among the best-preserved ancient copper production regions in the world. Moreover, located deep in the desert, the arid climate minimized the effect of erosion, while also leaving the sites bare of vegetation and thus easy to find, access, and research. The archaeological record of mineral exploitation in the southern Levant starts far before metallurgical technologies were introduced to the region – the green minerals were mined in large quantities already in the Pre-Pottery Neolithic and probably in smaller amounts as early as the Natufian (Bar-Yosef Mayer and Porat 2008), serving as raw material for the production of beads, pendants, and other ornaments at sites as far away from the mines as Yiftahel in the Lower Galilee (Garfinkel 1987). With the introduction of smelting technologies in the second half of the fifth millennium BCE, copper minerals were mined also for the production of copper metal; the well-studied record of the Aravah copper ore districts (Timna' and Feinan) indicates intermittent periods of exploitation, with peaks in the Early Bronze Age (III–IV [Ben-Yosef et al. 2016]), early Iron Age (Levy, Najjar, and Ben-Yosef 2014), Roman–Byzantine periods (Mattingly et al. 2007), and Islamic period (Jones, Najjar, and Levy 2018). The latest record of copper production in the Aravah is the Ayyubid (1187–1260 CE) site of Khirbat Nuqayb al-Asaymir in Feinan, whose copper has been linked to the intensification of the sugar industry at that time (Jones, Levy, and Najjar 2012).

Technology and Society: Copper Mining and Smelting in the Aravah Valley

The copper ore districts of the southern Levant constitute a "field laboratory" for the study of copper mining and smelting technologies, which, in turn, provides meaningful insights into broader questions, such as technological innovation and evolution, and the role of technology in society – or the anthropology of technology (cf. Lemonnier 1992 and Pfaffenberger 1992). While the early research of Rothenberg and the Aravah Expedition followed a simplistic view of technology (termed by Pfaffenberger [1992] "the Standard View"), recent

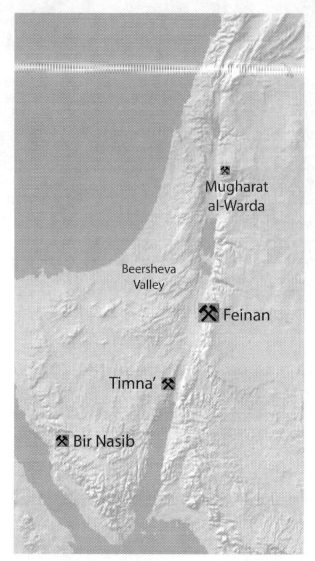

29.1. Location of main copper ore districts of the southern Levant and other places mentioned in the text. (Map by E. Ben-Yosef.)

research has demonstrated the complexity of technological practices related to copper production (e.g., Ben-Yosef, Tauxe, and Levy 2010) and the need for a holistic approach, including the utilization of anthropological models for better understanding the social aspects of technological records. For example, while evolution of copper smelting technologies in the southern Levant was understood as a unilinear process, from the use of "primitive" hole-in-the-ground furnaces to advanced shaft furnaces (Rothenberg 1990), detailed new studies with direct archaeomagentic dating of slag (Ben-Yosef et al. 2008) have demonstrated that simple technologies were practiced even after advanced technologies had been introduced to the region, reflecting discontinuity in the transformation of technological knowledge and/or marginal production systems operating simultaneously with the core industry but lacking the political and/or technological means to apply the more advanced methods. Similarly, the open-pits (*placer*) mines at Timna', dated by Rothenberg (2005) exclusively to the Chalcolithic based on the simple technology they represent, were found to be active also in the late second millennium BCE (Ben-Yosef 2018). Hence, "technological horizon" might be used *only* as a *terminus post quem* and also here only if the date of technological innovation is secure.

Beyond evolution processes and chronologies, the complexity of ancient technological practices includes various other aspects, which are the basis for inferring social meanings (cf. Costin and Wright 1998, and Costin 1991). When simplistic assumptions, such as "form follows function" and "necessity is the mother of invention" (Pfaffenberger 1992), are avoided, it is possible to isolate technological choices and past social realities; this is often done by utilizing the *chaîne opératoire* methodological tool[1] or the somewhat similar approach of *behavioral chain* (Schiffer 1976). Although these approaches are applicable to metallurgy (as they are to any ancient technology), there are only few archaeometallurgical studies that use them (Ben-Yosef 2010) and more should be encouraged, especially when the interface with society is one of the research objectives.

Iron Age Copper Production in the Aravah Valley: *Chaînes Opératoires* and *Socio-Technological Systems*

Intensive archaeological research in the ancient copper ore districts of the Aravah Valley (see Fig. 29.1) has been conducted during the last decades by various groups (e.g., Barker, Gilbertson, and Mattingly 2007; Hauptmann 2007; Levy, Najjar, and Ben-Yosef 2014; Ben-Yosef [ed.] 2018). Resulting in ample new technological data with associated sociocultural information, this research has enabled detailed studies into various aspects of the archaeometallurgy of copper. One such study (Ben-Yosef 2010) demonstrates the application of the *chaînes opératoires* methodological tool for gleaning social insights from technological data and their broader context. Based on materials from surveys and excavations of Iron Age (approximately 1200–586 BCE) mining and smelting sites in Feinan and Timna', detailed *chaînes opératoires* were constructed for this period (Fig. 29.2); differences in components (such as the one presented in Fig. 29.3) of these *chaînes* through time and/or space enabled identification of five distinct socio-technological systems, four of which were consecutive and one that probably existed throughout the period (Table 29.1). Hence, notwithstanding this study's technology-related building stones, its conclusions reach far beyond

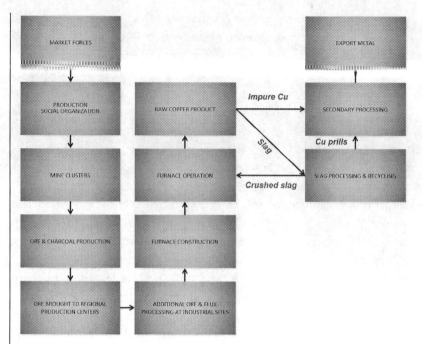

29.2. Generalized early Iron Age (twelfth–ninth centuries BCE) *chaînes opératoires* for copper production in the Aravah Valley (from Levy, Najjar, and Ben-Yosef 2014). When increasing detail resolution, at least five different *chaînes* can be constructed (for the entire Iron Age, see Ben-Yosef 2010: 881–954), which, in turn, enable identification of five distinct socio-technological systems (cf. Table 29.1).

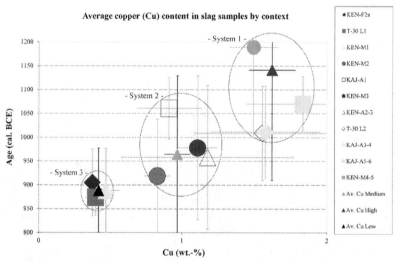

29.3. Copper content in slag from the Aravah Valley. For characterizing Iron Age smelting technologies, slag chemistry was analyzed by portable X-ray fluorescence device (pXRF [Ben-Yosef 2010: 769–880]). The results of dozens of slag samples (pulverized for averaging) from various contexts (see key in Ben-Yosef 2010) demonstrate improvement in efficiency (= less Cu) and standardization (= smaller standard deviation of the mean), reflecting three distinct socio-technological groups (cf. Table 29.1). Note the major shift in efficiency and standardization between Systems 2 and 3, attributed to Egyptian involvement. (Graph by E. Ben-Yosef.)

> technology and technological reconstructions, and provide insights on social organization and processes (as well as history, cultural identities, and more) in the Iron Age southern Levant.

THE DAWN OF METALLURGY IN THE LEVANT

Contrary to some previous suggestions, the southern Levant is not the cradle of extractive metallurgy. The first production of copper from the Aravah ore took place during the second half of the fifth millennium BCE (the Late Chalcolithic), several centuries *after* the first introduction of smelting technologies, which are now identified at sites around the ore-rich areas of central-east Anatolia (Roberts, Thornton, and Pigott 2009). This invention of smelting, and of copper in particular, was a substantial leap in the development of human control of fire and pyrotechnologies; the threshold conditions for a successful outcome do not allow for accidental discovery and imply deliberate research and experimentation by early societies that resulted in one of the more complex technologies in the history of humankind (Craddock 1995, with references). This complexity is also the main argument behind the common view today that this invention occurred only once in one location, from which the idea and the technological "know-how" disseminated to the rest of the Old World (Roberts, Thornton, and Pigott 2009). Although broadly accepted, this view is still not a consensus, and there are scholars who continue to follow Collin Renfrew (e.g., 1969) and others in suggesting independent innovations in multiple centers (e.g., Ruiz-Taboada and Montero-Ruiz 1999). In regard to the Late Chalcolithic southern Levant, the "diffusion of innovation" model should be adopted, as there is strong evidence for connections with Anatolia at this time (e.g., Yellin, Levy, and Rowan 1996) and probably even with Anatolian metallurgy, including trade with alloys and/or their minerals (e.g., Golden 2009, with references). A recent discovery of a late sixth-millennium BCE copper awl (with up to 7 percent by weight of tin) from Tel Tsaf (Garfinkel et al. 2014) indicates long-distance trade connections (probably with the Caucasus) and further supports the external origin of metallurgical knowledge.

The dawn of metallurgy in the southern Levant was an extraordinary phenomenon in the history of metallurgy of the region and beyond, with technological achievements that would not be paralleled until millennia later. These include not only the smelting of pure copper from the local ore but also sophisticated casting of complex objects, such as mace-heads, crowns, and scepters (e.g., the famous hoard of the Cave of the Treasure [Bar-Adon 1980]), by the lost wax technique (Goren 2008). The latter was done with imported copper alloys (with varying concentrations of arsenic/antimony/

TABLE 29.1. *Iron Age socio-technological systems in the Aravah Valley (after Ben-Yosef 2010).*

	System 1	System 2	System 3	System 4	System 5
Date (BCE)	1140–1000	1000–925	925–800	800–586	1300–586
Main sites*	Timna': Sites 30, 15; Feinan: KEN, KAG, KAJ	Timna': Sites 30, 34; Feinan: KEN, KAJ, KHI	Timna': Site 30; Feinan: KEN, Site 5	Feinan only (RAM Complex)	Timna': F2; Feinan: Fidan 630, ERS 23
Smelting technology (cf. Fig. 29.3)	Technological tradition similar to those used in Late Bronze Age Timna', possibly with some minor improvements	Improvement in efficiency (~1 wt.-% Cu in slag), possibly some improvement in standardization	Dramatic improvement in efficiency (~0.5 wt.-% Cu in slag) and standardization; accompanied by a new set of installations	No successful smelting (despite evidence for mining attempts)	Poor efficiency and standardization; application of simple technologies and "outdated" installations
General attributes	Intensification of copper production after Egypt left the Timna' Valley; social unification of Feinan and Timna' is evident; no substantial architecture; smelting took place in open sites; residence most probably in tents; small walls and stone-built installations	Large-scale production; substantial architecture appears, including defensive elements, reflecting regional instability and attempts to exercise power internally and externally; population is still essentially (semi-) nomadic	Large-scale production done at fewer sites (much more centralized organization of production); no defensive elements reflects stable period; population is still essentially (semi-) nomadic	A failed attempt at large-scale production; two fortresses and a massive tower directly associated with mining activities reflect regional instability – probably the reason for its failure; sedentary population (based at Buseirah)	Small-scale, "opportunistic" production; no architecture; smelting took place in marginal locations in a distance from the main smelting sites; nomadic population

* KAG = Khirbat al-Ghuweiba; KAJ = Khirbat al-Jariya; KEN = Khirbat en-Nahas; KHI = Khirbat Hamra Ifdan

nickel), which further testify to the extreme efforts invested in metallurgical practices at the time. This thriving metallurgy should be viewed in light of the social and cultural background of the Late Chalcolithic Ghassulian culture (Gilead 2011; Ben-Yosef et al. 2016), which represents advancements in other technologies (flint, pottery, agriculture), and a complex social structure, including stratification (or "inequality" [Levy 2006]) and specialization (possibly even with professional "guilds"). In this context, it is evident that Ghassulian metallurgy triggered and fulfilled social purposes, most probably through the medium of cult and rituals, rather than advancing agricultural and warfare technologies; these were still based on stone tools, while the so-called utilitarian metal artifacts were predominantly replicas used only in cultic contexts. In that respect, Ghassulian metallurgy is not different from early metallurgy around the world, which typically begins with nonutilitarian artifacts (such as ornaments) that bore symbolic meanings and played a role in social processes.

The Late Chalcolithic stands out in the history of metallurgy in the southern Levant also in regard to the organization of production, as this is the *only* period in which copper smelting took place far from the mines (Levy and Shalev 1989). The smelting workshops were found inside settlements in the Beersheva Valley, implying transportation of ore from Feinan, over 80 km to the southeast (Hauptmann 1989). This rather "inefficient" practice, together with the unique distribution pattern of specialized workshops in designated areas of particular settlements, also reflect the social background of the period and demonstrate well that social choices are an integral part of ancient technologies.

CONCLUSION

As archaeology *is* the study of ancient material culture, research into metals and associated technologies constitutes an essential component of archaeological practice. This research, broadly referred to as "archaeometallurgy," has the potential to shed light on core social and cultural issues in the history of humankind. In this chapter, we demonstrated this potential, focusing on archaeometallurgy's contribution to the social archaeology of the Levant, and its significant input into questions such as social structure and social processes.

The close association of archaeometallurgy with archaeometry, or "archaeological science" in general, and the emphasis on reconstruction of the chemical and physical processes (notably, in early archaeometallurgical research) might give the impression that archaeometallurgy is far from what is typically termed "social archaeology." However, even observations that seem only technical are in essence social, and the ultimate goal of archaeometallurgy has always been the study of ancient societies and social processes. This has been done predominantly by revealing links between society and technology, and between people and objects of unique qualities.

> ## Archaeometallurgy, Archaeological Science, and Social Archaeology
>
> Traditionally, archaeometallurgical research is strongly related to the type of studies broadly termed "archaeological science." This rapidly developing field refers to "the development and application in archaeology of techniques and concepts drawn from the natural sciences and engineering" (Martinón-Torres and Killick 2015) and, per that definition, is concerned more with research methods rather than methodologies. In fact, archaeological science does not pertain to any particular theoretical framework; as a result, its practitioners might base their research on any type of archaeological approach or brand of archaeological theory, including social archaeology. Thus, archaeological science does not necessarily imply a processual approach, and the term should not be confused with "scientific archaeology," which does express a conviction that archaeology should follow the natural sciences in methodology, research design, and validation of results.
>
> The significant contribution of analytical techniques to the study of ancient metals and their manufacturing technologies is evident (see above). With the advancement of science not only old techniques are constantly improving (and instruments becoming less expensive and more portable [see, e.g., Levy et al. 2010]), but also new techniques regularly become available. Therefore, the potential of archaeological science to provide new insights in archaeometallurgy is always growing – and as archaeology is essentially concerned with material, this potential exists in *all* of its branches, making archaeological science a promising research field within archaeology.

NOTE

1 For an overview of the concept and its application, see Sellet 1993.

REFERENCES

Albright, W. F. 1949. *The Archaeology of Palestine*. Pelican Books A199. Harmondsworth: Penguin.

Amri, Y. A. S. al- 2008. *The Role of the Iron Ore Deposit of Mugharet el-Wardeh, Jordan in the Development of the Use of Iron in Southern Bilad el-Sham*. PhD diss., Ruhr-Universität Bochum.

Bar-Adon, P. 1980. *The Cave of the Treasure: The Finds from the Caves in Naḥal Mishmar*. JDS. Jerusalem: IES.

Bar-Yosef Mayer, D. E., and Porat, N. 2008. Green Stone Beads at the Dawn of Agriculture. *PNAS* 105: 8548–51.

Barker, G.; Gilbertson, D. D.; and Mattingly, D. J., eds. 2007. *Archaeology and Desertification: The Wadi Faynan Landscape Survey, Southern Jordan*. Wadi Faynan Series 2; LSS 6. Oxford: Oxbow.

Ben-Yosef, E. 2010. *Technology and Social Process: Oscillations in Iron Age Copper Production and Power in Southern Jordan*. PhD diss., University of California, San Diego.

— 2018. The Central Timna Valley Project: Research Design and Preliminary Results. In *Mining for Ancient Copper: Essays in Memory of Beno Rothenberg*, ed. E. Ben-Yosef, 28–63. MSSMNIA 37. Winona Lake, IN: Eisenbrauns; Tel Aviv: Emery and Claire Yass Publications in Archaeology.

Ben-Yosef, E., ed. 2018. *Mining for Ancient Copper: Essays in Memory of Beno Rothenberg*. MSSMNIA 37. Winona Lake, IN: Eisenbrauns; Tel Aviv: Emery and Claire Yass Publications in Archaeology.

Ben-Yosef, E.; Gidding, A.; Tauxe, L.; Davidovich, U.; Najjar, M.; and Levy, T. E. 2016. Early Bronze Age Copper Production Systems in the Northern Arabah Valley: New Insights from Archaeomagnetic Study of Slag Deposits in Jordan and Israel. *JAS* 72: 71–84.

Ben-Yosef, E.; Tauxe, L.; and Levy, T. E. 2010. Archaeomagnetic Dating of Copper Smelting Site F2 in the Timna Valley (Israel) and Its Implications for Modelling of Ancient Technological Developments. *Archaeometry* 52: 1110–21.

Ben-Yosef, E.; Tauxe, L.; Ron, H.; Agnon, A.; Avner, U.; Najjar, M.; and Levy, T. E. 2008. A New Approach for Geomagnetic Archaeointensity Research: Insights on Ancient Metallurgy in the Southern Levant. *JAS* 35: 2863–79.

Ben-Yosef, E.; Vassal, Y.; van den Brink, E. C. M.; and Beeri, R. 2016. A New Ghassulian Metallurgical Assemblage from Bet Shemesh (Israel) and the Earliest Leaded Copper in the Levant. *JAS: Reports* 9: 493–504.

Childe, V. G. 1942. *What Happened in History: A Study of the Rise and Decline of Cultural and Moral Values in the Old World up to the Fall of the Roman Empire*. Pelican Books A108. Harmondsworth: Penguin.

— 1944. Archaeological Ages as Technological Stages. *JRAIGBI* 74: 7–24.

Costin, C. L. 1991. Craft Specialization: Issues in Defining, Documenting, and Explaining the Organization of Production. In *Archaeological Method and Theory*, Vol. 3, ed. M. B. Schiffer, 1–56. Tucson: The University of Arizona Press.

Costin, C. L., and Wright, R. P., eds. 1998. *Craft and Social Identity*. APAAA 8. Arlington, VA: American Anthropological Association.

Craddock, P. T. 1995. *Early Metal Mining and Production*. Edinburgh: Edinburgh University Press.

Dar, S. 1994. *The History of the Hermon: Settlements and Temples of the Itureans*. Tel Aviv: Hakibbutz Hameuchad (Hebrew).

Eliyahu-Behar, A.; Yahalom-Mack, N.; Shilstein, S.; Zukerman, A.; Shafer-Elliott, C.; Maeir, A. M.; Boaretto, E.; Finkelstein, I.; and Weiner, S. 2012. Iron and Bronze Production in Iron Age IIA Philistia: New Evidence from Tell es-Safi/Gath, Israel. *JAS* 39: 255–67.

Gale, N. H., and Stos-Gale, S. 2000. Lead Isotope Analyses Applied to Provenance Studies. In *Modern Analytical Methods in Art and Archaeology*, ed. E. Ciliberto and G. Spoto, 503–84. Chemical Analysis 155. New York: Wiley.

Garfinkel, Y. 1987. Bead Manufacture on the Pre-Pottery Neolithic B Site of Yiftahel. *JIPS* 20: 79*–90*.

— 1999. *Neolithic and Chalcolithic Pottery of the Southern Levant*. Qedem 39. Jerusalem: The Institute of Archaeology, The Hebrew University of Jerusalem.

Garfinkel, Y.; Klimscha, F.; Shalev, S.; and Rosenberg, D. 2014. The Beginning of Metallurgy in the Southern Levant: A Late 6th Millennium calBC Copper Awl from Tel Tsaf, Israel. *PLOS ONE* 9: e92591. http://journals.plos.org/plosone/article?id=10.1371/journal.pone.0092591 (accessed August 25, 2017).

Gilat, A.; Shirav, M.; Bogoch, R.; Halicz, L.; Avner, U.; and Nahlieli, D. 1993. Significance of Gold Exploitation in the Early Islamic Period, Israel. *JAS* 20: 429–37.

Gilead, I. 2011. Chalcolithic Culture History: Ghassulian and Other Entities in the Southern Levant. In *Culture, Chronology and the Chalcolithic: Theory and Transition*, ed. J. L. Lovell and Y. M. Rowan, 12–24. LSS 9. Oxford: Oxbow.

Golden, J. M. 2009. *Dawn of the Metal Age: Technology and Society during the Levantine Chalcolithic*. AAA. London: Equinox.

Goren, Y. 2008. The Location of Specialized Copper Production by the Lost Wax Technique in the Chalcolithic Southern Levant. *Geoarchaeology* 23: 374–97.

Gottlieb, Y. 2010. The Advent of the Age of Iron in the Land of Israel: A Review and Reassessment. *TA* 37: 89–110.

Hadas, G. 2004. A Pyrite and Limonite Mine near the Spring of 'En Gedi – A Second-Temple-Period Burial and Other Finds. *'Atiqot* 46: 5–14 (Hebrew; English summary on pp. 127*–8*).

Hauptmann, A. 1989. The Earliest Periods of Copper Metallurgy in Feinan, Jordan. In *Old World Archaeometallurgy: Proceedings of the International Symposium "Old World Archaeometallurgy," Heidelberg 1987*, ed. A. Hauptmann, E. Pernicka, and G. A. Wagner, 119–35. Anschnitt 7; Veröffentlichungen aus dem Deutschen Bergbau-Museum Bochum 44. Bochum: Deutsches Bergbau-Museum.

——— 2007. *The Archaeometallurgy of Copper: Evidence from Faynan, Jordan*. Natural Science in Archaeology. Berlin: Springer.

Jones, I. W. N.; Levy, T. E.; and Najjar, M. 2012. Khirbat Nuqayb al-Asaymir and Middle Islamic Metallurgy in Faynan: Surveys of Wadi al-Ghuwayb and Wadi al-Jariya in Faynan, Southern Jordan. *BASOR* 368: 67–102.

Jones, I. W. N.; Najjar, M.; and Levy, T. E. 2018. The Arabah Copper Industry in the Islamic Period: Views from Faynan and Timna. In *Mining for Ancient Copper: Essays in Memory of Beno Rothenberg*, ed. E. Ben-Yosef, 332–43. MSSMNIA 37. Winona Lake, IN: Eisenbrauns; Tel Aviv: Emery and Claire Yass Publications in Archaeology.

Key, C. A. 1980. The Trace-Element Composition of the Copper and Copper-Alloy Artefacts of the Nahal Mishmar Hoard. In *The Cave of the Treasure: The Finds from the Caves in Naḥal Mishmar*, ed. P. Bar-Adon, 238–43. JDS. Jerusalem: IES.

Killick, D., and Fenn, T. 2012. Archaeometallurgy: The Study of Preindustrial Mining and Metallurgy. *ARA* 41: 559–75.

Lemonnier, P. 1992. *Elements for an Anthropology of Technology*. Anthropological Papers 88. Ann Arbor: Museum of Anthropology, University of Michgan.

Levy, T. E. 2006. The Emergence of Social Inequality: The Chalcolithic Period in Palestine (ca. 4500–3600 B.C.E.). In *The Archaeological History of the Southern Levant*, ed. D. C. Hopkins, 1–46. Archaeological Sources for the History of Palestine 3. Boston: ASOR.

Levy, T. E.; Najjar, M.; and Ben-Yosef, E., eds. 2014. *New Insights into the Iron Age Archaeology of Edom, Southern Jordan: Surveys, Excavations, and Research from the University of California, San Diego–Department of Antiquities of Jordan, Edom Lowlands Regional Archaeology Project (ELRAP)*. 2 vols. MonArch 35. Los Angeles: The Cotsen Institute of Archaeology Press.

Levy, T. E.; Petrovic, V.; Wypych, T.; Gidding, A.; Knabb, K.; Hernandez, D.; Smith, N. G.; Schulz, J. P.; Savage, S. H.; Kuester, F.; Ben-Yosef, E.; Buitenhuys, C.; Barrett, C. J.; Najjar, M.; and DeFanti, T. 2010. On-Site Digital Archaeology 3.0 and Cyber-Archaeology: Into the Future of the Past – New Developments, Delivery and

the Creation of a Data Avalanche. In *Cyber-Archaeology*, ed. M. Forte, 135–53. BAR International Series 2177. Oxford: Archaeopress.
Levy, T. E., and Shalev, S. 1989. Prehistoric Metalworking in the Southern Levant: Archaeometallurgical and Social Perspectives. *WA* 20: 352–72.
Martinón-Torres, M., and Killick, D. 2015. Archaeological Theories and Archaeological Sciences. In *The Oxford Handbook of Archaeological Theory*, ed. A. Gardner, M. Lake, and U. Sommer. Oxford: Oxford University Press.
Mattingly, D. J.; Newson, P.; Creighton, O.; Tomber, R.; Grattan, J.; Hunt, C.; Gilbertson, D. D.; el-Rishi, H.; and Pyatt, B. 2007. A Landscape of Imperial Power: Roman and Byzantine *Phaino*. In *Archaeology and Desertification: The Wadi Faynan Landscape Survey, Southern Jordan*, ed. G. Barker, D. D. Gilbertson, and D. J. Mattingly, 305–48. Wadi Faynan Series 2; LSS 6. Oxford: Oxbow.
Meshel, Z. 2006. Were There Gold Mines in the Eastern Arabah? In *Crossing the Rift: Resources, Settlements Patterns and Interaction in the Wadi Arabah*, ed. P. Bienkowski and K. Galor, 231–8. LSS 3. Oxford: CBRL and Oxbow.
Pfaffenberger, B. 1992. Social Anthropology of Technology. *ARA* 21: 491–516.
Pigott, V. C., ed. 1999. *The Archaeometallurgy of the Asian Old World*. UMM 89; University Museum Symposium Series 7; MASCA Research Papers in Science and Archaeology 16. Philadelphia: University Museum, University of Pennsylvania.
Renfrew, C. 1969. The Development and Chronology of the Early Cycladic Figurines. *AJA* 73: 1–32.
Roberts, B. W., and Thornton, C. P., eds. 2014. *Archaeometallurgy in Global Perspective: Methods and Syntheses*. New York: Springer.
Roberts, B. W.; Thornton, C. P.; and Pigott, V. C. 2009. Development of Metallurgy in Eurasia. *Antiquity* 83 (322): 1012–22.
Rothenberg, B. 1990. Copper Smelting Furnaces, Tuyères, Slags, Ingot-Moulds and Ingots in the Arabah: The Archaeological Data. In *The Ancient Metallurgy of Copper: Archaeology – Experiment – Theory*, ed. B. Rothenberg, 1–77. Researches in the Arabah, 1959–1984 2; Metal in History 3. London: Institute for Archaeo-Metallurgical Studies.
 2005. Explorations and Excavations in the Mines of the Timna Valley (Israel): Paleomorphology as Key to Major Problems in Mining Research. *Glasnik Srpskog Arheološkog Društva* 22: 133–48.
Rothenberg, B., ed. 1990. *The Ancient Metallurgy of Copper: Archaeology – Experiment – Theory*. Researches in the Arabah, 1959–1984 2; Metal in History 3. London: Institute for Archaeo-Metallurgical Studies.
Ruiz-Taboada, A., and Montero-Ruiz, I. 1999. The Oldest Metallurgy in Western Europe. *Antiquity* 73 (282): 897–903.
Schiffer, M. B. 1976. *Behavioral Archeology*. Studies in Archeology. New York: Academic.
Scott, D. 2010. *Ancient Metals: Microstructure and Metallurgy*, Vol. 1. Los Angeles: Conservation Science Press.
Sellet, F. 1993. Chaine Operatoire: The Concept and Its Applications. *Lithic Technology* 18: 106–12.
Shalev, S. 2008. A Brief Outline Summary of Nonferrous Archaeometallurgy in Israel. *Israel Journal of Earth Sciences* 56: 133–8.
Trigger, B. G. 2006. *A History of Archaeological Thought*. 2nd ed. Cambridge: Cambridge University Press.
Tylecote, R. F. 1992. *A History of Metallurgy*. 2nd ed. Avon: The Institute of Materials.

Veldhuijzen, H. A. 2006. *Early Iron Production in the Levant: Smelting and Smithing at Early 1st Millennium BC Tell Hammeh, Jordan, and Tel Beth-Shemesh, Israel*. PhD diss., University College London.
——— 2009. Of Slag and Scales, Micro-Stratigraphy and Micro-Magnetic Material at Metallurgical Excavations. In *A Timeless Vale: Archaeological and Related Essays on the Jordan Valley in Honour of Gerrit van der Kooij on the Occasion of His Sixty-Fifth Birthday*, ed. E. Kaptijn and L. P. Petit, 155–66. Archaeological Studies Leiden University 19. Leiden: Leiden University Press.
Yahalom-Mack, N., and Eliyahu-Behar, A. 2015. The Transition from Bronze to Iron in Canaan: Chronology, Technology, and Context. *Radiocarbon* 57: 285–305.
Yellin, J.; Levy, T. E.; and Rowan, Y. M. 1996. New Evidence on Prehistoric Trade Routes: The Obsidian Evidence from Gilat, Israel. *JFA* 23: 361–8.

THIRTY

THE ARCHAEOLOGY OF MARITIME ADAPTATION

ASSAF YASUR-LANDAU

The landscape of the southern Levantine littoral is almost an ideal laboratory to test concepts of connectivity and adaptation to the maritime environment in Mediterranean micro-regions. The Akko Plain and the western Galilee, north of the Carmel, form a distinct micro-region, bordered by mountains to the south, north, and east. The coastal plain, stretching south of the Carmel ridge, is usually wide and borders the low hill country (Shephelah). The strongest maritime impact may have been felt in the least arable land between the sea and the mountains: the Carmel coast, stretching from the Sharon Plain in the south up to where Mount Carmel meets the Mediterranean Sea by Haifa (Rainey and Notley 2006: 36–8, 206). Connectivity, namely trade and other maritime interactions, may be presented as an adaptive strategy for risk management in the uncertainty of the Mediterranean climate, when used in tandem with the well-tested building blocks of the specialized Mediterranean economy, most of its elements existing from the Neolithic period: the cultivation of grains, vines, and olives rather than a single crop to maximize land use, thus enabling storage, and animal husbandry based on cattle, ovicaprids, and pigs (e.g., Broodbank 2013: 19–21, 170–8). While the southern Levant is hardly mentioned in Peregrine Horden and Nicholas Purcell's *The Corrupting Sea: A Study of Mediterranean History* (2000), it features prominently in studies of second–first-millennium BCE maritime networks (e.g., Broodbank 2013: fig. 9.1; Tartaron 2013).

Five decades of underwater and coastal archaeology in Israel (Galili, Raban, and Sharvit 2002: 933–43; Galili and Rosen 2008) have yielded impressive discoveries, resulting in studies of ship archaeology – mostly the Roman to modern periods (e.g., Pomey, Kahanov, and Rieth 2012) – of ancient harbors (e.g., Raban 1985; 1995b) and coastal settlements (e.g., Artzy 2006; Gilboa and Sharon 2008). At the same time, advances in the theoretical study of harbors and maritime interaction, as well as new approaches to maritime networks, continue to modify long-held views that consider ship archaeology, land archaeology, and harbor archaeology as separate disciplines (Tartaron 2013; Leidwanger et al. 2014; Preiser-Kapeller and Daim 2015). The introduction of geoarchaeological methods into the study of ancient harbors (e.g., Marriner et al. 2014) provides additional tools for the diachronic study of human impact on the coastal environment. It is beyond the scope of this chapter to present the numerous recent advancements in the archaeology of underwater, coastal, and harbor sites.[1] What this chapter will present, however, are some diachronic aspects of the intricate relationship between human communities and the sea in the long span between the Neolithic period and the end of the Iron Age, focusing on technological and, in some cases, social adaptations to life by the sea.

ADAPTIVE STRATEGIES IN THE MARITIME NEOLITHIC

The Neolithic revolution, including the introduction of agriculture and animal husbandry, and the domestication of cereals and legumes, as well as sheep, goats, and pigs, enabled the creation of stable communities residing in villages of growing sizes. The Neolithic lifestyle successfully met the challenges posed by the fickle Mediterranean climate by storing a variety of crops as a buffer for frequent dry years. Furthermore, the Neolithic cultural package was modified to accommodate life along the coasts of the Mediterranean in two major sea-related ways: First, the harvesting of maritime food resources, which was undertaken already in the Epipaleolithic period, became much more specialized during the Pre-Pottery Neolithic and was combined with coastal and deep-water fishing (Galili et al. 2002). The second form of adaptation was the incorporation of *connectivity*, a basic characteristic of the Mediterranean, into surprisingly complex maritime interactions: maritime migration and colonization, on the one hand, and the use of maritime networks for the procurement of exotic raw material, on the other. The end result has been aptly termed the "maritime Neolithic" (Broodbank 2006). The relative ease of maritime transport, once a suitable watercraft was available, enabled the permeation of the Neolithic lifestyle into the islands of Cyprus and Crete, as well as into coastal regions in the eastern Mediterranean (Horejs et al. 2015). The 9.2 ka BP climate event and the more severe one in 8.2 ka BP did not devastate the Levantine Neolithic cultures, likely because the Neolithic economy was resilient enough to survive such events (Flohr et al. 2016).

The Neolithic villages near the Carmel coast are an unusual archaeological example for the study of the maritime Neolithic. Now covered following a rise in sea level, they provide an exceptional wealth of organic finds that is missing from the terrestrial archaeological record. Of these, the best-explored site is 'Atlit-Yam, found near modern-day 'Atlit, at a depth of 8–12 m below sea level (bsl). The site covers ca. 40,000 m^2 of which ca. 70 percent has been exposed by the sea, enabling a detailed survey of most of the site and several small-scale excavations. A date within the ninth millennium BP in the Pre-Pottery Neolithic C was reached by analyzing radiocarbon samples retrieved from the site. The village includes domestic structures, dividing walls, burials, wells, and two megalithic structures, possibly of cultic nature. The wells were dug into the coastal aquifer, indicating the earliest example of architectural adaption to life in a coastal environment. The economy shows a combination between agriculture, collecting fruit from wild trees, raising domesticated animals, fishing, and some hunting. The botanic finds include domesticated species, such as wheat, barley, lentils, and flax, alongside wild fruit trees. The zooarchaeological assemblage includes domesticated sheep, goats, cattle, pigs, and dogs. Of the fish remains, 96 percent belonged to gray triggerfish, showing a preference in fishing practices. Additional evidence of fishing found at this site is fishing tackle, such as bone needles, hooks, and barbs, as well as groundstone net sinkers. Evidence of auditory exostosis, an ear pathology caused by diving in cold water, was found in some of the male skeletons buried at the site; this may be an indication of spear fishing (Galili et al. 2014: 183–9). While imports to these Carmel coastal sites include bitumen originating in the Dead Sea, there were no maritime imports, such as the Melian obsidian found at the Pre-Pottery Neolithic C Anatolian site of Çukuriçi Höyük (Horejs et al. 2015).

At least six Pottery Neolithic sites, belonging the Wadi Rabah phase of the Late Pottery Neolithic (seventh millennium BP), were found near the Carmel coast at depths of 1–6 m bsl. All sites show an expansion of the Mediterranean economy to include olives, as evidenced by the very large amounts of olive pits found at them. At Kfar Samir, a pit filled with large quantities of crushed olives, as well as a stone basin that may have been used for olive crushing, are evidence of olive oil extraction. A well found within this site, built of alternating courses of stones and branches, demonstrates the elaborate technique of well construction used in coastal areas (Galili et al. 2014: 189–97).

THE SECOND-MILLENNIUM BCE HARBORS AS LOCI OF MULTIPLE MARITIME INTERACTIONS

The transition into complex urban societies during the third and second millennia in the southern Levant opened new venues for maritime connectivity and adaptation. Unfortunately, little is known about maritime activity and adaptation in the Early Bronze Age on Israel's coast; besides a single Early

Bronze Age I Egyptian vessel with Nilotic bivalves found underwater in 'Atlit, there are no underwater finds relating to this period (Sharvit et al. 2002). This stands in contrast to the well-developed maritime policy of the Old Kingdom in Egypt that culminated in large-scale expeditions to procure raw materials. A notable import into Egypt was lumber from Lebanon, which was the basis for long-lasting connections with Byblos. Maritime transport in the Red Sea facilitated the commute and work of extensive mining expeditions in the Sinai Peninsula and possibly beyond; it was enabled by an impressive maritime infrastructure, seen in Wadi el-Jarf, where huge storage galleries and structures were found, as well as a massive mole (Tallet 2012).

The complex Canaanite societies in the second millennium grew accustomed to a reality in which maritime interregional interaction developed into a remarkable variety of co-occurring activities, fit for the growing social and economic needs of the local elites. Just how complex these interactions were can be seen in a unique harbor scene from the Tomb of Kenamun (TT 162), dating to the days of Amenhotep III (Davies and Faulkner 1947: pl. 8; Wachsmann 1998: fig. 14.6) (Fig. 30.1). The arrival of Levantine ships at the Egyptian port is followed by several scenes demonstrating different types of interactions on various scales with different participants:

1. Small-scale trade: Upon embarking, the sailors and merchants seen in the lower register are approaching a series of small shops in which Egyptians are selling textiles and sandals.
2. Large-scale bulk trade: The lower register also shows the import of Canaanite amphorae, bowls, and some finished products, such as a metal

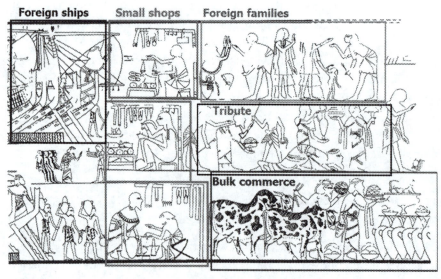

30.1. Interactions in a harbor scene, tomb of Kenamun (after Davies and Faulkner 1947: pl. 8). (Altered by A. Yasur-Landau. Courtesy of the Egypt Exploration Society).

statue of a bull and two very prominent, huge zebu bulls, indicating that livestock was indeed part of the bulk trade in the Bronze Age.
3. Tribute: The middle register shows a presentation scene in which Canaanite traders clad with heavy robes, standing among Egyptian officials, depicted as carrying metal vessels and other finished products, some bowing down.
4. Foreign families: In the top register, two women and a child face an Egyptian official. A Canaanite wearing a heavy robe is seated to the left, raising his hands toward another Egyptian official.

Besides these peaceful activities, maritime connectivity was used for purposes of war. For example, in the Amarna period, Byblos was attacked by the ships of Arwad (EA 101 [Rainey and Schniedewind 2015: 553]). Piracy and maritime raids were also a known phenomenon in the eastern Mediterranean even before the crisis years and the end of the Late Bronze Age. One example is the raids of the Lukka on Cyprus mentioned in the el-Amarna letters (EA 38 [Rainey and Schniedewind 2015: 1383]; Gilan 2013).

The image of Canaanites arriving at an Egyptian harbor and engaging in multiple forms of interactions is by no means limited to the Late Bronze Age and already appears in Middle Bronze Age literary sources. Thus, the last king of the 17th Dynasty, Kamose, boasts of raiding the Hyksos capital of Avaris:

> I haven't left a plank of the hundreds of ships [or 300?] of fresh cedar, which were filled with gold. Lapis, silver, turquoise, bronze axes without number. Over and above the moringa [more likely olive] oil, incense, fat. Honey, willow, bow-wood, sticks and their fine woods – all the fine products of Retenu – I have confiscated all of it. (Redford 1997: 14)

This inscription exposes a variety of co-occurring interregional interactions related to maritime activity, differing in duration and intensity. The first activity type is maritime trade, said to have originated in the Levant (*Retenu*). The massive presence of hundreds of ships in the harbor that functions as a gateway to the Mediterranean is a continuum of events formed by the coming and going of boats. By the time of the raid, Avaris had already been under Hyksos rule for a long time. The Hyksos phenomenon began with the arrival of people from the Levant in Tell el-Dab'a (and other Egyptian sites) as early as the 12th Dynasty. These included soldiers, merchants, workers, and captives from Egyptian raids, many of which, no doubt, through maritime interaction (Bietak 2010: 139–47).

THE MIDDLE BRONZE AGE (CA. 2000/1950–1550/1530 BCE): THE CREATION OF HARBOR COMMUNITIES

Connectivity had an important role in the renewal of urban life and complex societies in the southern Levant during the Middle Bronze Age (MB) I (twentieth–eighteenth centuries BCE). The rise along the Mediterranean coast of large fortified settlements, such as Ashkelon, Yavneh-Yam, Jaffa, Akko, and Achziv, is connected with maritime trade, as well as overland trade along the route connecting Egypt with the Lebanese coast. At the same time, smaller unfortified settlements, such as Tel Nami and Tel Dor, also appeared on the coast and may have served as emporia near bays used as anchorages. The urbanization of the coastal areas no doubt left a significant mark on the landscape, because the populations of such sites were involved in large-scale agricultural activities, including clearing natural vegetation and planting orchards in areas that are relatively scarce in arable lands (Kaniewski et al. 2014).

Egyptian literary evidence also points to social adaptation to maritime life and varying forms of interactions in the Middle Bronze Age. The 12th Dynasty early (Berlin) and late (Brussels) groups of Egyptian Execration Texts both mention the "Amu (Levantine) . . . of the harbor people" indicating that there was a class of people specifically related to activities in harbors (Rainey and Notley 2006: 52–3, 58).

The Egyptians, however, were much more interested, as this point, in connections with Lebanon and its rich lumber resources. The close connections between Egypt and Byblos demonstrated in the Mit Rahina Text on a maritime expedition to Lebanon in the days of Amenemhet II. The expedition brought back large quantities of silver, copper, bronze, lead, cedar, fig, sycamore, resin, weapons, and other commodities. Sixty-five men and women, mentioned among the commodities, were brought either as slaves or migrating artisans, shedding light on the role of maritime transport in human mobility during the Middle Bronze Age (Marcus 2007). Harbors in Ullasa and Byblos are mentioned in the tomb of Khnumhotep in Dahshur (Allen 2008).

The strongest indication of Middle Bronze Age maritime ties is the Cypriot pottery found at most coastal sites as early as the MB I and at many lowland sites in Israel during the MB II. These assemblages comprise mostly small- and medium-sized containers of the White Painted styles and are later complemented by container and bowls of the Red-on-Red/Red-on-Black style, as well as by other Middle Cypriot styles (Maguire 2009). It remains to be determined if Cypriot copper accompanied these ceramic imports. The Canaanite sphere of interaction during this period extended to the coast of Lebanon, as indicated by ridge-necked jars found in Ashkelon (Stager et al. 2008: 231) and the import of cedar wood found, for example, at Tel Nami and Tel Kabri (Lev-Yadun et al. 1996; Liphschitz 2002: 340).

Contact with the Aegean is rarer but still visible with a sherd of Cretan Kamares Ware found in Ashkelon (Stager et al. 2008: fig. 14.25), a pithos incised with Cretan Hieroglyphic signs from Tel Haror (Brandl, Oren, and Nahshoni 2014: fig. 7), the Aegean-style wall and floor paintings found in the MB II palace at Tel Kabri (Cline, Yasur-Landau, and Goshen 2011), the remains of *Lathyrus clymenum* found at Tel Nami (Kislev, Artzy, and Marcus 1993), and perhaps the resin from the *Liquidambar* tree, originating in western Anatolia, found at Tel Kabri (Koh, Yasur-Landau, and Cline 2014).

Two cultural innovations are tightly connected to maritime transport during the Middle Bronze Age; the so-called Byblian anchor and the transport storage jar. The maritime connections between Egypt and Lebanon were no doubt responsible for the widespread use of the Byblian anchor, named so as it was found in the MB I Obelisk Temple in Byblos. This type has a triangular shape with a rounded top, and a single hole is hewn in its top one-third. In many cases, a groove extends from the very top of the anchor to the hole, intended to hold the rope in place. More than forty such anchors have been reported; of these, two were found underwater at 'Atlit-Yam together with Middle Bronze Age storage jars (Galili, Sharvit, and Artzy 1994). Further confirmation of their dating to the Middle Bronze Age comes from examples of such anchors found at the Red Sea harbor of Mersa (Wadi Gawassis), active during the Egyptian Middle Kingdom (Fattovitz 2012: fig. 62). During the Late Bronze Age, this type of anchor was replaced by a heavier rectangular anchor of the type found in the Uluburun wreck (Pulak 1998). The occurrence of a single type of anchor in the vast area between Egypt and Lebanon points not only to the travel of boats between these areas but also to the transfer of maritime-related technology. It is intriguing that Canaanite jars were found in Mersa (Wadi Gawassis), indicating that Levantine commodities found their way as far as the Red Sea.

The second innovation is the use of transport storage jars, sometimes also named "Canaanite amphorae" or "maritime transport containers." These developed from domestic storage vessels in the beginning of the MB I. The search for a container that would hold liquids while withstanding the physical challenges of maritime voyage led to the creation of a jar with an oval body, a pointed base and two vertical handles. This would become the predominant maritime transport vessel in the eastern Mediterranean over one and a half millennia, from the Middle Bronze Age to the end of the Iron Age (Marcus 2007: 150, 162; Demesticha and Knapp 2016).

To date, no maritime facilities dating to the Middle or Late Bronze Age have been found in Israel. This stands in sharp contrast to Neopalatial Crete, where ship sheds were found in Malia, Poros, and Kommos (Raban 1991a; Tartaron 2013: 158–60), and also to Egypt, where artificial harbor basins were found at Tell el-Dab'a (Bietak 2017) and harbor storage facilities and related installations were found in the Red Sea harbors of Mersa (Wadi Gawassis) (Fattowitz 2012) and 'Ayn Sukhna (Tallet 2012). There are two possible reasons for this absence: One is that anchoring was practiced in bays that had no additional manmade protection or assisting facilities. The other is that natural processes left coastal and maritime installations buried under alluvial soil, coastal sands, or seawater. Such processes may have been the ca. 2 m rise in sea levels that occurred since the Middle Bronze Age (Sivan et al. 2001) or sedimentation of riverine anchorages. Thus, for example, at Akko, a geoarchaeological study established that the Bronze Age estuary of the Na'aman River created a bay between the southern part of the tell and the Treidl paleo-island – an eolianite hill, currently surrounded by alluvium. Protected anchoring was possible immediately south of the tell. This conforms to the ideas of Avner Raban on an anchorage located in Akko, Area P and on an adjacent gate. It is possible that the harbor basin and its associated structures are now covered by a thick layer of alluvial soil (Raban 1991b; Morhange et al. 2016).

An examination by the present author of two maritime modifications that were previously attributed to the Middle Bronze Age refuted this claim: The rock-cut channel south of Achziv was not created in the Middle Bronze Age. As aerial photos show, it first appeared during the 1960s in connection to the construction of the local Club Med (Raban 1995b: 144). A supposed quay in Yavneh-Yam is, in fact, a natural formation of beachrock.

At Tel Dor, a massive structure made of large, coarsely drafted stones and boulders was found on the coastline of the "Love Bay." It rests on top of the *kurkar* bedrock and is thus unlikely to have served as a quay – but was probably part of a coastal fortification. As the structure remains seem to have a corner, it may well have been a tower or part of a sea gate leading to an anchorage in the bay. Pottery associated with it is still being studied to determine whether it was constructed in the MB I, as argued by Raban (1995a: 301–3; 1995b: 145), or later in the Middle Bronze Age. A Cypriot-style three-hole anchor, characteristic of Late Cypriot (LC) I–IIIA coastal sites on Cyprus, was found in this bay in 2016 by the Dor underwater survey team, further supporting its use in the Bronze Age. Though no maritime installations have been found near it, Tel Nami, an unfortified site adjacent to the Neve-Yam bay and anchorage, was no doubt also connected with maritime activity. This site displays another adaptation to residence in a coastal area: a built well, dug into the coastal aquifer during the MB I. This rectangular stone-lined well indicates a considerably lower sea level in antiquity (Artzy 1995: 120–2). The nearby Neve-Yam bay yielded a group of fifteen Byblian anchors. Their total weight was 1,320 kg, and it is likely that they were used as ballast on a single boat. Most of these anchors were scattered along a 7.5 m axis in a limited area. This dimension would be the minimum length of the boat that carried the anchors; but it is more likely that the boat was considerably larger. A stone weight, an adze, and a chisel with a wooden handle found in the vicinity of the anchors may have also belonged to the same shipwreck (Galili, Sharvit, and Artzy 1994; Marcus 2007: 156).

SHIPWRECKS AND METAL CARGOES OF THE LATE BRONZE AGE (CA. 1550/1530–1200/1150 BCE)

The Late Bronze Age is characterized by a significant increase in imported pottery from Cyprus and, beginning in the fourteenth century BCE, also from the Aegean area. Cypriot pottery, as well as Late Helladic IIIA and IIIB pottery, is found virtually in every southern Levantine site (e.g., Yasur-Landau 2010: 194–200; Papadimitriou 2013; Greener 2015). The maritime import of ceramics, such as serving vessels and containers, was likely secondary in significance to the trade in metals. This is demonstrated clearly by the composition of the Uluburun cargo: Copper and tin comprised ca. 90 percent of the total value of the ship's cargo (Monroe 2010). Indeed, the strategic need for copper and tin in the maintenance of the Late Bronze Age economy required enhanced maritime transport to the Levantine coast.

The stretch of the Carmel coast where the Carmel ridge meets the sea and 'Atlit seems to be a hot spot of Late Bronze Age cargoes containing metal.[2] All cargoes are reported in areas north of Tel Nami and south of Shiqmona. Since these were the most significant Late Bronze Age coastal sites, the cargo find spots appear to be unrelated to any anchorage. Rather, it seems that the ships to which they belonged sunk when their attempts to circumnavigate the Carmel Mountains failed, perhaps because prevailing winds in this area are southwestern. It is possible, for example, that these ships were on their way from the south to the Akko Plain anchorages, such as Tell Abu-Hawam, never reaching their destination port. Ugaritic sources record similar events of wrecking and near wrecking: *KTU* 2.38 mentions a ship from Ugarit going to Egypt that was damaged in a storm and found refuge in Tyre. Another text, *KTU* 4.394, records the loss of a boat carrying a large amount of copper (Hoftijzer and van Soldt 1998: 334, 337).

As these ships had wrecked in relatively shallow water and were exposed to waves and currents, none of the hulls survived, and neither were ceramics found *in situ*. These wrecks are usually represented by finds of metals, as well as stone anchors, both of which sunk into the sand and were preserved. To date, the finds from the sites were collected through an intensive archaeological survey, while none was excavated, apart from trial excavations at the Hishuley Carmel site, they are still awaiting publication. The HaHotrim site, was located at a depth of 6 m, ca. 100 m from the coast, included several one-hole stone anchors, a fragment of an oxhide ingot, a small lead ingot with a hole, and several pieces of bronze objects, including a horse bit (Galili, Gale, and Rosen 2011: 67–8). The find in the Hishuley Carmel shipwreck site, 1.8 km north of HaHotrim (Galili, Gale, and Rosen 2011: 65–6), included eighteen one-hole stone anchors, fourteen of which were made from limestone found at a depth of 3–5 m bsl. The metal ingot assemblage includes fifteen tin ingots of various forms, weighing a total of 204 kg. Some of these ingots bore marks, and many were perforated to be carried by rope or weighed. Two copper oxhide ingots of a late type confirm the Late Bronze Age date of the assemblage. A lump of arsenic was also associated with this cargo along with socketed axes with Late Bronze Age parallels in Anatolia. The presence of these Anatolian-style weapons raises the possibility that there were armed Hittite soldiers or Anatolian mercenaries on the boat. Similarly, it was proposed that the Uluburun ship carried Mycenaeans, based on the presence of Mycenaean weapons in the ship's assemblage (Pulak 2005). Kfar Samir South is located only 900 m north of the Hishuley Carmel site, where a shipwreck was found at a depth of 3–4 m bsl. The assemblage from the wreck included a group of five stone anchors, one of which bears the incision of a scarab (Galili, Gale, and Rosen 2011: 66–7). Metal finds featured tin ingots of various sizes weighing a total of 80 kg. Other finds included a bronze sickle sword and five lead objects with perforated tops, which may have been small ingots or sounding weights. Kfar Samir North, 400 m north of Kfar Samir South, yielded one-hole stone anchors, pieces of copper oxhide ingots, and pieces of copper mixed with slag. Other finds from the sites were removed by looters (Galili, Gale, and Rosen 2011: 67).

The Yavneh-Yam anchorage, the first anchorage south of Jaffa, also provided evidence of maritime activity in the Late Bronze Age. Immediately east of a group of rocks blocking the anchorage from the west, more than thirty stone anchors were found, each with a biconical through-hole. In the center of the bay at a depth of 2–3 m bsl, a group of fifty-four gold objects and seventeen hematite weights was found. The metal objects were scrap gold in the form of granules and spills, and cut pieces of jewelry. The stone weights seem to have originated in various sets of weights, as they do not conform to a single standard. The gold items may have been collected for their intrinsic value and intended for use as currency by a merchant aboard a ship, likely together with the weights. A cylinder seal, a bronze ax, spearheads, and a bronze figurine of a smiting god were also attributed this assemblage, which bears resemblance to that of the Uluburun ship – the most important shipwreck of the Late Bronze Age found to date – which also contained weapons and scrap gold (Raban and Galili 1985: 329; Golani and Galili 2015).

The Carmel coast was also recently linked to part of the finds on the Uluburun ship. A petrographic analysis of the Uluburun anchors indicates that they originated from the eolianite (*kurkar*) of the Carmel coast. A significant percentage of the Canaanite amphorae found in the cargo were also found to originate petrographically in the Carmel region (Goren 2013).

These cargoes indicate the deep involvement of the southern Levantine coast in Late Bronze Age international trade by boats carrying metals. Sites in this region did not function merely as way stations on the route; they also provided the boats and their occupants goods and anchors. While the precise locus of these activities is not yet determined, it is likely to have been one of the two unfortified emporia of Tel Dor or Tel Nami, south of the Carmel, or Tell Abu-Hawam in the Akko Bay (Raban 1995b; Artzy 2006). This involvement is far greater than that elucidated by Egyptian sources, even by the el-Amarna letters, which provide much information about maritime activity along the northern Levantine coast, mainly in connection with Byblian correspondence, but very little on maritime connections with the southern Levant (e.g., EA 85, 98 [Rainey and Schniedewind 2015: 19]). Similarly, in the Ugaritic correspondence, there is rarely a mention of southern Levantine sites, apart from Ashdod, which is often mentioned but may not be the Ashdod located on the southern Canaanite littoral (Na'aman 1997: 609–11)

THE IRON AGE AND THE ADVENT OF HARBOR ARCHITECTURE

The renewal of large-scale maritime trade in the eleventh century BCE, after the twelfth-century crisis years, resulted in a new emphasis on the construction of harbors at coastal sites. One example is Tell Qasile, founded *ex nihilo* in the early eleventh century on the banks of the Yarkon River. The chosen location was ideal as an inner riverine harbor connecting the Mediterranean to the agricultural hinterland farther up the river. Tell Qasile also revealed evidence of trade with Egypt (Mazar 1985: 122; Gadot 2006; Ben-Dor Evian 2011).

The coastal site of Tel Dor yielded conspicuous evidence of trade with Egypt in the Iron Age I, including more than 750 Egyptian vessels and sherds, most of which belong to amphorae; this is the largest concentration of such pottery outside Egypt. Numerous bones of Nile perch were also found at the site, indicating that this fish was a traded commodity, too (Gilboa 2015). This strong connectivity brought unprecedented prosperity to Tel Dor. During the Iron 1b,[3] an ambitious building program was carried out on the southern edge of the tell, overlooking the south bay. It included the construction of the "Monumental Building," made of boulders with ashlar corners; the rounded "Bastion," built of boulders; and the so-called Sea Wall, which may have been built to retain the massive constructions to its north (Gilboa and Sharon 2008; Sharon and Gilboa 2013). It is likely that a similar, equally ambitious, building program was executed in the interface between the site and the sea.

Two massive parallel ashlar walls currently located on the waterline of the south bay and below it have been previously interpreted as quays. The northern one, closest to the tell, dates to the Iron 1b, and the southern, to the Late Bronze Age (Raban 1995a: 339–41). The bay was no doubt used for anchoring in the Bronze and Iron Ages, as indicated by underwater surveys that documented numerous anchors and pottery (Kingsley and Raveh 1996: 18; Lazar et al. 2018). However, underwater excavations by the joint Tel Dor

Land and Sea Project have demonstrated that the southern wall comprises a single course of flat rectangular ashlars with a maximum bottom elevation of ca. 0.6 m bsl. The northern wall, made of massive, wedge-shaped ashlar blocks that are as long as 2.5 m and laid as headers, has a maximum bottom elevation of ca. 1.1 m below the current sea level. It would have been too shallow for any boat to have anchored next to it, especially given that the sea levels were lower during the periods in question (Sivan et al. 2001). It is far more likely that these structures were the foundations of a massive coastal fortification and an adjacent ashlar paving. The date of this elaborate feature is provided by ceramic remains found between the stones of the walls and below them, which are no later than Iron 1b or transitional Iron Age 1b–2, and include fragments of imported Egyptian amphorae. It is likely that additional maritime features are buried under the sand and below the biogenic rock.

An east–west reef, running parallel to the ashlar walls, was thought previously to be a natural reef. In the renewed excavations, it was found to be made of biogenic rock that formed on an enormous accumulation of large ashlars – possibly a mole. The water depth south of this feature is 2.5–3 m deep, which would have been sufficient for anchoring boats in antiquity. Furthermore, a geophysical survey of the coast of Dor's south bay has uncovered additional buried features, possibly related to maritime activities (Lazar et al. 2018).

In the eighth century BCE, the Assyrian Empire emerged as a regional superpower and the overlord of the maritime city-states on the Phoenician coast and in the southern Levant. This raised the need to create new regulations for interactions between the maritime polities and Assyria, while providing the Phoenicians with extended trading rights on the coast of the southern Levant. In an inscription describing the events of 716 BCE, Sargon II argued that he "opened the sealed port of Egypt" (Rainey and Notley 2006: 236), reregulating trade on the boundary between Egypt and the Levantine coast. This Assyrian regulation entailed the foundation of new sites: Tell er-Ruqeish, south of Gaza, a heavily fortified site close to the coast, was probably founded by Sargon II and served as the main Assyrian harbor on the Egyptian border (Thareani 2016). The seventh-century BCE treaty between Esarhaddon, king of Assyria, and Baal, king of Tyre, clearly granted Tyre significant trade rights: "These are the ports of trade (KAR^{meš}) and the trade routes (KAŠKAL^{meš}) which Esarhaddon, king of Assyria, en[trusted] to his servant Baal: to Akko, Dor, to the entire district of the Philistines, and to all the cities within Assyrian territory on the seacoast, and to Gubla, the Lebanon, all the cities in the mountains" (Na'aman 1994: 3). The same treaty also provided rules for the salvage of cargo from a shipwreck. It stipulated that the cargo of a ship belonging to Baal or to the people of Tyre that is wrecked off the "land of the Philistines" or within Assyrian territory belongs to Esarhaddon, while the people on the boat should be returned to their countries unharmed (Parpola and Watanabe 1988: 25; Na'aman 1994: 3; 2009: 98–9; Rainey and Notley 2006: 281).

The port of 'Atlit reflects a more advanced concept of harbor construction than seen at Dor. Here, there are two sectors – a northwestern one and a southeastern one – each consisting of a mole and a quay that were likely built at the same time with no preceding harbor installations. The combination of moles and quays created two rectangular low-energy anchorages. The moles are constructed of ashlar headers with a fill of rubble, and the quays are built of ashlar headers. A fortification wall separated the harbor area from the rest of the Phoenician settlement. It is represented by the remains of a gate and a gateway paved with ashlar blocks. Raban suggested that the harbor was constructed during the eighth and seventh centuries BCE, during the period of Assyrian hegemony. He further suggested that one basin was Phoenician, while the other was, perhaps, an Assyrian emporium. Pottery from the bottom of the harbor basin includes complete late Iron Age storage jars, supporting Raban's notion, as well as large amounts of Persian-period pottery, indicating the harbor's heyday (Raban 1985: 31; 1996). Renewed excavations by Arad Haggi and Michal Artzy uncovered several pieces of wood inside the northern mole that were carbon dated and provide a *terminus post quem* in the ninth century BCE for the harbor's construction before the beginning of Assyrian domination; however, this is not currently supported by published pottery from the site. The harbor was sufficiently deep for boat anchoring: The bottom ashlar course of the northern mole in Area K1 was constructed at a depth of 4.2 m bsl. A layer of pebbles was found below this course, most of which were basalts, ophiolites, and gabbro, and none of which is local. These probably originated in the ballast of boats anchored in the bay of 'Atlit before the construction of the harbor (Haggi and Artzy 2007; Haggi 2009).

Besides the possible ascription of the Neve-Yam cargo of plano-convex copper ingots to the Iron Age, based on the attribution of their origin to the Aravah deposits (Yahalom-Mack et al. 2014), no other cargoes nor shipwrecks from this period were found in shallow water along the Israeli coast. Nonetheless, Iron Age I–III storage jars were discovered in underwater surveys in several locations, including Achziv and the Achziv islands (University of Haifa and IAA surveys), Shavei-Zion (Yasur-Landau and Ben-Shlomo 2012), 'Atlit (Raban 1996), Dor (Kingsley and Raveh 1996), and Caesarea's south bay (E. Galili, pers. comm., 2017). This dearth of evidence, compared with the wealth of data on Late Bronze Age cargo, may be far from coincidental, as it may simply reflect the difference in routes between the periods. It is not that shipwrecks were unheard of in the Iron Age. At the same time, the wrecks of the *Tanit* and *Elissa*, found at a depth of 400 m outside the territorial waters of

Israel, offer an important insight into maritime traffic during the mid-eighth century BCE. Their main cargo was amphorae, with at least 385 on the *Tanit* and 396 on the *Elissa*. The amphorae retrieved were coated with resin, meaning they probably contained wine. Galley wares included cooking pots, *mortaria*, a decanter, and an incense stand. These likely indicate massive exports of agricultural produce from the vineyards and orchards of the Levant to Egypt (Ballard et al. 2002).

EXPLORING THE FRAGILE INTERFACE

Ports and coastal settlements can be seen as liminal zones and loci of complex intercultural interactions, both economic and social, which can all be detected potentially in the archaeological record. For communities occupying these zones, fragility did not stop at the common risks of life in the eastern Mediterranean, such as drought, short- and long-term changes in climate, and anthropogenic risks like the predation of polities and empires. Changes in sea level (e.g., Sivan et al. 2001; Goodman-Tchernov and Katz 2016), the risk of tsunamis, and even severe winter storms (Goodman-Tchernov and Austin 2015; cf. Morhange et al. 2013) severely impacted maritime and coastal infrastructure, from wells and coastal walls to quays and moles. These may have required a series of long-term adaptations that are still far from understood. The continuous anthropogenic impact on the maritime environment has been demonstrated in the geoarchaeological studies conducted at the harbor sites of the eastern Mediterranean, mainly those of the northern Levantine coast (Marriner et al. 2014), and explained by a tripartite chronological typology:

- Phase 1: 8,000 to 6,000 BP; before direct human interference;
- Phase 2: 6,000 BP to the beginning of the Middle Bronze Age; proto-harbor phase, low human impact; and
- Phase 3: beginning in the Iron Age; toward artificial harbor basins and pronounced human impact.

The possible contradiction between the minimal anthropogenic impact on harbor basins in the Middle and Late Bronze Age and the existence of contemporary large coastal communities that were actively involved in maritime interactions pose a serious challenge to future research on human adaptation to the maritime conditions of the Mediterranean. This geoarchaeological challenge can only be taken up by utilizing more robust underwater and coastal archaeological field methods and theory. The starting point for future exploration of human adaptation to the Mediterranean is a comprehensive interdisciplinary exploration of sea, coast/port, and tell or settlement levels.

A unified archaeology of maritime connectivity will therefore combine methods of coastal ("dry") archaeology with those of underwater archaeology, as well as interdisciplinary methods of geoarchaeology and paleoclimatology, along with other methods aimed to reconstruct the full range of behavioral patterns: from sailing through activities in the port to the consumption of traded goods. Employing this interdisciplinary approach to research will also help bridge the methodological gap between underwater and tell archaeology in Israel, and the (mostly) tell-oriented land archaeology and the largely ship-wreck-oriented maritime archaeology.

NOTES

1 For a short status report on the study of harbors and anchorages in Israel, see Yasur-Landau et al. (in press).
2 In addition, Late Bronze Age anchors were reported from sites that did not yield metal finds and are thus not mentioned here. Of these, a notable site is Megadim, which yielded an anchor made from a reused Egyptian relief (Galili and Raveh 1988).
3 For the revised Iron Age chronology of Tel Dor, see Gilboa and Sharon (2008: 152).

REFERENCES

Allen, J. P. 2008. The Historical Inscription of Khnumhotep at Dahshur: Preliminary Report. *BASOR* 352: 29–39.

Artzy, M. 1995. Nami: A Second Millennium International Maritime Trading Center in the Mediterranean. In *Recent Excavations in Israel: A View to the West; Reports on Kabri, Nami, Miqne-Ekron, Dor, and Ashkelon*, ed. S. Gitin, 17–40. Colloquia & Conference Papers 1. Dubuque, IA: Kendall/Hunt.

2006. The Carmel Coast during the Second Part of the Late Bronze Age: A Center for Eastern Mediterranean Transshipping. *BASOR* 343: 45–64.

Ballard, R. D.; Stager, L. E.; Master, D. M.; Yoerger, D.; Mindell, D.; Whitcomb, L. I.; Singh, H.; and Piechota, D. 2002. Iron Age Shipwrecks in Deep Water off Ashkelon, Israel. *AJA* 106: 151–68.

Ben-Dor Evian, S. 2011. Egypt and the Levant in the Iron Age I–IIA: The Ceramic Evidence. *TA* 38: 94–119.

Bietak, M. 2010. From Where Came the Hyksos and Where Did They Go? In *The Second Intermediate Period (Thirteenth–Seventeenth Dynasties): Current Research, Future Prospects*, ed. M. Marée, 139–81. OLA 192. Leuven: Peeters.

2017. Harbours and Coastal Military Bases in Egypt in the 2nd Millennium B.C.: Avaris, Peru-nefer, Pi-Ramesse. In *The Nile: Natural and Cultural Landscape in Egypt; Proceedings of the International Symposium Held at the Johannes Gutenberg-Universität Mainz, 22 et 23 February 2013*, ed. H. Willems and J.-M. Dahms, 53–70. Mainz Historical Cultural Sciences 36. Bielefeld: Transcript.

Brandl, B.; Oren, E. D.; and Nahshoni, P. 2014. A Clay Door-Lock Sealing from the Middle Bronze Age III Temple at Tel Haror, Israel. *Origini* 36: 157–80.

Broodbank, C. 2006. The Origins and Early Development of Mediterranean Maritime Activity. *JMA* 19: 199–230.

2013. *The Making of the Middle Sea: A History of the Mediterranean from the Beginning to the Emergence of the Classical World.* London: Thames & Hudson.

Cline, E. H.; Yasur-Landau, A.; and Goshen, N. 2011. New Fragments of Aegean Style Painted Plaster from Tel Kabri, Israel. *AJA* 115: 245–61.

Davies, N. de G., and Faulkner, R. O. 1947. A Syrian Trading Venture to Egypt. *Journal of Egyptian Archaeology* 33: 40–6.

Demesticha, S., and Knapp, A. B. 2016. Introduction: Maritime Transport Containers in the Bronze and Iron Age Aegean and Eastern Mediterranean. In *Maritime Transport Containers in the Bronze–Iron Age Aegean and Eastern Mediterranean,* ed. S. Demesticha and A. B. Knapp, 1–16. Studies in Mediterranean Archaeology and Literature Pocketbook 183. Uppsala: Åströms.

Fattovitz, R. 2012. Egypt's Trade with Punt: New Discoveries on the Red Sea Coast. *BMSAES* 18: 1–59.

Flohr, P.; Fleitmann, D.; Matthews, R.; Matthews, W.; and Black, S. 2016. Evidence of Resilience to Past Climate Change in Southwest Asia: Early Farming Communities and the 9.2 and 8.2 ka Events. *QSR* 136: 23–39.

Gadot, Y. 2006. Aphek in the Sharon and the Philistine Northern Frontier. *BASOR* 341: 21–36.

Galili, E., and Raveh, K. 1988. Stone Anchors with Carvings from the Sea off Megadim, Israel. *Sefunim* 7: 41–7.

Galili, E., and Rosen, B. 2008. Marine Archaeology. *NEAEHL* 5: 1925–34.

Galili, E.; Gale, N.; and Rosen, B. 2011. Bronze Age Metal Cargoes off the Israeli Coast. *Skyllis* 11: 64–73.

Galili, E.; Horwitz, L. K.; Eshed, V.; Rosen, B.; and Hershkovitz, I. 2014. Submerged Prehistoric Settlements off the Mediterranean Coast of Israel. *Skyllis* 13: 181–204.

Galili, E.; Raban, A.; and Sharvit, J. 2002. Forty Years of Marine Archaeology in Israel. In *Tropis VII: 7th International Symposium on Ship Construction in Antiquity, Pylos 1999; Proceedings,* Vol. 2, ed. H. Tzalas, 927–61. Athens: Hellenic Institute for the Preservation of Nautical Tradition.

Galili, E.; Rosen, B.; Gopher, A.; and Horwitz, L. K. 2002. The Emergence and Dispersion of the Eastern Mediterranean Fishing Village: Evidence from Submerged Neolithic Settlements off the Carmel Coast, Israel. *JMA* 15: 167–98.

Galili, E.; Sharvit, J.; and Artzy, M. 1994. Reconsidering Byblian and Egyptian Stone Anchors Using Numerical Methods: New Finds from the Israeli Coast. *IJNA* 23: 93–107.

Gilan, A. 2013. Pirates in the Mediterranean – A View from the Bronze Age. In *Seeraub im Mittelmeerraum: Piraterie, Korsarentum und maritime Gewalt von der Antike bis zur Neuzeit,* ed. N. Jaspert and S. Kolditz, 49–66. Mittelmeerstudien 3. Paderborn: Schöningh.

2015. Dor and Egypt in the Early Iron Age: An Archaeological Perspective of (Part of) the Wenamun Report. *Egypt and the Levant* 25: 247–74.

Gilboa, A., and Sharon, I. 2008. Between the Carmel and the Sea: Tel Dor's Iron Age Reconsidered. *NEA* 71: 146–70.

Golani, A., and Galili, E. 2015. A Late Bronze Age Canaanite Merchant's Hoard of Gold Artifacts and Hematite Weights from Yavneh-Yam Anchorage, Israel. *JAEI* 7 (2): 16–29.

Goodman-Tchernov, B. N., and Austin, J. A., Jr. 2015. Deterioration of Israel's Caesarea Maritima's Ancient Harbor Linked to Repeated Tsunami Events Identified in Geophysical Mapping of Offshore Stratigraphy. *JAS: Reports* 3: 444–54.

Goodman-Tchernov, B. N., and Katz, O. 2016. Holocene-Era Submerged Notches along the Southern Levantine Coastline: Punctuated Sea Level Rise? *QI* 401: 17–27.

Goren, Y. 2013. International Exchange during the Late Second Millennium B.C.: Microarchaeological Study of Finds from the Uluburun Ship. In *Cultures in Contact: From Mesopotamia to the Mediterranean in the Second Millennium BC*, ed. J. Aruz, S. B. Graff, and Y. Rakic, 54–61. New York: The Metropolitan Museum of Art.

Greener, A. 2015. *Late Bronze Age Imported Pottery in the Land of Israel: Between Economy, Society and Symbolism*. PhD diss., Bar-Ilan University.

Haggi, A. 2009. Report on Underwater Excavation at the Phoenician Harbour, Atlit, Israel. *IJNA* 39: 278–85.

Haggi, A., and Artzy, M. 2007. The Harbor of Atlit in Northern Canaanite/Phoenician Context. *NEA* 70: 75–84.

Hoftijzer, J., and van Soldt, W. H. 1998. Appendix: Text from Ugarit Pertaining to Seafaring. In *Seagoing Ships & Seamanship in the Bronze Age Levant*, ed. S. Wachsmann, 333–44. College Station: Texas A&M; London: Chatham.

Horden P., and Purcell, N. 2000. *The Corrupting Sea: A Study of Mediterranean History*. Oxford: Blackwell.

Horejs, B.; Milić, B.; Ostmann, F.; Thanheiser, U.; Weninger, B.; and Galik, A. 2015. The Aegean in the Early 7th Millennium BC: Maritime Networks and Colonization. *JWP* 28: 289–330.

Kaniewski, D.; Van Campo, E.; Morhange, C.; Guiot, J.; Zviely, D.; Le Burel, S.; Otto, T.; and Artzy, M. 2014. Vulnerability of Mediterranean Ecosystems to Long-Term Changes along the Coast of Israel. *PLOS ONE* 9 (7): e102090. https://doi.org/10.1371/journal.pone.0102090 (accessed August 30, 2017).

Kingsley, S. A., and Raveh, K. 1996. *The Ancient Harbour and Anchorage at Dor, Israel: Results of the Underwater Surveys, 1976–1991*. BAR International Series 626. Oxford: Tempus Reparatum.

Kislev, M. E.; Artzy, M.; and Marcus, E. 1993. Import of an Aegean Food Plant to a Middle Bronze IIA Coastal Site in Israel. *Levant* 25: 145–54.

Koh, A. J.; Yasur-Landau, A.; and Cline, E. H. 2014. Characterizing a Middle Bronze Palatial Wine Cellar from Tel Kabri, Israel. *PLOS ONE* 9 (8): e106406. https://doi.org/10.1371/journal.pone.0106406 (accessed August 30, 2017).

Lazar, M.; Engolz, K.; Basson, U.; and Yasur-Landau, A. 2018. Water Saturated Sand and a Shallow Bay: Combining Coastal Geophysics and Underwater Archaeology in the South Bay of Tel Dor. *QI* 473A: 112–19.

Leidwanger, J.; Knappett, C.; Arnaud, P.; Arthur, P.; Blake, E.; Broodbank, C.; Brughmans, T.; Evans, T.; Graham, S.; Greene, E. S.; Kowalzig, B.; Mills, B.; Rivers, R.; Tartaron, T. F.; and Van de Noort, R. 2014. A Manifesto for the Study of Ancient Mediterranean Maritime Networks. *Antiquity Project Gallery*. http://journal.antiquity.ac.uk/projgall/leidwanger342 (accessed August 30, 2017).

Lev-Yadun, S.; Artzy, M.; Marcus, E.; and Stidsing, R. 1996. Wood Remains from Tel Nami, a Middle Bronze IIA and Late Bronze IIB Port: Local Exploitation of Trees and Levantine Cedar Trade. *Economic Botany* 50: 306–17.

Liphschitz, N. 2002. The Paleobotanical Remains. In *Tel Kabri: The 1986–1992 Excavation Seasons*, by A. Kempinski, 428–34. MSSMNIA 20. Tel Aviv: Emery and Claire Yass Publications in Archaeology.

Maguire, L. C. 2009. *Tell el-Dabʻa XXI: The Cypriot Pottery and Its Circulation in the Levant*. UZKÖAI 33; DG 51. Vienna: Austrian Academy of Sciences.

Marcus, E. S. 2007. Amenemhet II and the Sea: Maritime Aspects of the Mit Rahina (Memphis) Inscription. *Egypt and the Levant* 17: 137–90.

Marriner, N.; Morhange, C.; Kaniewski, D.; and Carayon, N. 2014. Ancient Harbour Infrastructure in the Levant: Tracking the Birth and Rise of New Forms of Anthropogenic Pressure. *Scientific Reports* 4: 5554. www.nature.com/articles/srep05554 (accessed August 30, 2017).

Mazar, A. 1985. *Excavations at Tell Qasile*, Vol. 2: *The Philistine Sanctuary; Various Finds, the Pottery, Conclusions, Appendixes*. Qedem 20. Jerusalem: The Institute of Archaeology, The Hebrew University of Jerusalem.

Monroe, C. M. 2010. Sunk Costs at Late Bronze Age Uluburun. *BASOR* 357: 19–33.

Morhange, C.; Giaime, M.; Marriner, N.; Abu Hamid, A.; Bruneton, H.; Honnorat, A.; Kaniewski, D.; Magnin, F.; Porotov, A. V.; Wante, J.; Zviely, D.; and Artzy, M. 2016. Geoarchaeological Evolution of Tel Akko's Ancient Harbour (Israel). *JAS: Reports* 7: 71–81.

Morhange, C.; Salamon, A.; Bony, G.; Flaux, C.; Galili, E.; Goiran, J.-P.; and Zviely, D. 2013. Geoarchaeology of Tsunamis and the Revival of Neo-Catastrophism in the Eastern Mediterranean. In *Overcoming Catastrophes: Essays on Disastrous Agents Characterization and Resilience Strategies in Pre-Classical Southern Levant*, ed. L. Nigro, 31–51. ROSAPAT 11. Rome: "La Sapienza" Expedition to Palestine & Jordan.

Na'aman, N. 1994. Esarhaddon's Treaty with Baal and Assyrian Provinces along the Phoenician Coast. *Rivista degli Studi Fenici* 22: 3–8.

―― 1997. The Network of Canaanite Late Bronze Kingdoms and the City of Ashdod. *UF* 29: 599–626.

―― 2009. Was Dor the Capital of an Assyrian Province? *TA* 36: 95–109.

Papadimitriou, N. 2013. Regional or "International" Networks? A Comparative Examination of Aegean and Cypriot Imported Pottery in the Eastern Mediterranean. *Talanta* 44: 92–136.

Parpola, S., and Watanabe, K., eds. 1988. *Neo-Assyrian Treaties and Loyalty Oaths*. State Archives of Assyria 2. Helsinki: Helsinki University Press.

Pomey, P.; Kahanov, Y.; and Rieth, F. 2012. Transition from Shell to Skeleton in Ancient Mediterranean Ship-Construction: Analysis, Problems, and Future Research. *IJNA* 41: 235–314.

Preiser-Kapeller, J., and Daim, F., eds. 2015. *Harbours and Maritime Networks and Complex Adaptive Systems: International Workshop "Harbours and Maritime Networks as Complex Adaptive Systems" at the Römisch-Germanisches Zentralmuseum in Mainz, 17.–18.10.2013, within the Framework of the Special Research Programme (DFG-SPP 1630) "Harbours from the Roman Period to the Middle Ages."* Römisch-Germanisches Zentralmuseum Tagungen 23; Interdisziplinäre Forschungen zu den Häfen von der Römischen Kaiserzeit bis zum Mittelalter in Europa 2. Mainz: Römisch-Germanisches Zentralmuseum.

Pulak, C. 1998. The Uluburun Shipwreck: An Overview. *IJNA* 27: 188–224.

―― 2005. Who Were the Mycenaeans aboard the Uluburun Ship? In *Emporia: Aegeans in the Central and Eastern Mediterranean; Proceedings of the 10th International Aegean Conference, Athens, Italian School of Archaeology, 14–18 April 2004*, Vol. 1, ed. R. Laffineur and E. Greco, 295–310. Aegaeum 25. Liège: Histoire de l'Art et Archèologie de la Grèce Antique, Université de Liège; Austin: Program in Aegean Scripts and Prehistory, University of Texas.

Raban, A. 1985. The Ancient Harbours of Israel in Biblical Times. In *Harbour Archaeology: Proceedings of the First International Workshop on Ancient Mediterranean Harbours, Caesarea Maritima, 24–28.6.83*, ed. A. Raban, 11–44. BAR International Series 257. Oxford: BAR.

———. 1991a. Minoan and Canaanite Harbours. In *Thalassa: L'Égée préhistorique et la Mer; Actes de la troisième Rencontre Égéenne Internationale de l'Université de Liège, Station de Recherches Sous-Marines et Océanographiques (StaReSO), Calvi, Corse, 23–25 avril 1990*, ed. R. Laffineur and L. Basch, 129–46. Aegaeum 7. Liège: Histoire de l'Art et d'Archéologie de la Grèce Antique, Université de Liège.

———. 1991b. The Port City of Akko in the MBII Period. *Michmanim* 5: 17–34.

———. 1995a. Dor-Yam: Maritime and Coastal Installations at Dor in Their Geomorphological and Stratigraphic Context. In *Excavations at Dor: Final Report*, Vol. 1A: *Areas A and C; Introduction and Stratigraphy*, ed. E. Stern, 285–354. Qedem Reports 1. Jerusalem: The Institute of Archaeology, The Hebrew University of Jerusalem in cooperation with the IES.

———. 1995b. The Heritage of Ancient Harbor Engineering in Cyprus and the Levant. In *Proceedings of the International Symposium "Cyprus and the Sea": Organized by the Archaeological Research Unit of the University of Cyprus and the Cyprus Ports Authority, Nicosia 25–26 September, 1993*, ed. V. Karageorghis and D. Michaelides, 139–89. Nicosia: University of Cyprus.

———. 1996. The Phoenician Harbour and "Fishing Village" at 'Atlit. *ErIsr* 25: 490–508.

Raban A., and Galili, E. 1985. Recent Maritime Archaeological Research in Israel – A Preliminary Report. *IJNA* 14: 321–56.

Rainey A. F., and Notley, R. S. 2006. *The Sacred Bridge: Carta's Atlas of the Biblical World*. Jerusalem: Carta.

Rainey, A. F., and Schniedewind, W. M. 2015. *The El-Amarna Correspondence: A New Edition of the Cuneiform Letters from the Site of El-Amarna Based on Collations of All Extant Tablets*. 2 vols. Handbook of Oriental Studies 1, The Near and Middle East 110. Leiden: Brill.

Redford, D. B. 1997. Textual Sources for the Hyksos Period. In *The Hyksos: New Historical and Archaeological Perspectives*, ed. E. D. Oren, 1–44. UMM 96; University Museum Symposium Series 8. Philadelphia: University Museum, University of Pennsylvania.

Sharon, I., and Gilboa, A. 2013. The SKL Town: Dor in the Early Iron Age. In *The Philistines and Other "Sea Peoples" in Text and Archaeology*, ed. A. E. Killebrew and G. Lehmann, 393–468. ABS 15. Atlanta: SBL.

Sharvit, J.; Galili, E.; Rosen, B.; and van den Brink, E. C. M. 2002. Predynastic Maritime Traffic along the Carmel Coast of Israel: A Submerged Find from North Atlit Bay. In *In Quest of Ancient Settlements and Landscapes: Archaeological Studies in Honour of Ram Gophna*, ed. E. C. M. van den Brink and E. Yannai, 159–66. Tel Aviv: Ramot.

Sivan, D.; Wdowinski, S.; Lambeck, K.; Galili, E.; and Raban, A. 2001. Holocene Sea-Level Changes along the Mediterranean Coast of Israel, Based on Archaeological Observations and Numerical Model. *Palaeogeography, Palaeoclimatology, Palaeoecology* 167: 101–17.

Stager, L. E.; Schloen, D. J.; Master, D. M.; Press, M. D.; and Aja, A. 2008. Stratigraphic Overview. In *Ashkelon 1: Introduction and Overview (1985–2006)*, ed. L. E. Stager, J. D. Schloen, and D. M. Master, 213–323. FRLLEA 1; HSMP. Winona Lake, IN: Eisenbrauns.

Tallet, P. 2012. Ayn Sukhna and Wadi el-Jarf: Two Newly Discovered Pharaonic Harbours on the Suez Gulf. *BMSAES* 18: 147–68.

Tartaron, T. F. 2013. *Maritime Networks in the Mycenaean World*. Cambridge: Cambridge University Press.

Thareani, Y. 2016. The Empire and the "Upper Sea": Assyrian Control Strategies along the Southern Levantine Coast. *BASOR* 375: 77–102.

Wachsmann, S. 1998. *Seagoing Ships & Seamanship in the Bronze Age Levant*. College Station: Texas A&M University Press; London: Chatham.

Yahalom-Mack, N.; Galili, E.; Segal, I.; Eliyahu-Behar, A.; Boaretto, E.; Shilstein, S.; and Finkelstein I. 2014. New Insights into Levantine Copper Trade: Analysis of Ingots from the Bronze and Iron Ages in Israel. *JAS* 45: 159–77.

Yasur-Landau, A. 2010. *The Philistines and Aegean Migration in the Late Bronze Age*. Cambridge: Cambridge University Press.

Yasur-Landau, A.; Arkin Shalev, E.; Zajak, P. R.; and Gambash, G. In press. Rethinking the Anchorages and Harbours of the Southern Levant 2000 BC–600 AD. In *Proceedings of the Conference "Harbours as Objects of Interdisciplinary Research – Archaeology + History + Geoscience," Kiel University, 1–2 October 2015*. Mainz: Römisch-Germanisches Zentralmuseum.

Yasur-Landau, A., and Ben-Shlomo, D. 2012. The Provenance of Storage Jars from the Shavei Zion Underwater Site. *R.I.M.S. News* 37: 22–3.

PART SIX

THIRTY ONE

THE IMPACT OF RADIOCARBON DATING AND ABSOLUTE CHRONOLOGY IN THE HOLY LAND

A Social Archaeological Perspective

FELIX HÖFLMAYER AND KATHARINA STREIT

SOCIAL ARCHAEOLOGY AND ABSOLUTE DATING EVIDENCE

At first glance, the quest for absolute calendar dates may seem rather detached from social archaeology and questions relating to more broadly defined fields, such as society, gender, ritual, economy, or statehood. However, in his inaugural lecture, Colin Renfrew (1973: 10) drew the connection between social archaeology and absolute dating evidence, that is, radiocarbon dating, discussing the example of the megalithic culture of Europe and its antecedence to the great civilizations of the ancient Near East. In the 1984 volume *Approaches to Social Archaeology*, absolute dating methods were mentioned, and a number of open chronological questions relating to social questions were formulated (Renfrew 1984: 169–75). Nevertheless, twenty years later in the *Companion to Social Archaeology*, absolute dating did not play a very prominent role, although Robert Preucel and Lynn Meskell claimed that "time is the central obsession of archaeology" (2004: 8). In current scholarship, it seems that often this "obsession" is being regarded as secondary to the study of social processes itself. Nonetheless, we would argue, and will try to show in this contribution, that absolute dating evidence is, in fact, the fundamental framework against which social processes can and should be studied. The question *when* is the prerogative of the questions *how* and *why*.

Only a secure absolute chronology provides a suitable framework for comparing societies with each other, and, more importantly, to trace "the social" and variations of it through time without the usual temporal and/or spatial limitations of a specific period or region. By applying a dense radiocarbon dating network as the necessary foundation for absolute time, we are able to track long-term changes in subsistence, economy, or statehood throughout the *longue durée*. Hence, it is possible to compare social developments in different civilizations according to a general chronological framework in order to identify patterns that may lead to a new understanding of social developments and the possible reasons that may have caused them.

Although the method of radiocarbon dating was developed as early as the late 1940s by Willard Frank Libby, it has only recently been consequently applied to the archaeology of the southern Levant. Scholars of the ancient Near East have been remarkably reluctant to accept radiocarbon as a dating method because: (1) historical chronologies of Egypt and Mesopotamia have been regarded as more precise and (2) some scholars found it difficult to accept that someone outside the field challenges long-held historical reconstructions and assumptions. Here is not the place to discuss these issues in great detail, but it should be emphasized that the application of radiocarbon dating within the archaeology of the southern Levant is still in its infancy. Only recent decades have seen the beginning of extensive radiocarbon dating programs that try to create the foundations for a radiocarbon-backed absolute chronology for the eastern Mediterranean Bronze and Iron Ages (an aim that was formulated more than twenty years ago [Bruins and Mook 1989; Bruins 2001]).

In this chapter, we will summarize the basic method of radiocarbon dating and discuss two case studies where radiocarbon dating has had a considerable impact on our understanding of social processes of the ancient Near East, the "collapse" of the first cities in the southern Levant at the end of Early Bronze Age III, and absolute dating evidence for the Iron Age along with the question of the historicity of the United Monarchy of David and Solomon.

RADIOCARBON DATING: THE METHOD

The method of radiocarbon dating has been described in great detail in articles and handbooks over the past sixty years, and there is no need for yet another in-depth introduction into this specific topic. Therefore, we will limit ourselves to a short overview of the method and its application as an introduction to our two case studies.[1]

The element carbon (C) consists of three isotopes, ^{12}C, ^{13}C, and ^{14}C (referred to as radiocarbon). While ^{12}C and ^{13}C are stable, ^{14}C is radioactive and decays according to a known half-life of ca. 5,730 years. Radiocarbon is produced by the bombardment of the earth's atmosphere with thermal neutrons that react with atmospheric nitrogen (^{14}N). Subsequently, ^{14}C oxidizes to $^{14}CO_2$ (carbon dioxide), gets mixed within the atmosphere, is absorbed by plants via photosynthesis, and finally enters animals and/or humans through ingestion of plants. As long as a given organism lives and continues exchanging carbon with the environment, the decaying ^{14}C is constantly replaced by fresh ^{14}C, so that the ratio of $^{12}C/^{14}C$ remains approximately in equilibrium with the environment. Once the organism dies and ceases incorporating (radio)carbon from its environment, ^{14}C decays over time, while the amount of stable ^{12}C remains constant. The less ^{14}C in relation to ^{12}C left in a given sample, the older it is, as more time elapsed from the point of time when the organism ceased taking up carbon from the environment (see also Bronk Ramsey 2008).

However, due to variations in the cosmic ray influx and the Earth's magnetic field, the production of radiocarbon in the upper atmosphere was not constant over time, resulting in varying $^{12}C/^{14}C$ ratios. Thus, the calculated date of an organic sample based on the measurement of the $^{12}C/^{14}C$ ratio and the half-life of radiocarbon differs from the true calendar age. The actual atmospheric $^{12}C/^{14}C$ ratio of a given calendar year can be reconstructed by measuring tree-ring sequences of known age (dendrochronology), that is, sequences that continue up to present time. Based on these tree-ring measurements, a calibration curve is being reconstructed that translates the "radiocarbon date" into a range of possible calendar dates (Stuiver and Suess 1966; Reimer et al. 2013).

Due to the irregular shape of the calibration curve, radiocarbon dates are expressed as probability distributions that can range over a century or more. In order to increase the precision of the results, a so-called Bayesian probability approach can be applied, that allows taking additional evidence (beside the measurement of the sample itself) into account. Within archaeology, this additional evidence is almost always the temporal sequence of samples according to archaeological stratigraphy. Using this additional information (also called *prior information* as it exists independent of and prior to the measurement of the sample in the laboratory), a mathematical model is created that calculates *posterior* probability distributions for the respective samples under the condition that the *prior* information (e.g., the stratigraphy of a given site) is correct. The result of such a model is an updated probability distribution on the timeline based on the measurements from the laboratory and the prior information entered into the model (Buck et al. 1991; Weninger et al. 2006; Bronk Ramsey 2009a).

CASE STUDY 1: DATING THE "URBAN COLLAPSE" OF THE EARLY BRONZE AGE II–III PERIOD

The Early Bronze Age (EB) II–III period saw the development of fortified settlements, population aggregation, craft specialization (including new agricultural techniques, such as olive and grape cultivation), and increasing social and economic differentiation. The result of the urbanization process was a settlement pattern that ranged from camps and small villages to fortified towns and very large fortified cities, some of which were more than 10 ha in size (Ai [et-Tell] or Tel Yarmouth), while others exceeded even 25 ha (Tel Beth Yerah) (Esse 1991; Ben-Tor 1992; Greenberg 2002; Philip 2003; Miroschedji 2009: 106; 2014).

This period also witnessed the first appearance of "palatial" and "temple" architecture, as exemplified at Tel Yarmouth (Miroschedji 1999) or Khirbet el-Batrawy (Nigro 2010), but one of the most characteristic features of the EB II–III period is probably the massive fortifications found at several sites, such as Khirbat as-Zeraqon (Douglas 2007), Tel Yarmouth (Miroschedji 1999), Tel Arad (Amiran et al. 1978; Amiran and Ilan 1996), and Khirbet el-Batrawy (Nigro 2012). The EB II–III period has usually been described as the "first urban period in the history of the Southern Levant" (Miroschedji 2009: 103, but see Chesson and Philip 2003, and Chesson 2015 who challenge the designation "urban").

The transition from the EB III to the EB IV (often termed "urban collapse" [cf. Miroschedji 2009]) was usually dated to ca. 2200/2300 BC and was thought to be a rather sudden event (Miroschedji 2009: 102, 109), being slightly earlier, but generally roughly contemporary to the end of the Akkad Empire in Upper Mesopotamia and the end of the pyramid-building Old Kingdom of Egypt.

The subsequent EB IV period (also called Intermediate Bronze Age) was designated as a non-urban interlude between the urbanized EB II–III and the second urbanized period of the southern Levant, the Middle Bronze Age (Palumbo 1991; Gophna 1992; Parr 2009; Prag 2014). There is a clear break in the settlement pattern; almost all of the EB IV settlements are new foundations, while the EB III cities have been abandoned or destroyed. Further, the EB IV settlements are of an entirely different character, usually small unfortified villages, such as 'Ein el-Hilu in the Jezreel Valley (Covello-Paran 1999; 2009). Only a few sites from this period retained their urban and fortified character, such as Khirbet Iskander in southern Jordan (Richard et al. 2010). In the southern Judean mountains and the Negev, it is generally believed that society returned to a (semi-)nomadic pastoral lifestyle, with people living in ephemeral settlements, probably connected to copper trade routes in the Negev, while burying their dead in burial grounds unconnected to their settlements, for example, at Jebel Qa'aqir in the southern Judean mountains (Haiman 1996; Dever 2014).

If social archaeology engages with questions of economy, statehood, and society, one would expect the late Early Bronze Age and its transformation from an urbanized world to rural seminomadic societies to be one of the key topics for the field. However, while recent scholarship has dealt *in extenso* with questions regarding the rise of urbanism, secondary state formation, the role of the landscape, population aggregation, storage, or socioeconomic inequality during the Early Bronze Age (e.g., Esse 1991; Philip 2003; Chesson and Goodale 2014; Chesson 2015), it was remarkably silent regarding interpretations of and models for the apparent "collapse" of urbanism at the end of EB III. The end of the first phase of urbanization was also absent in the list of "collapses" in Renfrew's *Approaches to Social Archaeology* (although he did include the collapse of the Egyptian Old Kingdom and the First Intermediate Period [1984: 370–2]).

Nevertheless, several possible scenarios have been proposed to explain the "urban collapse" of the Early Bronze Age.[2] Kathleen Kenyon and others argued that the collapse of the urbanized Early Bronze Age could be explained by the invasion of foreign tribes, specifically the Amorites (the so-called Amorite hypothesis [Kenyon 1966]). Suzanne Richard (1980: 25) proposed that the cessation of trade with Egypt might have been the trigger for the collapse of the Early Bronze Age economy and ultimately of the first urban centers. Benjamin Mazar (1968: 66) and Joseph Callaway (1978) thought that Egyptian military campaigns might have contributed to the end of the first cities in the southern Levant. Pierre de Miroschedji argued that the collapse of urban centers in the southern Levant might be found in "an analysis of the relationship between sedentary villagers and town dwellers, on the one hand, and nomadic pastoralists, on the other hand" (2009: 119), thus very much arguing along the lines of what is usually understood as "social archaeology." The most prominent explanation model in recent decades was the climatic crisis model. Harvey Weiss and others argued that a rapid climatic change occurring around 2200 BC (the so-called 4.2 ka BP event) and caused not only the end of the Akkad Empire in Upper Mesopotamia but also the collapse of the Early Bronze Age urban period in the southern Levant and even the end of the Egyptian Old Kingdom (Weiss et al. 1993; Rosen 1995; Weiss and Bradley 2001; Staubwasser and Weiss 2006). In order to test these hypotheses, an absolute chronological framework is obviously a *conditio sine qua non*.

Already in the mid-1980s, James Weinstein discussed the hitherto published radiocarbon record for the southern Levant from the Paleolithic onward (1984), but, at that time, margins of error were too large to allow any tight chronological control for the end of the Early Bronze Age. Later on, in the 1992 edition of Robert Ehrich's *Chronologies in Old World Archaeology*, Lawrence Stager published a comprehensive and updated list of radiocarbon dates for the Early Bronze Age (1992: 50–2) without discussing them in any detail.

The first dates that really challenged the long-held chronological synchronisms and absolute calendar dates came from Tell Abu en-Niaj and Khirbat as-Zeraqon. However, researchers argued that radiocarbon dating delivered calendar dates that were too high. Several dates for the EB IV site of Tell Abu en-Niaj turned out to be higher than the previously expected 2300/2200 BC date for the end of EB III (Bronk Ramsey et al. 2002: 82; Falconer, Fall, and Jones 2007). Also, the first dates for the EB II/III site of Khirbat as-Zeraqon in northwestern Jordan were remarkably high. Sixteen radiocarbon dates were published by Hermann Genz in 2002, many of which run on (potential long-lived) charcoal, but some on short-lived samples, such as olive pits or grain (2002: 9, table 1). Most dates fell to the late fourth or early third millennium BC and were considered too old for the expected calendar date range for the archaeological date of the site. Genz (2002: 7–10) argued that since many of the samples were run on charcoal, these samples might have come from construction timber and would thus be susceptible to the "old wood effect," the in-built age of charcoal samples originating from the inner rings of timber. In short, neither the results from Tell Abu en-Niaj nor the dates from Khirbat as-Zeraqon were considered reliable for dating the EB II–III period.

The first comprehensive sets of radiocarbon data were published only recently within the framework of the project ARCANE (Associated Regional Chronologies of the Ancient Near East) that aimed to redefine relative chronological phases for the third millennium BC. In 2012, Johanna Regev and her colleagues published two highly influential papers, the first on the radiocarbon sequence for one of the key sites for the Early Bronze Age, Tel Yarmouth (Regev, Miroschedji, and Boaretto 2012), and the second on the reevaluation of published radiocarbon data for the third millennium BC of the southern Levant (Regev et al. 2012). Tel Yarmouth is one of the many urban sites in the southern Levant that was abandoned at the end of the EB III period (Miroschedji 1988; 1993; 2000; 2013). The radiocarbon sequence for Tel Yarmouth covers the EB I–III periods, and modeled radiocarbon dates for the EB III (Strata Bd-2, Ja-3, G-3, and B-1 to 2) consistently fell to the first half of the third millennium BC (Fig. 31.1). Even the youngest samples of the latest (most recent) Stratum B-1 falls to around 2500 BC. One sample (RT-2965) was about 500 years younger than the rest of Stratum B-1 and can obviously be regarded as intrusive. Thus, the authors concluded that "EB III ended at the latest ~2450 BC, perhaps before 2500 BC" (Regev, Miroschedji, and Boaretto 2012: 505). A date of ca. 2500 BC for the end of EB III and thus for the end of the first phase of urbanization in the southern Levant was also substantiated by a comprehensive review of the already-published radiocarbon evidence by Johanna Regev and her colleagues (2012) (see Fig. 31.1).

These dates have essentially been substantiated at other sites throughout the region. Radiocarbon dates for the destruction of the late EB III palace storeroom of the urban site of Khirbet el-Batrawy in the upper Wadi az-Zarqa in Jordan also fell to the first half of the third millennium BC

RADIOCARBON DATING AND ABSOLUTE CHRONOLOGY 579

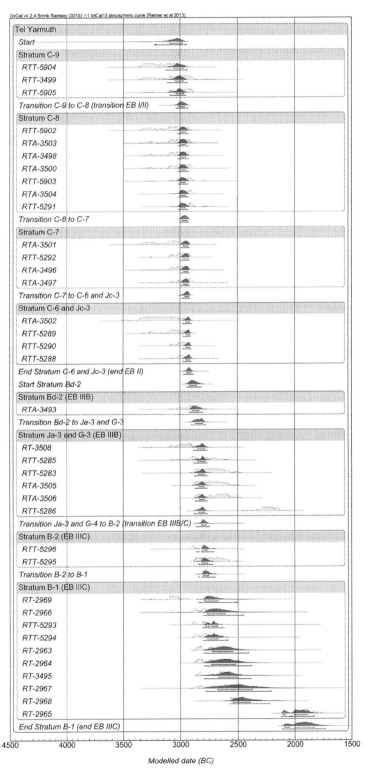

31.1. Modeled radiocarbon determinations for Tel Yarmouth based on stratigraphic information provided in Regev, Miroschedji, and Boaretto 2012. Modeling and calibration

(Nigro 2010; Höflmayer 2014: 130). In addition, new measurements of additional (short-lived) samples from Khirbat as-Zeraqon substantiated not only the high chronology for the Early Bronze Age but also the already-published results in Genz 2002. It could be shown that Khirbat as-Zeraqon was abandoned already early within the EB III period (as previously suggested by Genz [2002], based on the pottery). According to the radiocarbon evidence (samples published by Genz plus new measurements on additional short-lived samples conducted in recent years), the site was already abandoned during the twenty-ninth century BC (Höflmayer 2015; 2017).

A radiocarbon sequence of the Early Bronze Age site of Tell Fadous-Kfarabida on the Mediterranean shore of Lebanon is of special importance, as the stratigraphy of the site not only covers the EB I–III periods but also encompasses the post-urban EB IV period (Genz 2010; 2014; in press). Thus, a precise date for the transition from EB III to IV could be calculated (corresponding to the transition from Phase IV to V). Based on the Bayesian model shown in Fig. 31.2, the transition from EB III to IV at Tell Fadous-Kfarabida could be dated to ca. 2500 BC (Höflmayer et al. 2014; in press). Finally, the few EB IV radiocarbon dates from Khirbet Iskander, one of the few examples of a still-fortified urban center during the EB IV period, are consistent with the high Early Bronze Age chronology (Richard et al. 2010). A recent analysis of the radiocarbon dates of Tell Abu en-Niaj also concluded that the EB IV period should be dated to the second half of the third millennium BC (Falconer and Fall 2016).

Therefore, the date for the end of the EB III period had to be shifted to ca. 2500 BC (instead of 2200/2300 BC). This obviously has considerable impact on our picture of the Early Bronze Age ancient Near East and calls for a renewed investigation of possible scenarios and models of this transformation. Apparently, the end of EB III cannot be related to any climatic event occurring in ca. 2200 BC, and processes leading to the "non-urban" interlude of EB IV cannot be explained via any Egyptian military campaigns or the cessation of trade in the late Old Kingdom. In fact, the EB III period apparently ended some time during the height of the Egyptian Old Kingdom (probably the late 4th Dynasty [cf. Bronk Ramsey et al. 2010]). Also, the dates show that not all cities

---

31.1. (*cont.*) was done by Felix Höflmayer and Katharina Streit using OxCal 4.2.4 (Bronk Ramsey 2009a) against the IntCal13 radiocarbon calibration curve (Reimer et al. 2013) interpolated to yearly intervals (resolution = 1). In order not to "hand-pick" potential outliers, the "Outlier Analysis" of OxCal was applied, the "General" model for short-lived samples and the "Charcoal" model for charcoal samples. Outlier Analysis detects which individual samples are not consistent with the prior information (e.g., the sequence) or the other radiocarbon dates for their context, and incrementally reduces their contribution to the model outputs (meaning that outliers have a very limited impact on the posterior probabilities) (Bronk Ramsey 2009b).

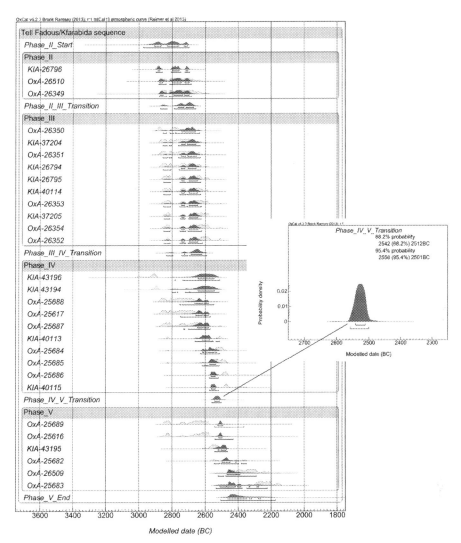

31.2. Modeled radiocarbon determinations for Tell Fadous-Kfarabida (after Höflmayer et al. 2014). (For details on modeling and calibration, see the caption for Fig. 31.1.) (Modeling by F. Höflmayer and K. Streit.)

collapsed at the same time. While Khirbat as-Zeraqon was abandoned already in the early third millennium BC, Khirbet el-Batrawy followed only later on during the first half of the millennium, while Tel Yarmouth continued as a fortified settlement until ca. 2500 BC and Khirbet Iskander in Jordan even into the EB IV period. Thus, one might envision the "collapse" of the first urbanization as a continuous decline rather than a sudden collapse (cf. also Greenberg 2017).

This is also in line with a scenario outlined by Graham Philip. He argued that many (walled) settlements might have been relatively short-lived or discontinued, and the landscape of EB II–III period in the southern Levant would probably have been spotted with occupied and abandoned settlements at any given time (Philip 2003: 114–15). Raphael Greenberg (2017) has called for individual histories of EB II–III sites, instead of applying a unitary model of Levantine urbanization, a view that is also shared by Timothy Harrison and Stephen Savage (2003).

Radiocarbon dating was able to demonstrate that all of these localized and individual collapses occurred over an extended time span, and the notion of the "collapse" of a homogenous urban EB II–III period is indeed misleading. Furthermore, we cannot relate the many individual "collapses" or urban centers to sudden climatic changes, as has been suggested previously. Instead, we might want to envision the "urban Early Bronze II–III" as a period of several short-lived urban projects, of which no one was enduring. The available radiocarbon record shows that urban projects materialized throughout the southern Levant over the first half of the third millennium BC, and by 2500 BC, most came to an end with only a few sites still retaining an urban character, such as Khirbet Iskander in Jordan. The phase of urban experimentation in the southern Levant is thus contemporary with the Egyptian Proto-Dynastic period and the height of the Old Kingdom. Sometime during the late 4th or early 5th Dynasty, the phase of urban experimentation in the southern Levant came to an end. This is the chronological framework in which we have to study "the social" of this phase in the eastern Mediterranean in general and the southern Levant specifically.

CASE STUDY 2: IRON AGE CHRONOLOGY, CHIEFDOMS, AND THE UNITED MONARCHY

While the first case study focused on the dating of events observed in the archaeological record, the second example demonstrates the importance of radiocarbon dating in the debate of historical chronologies and the reconstruction of the social history of the southern Levant.

Since the early days of archaeology in the southern Levant during the late nineteenth and early twentieth centuries CE, connections between archaeological finds and biblical texts have been proposed. As the main literary source of the southern Levant, the Bible dominated the perception of history and chronology in this region. Historical reports, such as the book of Kings, offer an account of the ascent of kings, and their respective reign lengths have been used to reconstruct absolute chronologies (e.g., van Seters 1997). However, the historical value of the Bible itself, and thus the reliability of its chronology, have been questioned: While scholars from the 1940s to 1960s established that the biblical account was highly valid (Albright 1932; Alt 1966), this maximalist approach has been criticized by the so-called Copenhagen School (Thompson 1999), which did not see any historicity within the Bible. Radiocarbon dating, as an independent line of evidence, played an essential role in the discussion (Levy and Higham 2005).

According to the biblical account, the "United Monarchy," established in the late eleventh century BC by Saul, saw a "golden age" under the rule of David and Solomon in the tenth century BC. Around 930 BC, the United Monarchy split into two: the kingdom of Israel in the north, which flourished greatly under the Omride dynasty of the ninth century BC, and was destroyed by the Assyrians in 721 BC; and the kingdom of Judah in the south, destroyed by the Babylonians in 586 BC (see, e.g., Mazar 1990 and Malamat 1979). In archaeological terms, the beginning of the United Monarchy is seen as the transition from Iron Age I to Iron Age II (Mazar 1990).

Since the late 1950s, archaeological research in the Holy Land was led by the assumption that the period between Saul and Solomon must have left substantial archaeological remains. Particularly, the fortifications commissioned by Solomon at Hazor, Megiddo, and Gezer, mentioned in 1 Kgs 9:15, guided the archaeological effort for this period. The six-chambered gates discovered by Yigael Yadin at Hazor Stratum X (Yadin et al. 1958) and his interpretation of the gates discovered earlier at Megiddo Stratum VA–IVB and Gezer Stratum VIII (Yadin 1958) were perceived as firm links to the biblical narrative and thus reliable evidence for the biblical account of a centralized political entity in the tenth century BC.

In the mid-1990s, Israel Finkelstein (1996) challenged the Solomonic date of Megiddo Stratum VA–IVB. Based on ceramic similarities of these strata with the site of Jezreel, the seat of the Omride dynasty, considered as a firm chronological peg, and by re-dating the Philistine Monochrome (Mycenaean IIIC:1b) Ware, Finkelstein suggested that Megiddo Stratum VA–IVB should be dated to the ninth century BC (to the Omride dynasty), while Stratum VIA would represent the tenth-century BC city (the Solomonic city). Shifting all strata that previously were regarded as Solomonic to the Omride period would leave the United Monarchy without any "royal" architecture at Megiddo, severely drawing into question the biblical account. According to Finkelstein, the account of King David should be understood as a later composition without any historical value. If King David existed as an historical person, he would have been more likely the chief of a local tribe and would not have ruled a centralized political entity. Finkelstein's suggestion has been rejected by Amihai Mazar (1997), based on different interpretations of the ceramic synchronisms between Megiddo and Jezreel, and opposite views regarding the re-dating of the Philistine Monochrome Ware, as well as stratigraphic considerations and possible links to the account of Shishak's destructions in the southern Levant. Mazar's high chronology has been further defended by Amnon Ben-Tor (2000) and Stager (2003) but was again rejected by Finkelstein (2005).[3]

With the stratigraphic debate reaching a deadlock, the demand for an independent absolute chronological dating methodology grew. Two pioneering radiocarbon dating projects were presented for Tel Dor (Gilboa and Sharon 2001; Sharon 2001) and at Tel Beth Shean and Tel Rehov (Mazar and Carmi 2001). In their radiocarbon sequence from Tel Dor, Ayelet Gilboa and Ilan Sharon (2001) collected twenty-two dates of the Iron Age strata that cover the Iron Age I–II transition. The authors concluded that the transition between Iron Ib and II occurred between 880–860 BC (Sharon 2001), significantly lower than Finkelstein's low chronology. Mazar and Israel Carmi (2001) published thirty-three dates from Tel Beth Shean and twenty from Tel Rehov. The authors did not reach a final conclusion on the dating of the Iron Age I–II transition, mainly because their radiocarbon results from the similar strata or loci scatter considerably. These two studies disappointed the high hopes for a "simple" answer to the dating question.

The inherent malady of radiocarbon dating in the period between ca. 1200 to 800 BC can be ascribed to the calibration curve. Iron Age radiocarbon ages (BP) fall to a plateau on the calibration curve; thus, calibrated calendar date ranges are particularly wide. Bayesian analysis provided a new approach, narrowing calibration margins based on statistical and thus objective grounds.

The first approach to achieve higher accuracy was "wiggle-matching," that is, determining the real age based on the measurement of the radiocarbon content with the help of logical deduction of the stratigraphic position of a set of samples and thus a resulting wiggle match (Bruins, van der Plicht, and Mazar 2003; Finkelstein and Piasetzky 2003; Mazar et al. 2005). As a result, wiggle-matching radiocarbon results follows the simple rule that "successive layers cannot have the same position on the calibration curve but, must follow each other in time" (Bruins, van der Plicht, and Mazar 2003: 316). However, the estimate for the duration of archaeological strata is subjective and thus debatable.

The second approach was to calculate transitional boundaries between Iron Age I and Iron Age II sites, combining radiocarbon dates from different sites (Sharon et al. 2007; Mazar and Bronk Ramsey 2008). While the boundary itself was calculated on statistical grounds, the results depend entirely on data selection, resulting in a vivid debate regarding the criteria and archaeological ascription of individual samples (Finkelstein and Piasetzky 2010). Further, a Bayesian model of samples originating from different sites is problematic, as there is no stratigraphic connection between the respective contexts.[4]

A different approach was the calculation of Bayesian models for single sites, for example, the sequence of samples from Tel Rehov analyzed in the laboratory at Groningen (Mazar et al. 2005). A model for Tel Rehov Areas C, D including all published radiocarbon dates is presented in Fig. 31.3. The results indicate a transition from Iron Age I to II (Stratum D3–C2) in the second half of the tenth century BC, thus in line with the low chronology.[5]

The discovery of Khirbet Qeiyafa (Garfinkel and Ganor 2009; Garfinkel, Ganor, and Hasel 2014), dated by the excavator to the early Iron Age II phase

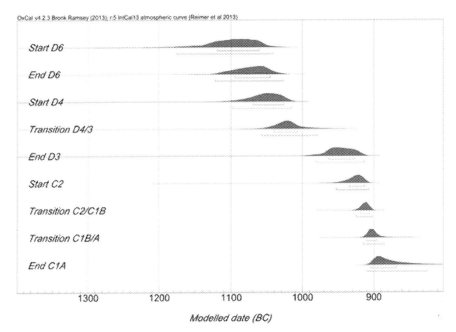

31.3. Modeled phase transitions for Tel Rehov based on dates to be published in Mazar and Streit in press. (Modeling by F. Höflmayer and K. Streit.)

in archaeological terms (Garfinkel and Kang 2011; for an alternative interpretation, see Singer-Avitz 2016), had a considerable impact on the Iron Age chronology debate. Khirbet Qeiyafa is a fortified site in the Elah Valley and displays many features of a Judean city, such as the "Judean city plan" with casemate walls and four-chambered city gates, evidence of writing (Misgav, Garfinkel, and Ganor 2009) and administration, dietary restrictions (exclusion of pork), as well as aniconic cult. Eleven short-lived samples are available from the Iron Age occupation (Garfinkel et al. 2012). Additionally, seventeen determinations from two laboratories have been measured for a cluster of olive pits uncovered *in situ* inside a broken jar from the Iron Age destruction layer (Garfinkel et al. 2015). A single phase model of all eleven available samples and the average of samples determined from the jar are presented in Fig. 31.4. According to the model, the end of this phase is calculated to 1007–962 BC at 68.2 percent and 1012–921 BC at 95.4 percent, indicating that this short-lived city was destroyed most likely sometime during the first third or the first half of the tenth century BC. The ethnic ascription, archaeological dating, stratigraphy, and radiocarbon dating have been contested.[6] Nevertheless, Khirbet Qeiyafa indicates the existence of a substantial central power in Judah in the early tenth century BC. Similar results for the Iron Age I–II transition have been produced at Megiddo (Toffolo et al. 2014).

Radiocarbon dating has shed new light on the heated debate of Iron Age chronology and is thus of major importance for assessing the historicity of the

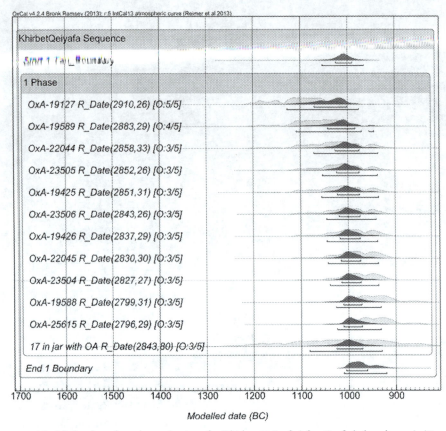

31.4. Modeled radiocarbon determinations for Khirbet Qeiyafa (after Garfinkel et al. 2015). (For details on modeling and calibration, see the caption for Fig. 31.1.) (Modeling by F. Höflmayer and K. Streit.)

biblical account that, for a long time, has been of prime importance to archaeologists and historians alike. The present discussion is about to leave the most basic question: Whether the biblical narrative is "right" or "wrong." Detailed radiocarbon analysis has shown that the transition from Iron Age I to II most likely did not take place at the same time throughout the southern Levant. Some sites, such as Khirbet Qeiyafa and Megiddo, provide evidence for an early transition in the first third of the tenth century BC, while the transition at other sites can be dated later. What becomes known as the "Judean assemblage" of city planning, ceramics, religion, and dietary preferences did start at the time the biblical narrative reported it. While this does support the reliability of the biblical account regarding a substantial political entity at this time, no conclusions regarding the historicity of the biblical King David can be reached at present. Nevertheless, the extensive radiocarbon dating projects of the last few decades provide a nuanced framework against which "the social" aspect of Iron Age archaeology can be studied.

CONCLUSIONS: SCIENCE AND SOCIAL ARCHAEOLOGY

A secure absolute chronology is the ultimate backbone of history. Radiocarbon dating provides an independent control of absolute time and dating, and should be used to reconstruct a chronological framework against which historical questions, including "the social," should be studied.

For Early Bronze Age urbanization and its "collapse," radiocarbon dating provided dates that were considerably higher than previously expected. The several theories that have been suggested to explain the transformation to the "non-urban interlude" of EB IV must be dismissed, and a new generation of scholars will have to study the potential factors that led to the end of the first cities and the social processes involved.

The case of the Iron Age is more complex. The question of absolute dating goes far beyond the simple problem of whether or not the Bible is right. The Iron Age debate is not only about archaeology and time; it is also about the interpretation of textual sources, and how we relate textual data to material culture. From a social archaeology point of view, the basic question can be compared to Early Bronze Age urbanization; however, this time we are dealing with the emergence of statehood (from a largely de-urbanized Iron Age I to an urbanized Iron Age II). The wide use and application of radiocarbon dating has shown that the picture of this transition is far more nuanced than could have been deduced from archaeology alone (or the biblical narrative). Now that a more detailed chronological framework is about to emerge, (social) archaeologists are called upon for new in-depth investigations and potential models to explain the varied picture of the Iron Age I to II transition.

In both cases, radiocarbon dating has shed new light on seemingly fixed archaeological/historical transitions, and the picture revealed is inherently more complex than previously expected. In both cases, we see more of a transformation instead of a clear break. Perhaps the famous statement by the Aegean prehistorian and excavator of Knossos Sir Arthur Evans is also applicable to biblical archaeology: "All is, in fact, transition" (1921: 30).

NOTES

1 For detailed explanations, see, e.g., Bowman 1995; Bronk Ramsey 2008; and Taylor and Bar-Yosef 2014.
2 For an overview, cf. Miroschedji 2009 and Höflmayer 2014; 2015; 2017.
3 For a summary of the debate, see Mazar 2005.
4 The succession of phases is entirely dependent on pottery analysis, whereas it cannot be assumed *a priori* that all transitions between pottery phases happened at exactly the same time throughout the region.
5 It should be noted that this result has been questioned by the excavator based on his stratigraphic interpretation and radiocarbon dates from different areas at Tel

Rehov, which point to a higher date for the Iron Age I to II transition (Mazar and Streit in press).
6 For a summary, see Garfinkel et al. 2015.

REFERENCES

Albright, W. F. 1932. *The Archaeology of Palestine and the Bible*. Richard Lectures 31. New York: Revell.

Alt, A. 1966. *Essays on Old Testament History and Religion*. Trans. R. A. Wilson, from German. Oxford: Blackwell.

Amiran, R., and Ilan, O. 1996. *Early Arad II: The Chalcolithic and Early Bronze IB Settlements and the Early Bronze II City; Architecture and Town Planning; Sixth to Eighteenth Seasons of Excavations, 1971–1978, 1980–1984*. Jerusalem: IES.

Amiran, R.; Paran, U.; Shiloh, Y.; Brown, R.; Tsafrir, Y.; and Ben-Tor, A. 1978. *Early Arad I: The Chalcolithic Settlement and Early Bronze City; First–Fifth Seasons of Excavations, 1962–1966*. Jerusalem: IES.

Ben-Tor, A. 1992. The Early Bronze Age. In *The Archaeology of Ancient Israel*, ed. A. Ben-Tor, 81–125. Trans. R. Greenberg, from Hebrew. New Haven, CT: Yale University Press.

———. 2000. Hazor and the Chronology of Northern Israel: A Reply to Israel Finkelstein. *BASOR* 317: 9–16.

Bowman, S. 1995. *Radiocarbon Dating*. 2nd ed. Interpreting the Past. London: British Museum Press.

Bronk Ramsey, C. 2008. Radiocarbon Dating: Revolutions in Understanding. *Archaeometry* 50: 249–75.

———. 2009a. Bayesian Analysis of Radiocarbon Dates. *Radiocarbon* 51: 337–60.

———. 2009b. Dealing with Outliers and Offsets in Radiocarbon Dating. *Radiocarbon* 51: 1023–45.

Bronk Ramsey, C.; Dee, M. W.; Rowland, J. M.; Higham, T. F. G.; Harris, S. A.; Brock, F.; Quiles, A.; Wild, E. M.; Marcus, E. S.; and Shortland, A. J. 2010. Radiocarbon-Based Chronology for Dynastic Egypt. *Science* 328 (5985): 1554–7.

Bronk Ramsey, C.; Higham, T. F. G.; Owen, D. C.; Pike, A. W. G.; and Hedges, R. E. M. 2002. Radiocarbon Dates from the Oxford AMS System: Archaeometry Datelist 31. *Archaeometry* 44: 1–150.

Bruins, H. J. 2001. Near East Chronology: Towards an Integrated ^{14}C Time Foundation. *Radiocarbon* 43: 1147–54.

Bruins, H. J., and Mook, W. G. 1989. The Need for a Calibrated Radiocarbon Chronology of Near Eastern Archaeology. *Radiocarbon* 31: 1019–29.

Bruins, H. J.; van der Plicht, J.; and Mazar, A. 2003. ^{14}C Dates from Tel Rehov: Iron-Age Chronology, Pharaohs, and Hebrew Kings. *Science* 300 (5617): 315–18.

Buck, C. E.; Kenworthy, J. B.; Litton, C. D.; and Smith, A. F. M. 1991. Combining Archaeological and Radiocarbon Information: A Bayesian Approach to Calibration. *Antiquity* 65 (249): 808–21.

Callaway, J. A. 1978. New Perspectives on Early Bronze III in Canaan. In *Archaeology in the Levant: Essays for Kathleen Kenyon*, ed. P. R. S. Moorey and P. J. Parr, 46–58. Warminster: Aris & Phillips.

Chesson, M. S. 2015. Reconceptualizing the Early Bronze Age Southern Levant without Cities: Local Histories and Walled Communities of EB II–III Society. *JMA* 28: 51–79.

Chesson, M. S., and Goodale, N. 2014. Population Aggregation, Residential Storage and Socioeconomic Inequality at Early Bronze Age Numayra, Jordan. *JAA* 35: 117–34.

Chesson, M. S., and Philip, G. 2003. Tales of the City? "Urbanism" in the Early Bronze Age Levant from Mediterranean and Levantine Perspectives. *JMA* 16: 3–16.

Covello-Paran, K. 1999. *The Rural Aspect of the Jezreel Valley during the Intermediate Bronze Age, in Light of the Excavations at 'Ein Helu (Migdal ha-'Emeq)*. MA thesis, Tel Aviv University.

――― 2009. Socio-Economic Aspects of an Intermediate Bronze Age Village in the Jezreel Valley. In *The Levant in Transition: Proceedings of a Conference Held at the British Museum on 20–21 April 2004*, ed. P. J. Parr, 9–20. PEFA 9. Leeds: Maney.

Dever, W. G. 2014. *Excavations at the Early Bronze IV Sites of Jebel Qa'aqir and Be'er Resisim*. SAHL 6; HSMP. Winona Lake, IN: Eisenbrauns.

Douglas, K. 2007. *Die Befestigung der Unterstadt von Ḫirbet ez-Zeraqēn im Rahmen der frühbronzezeitlichen Fortifikationen in Palästina*. ADPV 27 (3). Wiesbaden: Harrassowitz.

Esse, D. L. 1991. *Subsistence, Trade, and Social Change in Early Bronze Age Palestine*. SAOC 50. Chicago: The Oriental Institute of The University of Chicago.

Evans, A. J. 1921. *The Palace of Minos: A Comparative Account of the Successive Stages of the Early Cretan Civilization as Illustrated by the Discoveries at Knossos*, Vol. 1: *The Neolithic and Early and Middle Minoan Ages*. London: MacMillan.

Falconer, S. E., and Fall, P. L. 2016. A Radiocarbon Sequence from Tell Abu en-Ni'aj, Jordan and Its Implications for Early Bronze IV Chronology in the Southern Levant. *Radiocarbon* 58: 615–47.

Falconer, S. E.; Fall, P. L.; and Jones, J. E. 2007. Life at the Foundation of Bronze Age Civilization: Agrarian Villages in the Jordan Valley. In *Crossing Jordan: North American Contributions to the Archaeology of Jordan*, ed. T. E. Levy, P. M. M. Daviau, R. W. Younker, and M. Shaer, 261–8. London: Equinox.

Finkelstein, I. 1996. The Archaeology of the United Monarchy: An Alternative View. *Levant* 28: 177–87.

――― 2005. A Low Chronology Update: Archaeology, History and Bible. In *The Bible and Radiocarbon Dating: Archaeology, Text and Science*, ed. T. E. Levy and T. F. G. Higham, 31–42. London: Equinox.

Finkelstein, I., and Piasetzky, E. 2003. Comment on "^{14}C Dates from Tel Rehov: Iron-Age Chronology, Pharaohs, and Hebrew Kings." *Science* 302 (5645): 568.

――― 2010. The Iron I/IIA Transition in the Levant: A Reply to Mazar and Bronk Ramsey and a New Perspective. *Radiocarbon* 52: 1667–80.

Garfinkel, Y., and Ganor, S., eds. 2009. *Khirbet Qeiyafa*, Vol. 1: *Excavation Report 2007–2008*. Jerusalem: IES; The Institute of Archaeology, The Hebrew University of Jerusalem.

Garfinkel, Y.; Ganor, S.; and Hasel, M. G. 2014. *Khirbet Qeiyafa*, Vol. 2: *Excavation Report 2009–2013; Stratigraphy and Architecture (Areas B, C, D E)*. Jerusalem: IES; The Institute of Archaeology, The Hebrew University of Jerusalem.

Garfinkel, Y., and Kang, H.-G. 2011. The Relative and Absolute Chronology of Khirbet Qeiyafa: Very Late Iron Age I or Very Early Iron Age IIA? *IEJ* 61: 171–83.

Garfinkel, Y.; Streit, K.; Ganor, S.; and Hasel, M. G. 2012. State Formation in Judah: Biblical Tradition, Modern Historical Theories, and Radiometric Dates at Khirbet Qeiyafa. *Radiocarbon* 54: 359–69.

Garfinkel, Y.; Streit, K.; Ganor, S.; and Reimer, P. J. 2015. King David's City at Khirbet Qeiyafa: Results of the Second Radiocarbon Dating Project. *Radiocarbon* 57: 881–90.

Genz, H. 2002. *Die frühbronzezeitliche Keramik von Ḫirbet ez-Zeraqōn: Mit Studien zur Chronologie und funktionalen Deutung frühbronzezeitlicher Keramik in der südlichen Levante.* ADPV 27 (2). Wiesbaden: Harrassowitz.

——— 2010. Recent Excavations at Tell Fadous-Kfarabida. *NEA* 73: 102–13.

——— 2014. Excavations at Tell Fadous-Kfarabida, 2004–2011: An Early and Middle Bronze Age Site on the Lebanese Coast. In *Egypt and the Southern Levant in the Early Bronze Age*, ed. F. Höflmayer and R. Eichmann, 69–91. Orient-Archäologie 31. Rahden/Westf.: Leidorf.

——— In press. *Tell Fadous-Kfarabida I: The Site and Its Environment*, ed. H. Genz. ASORAR. Boston: ASOR.

Gilboa, A., and Sharon, I. 2001. Early Iron Age Radiometric Dates from Tel Dor: Preliminary Implications for Phoenicia and Beyond. *Radiocarbon* 43: 1343–51.

Gophna, R. 1992. The Intermediate Bronze Age. In *The Archaeology of Ancient Israel*, ed. A. Ben-Tor, 126–58. Trans. R. Greenberg, from Hebrew. New Haven, CT: Yale University Press.

Greenberg, R. 2002. *Early Urbanizations in the Levant: A Regional Narrative.* NAAA. London: Leicester University Press.

——— 2003. Early Bronze Age Megiddo and Bet Shean: Discontinuous Settlement in Sociopolitical Context. *JMA* 16: 17–32.

——— 2017. No Collapse: Transmutations of Early Bronze Age Urbanism in the Southern Levant. In *The Late Third Millennium in the Ancient Near East: Chronology, C14, and Climate Change; Papers from The Oriental Institute Seminar "The Early/Middle Bronze Age Transition in the Ancient Near East: Chronology, C14, and Climate Change," Held at The Oriental Institute of The University of Chicago, 7–8 March 2014*, ed. F. Höflmayer, 33–60. OIS 11. Chicago: The Oriental Institute of The University of Chicago.

Haiman, M. 1996. Early Bronze Age IV Settlement Pattern of the Negev and Sinai Deserts: View from Small Marginal Temporary Sites. *BASOR* 303: 1–32.

Harrison, T. P., and Savage, S. H. 2003. Settlement Heterogeneity and Multivariate Craft Production in the Early Bronze Age Southern Levant. *JMA* 16: 33–57.

Höflmayer, F. 2014. Dating Catastrophes and Collapses in the Ancient Near East: The End of the First Urbanization in the Southern Levant and the 4.2 ka BP Event. In *Overcoming Catastrophes: Essays on Disastrous Agents Characterization and Resilience Strategies in Pre-Classical Southern Levant*, ed. L. Nigro, 117–40. ROSAPAT 11. Rome: "La Sapienza" Expedition to Palestine & Jordan.

——— 2015. The Southern Levant, Egypt, and the 4.2 ka BP Event. In *2200 BC – Ein Klimasturz als Ursache für den Zerfall der Alten Welt? 7. Mitteldeutscher Archäologentag vom 23. bis 26. Oktober 2014 in Halle (Saale) [2200 BC – A Climatic Breakdown as a Cause for the Collapse of the Old World? 7th Archaeological Conference of Central Germany, October 23–26, 2014 in Halle (Saale)]*, Vol. 1, ed. H. Meller, H. W. Arz, R. Jung, and R. Risch, 113–30. Tagungen des Landesmuseums für Vorgeschichte Halle 12 (1). Halle (Saale): Landesamt für Denkmalpflege und Archäologie Sachsen-Anhalt.

——— 2017. The Late Third Millennium B.C. in the Ancient Near East and Eastern Mediterranean: A Time of Collapse and Transformation. In *The Late Third Millennium in the Ancient Near East: Chronology, C14, and Climate Change; Papers from The Oriental Institute Seminar "The Early/Middle Bronze Age Transition in the Ancient Near East: Chronology, C14, and Climate Change," Held at The Oriental Institute of The University of*

Chicago, 7–8 March 2014, ed. F. Höflmayer, 1–30. OIS 11. Chicago: The Oriental Institute of The University of Chicago.

Höflmayer, F.; Dee, M. W.; Genz, H.; and Riehl, S. 2014. Radiocarbon Evidence for the Early Bronze Age Levant: The Site of Tell Fadous-Kfarabida (Lebanon) and the End of the Early Bronze III Period. *Radiocarbon* 56: 529–42.

Höflmayer, F.; Dee, M. W.; Kutschera, W.; and Wild, E. M. In press. Radiocarbon Dates from Tell Fadous-Kfarabida. In *Tell Fadous-Kfarabida I: The Site and Its Environment*, ed. H. Genz. ASORAR. Boston: ASOR.

Kenyon, K. M. 1966. *Amorites and Canaanites*. Schweich Lectures 1963. London: Published for the British Academy by Oxford University Press.

Levy, T. E., and Higham, T. F. G., eds. 2005. *The Bible and Radiocarbon Dating: Archaeology, Text and Science*. London: Equinox.

Malamat, A. 1979. *The Age of the Monarchies: Political History*. World History of the Jewish People 4 (1). Jerusalem: Massada.

Mazar, A. 1990. *Archaeology of the Land of the Bible*, Vol. 1: *10,000–586 B.C.E.* ABRL. New York: Doubleday.

⎯⎯⎯. 1997. Iron Age Chronology: A Reply to I. Finkelstein. *Levant* 29: 157–67.

⎯⎯⎯. 2005. The Debate over the Chronology of the Iron Age in the Southern Levant: Its History, the Current Situation, and a Suggested Resolution. In *The Bible and Radiocarbon Dating: Archaeology, Text and Science*, ed. T. E. Levy and T. F. G. Higham, 15–30. London: Equinox.

Mazar, A., and Bronk Ramsey, C. 2008. 14C-Dates and the Iron Age Chronology of Israel: A Response. *Radiocarbon* 50: 159–80.

Mazar, A.; Bruins, H. J.; Panitz-Cohen, N.; and van der Plicht, J. 2005. Ladder of Time at Tel Rehov: Stratigraphy, Archaeological Context, Pottery, and Radiocarbon Dates. In *The Bible and Radiocarbon Dating: Archaeology, Text and Science*, ed. T. E. Levy and T. F. G. Higham, 195–255. London: Equinox.

Mazar, A., and Carmi, I. 2001. Radiocarbon Dates from Iron Age Strata at Tel Beth Shean and Tel Rehov. *Radiocarbon* 43: 1333–42.

Mazar, A., and Streit, K. In press. Radiometric Dates from Tel Rehov. In *Excavations at Tel Rehov*, ed. A. Mazar. Jerusalem: IES.

Mazar, B. 1968. The Middle Bronze Age in Palestine. *IEJ* 18: 65–97.

Miroschedji, P. de. 1988. Données nouvelles sur le Bronze ancien de Palestine: Les fouilles de Tel Yarmouth. *CRSAIBL* 132: 186–211.

⎯⎯⎯. 1993. Fouilles récentes à Tel Yarmouth, Israël (1989–1993). *CRSAIBL* 137: 823–47.

⎯⎯⎯. 1999. Yarmuth: The Dawn of City-States in Southern Canaan. *NEA* 62: 2–19.

⎯⎯⎯. 2000. Fouilles de Tel Yarmouth: Résultats des 11e, 12e et 13e campagnes de fouilles (1996–1999). *CRSAIBL* 144: 679–710.

⎯⎯⎯. 2009. Rise and Collapse in the Southern Levant in the Early Bronze Age. *Scienze dell'Antichità* 15: 101–29.

⎯⎯⎯. 2013. Fouilles de Tel Yarmouth: Résultats des travaux de 2003 à 2009 (14e–18e campagnes). *CRSAIBL* 157: 759–96.

⎯⎯⎯. 2014. The Southern Levant (Cisjordan) during the Early Bronze Age. In *The Oxford Handbook of the Archaeology of the Levant, c. 8000–332 BCE*, ed. M. L. Steiner and A. E. Killebrew, 307–29. Oxford: Oxford University Press.

Misgav, H.; Garfinkel, Y.; and Ganor, S. 2009. The Ostracon. In *Khirbet Qeiyafa*, Vol. 1: *Excavation Report 2007–2008*, ed. Y. Garfinkel and S. Ganor, 243–57. Jerusalem: IES; The Institute of Archaeology, The Hebrew University of Jerusalem.

Nigro, L. 2010. *In the Palace of the Copper Axes: Khirbet al-Batrawy; The Discovery of a Forgotten City of the III Millennium BC in Jordan.* Trans. M. Sala, from Italian. ROSAPAT 1. Rome: "La Sapienza" Expedition to Palestine & Jordan.

―――. 2012. *Khirbet al-Batrawy III. The EB II–III Triple Fortification Line, and the EB IIIB Quarter inside the City-Wall; Preliminary Report of the Fourth (2008) and Fifth (2009) Seasons of Excavations.* ROSAPAT 8. Rome: "La Sapienza" Expedition to Palestine & Jordan.

Palumbo, G. 1991. *The Early Bronze Age IV in the Southern Levant: Settlement Patterns, Economy, and Material Culture of a "Dark Age."* CMAO 3. Rome: University of Rome, "La Sapienza."

Parr, P. J., ed. 2009. *The Levant in Transition: Proceedings of a Conference Held at the British Museum on 20–21 April 2004.* PEFA 9. Leeds: Maney.

Philip, G. 2003. The Early Bronze Age of the Southern Levant: A Landscape Approach. *JMA* 16: 103–32.

Prag, K. 2014. The Southern Levant during the Intermediate Bronze Age. In *The Oxford Handbook of the Archaeology of the Levant, c. 8000–332 BCE*, ed. M. L. Steiner and A. E. Killebrew, 388–400. Oxford: Oxford University Press.

Preucel, R. W., and Meskell, L. 2004. Knowledges. In *A Companion to Social Archaeology*, ed. L. Meskell and R. W. Preucel, 3–22. Malden, MA: Blackwell.

Regev, J.; Miroschedji, P. de; and Boaretto, E. 2012. Early Bronze Age Chronology: Radiocarbon Dates and Chronological Models from Tel Yarmuth (Israel). *Radiocarbon* 54: 505–24.

Regev, J.; Miroschedji, P. de; Greenberg, R.; Braun, E.; Greenhut, Z.; and Boaretto, E. 2012. Chronology of the Early Bronze Age in the Southern Levant: New Analysis for a High Chronology. *Radiocarbon* 54: 525–66.

Reimer, P. J.; Bard, E.; Bayliss, A.; Beck, J. W.; Blackwell, P. G.; Bronk Ramsey, C.; Buck, C. E.; Cheng, H.; Edwards, R. L.; Friedrich, M.; Grootes, P. M.; Guilderson, T. P.; Haflidason, H.; Hajdas, I.; Hatté, C.; Heaton, T. J.; Hoffmann, D. L.; Hogg, A. G.; Hughen, K. A.; Kaiser, K. F.; Kromer, B.; Manning, S. W.; Niu, M.; Reimer, R. W.; Richards, D. A.; Scott, E. M.; Southon, J. R.; Staff, R. A.; Turney, C. S. M.; and van der Plicht, J. 2013. Intcal13 and Marine13 Radiocarbon Age Calibration Curves 0–50,000 Years cal BP. *Radiocarbon* 55: 1869–87.

Renfrew, C. 1973. *Social Archaeology: An Inaugural Lecture Delivered at the University, 20th March, 1973.* Southampton: University of Southampton.

―――. 1984. *Approaches to Social Archaeology.* Cambridge, MA: Harvard University Press.

Richard, S. 1980. Toward a Consensus of Opinion on the End of the Early Bronze Age in Palestine-Transjordan. *BASOR* 237: 5–34.

Richard, S.; Long, J. C., Jr.; Holdorf, P. S.; and Peterman, G., eds. 2010. *Khirbat Iskandar: Final Report on the Early Bronze IV Area C "Gateway" and Cemeteries.* ASORAR 14. Boston: ASOR.

Rosen, A. M. 1995. The Social Response to Environmental Change in Early Bronze Age Canaan. *JAA* 14: 26–44.

Seters, J. van. 1997. *In Search of History: Historiography in the Ancient World and the Origins of Biblical History.* Winona Lake, IN: Eisenbrauns.

Sharon, I. 2001. "Transition Dating" – A Heuristic Mathematical Approach to the Collation of Radiocarbon Dates from Stratified Sequences. *Radiocarbon* 43: 345–54.

Sharon, I.; Gilboa, A.; Tull, A. J. T.; and Boaretto, E. 2007. Report on the First Stage of the Iron Age Dating Project in Israel: Supporting a Low Chronology. *Radiocarbon* 49: 1–46.

Singer-Avitz, L. 2016. Khirbet Qeiyafa: Late Iron Age I in Spite of It All – Once Again. *IEJ* 66: 232–44.

Stager, L. E. 1992. The Periodization of Palestine from the Neolithic through Early Bronze Times. In *Chronologies in Old World Archaeology*, Vol. 2, ed. R. W. Ehrich, 22–60. 3rd ed. Chicago: The University of Chicago Press.

—— 2003. The Patrimonial Kingdom of Solomon. In *Symbiosis, Symbolism, and the Power of the Past: Canaan, Ancient Israel, and Their Neighbors from the Late Bronze Age through Roman Palaestina; Proceedings of the Centennial Symposium, W. F. Albright Institute of Archaeological Research and American Schools of Oriental Research Jerusalem, May 29–31, 2000*, ed. W. G. Dever and S. Gitin, 63–74. Winona Lake, IN: Eisenbrauns.

Staubwasser, M., and Weiss, H. 2006. Holocene Climate and Cultural Evolution in Late Prehistoric–Early Historic West Asia. *Quaternary Research* 66: 372–87.

Stuiver, M., and Suess, H. E. 1966. On the Relationship between Radiocarbon Dates and True Sample Ages. *Radiocarbon* 8: 534–40.

Taylor, R. E., and Bar-Yosef, O. 2014. *Radiocarbon Dating: An Archaeological Perspective.* 2nd ed. Walnut Creek, CA: Left Coast.

Thompson, T. L. 1999. *The Mythic Past: Biblical Archaeology and the Myth of Israel.* London: Basic Books.

Toffolo, M. B.; Arie, E.; Martin, M. A. S.; Boaretto, E.; and Finkelstein, I. 2014. Absolute Chronology of Megiddo, Israel, in the Late Bronze and Iron Ages: High-Resolution Radiocarbon Dating. *Radiocarbon* 56: 221–44.

Weinstein, J. M. 1984. Radiocarbon Dating in the Southern Levant. *Radiocarbon* 26: 297–366.

Weiss, H., and Bradley, R. S. 2001. What Drives Societal Collapse? *Science* 291 (5504): 609–10.

Weiss, H.; Courty, M.-A.; Wetterstrom, W.; Guichard, F.; Senior, L.; Meadow, R.; and Curnow, A. 1993. The Genesis and Collapse of Third Millennium North Mesopotamian Civilization. *Science* 261 (5124): 995–1004.

Weninger, F.; Steier, P.; Kutschera, W.; and Wild, E. M. 2006. The Principle of the Bayesian Method. *Egypt and the Levant* 16: 317–24.

Yadin, Y. 1958. Solomon's City Wall and Gate at Gezer. *IEJ* 8: 80–6.

Yadin, Y.; Aharoni, Y.; Amiran, R.; Dothan, T.; Dunayevsky, I.; and Perrot, J. 1958. *Hazor I: An Account of the First Season of Excavations, 1955.* Jerusalem: The Hebrew University of Jerusalem.

THIRTY TWO

ITINERANT OBJECTS
The Legal Lives of Levantine Artifacts

MORAG M. KERSEL

OBJECTS, LIVES, ITINERARIES, AND LAW

In 1986, Arjun Appadurai and Igor Kopytoff asked us to consider the "social lives of things" – arguing that objects are not static but wander in and out of different classifications of value and use over their duration. Initially focused on notions of commodification, value, and exchange, object biographies and the ideas of artifacts with lives and agency are usefully explored and employed (see, e.g., Winner 1980; Latour 1992; Mark 1994; Riggins 1994; Weiner 1994; Gosden and Marshall 1999; Dobres and Robb 2000; Knappett and Malafouris 2008; Dannehl 2009; Knappett 2013; Burström 2014; Maeir et al. 2015; and Robb 2015). Rather than a detailed account of the object and its constituent parts, biographies are used to reveal the relationships between objects and people (Gosden and Marshall 1999), understand the process of commodification and modes of exchange (Kopytoff 1986), and explain societal organization and human processes (Burström 2014). A variety of methods, including archaeological excavation and analyses, archival research, and ethnography, have been used to reconstruct the lives of artifacts. While the paradigm persists, there has been critique and subsequent reconsideration. Jody Joy suggests that a basic issue that prehistoric archaeologists have with object biographies is the quality of information available: "Put simply, unless the object under scrutiny has a recorded history, the evidence available is not sufficient to reconstruct a full life history, with a birth, life and death" (2009: 543). The best possible outcome for a prehistoric artifact is analogous evidence for production and contextual evidence of death, raising yet another issue with object biography: What constitutes death in this lifespan approach to reconstructing the past life of an artifact? Cornelius Holtorf (2002) proposes that in order to create a biography it may be necessary to work in reverse from death to production. In the edited volume of Hans Peter Hahn and Hadas Weiss (2013), authors highlight the shortcomings of object biography reasoning, which places the lifespan of an object on a straight path of a beginning, middle, and end. The desire to follow a pot from the ground to the consumer may assume a linear trajectory of production, distribution, and consumption (see Kersel 2006); however, the reality is a far more convoluted, enmeshed jumble of movement – a trip, which "traces the strings of places where objects come to rest or are active, the routes through which things circulate, and the means by which they are moved (Joyce and Gillespie 2015: 3).

In reaction to the concept of an object biography, scholars have expanded the trope to include a more comprehensive approach to the life and movement of objects, augmenting or even replacing the biography with an itinerary (see the examples in Joy 2009; 2015; Hahn and Weiss 2013; Mitcham 2013; and Joyce and Gillespie [eds.] 2015). Contributions to *Things in Motion: Object Itineraries in Anthropological Practice*, edited by Rosemary Joyce and Susan Gillespie, illustrate that the intertwined webs of objects and their movements are anything but straight, as there can be periods of stasis (Knappett 2013) and/or extensive movement. Routes suggest a journey, which may be without end and involve periods of non-movement. These trips may be filled with gaps, fragmented, and never ending.

> Examining the itineraries of things requires consideration of technologies for circulation; of *impediments and facilitators to movement*; of natural and cultural transformations along the way; of whether objects travel intact or incomplete, with others or alone; of the landscapes that result from the places linked through their travels; and of value of circulating objects for the production and reshaping of cultural relations that separate people, as well as for those that connect persons, places, and things across space and time. (Joyce and Gillespie 2015: 12 [emphasis added])

Laws and policies are created to facilitate and/or impede the movement of objects and as such are integral to the itinerary of a thing (Kersel 2017). As part of the bundling described by Webb Keane (2006: 201), "things always contain properties in excess of those which have been interpreted and made use of under given circumstances"; yet, rarely is law a factor in the analyses of an object's biography and itinerary.

An examination of ceramic vessels from Early Bronze Age (3600–2000 BCE) sites along the Dead Sea Plain in Jordan resulted in the notion that these vessels have extensive itineraries that are continually impacted by law. In their initial creation, varied uses, later deposition, unearthing, changing hands, crossing borders, and eventual final resting place in a collection, law affects a single pot at each stage of movement. *Follow the Pots* (http://followthepotsproject.org/) is interested in the lives and itineraries of Early Bronze Age pots from the graves of Bab adh-Dhra' and Fifa. These ceramic vessels have led lives as grave goods buried with various Early Bronze Age individuals; excavated archaeological artifacts and the object of scientific inquiry; looted objects, clandestinely excavated to fulfill a variety of motivations; collected items highly prized by individuals and institutions (foreign and local); and exhibited material on display in academic institutions, museums, and private homes. Using Joy's (2009; 2015) notion of a relational perspective to the examination of an object, the following is an ontological approach to the thing as it changes over time, takes various paths, and is affected and moved by external forces.

I want to extend Joy's (2015) thinking about objects and their lives by suggesting that the biography of an Early Bronze Age pot is comprised of its relationships with humans and law. "Objects are not just a product of society they are fundamental to it" (Thomas 1996: 141), and their morphing lives and itineraries make an examination of the lives of pots essential to our understanding of the past in the present. While the perfect path of a pot might have been to remain as a buried grave good with an ancient ancestor, by articulating the legal movement of a pot as a travel itinerary with a series of stops constituting the main stages in the life of a pot, it is possible to reconstruct how the various historic and contemporary legislative and policy efforts have shaped the life of a thing and, in turn, shaped our lives. Through the lens of law, the following will combine an examination of the biographies and the itineraries of Early Bronze Age pots from the Dead Sea Plain, Jordan.

THE LEGAL ITINERARY OF AN EARLY BRONZE AGE POT FROM TOMB GROUP A 72NW

Legal Itinerary Segment 1 – Pots Are Placed with People in Shaft Tomb A 72NW

During the Early Bronze Age (EB) IA (3600–3200 BCE) at the site of Bab adh-Dhra' (see Fig. 9.1) along the Dead Sea Plain in Jordan, hundreds of individuals were buried in single and multi-chambered shaft tombs. In Shaft Tomb A 72NW (Fig. 32.1), the skulls and long bones (secondary burial remains) of at least three individuals were buried in one of three chambers of an irregularly rounded shaft tomb (Schaub and Rast 1989: 132). Unusual in construction, the tomb had one rounded and two angular walls with squared corners (see Fig. 32.1). The thick stone slab blocking the tomb was not quite large enough

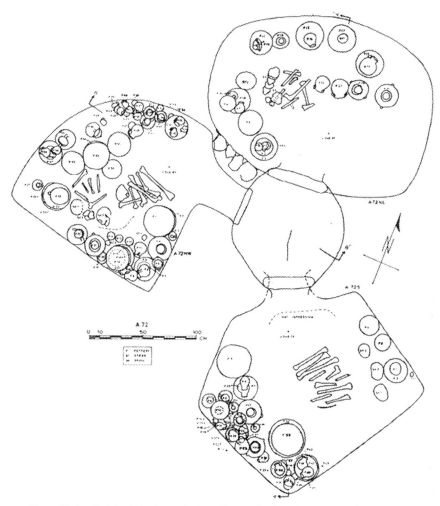

32.1. Plan of Bab adh-Dhra' Shaft Tomb A 72 (from Schaub and Rast 1989: fig. 76). (Courtesy of the Expedition to the Dead Sea Plain Project.)

to seal the entrance, necessitating the use of pebbled plaster to fill in the cracks. The burial consisted of a disarticulated bone pile in the center of the tomb on a reed mat (traces of a mat impression were evident). A minimum number of three people (complete skulls of two adults and a third fragmentary skull of a child) were buried with the typical mortuary toolkit of the EB IA: two basalt bowls, some carnelian beads, two limestone mace-heads, and sixty-three ceramic vessels. The majority of vessels were made of fine ware with thin walls and a reddish-orange slip, some burnished. Ceramic shapes included with the dead were wide deep bowls, small deep bowls, large ledge-handled jars, medium-sized loop-handled jars, and loop-handled juglets (Fig. 32.2). Meredith Chesson has proposed that a few of the forms have close parallels in the Jericho Proto-Urban A tombs, but similar groups, especially with the

32.2. A typical Early Bronze Age tomb group from Bab adh-Dhra' in the Royal Ontario Museum collection (reg. no. A 12). (Photo by M. M. Kersel, with permission from the Royal Ontario Museum.)

distinctive ware and decoration, are not yet known outside of the Bab adh-Dhra' area (1999; 2015).

Excavations by Paul Lapp in 1965 and 1966, and subsequent analyses by Chesson, R. Thomas Schaub, and Walter Rast suggest that there is little evidence for a permanent, full-scale domestic occupation of Bab adh-Dhra' during the EB IA. Data recorded by Lapp and further interpreted by Chesson, Rast, and Schaub support a seasonal or temporary campsite explanation for the archaeological remains in the eastern area of Cemetery A (http://expedition deadseaplain.org/). This lack of permanent EB IA habitational evidence led to the conclusion that during EB IA, the utilization pattern of the region was temporary. Periodic returns by pastoral groups to rebury their dead in an established burial ground seem likely (Schaub and Rast 1989; Chesson 1999; 2015). The occasional articulated burials recovered during the years of excavation at Bab adh-Dhra' can best be explained as associated with deaths that occurred during these visits or may belong to the end of this period when permanent occupation began (Chesson 1999; 2015). Despite the lack of written records, it is clear from the archaeological record that over the span of centuries at Bab adh-Dhra' people buried the dead in a particular manner with a specific mortuary toolkit (Baker 2012; Kersel and Chesson 2013). The purpose of these associated goods is unknown – perhaps they were intended for use in an afterlife? These lacunae in our understanding of the function of such artifacts reinforce Joy's (2009) assertion regarding problems encountered by prehistorians when reconstructing the biographies of objects. Clearly, during the Early Bronze Age, people brought their dead and the associated grave goods to the cemeteries at Bab adh-Dhra', an-Naqa, and Fifa (see Fig. 9.1). Presumably, these people did not envision that the burial vessels might be disinterred and redistributed but expected them to remain in Shaft Tomb A 72NW. What is not clear is whether they were following directives proscribed by traditional law on where and how to bury the dead during this period.

Legal Itinerary Segment 2 — Scenario A: The Pots Are Discovered in the 1920s

The mortuary goods buried with the dead in Shaft Tomb A 72NW remained undisturbed until the early 1920s, when William F. Albright and Alexis Mallon report the first incidents of looting at Bab adh-Dhra' (Albright 1924; Mallon 1924). During a survey of the southern Ghors, carried out as part of a search for the biblical cities of Sodom and Gomorrah, "Père Mallon discovered some cairns which the Arabs had opened, disclosing pottery of the Early Bronze Age" (Albright 1924: 6; Mallon 1924). While surveying, Albright and Mallon came into contact with these Early Bronze Age pots lying on the surface of the site, unearthed during looting. Their work was authorized under the legal permission of the British Mandate agent in charge of archaeology in Transjordan during this period. Between 1921 and 1946 (the latter is the date of the establishment of the Hashemite Kingdom of Jordan), Transjordan was closely tied to the British Mandate government and its laws (Corbett 2015). "Thanks to the efforts of Dr. Riza Tewfik Bey, former professor of Philosophy in the University of Constantinople and for a time Minister of Education in the Turkish Government, now Director of Antiquities in Transjordania, everything went smoothly and we were treated with courtesy and consideration by all the officials with whom we came into contact" writes Albright (1924: 3) in his account of the trip to the southern Ghors. British Mandate ordinances and rules were based directly on a succession of earlier Ottoman laws (1869, 1874, 1884 [see Shaw 2003; Kersel 2008; Özel 2010; Çelik 2011; 2016; and Eldem 2011]). This sequence of Ottoman legislative efforts was in response to increasing foreign archaeological interest in the area, the excavation of some high-profile sites and monuments, and the looting of archaeological material from the empire. Thus, it emphasized heavily the regulation of the movement of artifacts and monuments.

Prior to 1869, all governance of cultural heritage in the Ottoman Empire was based on Islamic law and local jurisprudence. The 1869 Turkish Bylaw on Antiquities (*Asar-ı Atika Nizam-namesi*) provided the first formalized "procedural and legal structure to regulate search, extraction, possession, and preservation of antiquities" (Eldem 2011: 314). The bylaw consisted of seven articles that established a series of requirements related to archaeology, artifacts, monuments, museums, and sites. Appearing first in the official Ottoman gazette (*Takvim-i Vekayi*) on February 13, 1869, and then in the foreign-language press the following month, the bylaw stated:

1. The new regulation requires that henceforth application for permission to excavate in any part of the empire shall be made to the Department of Public Instruction (under whose charge the museum is to be placed); and
2. Prohibits the exportation to foreign countries of any antiquities (ancient coins excepted) found in the course of such excavations, though they may be sold to private individuals resident in the empire, or purchased by the state.
3. Objects found on private property shall belong to the owner of the soil.
4. The right to remove antiquities is limited to such as are below the surface of the ground.
5. Those who disturb or damage memorials on the surface will be proceeded against.
6. Permission officially applied for by a foreign power can only be granted by special imperial written edict.
7. The last article provides for archaeological explorations at the expense of the state by persons competent to undertake such works, and those who are possessed of information calculated to promote the object in view are invited to communicate with the minister of public instruction. (*Levant Times and Shipping Gazette*, March 22, 1869, English summary of the 1869 Turkish Bylaw on Antiquities [Eldem 2011: 314])

Subsequent laws (1874, 1884, 1906) governing archaeology in the Ottoman Empire were based on this initial bylaw but added provisions. Edhem Eldem (2011: 282) suggests that the earlier 1869 bylaw may seem inconsequential in the development of cultural heritage legislation and policy, but it laid the groundwork for greater ministerial/museum oversight of cultural material and the future formation of a national ownership provision (Donkow 2004; Kersel 2010; Eldem 2011; Özel 2010). Using the 1869 bylaw as a springboard, the Ottoman authorities in Constantinople issued a series of laws, *Reglement sur les antiquities*, in 1874 (1874 law) that sought to regulate further the movement of artifacts, clearly articulating the principle of *partage* – the division of archaeological finds between the foreign excavators, the state, and the landowner. If, during the nineteenth century, an object was scientifically excavated from one of the Early Bronze Age sites along the Dead Sea, the pot could now be housed in Boston, Chicago, London, Melbourne, or Toronto as part of a *partage* arrangement. Or it could have been deemed "not needed for the national repository" and released to the thriving legal market in antiquities throughout the Ottoman Empire.

In the waning days of empire, the Ottoman government adopted a new law related to archaeology and antiquities. The 1906 decree took the national ownership provision further by declaring that all antiquities found in or on public or *private* lands were the property of the state and could not be taken out of country. As a result, "all newly discovered antiquities became state property by operation of law, ipso jure, at the time of discovery and no further act of acquisition was needed by the Ottoman government" (Özel 2010: 179). Personally held antiquities found prior to 1906 were grandfathered under the law and remained private property, sometimes making their way into the legal antiquities markets (see Kersel 2008; Çelik 2011; 2016; and Eldem 2011).

With the dissolution of the Ottoman Empire, the region comprising modern Israel, Jordan, and Palestine was ceded to the British after World War I, and the League of Nations passed The Palestine Mandate of the League of Nations in June 1922. The British Mandate period, often referred to as the "Golden Age of Archaeology," saw the establishment of an efficient, centralized colonial government and the improvement of transportation and communications throughout the region, as it became one of the most active centers of excavation and archaeological research in the world (see Silberman 1998; Bernhardsson 2005; Goode 2007; and Corbett 2015). The changes in oversight meant that the area Albright and Mallon surveyed in 1924 was under the jurisdiction of the British Mandate government. In their initial days of statehood, most postcolonial entities did not alter the basic institutional arrangements of colonial law and administration, which in this context resulted in British Mandate laws and ordinances retaining many of the characteristics of the earlier Ottoman laws and bylaws (Chatterjee 1993). In one of its first actions, the British Mandate government circulated an antiquities proclamation and then the 1920 Antiquities Ordinance, noting the importance of cultural heritage in the region and regulating archaeological excavations and surveys.

Under the conditions of their survey permit, based on the 1920 ordinance, it was legal for Albright and Mallon to pick up material from the ground in their survey area. As part of the itinerary of a pot from Shaft Tomb A 72NW, one of the vessels lying on the surface due to looting may have been collected by Mallon and Albright, and now may reside in a permanent collection in Jerusalem, the United States, or France. However, if the pot was not picked up as part of the 1924 survey, it may have passed through numerous hands over the years, which could include local acquisition by a looter for sale to a middleman, collector, foreigner, or museum.

In the 1920s, traveling from person-to-person or institution-to-institution, the Early Bronze Age vessel may have been subject to the 1929 Antiquities Ordinance of the newly established Department of Antiquities. Under this ordinance, the selling and buying of antiquities in Transjordan and Palestine was well articulated. The 1930 Antiquities Rules outlined formal procedures for excavation, survey, interpretation, the licensed trade in antiquities, and institutional acquisition of artifacts from this region. Jordanian families who had been in the antiquities business for decades were now required to apply and pay for a license to sell antiquities. This ordinance preserved many of the structural features, as well substantive policies, of the earlier Ottoman legislative efforts (Taha 2010; Kersel 2015a), creating a sense of legal continuity related to the management of cultural heritage.

Legal Itinerary Segment 3 – Scenario B: Paul Lapp Excavations in 1965 and 1967

In an alternate scenario, the mortuary goods buried with the Early Bronze Age ancestors remained undisturbed on the reed mat in Shaft Tomb A 72NW in Cemetery A. In response to a 1964 report asserting that the major source for the recent influx of Early Bronze Age vessels for sale in the antiquities shops in Jerusalem was the cemetery at Bab adh-Dhra', Paul Lapp (1966) mounted a rescue excavation at the site. In the late 1950s, Lapp, an archaeologist and director of the Jerusalem School of the American Schools of Oriental Research (now, the W. F. Albright Institute for Archaeological Research), noted a trickle, a stream, and then, by the mid-1960s, a flood of Early Bronze Age pots in the Jerusalem antiquities market (Saller 1964–1965; Lapp 1968). The unique pots were identified as coming from one of the Dead Sea Plain sites in the modern state of Jordan. During the 1965 campaign, Lapp excavated the northwest chamber of Shaft Tomb A 72, recovering one basalt bowl, two limestone mace-heads, a few carnelian beads, and sixty-three pots. He registered one of the buff-colored craters (Fig. 32.3) as no. 91431, noting that it had four rounded knobs and some decoration.

In 1946, British Mandate rule was nearing its end and the independent Hashemite Kingdom of Jordan was recognized. The first formal law enacted by the Jordanian state regarding antiquities was in 1953, which maintained many of the basic principles of the precursor Ottoman laws and British Mandate ordinances. The Antiquities Order No. 1 of 1953 [1953 law] laid the conditions for a sale in antiquities, as well as a permitting process for the excavation of sites and detailed a system of *partage* (Kersel 2015b). Under the 1953 law (part II), the Jordanian government could issue an excavation license to an applicant, and the pots recovered from these Early Bronze Age sites could be transferred out of Jordan as part of a division of excavated materials (*partage*). *Partage* artifacts remaining in Jordan that were not required for the national collection could be sold on the legal antiquities market in Amman. An excavated pot from Bab adh-Dhra' could be in an educational study collection, a museum, a private collection, a licensed antiquities shop (material considered duplicate could be sold by a licensed agent of the state on the legal antiquities market), or in a

32.3. Early Bronze Age vessel (Schaub and Rast 1989: fig. 85:1, reg. no. 91431 = OIM A35331) at The Oriental Institute from Bab adh-Dhra' Tomb Group A 72NW. (Photo by M. M. Kersel, with permission from The Oriental Institute.)

storeroom, awaiting study, analysis, and eventual publication. The excavated pots from Shaft Tomb A 72NW were placed in storage in Amman.

In 1970, Lapp died in a swimming accident off the coast of Cyprus, leaving the pots from Shaft Tomb A 72NW in limbo. Nancy Lapp, Paul's widow, was faced with thousands of vessels in storage after inheriting his legacy collections. In an archival letter from David McCreery (an archaeologist based in Amman) to Edward Campbell (ASOR representative), McCreery outlined an assessment of the stored pots in Amman. McCreary suggested the collection inventory was inadequate, that some of the pots were "missing," and the artifacts were at risk (David McCreery to Edward Campbell, Nancy Lapp, and R. Thomas Schaub, September 2, 1977, Nancy Lapp correspondence). Further correspondence between N. Lapp and the staff from the Jordanian Department of Antiquities indicated that storage space in Amman was at a premium, and tomb groups like Tomb Group A 72NW needed a "new home" (Nancy Lapp to Adnan Hadidi of the Jordanian Department of Antiquities, September 23, 1977, Nancy Lapp correspondence).

In response to the precarious storage situation of the Early Bronze Age pots, the Jordanian Department of Antiquities and ASOR (the Paul Lapp excavation sponsors) came up with an usual stage in the itinerary of the pots from Shaft Tomb A 72NW. In a December 1977 letter to The Oriental Institute of The University of Chicago, N. Lapp offered, on behalf of the Jordanian Department of Antiquities and ASOR, to sell Bab adh-Dhra' tomb group

A 72NW for the purposes of display and education (Nancy Lapp to The Oriental Institute, December 26, 1977, Nancy Lapp correspondence). Even though Jordanian Temporary Law N.12 of 1976 on Antiquities banned the trade in antiquities, the government could permit the transfer/sale of such material. This legal movement of pots satisfied a demand for teaching materials, freed up valuable storage space, and allowed the pots to increase interest in Jordanian archaeology, thus encouraging cooperative archaeological efforts between the United States and Jordan. The objects were to act as ambassadors on behalf of Jordan (Adnan Hadidi, the director of the Jordanian Department of Antiquities, to Nancy Lapp, August 15, 1977, Nancy Lapp correspondence). In the spring of 1978, The Oriental Institute acquired Tomb Group A 72NW, paying $6 USD per pot.

The pot traveled from the storage facility in Amman to the collection of The Oriental Institute in Chicago. As of 2018, the pot (see Fig. 32.3) from Shaft Tomb A 72NW remains a part of The Oriental Institute collection. After acquiring it in 1978, it was assigned Oriental Institute accession number OIM A35331, which corresponds to fig. 85:1 registration no. 91431 in the 1989 publication of the Lapp excavations at Bab adh-Dhra' by Schaub and Rast. Between April 3 and May 13, 2017, the pot (OIM A35331) was part of an exhibit about the ancient and modern movement of Early Bronze Age pots at the Neubauer Collegium at The University of Chicago. While an unconventional stage in the life of a thing, the controlled distribution of tomb groups permitted the Jordanians to decide how and where their cultural heritage was displayed and accessed in the public domain, allowing for greater contact with the material culture of the Early Bronze Age of Jordan.

Legal Itinerary Segment 4 – Scenario C: A Pot from Shaft Tomb A 72NW Sold in the Market Place in Jordan

Between 1965 and 1974, a Bab adh-Dhra' pot – one of a 1,000 excavated by P. Lapp – might not be considered necessary for the national repository, perhaps considered redundant (Bisheh 2001), and could legitimately make its way onto the legal antiquities markets in Amman. Demand, by both locals and tourists was vigorous, but 1974 saw a tightening of restrictions for the movement of archaeological materials with Jordan's ratification of the Convention on the Means of Prohibiting and Preventing the Illicit Import, Export and Transfer of Ownership of Cultural Property 1970 (also referred to as the 1970 UNESCO Convention). In ratifying this convention, Jordan agreed to abide by the principles outlined in the document and aid other countries in preventing the illegal movement of archaeological objects. At the same time, other member states agreed to protect against the illegal importation of Jordanian material across their borders. While the 1970 UNESCO Convention is not a law, it is a customary form of agreement between member states to protect against the illegal export/import of artifacts. Pots looted from the Early Bronze Age sites and illegally exported were now subject to seizure at the borders of the countries that had also implemented provisions of the 1970 UNESCO Convention.

The Temporary Law No. 12 of 1976 on Antiquities [1976 law] and the later Jordanian Antiquities Law No. 21 of 1988 (amended in 2004) along with the Regulations for Archaeological Projects in Jordan of 2015 make excavating without the permission of the Jordanian Department of Antiquities illegal. Any undiscovered artifacts below ground belong to the state (the people of Jordan). Additionally, the 1976 law banned the legal trade of antiquities in Jordan, but the Early Bronze Age sites were (and still are) being looted, and pots were (and still are) leaving the country illegally. Many of the looted items are for sale in the legally sanctioned Israeli antiquities market. In examining the biographies and itineraries of these objects, it is clear that they have legal and illegal stages, which constitute elements of their life stories. What kind of trip does a pot take to get from the ground in Jordan to the consumer in Israel?

Legal Itinerary Segment 5 – Scenario D: A Pot Illegally Excavated from Shaft Tomb A 72NW Sold on the Antiquities Market in Israel

In an different set of circumstances for Shaft Tomb A 72NW, instead of a systematic excavation by Paul Lapp, a looter made his way to Bab adh-Dhra' in the spring of 2014, armed with the standard tools (Fig. 32.4) – a long metal prod, a shovel, a flashlight, and a bucket. Using the metal prod, he poked holes in the surface until it hit a stone with a thud – a limestone slab indicating a burial chamber. Taking up a shovel, the looter dug down into the shaft until he came upon a chamber entrance. After pushing aside the long bones and skulls and leaving the undesirable mace-heads and carnelian beads, he recovered sixty-three pots and two basalt bowls. The removal of the pots without an excavation permit from the Jordanian Department of Antiquities is illegal. Under these conditions the items are not destined for academic study, but instead the itinerary of this pot may be dangerous, nonlinear, and precarious. Ethnographic interviews with looters reveal that while their motivations for looting are varied (boredom, employment, looking for gold), the end result is often the same – "big black cars from Amman and/or Kerak come to the sites and buy the pots for $4–7 USD" (Looters 3 and 15).[1]

Once in Amman, the pots may end up in private Jordanian collections, or they may be transferred to the legal market in Israel, traveling by back pack, in shipping containers, diplomatic vehicles and pouches, United Nations aid trucks, or by plane across an international border (see Kersel 2006). Illegally excavated artifacts often travel in the same well-established networks as arms, drugs, and humans (Efrat 2012). Global statistics on border inspections indicate

32.4. Looters' tools at the Early Bronze Age site of Fifa. (Photo by A. C. Hill. Courtesy of the Landscapes of the Dead Project.)

that approximately less than 10 percent of all material is stopped and checked, allowing for the movement of illegal material (Naím 2005). In a recent border interdiction at the King Hussein Bridge between Jordan and Israel, a car from the Norwegian Embassy was stopped and searched, based on an anonymous tip (Ben Zion 2016). During the incident, "[c]ustoms officials found 10 kilograms of ancient coins, statuettes, beads and other artifacts stowed in cardboard containers inside the car's paneling" (Ben Zion 2016). This search and seizure confirmed over ten years of ethnographic research on the movement of archaeological materials in diplomatic vehicles.

In Israel, the looted pots are assigned a registry number through a complex laundering process and can be legally sold and exported outside of the country (Kersel 2006). In 1948, like Jordan, the newly formed state of Israel adopted the existing British Mandate antiquities ordinances and rules regarding the care and handling of cultural heritage. It was some thirty years later that a new antiquities law was passed in order to protect archaeological monuments, sites, and objects. While Jordan rid themselves of the colonial influence of a state-sanctioned trade in antiquities in favor of laws curtailing the movement of objects outside of the new borders, Israel's Antiquities Law 5738 (1978) included a provision and guidelines for a legally licensed trade in antiquities (see Kersel 2008; 2010). Under the 1978 law, it is illegal to excavate any archaeological site without the permission of the relevant government agency, the IAA, established under Antiquities Authority Law 5749 (1989). Unfortunately, the 1978 law created a nonsensical situation, where the illegal

32.5. Buff-colored Early Bronze Age pots. (Photo by M. M. Kersel.)

excavation of antiquities is prohibited by law; however, the same law permits the legal sale of antiquities, even though some antiquities originate from illegal excavations in Jordan, Israel, the Palestinian Territories, and elsewhere.

Under the 1978 law, it is legal to sell, buy, and export artifacts in IAA-authorized shops. In order to comply with the licensing requirements, the dealer (Israelis and Palestinians) is required to submit an inventory of each item in their holdings, which should be comprised of pre-1978 dealer inventories, museum deaccessions, or inherited collections, which are grandfathered as eligible for sale. Until recently, the registry was typically a handwritten ledger or an Excel spreadsheet with vague descriptions of items like "buff colored pot" (Fig. 32.5), accompanied by an often hastily taken, blurry image. A tourist visiting a licensed shop (most of which are in the Old City) is mainly concerned with questions of authenticity: Is the pot real? Is it from the Dead Sea Plain in Jordan? Buyers assume that because they are making a purchase in a state-licensed shop, they are required to do nothing further as part of the transaction. Unclear in the process is the need for an export license to take the artifact outside of the country. Due to a poorly worded aspect of the 1978 law, the onus is on the tourist to ask the dealer for the export permit, which lists the items and their registry numbers. In order to receive an export license for a particular object, the dealer contacts the IAA with the registry number of each item being sold, and the IAA issues a license. If the tourist does not ask for the export license, and the dealer does not offer, the artifact leaves the shop, and there is no record of the sale. If there is no request for an export license and no record of the sale, the original registry number can be reused for a similar "buff-colored pot" allowing recently looted material to be laundered and enter the closed system in Israel. In order to close this gap in the 1978 law, the IAA instituted additional licensing guidelines in 2016, which required all licensed dealers to document their entire inventories online. Under this new rule, licensed antiquities dealers have to allocate every single artifact an identification number and associated picture, which will be stored in an electronic database with the IAA. Requiring an image to be attached to individual registry numbers should make it more difficult to launder newly excavated pieces with ambiguous descriptions and fuzzy images.

Back to our object itinerary, the Early Bronze Age pot from Bab adh-Dhra', illegally excavated in 2014, traveled from the Dead Sea Plain to the window of a licensed shop in Israel via a big black car, was issued a "used" registry number, and given a label indicating that it is from the "age of the patriarchs and matriarchs" (Fig. 32.6) and available for purchase. The itinerary of the pot does not end in the storefront. On a steamy August afternoon in 2014, an Australian tourist (Tourist 67) decides they have to have a pot from the "city of sin" (recall that Bab adh-Dhra' has been tentatively identified as biblical Sodom [Albright 1924: 6; Mallon 1924]). For $120 USD, the visitor buys the pot, asks for and receives an IAA export license with a distinct registry number, and then travels back to Melbourne. He is disappointed at both the airports in Israel and Australia that he is not asked to produce the export license allowing him to take the pot out of the country. The

32.6. Early Bronze Age pot from the "age of the patriarchs and matriarchs" in a Jerusalem shop window. (Photo by M. M. Kersel.)

pot now sits on the bookshelf in the home office of the tourist where he looks at it often, reminding him of a "very hot day in the Old City of Jerusalem" (Tourist 67).

Legal Itinerary Segment 6 – Object Death and the Journey's End?

In his consideration of the lives of things, John Robb (2015: 167) attempts to refocus the discussion by asking "what social task are they [things] intended to accomplish, and what characteristics (material and otherwise) enable them to do it?" This chapter expands Robb's thinking by demonstrating the impact that law has in determining the duties of things and in facilitating the carrying out of those duties. An 1874 Ottoman law allowed for unearthed objects to travel beyond the extent of empire in order to fill the coffers of museums. A 1976 Jordanian law encouraged objects to act as ambassadors on behalf of the kingdom by facilitating their transfer to educational institutions across the globe. A loophole in a 1978 Israeli law meant that a stage in the itinerary of an Early Bronze Age pot could be as a looted item legitimately presented for sale in a licensed shop with a reused registry number and available for purchase and export by individuals and institutions alike. A single pot can and does travel far and wide, movement that is facilitated, enhanced, or, at times, impeded by law.

CONCLUSION

An examination of the object biographies and itineraries of Early Bronze Age pots from Jordan allows for the simultaneous consideration of many life-stages or travel segments over a span of millennia. This enables what Joy (2015) refers to as a thicker analysis, turning the life of a thing into a rich narrative rather than a clinical listing of attributes. There is a durability and persistence of objects (Joy 2015) that allows them to move in and out of spaces, imbuing them with particular meanings and functions. Objects lay dormant, disappear, are reused, change contexts – their lives are filled with holes; for many, there is no direct progression from beginning, to middle, to end. While we may be able to argue for greater conformity at creation by the last stage in the life of a thing, there exists the greatest variation (Dannehl 2009). In its final resting place, a single Early Bronze Age pot can be a grave good, an excavated artifact, a looted object, a museum exhibit, an object of study, or a tourist's memento. When they reach their final resting places on bookshelves, in museum vitrines, in shaft tombs next to ancient ancestors, is the journey at an end? There is still room for debate on the notion of itinerant objects and their relationships to durability, stasis, continuity, agency, and law.

NOTE

1 Interviews were conducted after receiving Institutional Review Approval from the Ethics Review Boards at the University of Cambridge (2002–6), the University of Toronto (2007–9), Brown University (2009–10), and DePaul University (2010–present). Interviewees agreed to participate on the condition of anonymity and were each assigned aliases (i.e., Looter 7, Dealer 19, Tourist 95). Any direct citations are in quotes and attributed to that alias.

REFERENCES

Albright, W. F. 1924. The Archaeological Results of an Expedition to Moab and the Dead Sea. *BASOR* 14: 2–12.

Appadurai, A. 1986. Introduction: Commodities and the Politics of Value. In *The Social Life of Things: Commodities in Cultural Perspective*, ed. A. Appadurai, 3–63. Cambridge: Cambridge University Press.

Baker, J. L. 2012. *The Funeral Kit: Mortuary Practices in the Archaeological Record*. London: Routledge.

Ben Zion, I. 2016. Norway Launches Probe after Envoy's Driver Caught Smuggling Artifacts. *The Times of Israel*, June 6. www.timesofisrael.com/norway-launches-probe-after-driver-busted-smuggling-artifacts-from-jordan/ (accessed September 12, 2017).

Bernhardsson, M. T. 2005. *Reclaiming a Plundered Past: Archaeology and Nation Building in Modern Iraq*. Austin: University of Texas Press.

Bisheh, G. 2001. One Damn Illicit Excavation after Another: The Destruction of the Archaeological Heritage of Jordan. In *Trade in Illicit Antiquities: The Destruction of the World's Archaeological Heritage*, ed. N. Brodie, J. Doole, and C. Renfrew, 115–18. MIM. Cambridge: McDonald Institute for Archaeological Research.

Burström, N. M. 2014. Things in the Eye of the Beholder: A Humanistic Perspective on Archaeological Object Biographies. *Norwegian Archaeological Review* 47: 65–82.

Chatterjee, P. 1993. *The Nation and Its Fragments: Colonial and Postcolonial Histories. Princeton Studies in Culture/Power/History*. Princeton: Princeton University Press.

Chesson, M. S. 1999. Libraries of the Dead: Early Bronze Age Charnel Houses and Social Identity at Urban Bab edh-Dhra', Jordan. *JAA* 18: 137–64.

2015. Reconceptualizing the Early Bronze Age Southern Levant without Cities: Local Histories and Walled Communities of EB II–III Society. *JMA* 28: 21–79.

Çelik, Z. 2011. Defining Empire's Patrimony: Late Ottoman Perceptions of Antiquities. In *Scramble for the Past: A Story of Archaeology in the Ottoman Empire, 1753–1914*, ed. Z. Bahrani, Z. Çelik, and E. Eldem, 443–78. Istanbul: SALT.

2016. *About Antiquities: Politics of Archaeology in the Ottoman Empire*. Austin: University of Texas Press.

Corbett, E. D. 2015. *Competitive Archaeology in Jordan: Narrating Identity from the Ottomans to the Hashemites*. Austin: University of Texas Press.

Dannehl, K. 2009. Object Biographies: From Production to Consumption. In *History and Material Culture: A Student's Guide to Approaching Alternative Sources*, ed. K. Harvey, 123–38. Routledge Guides to Using Historical Sources. London: Routledge.

Dobres, M.-A., and Robb, J. E., eds. 2000. *Agency in Archaeology*. London: Routledge.

Donkow, I. 2004. The Ephesus Excavations 1863–1874, in the Light of the Ottoman Legislation on Antiquities. *Anatolian Studies* 54: 109–17.

Efrat, A. 2012. *Governing Guns, Preventing Plunder: International Cooperation against Illicit Trade*. Oxford: Oxford University Press.

Eldem, E. 2011. From Blissful Indifference to Anguished Concern: Ottoman Perceptions of Antiquities, 1799–1869. In *Scramble for the Past: A Story of Archaeology in the Ottoman Empire, 1753–1914*, ed. Z. Bahrani, Z. Çelik, and E. Eldem, 281–330. Istanbul: SALT.

Goode, J. F. 2007. *Negotiating for the Past: Archaeology, Nationalism, and Diplomacy in the Middle East, 1919–1941*. Austin: University of Texas Press.

Gosden, C., and Marshall, Y. 1999. The Cultural Biography of Objects. *WA* 31: 169–78.

Hahn, H. P., and Weiss, H., eds. 2013. *Mobility, Meaning and Transformations of Things: Shifting Contexts of Material Culture through Time and Space*. Oxford: Oxbow.

Holtorf, C. 2002. Notes on the Life History of a Pot Sherd. *Journal of Material Culture* 7: 49–71.

Joy, J. 2009. Reinvigorating Object Biography: Reproducing the Drama of Object Lives. *WA* 41: 540–56.

———. 2015. "Things in Process": Biographies of British Iron Age Pits. In *Biography of Objects: Aspekte eines kulturhistorischen Konzepts*, ed. D. Boschung, P.-A. Kreuz, and T. Kienlin, 125–41. Morphomata 31. Paderborn: Fink.

Joyce, R. A., and Gillespie, S. D. 2015. Making Things Out of Objects That Move. In *Things in Motion: Object Itineraries in Anthropological Practice*, ed. R. A. Joyce and S. D. Gillespie, 3–20. Santa Fe, NM: School for Advanced Research Press.

Joyce, R. A., and Gillespie, S. D., eds. 2015. *Things in Motion: Object Itineraries in Anthropological Practice*. Santa Fe, NM: School for Advanced Research Press.

Keane, W. 2006. Subjects and Objects. In *Handbook of Material Culture*, ed. C. Tilley, W. Keane, S. Küchler, M. Rowlands, and P. Spyer, 197–202. London: Sage.

Kersel, M. M. 2006. From the Ground to the Buyer: A Market Analysis of the Trade in Illegal Antiquities. In *Archaeology, Cultural Heritage, and the Antiquities Trade*, ed. N. Brodie, C. Luke, and K. Walker Tubb, 188–205. Cultural Heritage Studies. Gainesville: University Press of Florida.

———. 2008. The Trade in Palestinian Antiquities. *Jerusalem Quarterly* 33 (winter): 21–38.

———. 2010. The Changing Legal Landscape for Middle Eastern Archaeology in the Colonial Era, 1800–1930. In *Pioneers to the Past: American Archaeologists in the Middle East, 1919–1920*, ed. G. Emberling, 85–90. OIP 30. Chicago: The Oriental Institute.

———. 2015a. Fractured Oversight: The ABCs of Cultural Heritage in Palestine after the Oslo Accords. *JSA* 15: 24–44.

———. 2015b. Storage Wars: Solving the Archaeological Curation Crisis? *JEMAHS* 3: 42–54.

———. 2017. Object Movement: UNESCO, Language, and the Exchange of Middle Eastern Artifacts. In *The Routledge Companion to Cultural Property*, ed. J. Anderson and H. Geismar, 277–94. London: Routledge.

Kersel, M. M., and Chesson, M. S. 2013. Looting Matters: Early Bronze Age Cemeteries of Jordan's Southeast Dead Sea Plain in the Past and Present. In *The Oxford Handbook of the Archaeology of Death and Burial*, ed. S. Tarlow and L. Nilsson Stutz, 677–94. Oxford: Oxford University Press.

Knappett, C. 2013. Imprints as Punctuations of Material Itineraries. In *Mobility, Meaning and Transformations of Things: Shifting Contexts of Material Culture through Time and Space*, ed. H. P. Hahn and H. Weiss, 36–49. Oxford: Oxbow.

Knappett, C., and Malafouris, L., eds. 2008. *Material Agency: Towards a Non-Anthropocentric Approach*. Boston: Springer.

Kopytoff, I. 1986. The Cultural Biography of Things: Commoditization as Process. In *The Social Life of Things: Commodities in Cultural Perspective*, ed. A. Appadurai, 64–91. Cambridge: Cambridge University Press.

Lapp, P. 1966. The Cemetery at Bab edh-Dhra', Jordan. *Archaeology* 19: 104–11.

—— 1968. Bâb edh-Dhrâ', Perizzites and Emim. In *Jerusalem through the Ages: The Twenty-Fifth Archaeological Convention, October 1967*, 1–25. Jerusalem: IES.

Latour, B. 1992. Where Are the Missing Masses? The Sociology of a Few Mundane Artifacts. In *Shaping Technology/Building Society: Studies in Sociotechnical Change*, ed. W. E. Bijker and J. Law, 225–58. Inside Technology. Cambridge, MA: MIT Press.

Maeir, A. M.; Davis, B.; Horwitz, L. K.; Asscher, Y.; and Hitchcock, L. A. 2015. An Ivory Bowl from Early Iron Age Tell es-Safi/Gath (Israel): Manufacture, Meaning and Memory. *WA* 47: 414–38.

Mallon, A. 1924. Voyage d'exploration au sud-est de la Mer Morte. *Biblica* 5: 413–55.

Mark, V. 1994. Objects and Their Maker: Bricolage of the Self. In *The Socialness of Things: Essays on the Socio-Semiotics of Objects*, ed. S. H. Riggins, 63–100. Approaches to Semiotics 115. Berlin: De Gruyter.

Mitcham, C. 2013. Agency in Humans and in Artifacts: A Contested Discourse. In *The Moral Status of Technical Artefacts*, ed. P. Kroes and P.-P. Verbeek, 11–29. Philosophy of Engineering and Technology 17. Dordrecht: Springer.

Naím, M. 2005. *Illicit: How Smugglers, Traffickers, and Copycats Are Hijacking the Global Economy*. New York: Doubleday.

Özel, S. 2010. Under the Turkish Blanket Legislation: The Recovery of Cultural Property Removed from Turkey. *International Journal of Legal Information* 38: 177–84.

Riggins, S. H. 1994. Introduction. In *The Socialness of Things: Essays on the Socio-Semiotics of Objects*, ed. S. H. Riggins, 1–6. Approaches to Semiotics 115. Berlin: De Gruyter.

Robb, J. 2015. What Do Things Want? Object Design as a Middle Range Theory of Material Culture. *APAAA* 26: 166–80.

Saller, S. 1964–1965. Bab edh-Dhra'. *LibAnn* 15: 137–219.

Schaub, R. T., and Rast, W. 1989. *Bab edh-Dhrā' Excavations in the Cemetery Directed by Paul W. Lapp (1965–67)*. REDSPJ 1. Winona Lake, IN: Published for ASOR by Eisenbrauns.

Shaw, W. M. K. 2003. *Possessors and Possessed: Museums, Archaeology, and the Visualization of History in the Late Ottoman Empire*. Berkeley: University of California Press.

Silberman, N. A. 1998. Power, Politics and the Past: The Social Construction of Antiquity in the Holy Land. In *The Archaeology of Society in the Holy Land*, ed. T. E. Levy, 9–23. NAAA. London: Leicester University Press.

Taha, H. 2010. The Current State of Archaeology in Palestine. *Present Pasts* 21: 16–25.

Thomas, J. 1996. *Time, Culture and Identity: An Interpretive Archaeology*. Material Cultures. London: Routledge.

Weiner, A. B. 1994. Cultural Difference and the Density of Objects. *American Ethnologist* 21: 391–403.

Winner, L. 1980. Do Artifacts Have Politics? *Dædalus* 109 (1): 121–36.

THIRTY THREE

ARCHAEOLOGY, MUSEUMS, AND THE PUBLIC IN JORDAN

100 Years of Education

ARWA BADRAN

> *The chief mosaic, a most interesting map of Palestine and Jordan now preserved in the Greek Orthodox church ... There are several other mosaic [sic] in the town, all now in private houses, but arrangements have been made with the owners that visitors may inspect them if they wish.* (Harding 1967: 74)

G. Lankester Harding provides a glimpse into museological practices of the early twentieth century in Jordan. Cultural material held in private hands was, in many cases, archaeological remains found *in situ* under people's houses. Anyone can access these private collections with prior arrangement. Over the decades, however, private collections gradually moved into state ownership, particularly following the introduction of the Antiquities Law in the 1920s and the emergence of public museums in the 1950s. Developments in public access to material culture in Jordan were very different from those occurring in Western cultures. Going back just a few centuries, private collecting would have been strictly limited to the elite in Europe during the Renaissance, showing off their exotic collections to their close friends and family. Private collecting and access to these collections continued to be confined to the "privileged" until the emergence of public museums in the late seventeenth century. It was not until the last forty years that public accessibility received wider attention, becoming one of the most discussed topics in mainstream, relevant "Western" discourse. Archaeologists and museum professionals in Jordan are now beginning to rethink their approach toward public education.

This chapter examines the intersection of three disciplines, archaeology, education, and museums, within the Jordanian context over the past 100 years. Its synthesis is structured around the interplay of international and regional mainstream theories of archaeology, education, and museums. This intersection reveals an interesting insight into "local vs. international" in the production and shaping of museums and the use of archaeology for public education.

TEACHING WITH ARCHAEOLOGY, ENGAGING WITH INTERPRETATIONS

Approaches to investigating the past have varied since the emergence of modern archaeology in the nineteenth century, which is associated with the development of a systematic study of "prehistory" that differed from the antiquarianism of earlier times (Trigger 1989: 73). Prehistoric archaeology studied the history of humankind as evolutionary within which material evidence was studied and organized to describe prehistoric groups of people and define their cultures, an approach defined today as "culture history" (Greene 2002: 239). V. Gordon Childe, an influential scholar during the first half of the twentieth century, was not satisfied with merely describing cultures and went beyond culture description to tracing their origin (Renfrew and Bahn 2004: 37). He believed that characteristics of civilization were diffused into Europe from the Near East by the migration of people or trade (Renfrew and Bahn 2004: 37). This diffusionist approach was already common among archaeologists during the nineteenth century. However, Childe was different from his contemporary thinkers, as he (1957: 242–3) believed that indigenous developments took place in Europe (Renfrew and Bahn 2004: 37).

In the 1930s, interpretations using culture history were beginning to be challenged. Archaeology was starting to investigate the development of past communities from biological, ecological, political, and social point of views rather than investigating development through diffusion (Greene 2002: 243; Renfrew and Bahn 2004: 37). Archaeological work was influenced significantly by an ecological approach developed by Grahame Clark, who in the 1950s broke away from the culture history approach centered around artifacts and argued that many aspects of past human life can be understood through investigating human adaptation to the environment (Renfrew and Bahn 2004: 37). Parallel to the development of the ecological approach, scientific methods were also beginning to have a significant impact on archaeological investigation (Renfrew and Bahn 2004: 40). By the 1960s, a different approach to the interpretation of the past, known as "new archaeology," was fully developed as a reaction against the descriptive diffusionist approach of culture history (Shanks and Hodder 1995: 3).

New archaeologists, led by Lewis Binford, critiqued the aim of "traditional" archaeology to describe the origins and history of cultures, advocating instead that archaeology should explain and reconstruct communities' ways of living in the past (see Binford 1972: 78–100). New archaeology was considered an anthropological science that is interested in social reconstruction of the past with methods "modelled on the hard sciences" (Shanks and Hodder 1995: 3). In fact, new archaeology was perceived to have great potential to acquire positive knowledge about the past by using scientific methods, controlled observation, testing hypotheses, and forming logical arguments disconnected from the archaeologist's "subjectivity" in interpreting material evidence (Shanks and Hodder 1995: 4).

In the late 1970s, archaeologists influenced by structuralist schools of thought began suggesting that material culture could be regarded as a form of expression governed by hidden rules that generate cultural forms. They believed that culture could be explained by uncovering these rules (Johnson 1999: 91). These views, which were underpinned by a post-processual approach to interpretation, began challenging the scientific positivist outlook of "new archaeology" regarding the interpretation of the past (Shanks and Tilley 1987: 5; Johnson 1999: 98). They expressed doubts about the ability of "new archaeology" to investigate the beliefs and values of past communities.

By the mid 1980s, many voices within the archaeological community began questioning the "objectivity" of their discipline. In fact, long discussions about archaeology and "objectivity" in interpretation took place over four and a half days during the World Archaeological Congress, which was held in 1986 in Southampton, England. This was the first event of its kind in terms of the academic and nonacademic participation from different parts of the world (850 from 70 countries) and the focus drawn on subjectivity in interpretation and how the evidence of the past have been used and viewed by certain groups at different times (Ucko 1990: 10).

Post-processualists abandoned the aim of achieving "objectivity" in interpretation and began advocating for multiple interpretations (Renfrew and Bahn 2004: 49). Post-processualists argued, as part of the postmodern movement that encouraged variations of methods, that if there is no single truth out there to be discovered, then there is no single correct way of doing archaeology (Johnson 1999: 166–7; Renfrew and Bahn 2004: 49). Their views, which were identified as "relativism," argued that recognizing multiple interpretations would be challenging to single dominant interpretations used for political ends (Trigger 1995: 263). Relativism was heavily criticized in its "extreme" or "unrestrained" form that regarded all interpretations to be equally valid (Trigger 1995: 264; Johnson 1999: 172; Renfrew and Bahn 2004: 49). It was argued, however, that archaeologists should recognize some interpretations as being more valid than others. If interpretations cannot be either verifiable or detached from politics, archaeology is left for political manipulation instead of being a voice against politically undesired views of the past (Hodder 1991: 179; Johnson 1999: 170).

Along with the developments discussed above, many archaeologists have become increasingly aware of their responsibility toward providing the public with access to multiple interpretations of the past. There are many examples of approaches and programs that have been developed to increase public understanding of the interpretation of the past, whether it is through museums, archaeological sites, heritage centers, publications, the internet, awareness campaigns, and outreach (e.g., Stone and Molyneaux 1994; Jameson 1997; Beavis and Hunt 1999; Smardz and Smith 2000; Henson, Stone, and Corbishley 2004).

The relationship between archaeology and education was examined explicitly in 1986 during the World Archaeological Congress. The years to follow witnessed an increasing recognition among archaeologists for the potential of archaeology as an educational tool to enhance children's understanding of the past. As Peter Stone remarked:

> More recently, as archaeologists have seen their subjects used – and abused – for political and social advantage ..., many of them have accepted a wider role for archaeology. This wider role is also based on the acceptance that archaeology has an educational role, in that it is a subject that requires students to work critically and carefully, without accepting any single "true" version of the past. (1994: 17)

The potential of archaeology to teach pupils about cultural diversity, tolerance, and the commonality of humans and their values, which was in fact highlighted by Clark (1943) more than half a century ago, continues to be an important element of archaeological education today (e.g., Moe 2000; Pyburn 2000; Hodder and Doughty 2007). Furthermore, it has been indicated that archaeology has great potential to capture pupils' interest and engage them in an inquiry-based learning process, concerned with the interpretation of the past.

Archaeological discourse that occurred in the "West" during the twentieth century seemed to have been absent within the Jordanian context, if not in the Arab region as a whole. This is despite the fact that the benefits of using archaeology in formal education have been recognized early among Arab intellectuals. Yoram Meital (2006) examined the construction of national histories in Egypt during the first half of the twentieth-century and highlighted the role of Taha Husayn, an influential Egyptian scholar of that time, in criticizing the interpretation of the past in formal education that supported the legitimacy of the monarchy. By examining several of Husayn's works, specifically *The Future of Culture in Egypt* (1938), Meital (2006: 258) indicated Husayn's belief in the importance of recognizing ancient archaeological resources that have shaped Egyptian life, acknowledging their significant potential in defining the cultural and national identity of the present people of Egypt. Similarly, Iraqi scholars during the first half of the twentieth century resisted the single-state interpretation of the past in the education system. They advocated for an interpretation of a past in formal education that celebrates the diversity of the population of Iraq instead of state nationalistic narratives (Bashkin 2006). The importance of students' interpretations in challenging the curriculum interpreting the past was highlighted. Orit Bashkin (2006: 362) provided a valuable analysis of the writing of the Iraqi novelist Dhu al-Nun Ayyub, who suggested that students' exposure to resources about the past outside the classroom can lead to independent inquiry because it is more imaginative and interesting compared to the state version of the past.

Current debate in the Arab world regarding the potential of archaeology as a tool in formal education is generally lacking, although there are a handful of interesting studies worth mentioning. Researchers from Jordan, Egypt, and Libya argued that pupils' thinking and understanding of the past would be enhanced if it occurred through archaeological resources as opposed to memorizing the "facts" in traditional classroom education (Sarkaz 1977; al-Burai 1984; Abu Amma 1988; Malas 1997; al-Qaoud 2003). They indicated that learning through archaeological material can enhance pupils understanding of the past, foster their belonging to humanity, capture their interest, and engage them in an inquiry-based education (gathering information, reasoning, synthesizing) that develops their creative and critical thinking. Some of these researchers tested whether learning through the use of archaeological resources (sites and museums) would enhance pupils understanding and creative thinking in comparison to traditional classroom teaching (blackboard and textbooks) (e.g., Sarkaz 1977; al-Burai 1984; Abu Amma 1988; al-Qaoud 2003). Despite these valuable studies, the benefits of archaeology are hardly considered in education systems in the Arab region, where the single-state version of the past is much preferred by undemocratic political systems. In the case of Jordan, the past in the education system serves certain political agendas, focusing heavily on the Islamic period and the recent history of the country related to the Royal Hashemite family (see Badran 2011). The contribution of humanity to the present is almost completely ignored. In fact, prehistory is introduced to children for the first time in year 7 (age 12). Nowhere in the national curriculum are children exposed to the use of archaeology in interpreting the past. If anything, school textbooks and classroom teaching focus heavily on the benefits of archaeology as a source of income within the tourism industry (see Badran 2014).

MUSEUM AS LEARNING RESOURCES

Museums have acted as repositories of knowledge since their emergence. They have been commonly traced back to the third-century BC Greek *Mouseion* of

Alexandria, highlighting its purpose as a temple of the Muses as well as a philosophical institution (Burcaw 1983: 25–6; Abt 2011: 115). Displays for public knowledge during the past two millennia have been equally noted. Jeffrey Abt (2011), for example, referred to the display of statues and paintings of the powerful and the wealthy in public spaces during the Roman period and the displays of curiosities in the private houses and palaces of elite traders and collectors during the Renaissance. While these displays served the interest of certain individuals, the public had limited access and ownership of collections (Abt 2011: 117–22).

The late seventeenth century witnessed the establishment of many public museums (Pearce 1990: 15). Objects that were held for a long time in private residences were making their way to public display in museums. Nonetheless, museum collections never came into public ownership (Cameron 2004: 65). In addition, public access was still restricted in terms of the length of visitation, the number of visitors allowed at a time, and the process of obtaining tickets (Merriman 1991: 85; Abt 2011: 125–6). In the past 200 years, however, museums have undergone a significant shift in emphasis on public access, ownership, and education in a move away from the royal and elitist circles (Hooper-Greenhill 1991: 9; Merriman 1991: 1; Bennett 1995: 25–32; Cameron 2004).

Despite these advances, there were still some restrictions in terms of public access to collections and knowledge in museums (cf. Dana 2004). Shortly after World War II, museum professionalism and research increased, followed by a rigorous examination and revision of museums' practices toward enhancing public access to educational opportunities in museums (Roberts 1997: 5; Anderson 2004: 1). It was not until the 1970s, however, that debates grew significantly among museum commentators over the philosophy underlying the role of museums, and whether museums had actually detached from their history as elite institutions controlled by the dominant groups of society. Many began challenging the control museums had over the production of knowledge. It was argued that there is no universal truth or "objective" knowledge because knowledge is socially constructed and shaped by the values and interests of individuals (Weil 1990: 76–7; Roberts 1997: 2).

This shift in museum paradigm from being institutions of scholarship and authority to becoming public forums and multivocal was also accompanied by a deconstruction of the notion that knowledge is transmitted to passive, receiving museum users. Museum viewpoints on the public consumption of knowledge have been influenced by developments in education theory. Since the Enlightenment and until the early twentieth century, Western intellect was based on the organization of knowledge in a rational way (i.e., creating a network of subjects or disciplines with working relationships) independent from the learner (Hein 1996: 30). Learners were expected to absorb this knowledge, whereby their different levels of understanding were the only aspect taken into consideration (Hein 1996: 30). In education theory, this view on learning was referred to as "behaviorism." Museums followed the behaviorist model in their approach toward public education in theory and practice. The behaviorist model was considered in the thinking behind designing exhibitions with a "holding power" over visitors, while learning differences and the physical and social milieu within which learning occurs were largely ignored (Falk and Dierking 1992).

The twentieth century witnessed a significant shift in education theory away from the behaviorist model (Hein and Alexander 1998: 33–7). Education was gradually being acknowledged as learner-centered rather than subject-centered. It was argued that learning is not strictly an outcome of learned information. Rather, it is a process of constructing an understanding that occurs as individuals interact with the physical and social environment. This process occurs over a long period of time and is influenced by the different backgrounds, motivations, and learning needs of individuals. This view on learning, which was expressed by well-respected education theorists, such as John Dewey (1959), Jean Piaget (Helmore 1969), and L. S. Vygotsky (1978), underpinned constructivist theory (Hein 1996: 30–2). From a constructivist standpoint, knowledge was not an independent set of facts, rather ideas and meanings constructed by the learners (Hein 1996: 30–2). Museum researchers reflected on the use of constructivist theory within the museum context with references to Piaget's work (Helmore 1969) on child developmental psychology and how they construct their own understanding by interacting with the physical environment (Jensen 1994). Piaget's work has helped museums to better understand that children bring different experiences and conceptions with them to the museum, influencing what they learn (Helmore 1969). Equally, it helped museums to appreciate the importance of providing an environment that encourages active and hands-on learning.

Only Dewey's ideas relating to independent thinking of children have been considered to some extent in the education systems of the Arab world (see Rashdan and Hamshary 2003). Some debates in regards to learner-centered education had, however, occurred independently among Syrian and Iraqi intellectuals. Child-centered education was advocated by Sati al-Husri, Ali al-Tantawi, and Mahmud Ahmad al-Sayyid in the interwar period (1918–1939). They recognized that pupils construct their own understanding and emphasized the importance of allowing students' interpretations rather than only their teachers (Bashkin 2006: 354–5). It is also worth noting that significant research into education theory that supported deduction and reasoning instead of memorization in the Arab region can be traced to almost 1,000 years ago in medieval Islamic theory. Sebastian Günther (2006) provided an excellent review of some of the most famous medieval Islamic scholars who theorized about children's education. He refers to Abu 'Ali al-Husayn ibn Sina (known as Avicenna), for example, a leading philosopher and scientist who was influenced by Greek philosophy (mainly Aristotle) and the Qur'an (Günther 2006: 376). Ibn Sina believed that learning begins with the five senses: sight, hearing, touch, smell, and taste; that humans have a practical intellect that guides actions and a theoretical intellect that guides reasoning and thinking processes (Günther 2006: 377). Ibn Sina divided the theoretical intellects into four stages: the potential of acquiring knowledge, the ability to utilize knowledge to think, the ability to develop an intellectual activity to understand more complex ideas, and, finally, the ability to acquire this knowledge (Günther 2006: 377). Günther asserts that Ibn Sina's ideas are relevant to active learning, particularly to child learning that results from sensory experiences, which help "to stimulate children to identify, compare, and classify items as they explore the world around them" (2007: 377). Ibn Sina had, in fact, taken interest in child education and proposed that the emotional, physical, and intellectual development of children affects their learning (Günther 2006: 378). Effective education, Ibn Sina believed, relies on a method of teaching that is enjoyable and suits a child's level of intellect (Günther 2006: 378). This learner-centered approach toward education recommended by Ibn Sina was supported by other influential medieval Islamic thinkers, such as Abu Nasr al-Farabi and Abu Uthman al-Jahiz, who believed in the importance of reasoning (rather than memorization) in education and encouraged activities in the learning process guided by teachers (Günther 2006).

The development of museum practice in the Arab world failed to engage with local progressive thinking that advocated for child-centered education and public access to multiple interpretations, instead it held onto the concept of the "museum" as seen in the practices of collecting and preservation that seem to have been dominant in the region for a long time. Geoffrey Lewis (1984) traced museum practices of collecting and preservation in the Middle East back to the third-millennium BC Ebla archives, the sixth-century BC Nebuchadnezzar and Nabonidus collections of antiquities and restoration in their city, and even to the Islamic preservation of cultural property in the idea of al-Waqf. Nonetheless, the emergence of museums as public institutions did not materialize until mid-nineteenth century, with the establishment of the Museum of Egyptian Antiquities in Cairo by French Egyptologist Auguste Mariette. Following in the footsteps of Egypt, many other countries in the Arab region had their museums established during the colonial period. Bassey Andah (1997) explains that the colonial museum, like most European museums of that time, was more of a storehouse in which displays were deprived of their true essence in an inanimate setting. Museums have maintained that state of existence despite political independence – lack of relation with the native environment, located in the same place, managed the same way, and touching upon the interest of foreigners (Andah 1997).

JORDAN: ARCHAEOLOGY, MUSEUMS, AND PUBLIC EDUCATION

Andah's (1997) description of "the colonial museum" can be seen within the Jordanain context. After almost 70 years of independence, Jordanian archaeological museums are unable to break away from the "storage room" approach to displaying collections in the service of tourism rather than the local public. At the same time, the local museum practice seems distant from both the Arab progressive thinking on learning from the past, as well as the "Western" discourse on museum learning. This section provides an insight into the nature of public eduation provision within the heritage sector and its museums in Jordan.

Systematic uncovering and preservation of archaeological heritage emerged in Jordan with the founding of the Department of Antiquities after World War I. In the 1950s, the Bureau of Tourism was established and joined the Department of Antiquities a decade later to form the Ministry of Tourism and Antiquities.[1] This merger sought to facilitate the use of archaeology as a resource within tourism, contributing currently alongside a few other sources to the country's GDP (currently ca. 12–14 percent). The Department of Antiquities, however, acts as a separate body from the Ministry of Tourism and is designated by law as the sole official authority responsible for the excavation, discovery, survey, presentation, preservation, protection, and administration of the antiquities of Jordan (Department of Antiquities 2004: article 3:6). Under the supervision of the Department of Antiquities, local and foreign archaeologists are also involved in promoting and preserving the archaeology of Jordan through excavation, preservation, interpretation, and the management of sites. Archaeologists either work in the public sector under the Department of Antiquities or in the private sector with foreign teams that come to excavate in Jordan. Among the many foreign archaeological teams that excavate in Jordan, seven have permanent headquarters, such as ACOR, IFPO, and CBRL. Excavation, restoration, and site management activities are also undertaken by five state universities in Jordan that offer graduate and/or postgraduate degrees in archaeology as part of their research work and training of students.

Public awareness is briefly mentioned as part of the Department of Antiquities' responsibilities, in comparison to the elaborate list of tasks related to safeguarding antiquities (Department of Antiquities 2004: article 3a:7). The Department of Antiquities established the Archaeological Awareness Division in the early 1990s. Their work is mainly giving lectures at schools about the archaeology of Jordan and the importance of its preservation. Since 1998, the Department of Antiquities has published an annual magazine *Athar (Antiquity)* for the public that contains general topics about sites and excavations. The availability of *Athar* to the public is limited; a few thousand copies are printed annually. It is not available in shops, rather distributed free of charge to local authorities and libraries. The Ministry of Education receives 100 copies for its over 5,600 schools in Jordan. Generally speaking, *Athar* includes reports written by archaeologists for archaeologists, providing descriptive information on archaeological sites and findings using specialist language. For example, a short article in this magazine about excavation methods targeted to children reads:

> One of the most important forms to fill for recording the excavation is a paper for describing a phenomenon (Locus Sheet) [*sic*] ... the site is divided into four squares referring to a central point (Grid Point) [*sic*]. Each square is given a name according to its direction ... for example (Area N-E. squ 8/30) [*sic*] ... Squares are usually 25m² in size leaving space of one metre wide along two of the square sides, which is decided by the excavation supervisor. Hence, the size of this dirt partition (Balk) [*sic*] is 9m², equals 36% of the total square. (Tweiq 2002: 42)

There is a general absence of regular public programs provided on archaeological sites. Public engagement in archaeology is most commonly articulated in festivals for music, dance, and arts, such as the Jordan Festival (formerly, the Jerash Festival). There are tourist-targeted events as well, such as Petra by night and the Roman Army and Chariot Experience. The latter is organized privately on the hippodrome in the ancient city of Jerash and features the performance of Roman warfare techniques and a chariot race.[2] Presented in English and costing three times more than the entrance fee to the site itself, the show is a business opportunity run for tourists' pleasure. In 2010, local authorities were more than happy to "lend" the 2,000-year-old hippodrome to BBC's production team of the famous car program *Top Gear* to use its grounds as a race track for the sake of promoting Jordanian heritage to tourists abroad.

The management of archaeological sites by local authorities and stakeholders has always adopted a top-down approach to decision making and implementation for the satisfaction of tourists (Abu-Khafajah, al-Rabady, and Rababeh 2015). As a result, local communities have been alienated, perceived more or less as a passive population living in the vicinity of these sites (cf. Abu-Khafajah 2007). They are even seen as a threat to heritage rather than allies in its protection. Fences and guards have long become a common sight at archaeological sites to ensure no one comes near but those "trustworthy" government officials or interested tourists (Corbett and Ronza in press). These local practices are the legacy of earlier colonial attitudes. Bert de Vries (2013) traces the beginnings of community marginalization back to early archaeological exploration in Jordan and Greater Syria. He explains how "a disconnection between the people of past cultures and the people living on the land" was presupposed, admiring the ancients' achievements in monuments and literature while seeing the inhabitants as "the ignorant mismanagers of the decaying remnants of the glorious past" (Vries 2013: 132).

Most archaeological excavations still use local communities as cheap labor for digging and removing rubble. A few promising community-based projects emerged over the last decade as a response to these attitudes. The Temple of Winged Lions Cultural Resource Management Project, initiated by ACOR in 2009, for instance, follows a strategy of engaging local community as primary stakeholders in the management of the site and its preservation through employment and training (Corbett and Ronza in press). Another successful initiative is the Umm el-Jimal project, which uses views of the local community to inform future strategy, ensuring their participation in site preservation and maintenance. Some of the project outcomes were a virtual museum, an educational kit, and a cooperative society to implement a sustainable site management program (Vries 2013).

There is more attention given to public awareness and school education in Jordan by the non-governmental sector concerned with archaeology. The Associated School Project, founded by UNESCO in 1953, for example, has been implemented in Jordan with over 100 school members aiming to raise pupils' awareness on several issues, including world heritage. UNESCO has also initiated the Engaging Young People in Their National Tangible and Intangible Heritage in Jordan Project, which resulted in producing *I am Jerash*, an educational kit to compliment the national curriculum (see Badran 2013). UNESCO worked with the Friends of Archaeology and Heritage society, a local voluntary non-profit, non-governmental body established in the 1960s, on the production of the kit. The society aims to protect archaeological heritage and increase public awareness with a regular program of fieldtrips to heritage sites and museums, public lectures, heritage events, and awareness campaigns.[3] In the past, the Friends of Archaeology and Heritage managed the Museums with No Frontiers Project, which provided online educational tools for children.[4] The Friends of Archaeology and Heritage provides a small education service to interested schools, one of which is Al-Ahliyah School for Girls, which has the first and only archaeology club in Jordan, aiming to engage pupils in a process of investigation and learning about the past.

Archaeological museums have also taken an active role to increase public awareness of their past and heritage. There are eighteen archaeological museums, over half of which fall under the responsibility of the Department of Antiquities (Table 33.1). They are "the department extension that appears to the public."[5] The rest are either university museums dedicated mainly to research and teaching purposes or bank museums with limited public access due to security reasons. It was during and shortly after the British Mandate period (1918–1946) that archaeological museums in Jordan became the public institutions we know today. These developments marked the beginning of state ownership of the antiquities of Jordan, taking over from private collectors. The first archaeological display was set up in the Greek-Roman city of Jerash at the end of the 1920s by foreign

TABLE 33.1. *List of 18 archaeological museums in Jordan.*

	Museum	Administration
1	Umm Qais Museum	Public (Department of Antiquities)
2	Dar al-Saraya Museum	Public (Department of Antiquities)
3	Ajlun Archaeological Museum	Public (Department of Antiquities)
4	Salt Archaeological Museum	Public (Department of Antiquities)
5	Jerash Archaeological Museum	Public (Department of Antiquities)
6	Mafraq Archaeological Museum	Public (Department of Antiquities)
7	Jordan Archaeological Museum	Public (Department of Antiquities)
8	Madaba Archaeological Museum	Public (Department of Antiquities)
9	Karak Archaeological Museum	Public (Department of Antiquities)
10	Petra Archaeological Museum	Public (Department of Antiquities)
11	Aqaba Archaeological Museum	Public (Department of Antiquities)
12	The Lowest Point on the Earth Museum	Public (Department of Antiquities)
13	The Jordan Museum	Semipublic (Department of Antiquities & Board of Directors)
14	Ahli Bank Numismatics Museum	Private (Ahli Bank)
15	Central Bank Numismatics Museum	Private (Central Bank)
16	Yarmouk University Museum of Jordanian Heritage	University (Yarmouk University)
17	Mu'tah University Archaeological Museum	University (Mu'tah University)
18	University of Jordan Archaeological Museum	University (University of Jordan)

archaeologists excavating the site.[6] It was not until 1951 that the Jordan Archaeological Museum was founded by Harding, the British head of the Department of Antiquities at that time. The museum was the first public purpose-built museum and was also used as the Department of Antiquities headquarters (Harding 1967). It also represented the country's first national museum as a crucial symbol of an independent nationhood, a decolonization movement that has swept many newly independent nations around the world (Boylan 1990).

The museum today, with its 1950s showcases and floor, encompass a juxtaposition of an outdated museum and, yet, a truly unique masterpiece of its own time (Figs. 33.1 and 33.2). Since 1951 up to the present, twelve more archaeological museums opened their doors to the public. Local endeavors have played a significant role in the process out of true concern for the nation's archaeological heritage.[7] Lewis explains, "there is no evidence of Government policy to establish museums in the colonies [by Britain]; rather it was left for those in the colonies to take initiatives" (1984: 13). A lot of these museums echoed the purpose of the Department of Antiquities and its first official

33.1. The first display of Neolithic statues from 'Ain Ghazal, the oldest of their kind in the Near East, at the Archaeological Museum of Jordan. (Currently on display in the Jordan Museum.) (Photo by K. Barrow.)

archaeological museum – housing and protecting archaeological objects uncovered during excavations (Harding 1967; Curator D 2005).[8] These attitudes, which are imbedded in the colonial legacy, meant that the scope of their educational provision revolves around the idea of opening their doors to the public and placing their collections on display.

The one educational service that these museums rely heavily on is guided tours (see Badran 2012). They are usually the same in terms of structure and scope – it follows the content of the display. The Jordan Archaeological Museum's guided tours, for example, introduce pupils to the museum's chronological display, development in human life, the tools made, settlements,

33.2. Inside the Archaeological Museum of Jordan, the first purpose-built museum in the country. (Photo by K. Barrow.)

and husbandry. In the case of site museums, such as the Ajloun Archaeological Museum and Umm Qais Museum, guided tours are also used to introduce the history of the site to visitors. Apart from guided tours, less than half of the museums carry out lectures at schools. Their visits rely on the availability of staff and school requests rather than an organized schedule. Museum objects are not used for these lectures out of concern for their safety.

A handful of museums provide educational programs on an ad hoc basis beyond guided tours and school lectures. In 2007, the Jerash Archaeological Museum organized activities related to the Romans, such as making bread the Roman way using a replica oven and learning about Roman armor. Archaeological excavations were co-organized with a French archaeological team (IFPO), where pupils were introduced to the basics of excavating, such as how sites are selected, dividing the site into squares, stratigraphy, handling and packaging objects, and recording and drawing. In 2012, the Jerash Archaeological Museum took part in the UNESCO project, Engaging Young People in Their Tangible and Intangible Heritage and participated in piloting the *I am Jerash* educational kit. This involved engaging students in activities related to the museum collection, mainly drawing and describing pottery theater tickets and learning how to put on a Roman toga (Figs. 33.3 and 33.4). Another creative educational program was implemented in 2011 by the Kerak Archaeological Museum, which involved school children in a drawing competition of Kerak Castle. The drawings were exhibited in the

ARCHAEOLOGY, MUSEUMS, AND THE PUBLIC IN JORDAN

33.3. Students observing and discussing images on pottery theater tickets with their teacher at the Jerash Archaeological Museum in 2012. (© UNESCO)

33.4. Students trying on Roman togas with the help of their teacher at the Jerash Archaeological Museum in 2012. (© UNESCO)

museum, voting for the best to win free entrance to the castle and museum for a year. The drawings were then made into a calendar. Dar al-Saraya in Irbid is another influential museum that used to offer its central courtyard for school events, such as graduation, theater, annual festivals, modern art exhibitions, and drama, as well as celebrations on national occasions where lectures were given, arts and crafts were sold, and music was played. The above examples demonstrate the potential use of archaeological museums in Jordan for public learning. Unfortunately, these kind of activities are irregular and rely on individual efforts rather than an institutional policy.

One of the most recent archaeological museums to open to the public is the Jordan Museum. Less than 10 years old, the museum has so far managed to maintain the regularity of its educational programs, perhaps as it is the only archaeological museum that has educational policies and two education officers dedicated to such a task. The museum organizes regular lectures, exhibitions, and festivals that involve the display of arts and crafts, film shows, and traditional dances and drama. The museum has also been involved in large-scale projects. As part of the fourth EuroMed Heritage Programme, a project entitled "Solid Basis for the Future: Young People from Jordan and Lebanon Contribute to the Strengthening of Their Cultural Heritage" was launched. It aims to build knowledge and to strengthen young people's sense of belonging to heritage. In Jordan, the project involved training on various aspects of the documentation techniques for Jordanian tangible and intangible heritage. In addition, the museum hosted a UNESCO three-day workshop on risk planning for the whole local museum sector, which involved a simulation of a building fire and leading an organized operation to salvage objects from the museum's storage.

It is worth noting that the provision of education by archaeological museums in Jordan has been investigated and critiqued by a number of local and foreign museum commentators (see Tawfiq 1994; Badran 2001; 2010; 2012; al-Qaoud 2003; Malt 2005; al-Deek 2007; al-Shayyab and al-Muheisen 2008; and Kreishan 2011). It was suggested that if museums are to become effective in their educational mission, the following recommendations need to be considered by the sector: comprehensive planning, implementation, and evaluation of regular and variable educational program, the provision of educational material and learning spaces, the availability of specialized educators and the financial resources necessary to achieve quality educational provision to the various types of visitors, structured communication between the heritage and education sectors for building school–museum partnerships to facilitate learning and compliment the national curriculum, and most importantly, a vision, strategy, and network to support and guide the museum sector toward achieving quality in the provision of education.

WHAT WILL TOMORROW BRING?

Today's "Western" approach to museums and archaeological education is a culmination of engagement in scholarly debate and a reflection on the practice over several decades, an issue that has received less attention in the Arab region. Perhaps with the long periods of colonial rule, accompanied by political upheavals, local intellectual thinking and engagement in heritage discourse could not thrive. Colonialism, however, has most certainly left a legacy that defined past and current approaches to the provision of public archaeological education in the heritage sectors of the Arab region.

Recently, a change of attitude is noticeable in the Arab region, not least within the Jordanian context. There is increased interest in research on public engagement, archaeological education, and the use of museums as learning resources. There is an increase in public education initiatives, led by a workforce of foreign professionals working in the local heritage sector and Jordanian experts who recently obtained higher degrees from European and North American universities in the field of heritage and museums. This workforce of heritage experts is beginning to test new ideas and influence local attitudes. Jordanian experts, in particular, are beginning to actively engage in the global debate around heritage and the public through attending conferences, publishing, collaboration, and utilizing the internet to access relevant and the most up-to-date information.

After 100 years of excavation, recovery, and preservation, attitudes in Jordan are shifting toward heritage management with the public in mind. There is an ever-growing base of a new kind of professionalism, fed by several programs in heritage management and museum studies established at local universities. One cannot help to wonder, what trajectory will local museum practice take in the future? Will it be any different from the current "Western" model? If so, can it develop as an indigenous "good practice" in its own right – liberating local museum thinking and contributing to a multi-vocal international museum discourse?

NOTES

1 For more information, see www.tourism.jo/inside/AboutUs.asp?p=1.
2 For more information, go to www.jerashchariots.com/.
3 For more information, go to www.foah-jordan.org/.
4 For more information, go to www.discoverislamicart.org/learn/.
5 Interview with Dr. Fawwaz Khreisha, the head of the Department of Antiquities, June 2004.
6 Interview with the Mrs. Ayda Naghawy, the curator of the Archaeological Museum of Jordan, June 2004. They were the British School of Archaeology in Jerusalem and Yale University, headed by Carl H. Kraeling.

7 Interview with Mrs. Eman Oweis, the curator of the Jerash Archaeological Museum, June 2004.
8 Anonymity maintained as requested by the interviewee.

REFERENCES

Abt, J. 2011. The Origins of the Public Museum. In *A Companion to Museum Studies*, ed. S. Macdonald, 115–33. Blackwell Companions in Cultural Studies 12. Chichester: Wiley-Blackwell.

Abu Amma, F. 1988. *The Impact of Museums on the Achievement and Attitudes of Pupils Regarding Social Studies at Year Six of Elementary Education*. MA thesis, Ain Shams University, Cairo [Arabic].

Abu-Khafajah, S. 2007. *Meaning and Use of Cultural Heritage in Jordan: Towards a Sustainable Approach*. PhD diss., Newcastle University.

Abu-Khafajah, S.; al-Rabady, R.; and Rababeh, S. 2015. Urban Heritage "Space" under Neoliberal Development: A Tale of a Jordanian Plaza. *International Journal of Heritage Studies* 21: 441–59.

Andah, B. W. 1997. The Ibadan Experience to Date. In *Museums & Archaeology in West Africa*, ed. C. D. Ardouin, 12–23. Washington, DC: Smithsonian Institution Press; London: Currey.

Anderson, G., ed. 2004. *Reinventing the Museum: Historical and Contemporary Perspectives on the Paradigm Shift*. Walnut Creek, CA: AltaMira.

Badran, A. 2001. *The Communication of Archaeological Museums with Their Communities in Jordan*. MA thesis, Newcastle University.

——— 2010. *Archaeological Museums and Schools: Teaching Primary-Aged Children about the Past in Jordan*. PhD diss., Newcastle University.

——— 2011. The Excluded Past in the Jordanian Formal Primary Education: Introducing Archaeology. In *New Perspectives in Global Public Archaeology*, ed. K. Okamura and A. Matsuda, 197–216. New York: Springer.

——— 2012. *A Report on Engaging Young People in Their National Tangible and Intangible Heritage in Jordan*. Amman: UNESCO.

——— 2013. *Engaging Young People in Their National Tangible and Intangible Heritage in Jordan: UNESCO Project – Phase II*. Amman: UNESCO

——— 2014. Heritage Education in Jordanian Schools: For Knowledge or Profit? In *Public Participation in Archaeology*, ed. S. Thomas and J. Lea, 105–16. Woodbridge: Boydell & Brewer.

Bashkin, O. 2006. When Mu'awiya Entered the Curriculum: Some Comments on the Iraqi Education System in the Interwar Period. *CER* 50: 346–66.

Beavis, J., and Hunt, A., eds. 1999. *Communicating Archaeology: Papers Presented to Bill Putnam at a Conference Held at Bournemouth University in September 1995*. Bournemouth University School of Conservation Sciences Occasional Paper 4. Oxford: Oxbow.

Bennett, T. 1995. *The Birth of the Museum: History, Theory, Politics*. Culture: Policy and Politics. London: Routledge.

Binford, L. 1972. *An Archaeological Perspective*. New York: Seminar Press.

Boylan, P. 1990. Museums and Cultural Identity. *Museums Journal* 90 (10): 29–33.

al-Burai, I. 1984. *The Impact of Using Historical Remains on Achieving Educational Objectives of History Teaching in Elementary Education*. MA thesis, Ain Shams University, Cairo [Arabic].

Burcaw, G. E. 1983. *Introduction to Museum Work*. Rev. and exp. 2nd ed. Nashville, TN: American Association for State and Local History.

Cameron, D. F. 2004. The Museum, a Temple or a Forum. In *Reinventing the Museum: Historical and Contemporary Perspectives on the Paradigm Shift*, ed. G. Anderson, 61–73. Walnut Creek, CA: AltaMira.

Childe, V. G. 1957. *The Dawn of European Civilization. History of Civilization*. Rev. 6th ed. London: Routledge & Kegan Paul.

Clark, G. 1943. Education and the Study of Man. *Antiquity* 17 (67): 113–21.

Corbett, G., and Ronza, E. In press. Making Social Engagement Sustainable: Insights from the Temple of the Winged Lions Cultural Resource Management Initiative in Petra. In *Community Heritage in the Arab Region*, ed. A. Badran and S. Abu-Khafajah. New York: Springer.

Dana, J. C. 2004. The Gloom of the Museum. In *Reinventing the Museum: Historical and Contemporary Perspectives on the Paradigm Shift*, ed. G. Anderson, 13–29. Walnut Creek, CA: AltaMira.

al-Deek, A. A. 2007. *Assessment of the Educational Role of the Museum of Jordanian Heritage at Yarmouk University*. MA thesis, Yarmouk University.

Dewey, J. 1959. The School and the Society. In *Dewey on Education: Selections with an Introduction and Notes*, ed. M. Dworkin, 33–90. New York: Teachers College Press.

Department of Antiquities. 2004. *The Law of Antiquities: Law No. 21 for the Year 1988 and Its Amendments*. Amman: Jordan Press Foundation.

Falk, J. H., and Dierking, L. D. 1992. *The Museum Experience*. Washington, DC: Whalesback.

Greene, K. 2002. *Archaeology: An Introduction; The History, Principles and Methods of Modern Archaeology*. 4th ed. London: Routledge

Günther, S. 2006. Be Masters in That You Teach and Continue to Learn: Mediaeval Muslim Thinkers on Educational Theory. *CER* 50: 367–88.

Harding, L. G. 1967. *The Antiquities of Jordan*. New York: Praeger.

Hein, G. E. 1996. Constructivist Learning Theory. In *Developing Museum Exhibitions for Lifelong Learning*, ed. G. Durbin, 30–4. London: Stationery Office; Museums & Galleries Commission; Group for Education in Museums.

Hein, G. E., and Alexander, M. 1998. *Museums: Places of Learning*. Professional Practice Series. Washington, DC: Education Committee, American Association of Museums.

Helmore, G. A. 1969. *Piaget – A Practical Consideration: A Consideration of the General Theories and Work of Jean Piaget, with an Account of a Short Follow Up Study of His Work on the Development of the Concept of Geometry*. Oxford: Pergamon.

Henson, D.; Stone, P.; and Corbishley, M., eds. 2004. *Education and the Historic Environment*. Issues in Heritage Management. London: Routledge

Hodder, I. 1991. *Reading the Past: Current Approaches to Interpretation and Archaeology*. 2nd ed. Cambridge: Cambridge University Press.

Hodder, I., and Doughty, L., eds. 2007. *Mediterranean Prehistoric Heritage: Training, Education and Management*. MIM. Cambridge: McDonald Institute for Archaeological Research.

Hooper-Greenhill, E. 1991. *Museum and Gallery Education*. London: Leicester University Press.

Jameson, J. H., Jr., ed. 1997. *Presenting Archaeology to the Public: Digging for Truths*. Walnut Creek, CA: AltaMira.

Jensen, N. 1994. Children's Perceptions of Their Museum Experiences: A Contextual Perspective. *Children's Environments* 11: 300–24.

Johnson, M. 1999. *Archaeological Theory: An Introduction*. Oxford: Blackwell.

Kreishan, D. 2011. *The Role of Museums in Children's Education: A Case Study of Children's Museum in Jordan*. MA thesis, The Hashemite University [Arabic].

Lewis, G. 1984. Museums and Their Precursors: A Brief World Survey. In *Manual of Curatorship: A Guide to Museum Practice*, ed. J. M. A. Thompson, 5–21. Oxford: Butterworths.

Mulas, M. 1997. The Role of Museums in Education. *Education* 122: 157–65 [Arabic].

Malt, C. 2005. *Women's Voices in Middle East Museums: Case Studies in Jordan*. Gender, Culture, and Politics in the Middle East. Syracuse, NY: Syracuse University Press.

Meital, Y. 2006. School Textbooks and Assembling the Puzzle of the Past in Revolutionary Egypt. *Middle Eastern Studies* 42: 255–70.

Merriman, N. 1991. *Beyond the Glass Case: The Past, the Heritage and the Public in Britain*. Leicester Museum Studies Series. Leicester: Leicester University Press.

Moe, J. M. 2000. Archaeology and Values: Respect and Responsibility for Our Heritage. In *The Archaeology Education Handbook: Sharing the Past with Kids*, ed. K. Smardz and S. J. Smith, 249–66. Walnut Creek, CA: AltaMira.

Pearce, S. 1990. *Objects of Knowledge*. New Research in Museum Studies 1. London: Athlone.

Pyburn, K. A. 2000. Gatekeeping, Housekeeping, Peacekeeping: Goals for Teaching Archaeology in the Public Schools. In *The Archaeology Education Handbook: Sharing the Past with Kids*, ed. K. Smardz and S. J. Smith, 274–8. Walnut Creek, CA: AltaMira.

Qaoud, I. al-. 2003. The Efficiency of Using Educational Museum in Achievement and Developing Creative Feeling for the Basic Seventh Grade Students Learning History in Jordan. *Educational Research Center Journal* 11: 209–38.

Rashdan, A. Z., and Hamshri, A. A. 2003. *The Education System in Jordan 1921–2002*. Amman: Dar Safa [Arabic].

Renfrew, C., and Bahn, P. 2004. *Archaeology: Theories, Methods, and Practice*. 4th ed. London: Thames & Hudson.

Roberts, L. C. 1997. *From Knowledge to Narrative: Educators and the Changing Museum*. Washington, DC: Smithsonian Institution Press.

Sarkaz, A. 1977. *The Impact of Using Educational Resources for Teaching History at the Primary Level in the Libyan Arab Republic*. MA thesis, Tanta University.

Shayyab, A. al-, and al-Muheisen, Z. 2008. *Archaeology and Jordanian Museums*. Amman: Ministry of Culture [Arabic].

Shanks, M., and Hodder, I. 1995. Processual, Postprocessual, and Interpretive Archaeologies. In *Interpreting Archaeology: Finding Meaning in the Past*, ed. I. Hodder, M. Shanks, A. Alexandri, V. Buchli, J. Carman, J. Last, and G. Lucas, 3–29. London: Routledge.

Shanks, M., and Tilley, C. 1987. *Re-Constructing Archaeology: Theory and Practice*. New Studies in Archaeology. Cambridge: Cambridge University Press

Smardz, K., and Smith, S. J., eds. 2000. *The Archaeology Education Handbook: Sharing the Past with Kids*. Walnut Creek, CA: AltaMira.

Stone, P. G. 1994. Introduction: A Framework for Discussion. In *The Presented Past: Heritage, Museums and Education*, ed. P. G. Stone and B. L. Molyneaux, 14–28. OWA 25. London: Routledge in association with English Heritage.

Stone, P. G., and Molyneaux, B. L., eds. 1994. *The Presented Past: Heritage, Museums and Education*. OWA 25. London: Routledge in association with English Heritage.

Tawfiq, N. R. 1994. School Visits to Archaeological Museums in Jordan. In *Museums, Civilization and Development: Proceedings of the Encounter, Amman, Jordan, 26–30 April 1994*, 183–85. Paris: ICOM.

Trigger, B. G. 1989. *A History of Archaeological Thought*. Cambridge: Cambridge University Press.

1995. Romanticism, Nationalism and Archaeology. In *Nationalism, Politics and the Practice of Archaeology*, ed. P. L. Kohl and C. Fawcett, 263–79. Cambridge: Cambridge University Press.

Tweiq, S. 2002. The Alphabets of the Excavation. *Athar* 5: 42–3 [Arabic].

Ucko, P. 1990. Foreword. In *The Excluded Past: Archaeology in Education*, ed. P. Stone and R. MacKenzie, 9–24. London: Routledge.

Vries, B. de. 2013. Archaeology and Community in Jordan and Greater Syria: Traditional Patterns and New Directions. *NEA* 76: 132–41.

Vygotsky, L. 1978. *Mind in Society: The Development of Higher Psychological Processes*. Cambridge, MA: Harvard University Press.

Weil, S. 1990. *Rethinking the Museum and Other Meditations*. Washington, DC: Smithsonian Institution Press.

EPILOGUE

ASSAF YASUR-LANDAU, YORKE M. ROWAN, AND ERIC H. CLINE

Invoking the musical imagery of a mass, as was used to good effect in Norman Yoffee's conclusion to Thomas Levy's edited volume *The Archaeology of Society in the Holy Land* (1998), we are happy to note that this edited volume, like polyphonic choral music, weaves together the very distinct voices of the authors. Rather than dictate definitions or canonical theories, the thirty-three chapters presented here allow for just as many interpretations of social archaeology, some of which are very personal and (continuing the musical allusion), differ in the instruments, genre, style, and even basic musical tradition selected by the authors.

To us, this is a positive testimony of the health and vibrancy of the archaeological discipline after more than a century of scientific excavations, in which different voices can be heard as part of a multi-directional scientific enquiry. In lieu of a chapter-by-chapter summary, we wish to use this last section to present several observations based on these chapters, which connect the past, present, and possibly the future of social archaeology in the southern Levant. These, we hope, may present cross-sections of the fragmented and evolving archaeological landscape represented here.

As perhaps is to be expected from an archaeology of a region tightly connected to both (neo-) biblical and classical archaeologies, history and the critical use of literary sources play an important role in almost every chapter dealing with periods from the Bronze Age onward. Furthermore, scripts and the social contexts of their use, both cuneiform and alphabetic, are seen as a social phenomenon worth investigating within the context of social archaeology rather than history only. At the same time, while the works of prominent historians such as Mario Liverani and Nadav Na'aman are used by several scholars, the use of historical theory, such as that of the Mediterranean offered by Fernand Braudel, Peregrine Horden, and Nicholas Purcell, is still almost anecdotal. This restraint in using historical theory as a guideline for the creation of an archaeological narrative seems to be a good argument against any claim for a tyranny of the text, whether the Bible or classical sources, over archaeological investigation. However, a somewhat skeptical look at theoretical constructs is by no means an isolated phenomenon.

In general, it seems that most of the contributions to this volume do not use any theoretical terms as a *leitmotif* to guide their narrative about ancient society, although many quote theoretical works that illuminate parts of the arguments being made. Thus, for example, most authors are very much aware of the two decades of postcolonial critique of archaeology and anthropology, since many refer to authors using such theory in their work. However, the use of related terms such as "hybridity" and "entanglement" (e.g., Stockhammer 2012) seems to be rather rare. Even the term "materiality," with its clear theoretical connotations to the social interactions between humans and objects (e.g., Hodder 2012), appears in only four chapters. Furthermore, while the discipline of anthropology is mentioned in at least half of the chapters, and ethnography in more than a third, it may be that for many of the participants in this volume, anthropology has lost some of its appeal as a generator of theoretical constructs that can be used to tease social meaning out of material culture assemblages. At the same time, few archaeologists of historical periods in the southern Levant call anthropology their academic home.

One might argue that this stems from the fact that most of the contributors to this volume are active field archaeologists, a group traditionally skeptical of archaeological theory. Yet, this may only be a small part of the truth, for at the same time, connectivity, migration, and mobility are topics gathering momentum in the study of the Mediterranean and the ancient Near East, partly because they stem from the growing field of Mediterranean history and archaeology (e.g., Broodbank 2013) and partly because of the continued crises of forced and undocumented migration (Hamilakis 2016).

The term "ethnicity" was at the heart of social archaeology discourse of the Levant in the 1990s, with much focus and argument on the ethnic identity of the Israelites and the Philistines. It maintained much of its power in the pragmatic "Historical Biblical Archaeology" (e.g. Faust 2010; Yasur-Landau 2010). Here, in this volume, it seems to lose some of its appeal and is often replaced by the more general term "identity" and its derivatives. This may well be attributed to a postcolonial critique of archaeology on one hand, and the (perceived or real) lack of current theoretical models that can readily be used to point to and explain phenomena of group identity from material culture remains on the other hand. At the same time, it is very likely that we are facing a paradigm shift in the archaeology of identity motivated by increasingly prevalent DNA studies. Used primarily for the study of human and animal mobility, such studies may raise relevant questions on the relation between genetic makeup and ancestry, cultural ancestry, and material culture, as well as no less explosive questions of connections between past and present populations (e.g., Meiri et al. 2013; Lazaridis et al. 2017)

During the 1990s and even later, discussions of climate and environment were at the center of archaeological investigation that were only concerned with the prehistory of the Levant. Although such themes were presented in the introductory chapters of *The Archaeology of Society in the Holy Land*, they were nonetheless not integrated into many post-Chalcolithic discussions. Similarly, climate and environment did not play a major part in the historically centered negotiation of "biblical archaeology" (Levy 2010).

A change can now be seen in this volume, where environmental themes are discussed in a number of chapters concerned with eras that postdate the prehistoric periods. This most likely reflects new interests in environmental change as causing cultural change, requiring the integration of advanced methods of using numerous proxies to reconstruct ancient climate by way of archaeological data (Langgut et al. 2013; Knapp and Manning 2016). This interest in ancient climate, and the related potential challenges it poses by promoting truly synergic scientific research discourse, are unlikely to go away anytime soon, since contemporary climate change as well as sea level changes are at the very heart of public discourse today (not merely in archaeology).

As Levy notes in the foreword to the present volume, this has been produced in an era during which the "sciences," such as residue analysis, radiocarbon, zooarchaeology, geoarchaeology, palynology, and archaeobotany, are seen as integral parts of the archaeological investigation and therefore play a role in our reconstruction of ancient society (e.g., Yasur-Landau et al. 2015). Our decision to dedicate chapters to such scientific methods may be seen as an effort to place them on the front burner and underscore their importance. We hope that in future volumes of social archaeology, such methods will be even more integrated into the general archaeological practice as part of the initial research design, as so often is the case in prehistoric research.

Finally, a new and important venue of social archaeology that we see in this volume is the concern not only with past societies but also with the contemporary societies of the region. The modern social use of archaeology has been recognized for some time, whether for nationalist archaeologies or counterhegemonic resistance by the indigenous or disenfranchised people around the world who wish to reclaim control of their past and present (Preucel and

Meskell 2004: 9). Pertinent to this topic is the need for reflexive engagement with the public, especially in relation to the preservation and presentation of cultural heritage, as well as the related questions of ethics, legality, and the conservation of archaeological sites and finds. The ways in which ancient artifacts and sites are "owned," manipulated, and negotiated by modern countries, organizations, and communities involved in present-day agendas and tensions in the Middle East is a theme that is likely to remain relevant to archaeological investigations in this region for generations.

REFERENCES

Broodbank, C. 2013. *The Making of the Middle Sea: A History of the Mediterranean from the Beginning to the Emergence of the Classical World*. London: Thames & Hudson.

Faust, A. 2010. Future Directions in the Study of Ethnicity in Ancient Israel. In *Historical Biblical Archaeology and the Future: The New Pragmatism*, ed. T. E. Levy, 55–68. London: Equinox.

Hamilakis, Y. 2016. Archaeologies of Forced and Undocumented Migration. *Journal of Contemporary Archaeology* 3: 121–39.

Hodder, I. 2012. *Entangled: An Archaeology of the Relationships between Humans and Things*. Malden, MA: Wiley-Blackwell.

Knapp, A. B., and Manning, S. W. 2016. Crisis in Context: The End of the Late Bronze Age in the Eastern Mediterranean. *AJA* 120: 99–149.

Langgut, D.; Finkelstein, I.; and Litt, T. 2013. Climate and the Late Bronze Collapse: New Evidence from the Southern Levant. *TA* 40: 149–75.

Lazaridis, I.; Mittnik, A.; Patterson, N.; Mallick, S.; Rohland, N.; Pfrengle, S.; Furtwängler, A.; Peltzer, A.; Posth, C.; Vasilakis, A.; McGeorge, P. J. P.; Konsolaki-Yannopoulou, E.; Korres, G.; Martlew, H.; Michalodimitrakis, M.; Özsait, M.; Özsait, N.; Papathanasiou, A.; Richards, M.; Roodenberg, S. A.; Tzedakis, Y.; Arnott, R.; Fernandes, D. M.; Hughey, J. R.; Lotakis, D. M.; Navas, P. A.; Maniatis, Y.; Stamatoyannopoulos, J. A.; Stewardson, K.; Stockhammer, P.; Pinhasi, R.; Reich, D.; Krause, J.; and Stamatoyannopoulos, G. 2017. Genetic Origins of the Minoans and Mycenaeans. *Nature* 548: 214–18.

Levy, T. E., ed. 2010. *Historical Biblical Archaeology and the Future: The New Pragmatism*. London: Equinox.

Meiri, M.; Huchon, D.; Bar-Oz, G.; Boaretto, E.; Horwitz, L. K.; Maeir, A. M.; Sapir-Hen, L.; Larson, G.; Weiner, S.; and Finkelstein, I. 2013. Ancient DNA and Population Turnover in Southern Levantine Pigs — Signature of the Sea Peoples Migration? *Nature Science Reports* 3. www.nature.com/articles/srep03035 (accessed June 26, 2017).

Preucel, R. W., and Meskel, L. 2004. Knowledges. In *A Companion to Social Archaeology*, ed. L. Meskell and R. W. Preucel, 3–22. Oxford: Blackwell.

Stockhammer, P. W. 2012. Conceptualizing Cultural Hybridization in Archaeology. In *Conceptualizing Cultural Hybridization: A Transdisciplinary Approach; Papers of the Conference, Heidelberg, 21–22 September 2009*, ed. P. W. Stockhammer, 43–58. Transcultural Research — Heidelberg Studies on Asia and Europe in a Global Context. Heidelberg: Springer.

Yasur-Landau, A. 2010. Under the Shadow of the Four-Room House: Biblical Archaeology Meets Household Archaeology in Israel. In *Historical Biblical Archaeology and the Future: The New Pragmatism*, ed. T. E. Levy, 142–55. London: Equinox.

Yasur-Landau, A.; Cline, E. H.; Koh, A. J., Ben-Shlomo, D.; Marom, N.; Ratzlaff, A.; and Samet, I. 2015. Rethinking Canaanite Palaces? The Palatial Economy of Tel Kabri during the Middle Bronze Age. *JFA* 40: 607–25.

Yoffee, N. 1998. Conclusion: A Mass in Celebration of the Conference. In *The Archaeology of Society in the Holy Land*, ed. T. E. Levy, 542–8. London: Leicester University Press.

INDEX

[14]C *see* dating, radiocarbon

Abiba'al Inscription 376–77
acculturation 274, 297, 438, 450
Achaemenid Persian Empire 333, 393–405, 419
Acheulian period 9–24
Acheulo-Yabrudian complex 14–18
Achziv 558
Acre *see* Akko
acrophonic principle 374
adaptation 551–64
Aegean (region) 310–19, 556, 559–61
agency 78–79, 212, 411, 487, 594
agriculture *see* farming
Ahiram Inscription 376
Ahmarian culture 34–40
'Ain Difla 19
'Ain Ghazal 54, 76
'Ain Sawda 16, 18, 22
Akkad and Akkadians 576–77
Akkadian script and language *see* cuneiform
Akko 481, 483, 494, 496, 498–99, 558
Akko, Plain of 393–95
Akko-Ptolemais 418
alabaster 138, 169
Alexander the Great 381, 386, 410
alphabet, origins of 371–87
altars 314, 330, 404
Amarna letters, el- 247, 251, 254, 355, 375, 555, 561
Amon 293
Amorite hypothesis 577
amphitheaters 449–50
Amudian/Pre-Aurignacian culture 14
Anafa, Tel 414, 424
Anatolia 50, 53–55, 58, 74, 315, 442, 543, 560
Anaxikles 417
ancestor veneration 74, 78, 112, 230, 294, 331
anchors 557–61
Antioch 493
Antioch, county of 494
Antiquities Authority Law 5749 606
Antiquities Law 5738 606
Antiquities Order No. 1 of 1953 602
Antiquities Ordinance, 1920 601
Antiquities Ordinance, 1929 601
Antiquities Rules, 1930 602

Aphek 249–50, 254
apologetics 530–32
Arad, Tel 381, 383
Aramaic script and language 379–83, 399, 401, 421–22
Aravah Valley 289–90, 538–43
archaeobotanical remains 48–53, 108–10, 146–55
archaeological science *see* archaeometry
archaeology
  biblical 337–50, 354–64, 522–32, 582–87
  coastal settlement 551–65
  gendered 522–32
  maritime 551–65
  post-processual 3–4, 615–16
  processual 3–4, 614–15
  social 3–4
archaeometallurgy *see* metallurgy
archaeometry 545
architecture 291–92, 313
  cultic 295, 313–14
  domestic 71–72, 100–2, 439–42, 498–99, 525–27
  harbor 561–64
  monumental 70, 76, 89, 225, 227, 232, 234, 329, 359, 576
  shared 74–76, 102–4
Arqov/Divshon 37
Ascalon *see* Ashkelon
Ashdod 398
Asherah 382, 531
Ashkelon 248, 250, 398, 494
ashlar masonry 313, 561–63
assimilation 37, 310
Assyria and Assyrians 331–33, 344, 363–64, 562
'Atlit-Yam 553
Atlitian culture 37
Aurignacian culture 34–37
Avaris 555
Azarba'al Inscription 376
Azraq Oasis 20

Bab adh-Dhra' 169, 171, 173, 175–77, 199–214, 596–610
Babylon and Babylonians 320
Babylonian script and language 246, 249 *see also* cuneiform
Badia 100, 114–15

639

barley 51–53, 150–52, 299
baths 452–54
Be'er Resisim 188–89
behaviorism 610
Beidha 71–72
Bes 529
Besitun (Behistun) Inscription 380
beth 'av 341, 345–46, 349–50
Beth Shean 251, 267–68, 274
Beth Yerah, Tel 176
Bible, Hebrew 298, 301–2, 324, 328, 354–64, 528–32
biblical narrative 354–64, 582–83
Binyanei Ha'uma 444, 446, 448
bioarchaeology 199–214
biodistance 213
biographies, object 594–610
Bizat Ruhama 11
bowls, basalt 128–30
British Mandate period 599, 601–2
bronze 536–46
Bull Site 295
burial practices 58, 72–74, 111–12, 127–28, 134–39, 168–69, 190–91, 199–214, 230, 294, 315, 341–44, 349–50, 394, 442–43, 596–99
Busayra *see* Buṣeirah
Buṣeirah 332
Byblos 376
Byzantium and Byzantines 206, 458–73

Cadmus 384
Caesarea Maritima 447–53
Cairo Geniza documents 479–80
Canaan and Canaanites 163–79, 183–94, 224–40, 245–56, 265, 283–302, 310–20, 339, 357, 554–62
Canaanite amphorae *see* jars, transport storage
Canaanite script and language 371–87 *see also* Early Alphabetic writing
caves 134, 137, 349–50
cereals 47–60, 150
chaînes opératoires 112–13, 541–43
Chalcolithic period 100, 122–40, 146–55, 543–45
charcoal 578
chiefdoms 148, 297, 582
chipped-stone assemblages 31, 36–37, 128, 291
Christianity 458
chronology 30–31, 48, 98–100, 123–25, 164, 183–85, 284–88, 573–87
churches 495
cineraria 442
circuses 449–50
climate 177, 225, 284, 301, 539, 552, 564, 636
Coele-Syria 397–98, 413, 418
coins 393–406, 423–25, 498, 500
collapse 575–82
collective responsibility 345–46
colonialism 271, 447–53, 601–2, 620, 622, 629

communities 57, 67, 98–115, 177–79, 500, 514, 623
connectivity 551–65
conquest 283–302
Convention on the Means of Prohibiting and Preventing the Illicit Import, Export and Transfer of Ownership of Cultural Property 1970 604–5
copper 132, 192, 289, 328, 484, 536–46, 559
core-and-flake industry 11
core–periphery interaction 271–72
core area origin hypothesis 48–50, 60
courtyards 101–4, 110, 238, 439
craft specialization 90, 132, 171, 173, 178, 482, 486
Crusades 492–501
cult 57–58, 60, 76, 123, 132–34, 137–39, 191–92, 236, 294–96, 313–14, 328–31, 404, 415–17
cult stands 314
cultural heritage management 594–610, 613–29
cultural identity *see* ethnicity
culture history 614
cuneiform 236, 245–56, 374
Cyprus and Cypriots 54, 315, 556

daily life 174, 211–12, 438, 462–63, 470, 478–87, 525–27
Daliyeh, Wadi ed- 381, 410
Dan, Tel 224–40, 361, 422
Dan Stele, Tel 379
dating, radiocarbon 30, 284–88, 573–87
David 583
Dead Sea Scrolls 425
demography 208, 494
dental remains 169, 209–10, 213
determinatives 373
Dhiban 329
diet 209–10
differentiation 101, 168–70, 172, 175, 178, 311
diffusion 614
Diodorus Siculus 384–85
direct rule 271–73
diseases 210
DNA studies 213
domestication 53–55
Dor, Tel 558, 561
Dothan, Tell 199–214

Early Alphabetic writing 371–87
Early Bronze Age 163–79, 575–82
Early Roman period 438
Eastern Sigillata pottery 444
Ebal, Mount 295
Ebla 226
economic organization 48–55, 146–55, 163–79, 332–33, 343–45, 478–87, 514–16
Edicts of Cyrus 394
Edom and Edomites 403–5
education 245–56, 371–87

INDEX

Egypt and Egyptians 171, 192, 226, 246, 256, 265, 299–301, 528–29, 554–56, 577, 616
Egyptian scripts and language 373–74, 386
'Ein el-Hilu 187
'Ein Gedi 137–38
Eliba'al Inscription 376–77
elite emulation 271–73
Emar 250
'En Boqeq 471
Epipaleolithic period 31, 47–60, 69
equilibrium imperialism 273–74
Eshmunazar Sarcophagus Inscription 378
ethnicity 297–98, 310–20, 355, 393–406, 635–36
extensification 152

Fadous-Kfarabida, Tell 580
Fakhariyeh Bilingual Statue Inscription, Tell 379
family structures 71–74, 98–115, 341–44, 347–50, 471, 525–27
Faris, Khirbat 481
farming 47–60, 79, 122, 146–55, 298–99, 478–87, 511–12
feasting 107–11, 319
Feinan, Wadi 324–34, 478–87, 541
feminism 522–32
fertility
  human 528–30
  soil 153–54
figurines 104–6, 314, 395, 404, 528–29
fire 86–93, 108
forager–farmer transition 47–60
fortification systems 224–40, 576, 583
fortresses 471
Franks 492–501
Fustat see Cairo

gates 227, 238
Gath see Ṣafi/Gath, Tell eṣ-
gender 101, 104–7, 468–73, 482–83, 522–32
gender studies 524
Gerizim, Mount 400, 421–22
Gesher Benot Ya'aqov 12, 87
Gezer Calendar 377
Ghassulian culture 123, 545 see also Chalcolithic period
Gilat 138–39
Gilgamesh, The Epic of 249
glyptics see seals
Greece and Greeks 410–27, 438
Greek alphabet and language 318, 383–86, 417, 422
ground-stone assemblages 9–24, 29–41, 128, 291

Handmade Geometrically Painted Wares 484–87
Hazor 248
hearths 39, 86–93, 314
Hebrew script and language 379–83
Hellenistic period 393–406, 410–27, 438
Hermon, Mount 411–13

Herod the Great 426, 438
Herodotus 384
Ḥesi, Tell el- 254
Hezekiah 382–83
hippodromes 449–50, 622
Hishuley Carmel 559–60
Holy Sepulchre, Church of the 495
Homo spp. 9–24
house societies 103–4
houses *see also* architecture, domestic
  atrium 440–41
  four-room *or* quadripartite 292, 341, 347–49
hunter-gatherers 67, 89
hunting 55, 107, 111, 509–16
Hurrian language 246
husbandry 122, 125, 173, 291, 298–99, 362, 509–16, 526, 551–52

Ibn Jubayr 496
Ibn Sina, Abu 'Ali al-Husayn 619–20
iconography 137, 296, 399, 528–30
individuality 79
Intermediate Bronze Age 178, 183–94, 576
Iron Age 283–302, 310–20, 324–34, 337–50, 357–60, 371–87, 541–43, 561–64, 582–87
Iskander, Khirbet 186
Islam 619–20
Islamic period 478–87, 492–501
"Israelite house" *see* houses, four-room
Israel and Israelites 283–302, 337–50, 354–64, 522–32, 582–87
itineraries, object 594–610

Jaffa 267–68, 417
jars
  collared-rim *see* pithoi, collared-rim
  Gaza 445–46, 463
  Palestinian Bag 445–46
  transport storage 557
Jemmeh, Tell 253
Jerash 626
Jericho 173, 176–77
Jerusalem 340–41, 357, 360, 423, 480, 494
Jerusalem Haram documents 480, 483
Jews and Judaism 380, 394, 425–27, 438
Jordanian Temporary Law N.12 of 1976 on Antiquities 604
Judaea 438
Judah and Judahites 337–50, 402–3
Judea and Judeans 422–26

Kabri, Tel 89
Kahun 226
Karatepe Inscription 377
Kedesh, Tel 411–12, 418
Kenamun, Tomb of 554–55
Kerak Ware, Khirbet 176
Kfar Samir 560

kinship 178, 339
Kuntillet Ajrud 378, 382
lamps 446–47, 466

Late Bronze Age 245–56, 265, 284–88, 311, 355, 557, 559–61
Late Bronze Age/Iron Age transition 246, 310–20
Late Helladic period 315
Latin alphabet 386–87
law codes 249–50, 594–610
legions, Roman 444, 446–49, 622
legumes 151
Lejjūn, el- 471
Levallois techniques 16, 18, 20, 22
lexical lists 248–49
limestone 89
literacy 245–56, 371–87, 415–17
liver models 249–50

Marisa 405
maritime transport containers *see* jars, transport storage
Marj Rabba 146–55
markets 332–33
maternity 528–30
Megiddo 93, 228–32, 236–37, 359–60, 583
Merenptah Stele 357
Mesha Inscription 324–34
metallurgy 132, 150, 289–90, 317, 536–46, 559–61
Middle Bronze Age 224–40, 245–56, 555–58
milestones 451
mining 539–41
minimum number of individuals (MNI) 207–8
mints 393–406
miqveh (pl. *miqva'ot*) 426–27, 452
Moab and Moabites 324–34
"Moabite Bible" *see* Mesha Inscription
mosaics 441–42
Mousterian complex 18–24
mud bricks 92–93
Mujib, Wadi al- 327
multiregional hypothesis 50–51, 60
museums 613–29

Nahal Hemar Cave 76
Nahal Manayaheem Outlet 22
Nahal Mishmar Cave 132–34
names, theophoric 330, 402, 404–5, 421
Nami, Tel 558
Natufian period *see* Epipaleolithic period
Negebites *see* Edom and Edomites
Neo-Babylon and Neo-Babylonians 333, 346
Neolithic period 47–60, 67, 98–115, 512, 552–53
numismatics *see* coins
Nuqayb al-Asaymir, Khirbat 484

obsidian 114
Ohalo II 51
olives 151–52, 343

Omride dynasty 361–62
Ottoman Empire 599–601
ovens 526

Paleolithic period 9–24, 29–41, 86–88
partage 600, 602
Passover Letter 380
pastoralism *see* husbandry
patron deities 330
Persia and Persians 393–406
Philistia and Philistines 310–20, 398–400
Phoenicia and Phoenicians 395–400, 419–20
Phoenician script 375–79, 384–85
pithoi, collared-rim 289, 300
plaster, lime 89
plowing 153
pork 298–99
post-Wadi Rabah/pre-Ghassulian culture 125
pottery 108, 113, 130–31, 190, 267, 272, 288–89, 444–46, 460–66, 499, 556–57
    Philistine 315–16
Proto-Canaanite writing *see* Early Alphabetic writing
Proto-Sinaitic writing *see* Early Alphabetic writing
Pseudo-Scylax 397
pyrotechnology 86–93

Qeiyafa, Khirbet 584
Qesem Cave 15–16
queer theory 524–25

Rabah culture, Wadi 98–115, 125
ramparts, earthen 224, 227, 238–39
Rasafa, al- 22
regionalism 190
Rehov, Tel 584–85
relativism 615
ritual *see* cult
roads 450–51
Rome and Romans 386–87, 426–27, 438, 622

Ṣafi/Gath, Tell eṣ- 317
Samaria (city) 363
Samaria (region) and Samaritans 400–2, 421–22
scribes 245–56, 371–87
Sea Peoples 310–20
seals 173, 246, 251, 253, 291, 317, 418
secondary products revolution 126, 154
sedentism 56–57, 69–71
Seleucia and Seleucids 410–27
Sepphoris 440–42
Serapis 415–17
seren (pl. *seranim*) 318, 320
settlement patterns 19, 22–23, 56–57, 69–71, 113, 126, 185–90, 292–94, 326–28, 338–42, 346, 359, 492–93, 497–98, 576
Sha'ar Hagolan 101, 103, 110
Sharuhen *see* 'Ajjul, Tell el-
Shechem 357, 361

INDEX

Shephelah 337–50
shipwrecks 559–61, 563–64
Shiqmim 127–28, 146–55
Shkārat Msaied 71–72
Sidon 393–94, 397
Siloam Tunnel Inscription 382
smelting 539–41, 545
social organization 56–57, 80, 104, 112, 185, 296–97
socio-technological systems 541–43
socioeconomic organization 123, 188, 342, 344
spatial analysis 93, 106, 115, 516
spinning and weaving 126, 298, 471, 482–83
St. Stephen's Monastery 199–214
staple products 169
state 356, 361–64
sugar 483–84

Tabaqat al-Bûma 106, 112
Tabun Cave 13–14, 18–19
teeth *see* dental remains
Teleilat el-Ghassul 123
temples *see* architecture, cultic
Temporary Law No.12 of 1976 on Antiquities 605
textiles *see* spinning and weaving
theaters 449–50
Tiberias 495–96
Timna' 289, 527, 536, 541
tin 559
Tor Faraj 23
trade 176, 192, 396, 445, 451, 481, 551–65, 594–610
transcultural society 311
tribal kingdoms 356
tribes 356
Tsaf, Tel 146–55
Turkish Bylaw on Antiquities, 1869 599–600
Tyre 393–94, 397, 420, 496–97, 562–63

'Ubeidiya 10–11
Ugaritic script and language 374–75
United Monarchy 582–87
Ur III period 236
urbanization 163–79, 224–40, 576, 581, 587
'Uyun al-Qadim 12

villages 68–71, 228, 291–92, 478–87, 497
votive objects 253

Wad points, el- 40
walls 227, 238
warriors 239–40
watchtowers/booths 464
water management systems 154, 178, 238, 451
WE-2 20
wells 110
wheat 51–53, 150–52, 299
WHS 621 20
winepresses 466
women's studies 522–32
workshops 290, 482, 537, 545
writing systems 173, 245–56, 317–18, 371–87
WT-13 330–31

Yahweh 357, 378, 382
Yarmoukian 98–115
Yarmouth, Tel 175, 578
Yavneh-Yam 420, 463, 560
Yehimilk Inscription 376
Yotvata 471–73
Younger Dryas 69

Zenon 413–14
Zeraqon, Khirbat as- 580
zooarchaeological remains 53–55, 110, 509–16, 553

in the United States
& Taylor Publisher Services